MODERN ARCHITECTURE KUWAIT
1949–1989

MODERN ARCHITECTURE KUWAIT
1949–1989

ROBERTO FABBRI • SARA SARAGOÇA • RICARDO CAMACHO

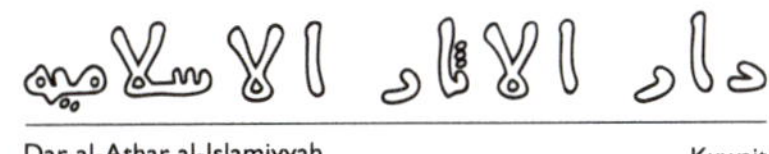

Dar al-Athar al-Islamiyyah

Kuwait

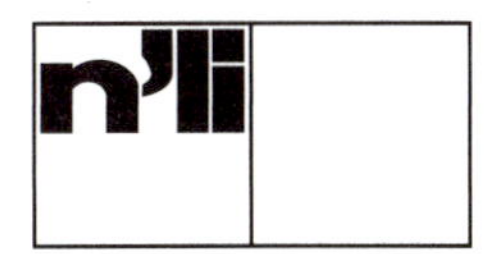

The Deutsche Nationalbibliothek lists this publication in
the Deutsche Nationalbibliografie; detailed bibliographic
data are available on the Internet at http://dnb.dnb.de

Modern Architecture Kuwait research and publication was
proudly supported by a grant from the Kuwait Foundation
for the Advancement of Science (KFAS) and
Dar al-Athar al-Islamiyyah, Kuwait (DAI).

RESEARCH TEAM:
Roberto Fabbri
Ricardo Camacho
Sara Saragoça Soares

RESEARCH COLLABORATION:
Noorah Al-Sabah, Fahed Ben Salamah, Fajer Al-Hendi,
Yousef Abdulaal, Samer Mohamed, Sarah Behbehani,
Khalid Al-Qamlas, Michael Kubo, Claudia Cagneschi,
Enrico Mambelli, Adal Albloushi, Yannis Kitanis,
Vladimir Deskov, the Arab Centre for Architecture,
Marisa Baptista, Ivan Rupnik.

PUBLICATION:
AUTHORS: Roberto Fabbri, Ricardo Camacho,
Sara Saragoça Soares
ENGLISH TEXT EDITING & PROOFREADING: Harvey Pincis
ARABIC TRANSLATION: Mohamed M. Moustafa
ARABIC TEXT EDITING: Ma'asuma Habib, Nadia Abdelsalam
BOOK DESIGN: Abdalla Abdelrahman
ILLUSTRATIONS: Yousef Abdulaal, Samer Mohamed and the authors
PHOTOGRAPHY: Nelson Garrido

© 2016 Niggli, imprint of Braun Publishing AG,
Salenstein, Switzerland
www.niggli.ch

ISBN 978-3-7212-0948-8

2nd edition 2021

Cover Image: Joint Banking Centre, Kuwait.

Photography by Nelson Garrido © 2015
Layout by Abdalla Abdelrahman

ACKNOWLEDGEMENTS

This research project and publication couldn't have been possible without the help and support of several people and institutions. First of all a special thanks goes to the Kuwait Fund for the Advancement of Science (KFAS) and to Dar al-Athar al-Islamiyyah (DAI); two Kuwaiti institutions that strongly believed in the project and supported the idea from the very beginning.

A personal thanks to Sheikha Hussah Sabah al-Salem al-Sabah, who is always curious and supportive of every project that explores the realm of Art.

The authors would like to express their sincere gratitude to the following institutions, organizations and firms for their help and support (*in alphabetical order*):

Al-Baptain Library, Aga Khan Trust for Culture, Aga Khan Visual Archive at MIT Libraries, Archivio di Stato di Roma, American University in Cairo, American University of Kuwait, Arab Centre for Architecture, Archives of American Art, Chadirji Foundation, CAT Group, Centre for Research Studies on Kuwait, Centro Archivi Fondazione MAXXI, Center for Gulf Studies, Cité de l'Architecture et du Patrimoine, Constantinos A. Doxiadis Archives at Benaki Museum, Croatian Academy of Arts and Sciences, Dissing+Weitling, ETH – gta archiv, Fondazione Franco Albini, Frances Loeb Library, GSD at Harvard University, Gulf Bank, Fundação Calouste Gulbenkian, McGill University, Montois Partners Architects, KEO International Consultants, Kuwait Oil Company, Kuwait Municipal Archives, Kuwait National Library, National Council for Culture, Arts and Letters, PACE, Royal Institute of British Architecture, Saudi Aramco World/SAWDIA, SSH International Consultants, Swedish Centre for Architecture and Design, The British Library, University of Guelph, United Real Estate Company, RIBA Collections at V&A, Vastu Shilpa Foundation – Sangath.

The authors would also like to take this opportunity to thank the following people for their interest and cooperation (in alphabetical order): Ali Hussain Al-Youha (NCCAL), Adnan A. Shihab-Eldin (KFAS), Abdullah Y. Al-Ghunaim (CSRK), Abdullah Al-Bishi (NCCAL), Abdulaziz Al-Kandari (AOK), Ala'a Ali-Reda (URC), Ala Hason (HKS), Alexandre Ragois (Cité de l'Architecture et du Patrimoine), Alia Farid, Andrea Schuler (AKAA), Angelo Bucci (Universidade de São Paulo), Annika Tengstrand (ARKDES), Amena Elezaby (PACE), Asseel Al-Ragam (KU), Blagoja Kolev, Brad Batcheller (KEO), Caecilia Pieri (IFPO), Carla Zhara Buda (Fondazione MAXXI), Catty Wilson, Claudine Abdelmassih (ACA), Charles Haddad, Dalal Al-Sayer, Dana Aljouder (PACE), Daniel Weiss (ETH-gta), Deema Al-Ghunaim (Madeenah), Elena Albricci (Fondazione Albini), Farah Al-Nakib (AUK – CGS), Filine Wagner (ETH – gta), François Pradal (French Embassy in Kuwait), Françoise Archambeau (MPA), Giota Pavlidou, George Arbid (ACA), Gustavo Ferrari, Helena Njiric (University of Zagreb), Hugo Ferreira, Ines Zalduendo (GSD, Loeb Library), Ioanna Theocharopoulou (SCE-Parsons), Ismail Rifaat, Ivana Nikšic Olujić (HAZU), Jad Cortas (Notre Dame University), Lobna Montasser (AKTC), Łucasz Stanek (MARC), Kata Gašpar (DAZ), Khushnu Panthaki Hoof (Sangath), Kurt Helfrich (RIBA), Paola Albini (Fondazione Albini), Par Lindstrom, Peter Mandl, Maath Alousi (Alousi Associates) Mafalda Aguiar (Fundação Calouste Gulbenkian), Marco Albini (Fondazione Albini), Marinella Celli (Università di Bologna), Martin Buxtorf, Naji Moujaes (PAD10), Nuno Barradas, Rania Ghosn (MIT), Rashid Binshabib (University of Oxford), Saad Al-Zubaidi, Samir Alnimr, Sarah Al-Rukhayyes, Sara Machado, Saša Begović (FGAG), Seng Kuan (Washington University in St. Louis), Shehab A. H. Shehab (NCCAL), Stig Egnell, Sue Lowry (RIBA), Takis Candilis, Tarek Shuaib (PACE), Valeria Carullo (RIBA).

Finally the authors would like to thank Dar al Athar al-Islamiyyah team for the invaluable help and support: Abdulkareem Al-Ghadban, Osama Al-Balhan, Katherine Baker, Zeinab Tarhini, Madoura Rao (Administration and Coordination), Ahmed Al-Najadah, Mais Al-Othman, Dalal Mussalam, Harvey Pinces, Ali Akashah (Media), Fahed Al-Najadah, Syed Hashim Ali, Mustafa Rabeea (Exhibitions), Susan Day (Educational Program).

ظهرت خلال العقود الأخيرة عشرات الكتب التي توثق معالم المدن في مختلف أنحاء العالم. وقد سجلت تلك الكتب التغيرات التي طرأت على أساليب العمارة، وما يتبع ذلك من اختلاف في أنماط السلوك وسبل المعيشة. وتحفل الدوريات العلمية أيضا بفيض من البحوث والدراسات المتعلقة بهذا الموضوع. وجميع تلك الأعمال العلمية التي صدرت بلغات مختلفة تقدم ثروة من المعلومات والمخططات والصور التي تساعد في فهم علاقة التطورات العمرانية بحركة السكان والتحولات الاجتماعية المختلفة.

وقد جاء هذا الكتاب في وقته المناسب، إذ تشهد مدينة الكويت اليوم تحولات كبيرة سببتها القرارات الخاصة بنظم البناء، التي أطلقت العنان للارتفاع الرأسي للمباني؛ فقد تغير المنظر العام لمدينة الكويت خلال العقدين الأخيرين، وأصبحت مباني النهضة الحديثة التي تمثل النمط المعماري للمدينة في الستينيات وما بعدها على وشك الاستغناء عنها وهدمها. وإننا نشكر للمؤلفين مساراعتهم في توثيق تلك المباني والمبادرة إلى الكتابة عنها وتعريف المختص والقارئ العام بها.

وإنني على ثقة كبيرة أن المؤلفين قد بذلوا جهودا كبيرة في جمع مادة الكتاب وإعداده، فلم يكن الأمر مقصوراً على العمل الميداني والمكتبي، بل إنهم حرصوا على إجراء العديد من المقابلات مع مهندسين ومعماريين كانت لهم إسهاماتهم العملية في الكويت وحصلوا من خلالهم مالم تحفظه لنا أرشيفات المستخدمين لتلك المباني اليوم.

وقد كان لمركز البحوث والدراسات الكويتية تجربة تكشف عن مقدار الصعوبات التي واجهت الباحثين في هذا الكتاب، وذلك حينما تم تكليف المصور المشهور يان آرثوس – برتراند بتصوير معالم مدينة الكويت لكتاب "الكويت من عليائها". فقد كان التصوير ميسرا وسهلا، ولكن المركز فوجئ بالنقص الشديد في الحصول على بيانات عدد من المعالم العمرانية، بل إن كثيرا من المؤسسات لم تكن تعرف شيئًا عن المعماري الذي صمم البناء ولا الفلسفة التي يهدف إليها، ومن ثم لم يتم استخدام المكان على النحو الأمثل.

نكرر الشكر للمؤلفين الثلاثة المشتركين في هذا العمل: فقد قدموا مرجعا مهما في موضوعه، سيحتل مكانته اللائقة في المكتبة الكويتية، ونرجو أن يكون ذلك سببا في اهتمام الدولة والأفراد على حد سواء بالمحافظة على الهوية المعمارية لدولة الكويت، ووضع القوانين اللازمة لتحقيق ذلك.

ونشكر لدار الآثار الإسلامية، ممثلة في مديرتها الشيخة الأستاذة حصة صباح السالم الصباح، رعايتها لهذا العمل وحرصها على إصداره على النحو المأمول.

أ.د. عبدالله يوسف الغنيم
رئيس مجلس الإدارة ورئيس مركز البحوث و الدراسات الكويتية

Several books were published in recent decades, documenting the urban environment in different parts of the world. These books have recorded the changes in architectural styles and their consequent effects on social behaviour and ways of living. Scientific journals are also rich with relevant studies. All these works published in different languages provide a wealth of information with plans and photographs that help in understanding the relationship between urban developments and various social transformations.

This book has come at the right time, as Kuwait City undergoes significant transformation caused by decisions related to building codes. These decisions allowed buildings to reach unprecedented heights in the history of architecture in Kuwait. The landscape of Kuwait City has changed in the last two decades, and the post-oil style of architecture constructed in the sixties which marks the era of modernity and welfare have become on the verge of being demolished. We thank the authors for their devoted effort in documenting those buildings, for their initiative and concern to write and to inform specialists and general readers about them.
I am very confident that the authors have made a great effort in the preparation of this book. Their process was not limited to field and office work, but they have conducted many thorough interviews with engineers and architects who have made their professional contribution to the urbanisation of Kuwait and whose experience and knowledge is hard to find in archival materials.

Reflecting on the amount of difficulties the researchers may have faced in the development of this book, I recall a situation we have encountered in the Center for Research and Studies on Kuwait when Yann Arthus-Bertrand, the famous photographer, was commissioned to produce aerial views for the book "Kuwait from Above." While the shooting process was well facilitated, we struggled to find access to any architectural information about a number of buildings, for instance the architects who designed them, or the intended philosophy or programme for the way it should function and operate. Consequently, an efficient use of these buildings is barely managed by the entities occupying them.

We reiterate our thanks to the three authors involved in this work; they have offered an important reference on this theme. The work will occupy a decent place in the Kuwaiti library, and we hope that this effort draws the attention of the State and individuals alike to preserve the architectural identity of the State of Kuwait and enact the necessary laws to achieve it.

Thanks to Dar al-Athar al-Islamiyyah, represented by its Director-General Sheikha Hussah Sabah Al-Salem Al-Sabah, for her academic patronage and her eagerness to issue it as hoped.

Dr. Abdullah Y. Al-Ghuneim
Director of the Center for Research and Studies on Kuwait

BUILDING LOCATOR
1949–1989

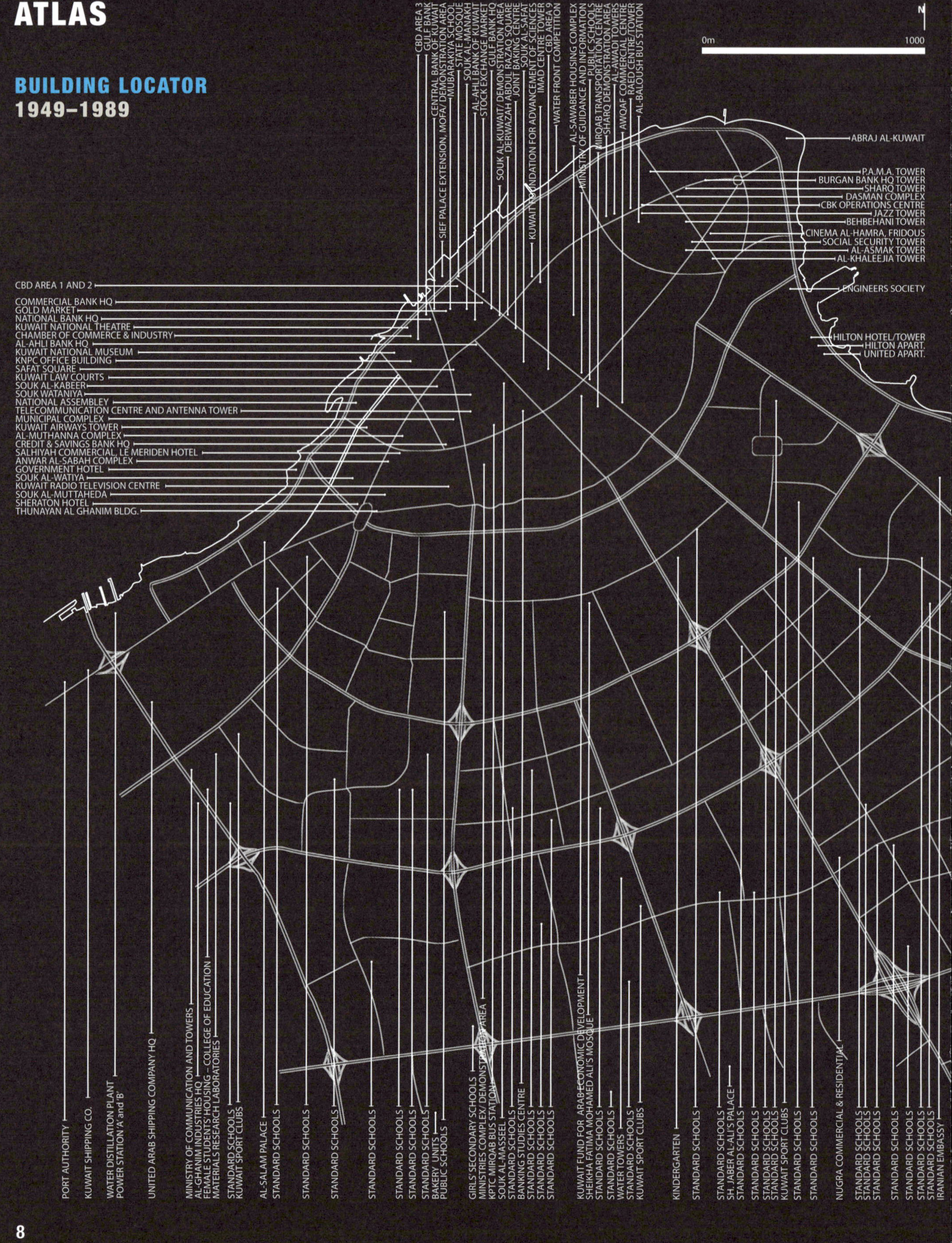

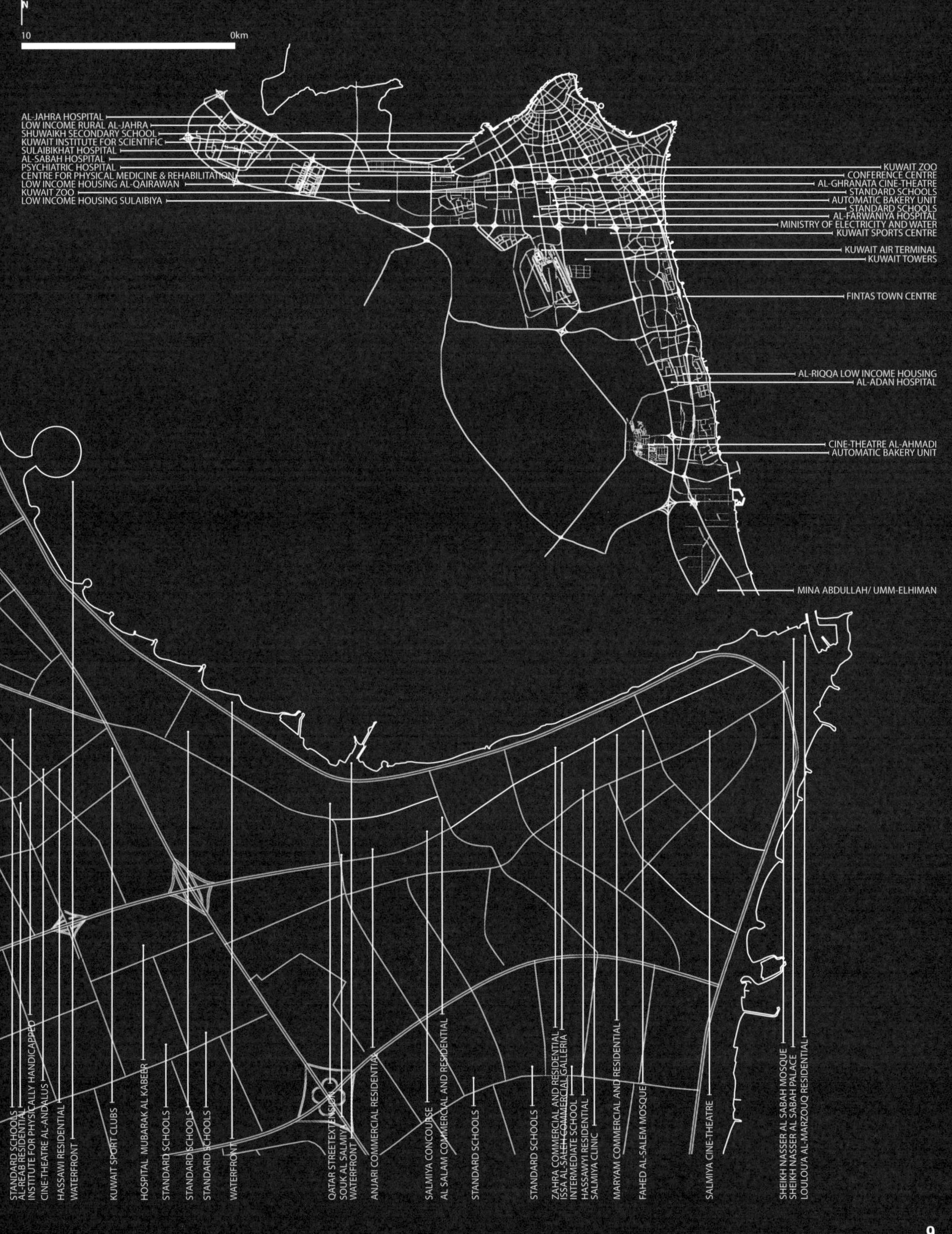

N
10   0km

AL-JAHRA HOSPITAL
LOW INCOME RURAL AL-JAHRA
SHUWAIKH SECONDARY SCHOOL
KUWAIT INSTITUTE FOR SCIENTIFIC
SULAIBIKHAT HOSPITAL
AL-SABAH HOSPITAL
PSYCHIATRIC HOSPITAL
CENTRE FOR PHYSICAL MEDICINE & REHABILITATION
LOW INCOME HOUSING AL-QAIRAWAN
KUWAIT ZOO
LOW INCOME HOUSING SULAIBIYA

KUWAIT ZOO
CONFERENCE CENTRE
AL-GHRANATA CINE-THEATRE
STANDARD SCHOOLS
AUTOMATIC BAKERY UNIT
STANDARD SCHOOLS
AL-FARWANIYA HOSPITAL
MINISTRY OF ELECTRICITY AND WATER
KUWAIT SPORTS CENTRE

KUWAIT AIR TERMINAL
KUWAIT TOWERS

FINTAS TOWN CENTRE

AL-RIQQA LOW INCOME HOUSING
AL-ADAN HOSPITAL

CINE-THEATRE AL-AHMADI
AUTOMATIC BAKERY UNIT

MINA ABDULLAH/ UMM-ELHIMAN

STANDARD SCHOOLS
AL-REAB RESIDENTIAL
INSTITUTE FOR PHYSICALLY HANDICAPPED
CINE-THEATRE AL-ANDALUS
HASSAWI RESIDENTIAL
WATERFRONT
KUWAIT SPORT CLUBS
HOSPITAL MUBARAK AL KABEER
STANDARD SCHOOLS
STANDARD SCHOOLS
STANDARD SCHOOLS
WATERFRONT
QATAR STREET EXTENSION
SOUK AL SALMIYA
WATERFRONT
ANJARI COMMERCIAL RESIDENTIAL
SALMIYA CONCOURSE
AL SALAM COMMERCIAL AND RESIDENTIAL
STANDARD SCHOOLS
STANDARD SCHOOLS
ZAHRA COMMERCIAL AND RESIDENTIAL
ISSA AL-SALEH COMMERCIAL GALLERIA
INTERMEDIATE SCHOOL
HASSAWYI RESIDENTIAL
SALMIYA CLINIC
MARYAM COMMERCIAL AND RESIDENTIAL
FAHED AL-SALEM MOSQUE
SALMIYA CINE-THEATRE
SHEIKH NASSER AL SABAH MOSQUE
SHEIKH NASSER AL SABAH PALACE
LOULOU'A AL-MARZOUQ RESIDENTIAL

0km

The Advisory Board, the international consultants invited for the "Urban Form Study of Old Kuwait City" and the Planning Committee of the Kuwait Municipal Council pose in a group picture in the courtyard of the Planning Department building. Undated, Spring 1970. Courtesy of Fondazione Franco Albini, Milan.

FRONT ROW, SEATED FROM LEFT TO RIGHT:

Reima Pietilä (1923–1993), *Invited Architect*; **Peter Smithson** (1923–2003), *Invited Architect*; **Colin Buchanan** (1907–2001), *Consultant for Kuwait Master Plan;* **Franco Albini** (1905–1977), *Advisory Group*; **Leslie Martin** (1908–2000), *Advisory Group*; **Hamid Shuaib** (1932–1994), *Assistant Under Secretary for Technical Affairs (Municipality)*; **Ahmad Al-Duaij** (1938–?), *Director-General of the Planning Board*; **Unidentified Housing Consultant**; **Lodovico Belgiojoso** (1909–2004), *Invited Architect*; **Gheorghios Candilis** (1913–1995), *Invited Architect*; **Raili Pietilä** (1926–), *Invited Architect*.

BACK ROW, STANDING FROM LEFT TO RIGHT:

Ghazi Sultan (1941–2007), Head of Counterpart Team (Municipality); **Unidentified Member of the Counterpart Team (Municipality)** ; **Unidentified Member of the Counterpart Team (Municipality)**; **Ian Haye**, Master Plan Consultant Working Team; **Unidentified Member of the Master Plan Consultant Working Team**; **Unidentified Member of the Master Plan Consultant Working Team**; **Raymond Story** (1941–2014), Director of the Master Plan Consultant Working Team; **Dr. Omar Azzam** (1930–), Advisory Group; **Puran Mehra**, Infrastructure Engineer of Master Plan Consultant Working Team; **Franklin Lee**, Master Plan Consultant Working Team; **Unidentified**; **Fahad Hassawi**, Head of Town Planning Department (Municipality); **Abbad Al Radi** (1944–) Master Plan Consultant Working Team; **Abdul Aziz Al Hamdan**, Head of Master Planning Department (Municipality); **Marco Albini** (1940–); **Unidentified**; **Abdalla Sabbar** (1939–), Master Plan Consultant Working Team; **Unidentified**; **Charles Haddad** (1934–), Division of Planning Projects (Municipality); **Unidentified Member of the Master Planning Department** (Municipality); **Kamal Al-Shaw**, Master Planning Department (Municipality); **Unidentified Member of the Master Planning Department** (Municipality).

MODERN ARCHITECTURE KUWAIT
The role of the building

In this period has grown the understanding that the building's action on the shaping of the territory and the spatial shaping of the territory itself should be at the centre of our work.[1]

(P. Smithson, 1996)

The undisputed literary cornerstone for those who would like to approach architectural studies about Kuwait is still Saba George Shiber's *The Kuwait Urbanization*.

Dated 1964, the book is a thorough and extensive reflection about the built environment of Kuwait during the period in which the author was involved as consultant in the Planning Board and participated in the international debate as one of the major critics of the Arab city's transformation.

On the one hand this collection of texts is a tool to advocate support for Shiber's thesis on city planning and his role played against the loose approach previously in place in Kuwait.[2] It describes the author's struggle to find solutions for the *original sin*: the demolition of the old traditional city. It also narrates his effort to suggest and implement a more organic city growth, a less scenographic approach and one which demonstrates a preference for the social use of space. On the other hand, it gives us a very clear picture of a capital city in the making, twelve years after the presentation of the First Master Plan to Sheikh Abdullah al-Salem al-Sabah, Amir of Kuwait. Shiber's sharp critiques certainly made an impression on his contemporary colleagues, even though his plans and projects were only partially implemented and in the following years, after his departure from Kuwait, the planning process took different directions.

While infrastructure, the road network and the new neighbourhood units were rigidly planned and implemented, the large scale projects for Kuwait

City—the old city centre—were never completely successful. The centre was progressively abandoned by the residents and transformed into an administrative and commercial district, and it now stands as a testimony of a non-completed vision.

The Western desire to explore the Middle East following the discovery of oil led to similar processes in a significant number of other small-sized cities in the region such as Doha or Dubai, and to the establishment of newly founded oil-towns. In the particular case of Kuwait, the formation of Ahmadi (1947–51), and its implementation through a corporate "Building Program" designed for the Kuwait Oil Company (KOC),[3] was a determinant in further approaching the city-state's redevelopment. The old coastal town was radically transformed by means of modern architecture in accordance with the population's social and economic aspirations. Its physical development assumed urban plans[4] and buildings that expressed the

Amir's political and social ambition to redistribute oil revenues and provide modern living conditions for all. From 1949, with the first commissions for power and water supply and distribution, modern architecture was able to translate these aspirations while displaying a particular setting of conditions that were new to the place. The Water Distillation Plant and Power Station in Shuwaikh and its distribution/ supply network, first opened in 1953, rendered two conditions that were particular to the preexisting mosques but not yet recognized as a planning tool: the potential role of the iconic building and the idea of the grid as a form of territorial control.

The construction of a city made of stand-alone buildings and a large highway network was then perceived as *a way to* Modernity. The rejection of the old buildings and urban conditions led finally to the demolition of the old town which had been progressively abandoned by the residents and replaced outside the city walls by neighbourhood units populated by, in Shiber's words "the modern and eclectic architecture of the omni-present villa."[5] Through the distribution of oil revenues, the State subsidised housing programs that allowed for "the assertion of an affluent individualism over all other urban form" and which "produced the (...) individual large house, set in a disproportionate building lot in relation to building bulk (...) that exposed the peripheral surface of the house to the harshness of the elements."[6] Such domestic culture became dominant, affecting the public building programs and transforming the city into a dense amalgamation of modern architectures which Shiber considered as structural misconceptions or paradoxes of good architecture. Referring to the new public buildings erected in Kuwait in the late 1970s, Lawrence Vale has written that "Most of these buildings [were] being treated like isolated islands in a sea of parking lots,"[7] highlighting how the lack of an organic urban connective ended up creating a cityscape made for cars more than for pedestrian circulation. In other words, citizens were estranged from the City. Modern Kuwait failed to integrate any earlier places or memories, lacking a clear urban identity, missing a *Genius Loci* and a civic sense of belonging.

To this day, the right of the City to take over land ownership for the purpose of providing land assets to its citizens, subsidised access to housing, and the aspirations for "a better future" dominate the social and economic spheres. Kuwait remains a merchant city where promises of industrialization and neoliberalism were defeated by the "affluent individualism" of its citizens and city officials devoted to the erection of their own modern monuments. Along with the exposure to the objective possibilities of new building forms, the citizens were seduced into the representation of glorified domestic industrial achievements, encouraged as a form of national pride. By their

size and volume, these exuberant buildings rapidly became dominant in the cityscape and were consequently represented in banknotes, stamps and postcards, projecting a hegemonic image of modernity.

Many of these buildings were produced by a certain elite of foreign architects and foreign-educated Kuwaitis who, during the 1970s, increasingly became aware of the modes of life, building materials and technologies particular to the region. The diversity of production sources, together with the strong motivation for experimentation, generated and continues to generate a series of remarkable architectural-urban models. The studies and the analytical schemes produced by these authors – including Hamid Shuaib, Ghazi Sultan, Alison and Peter Smithson, Candilis-Josic-Woods, Arthur Erickson, Luigi Moretti, and Jafar Tukan, large firms such as Pan Arab Consulting Engineers (PACE), BBPR Studio, Iraq Consult, The Architects Collaborative (TAC), Skidmore, Owings & Merrill (SOM), Doxiadis Associates, Ove Arup & Partners, VBB, Dorsch Consult, Energoprojekt, I. M. Pei & Partners, and more recently OMA, HOK, Fentress Architects, and AGI – offer substantive content to the debates on Arab town development in particular and urbanism and architecture in general.

"A Lost Identity"[8] for a "City of the Future"[9]

The emphasis on buildings and their material and technological performance has been the central object model to inform the architectural and urban design processes since the foundation of Ahmadi, the KOC oil town.

Ove Arup's final report for KOC on the desert sites at Ahmadi and Fahaheel, following a 16-day visit with Jane Drew in December 1946, identified the major challenges for the construction of the future city: the supply of coarse aggregate for concrete had to be collected from the desert by hand.

Arup wrote: "temperature range [is] from 36 to 118 in the shade, and sun temperatures up to 170. [The] preoccupations must be taken against the effects of heat expansion of materials."[10]

In the following year Drew, Maxwell Fry and Harry Ford published *Village Housing in the Tropics* and established some of the generalizations of their approach, later popularised by Alfred E. S. Alcock's albums *How to Build: To Size and Shape; Setting Out; Your Village.* However, in territories such as Kuwait, the efforts of MARS group members were more clearly exposed by the Head of the Civic Design Department at the University of Liverpool.[11] Prof. William G. Holford stated that in such contexts British architects should use British building technology but adopt the "indigenous crafts and materials [...] for decoration and embellishment of buildings."[12] The interest in promoting

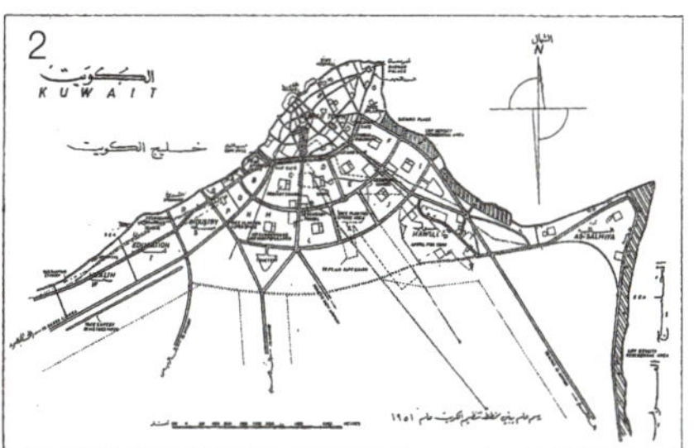

British construction industry *overseas* superseded Alcock's concerns regarding the lack of data to evaluate "the socio-economic status of those to be rehoused" and "the necessary knowledge and experience to forecast its future trends."[13]

From the Building Research Station in the United Kingdom, G. A. Atkinson defined the generic principles for Kuwait building design and John R. Harris was commissioned for the Building Research Laboratories in Kaifan (1952–54).[14] These laboratories would conduct an extensive program of research into the use of building materials in hot, dry climates over the coming years, leading to A. E. J. Morris's acknowledgement of "improvement in the design and detailing of construction projects in the Arabian Gulf and in many other similar parts of the world."[15]

In March 1961, Doxiadis formally introduced "The City of the Future" to Shiber through a letter that also included a questionnaire on Kuwait's urban characterisation. The reply was "as sketchy as the new image of Kuwait, in its fluid city shell." Shiber's questionnaire was mostly blank and it took three years more to finally send the completed volume of *The Kuwait Urbanization* to Doxiadis.[16]

Alison and Peter Smithson, who were called to Kuwait in 1968 to prepare urban form studies for the old city, preached for projects that could help to define a national identity. They called for buildings that, in their words, could carry that "quality" to differentiate Kuwait from other Arab cities, such as Cairo or Beirut. They envisioned buildings within the frame of the Arab urban tradition and adapted to contemporaneity, without variation taken from models in America, in Europe or in the Europeanised North Africa.[17] The urban form studies for the old city in the late 1960s catalysed the attention of major international designers working in synergy with local firms and local authorities. This enterprise left on the ground important examples of late modern architecture. As Kuwait gained independence and autonomy, the necessity of a new landscape to represent the freshly founded state grew high. A new urban environment was envisioned for a new state. Well-established international architects found the possibility here to expand their professional horizons and the challenge to compose an entire city, building by building, almost from scratch: an opportunity which was unfeasible, or at least less probable, in other parts of the world.

The extraordinary presence of important international designers, such as Alfred Roth, Pier Luigi Nervi, Basil Spence, and Jørn Utzon among many others, operating almost in the same period on a single city, was certainly a contribution in the desired new image of Kuwait. At the same time, like all such transformations that took place rapidly, it triggered criticisms of superimposing a different culture – and *taste* – onto local traditions. Such critiques, which are still largely diffused among the local population, do not consider that several renowned Arab designers were also involved in these years in the city's transformation, including Sayyed Karim, Mahmoud Riad, Dar al-Handasah, Hassan Fathy, Mohammed Makiya, and Rifat Chadirji, to name a few. Moreover, a new generation of young local architects emerged working side by side with these major international designers, which consequently impacted the work they were later able to accomplish independently on their home ground.

Kuwait always was, and still is, a crossroads between West and East. This strategic position is deeply reflected in the multicultural society that has developed over the last 60 years, a complex geography that can be drawn through the network of professional relations between the many actors involved in the city's transformation. The role of local institutions, the presence of numerous international consultants and contractors, and the growth of a local scene of designers and contractors are all fascinating aspects of this story.

About a Methodology

In light of such evidence there is ample support for the assumption that the phenomenon of Shiber's "fluid city shell" was no longer related to the implementation of large planning operations, though it has still substantial explanatory strength when it comes to the production of individual buildings. This, in turn, reinforces the conceptualisation of the architectural process as a mechanism of linkage through which architects, owners, contractors and contexts exert control over integral parts of the city's hierarchies, beyond the normative instruments of traditional planning.

"Modern Architecture Kuwait.1949–89," the MAK project, departs from this conceptualisation. These apparently uncorrelated works, described through mostly heretofore unknown information, are fundamental to providing tentative answers to a series of hypothetical questions: How were architectural design processes and practices developed from the early infrastructure of the 1950s to the invasion of 1990? How was architecture practiced in the absence of historical heritage, major local architectural references, strong morphological elements, or a strong urban footprint, and (occasionally) in the absence of adequate planning tools or their correct implementation?

The objective of MAK is to understand these dynamics of practice, rather than to produce a history of Kuwait's urban development. Consequently, the methods applied here concentrate the analysis on the multiple and built elements that compose the modern city, contextualizing the design practices and the architectural intentions behind them. Through the understanding of the territory as a *loose canvas* that allows the physical presence of these elements to be rendered in the urban landscape, it became clear that a survey of buildings was the principal subject of this investigation. The traditional methods of an urban-scale approach were inadequate to the task. Our investigation began therefore with architectural elements as pivotal subjects and with an intensive engagement with over 40 years of building production in Kuwait, including on-site visits, photographic surveys, archival research, and interviews with architects, planners, contractors, historians, and former city officials. This work was multiplied by extensive multidisciplinary and multimedia research using old city plans, building drawings, photographs, film footage, letters, legal documents, architectural and construction press, journals, popular press, and a range of other documents, including the portfolios and corporate profiles of design firms and contractors, in order to document every possible construction or building project comprised in those years. By focusing on the professional trajectories of these designers and by reading the presence of these buildings in the urban environment at the architectural scale, the research examines and analyses a selection of buildings which is finally presented here as an *architectural atlas*.

This repertoire of hundreds of buildings is revealed as a collection of *specimens*, selected for their specific qualitative aspects, as examples of particular design methodologies or typologies, or else for their different adaptations to the severity of local environmental conditions. The method applied here has been simultaneously read the differing chronologies and geographic linkages of urban and architectural practice in order to understand dynamics of change and innovation in terms of design principles, the city fabric and construction technology. As a result, a different

narrative from that of the chronological survey came to the forefront — what the building actually does, contrary to what it was intended or designed to do. In this way, the project pursues the value of the built object in the city beyond its function or program.

The final building selection involved a complex process of inclusion and exclusion. Some buildings are unequivocally – sometimes rhetorically – considered local landmarks, such as the National Assembly, the Abraj Al-Kuwait (the Kuwait Towers) or the State Mosque, while other types, such as single and multi-family dwelling units, exist in such numbers and diversity that they were impossible to account for and characterise in an overview study such as this and for that reason were excluded. With regard to housing, exceptions were made for certain mixed-use typologies, such as Hassawi

Residential and the Nugra and Dasman Complexes, that are relevant for their authors, their complexity of scale or their importance for understanding the city, as one can also argue in the cases of Al-Muthanna or the Rehab Complexes. The same approach gradually led the research into the systematic analysis of lesser-known projects, such as the Shuwaikh Power Station and Desalination Plant or the Kuwait Shipping Company offices, as well as unbuilt proposals such as the Sports Centre or the Low-Income Housing Schemes.

In this intricate realm, the availability of sources played a very important role in the selection of buildings. Despite the acknowledged efforts of some major local firms, it was not easy to gain access to primary sources in Kuwait, which are often dispersed or forgotten. Needless to say, some buildings could not be described here given the lack of these supports. On the contrary, the international projects, once discovered, were found to be well documented in archives, but these were scattered all over the world. It took the collaboration of several fellow researchers to collect these documents, creating a long-distance network of exchanges.

The research identified a selection of around 150 projects covering a span of 40 years. A major effort was invested in creating a timeline and biographical references of architects, planners and contractors that could put these projects in relation to the region's recent history as well as to the architectural

scene of the Middle East. In a second moment, local and foreign scholars and researchers were invited to develop further a critical understanding of the city and its buildings. These analyses will be published in a second volume of this project.

The Role of the Building

In the course of selecting and chronologically mapping the buildings, it became clear that the diversity inherent to architecture and urban practice in Kuwait were overdetermined by the city's history and geography of modernisation. The chronological organization of the buildings in four chapters in the book allows a reading across historical time of the interactive processes by which the city was gradually generated and, through authored projects, the city's image. Such an organization highlights the role of practices, and of urban architectural knowledge, in the process of generating the city.

I. Building as infrastructure

The first of these chapters reflects the first generation of the country's modern architecture and its foundational principles established by an elite group of British designers, contractors and officials. The core of this early development process was made of schools, power plants, hospitals,

administrative and governmental offices. Among these, the usage and the construction technique and material were dominant parameters. Although projects such as the Southwell Hospital in Ahmadi (1951–60), the Vocational Technical College (1953–54) in Shuwaikh and the Institute for the Physically Handicapped (1963–69) preceded later attempts by the Smithsons and Candilis, Josic and Woods to conceptualize low-rise, highly dense building types. Following Alison Smithson's publication on "How to Recognise and Read Mat-building" for the British Magazine *Architectural Design* in 1974 and their proposal for the Ministries Complex (1969–72), these typologies became popular references in many of the design briefs for schools and public institutions in Kuwait during the 1980s.

II. Building as national identity

The projects collected in the second section consider buildings but also some of the medium-scale urban schemes that best represent the *Pan-Arab Spirit* of the *"Al-Imara al-Haditha"* (modern architecture). The term coined by Ihsan Sherzad for Iraq is commonly used by local scholars and historians to refer to the work of Sayyed Karim in Kuwait and to Shiber's well-known "architectural control."[18] These principles express an ideal and mature Arab state seeking to establish its own national identity

through projects of often larger scale and international projection that could finally render the *City of the Future*. A fluid territory in which projects such as the Khaldiya Girls' Secondary School or the Governmental Hotel, for example, were allowed to change location or function within the span of a few years. Furthermore, Shiber's efforts to promote the revision of the First Master Plan through zoned and detailed urban plans led to the creation of the Central Business District Areas. In these areas Shiber called for the "rational building" of a "type of architecture suited for Kuwait."[19] The considerable number of buildings erected in these districts were either designed by Shiber and his team or through international design competitions, which diversified the design approaches from those discussed in the first chapter. For instance, the Grand Corniche and the redevelopment of the old city harbour area constituted proposals for the first large-scale development process that was open to urban design and in which Shiber pursued the ideal environment for this *City of the Future*.[20]

III. Building as cityscape

The complexity and experiences resulting from such operations prompted a new elite of city officials, such as Hamid Shuaib and Ghazi Sultan, to look into the city's historical layers and read them against the regulation plans. In the third chapter

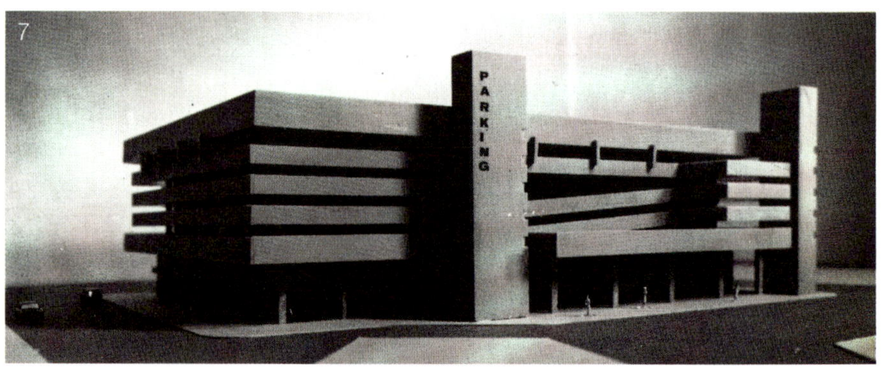

of *specimens* it becomes clear how the unstable environment of Kuwait's urbanisation made conventional methods of planning and urban homogenisation difficult to implement in subsequent years. In 1968 the invitation to Prepare Urban Form Studies for the Old City, given to Alison and Peter Smithson, Reima and Raili Pietilä, Candilis, Josic and Woods, and BBPR, and the multiple design competitions for Low-Income Housing Schemes, called for more agile and assertive techniques of intervention. What was expected from these proposed architectures was not simply a vision of future development but the actual capacity to generate physical impact in shaping the city's visual appearance, as well as the functionality of the cityscape itself.

The brief for Al-Riqqa Low-Income Housing, addressed to Jafar Tukan, requested "units of classic Arab design, in harmony with local architecture."[21] Meanwhile, Macklin L. Hancock called for an *Islamic-Arabic* inherited approach to "understand how this can be achieved [considering] materials which will help to keep maintenance costs low [and] effective solutions to technical problems unique to this part of the world."[22] During the 1970s practices such as Iraq Consult, PACE, KEO, KEG, and Sabah Abi-Hanna (later SSH) initiated a remarkable body of work related to the private development of mixed-used programs which sought, in their own ways, the aesthetic values identified by Hancock.

The functionality of this new cityscape required strategies that were architectural as well as urban. It required urban buildings that engaged the city at the level of the urban plan. In this sense, the Demonstration Areas, identified as consequences of the 1968 Urban Form Studies for the Old City fully expressed this condition: "The intention was to illustrate principles by actual buildings for known demands."[23] This initiative resulted in multiple modern souqs and high-rise buildings

scattered all across Kuwait City. The consultant to the Municipality, Roland Kluver, encouraged the idea of a *self-contained unit* in order to recover the residential component within the city centre.[24] The ambition of the late Sheikh Sabah Al-Salem Al-Sabah, was here finally rendered throughout different projects: "Kuwaitis are entranced by the fanciful idea of roofing over Kuwait and air-conditioning it all, with powerful planetariums projecting beautiful skies day and night. This little country has the money to think big."[25]

IV. Building as programme

Finally, during the 1980s, Kuwaitis' extensive interest in building construction became more of a business matter rather than a welfare policy. The celebration of the building boom uncritically offered the city up to market forces. The capitalization of formal and informal stock exchanges in Kuwait was by 1982 ranked third in the world, behind the US and Japan. But by the summer the Kuwait informal market stopped trading. The Souq Al-Manakh crash, still referred to until recently as "the greatest stock market bubble of all time," revealed the volatility of oil and the speculative finance economy prevalent in the country.[26] In the following year construction in Kuwait dropped by 50%, leading to the interruption of some of the undergoing projects, and eventually to the bankruptcy of contracting firms and designers such as TAC. Within this scenario, the fourth chapter covers the remaining interval of production until the Iraqi Invasion in 1990. This time frame of uncertainty represented a new beginning in urban policy, which eventually extended beyond the Invasion. As a result, architects and other building actors were forced to adjust to frequent changes and learned how to instrumentalise these changes in their own interest, claiming the autonomy of the discipline from the building function as an attempt to revive local tradition and culture. In

this way, the building program became the central argument to provide the spatial nature and capacity to evoke visual imaginaries and aspirations. The architecture elements are then defined by the choice of either parties and oscillated between exuberance and some disillusionment with the Modern. The Conference Centre in Bayan is a clear reference to this: the architecture of Sava Centar, the most modern convention centre at the time and once called the technological marvel of Tito in Belgrade, is here reinterpreted in a typology of the past claiming for other architectural roots than those being displayed in the city buildings. Initially without purpose the Conference Centre was the excuse to perform the scale and exuberance to which the country aspired.

Under the guidance of well-educated owners or client representatives, building practice often developed into personalized and emotional narratives, proper to a post-modern condition and well described by Krzysztof Wiśniowski, co-author of the Port Authority Headquarters. For this project Wiśniowski recalls the Centre Georges Pompidou being a strong reference in the client's requests, consequentially bringing more *analogical* arguments into the design process: "the four car ramps were [conceived] as mooring lines that secure a *Dhow*."[27] The Arab Organizations Headquarters Building in Shuwaikh, developed between 1982–90 by Mohamed

Makkiyah in association with Archicentre and completed in 1994 by PACE, is a good example of a design process initiated here and perpetuated to this day.

Mapping Modernity in Kuwait

Each *specimen* was dissected, analysed and presented here as part of the kaleidoscopic heritage of modern architecture in Kuwait. Time-wise, *Modernism* is conventionally situated in the first half of the 20th century and geographically placed, in most cases, in Europe or in the Americas. The definition of *Modern Architecture* is widely misused, often confused – for example with *contemporary* – and is not conducive to shaping a close classification, especially if it is understood that a real *modern movement* never really existed as one tight movement with a single agenda, but rather through multiple contingent collaborations, debates, and confrontations between architects and artists that often shared highly divergent points of view and approaches to design.

Marcel Breuer, whose studio was also involved in Kuwait at a later stage of his career, expresses in an undated note his concern regarding the word *modern*, for the multiplicity of meanings that it can trigger. He labelled it as an excellent sales term, and as such he tried to elaborate the concept in a way that seemed relevant for this research:

Now, if we use the term 'modern architecture' I mean something quite different. And I should say that I call the most modern architecture the one which longest remains 'modern'. [...] In the sense in which I use this term, modern design or architecture is not a form or a motif, but rather an instinct, or rather, a tendency. [...] As I mentioned before, not the outside characteristics are real significance of this movement but rather the fundamental instincts behind its

forms. Going down to the roots of our work, I see three basic principles: First: the direct approach. Second: the tendency for clarity. Third: the tendency to create with truthful elements; (or indifference to create with forms of illusion, or with decorative covering forms).[28]

These basic principles also suggest common characteristics among the varieties of different buildings, from different times and by different authors, that have been selected to compose this study. The Kuwaiti architectural context can perhaps be better inscribed in the frame of *other Modernisms*, borrowing the – nowadays frequently used – title of the Do.co.mo.mo (Docomomo International) Conference in Turkey 2006, which gave an impulse to reconsider less orthodox forms of Modernism.

Recovering a Lost Identity

Modernisation efforts were halted in 1990, and after the Invasion for the first time since the inception of the Antiquities Law in 1960,[29] conservation ideas began to take hold. Nevertheless, following the death of Saddam Hussein in late 2006, the country recovered its trust in a certain future and new initiatives for design and building started without the addition of any critique of the prior standards.

As with other cities in the region, the town centre of Kuwait has suffered a gradual deterioration in areas once characterised by their modern architecture, and today faces the challenge of conservation, confronted with the current processes of urban development. The residential urban periphery, although an urban fabric characterised by single-unit structures, includes a number of modern buildings of significant quality that have been modified or are at risk of demolition. In fact, the value of these modern structures is not always understood, so that often the buildings are demolished and replaced. This phenomenon

has been encouraged by an elite of politicians, scholars and even architecture and planning practitioners that have labelled these architectures as *foreign* and therefore implicitly indifferent to local history and building tradition. Only recently, under narratives of *nation building* through memory and identity, an emerging community of young, well-educated artists and professionals from the most varied sectors of society has started to project an *archaeological status* onto these buildings, urging for their preservation.

Among the major motivations for conducting this study are the lack of knowledge and common misconceptions of the architecture produced within this timeframe in Kuwait. Kuwaiti citizens often show disaffection and a low sense of belonging to these spaces, and the authorities have taken very few measures in the past to promote the conservation and restoration of this important heritage. Erasing this part of Kuwait's national history, as well as its international architectural heritage, is a major loss for the country, and a missed opportunity to investigate the country's recent past. The magnitude of this problem is easily demonstrated by the fact that since this study began at least three major buildings, all present in this book, have been demolished to create space for brand-new towers, while others have been deeply modified or covered with shiny aluminium cladding. While it is impossible not to feel a deep sense of loss every time a trace of the past has been erased, it is equally impossible to pursue preservation practice or policies without creating a proper baseline. This requires a scientific, systematic database similar, for instance, to Evangelia Simos Ali's survey of Kuwait's surviving pre-oil structures, conducted in the early 1980s.[30]

Two major goals can be ascribed to the survey presented here. First, to create the first database of the most significant modern architectural *specimens* in Kuwait, identifying the key players and distinctive features of relevance to both the culture of Kuwaiti citizens and a wider professional audience. Second, to reopen the discussion of building conservation decisions and an examination of emerging approaches related to the rehabilitation and adaptive reuse of modern architecture, nowadays suffering from a lack of recognition and an almost non-existent framework of legal protection. Contrary to the idea of fossilisation in a sort of a *modern archaeological park*, where every building becomes a *monument* to itself or a *museum*, compatible transformations can perhaps bring back life to the abandoned and re-establish new functions for the outdated.

A renewed architectural consciousness has emerged in recent years throughout the several publications, articles, exhibitions, conferences and lectures hosted both in academic and cultural contexts in Kuwait. These efforts have made modern architecture in Kuwait and the Middle East the main subjects of academic research for local and international scholars and research institutes, which MAK has acknowledged throughout this research.

A peak of this ongoing process can also be read in the participation of Kuwait in the last two architectural editions of *La Biennale di Venezia*, where the national pavilions were produced by local curators around the subject of national heritage. All of these combined efforts have been capped by the submission of *Abraj Al-Kuwait* to be listed as a UNESCO World Heritage Site. If successful, this will be the first nomination for the modern architectural and urban heritage of Kuwait. The blogosphere, a space in which a mass audience sharing comments and thoughts on the subject of the city in transformation becomes visible, has led to more tangible actions in the street, like the first public protest against the demolition of the old Chamber of

Commerce, in 2014. For those who are not familiar with the Gulf, this is not common.

In the authors' intentions, more than producing an exhaustive representation of 40 years of architectural practice in Kuwait, the aspiration is to deepen our knowledge of the city's built environment, with the declared intention of informing contemporary architectural and urban practice. A better understanding of this important heritage can open architects, planners and city officials to a different *way of doing*, providing not only a collection of information, documents and drawings, but a practical tool that could trigger a better use of these buildings.

1. Peter Smithson referring to 1978 in the foreword to Vidotto, Marco, *Alison + Peter Smithson. Obras y Proyectos. Works and Projects*, GG, Barcellona 1997, p. 8

2. Cf. Nasr, Joe, "Saba Shiber, 'Mr. Arab Planner.' Parcours professionnel d'un urbaniste au Moyen-Orient,» in *Géocarrefour*, v. 80, n. 3, 2005

3. Alissa, Reem, *Building for Oil: Corporate Colonialism, Nationalism and Urban Modernity in Ahmadi, 1946–1992*, University of Berkeley, 2012. Ph.D. diss.

4. Minoprio, Spencely, and P. W. Macfarlane. *Plan for the Town of Kuwait. Report to His Highness Shaikh Abdullah Assalim Assubah, C. I. E. The Emir of Kuwait. 1951*, Center for Research and Studies on Kuwait Archives

5. Shiber, Saba G., "Kuwait, the Growth of a Town," in *Middle East Forum*, Summer 1962, pp. 54–59

6. Ibid.

7. Vale, Lawrence, *Architecture, Power and National Identity*, 1992, Yale University Press, p. 259

8. Husayn, Habib; Sager, Saud, *Kuwait Architecture. A Lost Identity*, documentary, Dar al-Athar al-Islamiyyah, K.T.V. production, 1993

9. The City of the Future (COF) was the first research project launched by Constantinos A. Doxiadis with John G. Papaioannou in 1958 with the initial aim to compile an extensive survey on the urban environment involving 100 experts from different fields.

10. "Report on Kuwait," Ref. ARUP 7/45, *The Papers of Sir Ove Arup*, Churchill Archives Centre, Churchill College, Cambridge, UK

11. The English CIAM group, the Modern Architectural Research Group (MARS) established in 1933, emerged as a planning elite in the UK after World War II. Its members took leading roles in education, the development of post-war city plans and the preparation of new planning legislation. Among them were Maxwell Fry, Jane Drew, Ove Arup, Arthur Korn, William G. Holford, and Leslie Martin. "Modern Architecture Is Universal, Infinitely Adaptable" in *MARS, Modern Architecture*, London, n. 20, 1938

12. Foyle, Arthur M.(ed), *Conference on Tropical Architecture 1953: A Report on the Proceedings of the Conference Held at University College, London, March, 1953*, George Allen & Unwin, 1954

13. Alcock is quoted in a letter from G. A. Atkinson to William Holford, 19 May 1951, about the Volta River Survey Resettlement, cited in Holland, Jessica; Jackson, Iain, *The Architecture of Edwin Maxwell Fry and Jane Drew: Twentieth Century Architecture, Pioneer Modernism and the Tropics*, Ashgate Publishing Ltd., 2014

14. Atkinson ,George A., "West Indian Houses," in *Architectural Association Journal*, 67, February 1952, pp. 194–199

15. Morris, A.E. J, *John R. Harris Architects*, Hurtwood, Westerham, Kent 1984, p. 8

16. Correspondence between C. A. Doxiadis and S. G. Shiber, 04/03/1961– 24/01/1966, Ref.17854, C. A. Doxiadis Archive, Athens

17. Vidotto, Marco, 1997, *op. cit.*, p.138

18. The term was coined by Shiber in July 1960 for the municipality's control over the architectonic qualities of commissioned design projects through mediated discussions between architects, planners, and proprietaries. In some situations this control was formalised through regulations such as the Fahad Al-Salem Street façade code or the CBD areas building code. Cf. Shiber, Saba G., *The Kuwait Urbanization*, Kuwait Govt. Printing Press, Kuwait,1964

19. Shiber, Saba G., 1962, *op. cit.*

20. Shiber, Saba G., 1964, *op. cit.*

21. *Project Brief for Al-Rikka Low Income Rural Housing Scheme*, Credit & Savings Bank, Kuwait, 1966

22. Hancock, Macklin L., *Architectural Conception of Buildings in Accordance with Twentieth Century Islamic-Arabic Style*, Kuwait Municipality, Jan. 1969

23. "Proposals for Restructuring Kuwait," in *The Architectural Review*, v.156, Sep. 1974, pp. 178–182

24. Kluver was a Principal at TAC. See Biographical Notes

25. De Carvalho, George, "Everything Up to Date in Kuwait," in *Life Magazine*, Sep. 15 1965, p. 106

26. Kubo, Michael, "Oil-Slick: Middle Eastern Economy and Late-Modern Aesthetics," *Disappearing Non-West Conference*, Columbia, May 2012

27. Interview with Krzysztof Wiśniowski, Mar. 2014

28. Breuer, Marcel, *Defining Modern Architecture*, typescript, undated. Marcel Breuer Papers, 1920–1986. Series 6.1: Speeches and lectures, Archives of American Art, Smithsonian Institution

29. State of Kuwait, *Decree on the Antiquities Law*, n. 11, 1960

30. Ali, Evangelia Simos, *Kuwait Historical Preservation Study-Old Kuwait Town*, v. 1, Kuwait Municipality, Kuwait, 1988

IMAGE CAPTIONS:

1. Kuwait City, Jan.–Feb. 1977 (Tor Eigeland / Saudi Aramco World/SAWDIA)

2. Minoprio & Spencely and P.W. Macfarlane, Plan for the Town of Kuwait: Report to the Amir of Kuwait, November, 1951. (Kuwait Municipality Master Plan Department)

3. John R. Harris, Building Research Laboratories in Kaifan, 1952–54. (Architectural Design, Mar. 1957, v. 27, n. 3)

4. Sayyed Karim, Ahmadi Cinema,1962–65, Independence day celebrations, Jun. 1966. (KOC Archive, Kuwait)

5. Maxwell Fry and Jane Drew, Southwell Hospital in Ahmadi, 1951–60, and same authors, book cover of *Tropical Architecture in the Humid Zone*, Reinhold International Library Series, London, Batsford, 1956

6. Robert Wakim (Dar Al-Handasah), Kuwait Radio & Television Station, c. 1957 (CAT Archive, Beirut)

7. Rais & Tukan, Multi-Storey Car Park (Souq), proposal for United Realty Company, 1974 (Rais & Tukan Corporate Brochure, ACA Archive, Beirut)

8. Gulf Engineering Office (GEO), Souq Dawliyah under construction, Kuwait City, 1978 (E. Lach Archive, Wrocław)

9. Protest against the demolition of the Kuwait Chamber of Commerce Building, 2014

10. Sami Abdul Baki, Ministry of Finance, 1959–62 (*Al-Kuwait Magazine*, 1964)

TIMELINE
A chronological context for
architecture in Kuwait

YEAR	KUWAIT GENERAL	KUWAIT ARCHITECTURE	SPECIMENS	POP	MIDDLE EAST ARCHITECTURE
1945				90,000	New Gourna Village, Luxor, Egypt by Hassan Fathy
1946	Amir Sheikh Ahmad Al-Jaber Al-Sabah inaugurated the export of Kuwait's FIRST CRUDE OIL SHIPMENT Oil production began KOC and the Government initiated extensive water exploration programs	Kuwait Preliminary Building Programme by Jane Drew and Ove Arup			Ferdowsi University, Mashhad, Iran by Fry & Drew
1947	The Occupation of Palestine by Israel and end of British occupation of Iraq leading to the massive migration of refugees to Kuwait. Iraq (12,612), Palestine (12,488), Lebanon (6,006), Oman (4,732) for a total of 64,642 immigrants including 1,854 UK citizens First printing press established in Kuwait (Al-Ma'arif) J.D.Moody oil-prospection survey	Ahmadi Master Plan "Kuwait Building Programme – Housing, Municipal and Amenity Works: 1947–1951"			Sa'adat Nas'sajan Company's Factory, Yazd, Iran Al-Khobar City, Saudi Arabia by Aramco Amelieh School, Beirut, Lebanon by Said Hjeil
1948	Kazima published *Al-Baath* periodical Admiralty Chart showing limits of Kuwait's territorial waters	Power+Water Desalination Plant, Mina Al Ahmadi New Street in Kuwait City Centre completed			UNESCO Palace, Beirut, Lebanon, by Farid Trad, Alexis Boutros Faculty of Sciences and Literature, Istanbul University, Turkey, by Sedad Hakki Eldem and Emin Onat
1949	*The Arab of the Desert* by H.R.P. Dickson, Allen and Unwin Wilfred Thesiger visual survey (photographic)	Ahmadi General Hospital, housing, clinics and social amenities commission by Fry & Drew	**WATER DISTILLATION PLANT/ POWER STATION** in Fahaheel tendered		Madrasat Jaafariya, Baghdad, Iraq by Jafar Allawi
1950	Sheikh Ahmad Al-Jaber Al-Sabah died H.H. Sheikh Abdullah Al-Salem Al-Sabah became Amir First issue of *Al-Ra'id* periodical published			152,000	Heliopolis Hospital, Cairo, Egypt, by Mustafa Shawky and Salah Zeitoun Le Centre Lazarieh, Beirut, Lebanon, by André Leconte
1951	50/50 agreement on oil profit share Land Acquisition Policy (LAP) created British Royal Air Forces aerial photography survey Major public-works programme began Kuwait's infrastructure transformed Kuwait residents first enjoyed a high standard of living	Minoprio & Spencely and P.W. Macfarlane commissioned for the "Preliminary Study of Kuwait Urban Development" Plan for the Town of Kuwait Photographic survey of Kuwait by the Royal Air Force Government launched land acquisition programme Kuwait Development Board established	**SHUWAIKH SECONDARY SCHOOL** commission CAT Group to design and build **WATER DISTILLATION PLANT/ POWER STATION** in Shuwaikh commissioned		Baghdad Railway Station, Iraq by J.M. Wilson & H.C. Mason
1952	Development and Welfare Board established The National Bank of Kuwait established Case, Paul Edward, *Boom Time in Kuwait*, The National Geographic, Dec. Kuwait Science and Natural History Museum established	Kuwait Master Plan by Minoprio & Spencely and P.W. Macfarlane Tripe & Wakeham Partnership to design palace for one of the ruling family members Shuwaikh Harbour and Jetty by Sir William Halcrow	**PUBLIC SCHOOLS PROGRAM** commissioned Tripe & Wakeham Partnership to design John R. Harris appointed for the design of **KUWAIT RESEARCH LABORATORIES**	160,000	Qatar State Hospital Design Competition, winning entry by John R. Harris Rue des Banques, Beirut, Lebanon Martyrs' Monument, Beirut, Lebanon, commission won by Sami Abd Al-Baqi
1953	First issue of *Al-Imam* periodical The Kuwait Investment Authority (KIA) founded as the world's first sovereign wealth fund	First power station inaugurated	**KUWAIT RESEARCH LABORATORIES** completed **POWER STATION A** inaugurated		AUB Alumni Club Building, Design Competition
1954	Kuwait National Airways founded reorganization of Public Works Dept, Municipality and Health Department ; Major General Hasted, British Political Agency resigned Hadama: destruction of the mudbrick structures by heavy rainfall. 2000 homes destroyed Kuwait National Cinema Company founded First issue of *Kuwait Al-Youm* official gazette	Dasmah Neighbourhood Unit Plan and Construction, Minoprio & Spencely and P.W. Macfarlane Shuwaikh Neighbourhood Unit construction Ahmadi "Arab Village" construction began Ministry of Public Works and Social Affairs appointed its first planning adviser Sheikh Jaber Abdullah Al-Sabah founded a zoo in Salwa Park Demolition and removal of the 3rd Kuwait City wall was agreed upon preserving the gates	**SULAIBIKHAT HOSPITAL** commissioned John R. Harris **CINEMAS**, first inaugurated **PUBLIC SCHOOLS PROGRAM** Completion of Central Kitchen design by Tripe & Wakeham Partnership	250,000	Town Plan for Ummaidieh, Iran, by Fry & Drew National Bank of Iraq, Design Competition for Baghdad by Alvar Aalto and Gio Ponti, William Dunkle Rifat Chadirji residence, Baghdad, Iraq, by Rifat Chadirji Dar Al-Sayad, Lebanon by Karl Chayer, Wassek Adib, and Bahije Makdissi

YEAR	KUWAIT GENERAL	KUWAIT ARCHITECTURE	SPECIMENS	POP	MIDDLE EAST ARCHITECTURE
1955	Construction of Kaifan Neighbourhood Construction of Shamiyah Neighbourhood Oil discovered in Al-Rawdatain field Kuwait Chamber of Commerce and Industry established	The Council of Construction established Fahaheel Road Completed American Mission Hospital (Mylrea Memorial or Men's Hospital) opened	**SHEIKH JABER AL-ALI PALACE** commissioned Farmer & Dark to design		Arab League Headquarters, Cairo, Egypt by Mahmoud Riad Abboud Tower, Baghdad, Iraq by Abdullah Ihsan Kamil Senate house of Iran, Tehran by Heydar Ghiai and Mohsen Foroughi Museum of Modern Art in Tehran, Iran Competition Entry by B. Khatiblou, M. Foroughi and A. Farmanfarma Collège Protestant Français, Beirut, Lebanon by Michel Écochard, Claude Lecoeur Pan American Building, Beirut, Lebanon by George Rayes, Theo Kanaan & Assem Salam Hilton Hotel, Istanbul, Turkey, by SOM
1956	Construction of Faiha Neighbourhood Government Possession Council established *Kuwait And Her Neighbours*, by H.R.P. Dickson, Allen and Unwin Kuwait News Agency established Mass arrival of Palestinian refugees British Council established in Kuwait Proclamation of the achievement of Kuwait Oil industry in Khafji (Saudi Arabia) started with Pan Petroleum Trading Company Ltd (future Arabian Oil Company)	KOC Display Centre in Ahmadi founded *Plans of Towns in Kuwait. GSGS 4879, Kuwait Town*, published by D. Survey, British War Office and Air Ministry	**PUBLIC SCHOOLS PROGRAMME** inaugurated in Sallahiddine, Salmiyah, Al Siddiq, Jahrah, Magwa, Tarik, Muhallab **MUNICIPAL COMPLEX** commissioned		Baghdad Master Plan by Minoprio, Spencely & MacFarlane Daftar Dar Building, Baghdad, Iraq by Abdullah Ihsan Kamil Riyadh Ministry buildings, Saudi Arabia by Sayed Karim Middle East Technical University, Faculty of Architecture, Turkey established Sports Complex and Gymnasium, Baghdad, Iraq proposal by Le Corbusier
1957	Demolition and removal of the 3rd Kuwait City wall 11,659 shanty homes surveyed in Kuwait The Social Affairs Department conducted 1st population census National Museum established O'B. Perry and B.H. Al-Refai oil-prospection survey Kuwait Olympic Committee established 55 state-schools, including four mixed kindergartens built	Development of Fahad Al Salem St. Sheikh Fahad Salem Al-Mubarak Al-Sabah Director of Public Works and the Municipality Kuwait National Museum established **RIFAT CHADIRJI** commissioned to design Hammad Villa in Salmiya Di'iya Neighbourhood Unit construction Kuwait's First Demography Report **FINTAS DEVELOPMENT PLAN** by Minoprio & Spencely and P.W. Macfarlane **"Architecture in the Middle East," by RAGLAN SQUIRE in Architectural Design** Dar Al-Handasah comissioned for Power Station 'C' Palace of Sheikh Abdullah Al-Jaber Al-Sabah converted in Kuwait National Museum	**THUNAYAN AL-GHANIM BUILDING** commissioned Sayed Karim to design **SHUWAIKH SECONDARY SCHOOL** completed **GOVERNMENT PRINTING PRESS** proposal by Sayed Karim (Ministry of Guidance and Information) **GIRL'S SECONDARY SCHOOL** first proposal for Bneid Al-Gar **WATER DISTILLATION PLANT** distillated water for a population of 200,000	206,473	Carlton Hotel, Beirut, Lebanon by Karol Schayer & Wassek Adib with Bahij Makdisi Nile Ritz Carlton, former Nile Hilton, Cairo, Egypt by Welton Becket and Mahmoud Riad Nile Ritz Carlton, former Nile Hilton, Cairo, Egypt by Welton Becket and Mahmoud Riad Baghdad University Campus Master Plan, Iraq, by TAC with Hisham A. Munir Iraq National Museum of Archeology, Iraq by Werner March Khan Pasha Building, Baghdad, Iraq by Abdullah Ihsan Kamil Hebrew University Synagogue, Jerusalem, by Heinz Rau and David Reznik Plan for Sadr City and Mosul, Iraq by Doxiadis Associates Ministry of Finance, Doha, Qatar by John R. Harris Villa Nemazee, Tehran, Gio Ponti College Protestant, Lebanon, by Michel Ecochard and others Anadolu Club, Buyukada, Istanbul, Turkey, by Turgut Cansever and Abdurrahman Hanci
1958	First Housing Committee established First issue of *Al-Arabi* magazine published 1st Arab Art Exhibition (first pan-Arab art exhibition) Oil-concession agreement with the Japanese Arabian Oil Company (AOC) Kuwait Postal Service established with the release of three stamps depicting Sheikh Abdullah Al-Salim Al-Sabah Gamal Abdel Nasser meeting with Sheikh Abdullah in Damascus Danish Archaeological Expedition in Failaka island	Qadisiya Neighbourhood Unit construction Completion of the Main Roads defined by the First Master Plan *Plans of towns in Kuwait. GSGS 4879, Mina Al-Ahamdi* published by D. Survey, British War Office and Air Ministry	**MUBARAKIYA SCHOOL** Renovation and expansion commissioned Sayed Karim to design **CINEMAS** Al-Firdous and Al-Hamra atributed to Sayed Karim constructed **GOVERNAMENTAL HOTEL** near Jahra Gate proposal by Raglan Squire & Partners **PSYCHIATRIC HOSPITAL** completed		Nasr City, Cairo, Egypt by Sayed Karim University of Baghdad, Iraq, proposal by The Architects Collaborative (TAC) Sadr City, Baghdad, Iraq by Constantinos Doxiadis Ministry of Planning HQ, Baghdad, Iraq, by Gio Ponti Civic Centre, various buildings, Baghdad, Iraq by Willem Dudok Cinema Hamra, Beirut, Lebanon by George Reys and Theo Kanaan

YEAR	KUWAIT GENERAL	KUWAIT ARCHITECTURE	SPECIMENS	POP	MIDDLE EAST ARCHITECTURE
1959	Construction of Shaab Neighbourhood 2 March 1959, *Life Magazine, Outsiders blow up a storm in Kuwait* Free Atelier (evening open art studios) established Palestinians met in Kuwait and formed Fatah Kuwait took over the entire responsibility of its postal service; a full range of internationally valid stamps released	Completion of 3 Ring Roads, 8 Neighbourhoods and Shuwaikh Port **WATER DISTILLATION PLANT/ POWER STATION**, Safat Square Water Reservoir Towers and Bader Al-Mailam Mosque first Kuwaiti buildings displayed on first national commissioned stamp collection	**MINISTRY OF GUIDANCE AND INFORMATION** construction started **THUNAYAN AL-GHANIM BUILDING** completed **AL-SABAH HOSPITAL** Master Plan commissioned to Dorsch Consultants Arab Contractors commenced work for the **MUNICIPAL COMPLEX** three units		Gachsaran New Town, Iran by Fry & Drew Baghdad Faculty of Architecture established Socialist Union Building, Cairo, Egypt by Mahmoud Riad Melli Bank, University of Tehran Branch, Tehran, Iran by Jørn Utzon Shell Building, Beirut, Lebanon by Karl Chayer, Wassek Adib, Bahije Makdissi
1960	Gulf Bank established Commercial Bank of Kuwait (CBK) established Kuwait National Petroleum Company (KNPC) established Credit Bank established under Law No. 40 to facilitate real-estate credit Iraq, Iran, Kuwait, Saudi Arabia and Venezuela formed OPEC Potable Water found in the Dibdibba Formation (Al-Rawdatain) Al-Arabi, Kuwait and Qadsiya Sport Clubs founded	Antiquities Law promulgated by Amiri Decree No. 11 **GEORGE SABA SHIBER** hired by the Department of Public Works Central Business District (CBD) Zoning Plans started **AHMADI HOSPITAL** inaugurated, designed by Maxwell & Drew **GEORGE SABA SHIBER** established guidelines on *Architectural Control* **CENTRAL BUSINESS DISTRICT (CBD)** zoning plan 11 areas, approved by the Supreme Council, Municipal Council, and Development Board Municipality Intermediate Plan (First Master Plan Revision) Baladiya Garden "Hadikat al Baladiya" initiated "The New Metropolis in the Arab World" symposium in Cairo	**KUWAIT NATIONAL MUSEUM** Design Competition **ANWAR AL-SABAH COMPLEX** completed **SHEIKH JABER AL-ALI PALACE** completed		Abadan and Tehran Airports by Brian Colquhoun and Partners Iran Oil Workers Housing by Fry & Drew Cairo International Stadium, Egypt by Werner March United States Embassy, Baghdad, Iraq, by Sert, Jackson and Gourley Agriculture City, Saudi Arabia by Kisho Kurokawa Civic Centre, Baghdad, by Josep Lluís Sert
1961	Kuwait Independence declared along with Qatar and Bahrain The Kuwait Fund for Arab Economic Development, (KFAED) established Kuwait Television began broadcasting Construction of Khaldiya Neighbourhood The Anglo-Kuwait Agreement of 1899 formally withdrawn Kuwait joined the Arab League 20 July Iraq demanded dominion over Kuwait Kuwaiti vote opposed Iraq's annexation plans Land Valuation Committee established *Al-Rai Al-Aam* newspaper founded British troops landed in Kuwait to aid against Iraqi threats Soviets vetoed a UN seat for Kuwait, pleasing Iraq *Kuwait Times* daily newspaper founded 99 state-schools built	**SABAH ABI-HANNA** established local private architectural practice Development of the first CBD areas **CENTRAL BUSINESS DISTRICT (CBD)** implementation commenced; Areas 1,2,3 and 9 designed and built **SHUWAIKH SECONDARY SCHOOL** featured in 35 and 90 Fils stamp	**AL-SALAM PALACE** started construction **NATIONAL BANK HQ** in CBD Area 3 **WATERFRONT** Design Competition **FAHED AL-SALEM MOSQUE** commissioned by Sheikha Badriya Al-Sabah to Sabah Abi-Hanna **GIRL'S SECONDARY SCHOOL** proposal changed location to Khaldiya	321,621	Morvarid Palace, Mehrshahr, Iran by Frank Lloyd Wright Foundation and Wesley Peters Riyadh Bus Terminal, Saudi Arabia Dhahran Civil Air Terminal, Saudi Arabia by Minoru Yamasaki Phoenicia Hotel, Beirut, Lebanon by Edward Durell Stone, F. Dagher and Rodolphe Elias Collège Notre-Dame de Nazareth's Kindergarten, Lebanon by Jacques Liger-Belair Hopital du Sacre Coeur, Beirut, Lebanon, by Michel Ecochard and Henri Edde

YEAR	KUWAIT GENERAL	KUWAIT ARCHITECTURE	SPECIMENS	POP	MIDDLE EAST ARCHITECTURE
1962	First National Assembly First Constitution of Kuwait Kuwait Transportation Company established, later to become Kuwait Public Transportation Company (KPTC) An Amiri Decree issued providing for the division of the country into three Governorates *Cadillacs and Coca-Cola, Experiments of a Swiss Engineer in Kuwait, (53° in the Shade, 82° in the Sun)* by John Henry Muller Kuwait passed a law requiring women to get their husband's signature to obtain a passport Concessioned area for oil-prospection reduced to half	**PLANNING BOARD** established by Amiri decree **KUWAIT SOCIETY OF ENGINEERS** (KSE) formed with H.H. Sheikh Salem Ali Al-Salem Al-Sabah as first Honorary President Model proposal for CBD Area 11 to include high-rise buildings H.H. Sheikh Salem Ali Al-Salem Al-Sabah first Minister of Public Works **CENTRAL BUSINESS DISTRICT (CBD)** plot auctioned for acquisition Magwa Plan by **GEORGE SABA SHIBER** **MUNICIPAL COMPLEX** temporarily accommodated the seat of the Majlis Al-Ummah – the National Assembly UN consultant Dr. Jacob Taysi, study on housing in Kuwait To commemorate the Golden Jubilee (1912–62) **MUBARAKIYA SCHOOL** featured on stamps	**CBD AREA 2** first buildings erected **MINISTRY OF GUIDANCE AND INFORMATION** inaugurated w/Printing Press **AL-SABAH HOSPITAL** Master Plan completed including main buildings **KUWAIT INTERNATIONAL AIRPORT** commission Sir Frederick Snow & Partners to design new terminal and runway **MUNICIPAL COMPLEX** inaugurated		Rashid Karami International Fair, Tripoli, Lebanon, by Oscar Niemeyer Royal Tehran Hilton Hotel, Iran by Heydar Ghiai & Raglan Squire
1963	H.H. Sheikh Sabah Al-Salem Al-Sabah nominated Prime Minister Iraq renounced its claim laid to Kuwait Kuwait became the 111th member of the UN World Bank Report on Kuwait Demography Construction of Idailiya (Adeliya) West Neighbourhood First parliamentary elections held First elected National Assembly convened Kuwait became a member of United Nations Organization	Planning Department transfered from Ministry of Public Works to Kuwait Municipality **MUNICIPAL COMPLEX** displayed on Kuwait Constitution commemorative stamps	**INSTITUTE FOR PHYSICALLY HANDICAPPED** first design proposal by Barlett & Gray Architects **GULF BANK** in CBD Area1 design and build **KUWAIT STADIUMS** Mahmoud Riad commissioned for Kuwait Sports Club **STANDARD SCHOOLS** built in various locations **CBD AREA 9** first building erected		East Baghdad, Iraq by Constantinos Doxiadis Isa Town, Bahrain Nader Shah Mausoleum in Mashhad, Iran by Houshang Seyhoun Omar Khayyám Mausoleum, Nishapur, Iran by Houshang Seyhoun Town Hall, Bat Yam, Israel by Alfred Neumann, Zvi Hecker & Eldar Sharon Artisans House, Beirut, Lebanon by Pierre Neema First issue of the *Journal of the Order of Engineers of Beirut: Al Mouhandess* Al-Khulafa Mosque, Baghdad by M. Makiya Mixed-use Strand Buiding, Beirut, Lebanon by Dar Al-Handasah
1964	Construction of Sulaibikhat Neighbourhood Common Market of Iran, Jordan, Kuwait and Syria established Kuwait participated in the global campaign to save the Nubian Monuments by issuing a set of three stamps highlighting the campaign *Al'Asifa* first Kuwaiti produced film	**GEORGE SABA SHIBER**, *The Kuwait Urbanization. Documentation Analysis Critique*, published by Kuwait Govt. Printing Press **GEORGE SABA SHIBER** departed as Municipality Head of Planning Rumaithiya Neighbourhood Plan and construction by **VBB** **KUWAIT ENGINEERS OFFICE (KEO)** established	**KNPC OFFICE BUILDING** started construction in CBD Area 3 **INSTITUTE FOR PHYSICALLY HANDICAPPED** awarded to Energoprojekt Co. for construction **CBD AREA 9** is completed **SULAIBIKHAT HOSPITAL** completed **AL-SALAM PALACE** completed		Pahlavi University, Shiraz, Iran, Fry & Drew Baghdad Gymnasium, Iraq by Le Corbusier First National City Bank, Dubai, by Anthony Irving and Gordon Jones King Fahd University of Petroleum & Minerals, Dhahran, Saudi Arabia by CRS The Khulafa Central Mosque, Baghdad, Iraq by Mohamed Makiya completed Social Security Offices Istanbul, Turkey by Sedad Hakki Eldem
1965	Sheikh Sabah Al-Salem Al-Sabah accession as Amir Kuwait and Saudi Arabia signed an agreement on the partition of the Neutral Zone Construction of Idailiya (Adeliya) East Neighbourhood Construction of Mansouriya Neighbourhood Planning Board of Kuwait initiated first population census Credit & Savings Bank replaced the Credit Bank Kuwait housing stock: 67,517 units Provisions of the Arab Common Market entered into force	**ALFRED ROTH** appointed by UNESCO to assess the condition of school buildings in Kuwait **GHAZI SULTAN** established the Architectural Dept. at **KUWAIT ENGINEERING OFFICE (KEO)** **HAMED SHUAIB** appointed Head of Planning **AHMADI CINETHEATRE** completed Shuwaik Port started operation Jugomont system proposal for KOC Resort in Mina-Abdullah MACKLIN L. HANCOCK/Project Planning Associates submitted the Kuwait Waterfront Development Plan; a new coast line is established	**AUTOMATIC BAKERY UNITS** construction began in various locations **GIRL'S SECONDARY SCHOOL** completed A scheme of 33 **WATER TOWERS** commissioned to VBB including the **ABRAJ AL-KUWAIT** complex	467,339	Veterinary College, Baghdad, Iraq, Rifat Chadirji (Iraq Consult) Ministry of Municipal and Rural Affairs, Baghdad, Iraq by Rifat Chadirji (Iraq Consult) Waqaf HQ, Baghdad, Iraq by Rifat Chadirji (Iraq Consult) Iraq Consult Bureau, Baghdad, Iraq Telecommunication Building, Tehran, Iran by AFFA Abdol Aziz Farman Farmaian & Zoker & Partners Israel Museum, Jerusalem, by Al Mansfeld and Dora Gad

YEAR	KUWAIT GENERAL	KUWAIT ARCHITECTURE	SPECIMENS	POP	MIDDLE EAST ARCHITECTURE
1966	Kuwait University founded Construction of Omariya Neighbourhood Arabian Oil Company (AOC) established Kuwait Institute for Scientific Research (KISR) under article 28.B of the AOC-Kuwait Concession Agreement of 1958	Kuwait University established on the site of Khaldiya **GIRLS' SECONDARY SCHOOL** **ALFRED ROTH**: Kuwait's Schools Report for UNESCO To commemorate the inauguration of the WHO headquarters in Geneva (Le Corbusier) Kuwait issued a set of two stamps To commemorate the inauguration of the new **MINISTRY OF GUIDANCE AND INFORMATION** Kuwait issued a set of four stamps	**SHERATON HOTEL** inaugurated **CENTRAL BANK OF KUWAIT** commissioned Arne Jacobsen **LOW-INCOME AND RURAL HOUSING** Project promoted by Kuwait Municipality **CHAMBER OF COMERCE & INDUSTRY** completed		Al-Mustansiriya University, Baghdad, Iraq by Qahtan Awni Baghdad Stadium, Iraq by Francisco Keil do Amaral Federation of Industries, Baghdad, Iraq by Rifat Chadirji (Iraq Consult) American University of Beirut, Faculty of Architecture National Museum of Aleppo International Competition Broumana High School, Lebanon by Assem Salam Turkish Historical Society, Ankara, Turkey, by Turgut Cansever and Ertur Yener
1967	(ABK) Ahli Bank of Kuwait established Construction of Badawiyah Neighbourhood Construction of Sabahiya Neighbourhood Kuwaiti Art Society established Under KISR, AOC conducted the first survey on Kuwait's agriculture and fishery potential 1st Arab Cities Organization Conference held in Kuwait Arab Towns Organization (ATO) established in Kuwait 3rd Arab Labour Ministers' Conference held in Kuwait	Municipality Development Plan by Town Planning Department Rural Housing project Developed by Kuwait Municipality **ADVISIORY BOARD** established with the Prime Minister, Minister of Public Works Minister (in charge of Municipality) and Director General of the Planning Board Assistant Director for the technical Affairs (Hamed Shuaib) and three independent advisors, Dr. Omar Azzam, Prof. Franco Albini and Prof. Sir Leslie Martin	**FEMALE STUDENTS HOUSING** proposal by Energoprojekt Co. with IMS Systems **KUWAIT INTERNATIONAL AIR TERMINAL** initiated **KUWAIT INTERNATIONAL AIR TERMINAL** interrupted and commissioned to Pacific International Consultants **INTERMEDIATE SCHOOL FOR GIRLS** commissioned to Alfred Roth		Tobacco Monopoly HQ, Baghdad, Iraq by Rifat Chadirji (Iraq Consult) Tractor Assembling Plant Administration Bldg., Tabriz, Iran by Pirraz Consulting American Life Bldg, Beirut, Lebanon by Anthony Irving and Victor Tarazy
1968	Construction of Abdullah AlSalem Neighbourhood Construction of Nuzha Neighbourhood	Through initiative of **ADVISIORY BOARD**, Government invited four architects to enter a competition Colin Buchanan and Partners commissioned to work on the Second Master Plan **PAN ARAB CONSULTING ENGINEERS** (PACE) established by Hamed Shuaib and partners began its operation in association with **IRAQ CONSULT**, owned by Rifat Chadirji and partners MACKLIN L. HANCOCK/Project Planning Associates submitted report to provide coastal road extending both sides of the town, relocation of the Dhow Harbour and the development of Waterfront	**HASSAWI RESIDENTIAL COMPLEXES** commissioned **FOUR "URBAN FORM STUDIES FOR THE OLD CITY"** design competition **KUWAIT SPORTS CENTRE** competition **FAHED AL-SALEM MOSQUE** completed **KUWAIT SOCIETY OF ENGINEERS** design competition for Headquarters Kenzo Tange + URTEC appointed to design **KUWAITY EMBASSY AND CHANCHELLERY** in Japan **LOW-INCOME AND RURAL HOUSING** Design competition **AL-AHLI BANK** first HQ commissioned **COMMERCIAL BANK OF KUWAIT** main office commissioned Decision to build a new **NATIONAL ASSEMBLEY** including site selection		Al-Maktoum Hospital expansion, Dubai, UAE by John R. Harris National & Grindlays Bank, Muscat, Oman by John R. Harris Azadi Olympic Sports Complex, Tehran, Iran Niavaran Palace Complex, Tehran, Iran by Mohsen Foroughi Takhti Stadium, Tehran, Iran by Jahangir Darvishbani Ministry of National Defense, Beirut, Lebanon by Andre Wogenscky and Maurice Hindi Maison de l'Artisan, Beirut, Lebanon by Bureau d'Etudes (CETA) Social Security Complex, Zeyrek, Istanbul, Turkey by Sedad Eldem
1969	Central Bank of Kuwait established Demarcation Agreement of the Neutral Zone Kuwait-Saudi Arabia signed Sultan Gallery inaugurated in **THUNAYAN AL-GHANIM BLDG.** 1st communication satellite earth station opened	**PAN ARAB CONSULTING ENGINEERS** (PACE) terminated association with **IRAQ CONSULT** Kuwait Municipality Conference on construction materials and low maintenance Hancock, Macklin L., *Architectural Conception of Buildings in Accordance with Twentieth Century Islamic-Arabic Style* paper delivered at Kuwait Municipality Conference Team 10 meeting in London, A+P Smithson presented the **Kuwait Urban Study** under the theme of "Advocacy Planning: Open Design" The Kuwait Second Master Plan, **POPULATION ESTIMATE: 1,250,000** Artificial island for oil tankers in front of Mina Al-Ahmadi shore inaugurated	**HILTON HOTEL** built in Bneid Al-Gar **GULF BANK HQ** new location and design commissioned **INSTITUTE FOR PHYSICALLY HANDICAPPED** completed Following the submission of Design entries for the "Urban From Studies for the Old City" **FOUR DEMONSTRATION AREAS** area commissioned	700,000	Rafidain Bank branch, Baghdad, Iraq by Rifat Chadirji (Iraq Consult) Sheikh Rashid Hospital, Dubai, UAE by John R. Harris & Partners National Bank of Dubai, Deira branch, UAE by John R. Harris & Partners Main Entrance Gate of Tehran University, Iran by Archen Consulting Shiraz Art Museum, Iran by Alvar Aalto Synagogue at Officers School Training Base I, Israel by Svi Hecker College des Freres Mont La Salle, Ain Saade, Lebanon by Raoul Verney Faculty of Sciences, Lebanon by Andre Wogenscky and Maurice Hindie

YEAR	KUWAIT GENERAL	KUWAIT ARCHITECTURE	SPECIMENS	POP	MIDDLE EAST ARCHITECTURE
1970	Demarcation Agreement of the Neutral Zone Kuwait-Saudi Arabia ratified 21,208 shanty homes surveyed in Kuwait	Paolo Portoghesi proposal for unnamed Satelite Town in Kuwait **KUWAIT SECOND MASTER PLAN** *Kuwait: The Long Term Strategy,* 1st report by Colin Buchanan and Partners Shanty Town clearance scheme "Housing Replacing Shanties Project" or "Al-Masakin Al-Badilah Lil Ashish" (in Arabic) "Technical Note OA 18: New Housing: The Bedouin Sector" by Alfred Neumann & Zvi Hecker First pre-fab Jugomont system building erected in Hawally **KUWAIT SECOND MASTER PLAN** *Kuwait: The Short Term Strategy,* 2nd report by Colin Buchanan and Partners	**KUWAIT SPORT CLUBS** commissioned to IRAQ CONSULT **CREDIT & SAVINGS BANK MAIN OFFICES** Design Competition **SALEM AL MUBARAK STREET** consolidated area known as Old Salmiya **INTERMEDIATE SCHOOL FOR GIRLS** in Rumaythiya completed **HASSAWI RESIDENTIAL COMPLEXS** completed		Sabbag Center, Beirut, Lebanon by Alvar Aalto with Alfred Roth Saudi Arabia-Bahrain causeway by Christiani and Nielsen Pcl. Engineering InterContinental Tehran Hotel, Iran by Neal Prince Medical City, Baghdad, Iraq by Hisham Munir Basilique Notre-Dame du Liban, Beirut, by Pierre el-Khoury Centre Gefinor, Beirut, Lebanon by Assem Salam Middle East Technical University, Ankara, Turkey, by Behruz and Altug Çinici Sarkis Armenian Cathedral, Tehran, Iran, by Mirza Koutchek
1971	The Union of Consumer Cooperative Societies (Co-op) launched	**MACKLIN L. HANCOCK**/Project Planning Associates commissioned for Ras Al-Ardh Ferry Terminal and the sea clubs of Blajat Street, Hilton Sea Club, Paradise Cove Sea Club, Fahaheel Sea Club & Fishing Harbour **KUWAIT SECOND MASTER PLAN:** Plan for Kuwait Town and Plan Implementation by Colin Buchanan and Partners **SALMIYA CONCOURSE** (Salmiya District Centre) first proposal by L.G. Mouchel and Partners, Derek Lovejoy and Partners, Hoare Lea and Partners and TEST Technical Studies Bureau **SALEM AL MUBARAK STREET**, with participation of Maath Alousi for Architecture Colin Buchanan and Partners, Fintas-Egaila Township Report Rural Housing project implementation started	**KUWAIT SHIPING COMPANY HQ** Competition, project awarded to PACE **UNITED HOUSING PROJECT** commissioned **LA'ALA MARZOUQ** completed **AL-REHAB COMMERCIAL COMPLEX** commenced construction **NATIONAL ASSEMBLEY** Design Competition **COMMERCIAL BANK OF KUWAIT** completed		Central Post, Telegraph and Telephone HQ, Baghdad, Iraq by Rifat Chadirji (Iraq Consult) Dubai International Terminal 1, UAE by Page and Broughton Dubai Second Master Plan, UAE by John R. Harris & Partners Qatar Development Plan by George Candilis
1972	Khalid Yousuf Al-Marzouq established Kuwait Real Estate Co. Kuwait has the highest rate of population increase in the world *Desert Cloud* by Graham Stevens Statue of Sheikh Abdullah Al-Salem by Sami Mohammad for newspaper *Al-Rai Al-Aam* owner *Al-Qabas* Arabic-language daily newspaper founded	**SABAH ABI-HANNA** and Salem Al-Marzouk established **SSH** Colin Buchanan "Report on the Problem of the Oil Surveys" Second Kuwait Master Plan **KUWAIT SECOND MASTER PLAN** Final study defined Action Area 1 Fintas/Egaila Rural Rehousing intervention and Area 2 Kuwait City Centre and Vehicular Traffic resolution.	**KUWAIT AIRWAYS HQ** completed **FOUR DEMONSTRATION AREAS** design proposals submitted **KINDERGARTEN IN MANSOURIYA** **NATIONAL ASSEMBLEY** Utzon Design awarded and construction commenced **SHUWAIKH SECONDARY SCHOOL** converted to Kuwait University **SHEIKHA FATMA MOHAMED ALI MOSQUE** commissioned **PSYCHIATRIC HOSPITAL** expanded **CENTRAL BANK OF KUWAIT** constructon commenced		Électricité du Liban HQ, Beirut, Lebanon by CETA Old Central Souq, Abu Dhabi, UAE by Abdulrahman Makhlouf British Embassy, Dubai, UAE Tehran City Theater, Iran by Amir Ali Sardar Afkhami Riyadh Master Plan, Saudi Arabia by Doxiadis Associates Eskan's residential towers, Tehran, Iran by Solel Boneh Shomal House, Mazandaran, Iran, by Ali Akbar Saremi General Organization for Social Insurance Building, Riyadh, Saudi Arabia by Omrania & Associates
1973	United Realty Company (URC) established National Real Estate Company (NREC) established National Council for Culture, Arts and Letters (NCCAL) established OPEC, the Arab oil-producing nations, met in Kuwait and announced total embargo of Western nations and Japan Law No. 14 established the Constitutional Court Industrial Bank of Kuwait established	**ISSA AL-SALEH COMMERCIAL GALLERIA** in **SALAM AL MUBARAK ST**, designed by SSH opens *Kuwait, a Salutary Tale* by Karim Jamal published in *The Architect's Journal* **SOUQ AL-KUWAIT** collapsed during construction	**SOUQ AL-MANAKH and Souq AL-SAFAT** tendered by Kuwait Investment Co. **SOUQ AL-KUWAIT and Souq AL-KABEER** tendered by Kuwait Real Estate Co. **SOUQ AL-MUTTAHEDA AND AL-MASEEL** tendered by URC **SIEF PALACE EXTENSION** commissioned **AL-REHAB COMMERCIAL COMPLEX** completed **KUWAIT FUND FOR ARAB ECONOMIC DEVELOPMENT** Phase I completed **KUWAIT SHIPING COMPANY HQ** completed **AL-JAHRA CINETHEATRE** completed		John Bonnington and Partners commissioned to design Doha Zoo, Qatar "Architecture for the Poor: An Experiment in Rural Egypt" by Hassan Fathy translated into English Convalescent Home (adapted for a hotel), Tiberias (Sea of Galilee) by Arieh Sharon – Eldar Sharon and Associates

| --- | --- | --- | --- | --- | --- |
1974	National Housing Authority (NHA) established Department of Illegal Dwellings established "Popular Housing" programme for re-settlement expanded Attack on the Japanese Embassy in Kuwait End of the Oil Embargo *Al-Watan* Arabic-language daily newspaper founded	"Proposals for Restructuring Kuwait," published in *Architectural Review* "Kuwait," by GHAZI SULTAN published in *The Architect's Journal*	New **GULF BANK HQ** completed **HILTON HOTEL** extention commissioned to PACE **SOUQ AL-WATANIYA & SOUQ AL-WATIYA** tendered by NREC **SHEIKH NASSER PALACE** completed **AL-AHLI BANK** first HQ completed **HILTON HOTEL** extention completed		Doha International Airport Terminal Design Competition Shushtar New Town, Khuzestan, Iran proposal by Kamran Diba and others Architecture School, University of Damascus, Damascus, Syria proposal by Mohamed Bourhan Tayara
1975	Kuwait Oil Company (KOC) nationalised Ministry of Housing Affairs established Average Kuwaiti household size was 8.14 people/home Legislation to introduce conscription approved 21,208 Shanties surveyed Arab Art Exhibition 4th Kuwait Fine Art Exhibition Civil Service Law	Mohammed Al-Sanan established INCO Planning Board concluded relation with Peter and Alison Smithson for the design of **MINISTRIES COMPLEX** Ras Al-Ardh Ferry Terminal and the sea clubs of Blajat Street, Hilton Sea Club & Paradise Cove Sea Club, Fahaheel Sea Club & Fishing Harbour completed United Pre-Fab Building Company builds **SOUQ AL-MUTTAHEDA AND AL-MASEEL** **SSH** commissioned to design **SOUQ AL-SALMIYA** International Design Competition for Tourist Development Complex – Um Qasaba, Fahaheel National Housing Authority controlled the State housing development Ain Baghze for 26000 in Hadlan commissioned to Pacific Consultants International	**SOUQ AL-MANAKH and SOUQ AL-SAFAT** completed **NUGRA COMMERCIAL AND RESIDENTIAL COMPLEX** construction of Phase I commenced **ANWAR AL-SABAH COMPLEX** Phase II Design Competition **DASMAN COMPLEX** commissioned by NREC **CREDIT & SAVINGS BANK MAIN OFFICES** completed **UNITED HOUSING PROJECT** in Bneid Al-Gar completed		Mayor's Office in Baghdad, Iraq by Hisham Munir Regional Command Council for Ba'ath Arabic Socialist Party, Baghdad, Iraq by Rifat Chadirji (Iraq Consult) Safa Park, Dubai, UAE Hotel and Lift Station, Mount Tochal- Tehran, Iran by Marcel Breuer, Damavand College, Tehran, Iran by Frank Lloyd Wright Foundation Institute of Public Administration, Riyadh, Saudi Arabia by TAC "The tower at Doha, Qatar», by George Candilis Hilton Beirut, Lebanon by Louis, Sami and Jade Tabet
1976	Kuwait Foundation for the Advancement of Sciences (KFAS) established United Arab Shipping Company (UASC) founded Touristic Enterprises Company established First Integrated Law for Social Security issued Future Generations Fund signed into law Amir suspended National Assembly, said it is not acting in the country's interests Mina Al-Ahmadi Gas project initiated *Al-Anbaa* Arabic-language daily newspaper founded	Riggae Low-Income Housing PACE developed design for **GOLD MARKET** in conjunction with **SHEIKH FAHED MOSQUE**. A first attempt for the regeneration of the Old city core Michael Carapetian Associates developed housing scheme never built **ZAHRA COMPLEX** in **SALAM AL-MUBARAK ST.** commissioned to Ghazi Sultan and KEO **AL-ASMAK TOWER** in Sharq construction commenced "Destruction of the Middle East?" by Karim Jamal in *The Architect's Journal* Private Sector and Land Owners put pressure to increase FAR in the City Center	**SHERATON HOTEL** extension by TAC **JOINT BANKING CENTRE** Design competition 1st Prize awarded to SOM **SOUQ AL-KABEER** completed **KUWAIT LAW COURTS** Design Competition Riqqa City **LOW-INCOME AND RURAL HOUSING** occupied **CENTRAL BANK OF KUWAIT** completed by Dissing & Weitling First **WATER TOWERS** completed **SHEIKHA FATMA MOHAMED ALI MOSQUE** completed 21km **WATERFRONT** Design Competition **BANKING STUDIES CENTRE** design commissioned to Maath Alousi **GOLD MARKET** commissioned to PACE Marcel Breuer Associates presented proposal for **MIDEAST MARKET PROJECT** **SOUQ AL-KUWAIT** completed **KUWAIT STATE MOSQUE** design competition		Bateen Mall, Abu Dhabi, UAE Pearl Tower, Dubai, UAE Dubai Third Master Plan, UAE by John R. Harris & Partners Habitat Tehran, Iran by Moshe Safdie Habitat East-Village, Iran by Justus Dahinden and Associates Mashad Commercial Center, Mashad, Iran by Dariush Borbor Hotel Tehran, Iran by Kenzo Tange Carpet Museum of Iran, Tehran, by Abdol Aziz Farman Farmaian Pahlavi National Library Competition, Tehran, Iran Ministry of Interior, Qatar by Triad CICO Doha Club, Qatar by Triad Cico Conference Center and Hotel, Mecca, Saudi Arabia by Rolf Gutbrod and others Office Complex for the Heir Apparent, Riffa, Bahrain by M. Makiya Prototype Kindergarten, Sharjah, UAE by Jafar Tukan and George Rais

YEAR	KUWAIT GENERAL	KUWAIT ARCHITECTURE	SPECIMENS	POP	MIDDLE EAST ARCHITECTURE
1977	Kuwait Finance House (KFH) established Sheikh Sabah Al-Salem died, Jaber Al-Ahmad Al-Jaber new Amir Burgan Bank established *Arab Times* daily newspaper founded	**KMPR1** First Review of the Second Kuwait Masterplan by Shankland Cox Partnership in association with SSH PACE and SOM commissioned for Kuwait Hyatt Regency Hotel First Holiday Inn Hotel commenced construction *Mirqab Action Area Plan*, developed by Perkin & Wills International + De Leuw, Catter International Inc. Salmiya Urban Plan regulated **SALEM AL-MUBARAK STREET** buildings capacity, typology and use Anjari, Maryam and Al-Salam Residential and Commercial complexes in **SALEM AL-MUBARAK STREET** commenced **SALMIYA CONCOURSE** for Kuwait Municipality by L.G. Mouchel and Partners, Derek Lovejoy and Partners, Hoare Lea and Partners and TEST Technical Studies Bureau **SALEM AL-MUBARAK STREET** Krzysztof Wisniowski, Andrzej Bohdanowicz, Jan Urbanowicz and Boris Bohdanowicz with Victor Shiber proposal for Sabah Al-Salem City Project Jahra City Centre proposal by Devecon **ABRAJ AL-KUWAIT** featured in 30 Fils stamp	**ABRAJ AL-KUWAIT** completed **AL-SAWABER HOUSING COMPLEX** Design Proposal **OFFICE TOWERS** start being built in **SHARQ** **KUWAIT SPORT CLUBS** completed **IRANIAN EMBASSY** Design Competition **HILTON AREA APARTMENTS** Design awarded to I.M. Pei & Partners **CREDIT & SAVINGS BANK MAIN OFFICES** façade commissioned to PACE **ANWAR AL-SABAH COMPLEX** Phase II, Ghazi Sultan awarded first prize, construction commenced **KUWAIT NATIONAL THEATRE** Design Competition		Intercontinental Hotel, Muscat, Oman by Pierre el Khoury & BAU Design for National Commercial Bank, Jeddah, Saudi Arabia by SOM Palace of the Amir reconstructed into National Museum, Doha, Qatar by Michael Rice and Anthony Irving Bank Street, Dubai, UAE Bushehr New Town, Iran by Dan Eytan Tehran Museum of Contemporary Art, Iran by Kamran Diba and others Lassa Tyre Factory, Izmit, Turkey by Dogan Tekeli and Sami Sisa Yarmouk University, Amman, Jordan proposal by Kenzo Tange Associates and others
1978	Law established banning shops in residential areas Kuwait Regional Convention for Co-operation on the Protection of the Marine Environment from Pollution with Bahrain, Iran, Iraq, Kuwait, Oman, Qatar, Saudi Arabia and the UAE "Al-Nasheed Al-Watani" became Kuwait's official anthem replacing the "Amiri Salute"	**BEHBEHANI TOWER** in Sharq commissioned to PACE Kuwait Real Estate Development Co. commissioned the design for the highest tower in Sharq, 21 storeys-high, named after **BURGAN BANK HQ TOWER** and recently renamed WATANIYA HQ TOWER ALGHANIM INDUSTRIES commissioned design for new HQ with Computer Center Sabah Al-Salem City Project, planned for 60,000: construction commenced Housing Co-opeartive Society for Egyptians Working in Kuwait "Traditional Architecture in Kuwait and the Northern Gulf," by Ronal Lewcock & Zahra Freeth, *Art and Archeology Research Papers*, London *Engineering & Architecture in the 21st Century*, published with Dr. Riyad Al-Nakib diagrams: *Kuwait of the Future in Pictures*	**WATERFRONT** Design Competition awarded to Ghazi Sultan, KEO, Sasaki Associates, construction commenced **STOCK EXCHANGE** Design Competition Ministry of Islamic Affairs commissioned mixed-use **AWQAF COMMERCIAL COMPLEX** to Hassan Mansour and Son **AL-SABAH HOUSE** commissioned to Hassan Fathy Arthur Erickson Associates commissioned for **FINTAS TOWN CENTER** **MINISTRIES COMPLEX** awarded to Energoprojekt Co. **ALGHANIM INDUSTRIES** commissioned the design for new HQ **KUWAIT FUND FOR ARAB ECONOMIC DEVELOPMENT** Phase II completed **KUWAIT RADIO TELEVISION CENTRE** awarded (present Ministry of Information)		Blue Souq, Sharjah, UAE, by Michael Lyell Associates Cultural Center Garden of Niavaran, Tehran, Iran by Kamran Diba New Dubai Hospital, Dubai, UAE by John R. Harris & Partners Dubai Town Hall Complex, UAE by Pacific International Consultants Industrial Credit Bank, Tehran, Iran by I. M. Pei & Partners Saudi Arabia Monetary Agency HQ, Riyadh by Minoru Yamasaki Qavam-os- Saltaneh House (now Abguineh Glass and Ceramics Museum), Tehran, Iran by Hans Hollein Turkish Language Society, Ankara, Turkey, by Cengiz Bektas
1979	Ministerial Committee for Housing recommends production of high-rise apartment housing stock Kuwait Prize established by KFAS Queen Elizabeth II visit to Kuwait Duke of Edinburgh visited a dhow-building yard at Doha Village	Operated by Tourism Enterprise Company **ICE SKATING RINK** completed **AL-ASMAK TOWER** in Sharq construction commenced PACE commissioned for Imad and Raed Centre Towers in Sharq Jahra City Centre proposal by Michael Lyell Queen Elizabeth II official visit to **ABRAJ AL-KUWAIT** Queen Elizabeth II received by the Amir at the **AL-SALAM PALACE**	**SOUQ AL-MUTTAHEDA AND SOUQ AL-MASEEL** completed **AL-MUTHANNA COMPLEX** developed for Kuwait Finance House (KFH) **KOC COMPUTER & TRAINING CENTRE** tendered for Design Competition **KUWAIT INSTITUTE FOR SCIENTIFIC RESEARCH** comissioned to PACE and TAC Stanko Kristl IMOS proposal for **KUWAIT REHABILITATION CENTER** **COMMERCIAL BANK OF KUWAIT OPERATIONS CENTRE** awarded **AL-AHLI BANK HQ** new HQ comissioned **DERWAZAH ABDUL RAZAQ SQUARE** Design Competition **MUBARAKIYA SCHOOL** converted to Central Library **SOUQ AL-WATANIYA** completed		UAE Embassy in Oman, Muscat by Maath Alousi World Trade Center, Dubai, UAE by John R. Harris & Partners National Bank of Dubai, UAE by John R. Harris & Partners The General Post Office, Doha, Qatar by Twist + Whitley Architects

YEAR	KUWAIT GENERAL	KUWAIT ARCHITECTURE	SPECIMENS	POP	MIDDLE EAST ARCHITECTURE
1980	Kuwait hosts AFC Asian Cup The World Bank Report on housing in Kuwait The World Bank Report concluded that 80% of new families would require public housing *Modern Kuwait* by David Sapsted, Macmillan London Iran-Iraq War: Kuwait supported Iraq strategically and financially Tareq Rajab Museum opened Kuwait Petroluem Corporation established	Aga Khan Award for Architecture: Kuwait and Water Towers Public Institute for Social Security Tower in Sharq awarded to PACE **TELECOMMUNICATION CENTRE** featured in One Dinar Notes	**ALGHANIM INDUSTRIES HQ** completed PACE awarded to design of **UNITED ARAB SHIPPING COMPANY HQ** **BAYAN CONFERENCE CENTER** competition Alfred Roth design proposal for **HOTEL INTERCONTINENTAL PROJECT** **NUGRA COMMERCIAL AND RESIDENTIAL COMPLEX** pedestrian bridge **SHEIKH NASSER AL-SABAH MOSQUE** design commissioned **LE MERIDIEN HOTEL** and Salhiya Commercial Complex completed	1,350,000	Qatar University by Kamal El-Kafrawi and Ove Arup Ministry of Information and National Theatre, Doha, Qatar by Triad CICO and James Connell Zayed Sports City Stadium, UAE Shushtar New Town, Shushtar, Iran by Daz Consulting Saudi Fund for Development Building, Riyadh by Urbahn and Coile International *Design Primer for Hot Climates* by Allan Konya
1981	"Housing Service in the State of Kuwait" study by Al-Tehaih, submitted to the Amir Gulf Cooperation Council established National Assembly recalled	**MINISTRIES COMPLEX** Water Fountain awarded to Ja'afar Islah Khaleejia Complex Tower in Sharq commissioed to PACE Ahmadiah Contracting commenced construction of Sharq Tower, the highest with 23 stories Al-Massaleh Tower, first unit of **HILTON AREA APARTMENTS completed**	**KUWAIT ZOO EXTENSION AND RENOVATION** design proposal by John S. Bonnington Partnership **KUWAIT INTERNATIONAL AIR TERMINAL** completed **SHEIKH NASSER AL-SABAH MOSQUE** completed New **TELECOMMUNICATION CENTRE AND ANTENNA TOWER** tendered **SAFAT SQUARE.** Design Competition **MINISTRY OF COMMUNICATION TOWERS** tendered for different locations **FEMALE STUDENTS' HOUSING – COLLEGE OF EDUCATION** completed		Cultural Foundation, Abu Dhabi, UAE by TAC Basra International Hotel, Iraq by TAC 1980 Hajj Terminal, Jeddah, Saudi Arabia by SOM National Library and Cultural Centre, Abu Dhabi by The Architects Collaborative (TAC)
1982	Souq Al-Manakh (informal Stock Market) collapsed erasing $94 billion in paper wealth	**ZAHRA COMPLEX** in **SALAM AL-MUBARAK ST.** inaugurated Raed Centre Tower in Ahmad Al-Jaber St. completed Behbehani Tower completed, highest in Kuwait PAMA Tower in Sharq commissioned **ORGAN TRANSPLANT CENTRE** design commissioned to KEO Ahmed Al-Jaber Commercial Complex design proposal by SOM New Wafra Town commissioned to Dar Al-Handasah Al-Qurain City design proposal by Jerzy Plesner, Kuba Chojnacki, Tadeusz Cukier, Artur Jasinski Kuwait Society of Engineers Study on Housing	**MINISTRIES COMPLEX** completed **KUWAIT FOUNDATION FOR THE ADVANCEMENT OF SCIENCES** new HQ commissioned to PACE and TAC **GOLD SOUQ** completed **AWQAF COMMERCIAL COMPLEX** completed **BEHBEHANI TOWER** completed		Gulf International Bank, Manama, Bahrain by Gibb, Petermuller and Partners Doha Zoo, Qatar by John S. Bonnington Partnership Doha Sheraton Hotel, Qatar by William Pereira Al Khayriyya Complex, Riyadh, Saudi Arabia by Kenzo Tange Salam Plaza, Doha, Qatar Unknown Soldier Monument in Baghdad, Iraq by Marcello D'Olivo and Hisham Munir East Talpiot Housing Development, Jerusalem, by Y. Rechter – A. Rechter

YEAR	KUWAIT GENERAL	KUWAIT ARCHITECTURE	SPECIMENS	POP	MIDDLE EAST ARCHITECTURE
1983	Bubiyan Bridge opened American Embassy in Kuwait bombed French Embassy in Kuwait bombed Explosion in Shuaibia Petro-Chemical Plant Explosion in Kuwait's main water desalinisation plant Kuwait International Air Terminal Control Tower bombed	Alssarrafeen Square and Souq Al-Amir Visual Survey for Kuwait Municipality Stephan Gardiner published *Kuwait: The Making of a City* Imad Tower in Sharq completed Burgan Bank HQ Tower completed Public Institute for Social Security completed Sharq Tower completed, highest in Kuwait Soor Gardens (formerly designed Project Planning Associates) implemented by TEC under the name Musical Fountain **KMPR2** Revision of Kuwait Master Plan by Colin Buchanan and Partners & OAP/KEB	**KUWAIT NATIONAL MUSEUM** inaugurated **JOINT BANKING CENTRE** completed **KUWAIT LAW COURTS** completed **MIRQAB TRANSPORTATION CENTRE** proposal by WS Atkins **KOC COMPUTER & TRAINING CENTRE** completed winning proposal by T+W **KUWAIT INSURANCE COMPANY** proposal by Arthur Erickson Associates **SIEF PALACE EXTENSION** completed, including the Ministry of Foreign Affairs (MOFA) **KUWAIT INSTITUTE FOR SCIENTIFIC RESEARCH** completed		National Commercial Bank, Jeddah, Saudi Arabia by SOM and others Front Jordan Residential Buildings, Tehran, Iran by Feridoun Mirjalali Doha Corniche, Qatar by Llewelyn-Davies and Shankland Cox King Khaled International Airport, Riyadh, Saudi Arabia, by HOK + 4 Consortium Mayor's Office, Baghdad, Iraq by Hisham Munir
1984	Wafra Real Estate Company (WRE) established NHA committed to building 5,800 dwellings/year Gulf Cooperation Council (GCC) members agreed on the creation of a two-brigade (10,000 troops) Peninsula Shield Force, based in Saudi Arabia near the Kuwaiti and Iraqi borders	Entertainment City inaugurated Khaleejia Complex Tower in Sharq completed PAMA Tower in Sharq completed Project Planning Associates initiates the planning works for the Khiran Coastal Development for the Ministry of Public Works	**PORT AUTHORITY HEADQUARTERS** Design Competition **HILTON HOTEL** extention commissioned to PACE, inaugurated **MINISTRY OF PUBLIC WORKS & MINISTRY OF ELETRICITY AND WATER** awarded to TAC		Ministry of Foreign Affairs, Riyadh, Saudi Arabia by Henning Larsen United Gulf Bank, Bahrain by SOM Arab Gulf University, Bahrain by Kenzo Tange Wafi City, Dubai, UAE by John R. Harris & Partners Inter-Continental Hotel, Abu Dhabi, UAE by Makiya Associates King Faisal Foundation, Riyadh, Saudi Arabia by Kenzo Tange + Urtec Abi Nawas Development, Baghdad, Iraq by Planar, and Skaarup & Jespersen
1985	Kuwait houses number 228,815 units Immigrant labour constituted about 81% of Kuwait's manpower Failed assassination attempt made on Sheikh Jaber Al-Ahmad Al-Jaber Al-Sabah The Government announced plans to construct military bases on the islands of Bubiyan and Warba Bubiyan declared war zone, access to the island restricted	**AL-MUTHANNA COMPLEX** sales campaign launched on TV	**AL-MUTHANNA COMPLEX** completed **MUBARAKIYA SCHOOL** converted to National Library **NATIONAL ASSEMBLEY** completed **HOSPITALS: MUBARAK AL-KABEER, AL-ADAN, AL-JAHRA** completed		Qatar University, Doha by Kamal El-Kafrawi Central Bank of Iraq, Baghdad, Iraq by Dissing + Weitling Tuwaiq Palace, Saudi Arabia by OHO joint venture with Frei Otto & Buro Happold Al-Thawra Hospital, Sana'a, Yemen by Heinle, Wischer and Partner
1986	National Assembly Dissolved Annual Statistical Abstract Domestic security concerns, particularly about Iran's perceived influence over the Shi'ite minority, prompted the deportations of thousands of expatriates, many of them Iranian Explosions occurred in the Mina Al-Ahmadi UK, Belgium, Italy and France ordered minesweepers to the Persian Gulf	Khiran Resort construction initiated under TEC Sharq Al-Sief Area Planning and Schematic Design for Kuwait Municipality by BBPR and KEO Al-Awadi Towers and the Jazz Tower by Arab Consultants completed Ta'meer Complex of **HILTON AREA APARTMENTS** completed 20 Dinars Note featured **KUWAIT LAW COURTS** and **STOCK EXCHANGE MARKET**	**STOCK EXCHANGE MARKET** completed **DERWAZAH ABDUL RAZAQ AND SAFAT SQUARE** completed **AL-BALOUSH BUS STATION** Design awarded to INCO **KUWAIT FOUNDATION FOR THE ADVANCEMENT OF SCIENCES** completed **BAYAN CONFERENCE CENTER** inaugurated by H.H. the Amir **COMMERCIAL BANK OF KUWAIT AHMAD AL-JABER – OPERATIONS CENTER** completed **AL-AWADHI TOWER** completed		Ministry of Justice and Islamic Affairs, Manama, Bahrain by CRS Architects Rifat Chadirji published *Concepts and Influences: Towards a Regionalized International Architecture* French Cultural Centre, Damascus, Syria, by Jose Oubrerie and others Doha Zoo, Qatar by John S. Bonnington Partnership completed Corniche Mosque, Jeddah, Saudi Arabia, by Abdel Wahid El-Wakil Etisalat Headquarters, Abu Dhabi, UAE, proposal by Arthur Erickson Associates

YEAR	KUWAIT GENERAL	KUWAIT ARCHITECTURE	SPECIMENS	POP	MIDDLE EAST ARCHITECTURE
1987	US offered military protection to Kuwaiti ships in the Persian Gulf US began its policy of escorting re-flagged Kuwaiti tankers up and down the Persian Gulf to protect from attack by Iran British government sold the last of its shares in BP, Kuwaiti Government bought 22% of total shares Amir of Kuwait dissolved Parliament	"An Architect from Kuwait," *Albenaa*, by GHAZI SULTAN *Kuwait Al-Madhi*, by Sulaiman Al-Awadi *Kuwait Municipality: Kuwait Town Master Plan Review and Updating*	**TELECOMMUNICATION CENTRE AND ANTENNA TOWER** construction commenced **NUGRA COMMERCIAL AND RESIDENTIAL COMPLEX** completed		King Fahd Stadium, Saudi Arabia by Ian Fraser, John Roberts and Partners Al-Ghadie Mosque, Tehran, Iran by Jahanguir Mazlum Demir Holiday Village, Bodrum, Turkey by Turgut Cansever
1988	*Baladiyat Al-Kuwait Fi Khamseen A'men*, by Najat Al-Jassim, Baladiyat Al-Kuwait PM Margaret Thatcher forced Kuwait to sell over half their stake in BP Iraq re-asserted its claim to Kuwait following cease-fire declared with Iran	*Kuwait Municipality: Historical Preservation Study; Old Kuwait Town*	**AL-BALOUSH BUS STATION** completed **WATERFRONT** implementation is completed and followed by Phase 5 competition **AL-AHLI BANK HQ** new HQ completed		National Museum of Bahrain, Manama by Krohn & Hartvig Rasmussen+Cowiconsult Abu Dhabi Commercial Bank HQ Abu Dhabi National Oil Company HQ Jolfa Residential Complex, Isfahan, Iran by Tajeer Architects Museum, Dubai, UAE proposal by Mohamed Makiya
1989	Statue of Sheikh Sabah Al-Salem by Sami Mohammad for newspaper *Al-Rai Al-Aam* owner	Philip Johnson and John Burgee commissioned by Kuwait Investment Office for KIO Towers in Madrid, Spain "Design for the Arabian Gulf Region" in *Architecture + Design:India*, by GHAZI SULTAN "Urban Development in Kuwait," in *Alam Al-Bena*, by HAMID SHUAIB Shakland and Cox and W.S. Atkins commissioned to work on the third review of Kuwait Master Plan	**AL-SAWABER HOUSING COMPLEX** partially completed		Ministry of Interior, Riyadh, Saudi Arabia by Archisystems and Musalli, Shakir and Mandilli Hebrew Union College, Jerusalem by Moshe Safdie and Associates The Spiral, Tel Aviv by Zvi Hecker National Museum, Manama, Bahrain by Krohn & Hartin Rasmussen Grand National Assembly Mosque, Ankara, Turkey by Behruz and Can Çinici French Embassy, Muscat, Oman by Architecture Studio
1990	Iraq complained to OPEC, accused Kuwait of stealing its oil from a field near the border Iraq invaded and then annexed Kuwait			2,141,465	Sheikh Zayed Road, Dubai, UAE
1991	Kuwait Liberated	"Kuwait's Post-War Reconstruction" in *MINAR*, by Huda Al-Bahar Kuwait Emergency and Recovery Office attributed a contract for oil industry recovery and overall infrastructures rehabilitation and reactivation to USACE (US Army Corps of Engineers) W.S. Atkins held conference in London to present Kuwait reconstruction plan Planning for Reconstruction and Development in Postwar Kuwait, by Derrick Hartley presented at MEED conference in association with the United Bank of Kuwait			

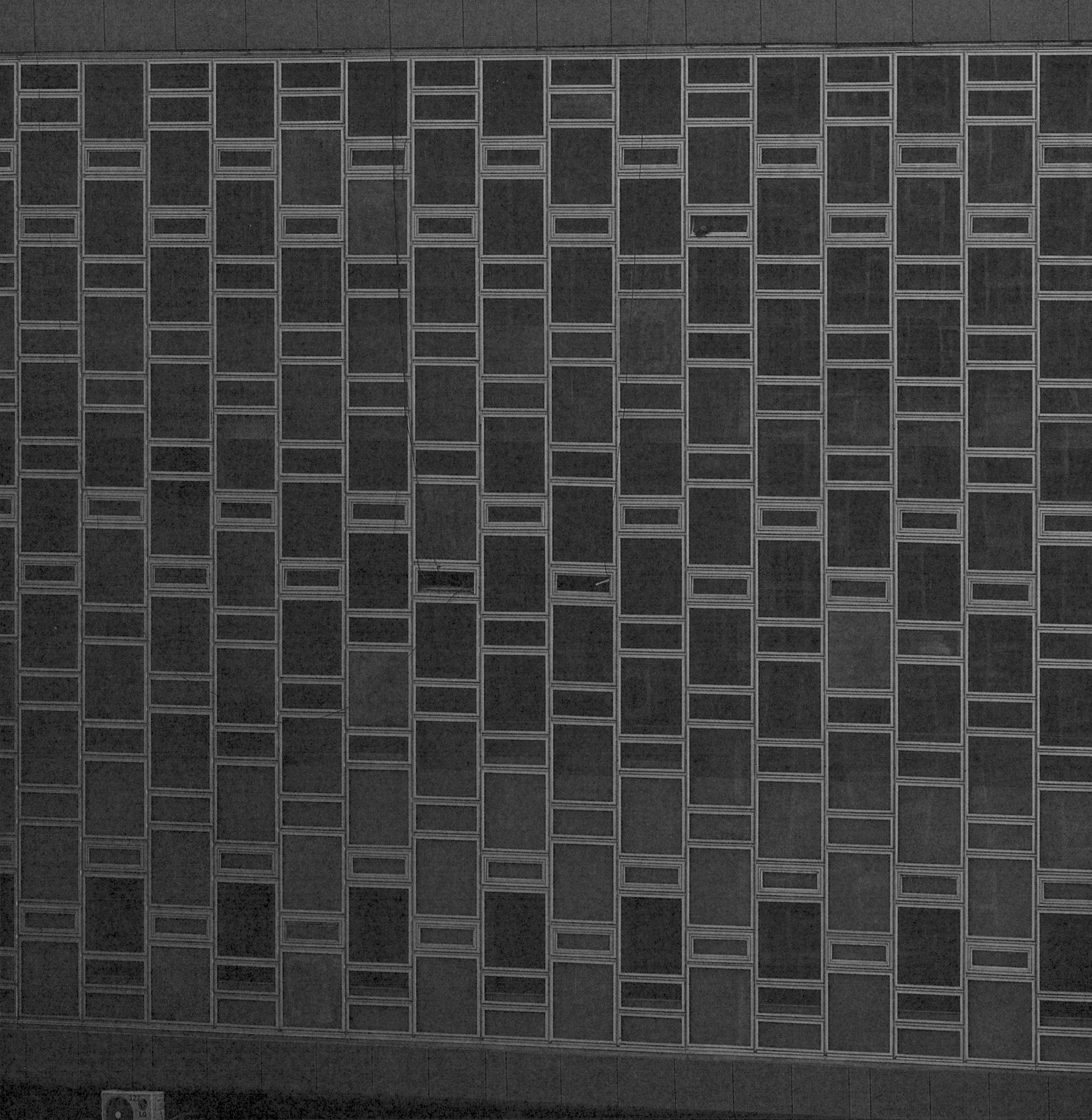

SPECIMENS I
Building as infrastructure
1949–1960

WATER DISTILLATION PLANT AND POWER STATION A AND B

SHUWAIKH PORT
1956–1962

DESIGNERS • Ewbank & Partners Ltd
(lead consultant);
Farmer & Dark, Architects (architect);
John Taylor & Sons (services)
CLIENT • H.H. the Amir of Kuwait
CONTRACTOR • Richard Costain
(Middle East) Co. Ltd.; Kuwait Austrian
Engineering Co. (Overseas AST Co. Ltd.)

MODIFIED

Three years after the inauguration export of Kuwait's crude oil shipment (1946), Ewbank & Partners Ltd were appointed by the Amir to design a major complex in Mina al-Ahmadi Port.[1] The scope of the work encompassed two schemes: the provision of drinking water and the provision of electricity. The same program in 1951was awarded to the consultants for Kuwait City's Shuwaikh Port.

The power station and distillation plant programmes included the installation of turbines, pumps and switchgear and the creation of administration areas.

The structural resolution of the scheme with steel framing for a large span allowed for construction of the units with flexibility and speed. The heavy brick walls insulated the thermal capacity and dampened turbine noise in the power plant. The brick façade was developed into a decorative and ornamental feature associated with the recessed ground floor with painted façade tiles. A relevant feature in the distillation plant was the tower, made from Amarah brick that stood as a main element for the whole complex.

The first power station was inaugurated in 1953.

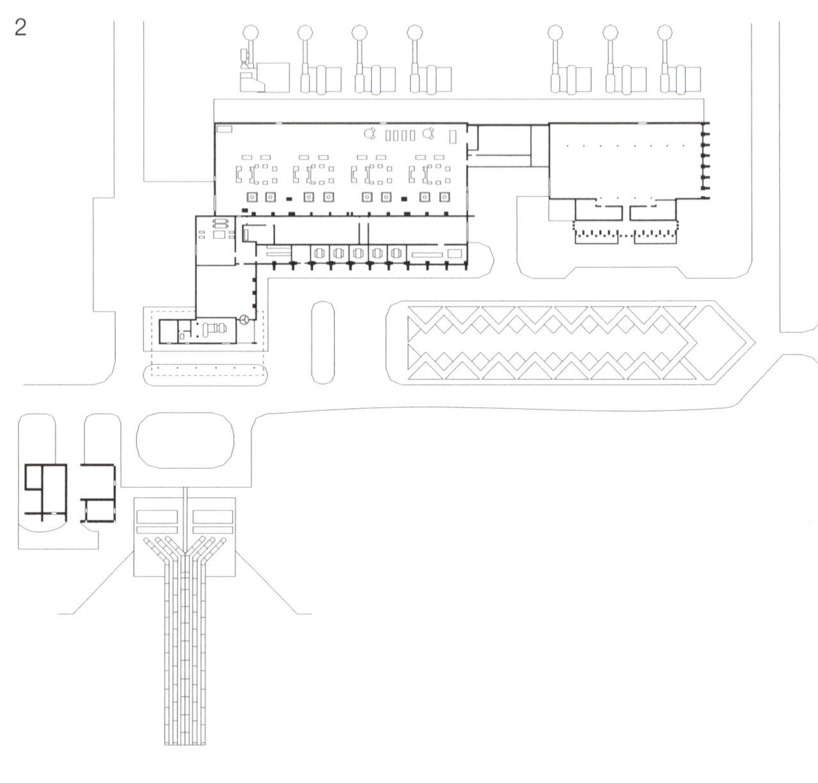

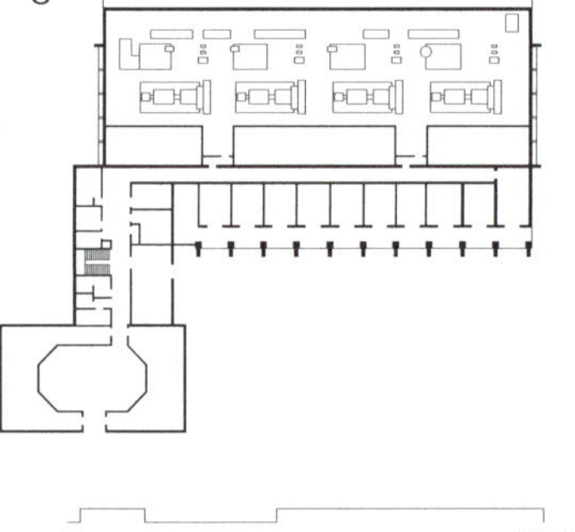

1. Aerial view, undated
2. Power station, ground floor plan
3. Power station, first floor plan
4. View of the entire forecourt, 1954
5. Power station, control room, north elevation, 1954
6. Kuwait Town power station, perspective, 1954
7. Kuwait Town distillation plan, perspective, 1951

SHUWAIKH SECONDARY SCHOOL

SHUWAIKH
1951–1957

DESIGNER • Contracting and Trading Co. (lead consultant)
CLIENT • Ministry of Public Works; Council for Education
CONTRACTOR • Contracting and Trading Company (CAT); Ahmadiah Contracting & Trading Co.

MODIFIED

One of the first large-scale projects in Kuwait, this high school has been for years at the cutting edge of the regional education system. Strategically located in the Educational Zone in the First Master Plan, with sport facilities, a diplomatic club and separate residences both for teachers and students, it used to attract people from all over the Middle East for study or work. Several different technical curricula were offered, thanks to the ample space allocated for laboratories.[2]

The main building's classic layout is based on a central symmetrical axis. Two-storey, curved wings converge on the central portal and the front is enveloped in a shallow arcade. On the other end, the wings continue orthogonally and meet at the very back, again on the central spine, to enclose a vast courtyard. The central axis is therefore punctuated by a sequence of higher buildings: the domed entrance, the assembly hall and the clock tower, the latter close to the shore.

Unfortunately, the author of this important project is unknown, but the general layout and some architectural features, have a very close resemblance to the 1939 Abadan Institute of Technology, built in Iran by Wilson and Mason. The British firm was very active in Kuwait from the mid 1940s, having designed, among other projects, two mosques in Ahmadi and a guest house for H.H. the Amir.

Since 1972 the building has been part of Kuwait University. This new function forced several additions to the original plan which changed the original layout.

1

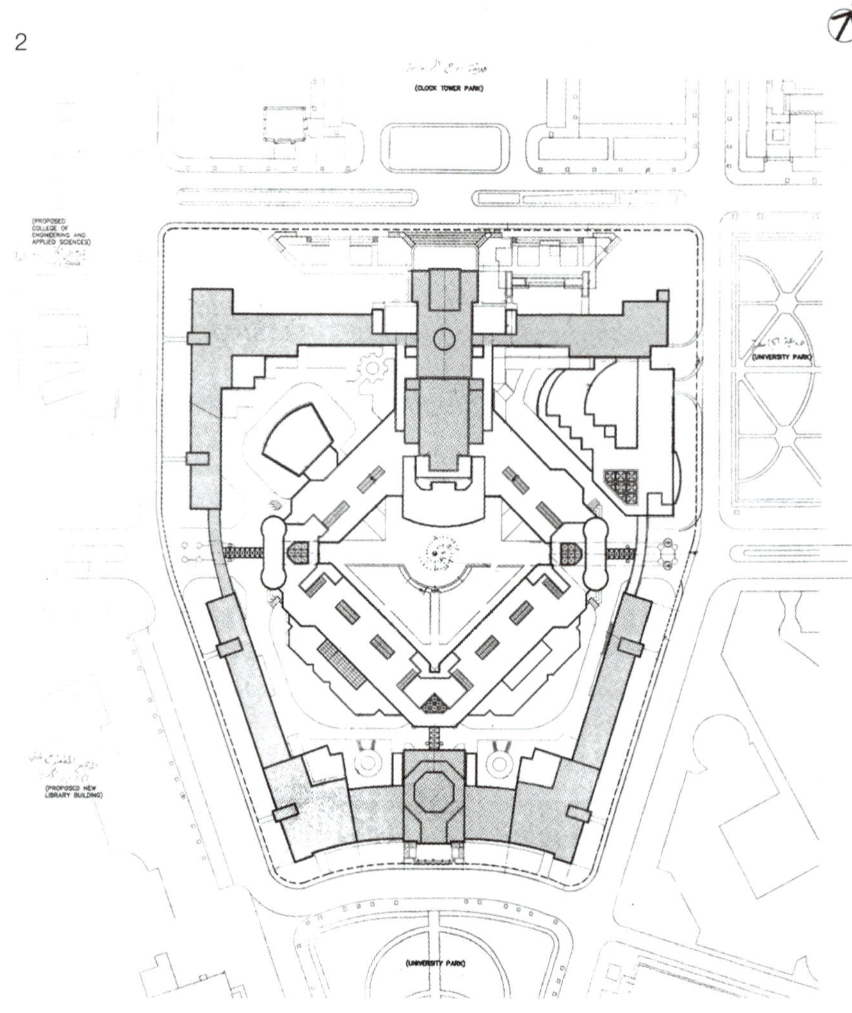

2

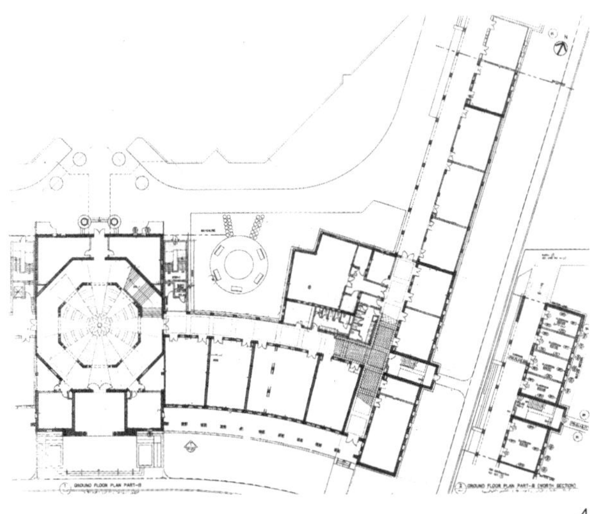

4   5

1. Clock tower, undated
2. Site plan, with 1994 additions to the courtyard
3. Aerial view, undated, circa 1960
4. Plan detail, entrance and right wing
5. Site under construction

PUBLIC SCHOOLS

VARIOUS LOCATIONS
1952–1956

DESIGNERS • Tripe And Wakeham
Partnership
CLIENT • Ministry of Public Works;
Council for Education
CONTRACTOR • Various

MODIFIED

1

A National Educational Programme
was among the first priorities in the
early stages of Kuwait's modernisation.
Between the years 1952 to 1956, while
Shuwaikh Secondary School was under
construction, Tripe and Wakeham were
commissioned to design a Technical
College, several elementary schools
and nurseries, as well as the Ministry
of Education Central Kitchen with a
capability of supplying 10,000 meals
for all government schools in 1954.

The Technical Vocational College in
Shuwaikh (1953–54), with David Oakley
(1927–2003) as part of the design team,
worked as a compound of several
blocks: 6 dormitory blocks for 250
resident students out of a total of 750,
3 laboratory blocks to teach mechanical
and electrical engineering, physics,
science, metallurgy and automobile
studies and 4 workshop blocks related
to repair and maintenance.

The first elementary schools to be
implemented were in Sallahiddine,
Shamiyah and Al-Siddiq, each of them
to cater to 800 pupils and 30 resident
teachers; the nursery schools of Jahrah
Gate, Magwa, Tarik and Muhallab, were
planned for 105 pupils (15 per class).
These schools were developed under
a regular 3m grid made with standard
precast reinforced concrete elements,
solving time and local resource issues.
In this first phase, no air-conditioning
was contemplated, demanding
an architecture that responded to
conditions of extreme heat. Shade
and ventilation were therefore main
concerns, so the building width was
no more than one room in thickness;
the windows were north-east oriented;
concrete *mashrabiah* screens were
used as was the use of bright colours
relating to desert tones and shaded
walkways, walls and roofs were built as
well as ventilated false acoustic board
ceilings. The materials used in finishing
were chosen for durability and low
maintenance. On the walls the common
use of Baghdad brick was mixed with
travertine stone or decorative ceramic
tiles in some specific situations, and
the floors were laid with locally made
terrazzo tiles.[3]

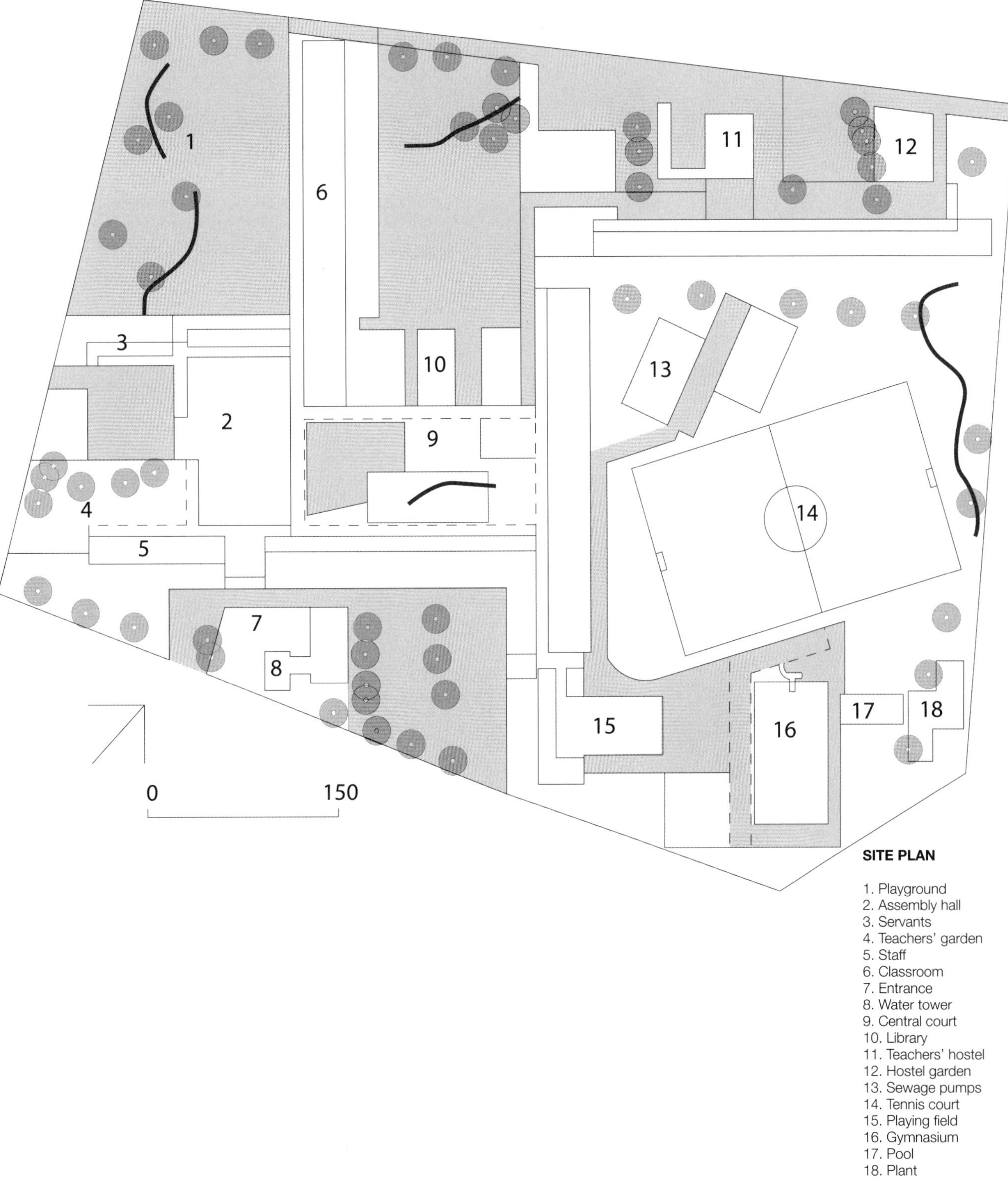

1. Al-Muhallab school, view of the courtyard
2. Site plan of a typical school

3

4

5

6

7

3. *Al-Siddiq Elementary School, detail of the staircase*
4. *Shamiyah school, 1957*
5. *Outdoor class activities*
6. *Detail of the ceramic screen*
7. *Al-Siddiq Elementary School*

SULAIBIKHAT HOSPITAL

SULAIBIKHAT
1954–1964

DESIGNERS • John R. Harris Architects; Scott & Wilson, Kirkpatrick & Partners (structure); Hoare Lea And Partners (services)
CLIENT • Ministry of Public Works
CONTRACTOR • Consolidated Contractors Co. (CONCO)

MODIFIED

1

This hospital, also called the Women's Hospital, was built in the Sulaibikhat area, the "health zone" as defined in the Master Plan. The young British architect John R. Harris was appointed in 1952 to design the Kuwait Research Laboratories in what was his first work outside the UK. This project kept the newly formed office in the country and was significant for the understanding of material behaviour in hot climates. After winning the project for a hospital in Doha (1952–1957) he was commissioned for the Chest Diseases Hospital in Kuwait, later converted to the Maternity Hospital. The complex is comprised of 11 interconnected pavilions with different numbers of floors creating a diagonal, parallel to the coast. The three longest and tallest, four-storey blocks for the wards, at the North boundary facing the Gulf, as well as the (demolished) Physiotherapy and Occupational Therapy Centre with its distinctive circular plan and zig-zag concrete roof.

The block units are comprised of concrete pre-fabricated façade panels creating a rational performance in the building display and use, and are clad in locally made sand-lime bricks interrupted by vertical aluminium windows from floor to ceiling, with intentionally exposed downspouts draining concrete water channels.[4] The public entrances, lying on an east-west axis, are covered by concrete canopies.

1. Scale model, Physiotherapy Centre in foreground
2. Ground floor plan

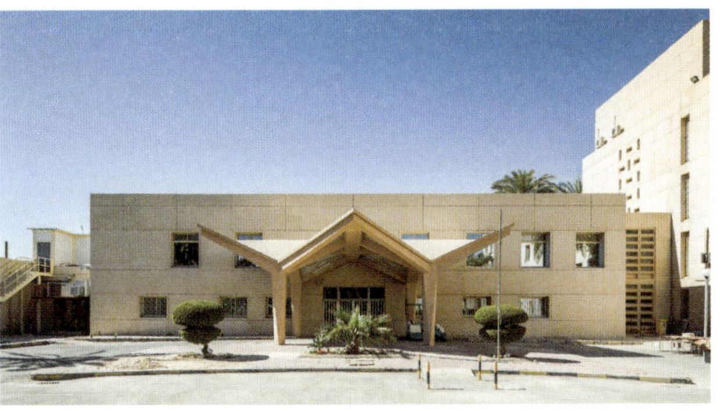

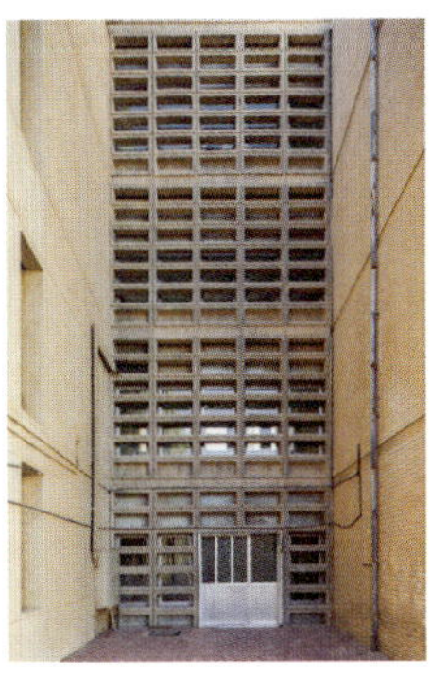

2

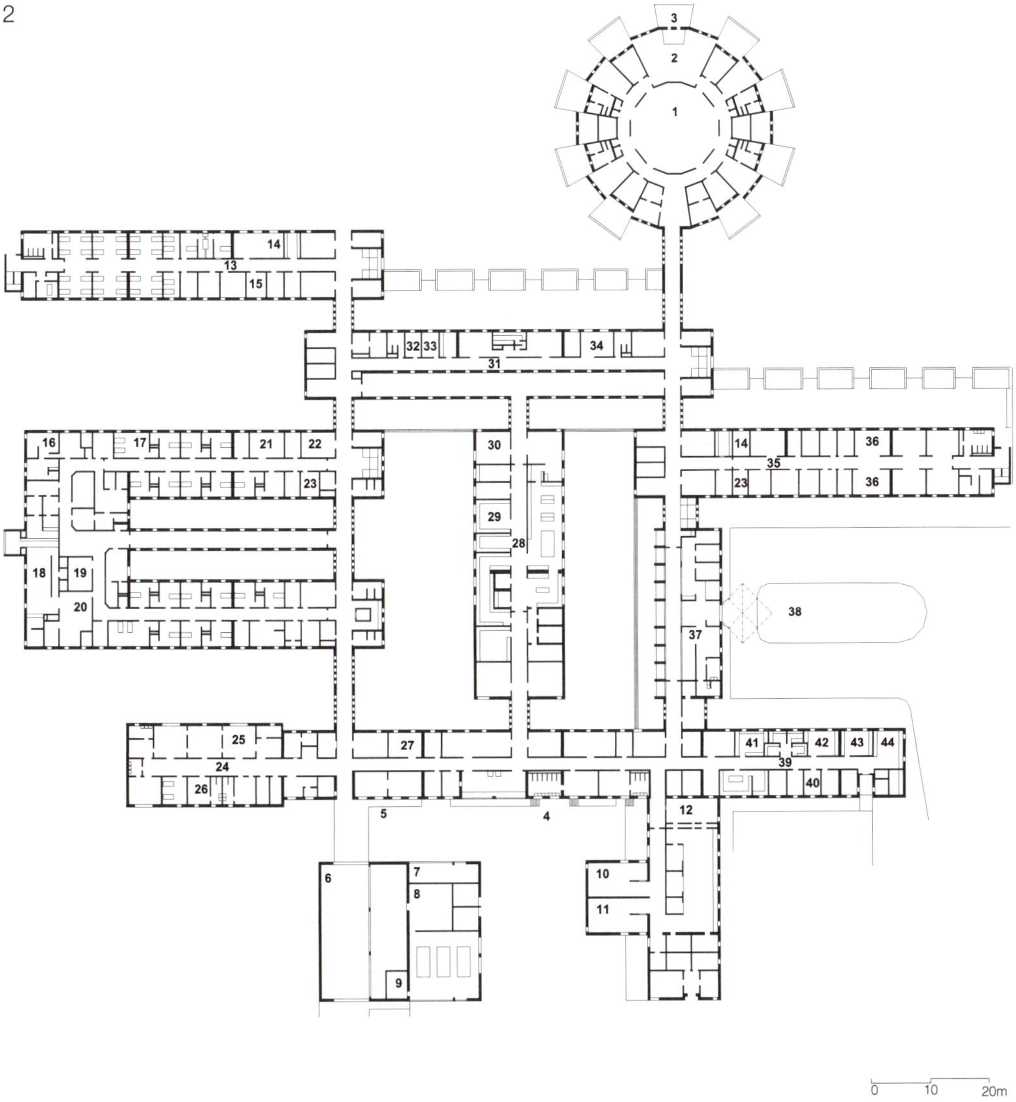

GROUND FLOOR PLAN

1. Physiotherapy & Occupational Therapy Centre
2. Lecture hall
3. Terrace
4. Service yard
5. Engineer's loading
6. Air conditioning plant
7. Transformer bay
8. Switch room
9. Incinerator
10. Clean laundry
11. Dirty laundry
12. Sterile side
13. 30-bed ward
14. Day and dining room
15. Treatment
16. Doctor's bed-sitting room
17. Labour ward
18. Concourse
19. Air conditioning
20. Dispensary
21. Small operations
22. Air conditioning
23. Doctor
24. Theatre suite
25. Theatre
26. Doctors
27. Oxygen store
28. Kitchen
29. Diet kitchen
30. Staff dining
31. X-ray treatment
32. Radiologist
33. Radiographer
34. Physiotherapy
35. 30-bed ward
36. 4-bed bay
37. Reception
38. Main entrance
39. Pathology department
40. Pathologist
41. Serology
42. Bacteriology
44. Biochemistry
44. Post mortem

SHEIKH JABER AL-ALI'S PALACE

SURRA
1955–1960

DESIGNER • Farmer & Dark Architects (John Barton, principal)
CLIENT • Sheikh Jaber Al-Ali Al-Sabah
CONTRACTORS • Contracting and Trading Co. (CAT)

MODIFIED

Contemporary of Prince Akihito's palace in Japan and the Planalto Palace in Brasília, Sheikh Jaber Al-Ali's palace is no longer in use. The magazine article, together with the pictures by Reginald Hugo de Burgh Galwey, remain the sole sources of information. According to these sources the palace stands on a site levelled to provide a plateau 7.5 m above the surrounding area that was extensively planted to relieve the aridity.[5]

A controlled garden layout containing two courtyards, fountains and a pool gives a "feeling of coolness" to the approach of the palace's main entrance. From this point, the entrance gives way to a gallery, large salon, anteroom and dining hall. Along the first floor a long gallery balcony of teak balustrade with panels of coloured armoured glass lead to the guest suites and command a view of the city. This volume is covered by a parabolic roof finished in copper.

The polychromatic façades with extensive use of tiles, mosaic and marble were a way to achieve the "required feeling of opulence" with unskilled labour avoiding elaborate detail. However, the use of anodised aluminium grilles and teak sliding shutters provide a feeling of refinement.

1

2

3

5

4

6

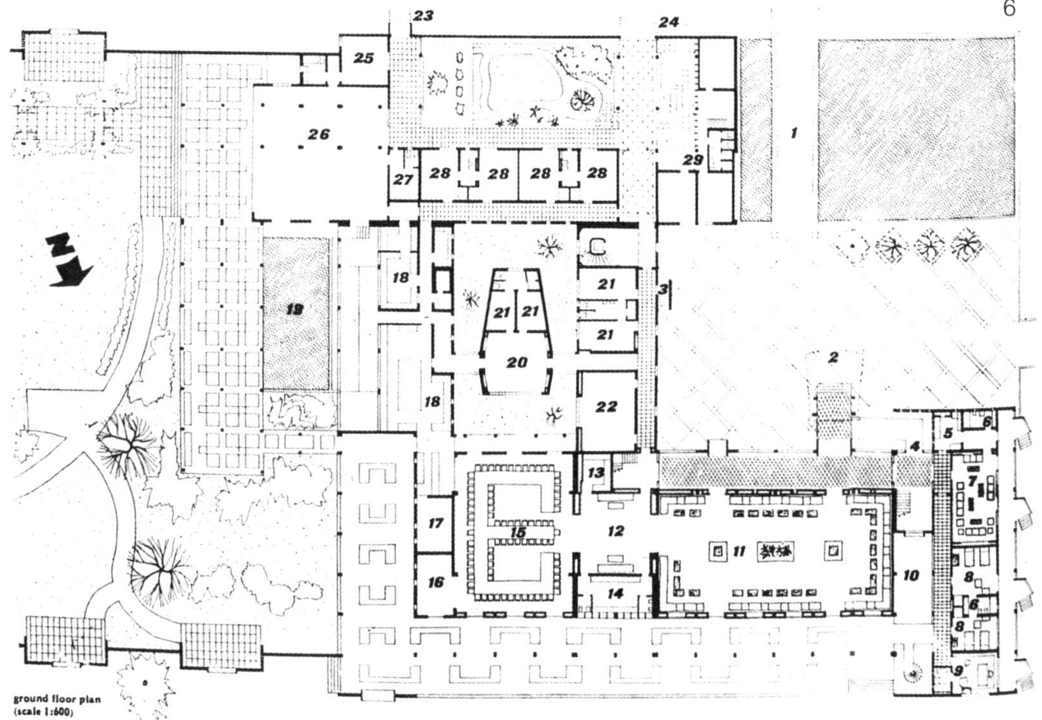

GROUND FLOOR PLAN

1. Bridge
2. Entrance porch
3. Servants' entrance
4. Guests' entrance
5. Guests' kitchen
6. Guests' bathroom
7. Guests' reception
8. Guests' bedrooms
9. Office
10. Patio
11. Salon
12. Ante room
13. Coffee kitchen
14. Wash room
15. Banqueting room
16. Furniture store
17. Projection room
18. Kitchens
19. Swimming pool
20. Servants' dining room
21. Servants' bedrooms
22. Servants' sitting room
23. Entertaining entrance
24. Harem entrance
25. Reception
26. Sheikh's dining and sitting room
27. Wash room
28. Bedrooms

THUNAYAN AL-GHANIM BUILDING

JAHRA GATE
1957–1959

DESIGNER • Sayyed Karim
CLIENT • Yusif Ahmed Al-Ghanim
CONTRACTOR • Unknown

IN USE

1

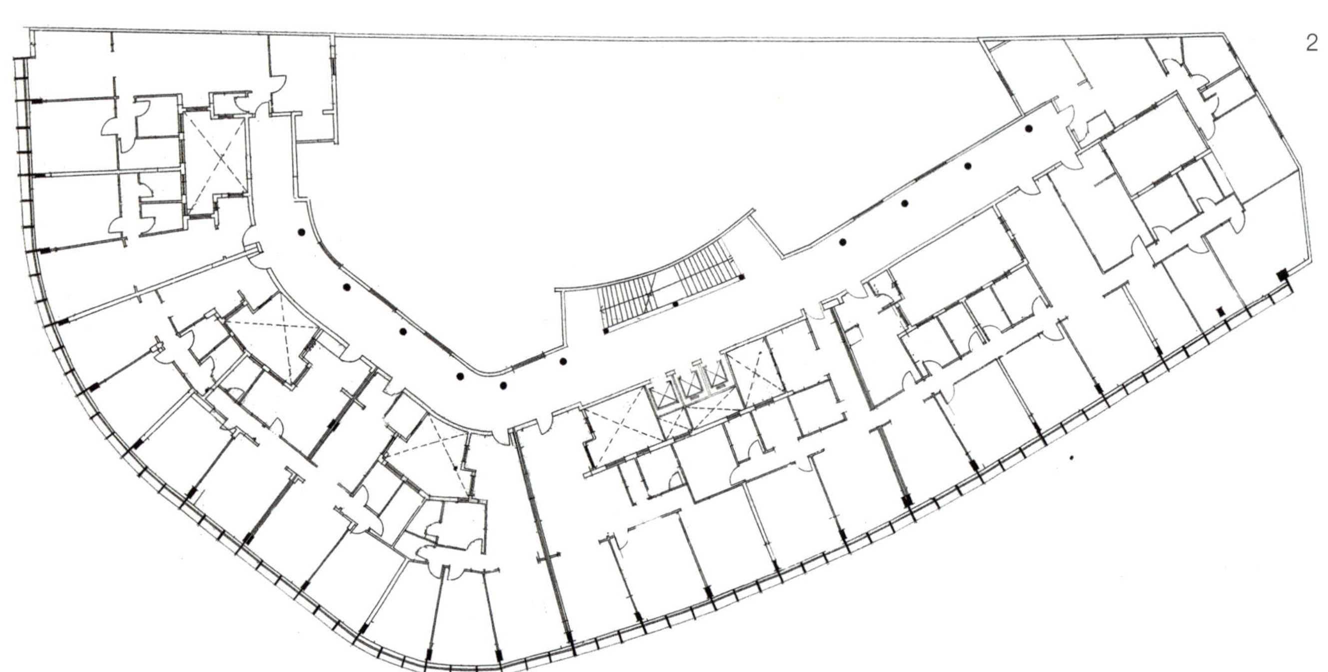

2

The Land Purchase Policies, as a consequence of the First Master Plan, encouraged the emergent private sector to invest in the construction of mixed-use buildings. The development pressure along Fahad Al-Salem St. during the 1950s, together with the demolition of the city's Third Wall and the completion of the First Ring Road, established the context for this commercial and apartment building, later converted into offices.[6]

The location and plot geometry facing Jahra Gate[7] at the entrance to the first modern avenue in the city, Fahad Al-Salem St., was and still is a fundamental condition for the complex display. The boomerang shaped plan expresses the building's volume which is mapped by a square pattern screened modulation and which provides shading and animates both shadows and light.

The rear façade features a passageway with a dominant staircase that distributes the flow of people along the top four floors to the different apartment units grouped in pairs around vertical shafts. The 48 units facing the main façade cantilever outside the commercial ground floor, allowing a covered arcade that later is extended beyond the building, all the way to Safat Square.

With this, the first multi-storey building in Kuwait, the important local Al-Ghanim family began their involvement in construction and development.

3

4

1. Scale model, circa 1957
2. Typical floor plan
3. Front view
4. Detail of the staircase

MINISTRY OF INFORMATION AND GUIDANCE

MUBARAK AL-KABEER ST.
1959–1962

DESIGNER • Sami Abdul Baki
with Ernst Van Drop
CLIENT • Ministry of Public Works
CONTRACTOR • Al-Shaya
Construction Co.

IN USE

Today's Headquarters of the National Council of Culture, Arts and Letters is an urban reference at the entrance of the central artery of Mubarak Al-Kabeer St. that leads to Sief Palace.

Initially it was conceived by Sayyed Karim to be an office building with a printing press incorporated into a four-storey building. The programmatic challenge and the free placement of the building on a corner plot produced a particular result where the concept of flow and organic dynamism are the main generators of form. The scheme was never implemented; only the position and the planimetric distribution of programme were kept in the building whose construction was started in 1959.[8]

When approached from the south, the rhythm of the façade is felt by the geometric regular concrete elements. The protective grid blocks the harsh sunlight, reinforcing its regular and horizontal volume. The recessed ground is emphasised by bold-coloured decorative tiles combining symbols of the old and new city. The main entrance is defined by a vertical white tile band background of an abstract composition that combines lines and geometric shapes with iconographic elements.

The inside of the public lobby features porcelain murals that are themed with images taken from Failaka in the Hellenistic era.

Before today's use, it functioned as the Ministry of Guidance and Information and also housed the first printing press in the country.

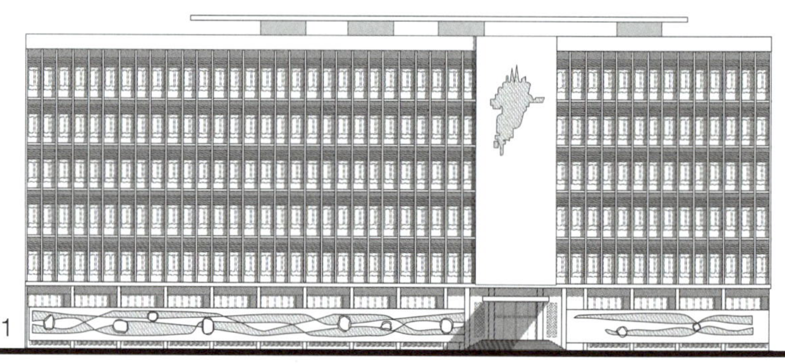

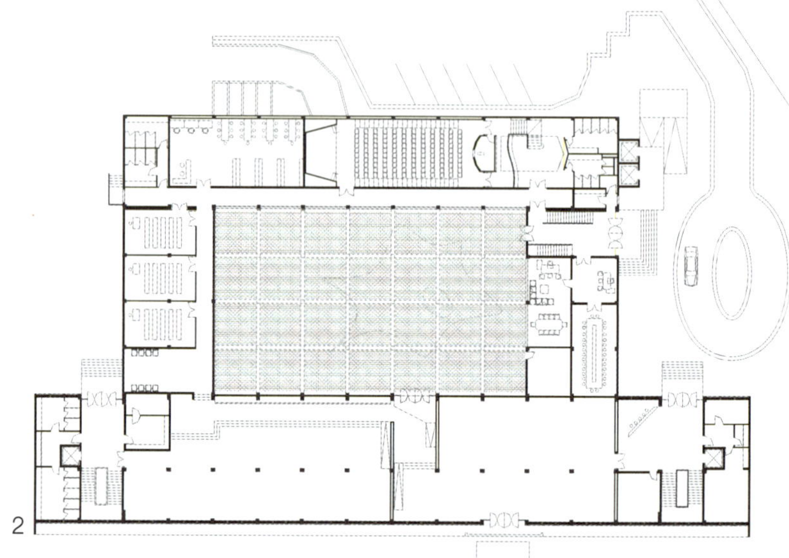

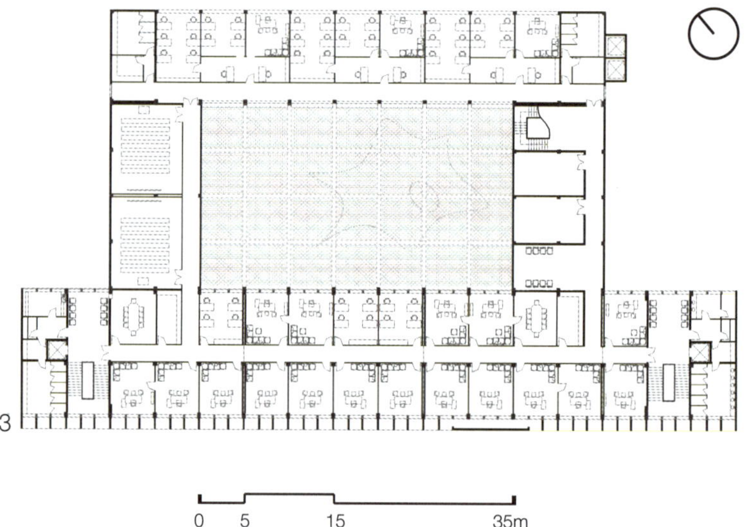

4
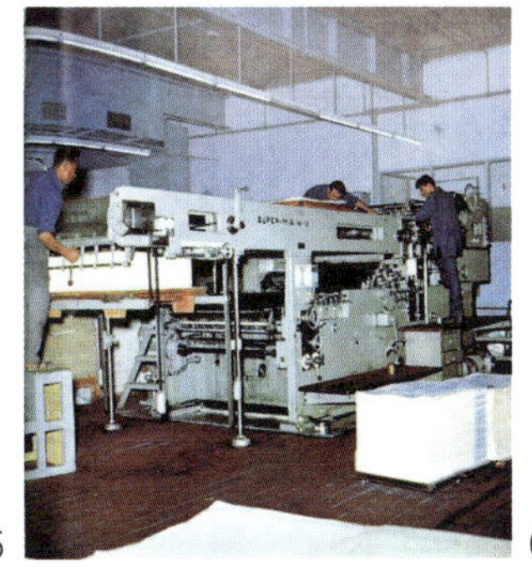
5

6

1. Main elevation
2. Ground floor plan
3. First floor plan
4. Detail of the ceramic mural, entrance lobby
representing Failaka vestiges
5. Printing machines "Superman IV", 1965
6. Printing area, 1965

GIRLS' SECONDARY SCHOOL

KHALDIYA
1962–1966

DESIGNER • Rambald von Steinbüchel-Rheinwall
CLIENT • Ministry of Public Works
CONTRACTOR • Overseas AST Co. Ltd.

IN USE

1

2

This school complex was awarded to an Austrian architect with offices in Frankfurt, following the completion of the Public Schools building programme in 1956 and the Boys' Secondary School in Shuwaikh.

The project's location as identified by Shiber in Bneid Al-Gar dates from 1957.[9] Upon his suggestion in 1961, the Education Department accepted to transfer the project, ready for tender, from that site to its actual location in Khaldiya.

The school was then built for 1,000 girls, 350 residents and teaching staff, comprising an auditorium seating 1,600 persons, along with a music centre and a detached area for sports including a swimming pool as part of the larger goal to provide the country with all kinds of recreational and sports facilities. This motivated the clear separation between the school's teaching programme and the sports facilities with direct access to the Airport Motorway.[10]

The swimming pool is arranged in a strongly designed zig-zag concrete pattern, interrupted by triangular windows running the full height of the building, allowing natural illumination and cross ventilation. Swimmers' access to the pool is through the gymnasium's lower level entrance while spectators' access is at the upper level by means of two external staircases.

Despite the fact that the residential area is quoted as a reference point of good climatic practice,[11] Alfred Roth criticises its climatic negligence in the 1966 report.[12] The article uses pictures of the three-bar residential units to showcase the building complex as an environmentally efficient scheme with protection from sandstorms and sun, vertical and cross circulation of air and double roof layers.

The music centre is a hinge connecting these units with the auditorium. In both there is an insistence on ramps as means of external circulation connecting the buildings and façade performance. The centre and auditorium with their organic shape and external lobby area with a complex system of ramps define an overall composition organised in terms of straight axial symmetry and connected

3

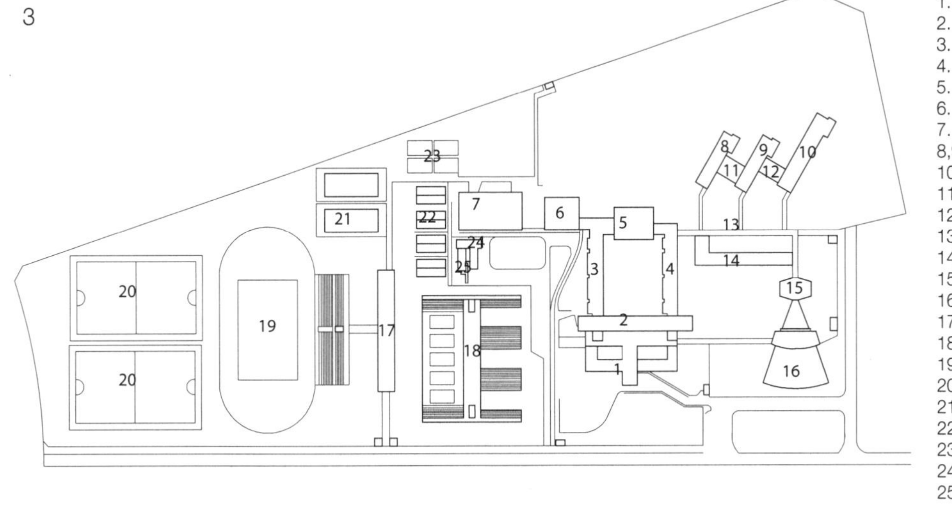

SITE PLAN

1. Main entry with administration
2. Classroom block
3. Science classrooms
4. Domestic science classroom
5. Dining room, exhibition space
6. Main kitchen, gymnasium
7. Covered swimming-pool
8,9. Staff living quarters
10. Students' living quarters
11. Girl guides
12. Pupils' workroom
13. Covered ways
14. Infirmary
15. Music room
16. Auditorium / main hall
17. Showers and WC
18. Tennis courts with grandstand
19. Stadium, ice hockey rink, grandstand
20. Handball pitch
21. Basketball pitch
22. Handball pitch
23. Volleyball pitch
24. Transformer building
25. Pumping station

4

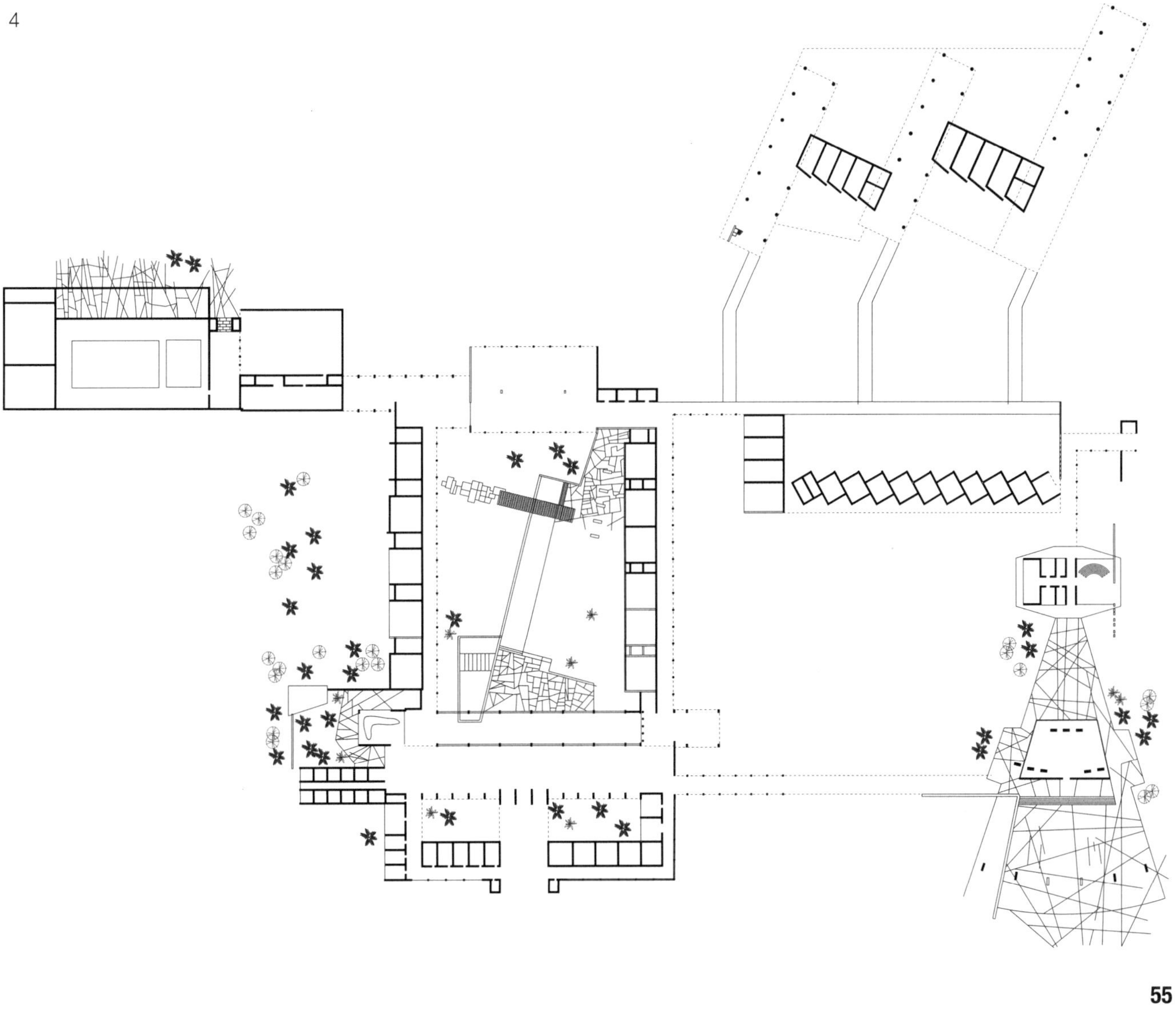

5

to the school main area by two long covered walkways.

The main programme of the school was comprised of administration, classrooms and dining hall, including a courtyard which no longer exists. The classrooms are open towards the north and all elements facing south and east are protected by either vertical or horizontal sun-breaks. Towards the south-east, the infirmary rooms are arranged in a non-orthogonal way following the sun's orientation.

The use of colour throughout the complex is of major relevance considering the relationship between the author and the *Deutscher Werkbund*, and his involvement in the exhibitions; *Sezession Graz* and *Berliner Bauausstellung*.[13]

The ambitious programme of the school together with the free plan of the campus may have influenced the conversion of the campus into a university in 1966.

6

1. Aerial view of the complex, circa 1968
2. Auditorium / main hall, side view
3. Site plan
4. Ground floor plan
5. Swimming pool, side view
6. Swimming pool, internal view
7. Former students' dormitories
8. Students' dormitories, staircase
9. Students' dormitories, external ramps

MUBARAKIYA SCHOOL

MUBARAKIYA
1957–1958

DESIGNER • Sayyed Karim
CLIENT • Ministry of Public Works
CONTRACTOR • Unknown

RENOVATED IN 2011

1

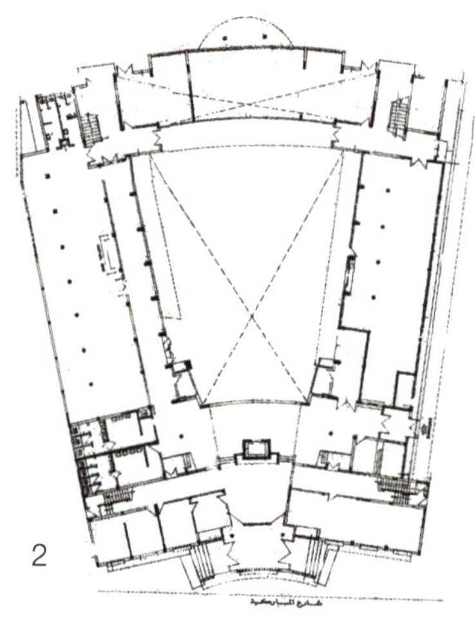

2

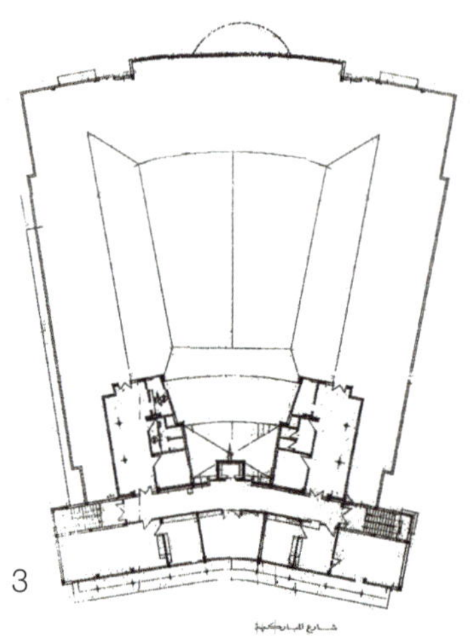

3

Built over the first known school in the country (1912) and inserted into the existing old fabric, the new secondary school for boys revitalised the site, introducing a new building scale and usage stock.

The main entrance on the west façade is raised from the street and covered by a thin shading slab. The upper floors cantilever, with thin concrete horizontal shading and vertical panels similar to those of contemporary buildings like the Thunayan Al-Ghanim and the Ministry of Information and Guidance. Behind the entrance, twin classrooms opened to an arcade facing the central courtyard. Opposite to the main façade, a circular auditorium enclosed the court.

Gradually the site acquired various uses after the school closed down, hosting the Central Library in 1979, the National Library between 1985 and 2011 and at present, the History of Education Museum.

Despite the changes in the internal space, this might be one of the few successful examples of adaptive re-use and modern structure preservation in the country.

1. Classrooms wing elevation, detail
2. Ground floor plan
3. First floor plan
4. View from Saud Bin Abdulaziz Street, 1958
5. Aerial view, circa 1971

CINEMAS

AHMADI
SHARQ
HAWALLY
JAHRA
SALMIYA
KHAITAN
1954–1973

DESIGNERS • Sayyed Karim;
Iraq Consult; Pace
CLIENT • Kuwait National Cinema Co.
CONTRACTORS • Various

*DEMOLISHED /
UNDER THREAT OF DEMOLITION*

The cinema building typology is among those referenced in the "Kuwait Building Programme" for Ahmadi. However, the first proper cinema building in that town, with a capacity for 1,200, was only inaugurated in 1966. Meanwhile The Kuwait National Cinema Company was established in 1954. One year later, Al-Sharqia Cinetheater was inaugurated with a capacity for 1,000 cinemagoers. The designer is unknown, but it is noted to be the first cinema in Kuwait City.[14]

In the same period, several other cinema projects were attributed to the Egyptian architect Sayyed Karim: Al-Firdous and Al-Hamra, both built in 1958 with pre-stressed concrete beams and located in the same area.[15] Cinema Al-Andalus, built in Hawally two years later had comprehensive similarities to the previous two and can be attributed to the same designer.[16] These buildings have the use of façade-shading geometrical elements within complex and articulated masses in common.

In the following years, 25 new cinemas were built around Kuwait, including Al-Jahra CineTheatre for 500 cinemagoers by PACE in collaboration with Iraq Consult, which was completed in 1973. The building is a regular and cubical volume textured by brick wall panels, revealing aluminium-framed fenestrations.

1

2

3

4

1. Salmiya Cinema, 1974
2. Al-Andalous Cinema, Hawally, 1974
3. Al-Andalous Cinema, Hawally, 1974
4. Al-Andalous Cinema, interior

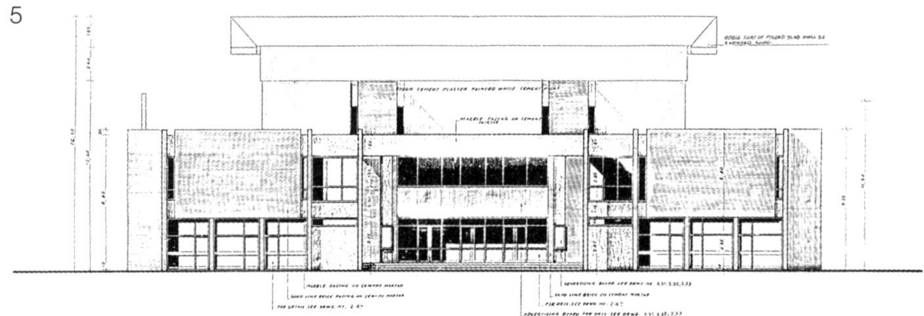

NORTH EAST ELEVATION
SCALE 1:100

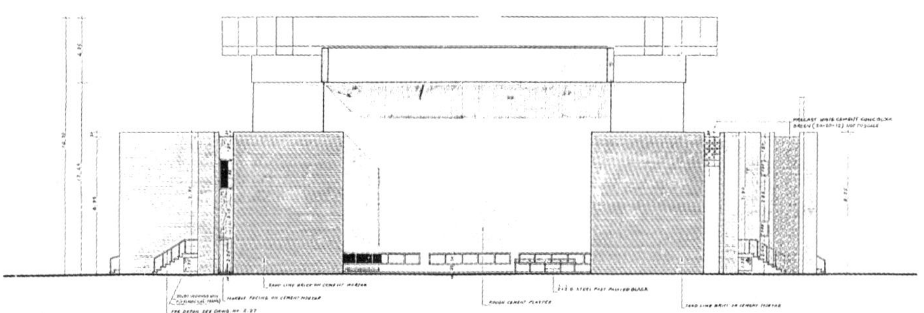

SOUTH WEST ELEVATION
1:100

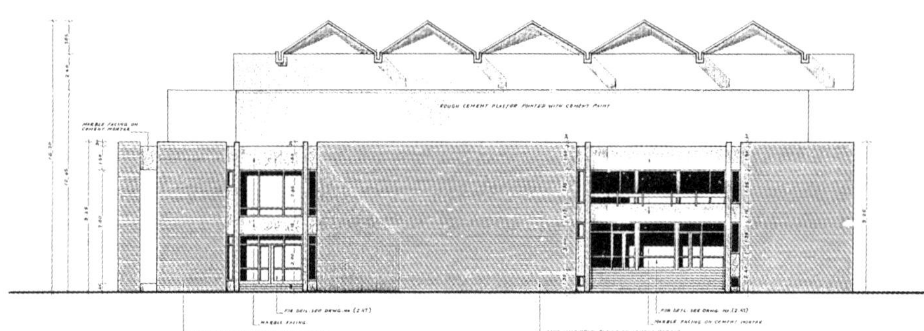

NORTH WEST ELEVATION
1:100

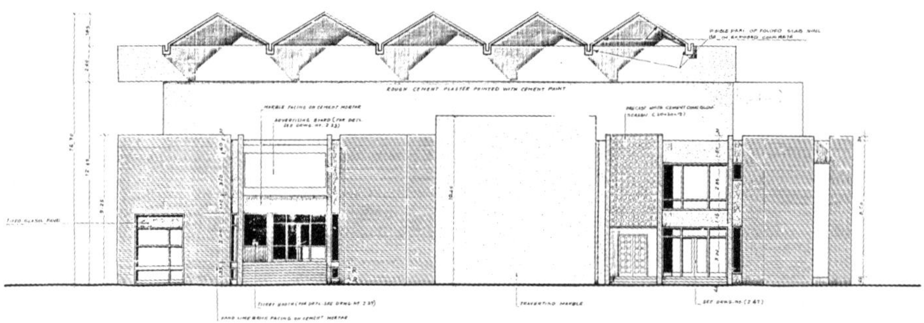

SOUTH EAST ELEVATION
SCALE 1:100

6

7

AL-JAHRA CINETHEATRE, 1969–1973

5. Elevations
6. General view
7. Front view

8

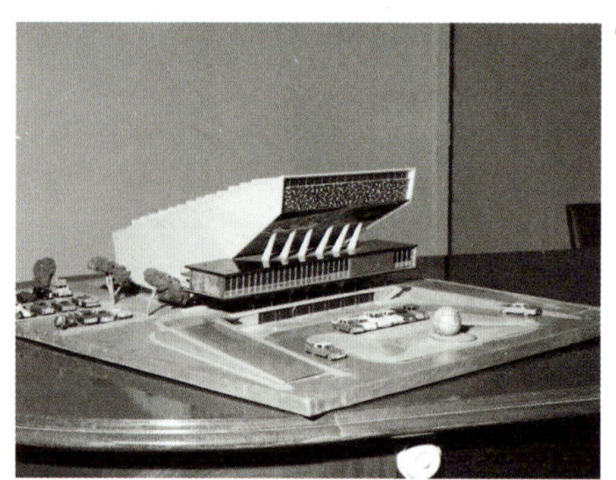

9

8. Gharnata Cinema, Khaitan, 1971
9. S. Karim, Ahmadi Cinetheatre,
1962–1965, scale model, January
1963 and aerial view, 1966
Contractor: Ahmadiah
10. S. Karim, Al-Hamra Cinema,
Sharq, 1958

GOVERNMENT HOTEL

GREEN BELT
1958

DESIGNER • Raglan Squire & Partners
CLIENT • Kuwait Development Board

UNBUILT

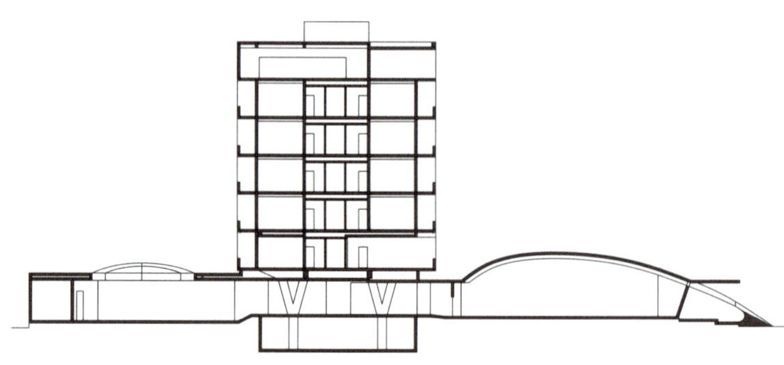

1. Scale model, circa 1958

While Kuwait was intensifying commercial exchanges, the necessity for a proper hotel increased. It is known that accommodation was available in the city centre since the late 1940s, though the existing lodging was not considered appropriate for the kind of businessmen or delegations that Kuwait was trying to attract. Consequently, the international British firm, Squire, was consulted to design a first-class hotel directly sponsored by the State. Squire's firm had other commissions in the country (i.e. several police stations and the American Embassy), but he was probably selected because of his connection with Hilton Hotels: for which he designed hotels in Manama, Cyprus and Tehran.

The first proposal was a patio typology, a large quadrilateral embracing a semi-covered garden, presented as an "old Turkish concept" in the designer's words.[17] However the client preferred a more western type of building with open plans and a ground floor able to accommodate receptions, restaurants, shops, meeting rooms, etc. The final version was a linear block with deep balconies punctuated by vertical fins as protection from direct sunlight.[18] Particular care was put into the structural design, preventing concrete dilating in the extreme heat, and into the proposed finishes: marbles, travertines, teak and coloured mosaic tiles for the parapets. The building was praised by Shiber as an example of simplicity against the eclecticism spreading in town, but nonetheless he suggested relocating it, so as not to interfere with the city park known as the Green Belt.[19]

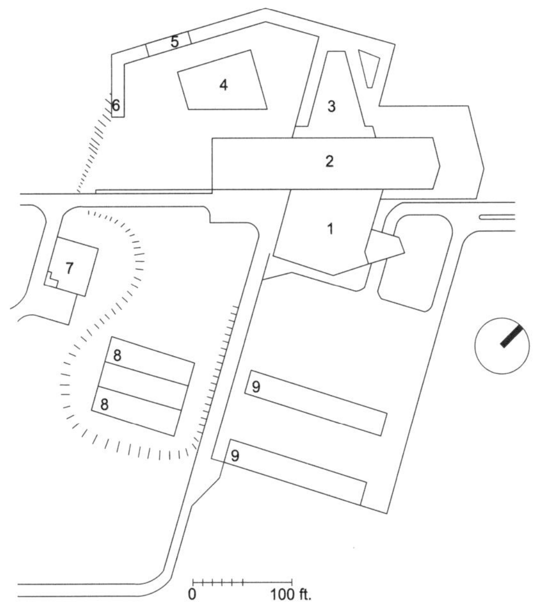

SITE PLAN

1. Entrance foyer
2. Main hotel block
3. Restaurant
4. Swimming pool
5. Changing rooms
6. Pool play room
7. Manager's bungalow
8. Staff quarters
9. Garages

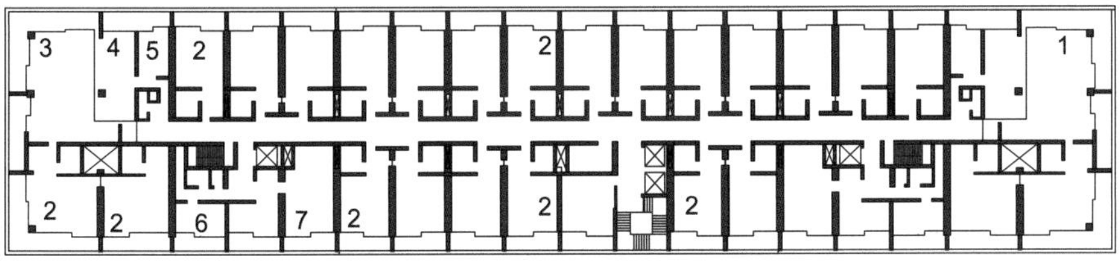

TYPICAL FLOOR PLAN

1. Private suites
2. Bedrooms
3. Living room
4. Dining area
5. Kitchen
6. Servants
7. Housekeeping

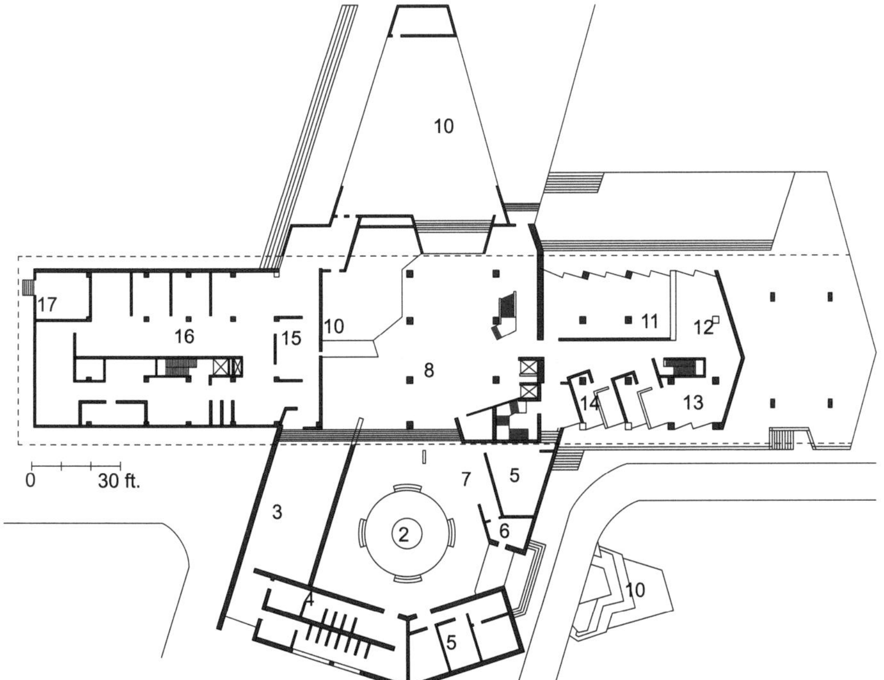

GROUND FLOOR PLAN

1. Entrance
2. Pool
3. Private dining rooms
4. Cloakroom
5. Administrative offices
6. Porter
7. Receptions
8. Main lounge
9. Tea lounge
10. Restaurants
11. Waiting room
12. Beauty salon
13. Men's hairdressing
14. Shops
15. Washing up
16. Cooking area
17. Garden equipment store
18. Fountain

PSYCHIATRIC HOSPITAL

SULAIBIKHAT
1954–1958

DESIGNER • Unknown
CLIENT • H.H. the Amir of Kuwait
CONTRACTOR • Unknown

IN USE

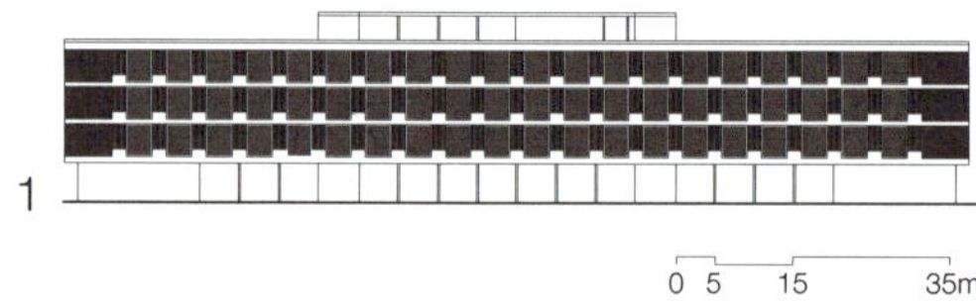

1

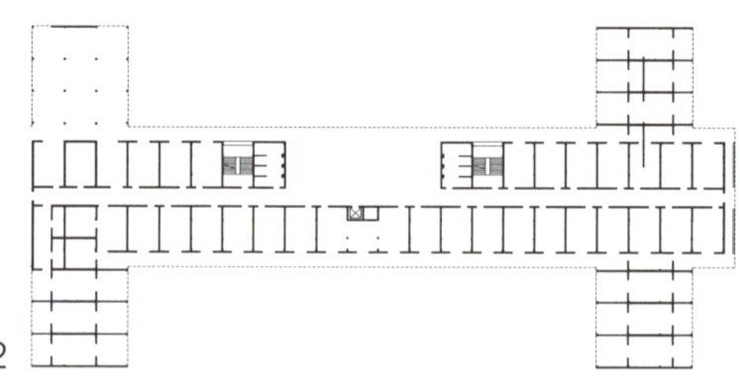

2

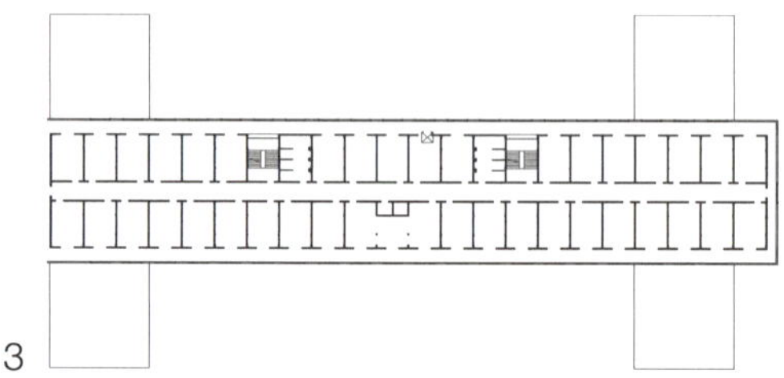

3

The complex, located in Sulaibikhat and disconnected from the rest of Al-Sabah Hospital, is known as the former Psychiatric Hospital. The date of the first reference to the earliest hospital in this area is not precise, but does date between 1954 and 1958. Different publications refer to it as a T.B. Sanatorium, Hospital for Nervous Diseases, Psychiatric Hospital, an Infectious Diseases Hospital or simply refer to its location. However, in 1957 the "Health Statistics" of Kuwait Ministry of Health reported an increase of beds from 611 to 1,322 that could eventually fit in this complex. The later reference to the building description refers to a "pavilion style" with a capacity for 200 beds later expanded to double the size.[20]

Specialised medical literature refers to a large increase in mental health and psychological services[21] that were started at the hospital in 1972 and that may have resulted in the building expansion. To this day the complex is distributed along two wings connected by covered pedestrian paths leading to admission and emergency care, clinical medical services, functional diagnostics, laboratory medicine, nuclear medical therapy, physical therapy, administration and management offices, archives, library, education and training, child care centre, and staff housing.

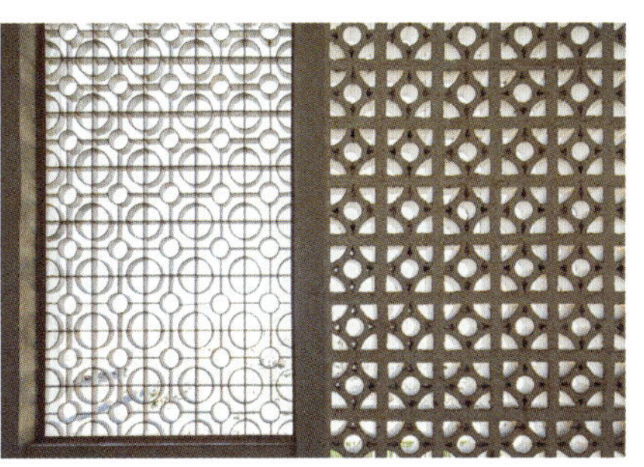

1. Typical elevation
2. Ground floor plan
3. Typical patient rooms floor plan

AL-SABAH HOSPITAL

SULAIBIKHAT
1958–1982

DESIGNERS • Dorsch Consultants (planning and services); Scott & Wilson, Kirkpatrick & Partners; KEO
CLIENT • The State of Kuwait
CONTRACTOR • Contracting And Trading Co. (CAT); Overseas AST Co. Ltd; Consolidated Contractors Co. (CONCO)

UNDER THREAT OF DEMOLITION

1

2

The Hospital Master Plan was completed in 1959.[22] Following this, a series of buildings consolidated the complex, including three central units with a capacity for 600 beds dedicated to specialised treatment and admitting inpatients and casualties, with segregation in maternity, surgical, and paediatric care; nurses' and doctors' hostels; staff accommodation; the college of nurses and medical store.[23]

Who the authors of the initially proposed architectural scheme were and who implemented the majority of the work up to the late 1960s is not known; the exception being the medical store that Scott & Wilson, Kirkpatrick & Partners built between 1963–65, already part of the campus axonometric layout published in *Al-Kuwait* in 1959. The nurses' hostel units 1 and 2 (later expanded to two more) are also part

of this scheme, together with the staff accommodation.

Later the campus was expanded towards the south to include the Organ Transplant Centre (KEO, 1982), the Kuwait Cancer Control Centre buildings, including the Hussain Makki Juma building for Specialized Surgery and the Sheikha Badriya Al-Sabah Medical Oncology Building.

3

4

5   6

1. Surgery Inpatient Unit, circa 1966
2. Former Maternity Hospital and outpatients, 1962
3. Nurses' school, interior, 1972
4. Al-Kuwait magazine, cover, 1964
5. Aerial view of the compound, 1968
6. Nurses' school, 1972

7

8

9

10

7. Former Marternity Hospital, outpatients admission
8. Dispensary
9. Former Marternity Hospital, side elevation
10. Nurses' hostel
11. Kuwait Cancer Control Centre, detail of the precast sun-breakers
12. Kuwait Cancer Control Centre, entrance

13

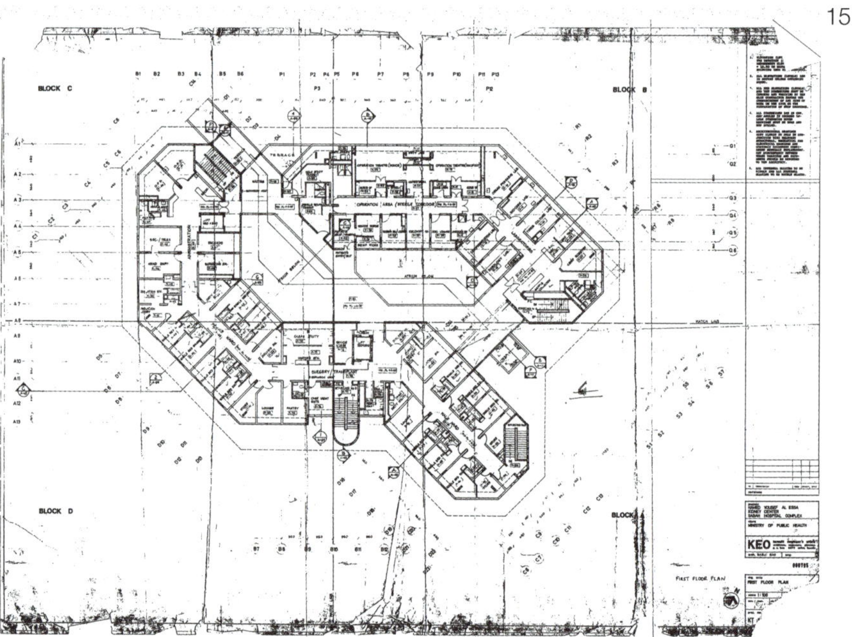

14

15

74

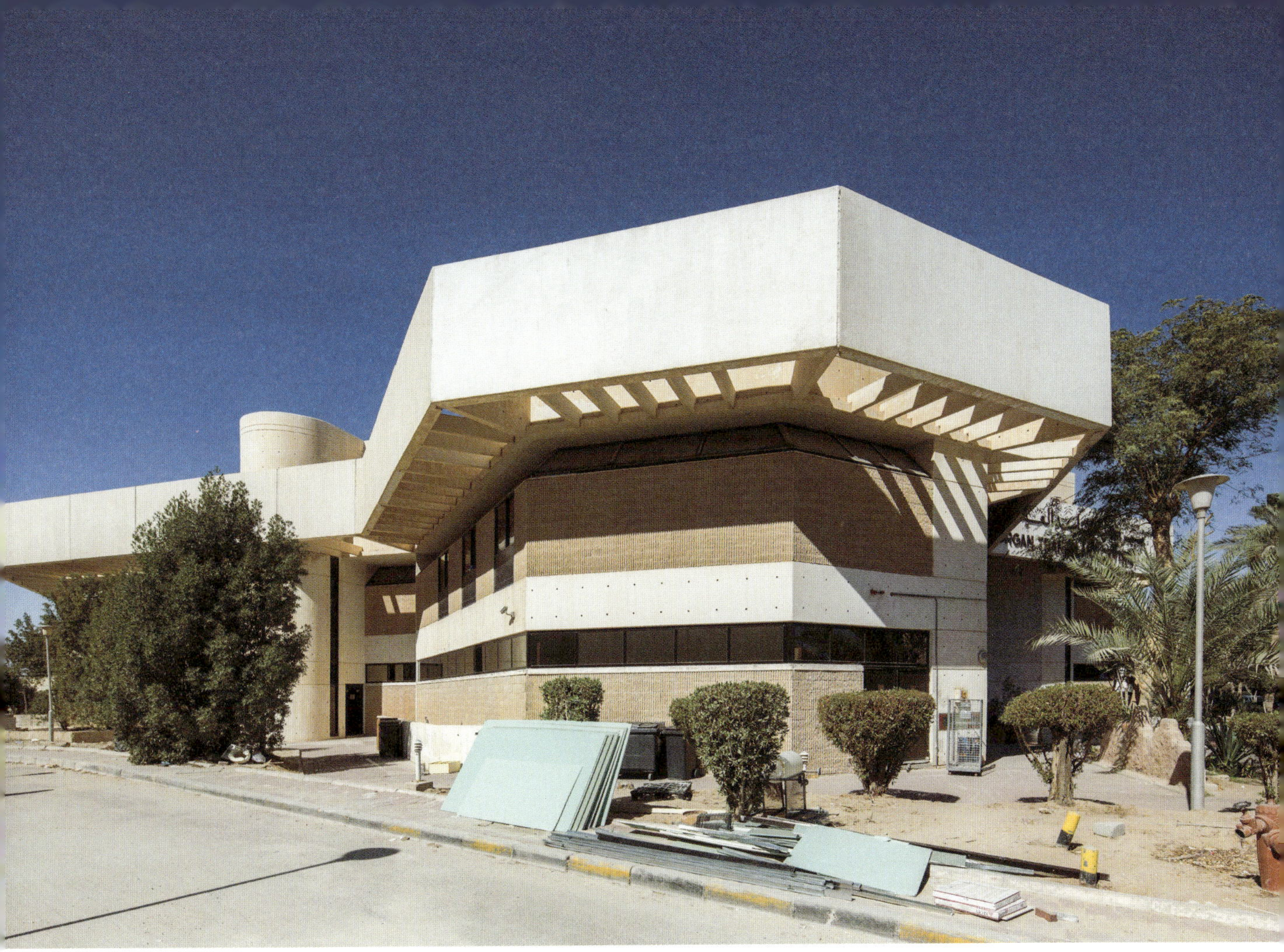

16

17

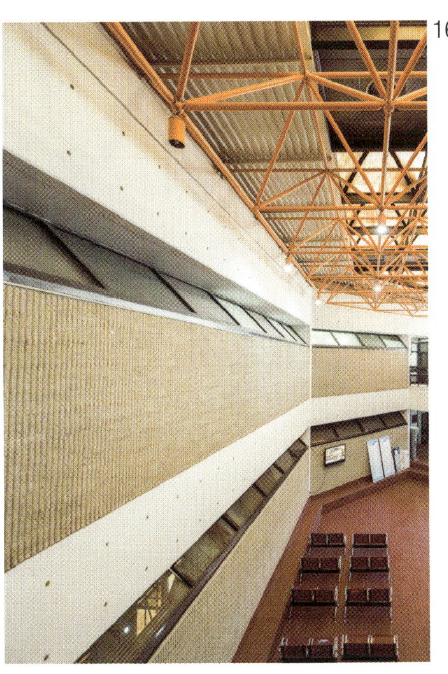

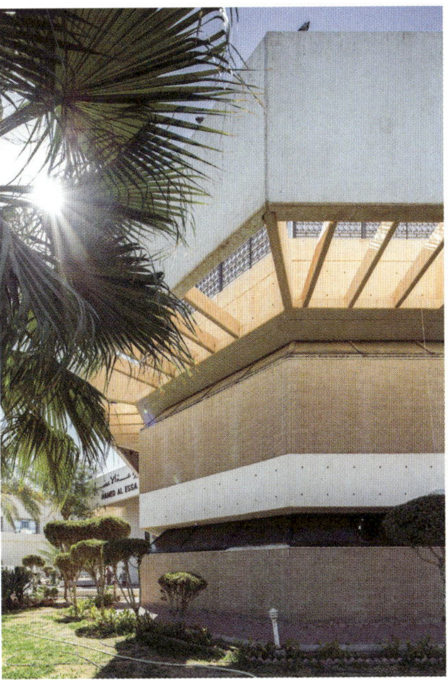

SHEIKHA BADRIYA AL-SABAH MEDICAL ONCOLOGY BUILDING:

13. East elevation
14. Main entrance
15. Ground floor plan

ORGAN TRANSPLANT CENTRE:

16. Interior
17. Detail of the façade

MUNICIPAL COMPLEX

ABDULLA AL-SALEM ST.
1959–1962

DESIGNER • Sami Abdul Baki
CLIENT • Ministry of Public Works
CONTRACTOR • Osman Ahmed
Osman & Co. (Arab Contractors)

MODIFIED

1

Today's Municipality complex, also known as the *Baladiya*, was awarded to an Arab architect and contractor following Sheikh Fahad Al-Salem directions.[24]

Once finished, this building simultaneously accommodated the temporary seat of the *Majilis al-Ummah* – the National Assembly, hosted for the first time after the December 1962 elections.

Conceived in three similar autonomous units (A, B, C), with a common underground parking, they were among the first reinforced concrete structures in the country.

Instead of the heavy use of concrete shaded fenestration, generically labelled as *Al-imara al-haditha*,[25] here the building is covered by the newest façade technology, following references to the International Style.

The top façades are covered with sea blue tiles and coloured smaller mosaics. The main entrance is defined by a freestanding arch.

Along with the Ministry of Guidance and Information, these buildings were the symbols of an up-and-coming new city and until now, act as urban references.

2

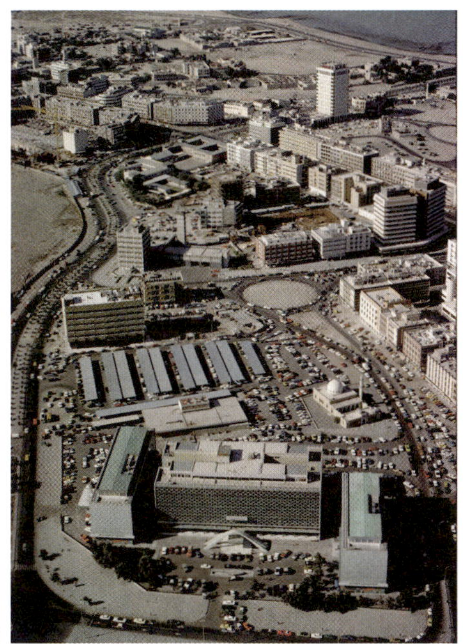

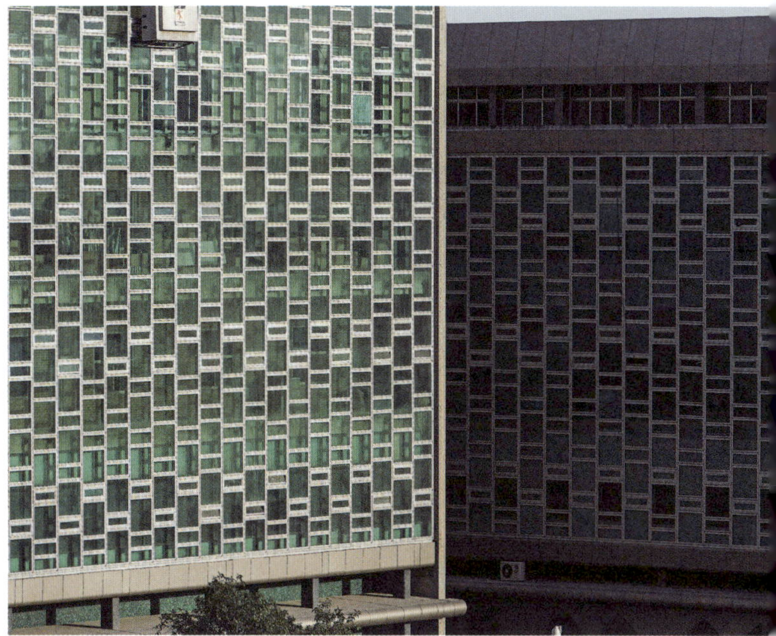

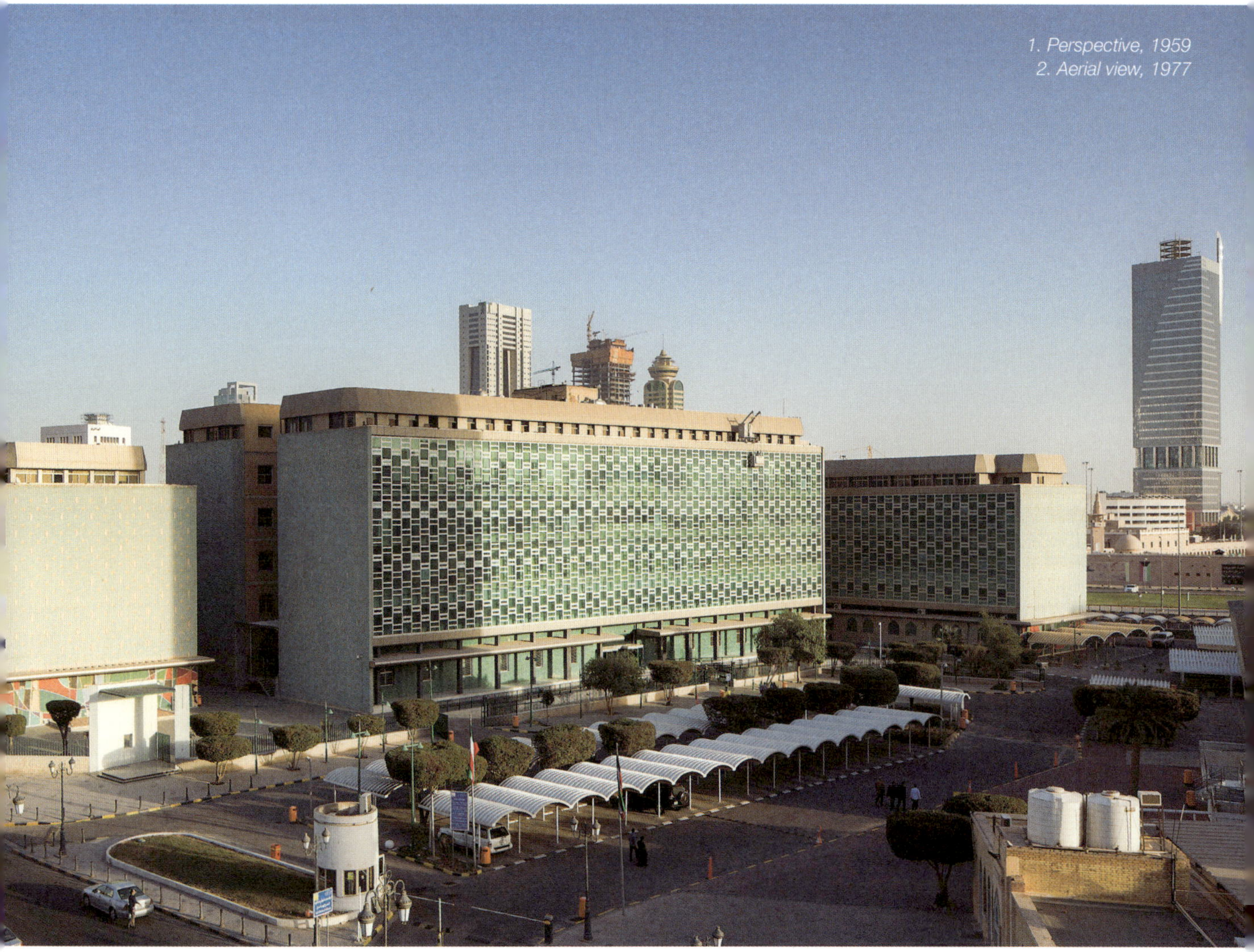

1. *Perspective, 1959*
2. *Aerial view, 1977*

ANWAR AL SABAH COMPLEX, PHASE I AND II

SALHIYA
1975–1981

DESIGNERS • Ghazi Sultan with KEO;
CLIENT • United Realty Co.
CONTRACTOR • Musaad Al-Saleh & Sons Co.

UNDER THREAT OF DEMOLITION

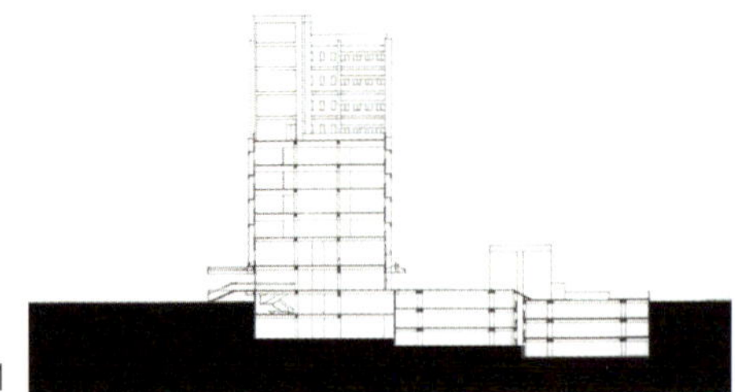

1

2

The important reference point of the city's early modernisation, Fahad Al-Salem Street became an attractive area for private development in 1960.[26] Ruling family members were among the first investors. Popularly known as the "Al-Sabah Complex," the residential and commercial unit was built under Shiber's design guidelines.[27] Three building blocks are unified by a single façade system, a common commercial arcade facing the street and a pergola connecting the backyard. The complex is in a state of advanced degradation, but is still in use for retail and residential purposes.

Almost fifteen years later the backyard became part of an international competition. The winning proposal of a massive sandstone-clad complex was built. Incomplete, it remains unoccupied today.

3

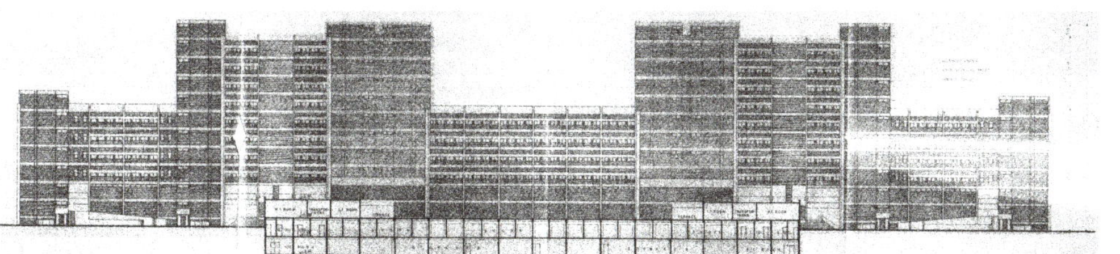

5

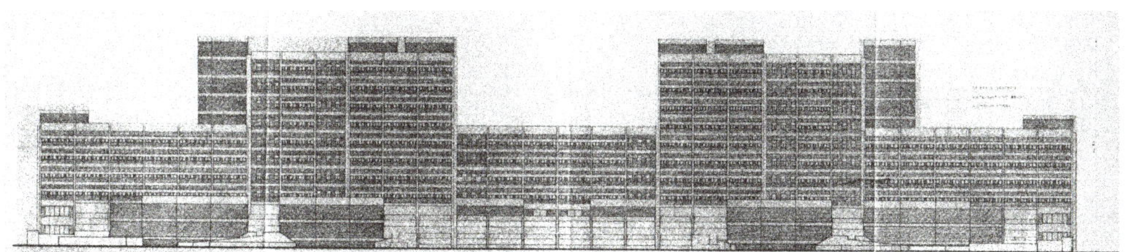

1. Phase II, sections
2. Phase I, front view from Fahed Al-Salem Street
3. Phase II, south elevation
4. Phase I, view of the rear façade
5. Phase II, elevations

AL-SALAM PALACE

ARABIAN GULF STREET
1961–1964

DESIGNER • Medhat El-Abd
CLIENT • Sheik Saad Al-Abdullah Al-Sabah
CONTRACTOR • Unknown

UNDER RENOVATION

Facing the city waterfront at the end of the Second Ring Road, the Amir's Guest Palace was once surrounded by extensive formal gardens and enclosed by an expressive boundary brick wall, only interrupted by two steel gates and flanked by sentry posts. The plan's alignment, perpendicular to the sea, defines the building's internal organization and entry points.

The core of the palace is a central, circular, enclosed court of triple height, with all walls radiating about or from the centre of this space, covered by a spired plate roof with a domed freestanding concrete slab. The external composition is crafted between opaque surfaces and grids working as geometric ornamentation. Inside, a fountain aligned with a large chandelier emphasises the centre of the formal noble reception room, with its perimeter defined by a loop of elliptical elements running to the full height of the core. The combination of different materials improves the plasticity of the whole: the original interior finishes included walnut and mahogany veneer plywood paneling, glass mosaics, stone and ceramic floor tiles and painted plaster walls and ceilings.

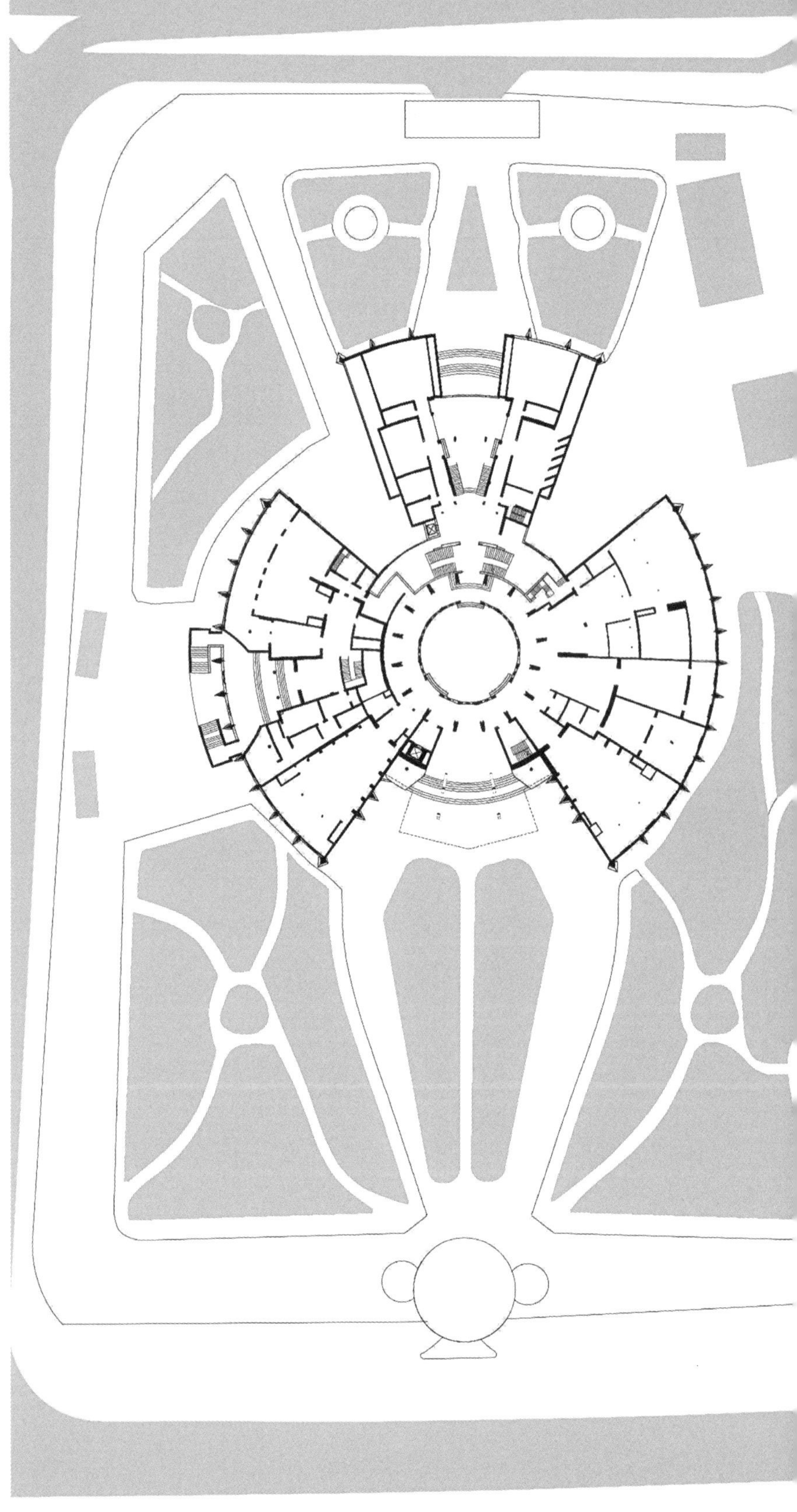

1

2

3

4

5

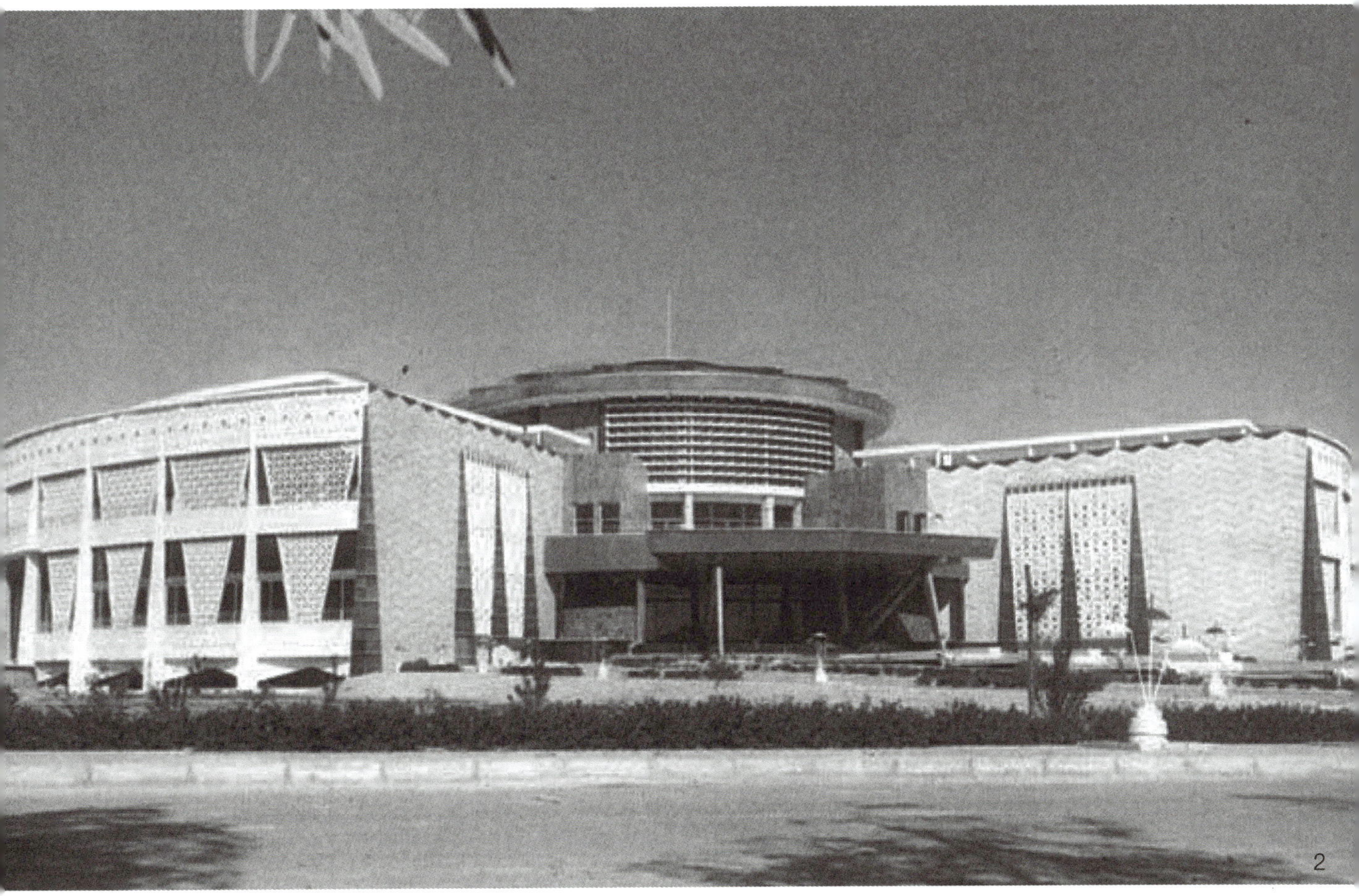

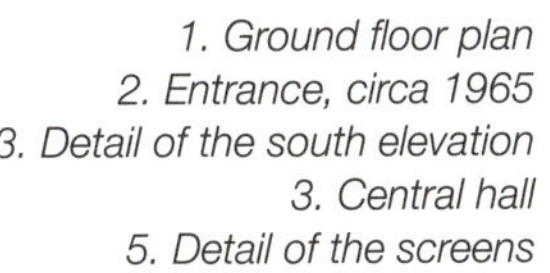

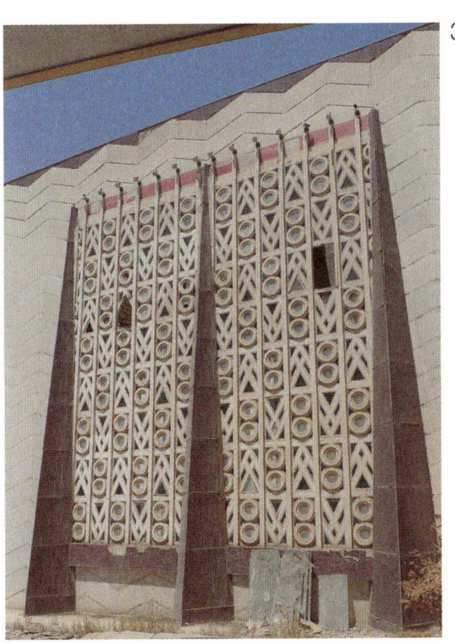

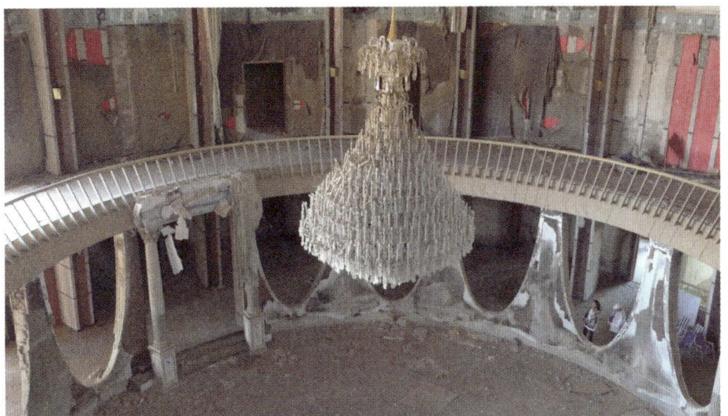

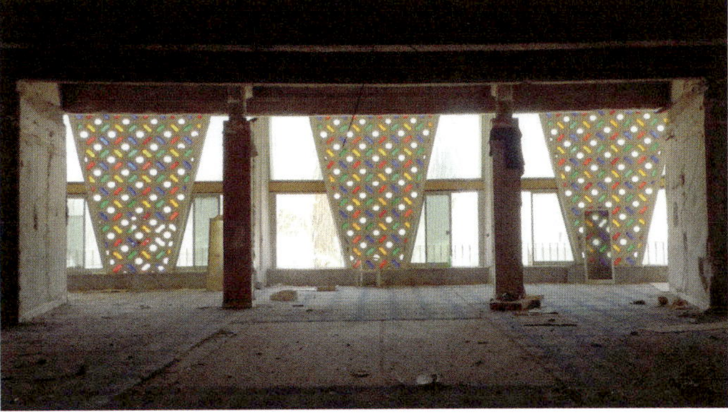

1. Ground floor plan
2. Entrance, circa 1965
3. Detail of the south elevation
3. Central hall
5. Detail of the screens

NOTES

1. "Civil Engineering Contracts", in *The Engineer*, Dec 20 1957

2. Abuhamdeh, Said, "Kuwait", in *Middle East Forum*, April 1958, p.19

3. "Schools at Kuwait", in *Architectural Design*, Mar. 1957, v. 32, p. 94

4. Cf. "Women's Hospital, Kuwait", in *Architectural Review*, Apr. 1969, v. 145, n. 866, pp. 291–294

5. "Palace in the Persian Gulf", in *Architectural Review*, Dec. 1960, pp. 424–428

6. Cf. "Architecture in the Middle East", in *Architectural Design*, Mar. 1957, v. 27, p. 75, 87

7. The Jahra Gate of the old mud wall was the main entrance between the desert and the city, giving to this building an important cultural meaning: the New behind the city walls ruins.

8. The first known proposal for this site from 1957 by Sayed Karim gives the Press and Publications Department of the Government as client.

9. Shiber, Saba G., "Saving the Green-Belt of Kuwait", March 1961, in *The Kuwait Urbanization*, Government Printing Press, 1964

10. "Sekundärschule für Mädchen in Kuwait", *Bauen + Wohnen*, n. 20, 1966, pp.144–145

11. "Sekundärschule für Mädchen in Kuwait", *Bauen + Wohnen*, n. 20, 1966, pp.144–145

12. Alfred Roth, *The School Buildings of Kuwait*, report, 1966

13. After working for Hans Poelzig and Peter Behrens, Rambald von Steinbüchel-Rheinwall became a member of *Deutscher Werkbund* and took part in the exhibition *Berliner Bauausstellung* in 1931 about *"Sun, Air and House for All."* Two years later, as the artistic director of Graz municipality, he took part in the *Sezession Graz*.

14. Al-Ghunaim, Abdullah Y. (ed.), *Kuwait in Postcards,* Centre for Research and Studies on Kuwait, Kuwait, 2009

15. Abuhamdeh, Said, "Kuwait," in Middle East Forum, Apr. 1958, pp. 20–21

16. Alissa, Reem, *Building for Oil: Corporate Colonialism, Nationalism and Urban Modernity in Ahmadi, 1946–1992*, Ph.D. dissertation, UC Berkeley, 2012

17. "Hotel in Kuwait," in *Architectural Design*, Nov. 1958, v. 28, pp. 460–461

18. "Grande albergo a Kuwait", in *Domus*, Mar. 1959, n. 352, p. 6

19. Shiber, George "Saving the Green Belt" in *The Kuwait Urbanization*, Kuwait Govt. Printing Press, 1964, pp. 378–379

20. French, Geoffrey E. Hil, Alan G. "Kuwait: Urban and Medical Ecology. A Geomedical Study", in *Medizinische Länderkunde Geomedical Monograph Series*, v. 4, 1971

21. Al-Motawa, M., Ayoub, A., & Horan, H., *Psychiatric Nursing in Kuwait*, Kuwait, 1987

22. "Kuwait State Development Projects," in *The Kuwaiti*, 26 March 1959

23. French, Geoffrey E. Hil, Alan G., "Kuwait: Urban and Medical Ecology. A Geomedical Study", in *Medizinische Länderkunde Geomedical Monograph Series*, Volume 4, 1971

24. Head of the Department of Public Works and Kuwait Municipality

25. Sayyed Karim's expression to translate the International Style or Modern Architecture as referred to by local authors: Al-Ragam, "Towards a Critique of an Architectural Nahdha: A Kuwaiti Example"; Alissa, "Building for Oil: Corporate Colonialism, Nationalism and Urban Modernity in Ahmadi, 1946–1992."

26. Cf. Mueller, John, Henry, *Cadillacs and Coca-Cola; 53° im Schatten, 82° an der Sonne. Erlebnisse eines Schweizer Ingenieurs in Kuwait*, Zürich, Schweizer Druck- und Verlagschaus, 1962

27. Fahad Al Salem Street built in the first years of post-1952 urban development with no building regulations or guidelines. After Saba George Shiber's arrival in Kuwait, from July 1960 the Municipal Council initiated "architectural control". Cf. Shiber, Saba George, *The Kuwait Urbanization: Documentation, Analysis, Critique*, Kuwait Govt. Printing Press, 1964

SPECIMENS II
Building as national identity
1961–1970

KUWAIT NATIONAL MUSEUM COMPETITION

JIBLA
1960

PARTICIPANTS • Hans Asplund; Zdravko Bregovac; Ignazio Gardella; Karim Sayyed; Affonso Reidy; Michel Écochard (with Pierre Lajus)
CLIENT • Ministry of Education

UNBUILT

The museum programme was established in 1960 by Selim Abdul-Hak of UNESCO at the request of the Government of Kuwait.[28] Consequentially the first international architectural competition of Kuwait was held by the Ministry of Education, inviting the following architects: Hans Asplund (Stockholm), Zdravko Bregovac (Opatija), Ignacio Gardella (Milan), Sayyed Karim (Cairo), Affonso Reidy (Brazil) and the winner Michel Écochard (Beirut, Paris).

All the competitors had to follow precise guidelines and direct their design to incorporate the following topics: (1) Land of Kuwait; (2) Man of Kuwait; (3) Kuwait of today and tomorrow; (4) Cultural Section, which included administration, temporary exhibitions, and various conference rooms, a library and cafeteria; (5) Planetarium; to show the ancient instruments of observation.

2

1

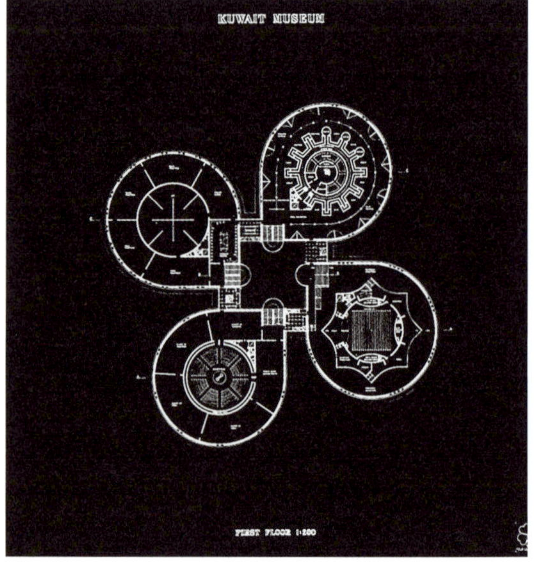

4

3

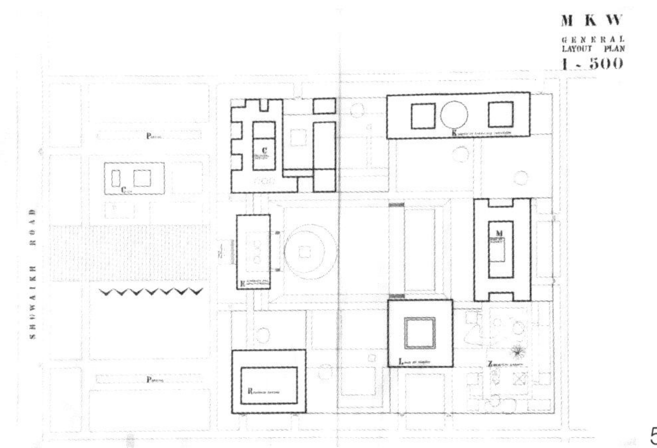

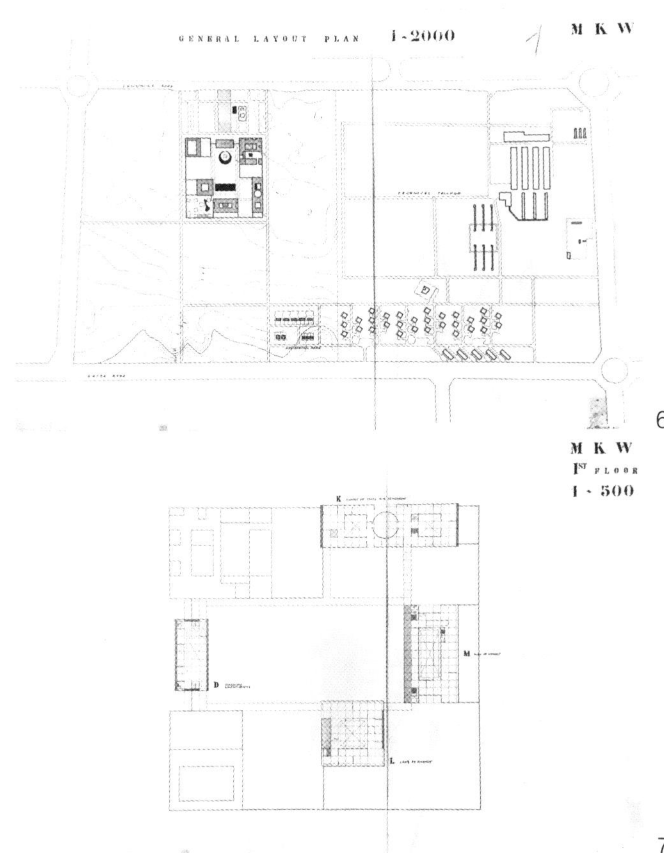

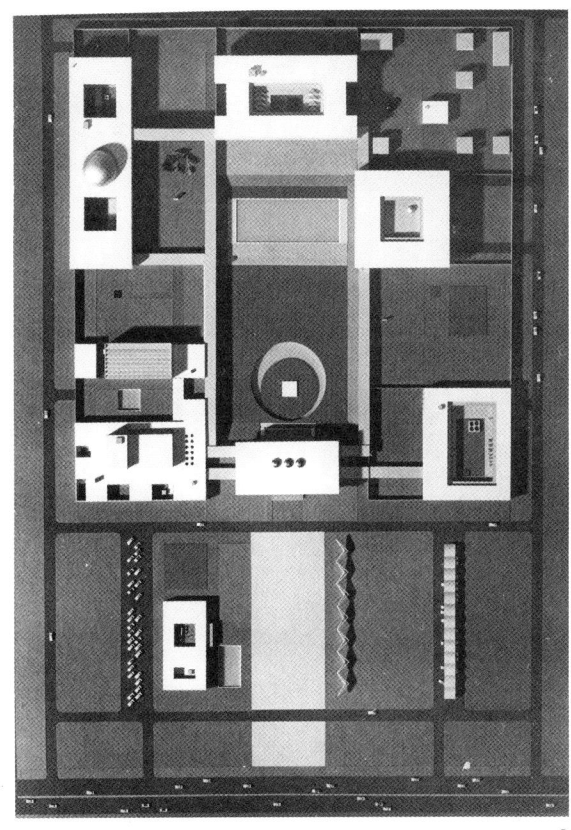

H. ASPLUND'S PROPOSAL:

1. General perspective
2. Site plan
3. First floor plan
4. Interior perspective

Z. BREGOVAC'S PROPOSAL:

5. General layout plan
6. Site plan
7. First floor plan
8. Scale model, top view
9. Scale model

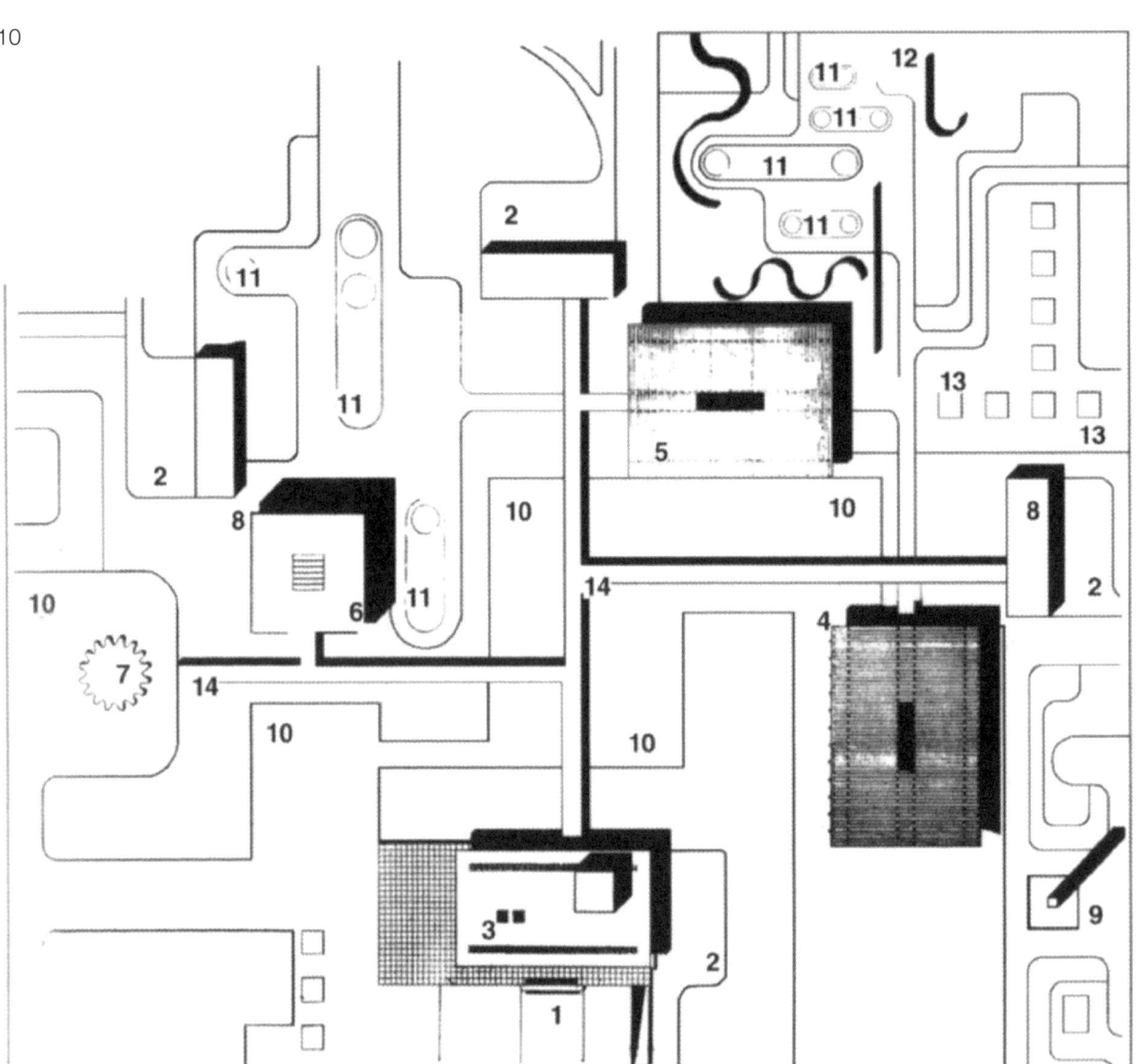

The Asplund proposal explores the imaginary of an oasis in the desert. The vast 1 km² plot is left almost empty, surrounded by a line of trees leading to a central access with a large water feature inviting visitors to approach the museum in a very formal procession. The required programme was distributed over four composed polygons joined in a plan to generate an open courtyard.

With a very different approach, the Brazilian architect, who won the third place, distributed the programme over the totality of the plot. The main buildings together with the planetarium are linked by covered passages crossing the water features that surround them. The remaining area is occupied by complementary service buildings and landscape features like fountains, gardens, and flowerbeds, keeping a deep connection amongst buildings through their glass curtained walls. The entrance to the Cultural Section appeared elevated from the ground giving access to a 20 m high atrium that would also work for temporary exhibitions. The planetarium, shell-shaped, was semi-buried, giving the idea of emerging from the water.

Bregovac, who won second prize, introduced an organised scheme of horizontal pavilions interspersed with several courtyards and gardens, which together make up a square around a main open patio. The planetarium appeared like a dome in the "Kuwait of Today and Tomorrow" section block.

SITE PLAN

1. Entrance
2. Parking lot
3. Cultural and Administrative sector
4. Section: Land of Kuwait
5. Section: Man of Kuwait
6. Section: Kuwait of Today and Tomorrow
7. Planetarium
8. Offices, laboratories and deposit
9. Water tank
10. Lake
11. Flower beds
12. Gardens
13. Reconstruction of ancient fountains
14. Covered passages

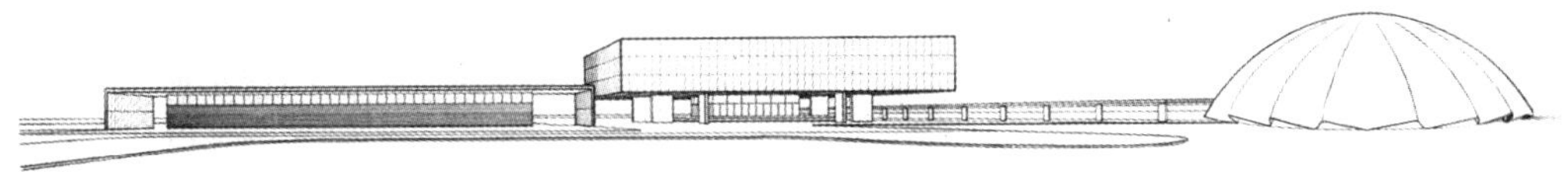

12

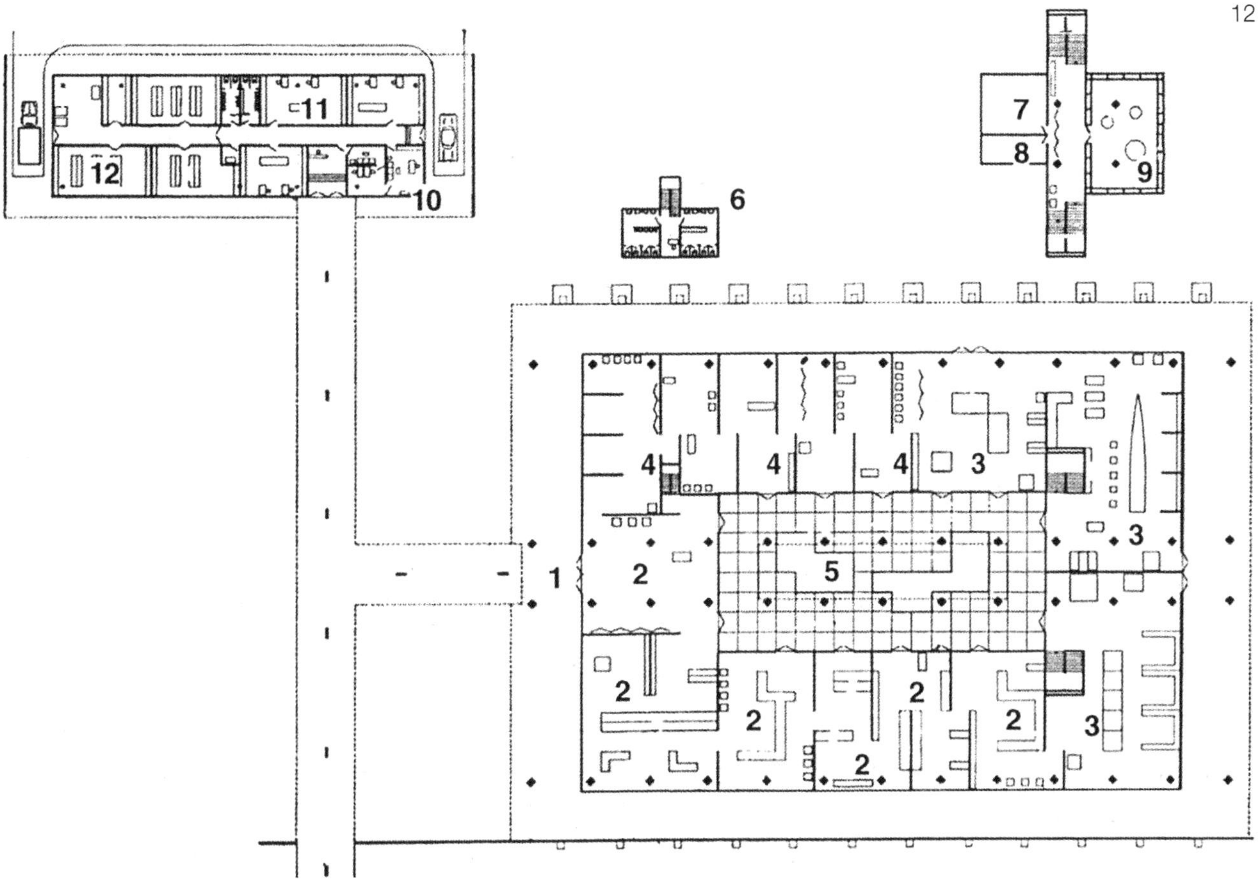

GROUND FLOOR PLAN
Department of Men

1. Entrance
2. Archeaology & History
3. Ethnography and Folklore
4. Kuwait Art
5. Patio
6. Lavatories
7. Air conditioning
8. Electric & mechanic installation
9. Gallery of Pearls
10.Office
11. Laboratory
12. Deposit

A. REIDY'S PROPOSAL:

10. Site plan
11. Perspective view
12. Ground floor plan: Department of Kuwait Man, site plan

KUWAIT NATIONAL MUSEUM

JIBLA
1960–1983

DESIGNERS • Michel Écochard (architect); André de Villedary (associated architects); Pierre Saddy (associated architects); Zygmunt Soltan (associated architects); Nikos Chatzidakis (structure)
CLIENT • Ministry of Public Works
CONTRACTOR • Unknown

UNDER RENOVATION

Following the establishment of the Kuwait National Museum in 1957 and the emergence of a national sovereignty, an international competition was launched for a new museum to be implemented in a one-square-kilometre park and to include a planetarium and four distinct departments: (1) Land of Kuwait; (2) Man of Kuwait; (3) Kuwait of Today and Tomorrow; (4) the Cultural Section.[29]

The Ministry of Education on the advice of UNESCO, selected Michel Écochard's proposal out of six entries.

The winning project was in some ways similar to what was to be built twenty years later, but with a more complex design: the layout was based on four departments geometrically aggregated around a square piazza, with a series of minor volumes and enclosed courts, which were not part of the final solution.[30]

The solution was in fact four interconnected two-storey pavilions (and the planetarium) linked by suspended bridges. The experience offered to the visitor was a continuous free-flow through different sectors around the central garden/courtyard, shielded from the heat by a three dimensional frame-structure of identical tetrahedral elements. The paths were fluidly intersecting ramps, platforms and double height spaces, offering different perspectives of the exhibitions together with sea and garden views provided by the bridges and the main

1

2

3

fenestrations. The façade composition was modulated by large panels, made of concrete frames and filled by red brick.

The museum was severely damaged during the 1990 Invasion and the collection of artefacts was looted. Since then, the museum has been only partially functional. A series of technical assessments and renovation works has taken place and is still continuing under the guidance of the National Council for Culture Arts and Letters in collaboration with UN agencies.

1. Courtyard, detail of the structure, circa 1987
2. Scale model
3. Aerial view, undated
4. View of the covered courtyard, circa 1987
5. Axonometric view
6. Site plan

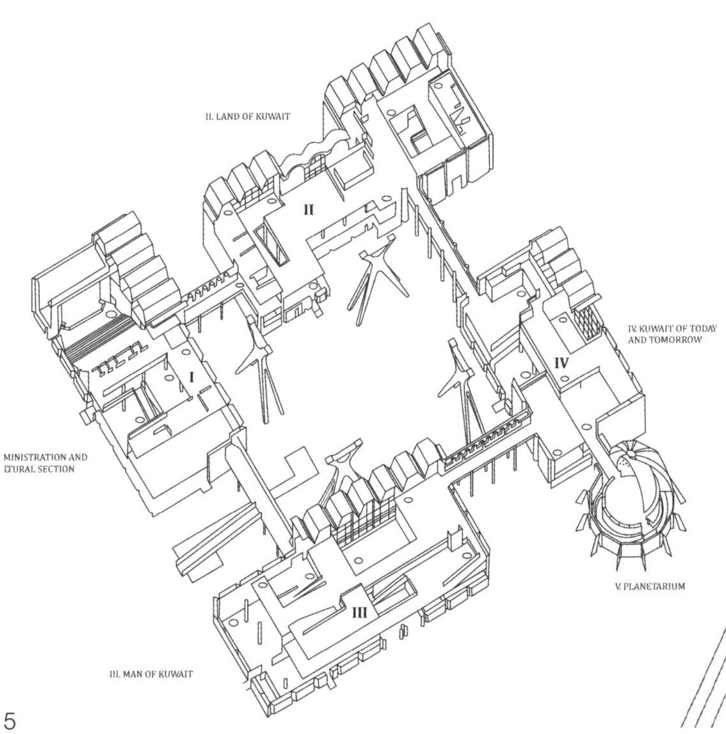

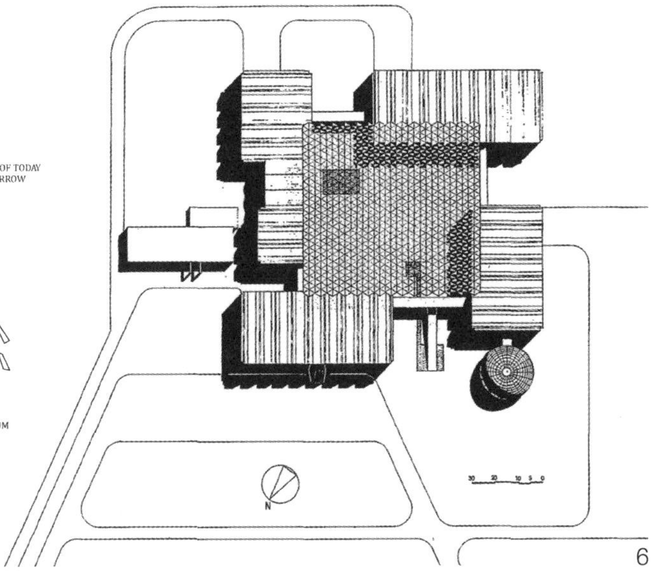

7

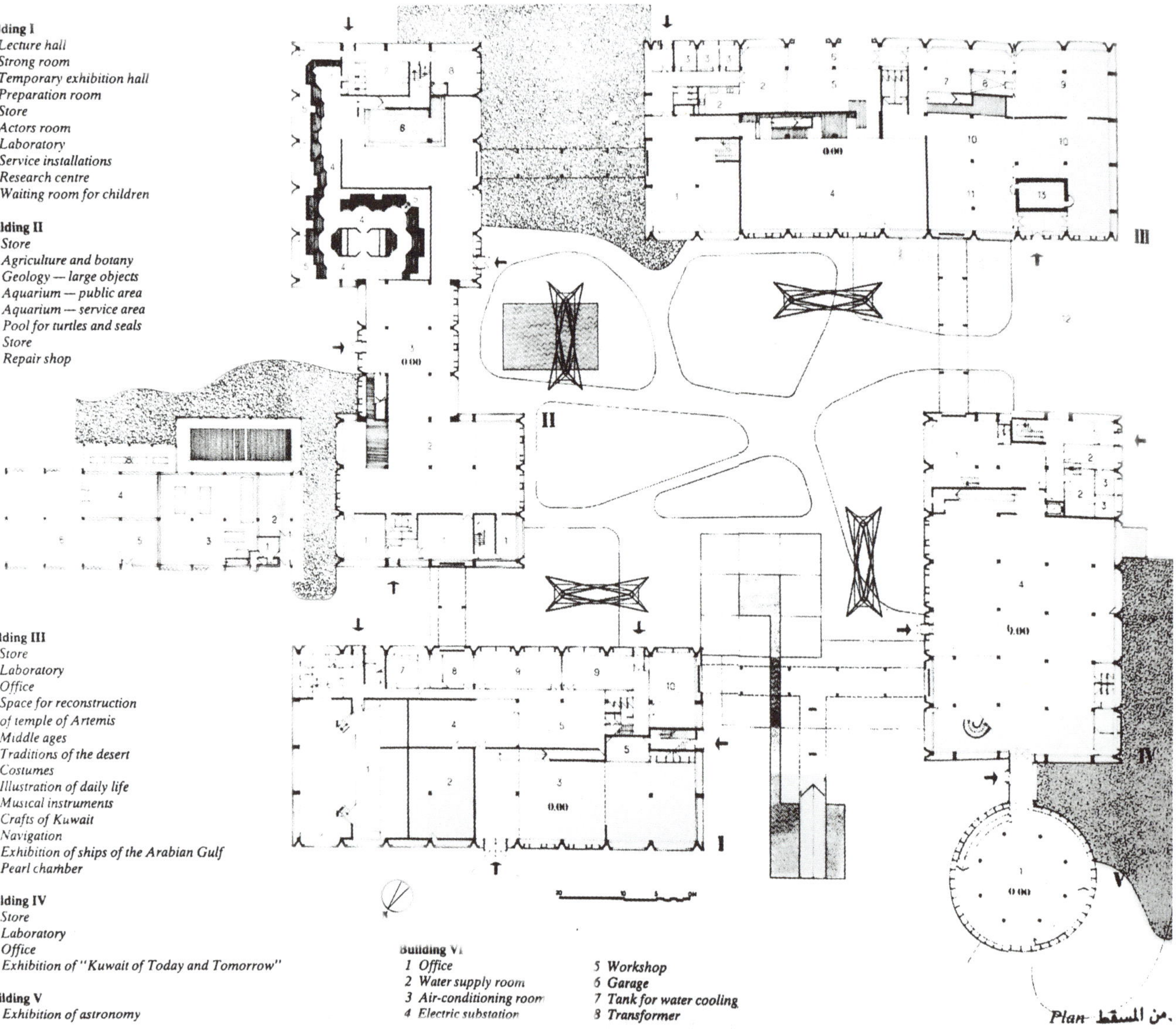

Building I

1 Lecture hall
2 Strong room
3 Temporary exhibition hall
4 Preparation room
5 Store
6 Actors room
7 Laboratory
8 Service installations
9 Research centre
10 Waiting room for children

Building II

1 Store
2 Agriculture and botany
3 Geology — large objects
4 Aquarium — public area
5 Aquarium — service area
6 Pool for turtles and seals
7 Store
8 Repair shop

Building III

1 Store
2 Laboratory
3 Office
4 Space for reconstruction
  of temple of Artemis
5 Middle ages
6 Traditions of the desert
7 Costumes
8 Illustration of daily life
9 Musical instruments
10 Crafts of Kuwait
11 Navigation
12 Exhibition of ships of the Arabian Gulf
13 Pearl chamber

Building IV

1 Store
2 Laboratory
3 Office
4 Exhibition of "Kuwait of Today and Tomorrow"

Building V

1 Exhibition of astronomy

Building VI

1 Office
2 Water supply room
3 Air-conditioning room
4 Electric substation
5 Workshop
6 Garage
7 Tank for water cooling
8 Transformer

Plan من المسقط

7. Ground floor plan
8. View of the courtyard
9. Main access ramp to Building IV: Kuwait
of Today and Tomorrow.

WATERFRONT COMPETITION

KUWAIT CITY
1961

DESIGNERS • Scott & Wilson,
Kirkpatrick & Partners with John R. Harris;
Macklin L. Hancock/Project Planning
Associates Ltd.;
Rendell, Palmer & Tritton;
Coode & Partners;
Associated Maritime Consultants
CLIENT • Kuwait Development Board

UNBUILT

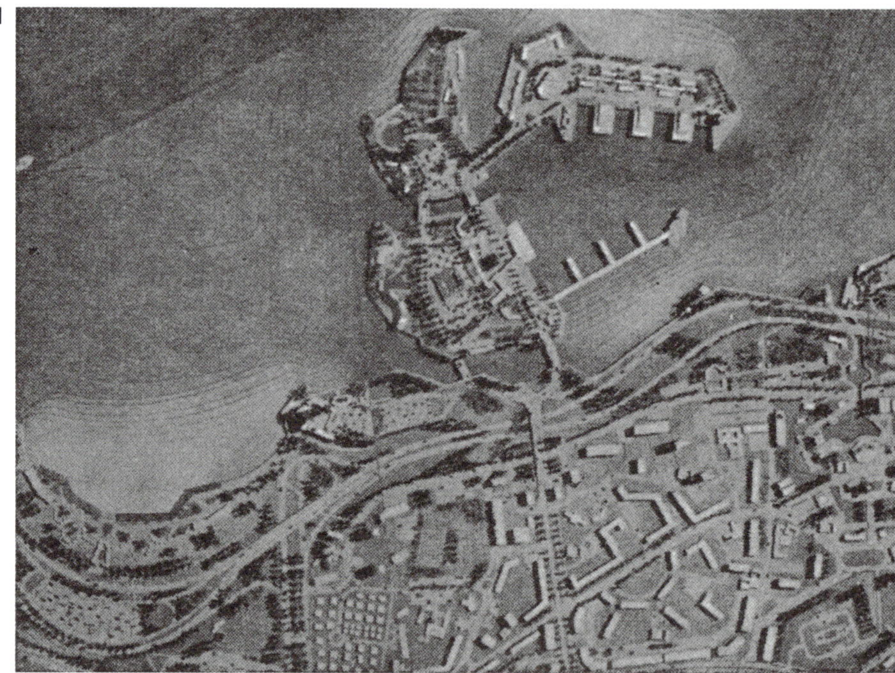

The "Grand Corniche" for the
redevelopment of the former harbour
area, by then filled with the demolished
material of the old town, reclaiming new
land from the sea, became the premise
for a Waterfront Design Competition
in 1961. The 1951 Master Plan had
defined several aspects of the city's
development, but not the seafront.
Even so, the necessity to relieve
congested areas around the Sief Palace
and relocate the fishing harbour and
docks appeared as a priority, triggering
the call for the competition.

Of the five firms that participated in the
1961 competition, only two proposals
are available. The British firm Scott &
Wilson was an engineering company
very active in vehicular infrastructure
and valued the input of Cyril Kirkpatrick,
for many years, head of the Port of
London Authority. Their proposal was
a long and curvy strip of reclaimed
land, circumscribed by a ring road from
Dasman to the Port of Shuwaikh. This
project identified different functional
zones that were developed in tri-
dimensional concepts with the help of
John Harris, a few years before their
collaboration on the Women's Hospital.
The project introduced the key idea of
the stepped sea wall to make the shore
always reachable from the promenade
and providing seating for leisure time. [31]

The second entry was presented by the
Canadian architect, Hancock, who had
experience with large settlement design
and landscaping, aspects which were
very evident in his proposal. Hancock's
design is in fact less structured and
more fluid. It configured an artificial
lagoon in front of the Sief Palace (which
was later implemented in the 1990s)
and a large deep-sea floating harbour.
This proposal won the competition,
but being considered "unnecessarily
extravagant" by the Waterfront
Committee, it went through several
rounds of reviews. In 1964, according

to Shiber, the project was still with the
Ministry of Public Works.

Despite it never being implemented,
the competition had foreseen several
further developments: such as the
realisation of the Gulf Road and the
allocation of certain functions (hotels,
ports, public buildings, etc.) It also
paved the way for the 1976 Waterfront
Project, which, when realised, reshaped
the relationship between Kuwait and its
coastline.

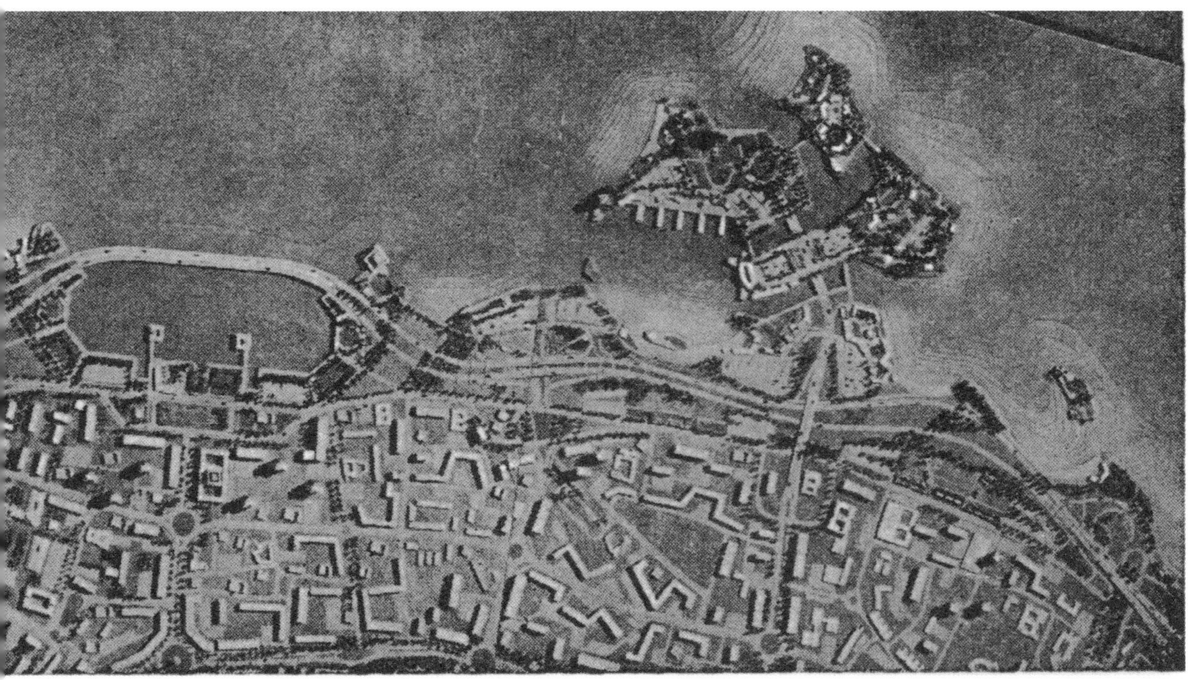

2

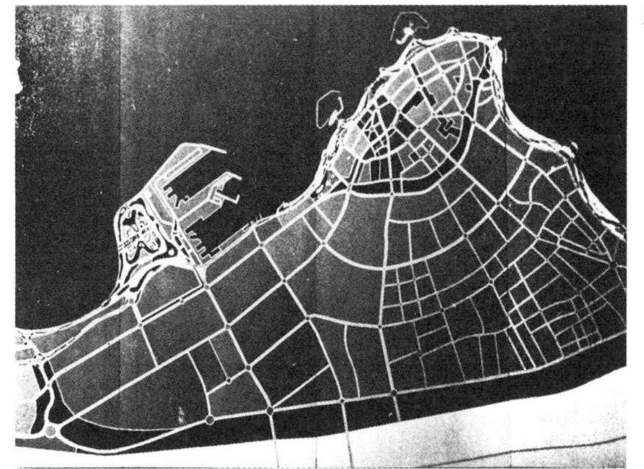

MACKLIN L. HANCOCK/
PROJECT PLANNING ASSOCIATES LTD.:

1. Scale model, details and plan of the project
2. Waterfront Development plan by Project Planning
Associates Ltd., 1964–1967 (the Corniche Scheme)

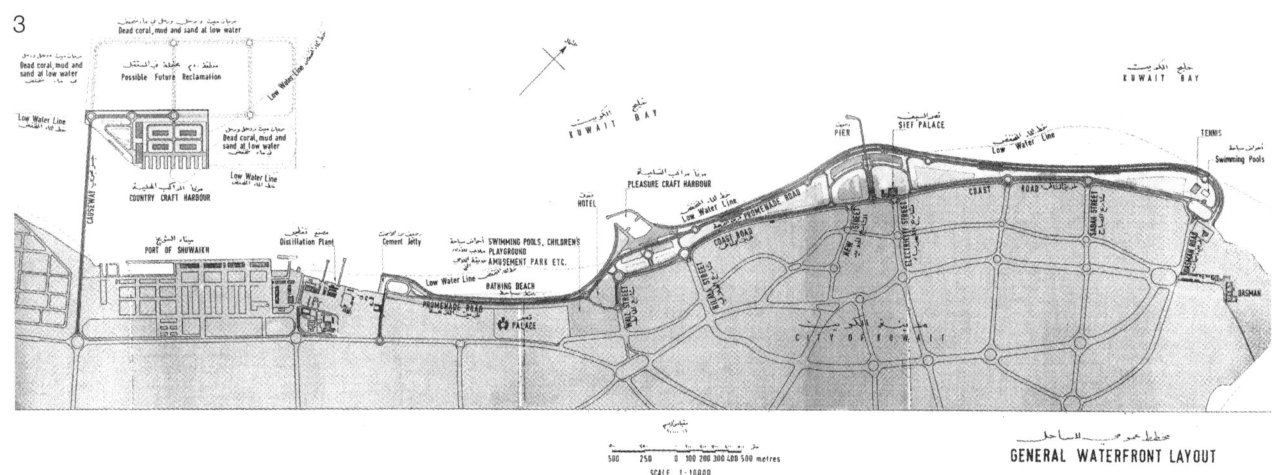

SCOTT & WILSON, KIRKPATRICK
& PARTNERS WITH J.R. HARRIS:

3. Project plan and perspective views

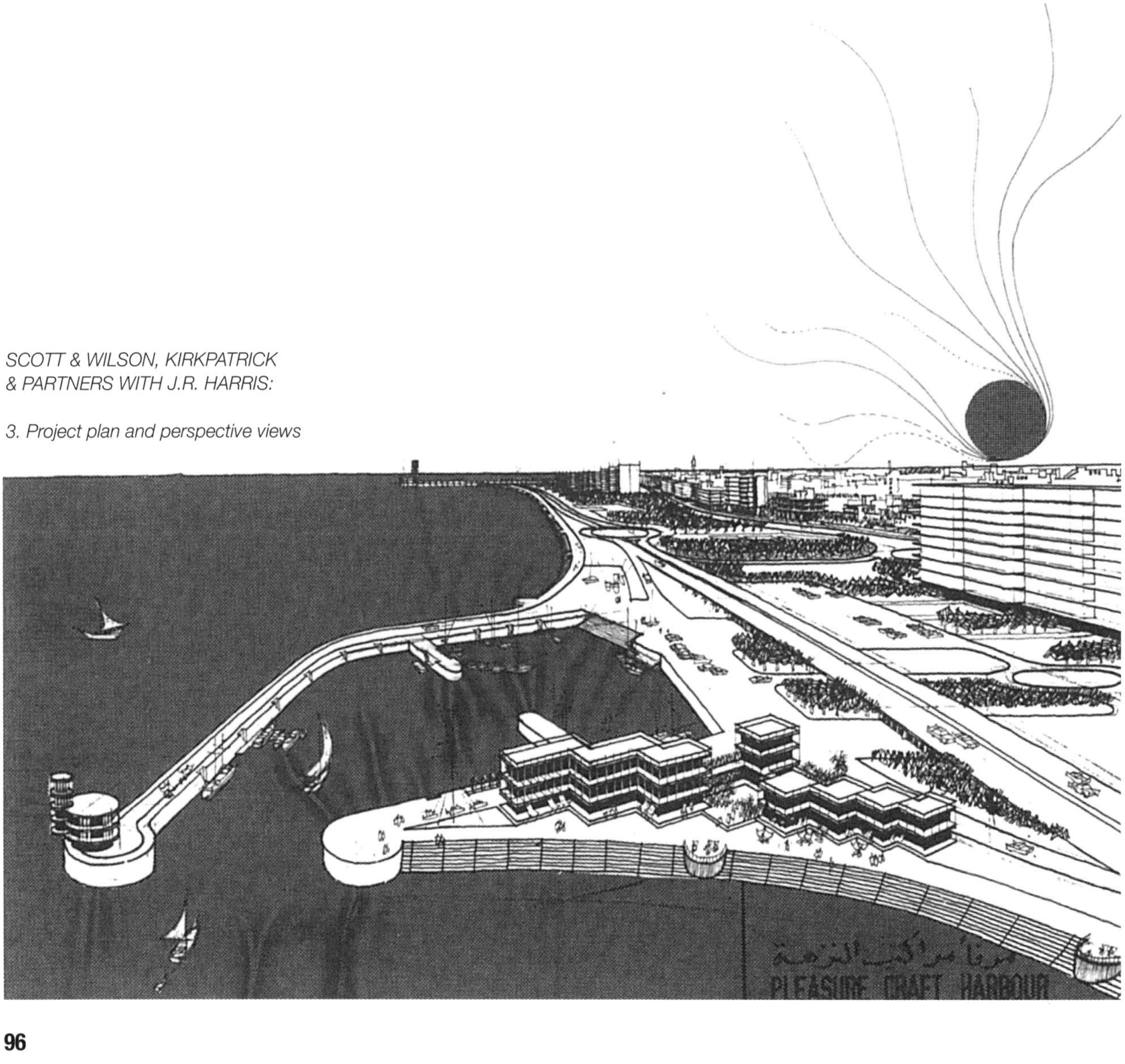

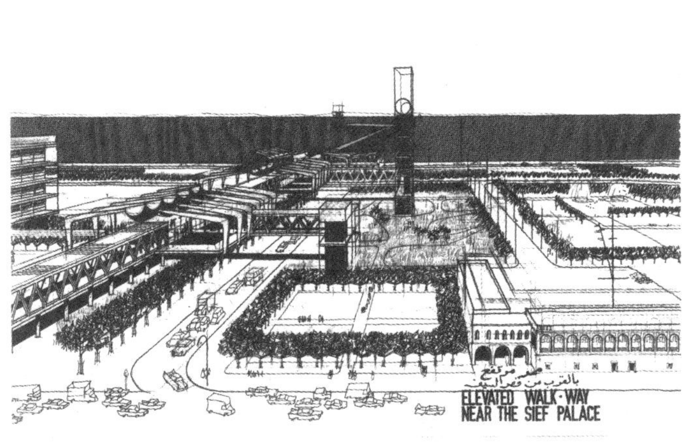
بالقرب من قصر السيف
ELEVATED WALK·WAY
NEAR THE SIEF PALACE

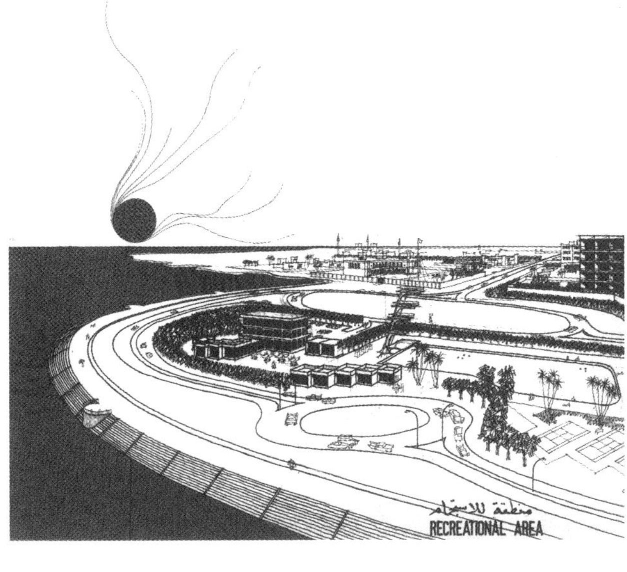
منطقة للاستجمام
RECREATIONAL AREA

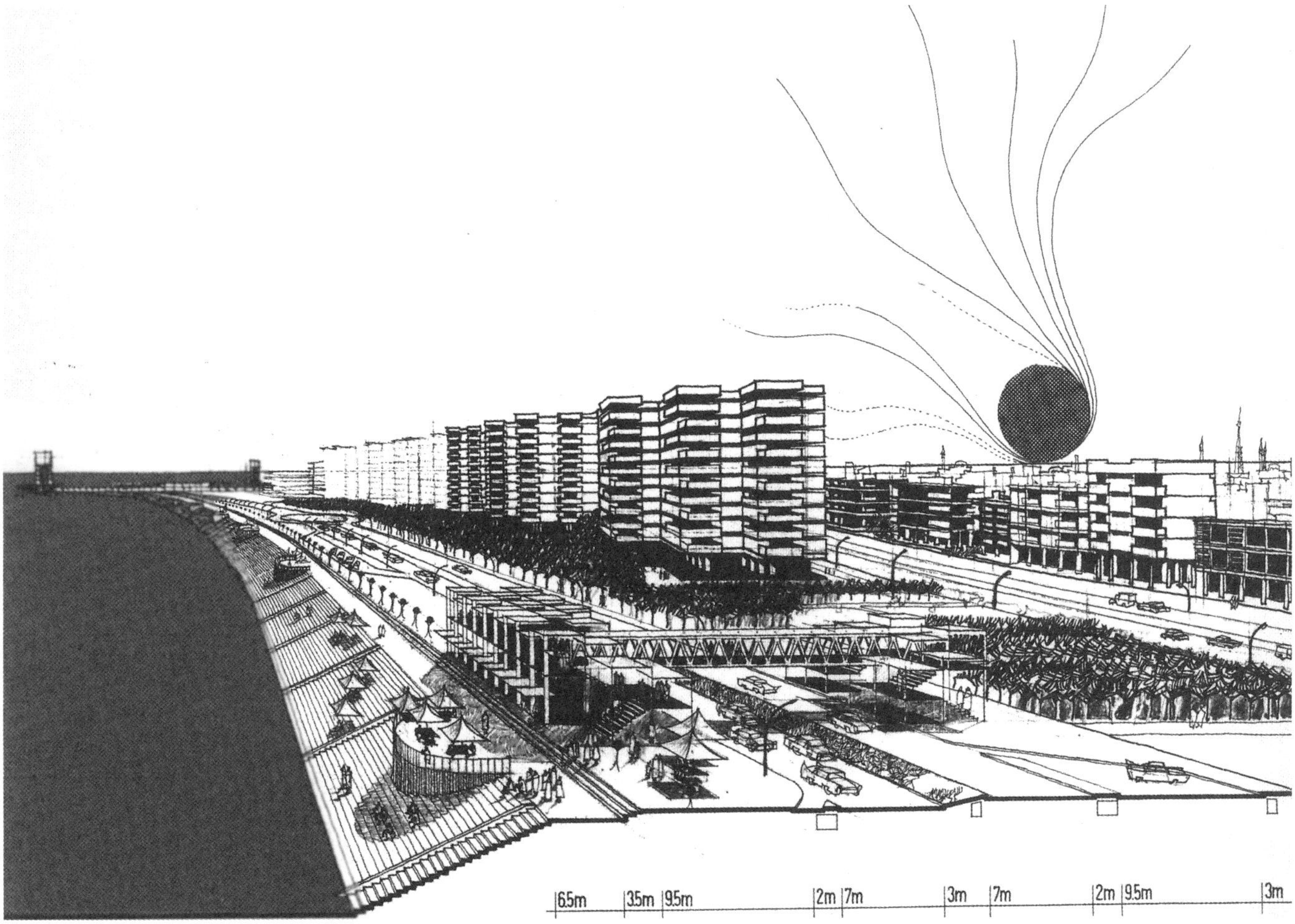

6.5m 3.5m 9.5m   2m 7m   3m 7m   2m 9.5m   3m

CBD
AREA 1/AREA 2

CENTRAL BUSINESS DISTRICT, SIEF
1961–1965

DESIGNER • Municipality Planning Department
(Saba George Shiber, principal)
CLIENT • Kuwait Municipality
CONTRACTOR • Various

MODIFIED

1

The Central Business District Areas 1 and 2 were the next to be developed, after Area 3 and according to the same guidelines. Here the main concern was to establish a relationship with the surroundings through a three-dimensional concept and architectural control of the buildings.

The Area 1 plan, publicly auctioned in October of 1962, had three blocks of one floor, two blocks of two with a mezzanine, and a multi-storey building for a hotel that was later remodeled into offices. In contrast with the plan, the two existing mosques were demolished and replaced by a bigger one in the central square.[32]

Contiguous to Area 1, Area 2 recalls the *Kaysariyat Al-Amir*, once the offices of important merchants of the old city, with the new group of buildings making a total of 170 offices designed around a common square and according to the *Kaysariya* typology.[33]

These long, linear blocks stand out with a cantilevered first floor with square framed openings of equidistant distribution and by the main entrances assuming the entire height of the two floors above ground, leading to an internal street. In the late 1970s, the Central Bank of Kuwait occupied one of the corners of the area.

Elevated from the Arabian Gulf Street, Area 1 and 2 assumed an important role in the urban context by forming a relationship between the souq area and the sea.

2

3

AREA 1:

1. Axonometric view
2. Kuwait Insurance Company building by
Saba Abi Hanna, circa 1965

AREA 2:

3. Merchants Markets
4. Site plan
5. Internal view
6. Side entrance
7. Front entrance, undated
8. Site view, undated
9. Aerial view

CBD AREA 3

CENTRAL BUSINESS DISTRICT, JIBLA
1961–1965

DESIGNER • Municipality Planning Department
(Saba George Shiber, principal)
CLIENT • Kuwait Municipality
CONTRACTOR • Various

MODIFIED / DEMOLISHED

1

2 3

Area 3 was the first area to be implemented in the Central Business District out of a total of eleven under Saba George Shiber, originally as coordinator and eventually as urban planner.[34] The zoning plans implementation strategy by Shiber for the CBD was a fundamental step towards the post-1952 city development.[35] Zoning plans were generators of new building and urban typologies, promoting schemes that had the capacity to instigate new relationships between the general scheme and the details. These relationships were not only drawn up but also regulated by the "General Unifying Regulations" which established the following: all buildings should have the same height; the exiting mosques were to be integrated; all buildings were to have four façades and to be connected by covered passages.[36] Nevertheless, these rules were not enough to create uniformity since in some cases a single plot contained three multi-owned parcels, with three different architects. The Municipality imposed meetings with the private architects at a preliminary stage of the project, based in a relation of "conformity, co-operation and guidance" searching for the best "aesthetic standards of architecture." [37]

Initially thought of as a bank area, the first two buildings were the National Bank of Kuwait and the British Bank of the Middle East. Later on, other functions joined including the Chamber of Commerce and Industry, Kuwait National Petroleum, Kuwait Airways, and 24 shops for money changers.

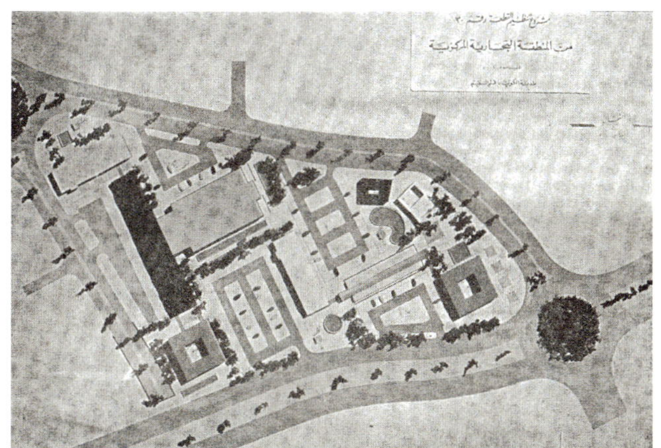

6

1. Graphic feature highlighting the former bank district, 1968
2. Aerial view, circa 1968
3. British Bank of the Middle East, 1968
4. Area 3, first scale model after the Municipal Council approval, 1961
5. Area under construction, circa 1963
6. Kuwait Airways Corporation offices, 1964

NATIONAL BANK HEADQUARTER

CENTRAL BUSINESS DISTRICT, AREA 3
1961–1963

DESIGNER • Design Construction Group (Antony Irving and Gordon Brown)
CLIENT • National Bank of Kuwait
CONTRACTOR • Unknown

MODIFIED

The National Bank of Kuwait was initially a citizens' initiative and then established by an Amiri decree in 1952. The first office was opened in Safat Square, but very soon the necessity for a proper headquarters emerged. It was probably one of the first buildings constructed in the newly planned CBD-Area 3 and the design was given to the Lebanese-based firm Design Construction Group, also the designers of the early Gulf Bank and Commercial Bank buildings. Similar to these examples, NBK is a simple linear block with a recessed ground floor and a solid crown. All the emphasis was given to the geometric pattern generated by the shading devices, intended to screen the office floors, in this case, the steady rhythm created by the repetition of vertical concrete fins of different depths. The firm, as usual, dedicated equal care to the design of the interiors defining both surfaces and furniture.

The building is still operative, although the external screen has been removed in favor of a more conventional stone cladding, which completely alters its appearance.

1

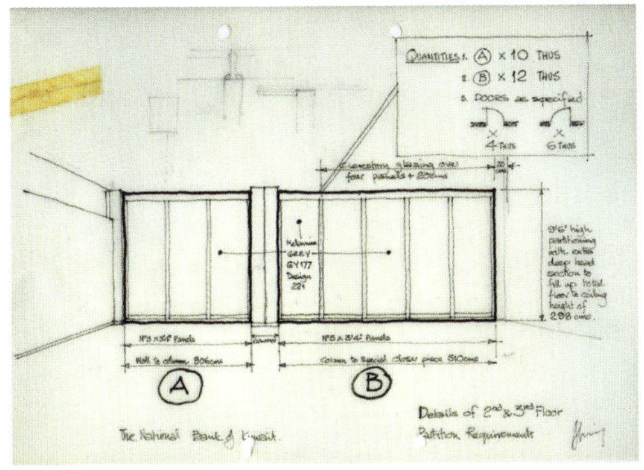

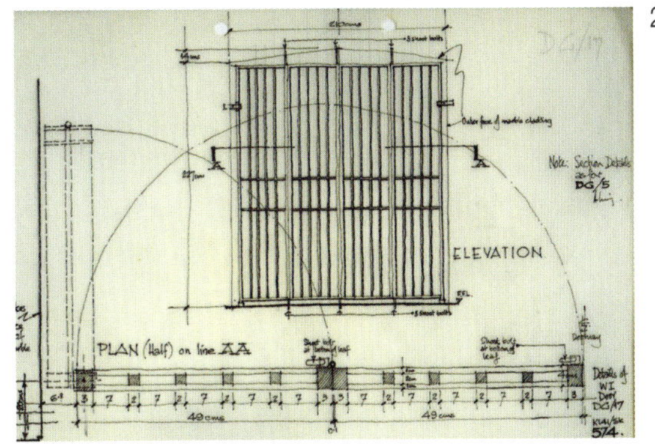

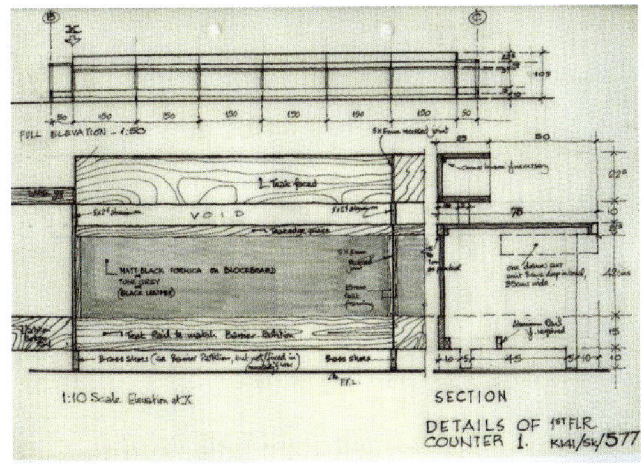

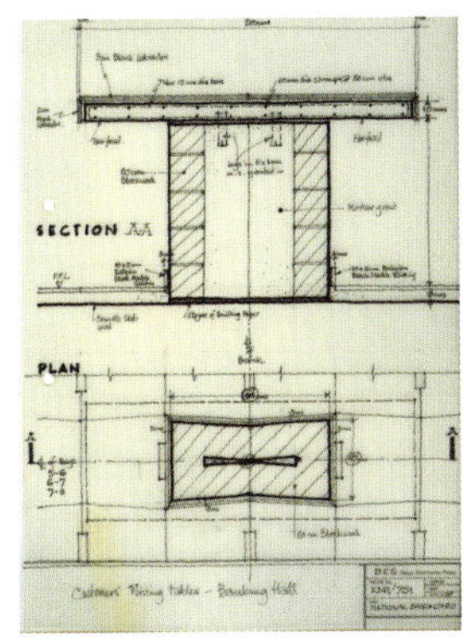

1. West elevation, circa 1963
2. Project details, 1961
3. South elevation, circa 1963
4. View of the building after the renovation work

GULF BANK

CENTRAL BUSINESS DISTRICT, AREA 1
1961–1963

DESIGNERS • Design Construction Group (Antony Irving and Gordon Brown)
CLIENT • Gulf Bank
CONTRACTOR • Unknown

MODIFIED

Designed in 1963 by the British architects Tony Irvine and Gordon Jones of the Design Construction Group, the building follows Shiber's regulations and urban guidelines for the Central Business District commercial areas. Located in Area 1 the multi-owned building comprises a regular office floor structure in two-storeys above ground, divided into three autonomous properties. One of those is the bank headquarters. The bank entrance, placed at one of the short ends, is the only interruption in a repetitive façade system. This entrance, clad in stone, can be related to other similar projects by the same designer.[38]

The long building is unified at the first floor by the pre-moulded concrete screen painted in white, with reference to Arabic motifs also common to other structures in the CBD Areas 1, 2 and 3, emphasise the visual identity of the building.

The hexagonal pattern with metallic strips works as a sunscreen in the continuous façade made of bracketed concrete panels. The recessed ground floor raised from the street level is indented to create an external colonnade providing solar protection to the customers.

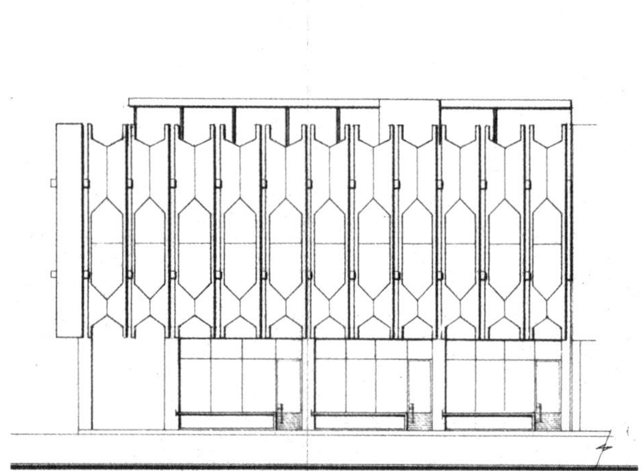
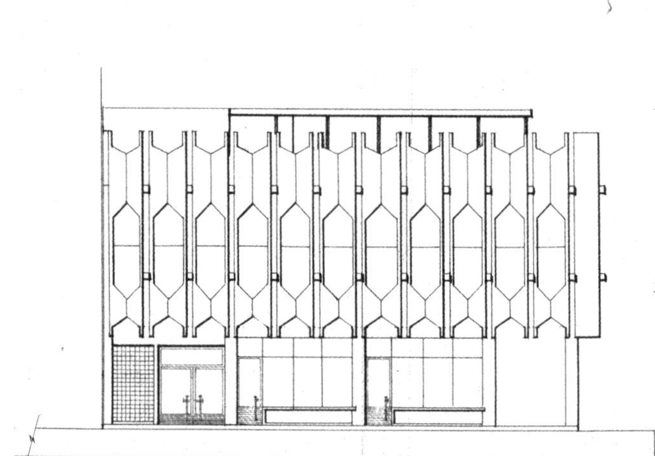

1

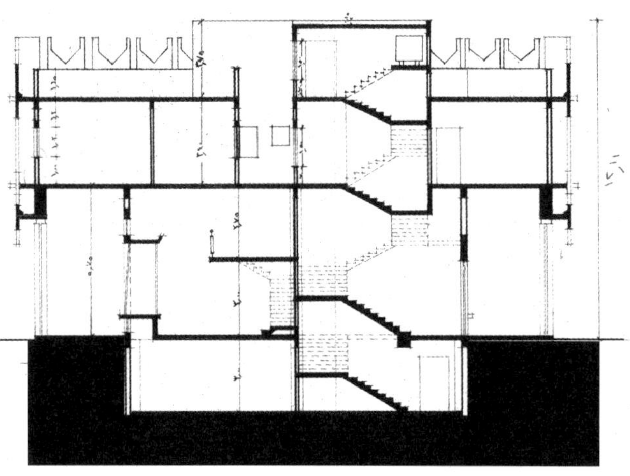
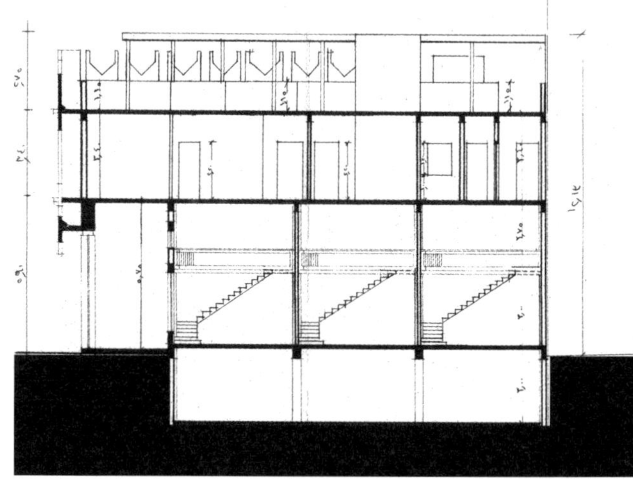

2

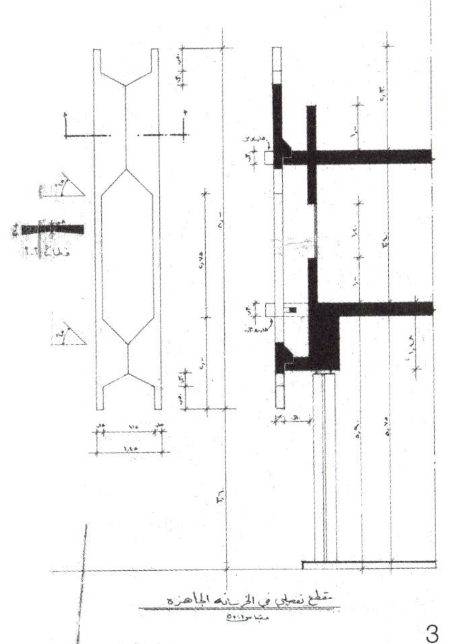

1. Front elevations
2. Sections
3. Project details
4. Actual detail of the façade
5. View from Abdullah Al-Salem Street, 1972

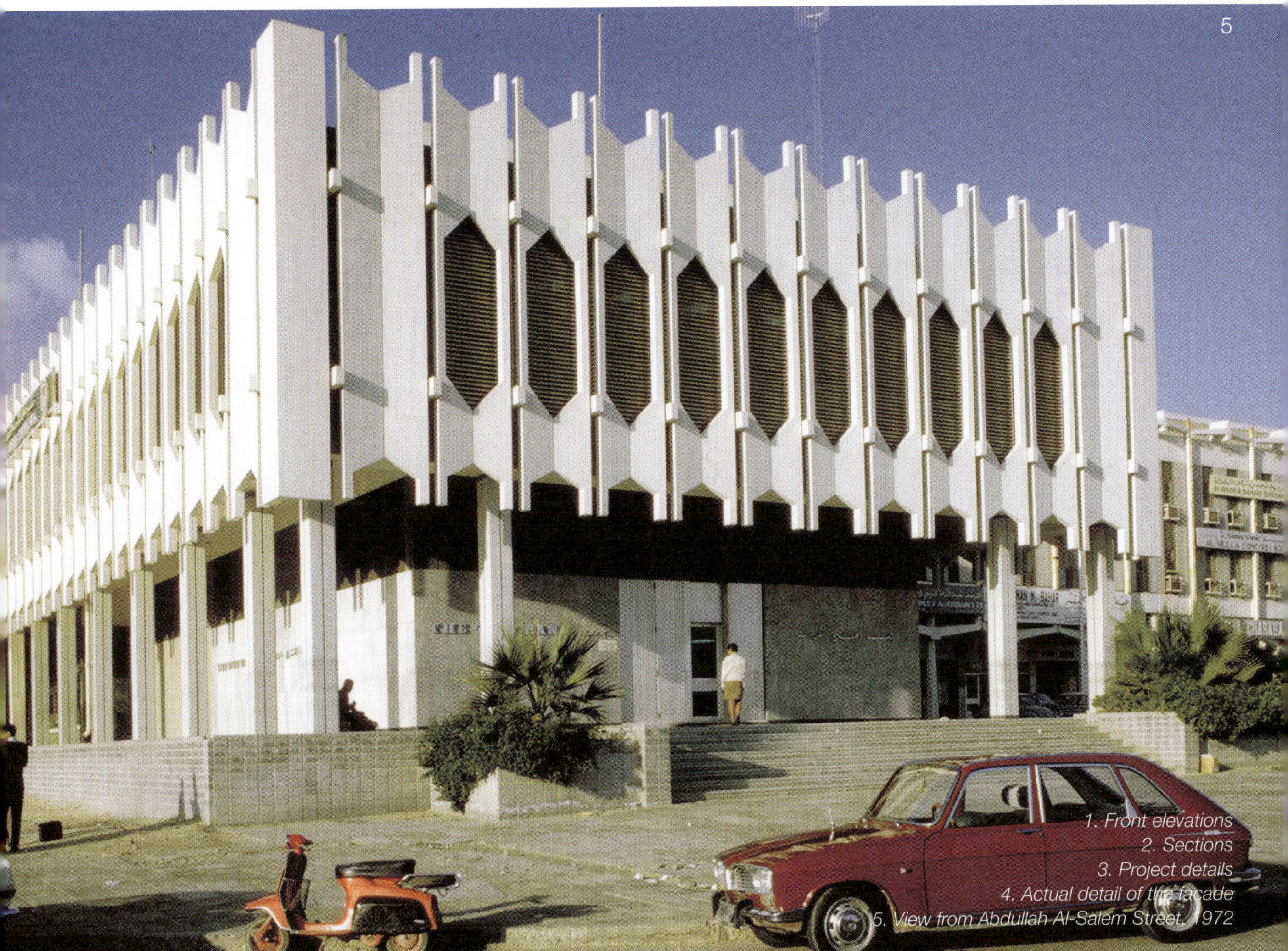

KNPC OFFICE BUILDING

CENTRAL BUSINESS DISTRICT, AREA 3
1964–1965

DESIGNER • Dar Al-Handasah (Ghassan Klink, principal)
CLIENT • Kuwait National Petroleum Company
CONTRACTOR • Unknown

RENOVATED IN 2013

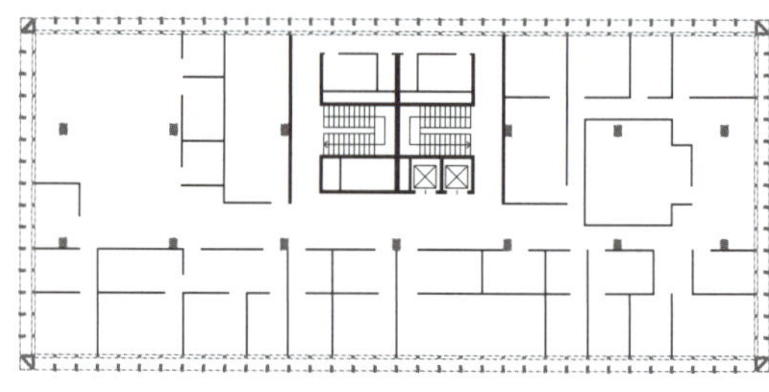

1

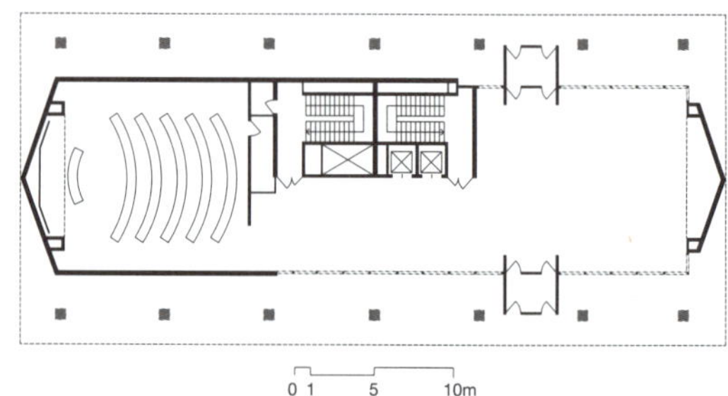

2

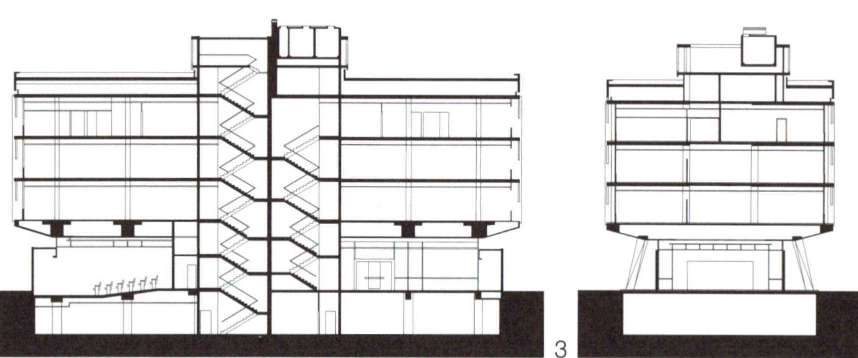

3

In 1964 Dar Al-Handasah won the international competition for the design of two key buildings in the Central Business District, Area 3. One was the Chamber of Commerce and Industries and the other was the contiguous headquarters for the National Petroleum Company.

KNPC was founded in October 1960 and after a few years established its headquarters in the city.

Three office levels and one mechanical floor on the rooftop accommodate the essential functions, leaving an open space at the ground level for reception areas, including an exhibition hall and a small auditorium. A double row of external, tilted pillars bear, together with the central core, a thick concrete slab. The latter sustains the planted supports for the three upper floors.

This structure, not common in Kuwait at that time, allows full flexibility in internal distribution at all levels and an independent façade design. The elevations are composed and modulated by the juxtaposition of geometrical brise-soleil. These peripheral elements are closely spaced, providing an efficient sun protection and, in the designers' words, an "oriental character." [39]

4

1. Typical floor plan
2. Ground floor plan
3. Sections
4. General view, circa 1965

CHAMBER OF COMMERCE & INDUSTRY

CENTRAL BUSINESS DISTRICT, AREA 3
1964–1966

DESIGNER • Dar Al-Handasah (Ghassan Klink, principal)
CLIENT • Chamber Of Commerce and Industry
CONTRACTOR • Unknown

DEMOLISHED

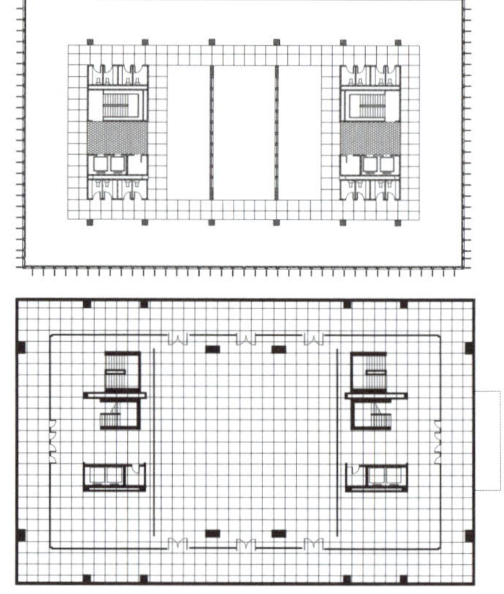

1

2

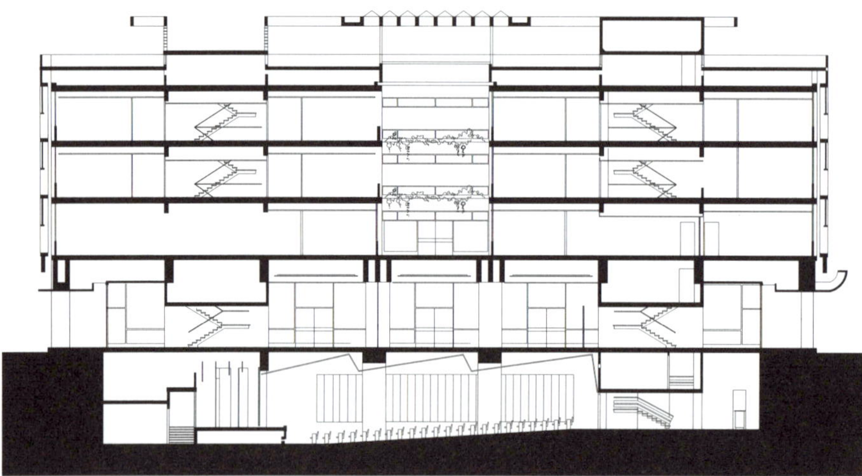

3

Under the guidance of Shiber, an international competition was held and subsequently won by Dar Al-Handasah, the young Lebanese firm leaded by Kamal Shair.

Located in the CBD Area 3, the multi-storey building combines an open ground floor plan with a typical flexibly designed office space lifted from the ground. The ornamented façade and the central full-height hall integrate modern building technology with the aesthetic and typological principles of Arab culture.

The main ground floor access is formed by a recessed aluminium box with a gold finish and is detached from the concrete primary structure. Above, the office stores are enclosed by perforated pre-cast concrete façade panels decorated with small painted gold metal pieces. The central element is covered with acrylic pyramidal skylights collecting natural light for the interior. Placed in the space between the cores was a basement auditorium with seating for 1,000 people.[40]

After the new headquarters was built in 1999, the building was abandoned despite its good condition and strong presence at the entrance of the old souq. In 2014 it was demolished and caused the first public demonstration against the destruction of the country's modern heritage.

4

5

1. Typical floor plan
2. Ground floor plan
3. Cross section
4. Façade detail, 1972
5. Internal view, before demolition
6. View from Ali Al-Salem Street, 1972

6

SHERATON HOTEL AND EXTENSION

JAHRA GATE
1964–1978

DESIGNERS • Dar Al-Handasah
(Sami Khoury, principal; 1964–65);
TEST (c.1973); TAC with PACE (1975–78)
CLIENT • Ahmed Al-Fahed; Oriental
Hotel Co.; Eastern Hotels Co.
CONTRACTORS • CAT; Contracting
And Trading Co. (CAT,1964–66);
Hanyang Coorporation (1976),
Al-Rumaihi Co.;
Al-Hani Construction & Trading Co.
(1975–78)

RENOVATED IN 1992

1

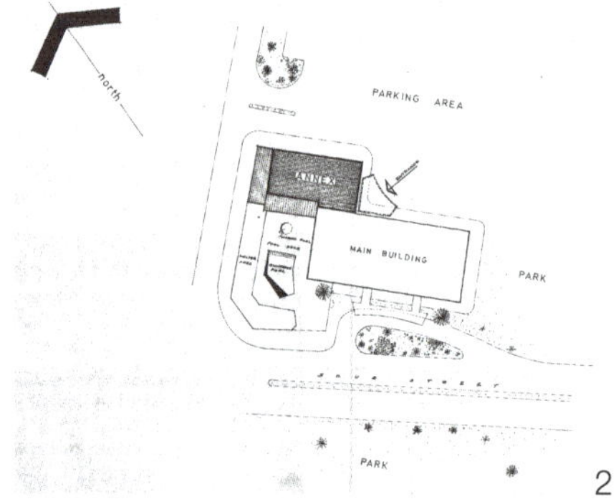

2

An attempt to build a Government
Hotel failed in the late 1950s.
Nonetheless, urban plans, such as the
1961 Waterfront Project, showed that
the strip of land between the Jahra
Roundabout and the sea had been
dedicated to hotel development. In
the same years, a local investment
group succeeded in signing a deal to
build the first Sheraton Hotel outside
of the United States. This was the right
occasion to solve Kuwait's chronic lack
of luxury accommodation for incoming
delegations and businessmen.

The ten-storey building accommodated
144 rooms and 12 suites, plus public
spaces, restaurants and shops.[41]
Six typical floors dedicated to guest
rooms were shaped in a rectangular
plan with saw-tooth indentations,
all along the four sides of the
building.[42] This surface, embellished
with metal *mashrabias,* became the

architecturally distinctive feature of
the Kuwait Sheraton. H.H. the Amir
inaugurated the hotel in 1966, but
work continued due to the pressing
need for extra accommodation. This
process culminated in 1976 with the
submission by the American firm TAC
of a completely new building following
the construction of a trapezoidal
swimming-pool and restaurant
designed by TEST a few years earlier.
TAC's project is an unadorned prism
clad with clear stone interposed with
bronze-glazed flush windows. Being
understated, it created the perfect
neutral backdrop for the main building.

The hotel was severely damaged during
the Invasion and the interiors were
fully compromised. In the aftermath
of Liberation, the Sheraton was
completely renovated, preserving the
external overall appearance.

3

1. Front view, late 1960s
2. Site map
3. Façade detail

NEXT PAGES, HOTEL EXTENSION:

4. Elevation and section
5. Section
6. Typical floor plan

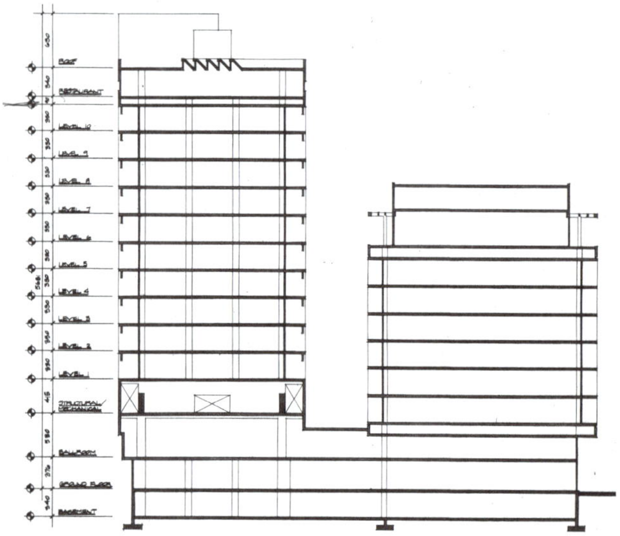

4

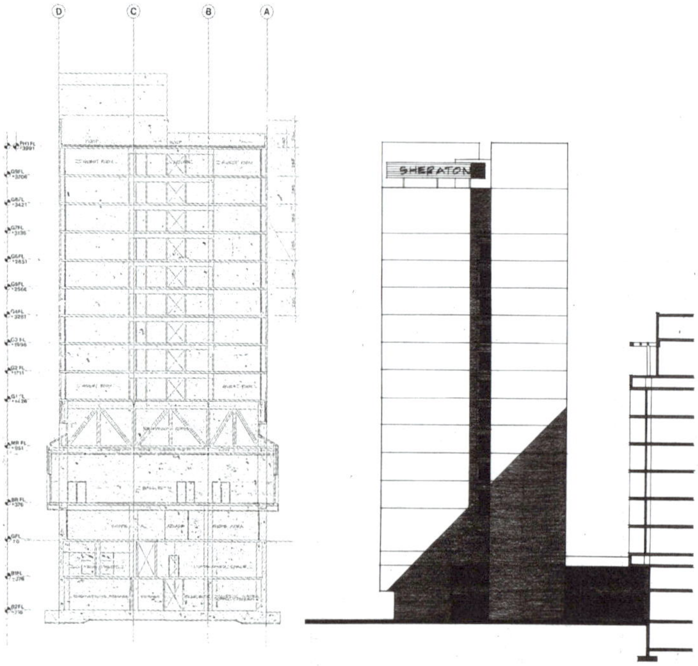

5

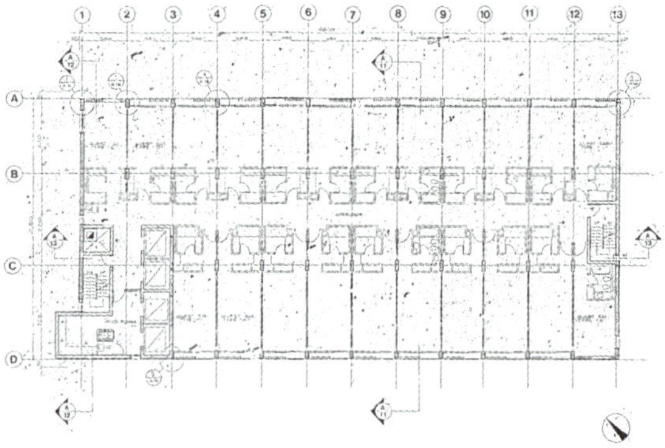

6

CBD AREA 9

CENTRAL BUSINESS DISTRICT, MIRQAB
1961–1975

DESIGNER • Municipality Planning Department
(Saba George Shiber, principal)
CLIENT • Kuwait Municipality
CONTRACTOR • Various

DEMOLISHED / MODIFIED

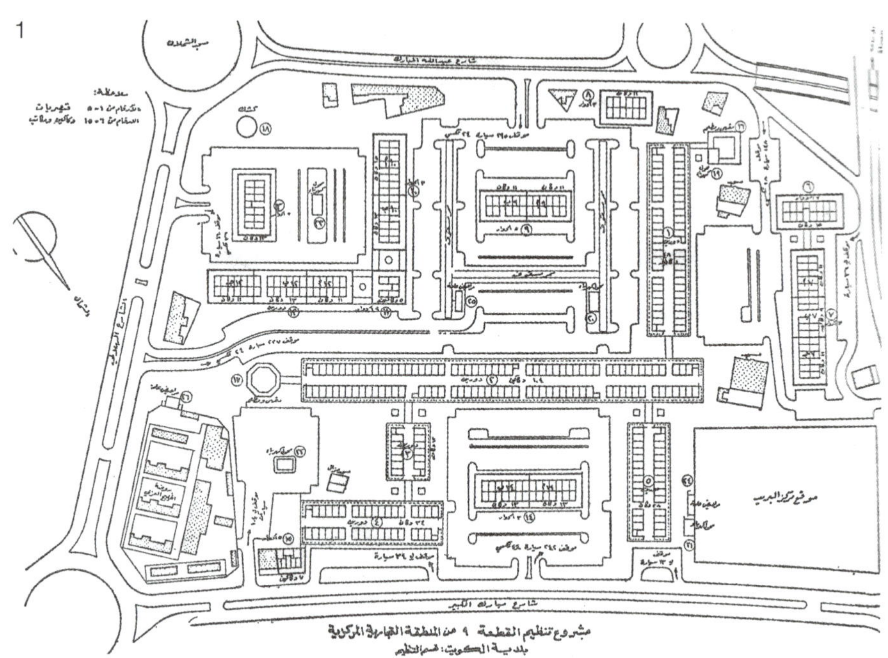

1

Area 9 was the last one to be developed under Saba George Shiber's guidance, after Areas 3, 2 and 1. All remaining planned CBD Areas did not emerge until the following two decades. As in other areas, the urban plans and respective regulations were finalised in 1961. After the demolition of the pre-existing building and the completion of basic services and road works, the different plots were listed for public auction on the 19th and 20th of January, 1963. A private initiative was offered with land for commercial development. The plan dictated a rational building distribution organised by two main squares. The motor-vehicle traffic was to be restricted to parking and taxis, the existing mosques were to be maintained, as the covered galleries were essential to protect visitors from the hot weather.

Muhammad Kumaikh, Abdullah Jassim Shehab and Muhanna Abdulrahman Muhanna and Co. were among the first private developers in Area 9;[43] however, the Association of Cloth Merchants had a major impact on the area, developing several shopping galleries, popularly known as the textile market. By 1964, the area was the newest and biggest shopping area in the city with a total of 450 shops.[44] These long corridor buildings interconnected, defining a new and modern urban experience similar to that of the old souq, establishing the commercial motivation and future for the whole area, which today is known as *blokat* (fabric market).

The central element in the plan is one of the covered shopping galleries (n. 2) which serves as a main axis towards the existing mosque. The flow is extended to Buildings n. 1, 3, 4 and 5, all interconnected as an Arab bazaar, designed to bring the traditional way of shopping into the first modern covered market. Decorated by geometric motifs, the buildings had three floors above ground and a basement floor for warehousing, which was accessible directly from the outside and illuminated and ventilated by openings in the ceiling. On the ground floor the sequence of rectangular fabric stores face a lofty central passageway. This is a covered street with a 7 m high ceiling supported by roof beams in a geometric rhythm, which created a disciplined alternation of concrete structures and natural illumination from glass screens. The mezzanine also belongs to the shop and the upper gallery is usually a tailors' workshop.

Besides these, other relevant elements are the mixed-use typologies designed by Sabah Abi-Hanna for the same association (n. 3 and n.4), the higher elements of the structure (n.13), the KIC apartment building designed by Dar Al-Handasah and numbers 11 and 8 which, with similar façades, were the last to be demolished along with the former Ministry of Defense. In the middle of the main squares, two similar buildings were later implemented with compact volumes and a concrete louvered linear façade-shading element.

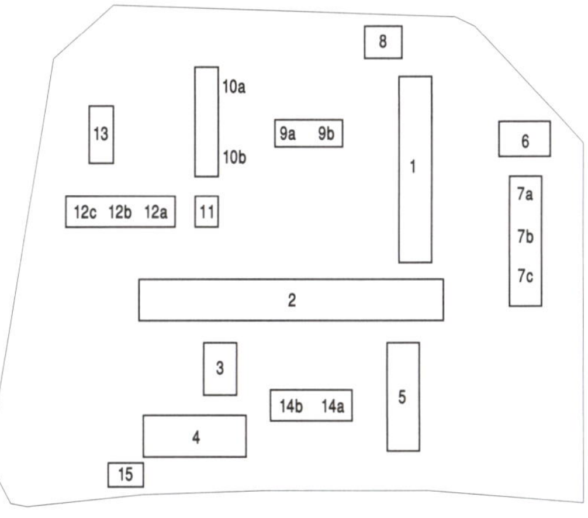

SITE PLAN

Building 1, 2, 3, 4, 5: Covered Market or Qaysariyah, 1965
Client: Association of Cloth Merchants
Building 8, 11: Offices of the Ministry of Commerce and Industries, 1965
Designer: Dar Al-Handasah
Building 9 a, b: Loulou Al-Masseel Building
Building 10 a: Mr. Muhanna Abdulrahman Muhanna and Co., 1968
Designer: Yousif Sha't and Esam Fahmy Al-Tarzy
Building 10 b: Jawharat Al-Khaleej Building (Jewel of the Gulf), 1963–67
Designer: Abdulhadi Darweesh Abu Al-Afiya
Building 12 a, b, c: Covered Market
Building 13: KIC apartment building,
Designer: Dar Al-Handasah
Building 14: Mr. Muhammad Kumaikh and Abdullah Jassim Shehab Building, 1967

1. Plan of the final layout, 1963
2. Façade detail of the Covered Market (Building 5)

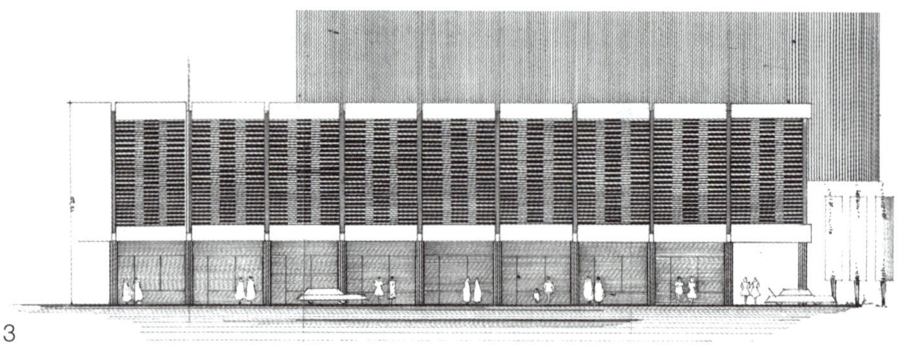

3

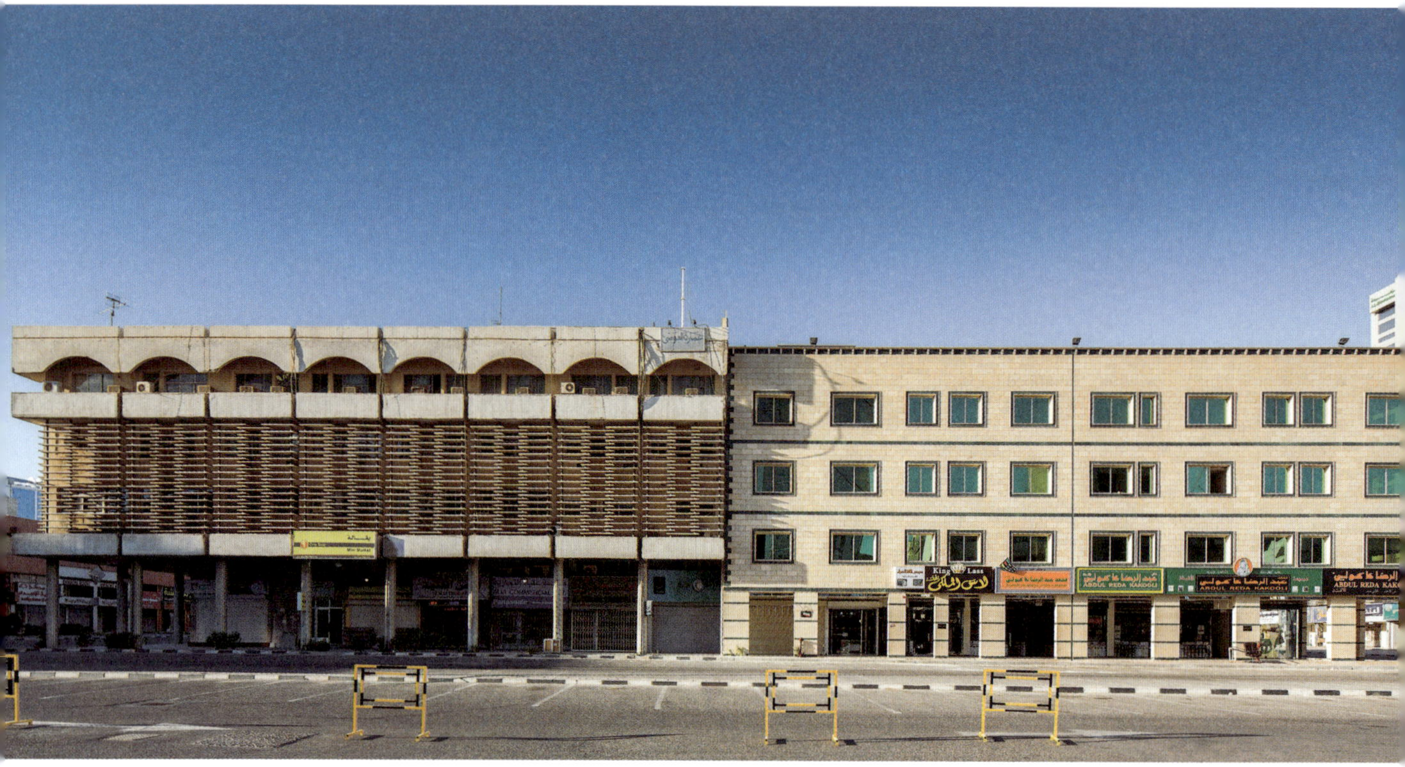

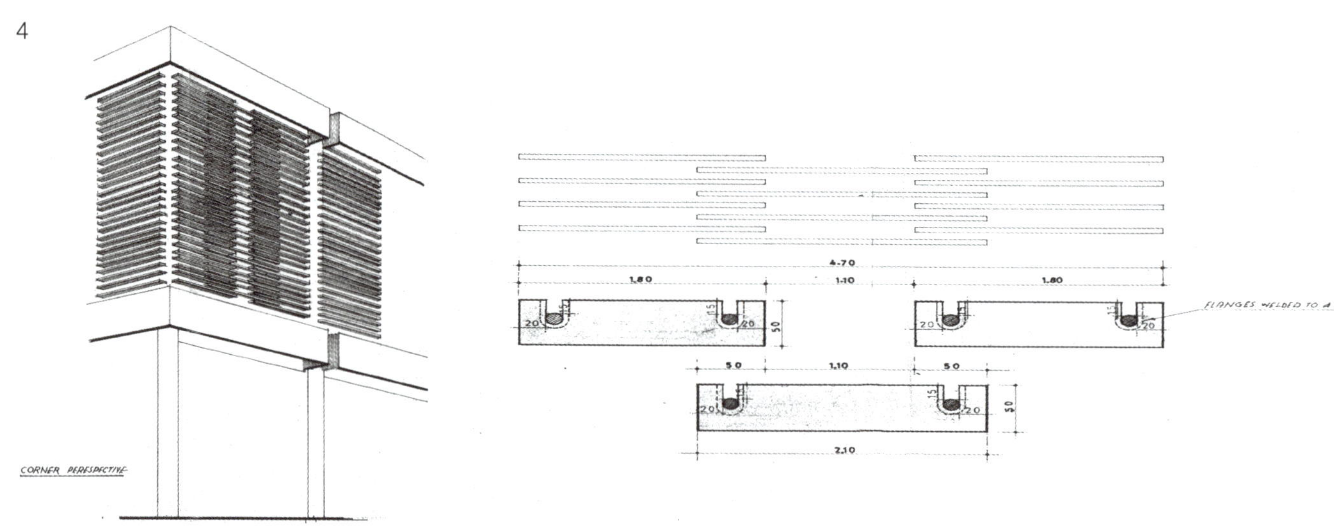

4

CORNER PERESPECTIVE

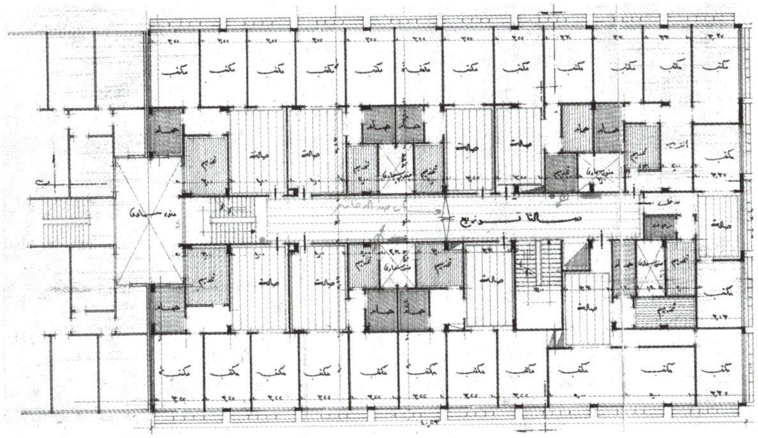

5

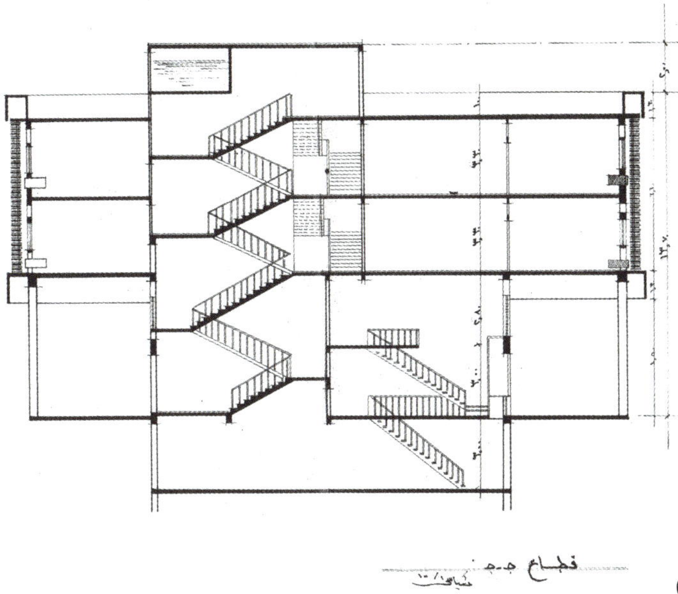

6

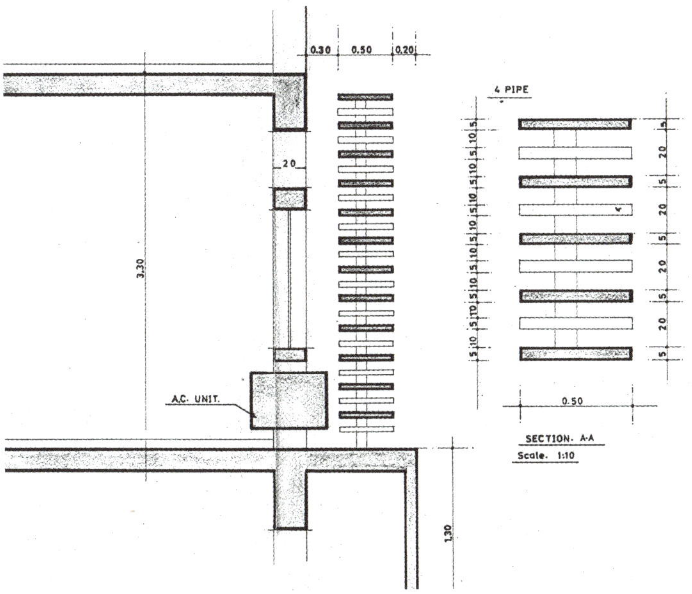

7

MR. MUHAMMAD KUMAIKH
AND ABDULLAH JASSIM SHEHAB BUILDING:

3. Elevation
4. Façade details
5. Typical floor plan
6. Section
7. Interior, 1969

8

9

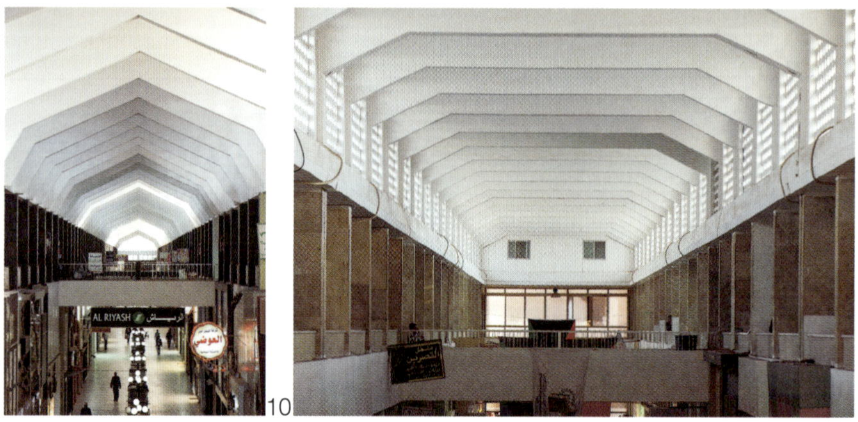

10

8. Façade detail of the Covered Market (building 2)
9. Aerial view, 1969
10. Covered Markets, internal view of the galleries
11. Prime Minister Diwan, north-west elevation

12

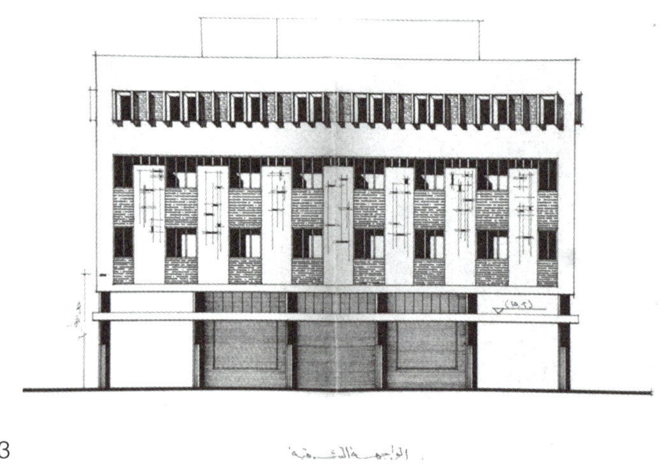

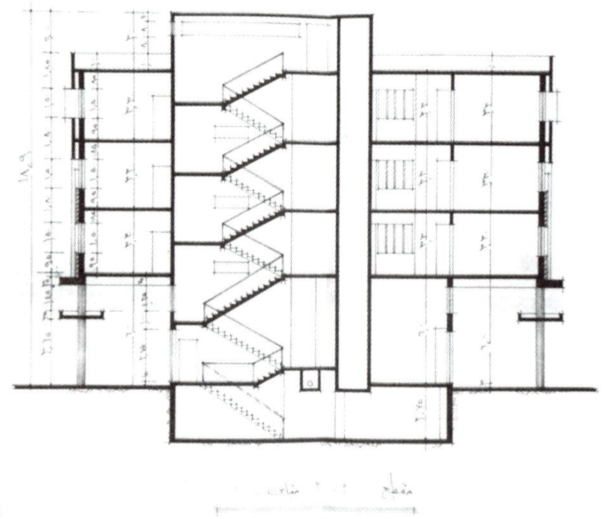

13

12. Former Ministry of Defence, 1965
13. Jawharat Al-Khaleej Building (n. 10 A),
project by Abdulhadi Abulafia, 1967
14. Kuwait Investment Company, residential and
commercial building, by Dar Al-Handasah, built in 1967

INSTITUTE FOR PHYSICALLY HANDICAPPED

HAWALLY
1963–1969

DESIGNERS • Bartlett & Gray
Architects; Norris & Partners (engineers)
CLIENT • Ministry of Public Works;
Ministry of Education
CONTRACTOR • Energoprojekt
Engeneering and Contracting

MODIFIED

Following the urbanisation of eastern Hawally with low-income housing schemes and the construction of Cairo Street during the late 1950s, an architectural firm from Nottingham was commissioned to develop an 8 ha site. The complex was intended to host 640 children of both sexes and accommodate 400 boarders. Strict segregation by gender, together with individual facilities for training and education of the deaf, blind or mentally handicapped children were required.

According to the written sources, apart from the spatial segregation of gender a "cool relaxing teaching" experience was obsessively pursued.[45] This was believed to be the most conducive condition to a child's mental and physical stimulation in this climate.

The *mat-building* scheme explores shade and elaborates on solar research. The external circulation, play areas and internal façades are partially shaded. Being confined to courtyards, these areas are also protected from sand and dust. Louvres are used vertically and placed with accuracy. Two *heliodons* built at the Building and Civil Engineering Dept. of Nottingham Technical College were brought to test the sun incidence reproducing the *sciagraphic* conditions of Kuwait.

The building's precast concrete roof is ribbed, echoing the vertical elements. Carefully defined, the designer aims that all external finishes be as smooth as possible to prevent staining from the combination of dust, sand and rain. After conversion into another educational facility, the building façades were plastered in a grained pre-blended mix, which stains easily.

1

2

3

4

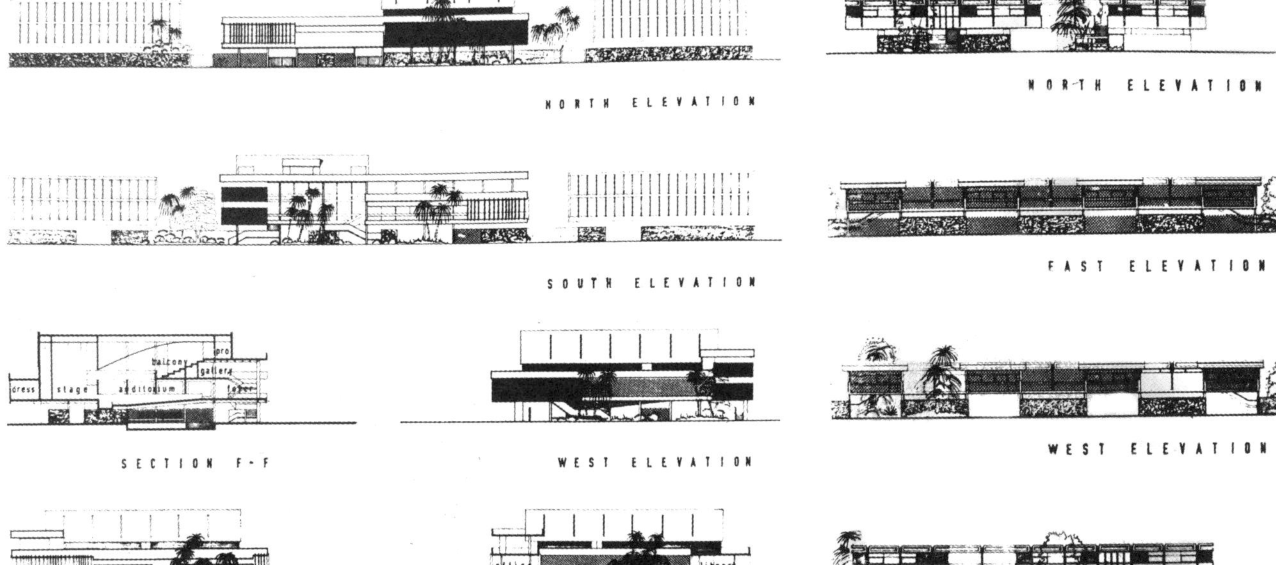

1. Drawing showing the handy crafts room seen from one of the courtyards of the female section of the Special Collective Institute
2. View of classroom court in the Female Institute, featuring Tamarisk trees
3. Collage of the view of the classrooms and dormitories of the Female Institutes
4. Aerial view, circa 1971
5. Elevations and sections of the Assembly Hall and Entrance Court of the institute
6. Elevations of the handy crafts section
7. Ground floor plan of the handy crafts section
8. Ground and first floor plans of the Institute for Mentally Deficient Girls

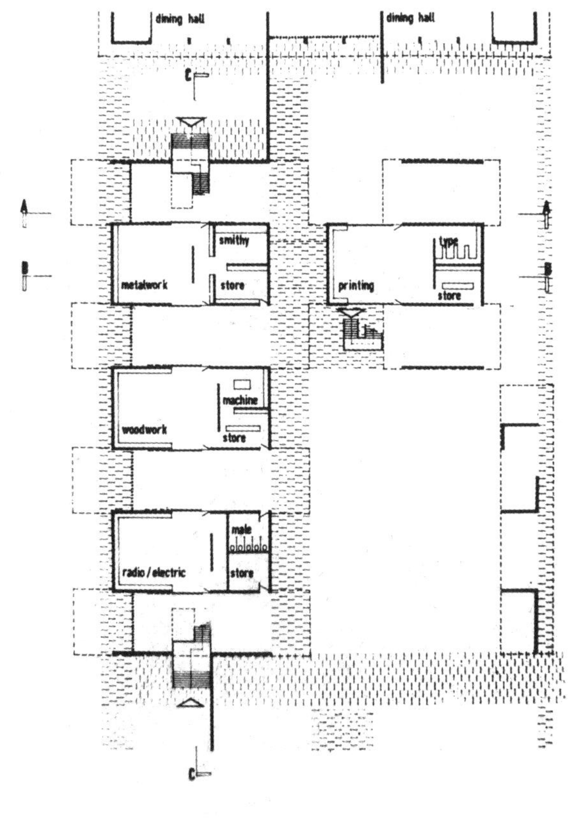

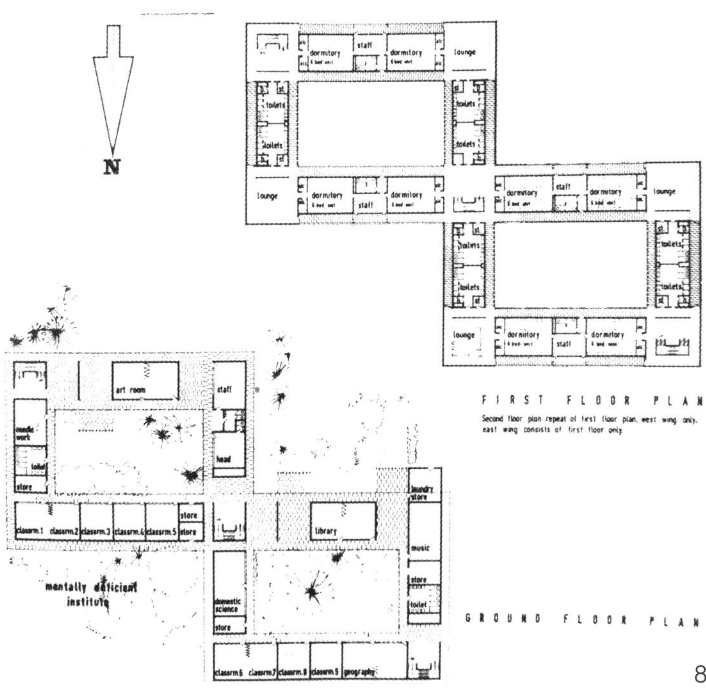

STANDARD SCHOOLS

VARIOUS LOCATIONS
1963

DESIGNERS • Ministry of Public Works; revised by Alfred Roth
CLIENT • Ministry of Education; Ministry of Public Works
CONTRACTOR • Various

DEMOLISHED / MODIFIED

In the early 1960s, the population was rapidly growing in number and so were children of school age. Therefore, the Ministries of Education and Public Works developed a standard design that was quick to build and economical. It was an E-shaped plan on three levels. Three classrooms were allocated to each wing, with services and staircases, while the front hosted the reception, administration, teachers' rooms, laboratories and verandas. All the functional spaces were grouped in the centre and served by peripheral balconies generated by a concrete-frame envelope: a characteristic feature that punctuated the façades and offered shade.

In 1965, Alfred Roth praised the clarity and the practicality of this typology and proposed solutions for improving the building's performance. This was done mostly by reducing redundant spaces: lower ceiling height; new dimensions for the classrooms and re-arrangement of their position in plan. In addition, reduction of the number of levels for the wings, plus the introduction of louvres and soft landscaping.[46] This type was replicated in almost every residential neighborhood and it has been in use until very recently.

1. Neighborhood centre in Qadsiya, bird's eye view of the standard school building at the top right corner, mosque and clinic in foreground and complex with public offices, library and shops in a central position, undated, circa 1968
2. Girls' Intermediate School in Qurtuba, 1965
3. Typical plans, revised by A. Roth, 1965

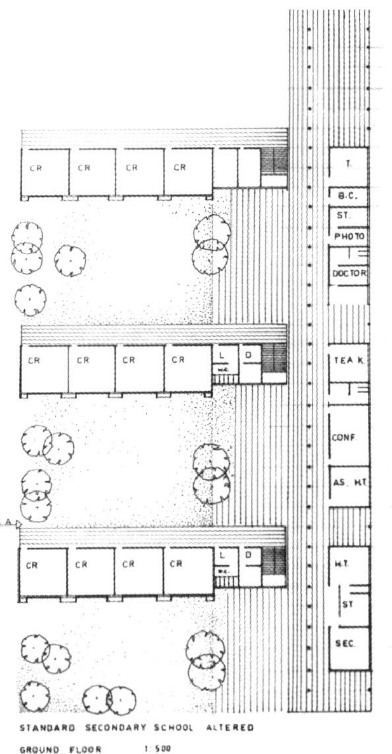

STANDARD SECONDARY SCHOOL ALTERED
GROUND FLOOR   1 : 500

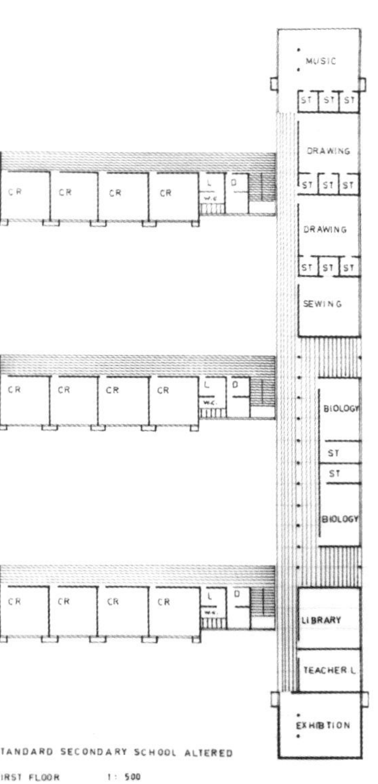

STANDARD SECONDARY SCHOOL ALTERED
FIRST FLOOR   1 : 500

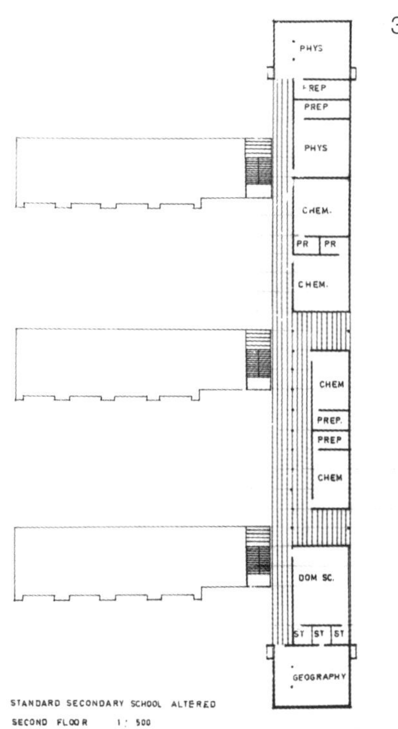

STANDARD SECONDARY SCHOOL ALTERED
SECOND FLOOR   1 : 500

FAHED AL-SALEM MOSQUE

SALMIYA
1961–1968

DESIGNER • Sabah Abi-Hanna
CLIENT • Sheikha Badriya Al-Sabah
CONTRACTOR • Unknown

IN USE

One of the first works of the young Lebanese architect Sabah Abi-Hanna, it was focused on the detailed requests and visual inspirations of the client, taken from her travels to Egypt.[47] This geographical reference may explain the thick, solid masses and the geometry of the minarets. The mosque has a common layout: a square plan, with a covered *sahan* that leads to the prayer room. Nonetheless, some features make it singular such as the entrance, which is accentuated by a series of arches protruding from a square recess in the flat front wall. These elements are repeated on the side doors, in a system that forms a sort of transept. These kinds of narthexes and the crowning friezes, which run all around the building, are the only tri-dimensional bodies meant to break the monotone volume of the building.

Also remarkable is the combination of traditional materials such as the limestone cladding with more advanced reinforced fiber composites intended for the main dome of the prayer hall.

1. Entrance
2. Detail of the minarets
3. View of a minaret from the Sahan
4. General view, circa 1970
5. View of the Prayer Hall
6. Detail of the Prayer Hall wall

LOW-INCOME AND RURAL HOUSING PROJECTS

SULAIBIYA, MINA ABDULLAH, AL-RIQQA
1968–1969

FINTAS, AL-RIQQA, NEW WAFRA
1966–1976

DESIGNERS • Luigi Moretti with Arab Consulting Office; Dar Al-Handasah; Thurfjell Consult; Jafar Tukan with KEB; Kazim Kenan for CAT; Pacific Consultants International with Toshikagaku Institute; Colin Buchanan and Partners
CLIENT • Saving and Credit Bank
CONTRACTOR • Unknown

UNBUILT / MODIFIED

When the former desert population, the Bedouins, started becoming more sedentary, a number of temporary shelters were erected on vacant lots, mostly close to their workplaces or near the oil fields. The situation rapidly showed the need for government intervention and help. [48]

The migration from rural to vacant urban areas, together with the massive influx of foreign migrants, also mostly originating from rural environments, characterised the nature of these spontaneous settlements.[49]

From 1966, a joint effort by the different housing authorities and the planning consultants suggested several sites for agricultural settlements at the edges of the urban areas, in particular towards the north-west (Jahra), and the south (Mina Abdullah or Umm-Elhiman). The outcomes of this initiative were not developed further, but ten years later two other projects were partially implemented with similar purposes for the same locations. One of those, an *Agricultural Town* model, was developed under the World Bank by the Swedish practice of Jan Thurfjell, T-Consult, previously known for large pre-fabricated housing schemes in wood. [50]

The *Agriculture Town* was in concept very similar to Kisho Kurokawa's *Agriculture City* in Saudi Arabia (1960–61). It was based on the principle of autonomous squatters providing employment and housing, by reclaiming empty areas of the desert not suitable

3

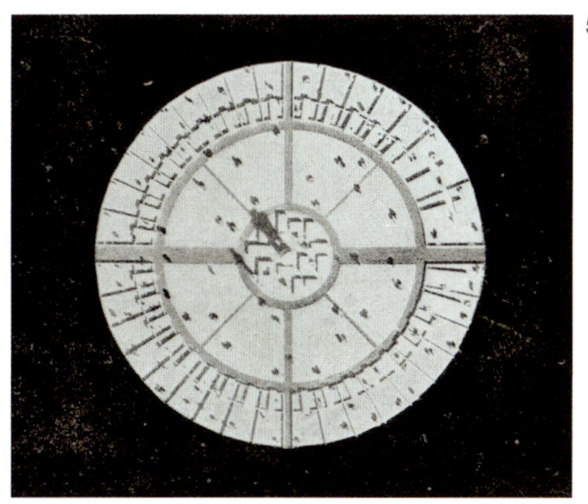

4

5

1. Site survey of existing shanty settlements in Kuwait, 1965
2. J. Tukan, Al-Riqqa aerial view, 1977
3. J. Tukan, Al-Riqqa aerial view, 1977
4. J. Tukan, view of the housing unit, 1976
5. T-Consult, Agricultural Town, view of the model, 1964

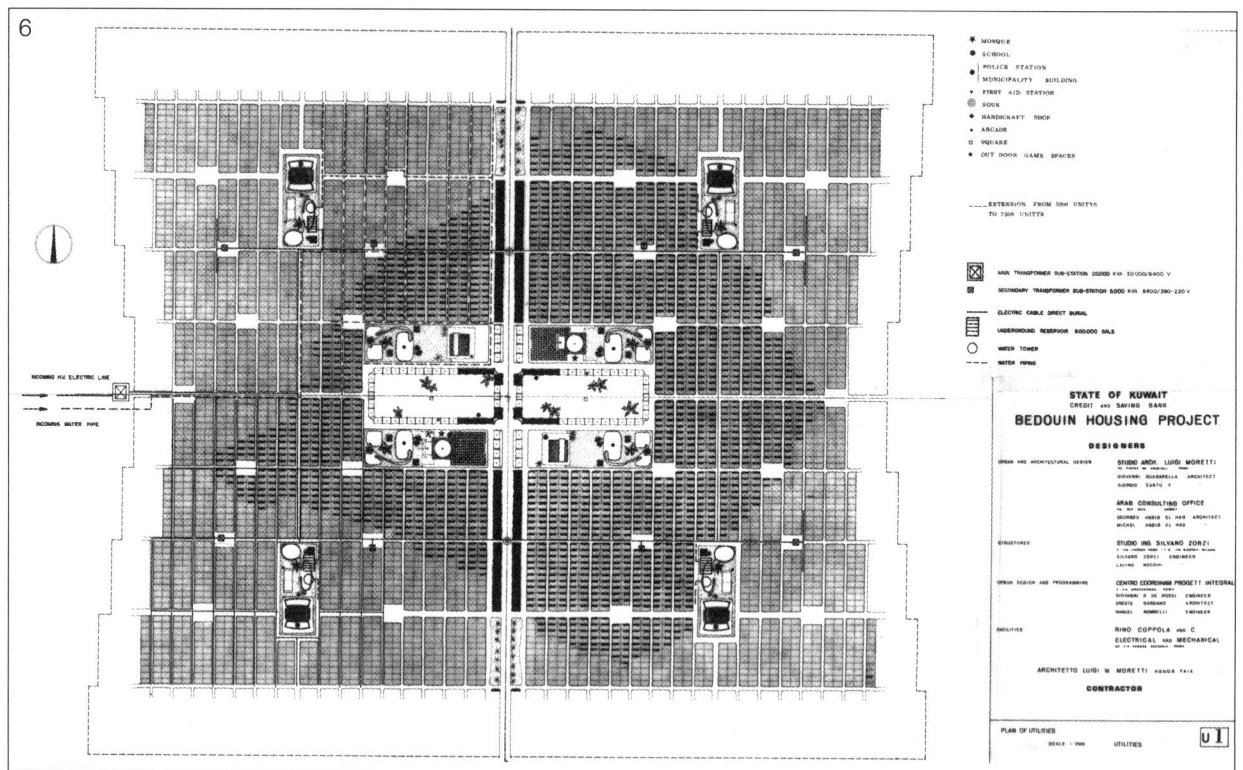

for mineral exploration, and also by pursuing the pending resolution of the neutral-zones.[51]

In 1968 the State of Kuwait promoted an international competition for rural houses. The competition brief identified two marginal areas at the eastern and southern limit of the city. Identical enclosed plots of 150 square metres each, should have been assembled in a village form to give home to 10,000 people: a simple linear typology of 50 m^2 of double bedroom units was suggested as a plausible solution.[52] Luigi Moretti's answer to the rigid requirements was a clear plan based on a rectangular module with a hierarchic definition of streets and squares. He focused the proposal on a better climate performance of the units. He suggested insulating sandwich panels and a curved roof system detached from the buildings, in order to trigger natural ventilation. The same elements were used to add some architectural quality to the rigid boxes and to the fences, which identified private and public areas. However, again, this proposal was not implemented.

An exception was Al Riqqa Low-Income Housing scheme. As a consequence of the Rural Housing project from the 1966 Municipality Plan, it was built between 1971 and 1973. The large development

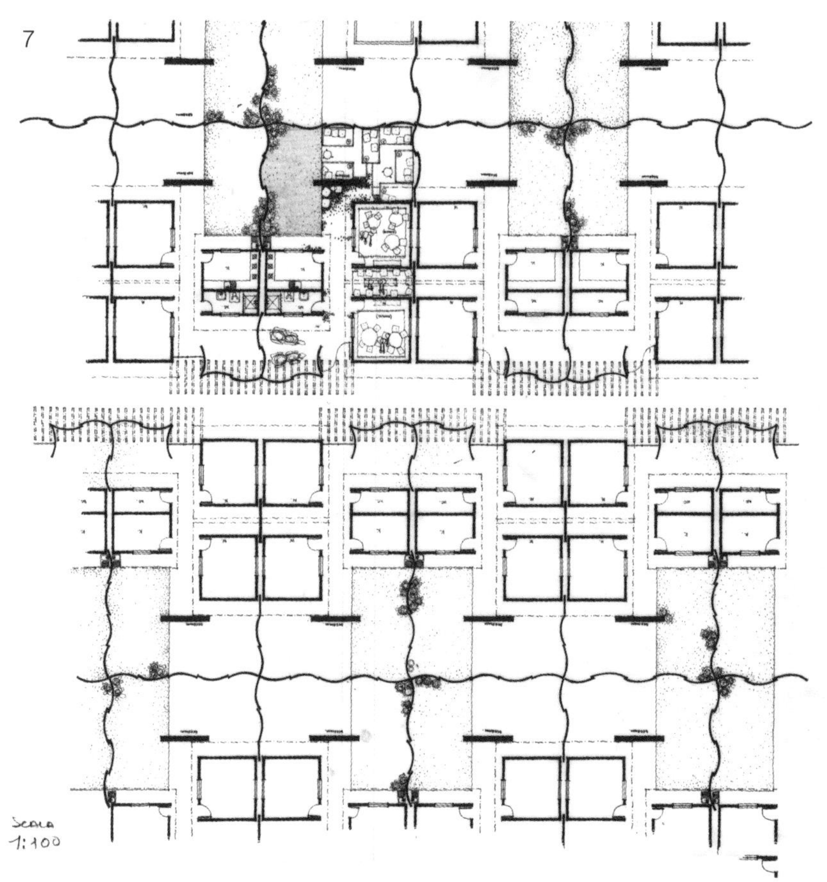

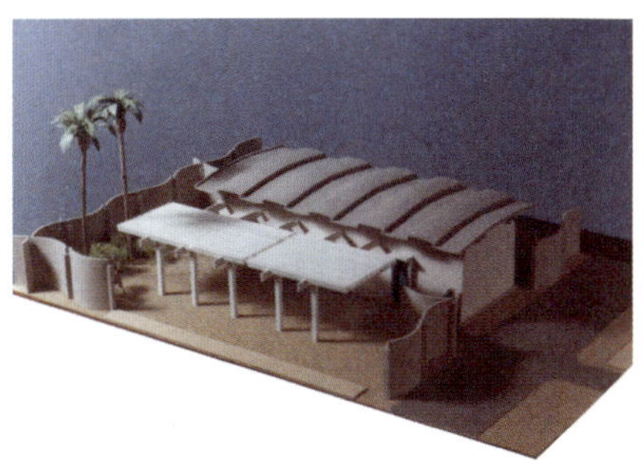

for 2,330 units was comprised of two-storey semi-detached homes with a substantial integration of pre-fabricated concrete elements. Developed by the Jordanian architect Jafar Tukan in collaboration with Kuwait Engineering Bureau, the houses were to be distributed in 1976. The brief received by Tukan, requesting 40% of the surface to be considered as open area for agricultural development, bears similarity with the above-described projects and to Dar Al-Handasah's New Wafra Town, built in the former neutral-zone at Kuwait's southern border in 1976–78.[53]

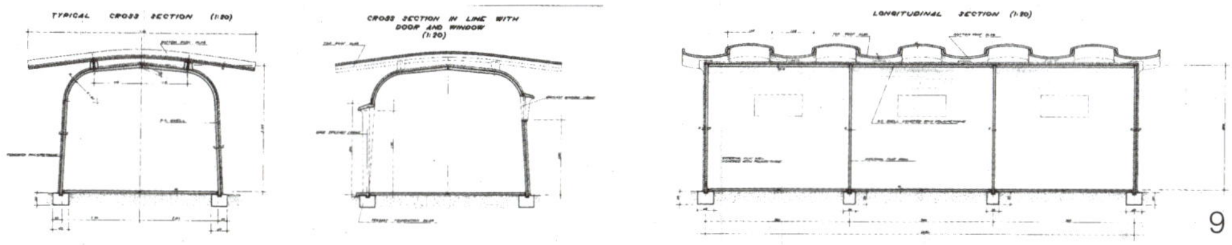

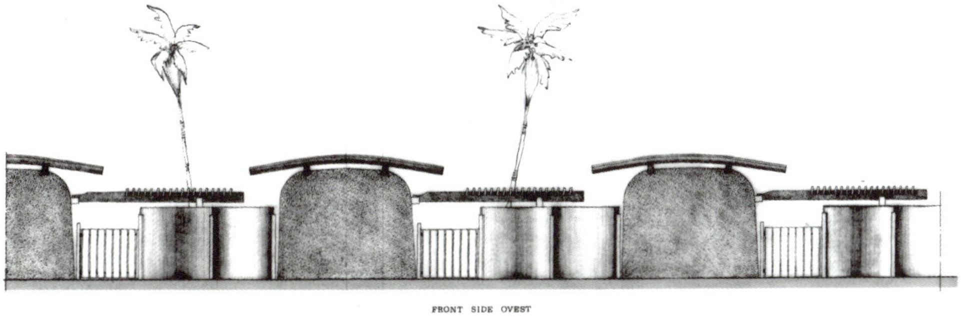

L. MORETTI, BEDOUIN HOUSING PROJECT, 1969:

6. Site plan
7. Units aggregative system
8. Scale model
9. Sections
10. West elevation
11. North elevation
12. Sketches

HASSAWI RESIDENTIAL COMPLEXES

HAWALLY & SALMIYA
1968–1973

DESIGNERS • Iraq Consult with PACE
CLIENT • Mubarak AbdulAziz Al-Hassawi
CONTRACTOR • Abdulhamid Al-Essa

UNDER THREAT OF DEMOLITION

The first large built project of Rifat Chadirji in Kuwait, after the completion of M. Al-Hamad residence in 1967, is the result of a two year association between his office, Iraqi Consult and the new local design firm, Pan Arab Consulting Engineers.

The mixed-use complex with a commercial arcade along Beirut Street and nine residential blocks of six-storey height, reflect the aesthetic and material concepts and influences proposed by the author as a modern regionalised architecture.

The expression of architectural elements is manifested through raw materials such as the brick façade, together with the latest in building technology, generating a strong visual composition: verticality, free-standing arcades and small openings meticulously organised. In this specific case, Chadirji affirms as influences the Jumah Congregational Mosque (Iran) and Al-Aqsa Mosque (Jerusalem) through their physical existence but also emotional condition, highlighting the argument of the intermediate semi-private communal spaces in between the residential units.[54] The cross circulation between these and the commercial arcades were fundamental to promoting neighborhood social activity and importantly humanising the space. At the same time and for the same client, another project would be built in Salmiya, following the same principles and with very similar results in façade design. Addressing the topography, a wall delineates the perimeter of the plot, creating a platform that underpins the four exclusively residential blocks. Car parking was allocated to the ground level in one of the corners of the plot.

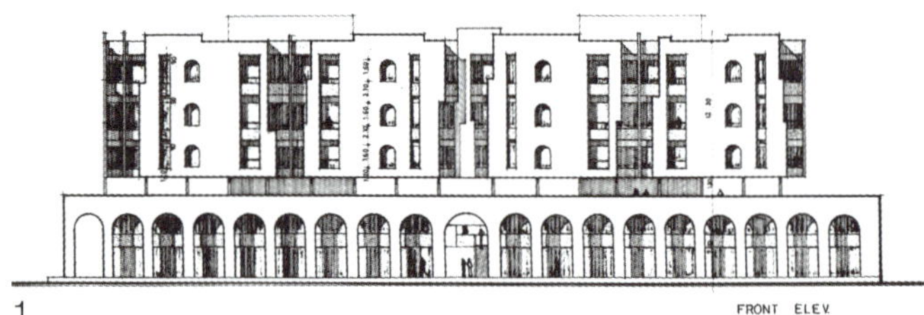

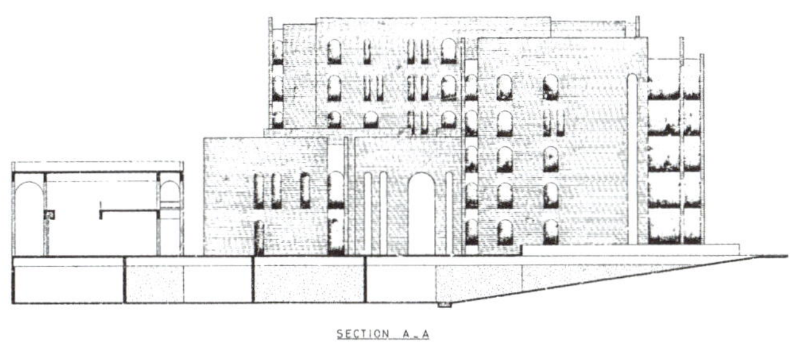

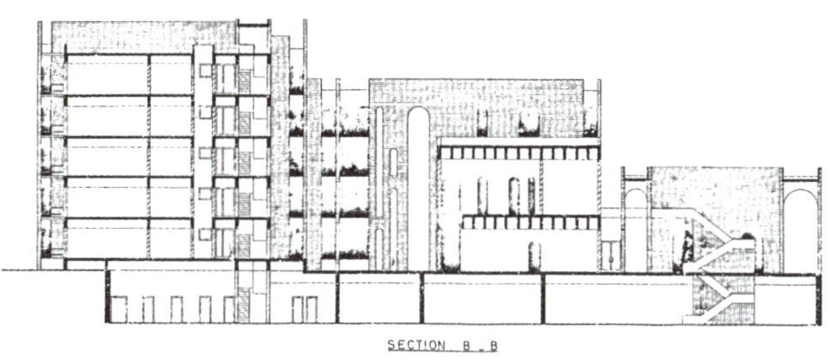

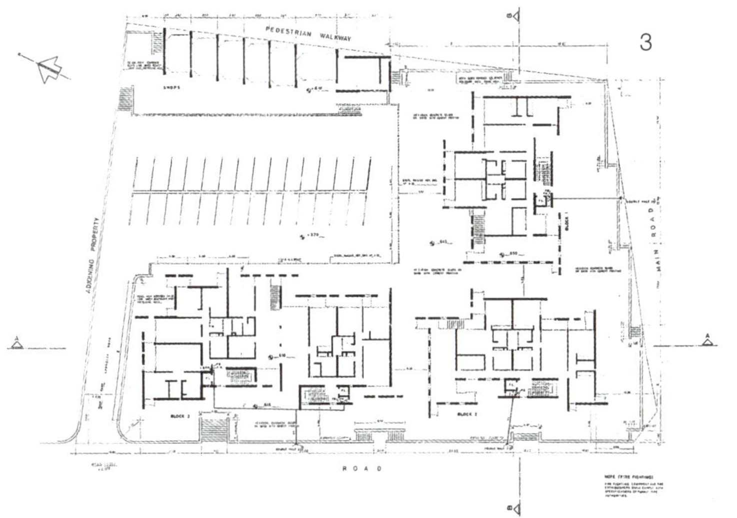

1. Al-Andalous Complex, front elevation
2. Al-Andalous Complex,
sections through the courtyard
3. Aziziya Complex, ground floor plan
4. General view, undated

135

KUWAIT SOCIETY OF ENGINEERS

BNEID AL-GAR
1968

DESIGNERS • Ghazi Sultan (1st Prize entry), PACE (lead consultant); Luigi Moretti with Arab Consulting Office (competition entry); Iraq Consult (competition entry)
CLIENT • Kuwait Society of Engineers
CONTRACTOR • Unknown

MODIFIED

In 1968 the Society of Engineers issued an international competition for their new head office, to be located on the Gulf Road, next to the American Embassy and the old Hilton Hotel. The empty plot was sufficient to accommodate the administrative offices, a club for 900 members and a park.

Moretti proposed a free aggregation of independent volumes: four fluid shapes in a lush garden. The administration cluster housed the offices and a large circular library, while the club was formed through the curved volume of the assembly hall, the restaurant and the commercial/recreational area. This proposal was not implemented; nonetheless it seems almost easy to imagine these blocks with the thick, raw, off-white plaster typical of his constructions at that time.

Chadirji's proposal was very different. It was a chessboard of rooms, some enclosed, some open-air among vegetation and trees. The elevations offered a forest of brick arches and curved walls, revealing unexpected pathways among the build volumes.

The erected project was designed by Ghazi Sultan in 1971, in collaboration with PACE and KEO; the park was cancelled and the functional programme reduced. The outcome was a combination of two linear blocks, connected by the smaller volume of the staircase. The concrete frame was exposed, highlighting by chromatic contrast the white brickwork. The slanted roof, an unusual feature in the area, added dynamism to a somewhat rigid composition.

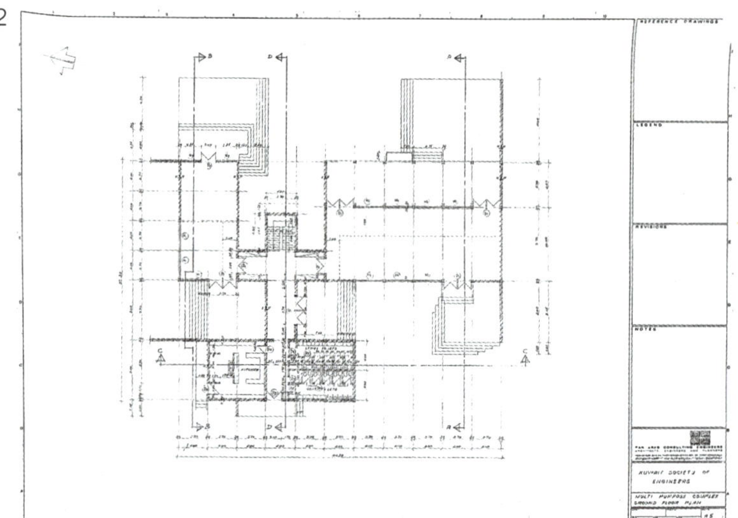

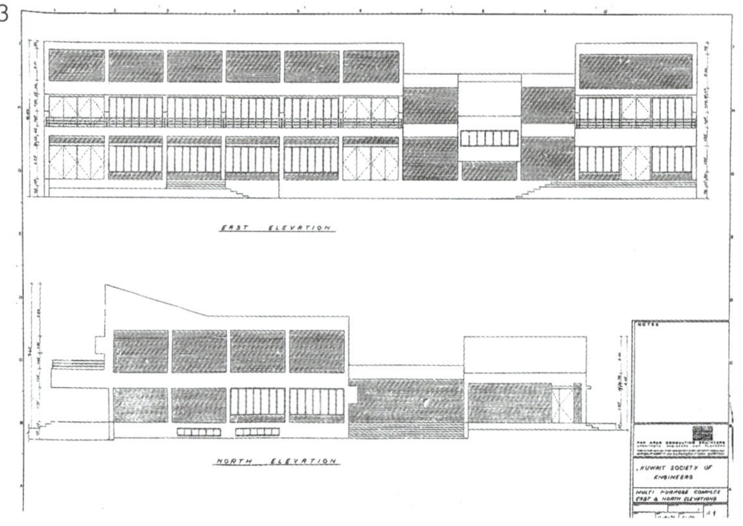

5
6

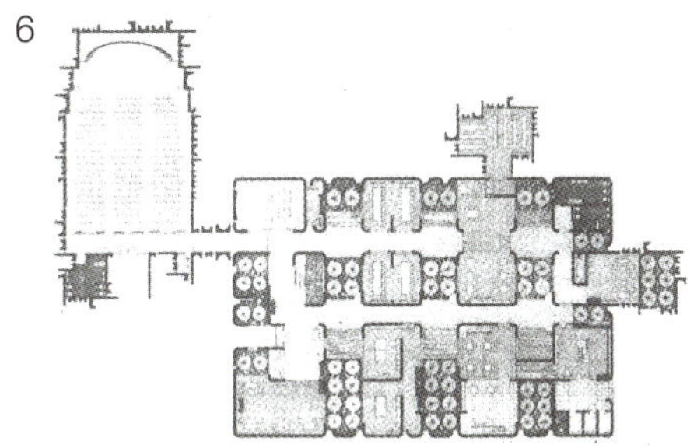

G. SULTAN, PACE, KEO PROJECT:

1. View of the courtyard
2. Ground floor plan
3. Elevations
4. View of the entrance

R. CHADIRJI'S PROPOSAL:

5. Ground floor plan
6. Elevations

7

KUWAIT SOCIETY OF ENGINEERS
SNEID EL KAR
KUWAIT
ARCHITECTS
ARAB CONSULTING OFFICE
ARCHITECT GEORGES HABIB ELHAG
ARCHITECT MICHEL HABIB ELHAG
CENTRO COORDINAMENTO PROGETTAZIONE INTEGRALE
ARCHITECT G. DE ROSSI
ARCHITECT O. GARGANO
ARCHITECT LUIGI W. MORETTI F.A.I.A.
3
GROUND FLOOR PLAN
scala 1:200
A ENTRANCE DRIVE WAY
B CLUB MAIN ENTRANCE
C DIRECTION MAIN ENTRANCE
D SERVICE ROAD
E TRUCK RAMP
CLUB
1 PARKING
2 HALL
3 STAIR TO BASEMENT
4 DRESSING ROOM
5 CONTROL AND RECEPTION
6 PATIO
7 CINEMA
8 TOILET
9 PRIVATE PROJECTION ROOM
10 AUDITION ROOM
11 LISTENING-BOX
12 MIXAGE
13 PLAY ROOM
14 TOILET
15 STAIR TO GRILL
16 RESTAURANT
17 TERRACE
18 SWIMMING POOL
19 BASKET
20 TENNIS
DIRECTION
1 ENTRANCE FOYER
2 STAIRS TO 1ST FLOOR
3 RECEPTION
4 SECRETARIAT
5 PRESS
6 UTILITIES
7 BOOKKEEPER
8 DRESSING ROOM
9 TOILET
10 CONFERENCE AND RECEPTION ROOM
11 TERRACE

8

SECTION A-A
SECTION B-B
SECTION C-C

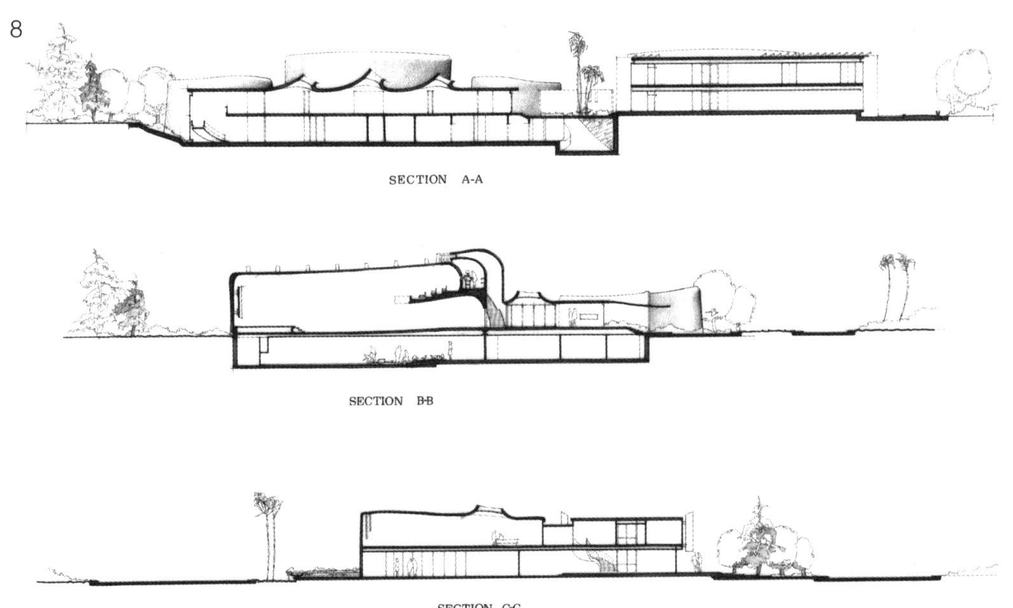

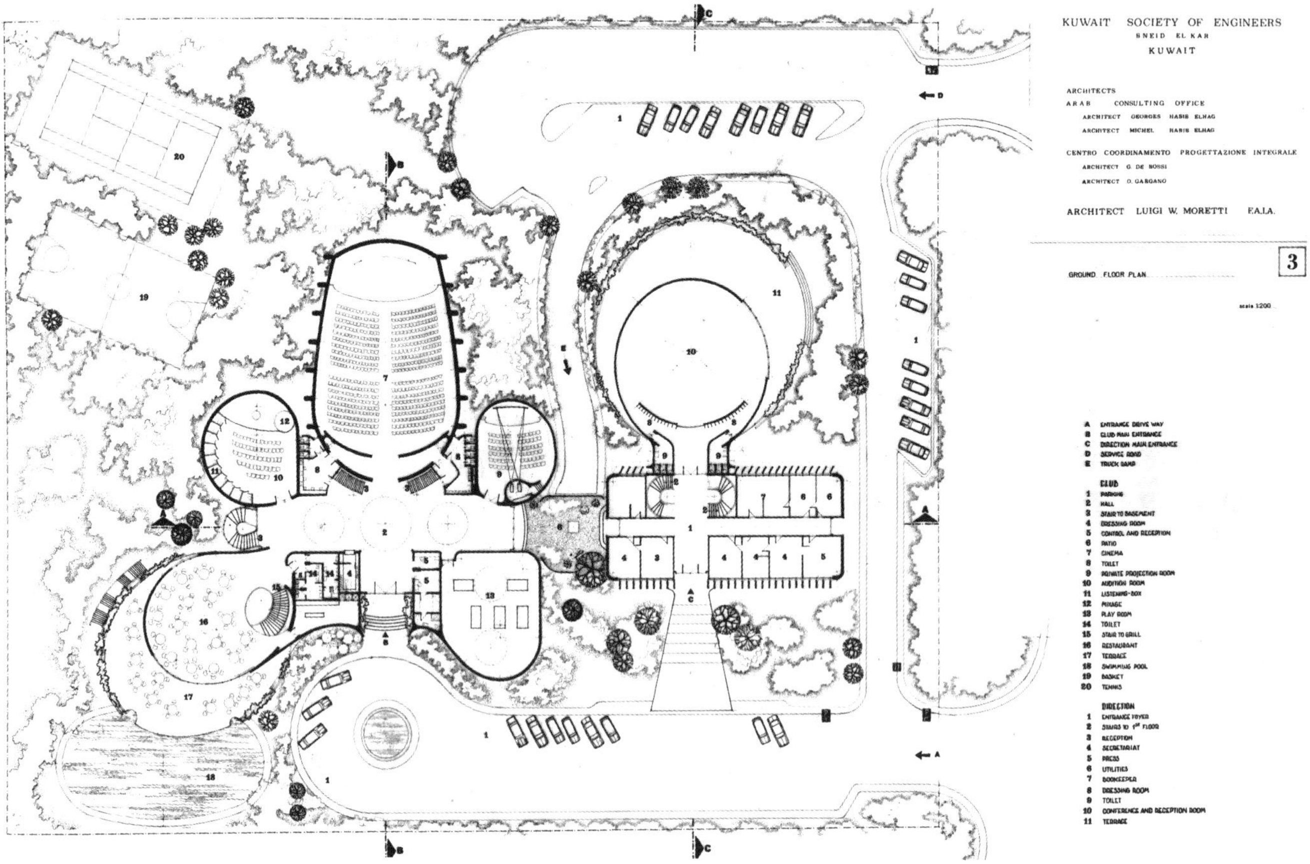

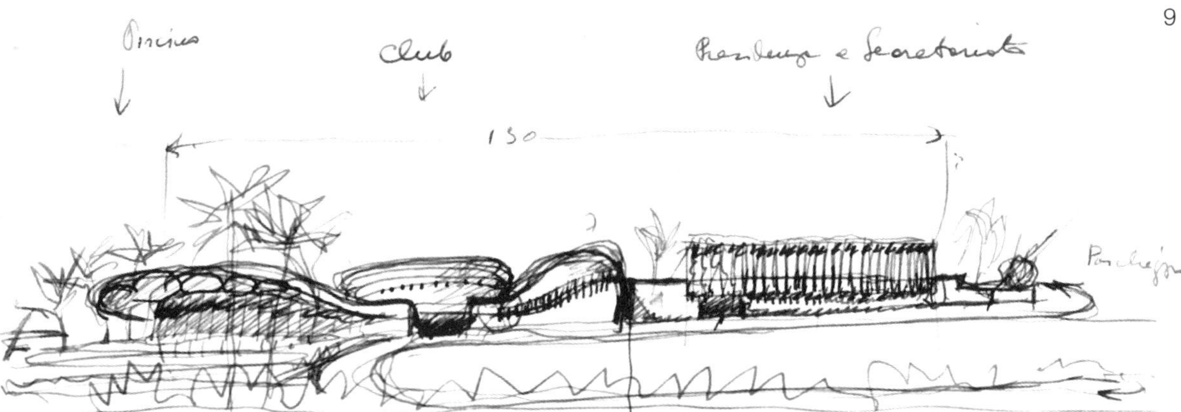

L. MORETTI'S PROPOSAL:

7. Site plan
8. Sections
9. Sketch by the designer
10. Scale model

INTERMEDIATE SCHOOL FOR GIRLS

RUMAITHIYA
1967–1970

DESIGNER • Alfred Roth
CLIENT • Ministry of Education;
Ministry of Public Works
CONTRACTOR • Unknown

MODIFIED

Alfred Roth was appointed in 1965 by UNESCO to assess the condition of school buildings in Kuwait. This initial survey led to further collaborations with the Ministry of Education in order to develop specific school types for the persistent need of updated educational facilities. The first commission was for a secondary school for girls as a demonstrative prototype in the new neighborhood of Rumaithiya. Roth's reflection started from the role of the school in the community and its location as a pivotal point in the neighborhood unit, together with the mosque and the civic centre.

He designed an introverted building, a courtyard school. All the main didactical and recreational activities revolved around this central void. It was the main distribution hinge as well as the key climate control tool. Initially, in fact, the school was not air-conditioned. Thus the only possible solution was to trigger natural cross ventilation from the courtyard to the outside through channels cut between the concrete slabs and the beams.[55]

As a prototype, the building was initially designed to be prefabricated, but the technology needed was not available in Kuwait at that time; therefore it was chosen to be cast on-site and faced with limestone bricks. This specific design was not reproduced elsewhere as initially conceived, but several elements, including the courtyard, were adopted in many other schools in the following years.

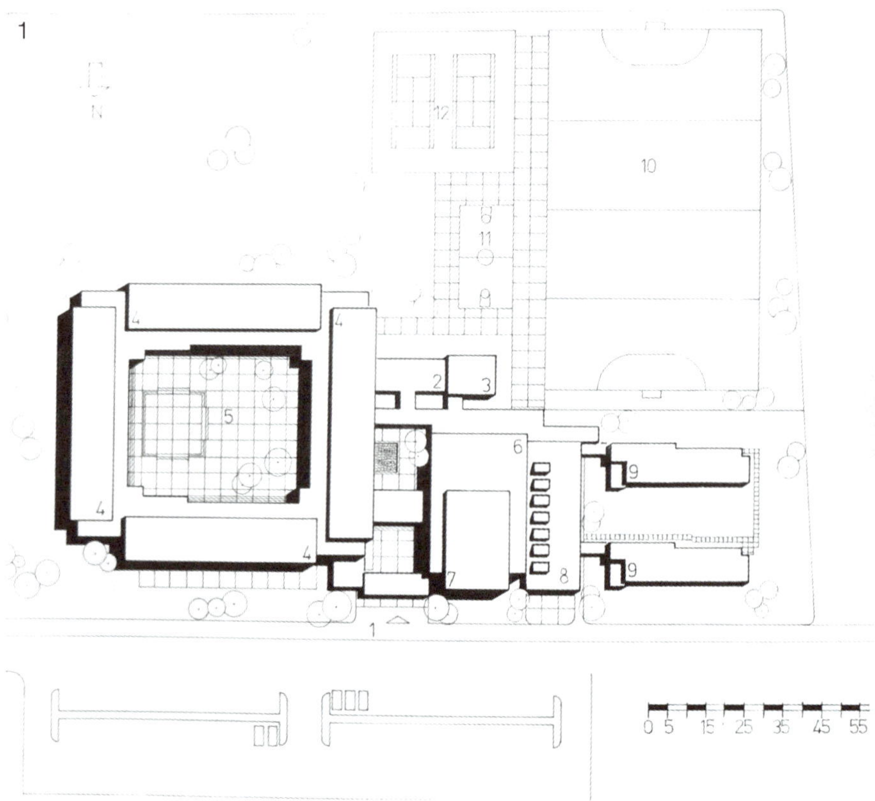

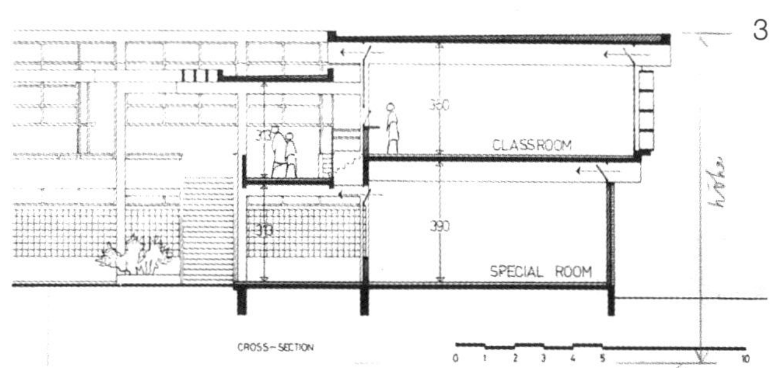

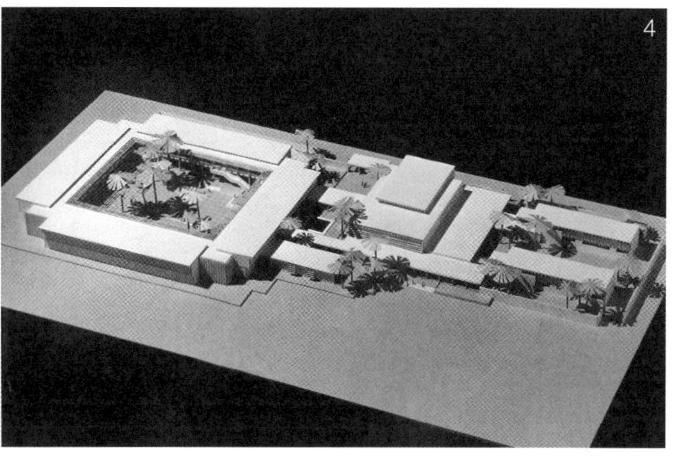

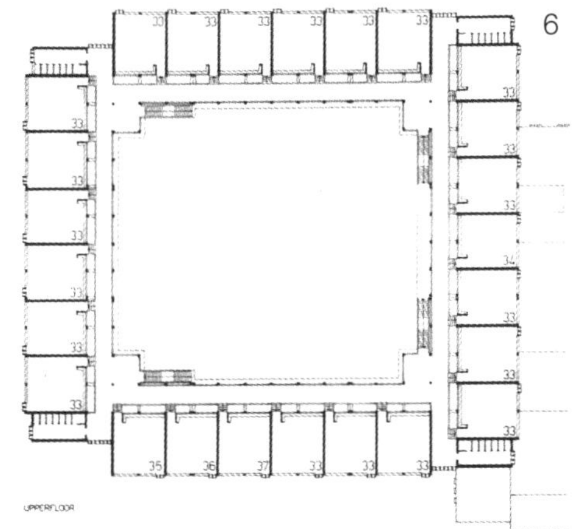

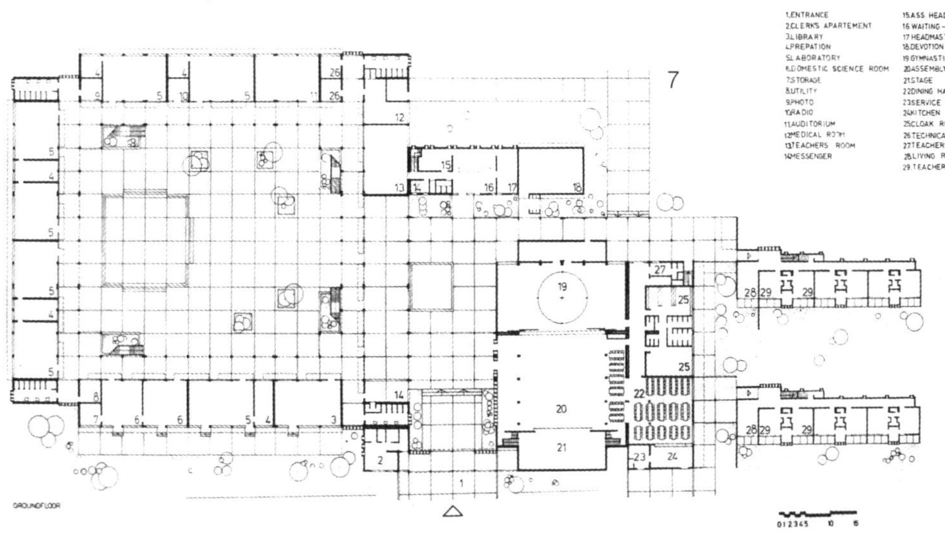

1. Site plan
2. South elevation
3. Section
4. Scale model
5. View of the main courtyard
6. First floor plan
7. Ground floor plan

141

EIGHT AUTOMATIC BAKERY UNITS

VARIOUS LOCATIONS
1961–

DESIGNER • Unknown
CLIENT • Kuwait Flour Mills Company (KFMC)
CONTRACTOR • Richard Costain (Middle East) Co. Ltd.; various others

IN USE

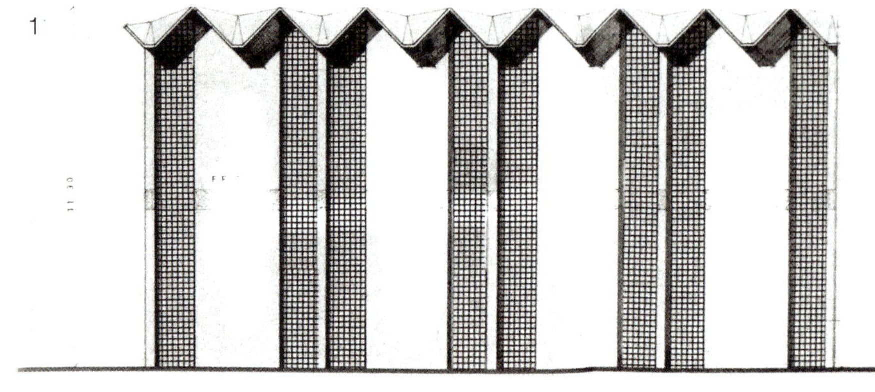

An integrated system of flour production and storage and also baking and packing the bread, was implemented through the years and distributed throughout the city. In 1965, the central unit for flour started its operation in Shuwaikh Port and eight prototypical projects were implemented as neighbourhood units for bread production.[56]

The materials used in the prototype construction were chosen with special regard to the harsh climatic conditions to make food production and storage practical. The building complex had to respond to the functional pragmatism of a modern automatic wheat mill with packaging and storage of the sacks and advanced equipment to load into transport vehicles for delivery.

The storage silo, 8 m in height, was used as a main reference point, standing in the monotonous townscape of the residential neighbourhoods. This large volume covered in brick, dominates a large packing hall that leads to the loading area. A small retail outlet serves as local bread distribution. The hall, built in a precast concrete frame and filled with exposed brick partitions, reflects a construction system that became common practice in Kuwait during this period.

1. Proposal for side elevation
2. Production areas, bread baking
and packing automated process, 1969

FEMALE STUDENTS' HOUSING – COLLEGE OF EDUCATION

KAIFAN
1979–1981

DESIGNER • Energoprojekt Engeneering and Contracting, Sector of Architecture and Construction
CLIENT • Kuwait University
CONTRACTOR • Energoprojekt Engeneering And Contracting

IN USE

1

The complex is dominated by a residential building with a central tower articulating three equal alleys of six floors each, comprising a total of 300 room units and a ground floor with common facilities. The tower element with blind concrete façades on top and vertically continuous concrete panels shading the building's central core in a glass curtain-wall, is the central element of the building. In addition, the complex includes three major detached buildings: a sports-hall, the central kitchen for the college and a greenhouse.

While we have no confirmed date for the project development and construction, it is known that this project was developed in parallel with the Ministry of Communication Tower. However Dr. Petar Perović, a structural engineer working for the Energoprojekt, makes a reference to this project dating back to 1967–68 and to the use of IMS systems pre-stressed reinforced concrete walls, façade panels and slabs.[57] This defined the final image of the building, dominating all façade partitions and proportions. The façade is partitioned into regular units and includes shading panels and a single aluminium framed window.

144

1. Commercial advertisement from Al-Bahar
Construction Company for prefabricated
IMS System in Kuwait, 1970
2. Residential building in Maidan Hawally,
implementing the IMS U51 System, circa 1974

CENTRAL BANK OF KUWAIT

CENTRAL BUSINESS DISTRICT – AREA 2
1966–1976

DESIGNERS • Arne Jacobsen; Dissing + Weitling
CLIENT • Ministry of Public Works
CONTRACTOR • Al-Hani Construction & Trading Co.

MODIFIED

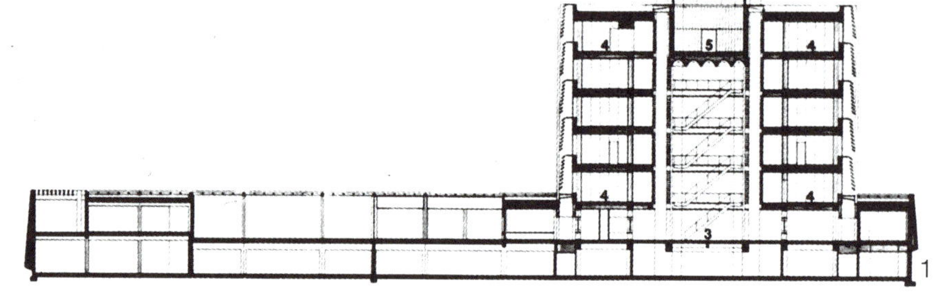

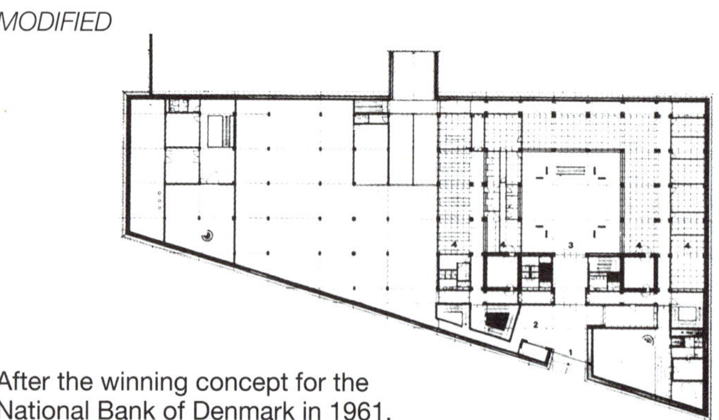

After the winning concept for the National Bank of Denmark in 1961, Arne Jacobsen was commissioned to design the Central Bank of Kuwait. It was one of Jacobsen's last projects and was built after his death under the supervision of Hans Dissing and Otto Weitling (1973–1976).

Located in Area 2 of CBD, the building consists of two main volumes, one inscribed in the other: The lower one acts as an opaque podium of grey stone and follows the perimeter of the plot, in what seems to be a reference to the old city wall. The second one, in a square shape, protrudes from the podium five stories high.[58]

The aluminium louvers on the façade shade the glazed curtain protecting the building from the sun. Inside, the offices are distributed around a central courtyard, and like the Bank of Denmark the staircase under the customized artificial light is the centrepiece.

Very few elements remain from the original building of Arne Jacobsen, identifiable only by the main entrance punctuated by the golden dome. Only nine years after its completion, the building was altered in order to get closer to what was the original intention of a more Islamic architectural structure.

1. Section
2. Ground floor plan
3. Typical floor plan
4. West elevations, after the renovation
5. View of the skylight
6. Interior, view of the balconies overlooking the Central Hall
7. West elevation, before the renovation

AL-AHLI BANK

MUBARAKIYA (CBD AREA 5)
1968–1974

DESIGNERS • Thurfjell Consult with PACE
CLIENT • Al-Ahli Bank of Kuwait
CONTRACTOR • Ahmadiah Contracting & Trading Co.

DEMOLISHED

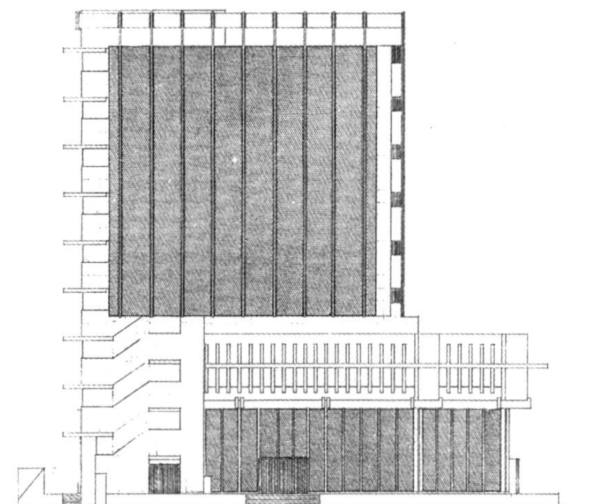

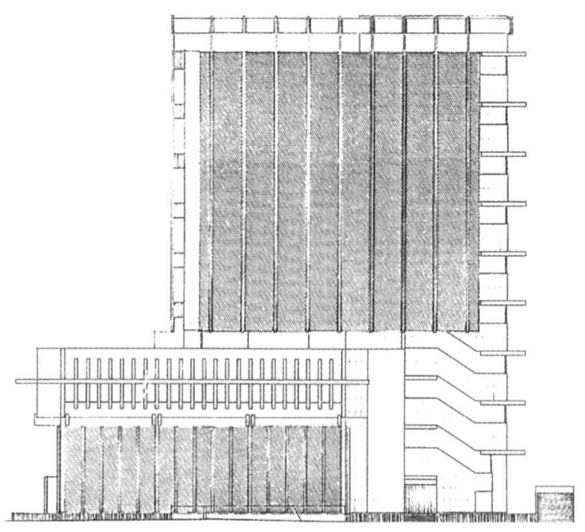

1

The international practice of Jan Thurfjell,[59] Theme Consult (T-Consult), well-known for large pre-fabricated housing schemes, was among the first design associates of PACE.[60] This project was developed together at a critical moment for the old city core development. This initiative might have eventually triggered future development of an area that became the city's financial centre in the following years.

Meant to be the highest building in the city with 10 floors above ground,[61] its impact could have been bigger; however, the construction took so long that other similar volumes were built during those years. With a total area of 10,800 m^2 and two underground floors for parking, the building's main programme related to banking with typical open-plan office floors and a curtain façade in the upper floors, with the main branch on the ground, mezzanine and first floors.

The lower element, detached from the street by an elevated platform in black marble, assumed the role of a podium, dealing with plot geometry and boundary relations. The tower, with the staircase as a reference element, was covered with an aluminium louvered façade system.

2

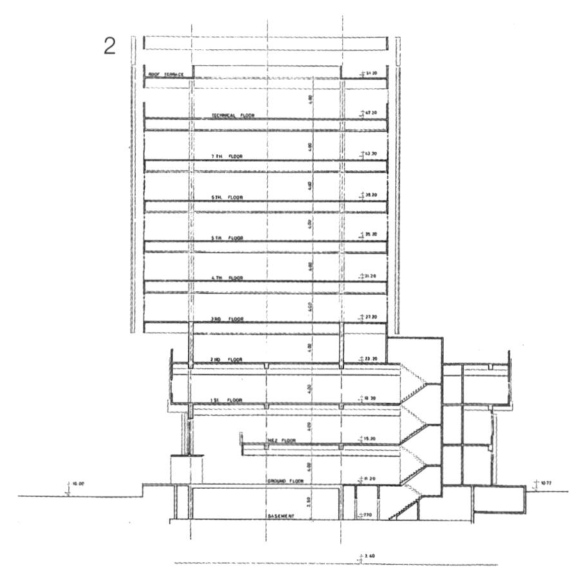

1. Elevations
2. Section
3. View from Oman Street, circa 1975
4. View of the interior, under construction

COMMERCIAL BANK OF KUWAIT

MUBARAKIYA (CBD AREA 5)
1968–1971

DESIGNERS • Design Construction Group
(Antony Irving and Gordon Brown); KEO
CLIENT • Commercial Bank of Kuwait
CONTRACTOR • Unknown

MODIFIED

By the time the project was commissioned, Tony Irving's team was a well-known reference in bank head offices design considering the completion of the respective headquarters of the National Bank of Kuwait and Gulf Bank. In both projects, the chief architect was Brian Broughton, who in 1965, joined Ghazi Sultan in the establishment of the architects' department at KEO.

The Commercial Bank ten storey-high tower followed the exception given to Al-Ahli Bank in exceeding the height previously allowed by regulation of CBD Area 5, becoming another important vertical element shaping the area.

The similarities with Al-Ahli Bank are in the footprint, in the podium with two floors for the main branch, in the basement for safe deposits and in the office floors wrapped in a glazed curtain façade, shaded with aluminium mesh.[62] The second skin of meshed façade was an experimental theme using various shapes and material as a modern reinterpretation of the more traditional wooden *mashrabiah* (lattice work). In the majority of the cases, this led to a complication in maintenance and ultimately to the complete re-placement of these external fixtures with plain stone cladding. This was also the destiny of the Commercial Bank, which was enveloped in a new skin of grey granite and reflective glass glazes, strongly affecting its initial aesthetic coherence and making it unrecognisable.

1

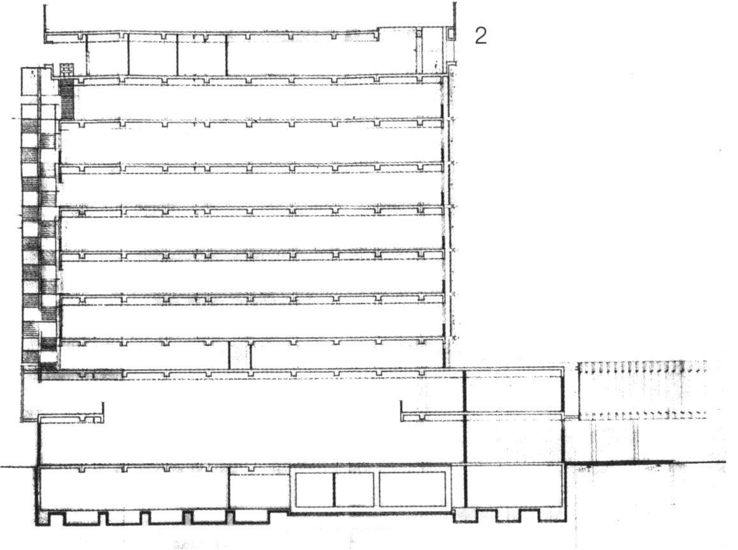

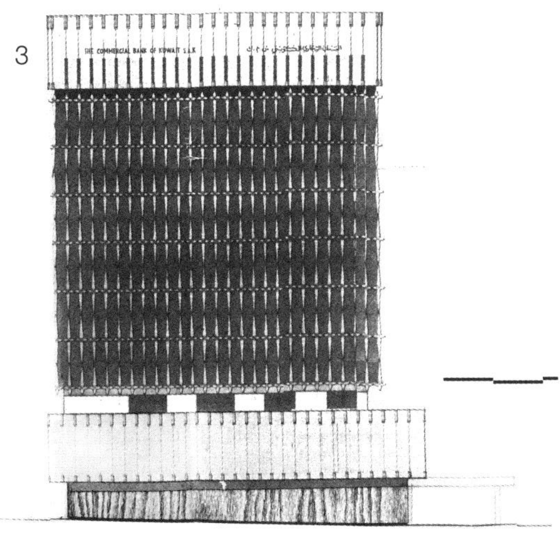

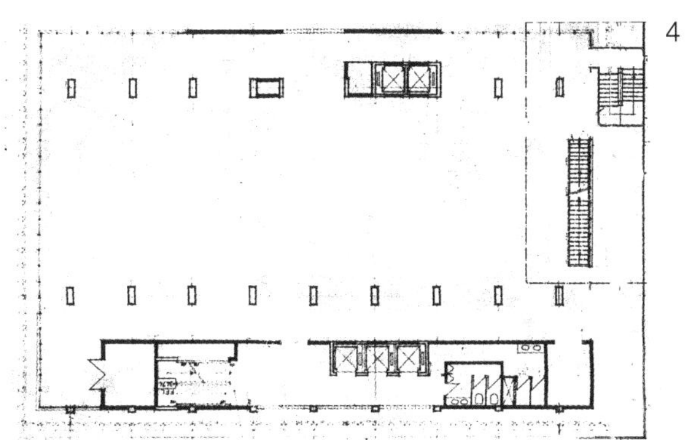

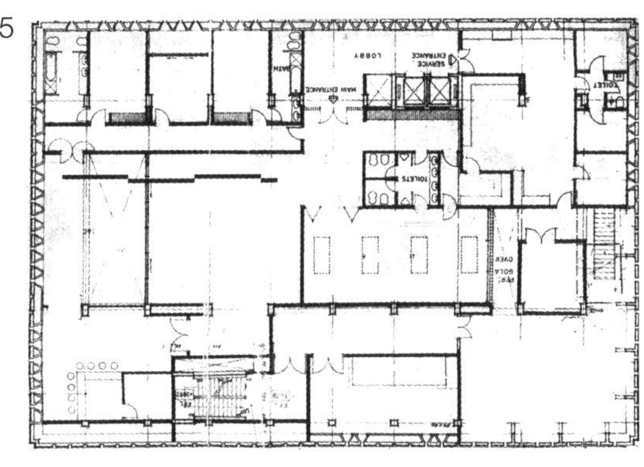

1. Side view, circa 1972
2. Section
3. Side elevation
4. Ground floor plan
5. Typical floor plan

EMBASSY OF THE STATE OF KUWAIT AND CHANCELLERY

TOKYO (JAPAN)
1968–1970

DESIGNER • Kenzo Tange + URTEC
CLIENT • State of Kuwait
CONTRACTOR • Unknown

UNDER THREAT OF DEMOLITION

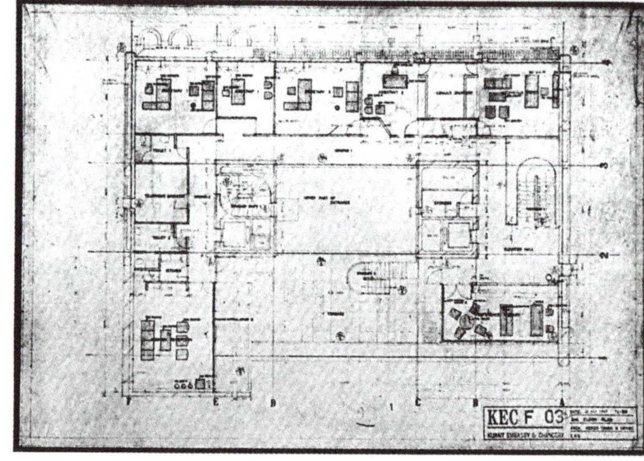

1

2

In the same years of the Sport Centre and that of the Airport competition, Tange was appointed to design the Kuwait Embassy in Tokyo: a building for diplomatic offices and for the Ambassador's residence. The project did not try to establish any bridge or reference to the Gulf state's national identity, neither in form, nor in material. It is instead a further investigation of architecture as a self-sufficient, repeatable fragment in (Japanese) cities; it is a vertical dwelling as an answer to a densely built environment.[63] The building, on a much smaller scale, has more to share with the Shizuoka Centre (1967) or the Yamanashi Centre (1966), then with any other Arab inspired architecture.

Similar to these exempla, the Embassy has two vertical cores, two pivotal distributive centres, which hinge a series of suspended and scattered volumes. The composition is all about negative space. The void is the carving tool that moulds and defines the volumes. The same type of spatial ambiguity can be read in the interiors, where public spaces often seamlessly flow into private spaces.

3

4

1. *Third floor plan*
2. *General view*
3. *View of the open courtyard*
4. *View of the covered piazza*
5. *Section*
6. *Plan diagrams*

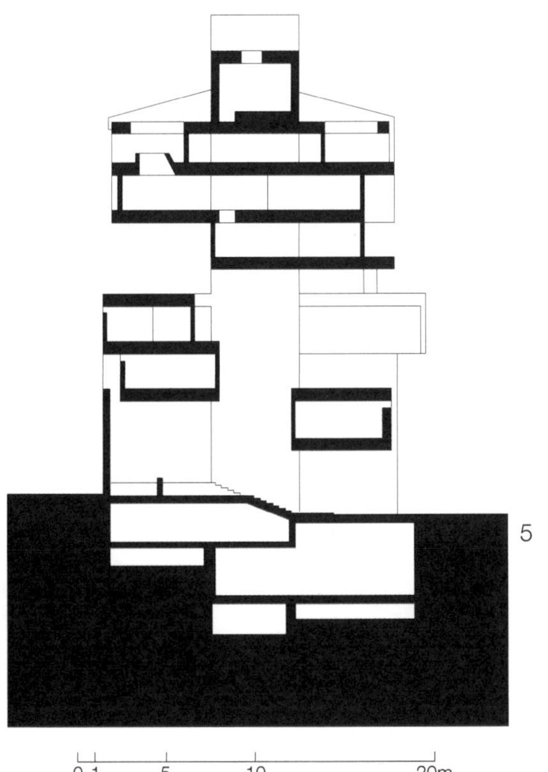

5

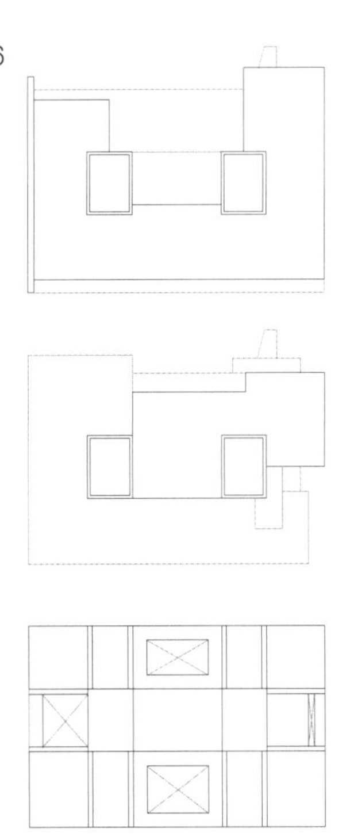

6

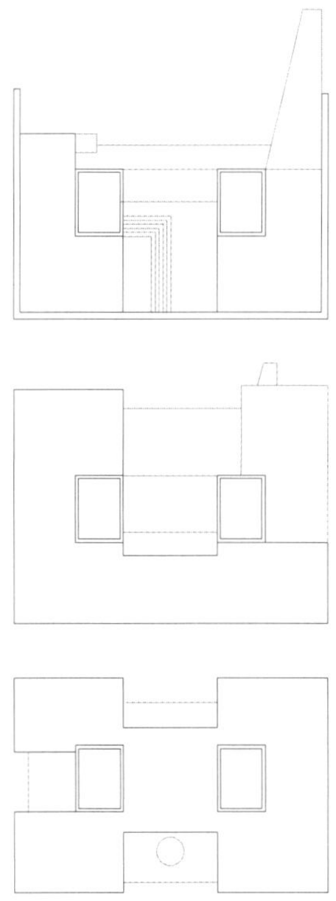

0 1   5   10   20m

153

KUWAIT INTERNATIONAL AIR TERMINAL

FARWANIYAH
1967–1981

DESIGNERS • Pacific Consultants International (lead consultant); Kenzo Tange + URTEC (architect); KEO (engineering)
CLIENT • State of Kuwait
CONTRACTORS • Ballast Nedam Group NV and Solico Contracting Co. L.L.C. (General contractor); Enrico Romagnoli Spa; Al-Hani Construction & Trading Co; Higgins and Castle; Bronswerk Heat Transfer; International Aeradio Ltd; FMC Corporation; Stanray Corporation; Lamson Engineering Company Ltd.

MODIFIED

In 1962, the British contractor Sir Frederick Snow & Partners was appointed to the construction of the new airport.[64] The work was later stopped and the contract interrupted, leading to a major international legal action. Consequently, the Japanese Pacific International Consultants took over and suggested the name of Kenzo Tange as lead architect for the terminal building.

The design, deliberately inspired by an aircraft's shape, was meant to be – in the client's request and in the vision of the Japanese master – a strong visual landmark in an empty desert plot, far away from the urban centre.[65] The plan and the sleek profiles clearly alluded to the dynamic silhouette of jets, while the steel clad ceiling and walls resembled the fuselage, bringing inside the same *airborne experience*. The symmetrical structure, with the two overlay levels, determined with clarity the different areas related to the phases of embarking and disembarking. The building's plan was initially conceived to allow future extensions of the wings, to accommodate more travellers and boarding decks. In the late 1990s, the airport was massively renovated, without following the original expansion scheme, rather preferring additional volumes on the longitudinal axis. These works also altered the interiors, introducing materials and shapes in contrast to the original concept.

1

2

3

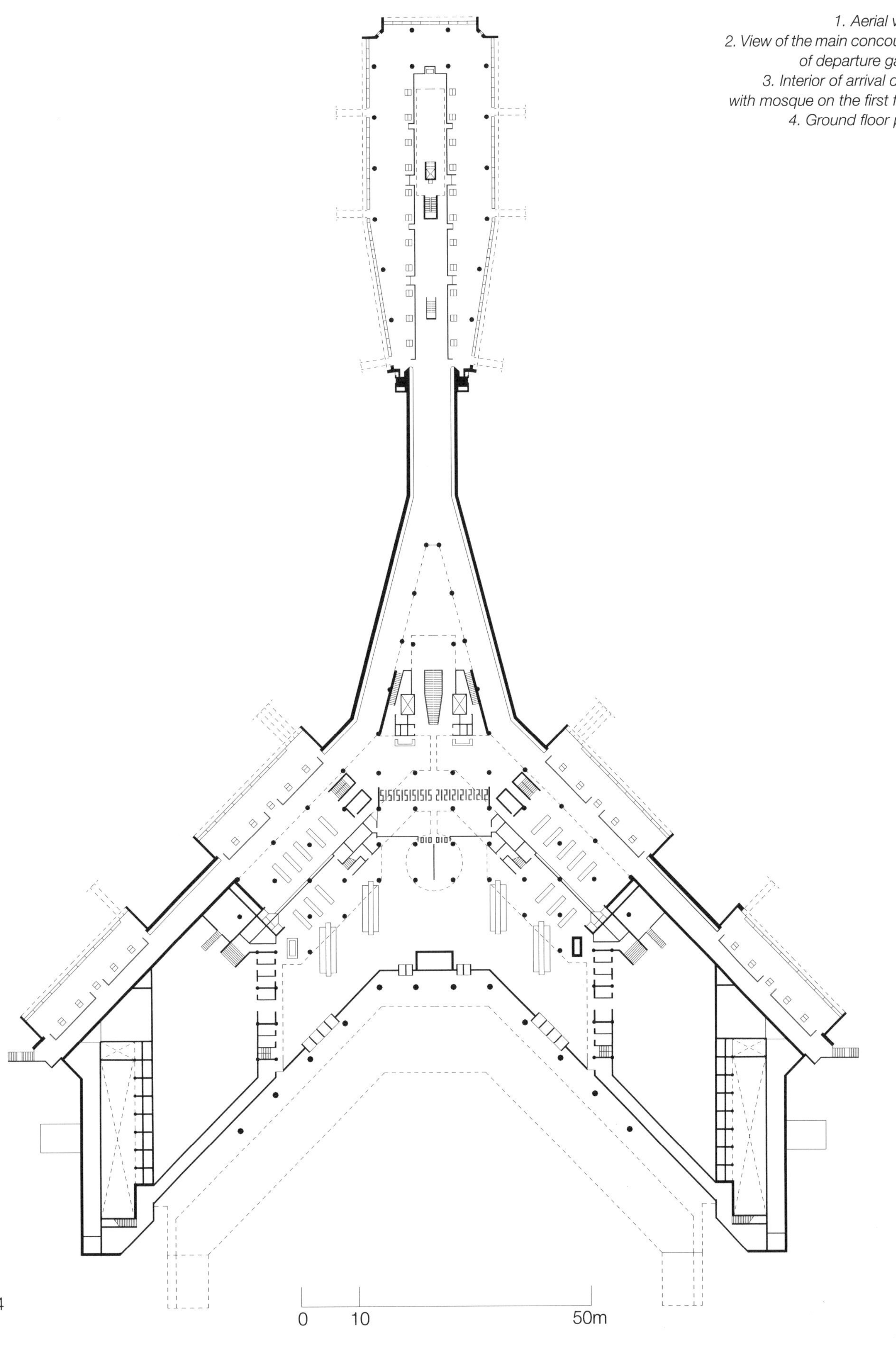

1. Aerial view
2. View of the main concourse
of departure gates
3. Interior of arrival deck
with mosque on the first floor
4. Ground floor plan

4

KUWAIT SPORTS CENTRE

SABAH AL-SALEM
1968

DESIGNERS • Kenzo Tange + URTEC
with Frei Otto; Studio Nervi;
Felix Candela with Emilio Perez Piñero;
Lloyd, Morgan & Jones
CLIENT • Ministry of Planning of Kuwait

COMPETITION / UNBUILT

1

The international competition for three stadiums in early 1968 is one of the first outcomes of the triumvirate of Martin, Albini and Azzam as advisors to the Planning Board. All of the invited firms had vast experience in Olympic stadium design. The competition brief describes a large sport complex with detailed requests: the football stadium with a minimum of 40,000 seats, an Olympic swimming pool, the multipurpose court, various training pitches together with large parking lots and reception areas.[66]

Nervi's proposal is a rigid cruciform plan with the main pitch at the centre and the other facilities at the periphery. It pays particular attention to vehicular and pedestrian distribution. The interstitial areas are shaded walkway and radial parking lots. Nervi uses his vast experience in reinforced concrete to shape the main arena introducing, this time, a space frame system (Triodetic system by Vickers Ltd.) to create an ambitious translucent dome, 300 m in diameter.[67] The entry from Lloyd, Morgan & Jones, with the engineering group Wilson, Morris, Crain and Anderson refers to their masterpiece, the Astrodome, inaugurated in 1965 as the world largest vaulted stadium at that time. Similar to the project in Houston, they created low drums supporting a radial ribbed dome.

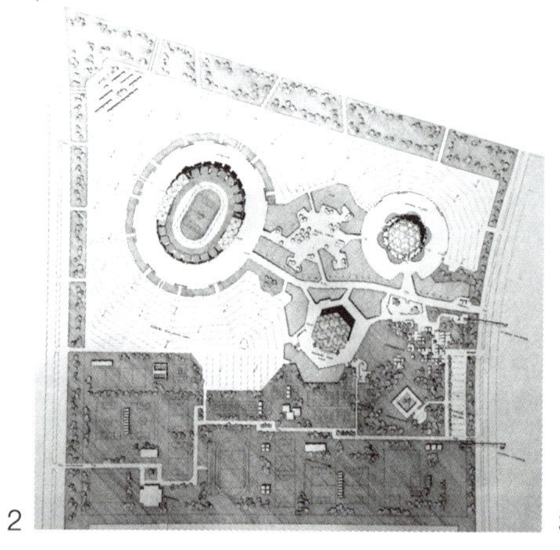

2

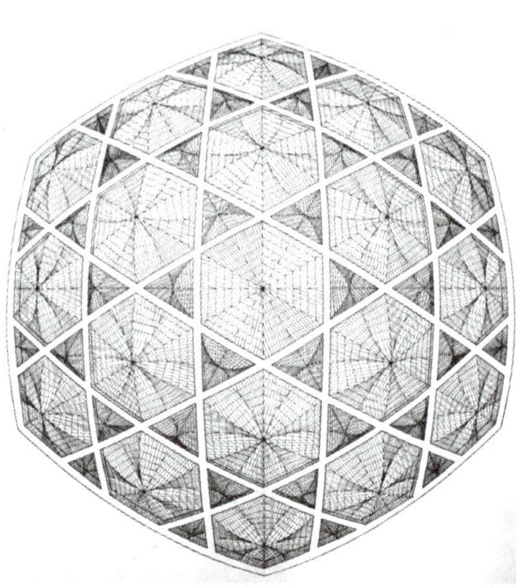

3

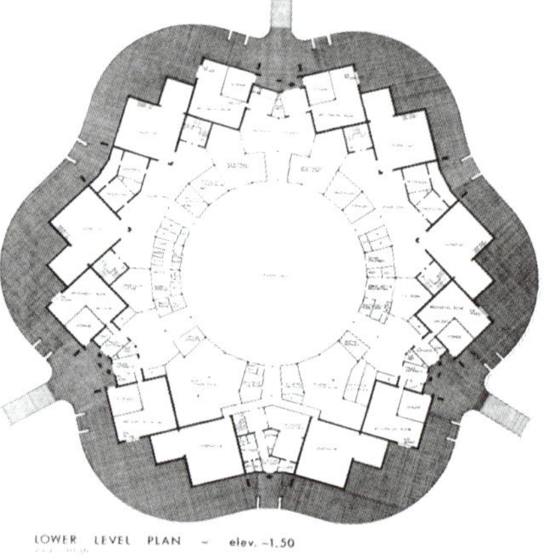

LOWER LEVEL PLAN – elev. –1.50

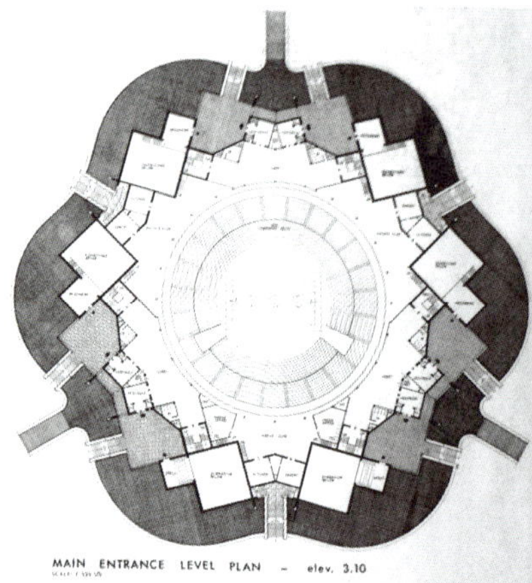

MAIN ENTRANCE LEVEL PLAN – elev. 3.10

4

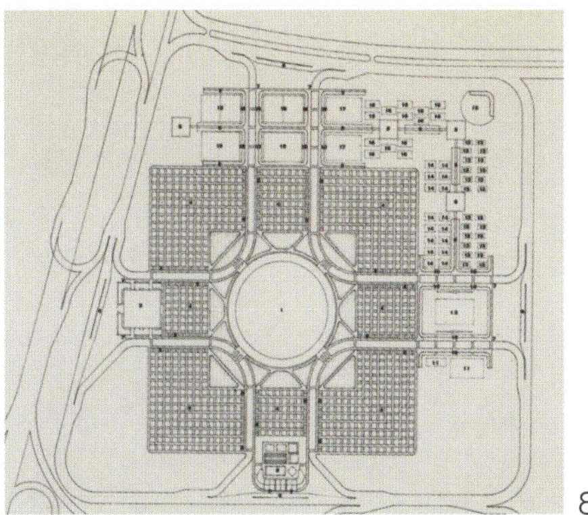

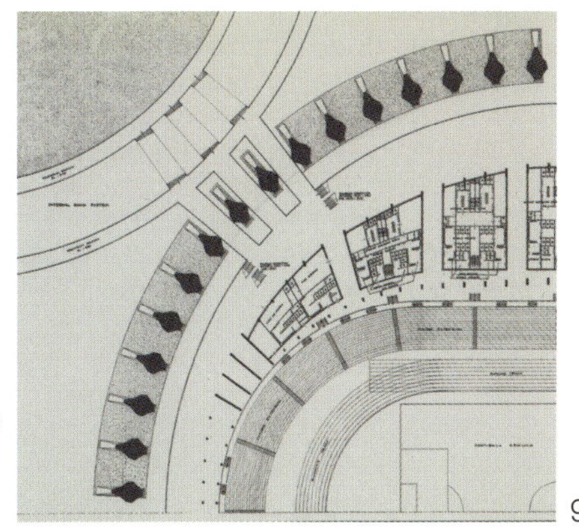

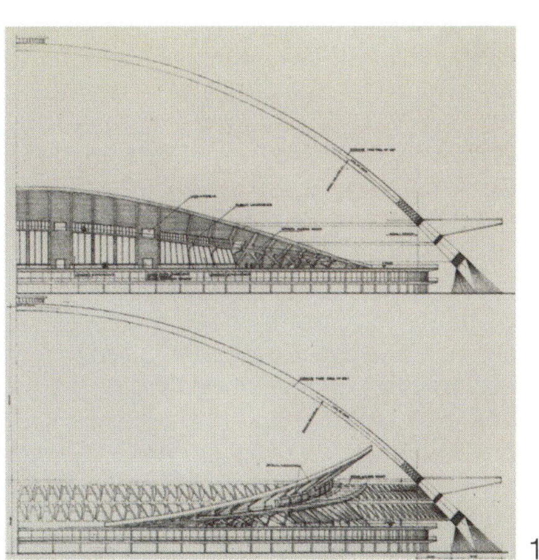

F. CANDELA PROPOSAL:

1. Main stadium, sketch by the designer
2. Site plan
3. Sport Palace, structure of the dome
4. Sport Palace, plans

P.L. NERVI PROPOSAL:

5. Main Stadium, scale model
6. Structural detail, scale model
7. Sports Centre location
8. Site plan
9. Ground floor plan, detail
10. Section of the dome

Candela's proposal is similar to the American firm's entry in the free plan and in the loose aggregation of the volumes. However, in the Sports Palace he opted for a concrete shell reinforced with external steel ribs, similar to the experimental one in his Palacio de los Deportes for the Games in Mexico City '68. Tange's proposal opts for open arenas, partially shaded without involving the complication of air-conditioning. The plan was linear and simply based on one major axis, which distributed all the facilities. The central spine was not only the main connector, but also the planted green area. When this scheme was set, Frei Otto was involved to solve the problematic issue of the large shading devices. During the same years, in fact, the German engineer was developing a new solution for the Pavilion at Expo '67 and for what would be the Olympic Stadium of the 1972 Games in Munich. In Kuwait he proposed a similar design: tensile membrane structures shaped by three consecutive steel arches.[68] This technique was relatively new at that time and gave a lighter weight and a more contemporary appeal to the entire project. The practical advantages of this solution, which primarily did not require the use of an expensive air-conditioning system, were well received by the jury and it was awarded the first prize. Sadly, none of the entries were ever implemented.

11
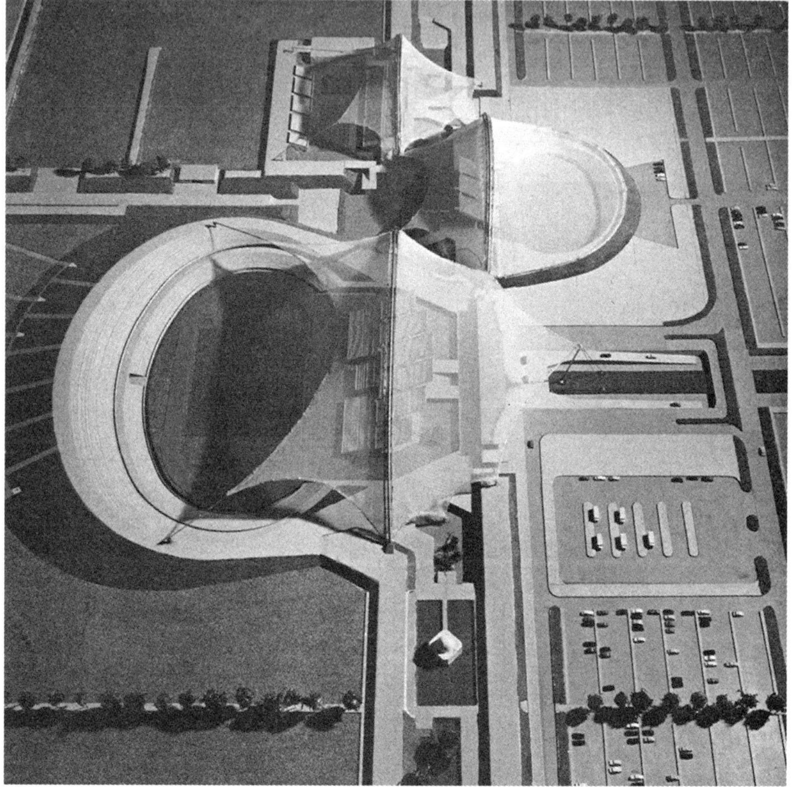

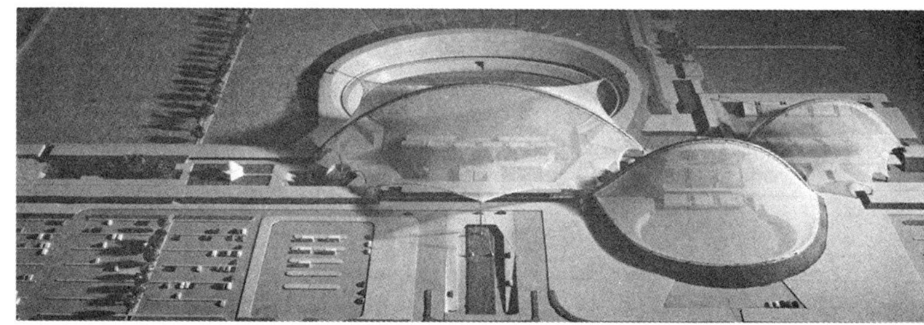

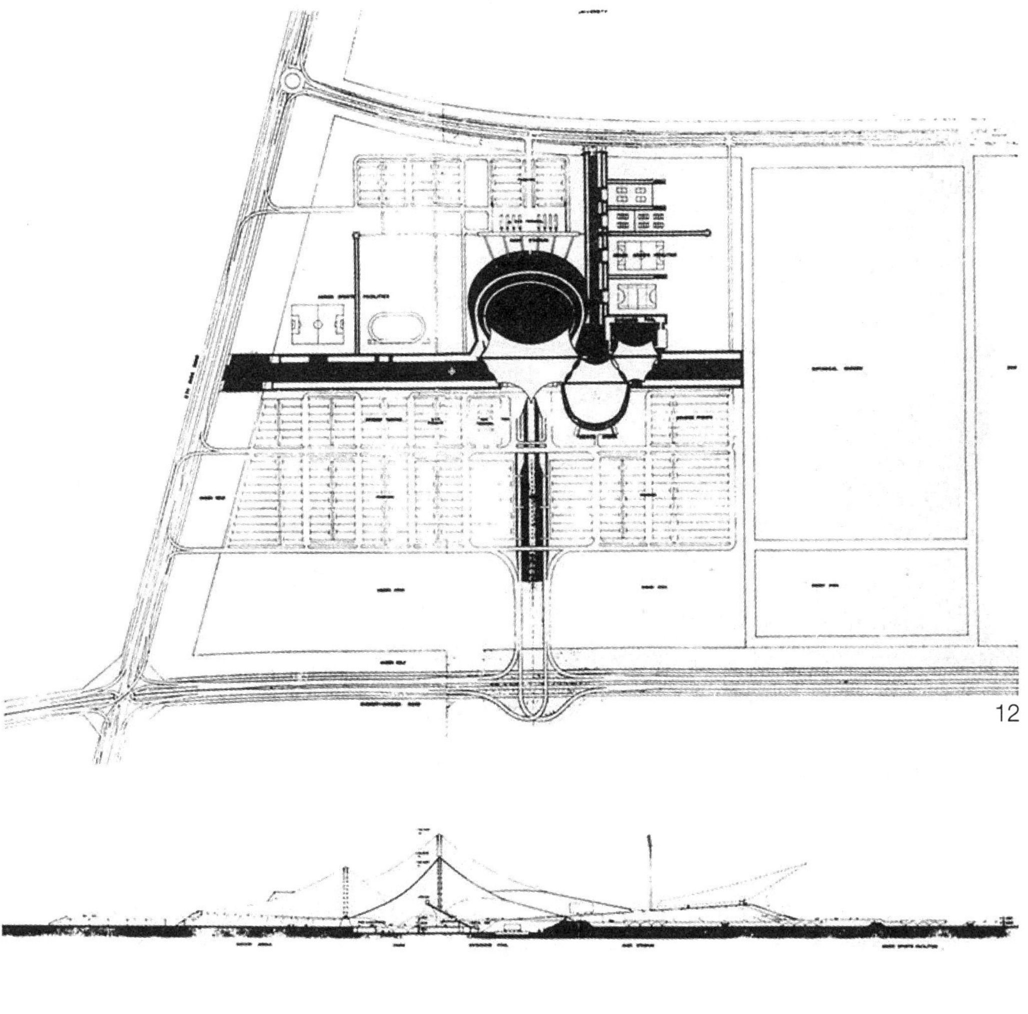

12

13

WATER TOWERS

VARIOUS LOCATIONS
1965–1976

DESIGNER • VBB (AB Vattenbyggnadsbyrån)
CLIENT • Ministry of Electricity and Water
CONTRACTOR • Various

IN USE

1

After the first advancements in water desalinisation, the distribution of water became an element of display through the installation of several exposed steel structured towers all over the old city.[69] With the rapid urbanisation of the country, the system became redundant due to two main challenges: the technology of construction, the rapid implementation and the water pressure requirement. Together with Kuwait Towers (Abraj al-Kuwait), the Water Towers were part of the attempt to establish a modern system of water distribution.

The structural challenge of the height became the main design parameter for VBB's chief architect Sune Lindström and his team while implementing the first 31 towers. As in Örebro,[70] the formwork of the inverted conical top was made with prefabricated elements assembled on the ground and afterwards placed for the actual pouring, with the shafts being built with reinforced concrete, cast in place. This prototypical design is still being used to this day, consolidating the Towers role in the City's and country's landscape.

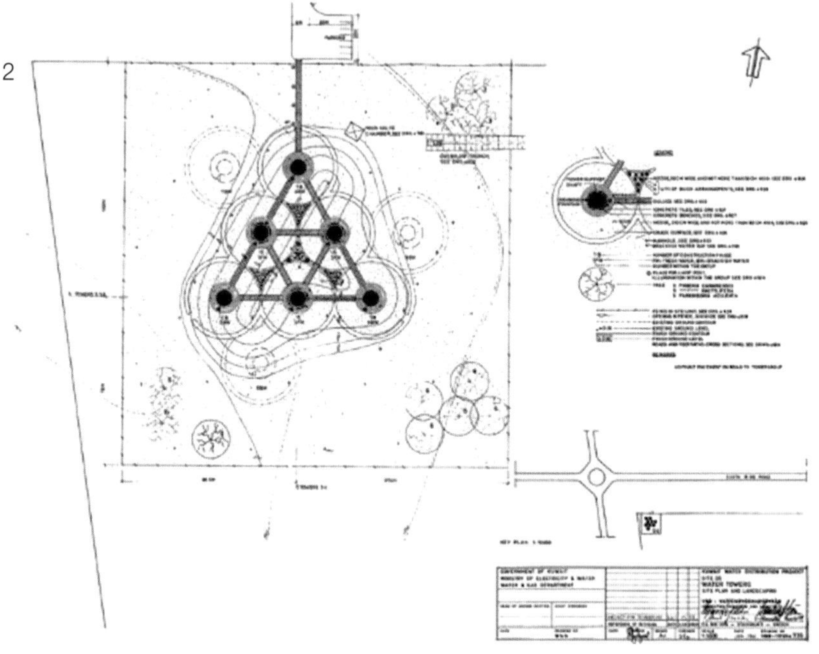

2

4. Towers under construction

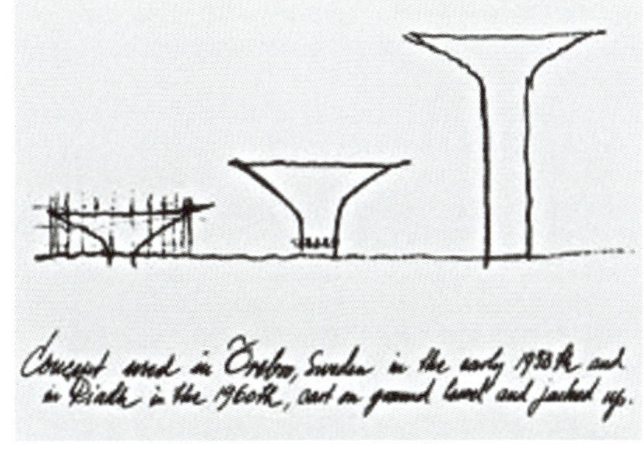

3. Construction system, sketch

5. View from the rooftop

1. Elevations and sections
2. Site plan
3. Construction system, sketch
4. Towers under construction
5. View from the rooftop

ABRAJ AL-KUWAIT

DASMAN, GULF ST.
1965–1977

DESIGNERS • VBB, AB Vattenbyggnadsbyrån (architect and engineer, Sune Lindström principal); Bjørn & Bjørn Design - Malene Bjørn (architect associate); Fuller & Sadao Inc. (façade)
CLIENT • Ministry of Electricity and Water
CONTRACTORS • Energoprojekt Engineering and Contracting (UNION Engineering)

UNDER RENOVATION

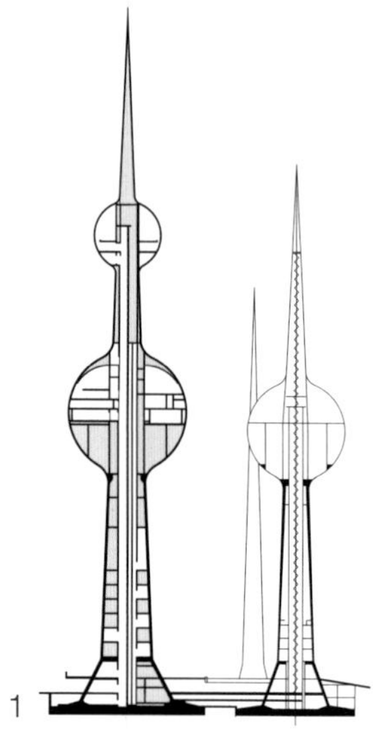

1

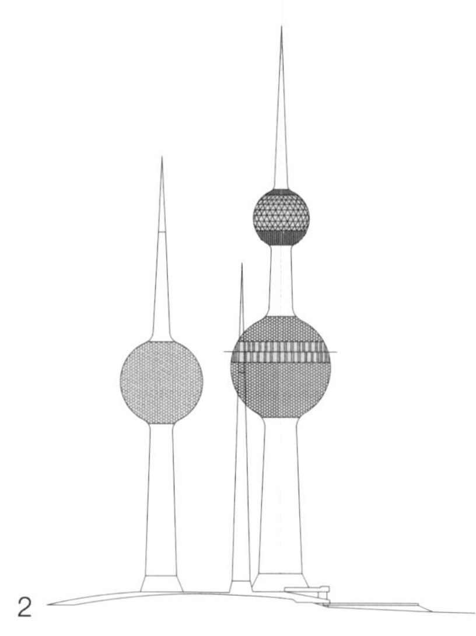

2

Recipient of first Aga Khan Award for Architecture in 1980,[71] and presently listed as a tentative UNESCO World Heritage Site,[72] these water reservoir and observation towers are today the most representative piece of the country's modernisation.

From among other proposals, the Amir selected an unified composition of three spikes, two of those with spheres, implemented in a circular perimeter of a green landscape base in reclaimed land off the coast.[73]

Of different heights, they comprise different functions: the tallest of 185 m has two spheres and hosts a dual programme of water reservoir and public facilities; the restaurant and the above viewing sphere allow a full view of the city, sea and desert, as its platform rotates 360° every half-hour.[74] The visitors' access is at sea level through the base of the tower, inviting the public around the slopes, and across ramps and stairs with elegant balustrades. The second tower, with one sphere, is exclusively a water reservoir. The third and smallest one, like a white needle, is purely sculptural and holds a floodlight system illuminating the other towers. The spheres are decorated by 41,000 enamelled steel disks.

The Kuwait Towers, or *Abraj Al-Kuwait*, alludes to an Islamic context, recalling minarets and tiled domes, in conjunction with the latest 20th century technology.[75]

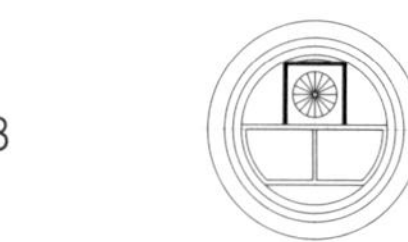

3

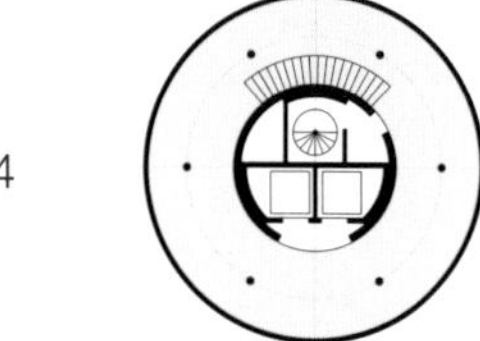

4

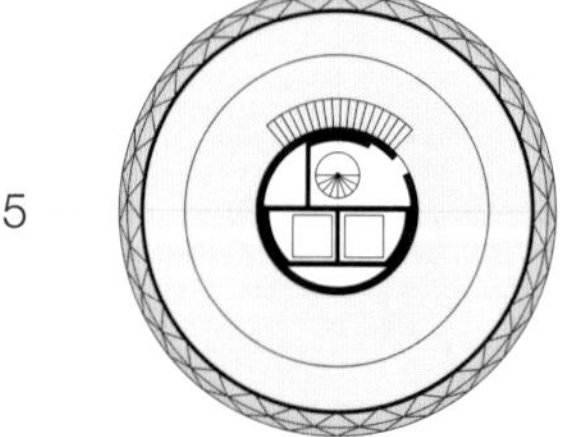

5

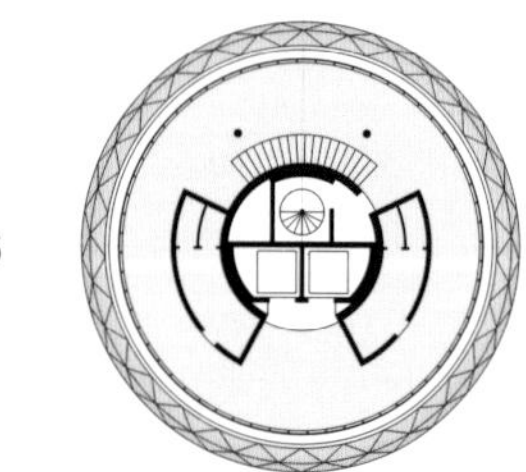

6

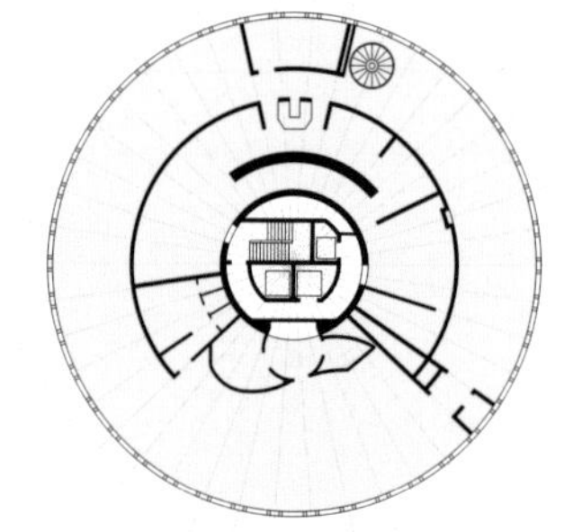

7

9

1. Section
2. Elevation
3. Typical floor section of the tower trunk
4. Plan of the access to the observation platform
5. Plan of the observation platform
6. Plan at the services level
7. Plan at the restaurant level
8. Project variations, scale model
9. Aerial view, 1977

FOUR "URBAN FORM STUDIES FOR THE OLD CITY"

KUWAIT CITY
1969

DESIGNERS • Alison and Peter Smithson; Reima and Raili Pietilä; Candilis, Josic, Woods (Georges Candilis, Principal); BBPR
CLIENT • Kuwait Municipality

UNBUILT

Four groups of architects were invited to "prepare urban form studies for the old city" in direct coordination with local architects, with the Advisory Board, and with Colin Buchanan's team.[76] Since then, this debate has become an ideal method for city generation in the uncertain context of Kuwait land ownership and development. All architects involved were aware of the inefficiencies of normative planning procedures in the context of rapid growth and administrative disorganization. BBPR started a detailed analysis of the old city core considering the re-arrangement of residential stock and the definition of circulation hierarchies between pedestrians and vehicles from the line of the second city wall to the seafront. The seafront proposal, which suggested a complex of six islands to anchor a car viaduct and an elevated "transverse pedestrian walk" recalled the images and content of John R. Harris sketches for the 1961 competition. Candilis' group proposed the activation of this urban fabric by the introduction of *habitat* units. A perfect grid of 6 x 8 m organised a common reference between the existing elements and inserted units. The grid is justified for its structural economy and flexibility to facilitate the planning of larger units. The Smithsons, apart from the proposed grid, referenced in the existing mosques, suggested "a city with low profile" by the sea.[77] A complex system of shaded surfaces and protective buildings were designed to re-establish the "old town environment." The *maidan* and the Green Belt were to provide new centralities to solve congestion problems. Reima Pietilä considered in detail two scalar extremes, the larger definition of a transportation system accomodating city expansion and the production of a new generic city fabric.

1   THE FUTURE DEVELOPMENT OF THE OLD CITY OF KUWAIT   SOLUTION EXCLUDING THE UNIVERSITY   1:5000   A9

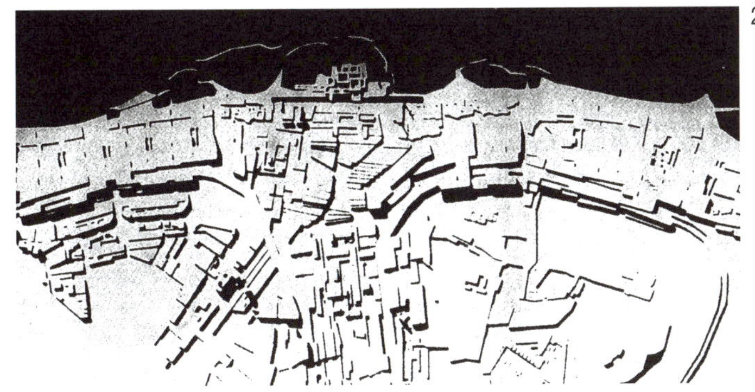

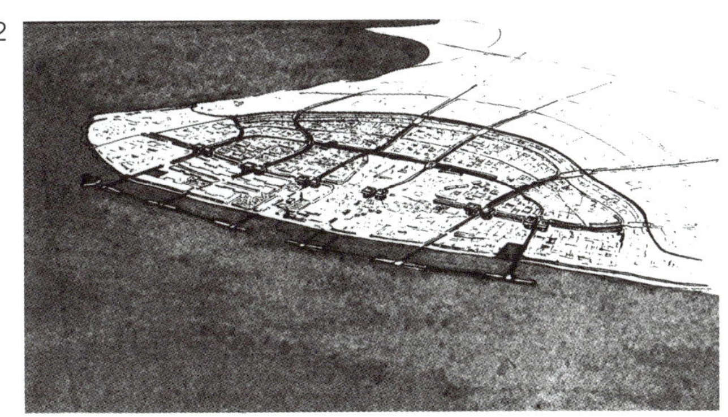

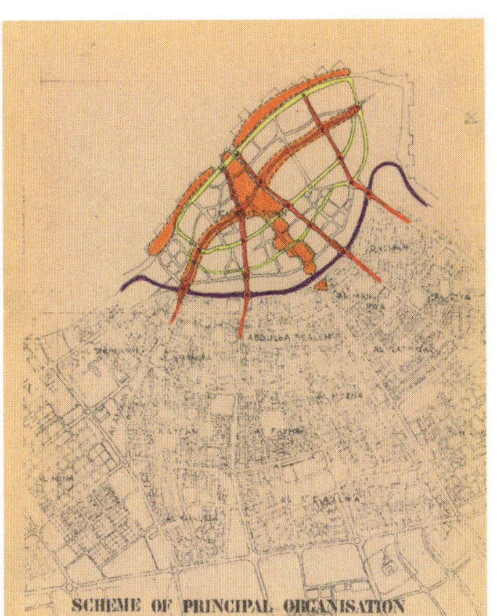

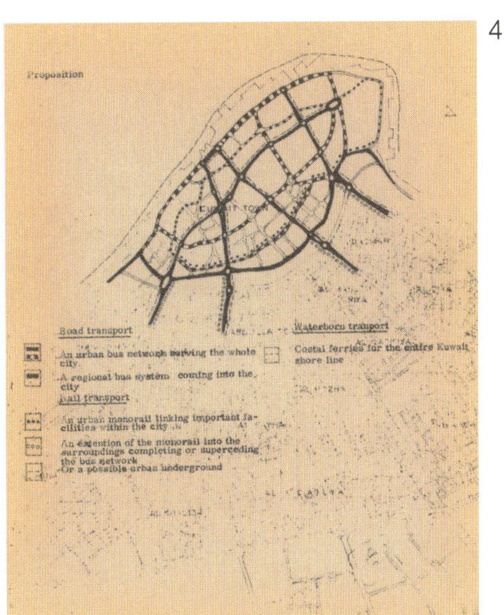

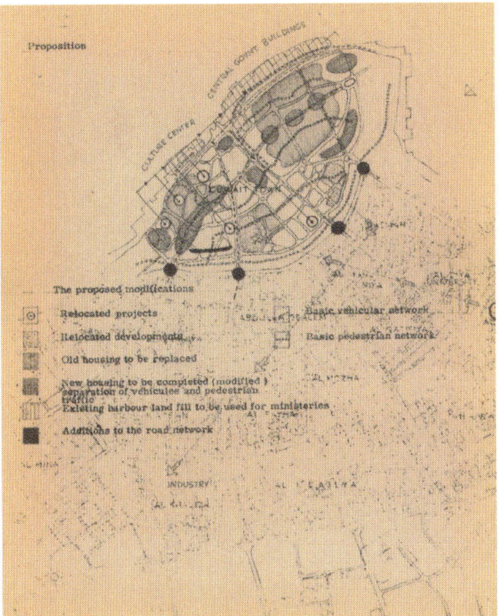

1. BBPR, Parallel Scheme Solution A, detailed plan
2. R. and R. Pietilä, New Central City Area, scale model
3. BBPR, Symmetrical Scheme Solution B, Minimum Solution of the Seafront, general view of the city from the sea
4. G. Candilis, Reflections on the Development of the "City of Kuwait", Scheme of Principal Organisation; Transportation; Decentralisation of Activities; Redevelopment

مدينة الكويت القديمة
KUWAIT OLD CITY
GROUND

5

KUWAIT OLD CITY   PERSPECTIVE IN ORANGERIE
69

6

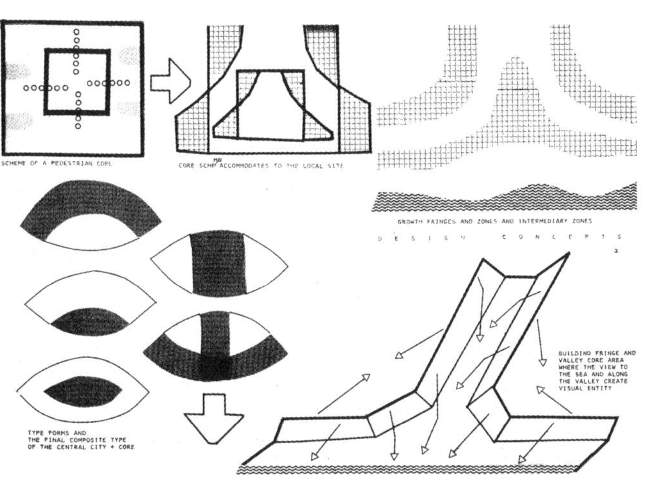

*A. AND P. SMITHSON'S. KUWAIT OLD CITY
URBAN FORM STUDY, 1969:*

5. Plan at ground level
6. Perspective in Orangerie Maidan (Amir's Pavilion)

R. AND R. PIETILÄ. NEW CENTRAL CITY AREA:

*7. Visualisation of the relation of physical and functional form of new
city to old physical pattern of Kuwait Town*
8. Capital core, scale model
9. Behaviours of 100,000 people moving by feet in the core of Kuwait

7

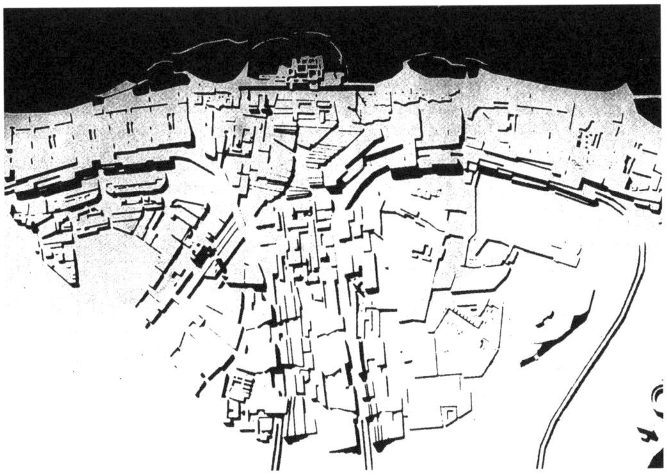

8

9

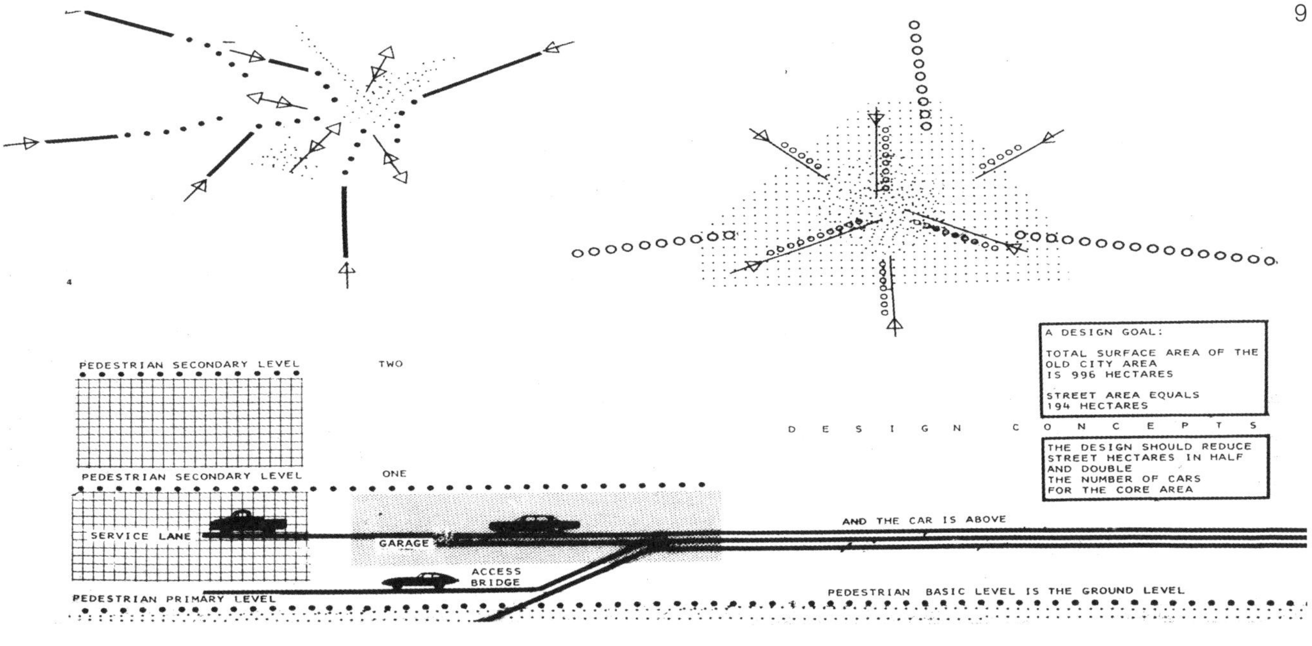

FOUR DEMONSTRATION AREAS

KUWAIT CITY
1969–1972

DESIGNERS • Alison and Peter Smithson; Reima and Raili Pietilä; Georges Candilis Architect (Candilis, Josic, Woods); BBPR
CLIENT • Kuwait Municipality

UNBUILT

The "demonstration areas," taken out of the 1969 studies for the "Urban form of the old city," were intended "to illustrate principles by actual buildings for known demands."[78]

The preliminary work on the Second Master Plan provided the essential context for the first studies developed by the different groups of architects. The Smithsons developed a mat-building as a large scheme for Government offices in Mirqab; the *pilotis* organise the programme and circulation under a freestanding roof. BBPR who studied the pedestrian scale of the old core in detail, developed a zoning plan for the area taking preservation and uses into consideration. The Candilis' team appointed for construction of a critical vacant site, proposed three housing typologies condensed into superblocks: flats, *maisonettes* and servant-shared units. In these, traditional and local family domesticity and routines were a major argument, relegating the habitat experiment to an abstract state of mind.[79]

Reima Pietilä developed a detailed and sensitive proposal for the restoration and extension of the State Ruler's Sief Palace that was finally built. A few authors refer to the Kuwait National Assembly competition of 1972 as a fifth demonstration area, based on the context of this brief and the site selection map available in the Second Master Plan.

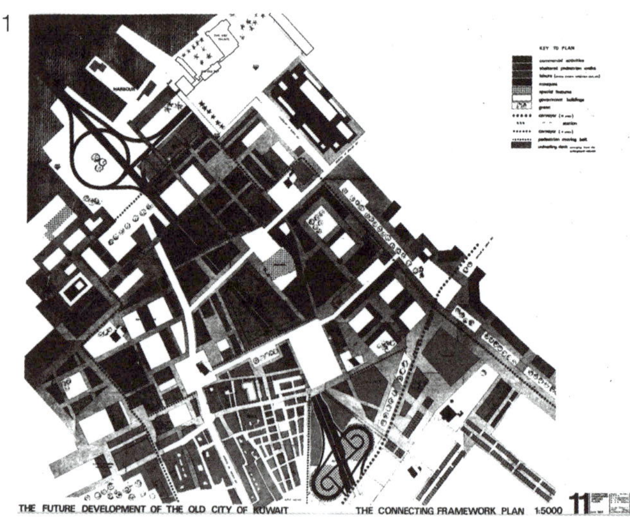

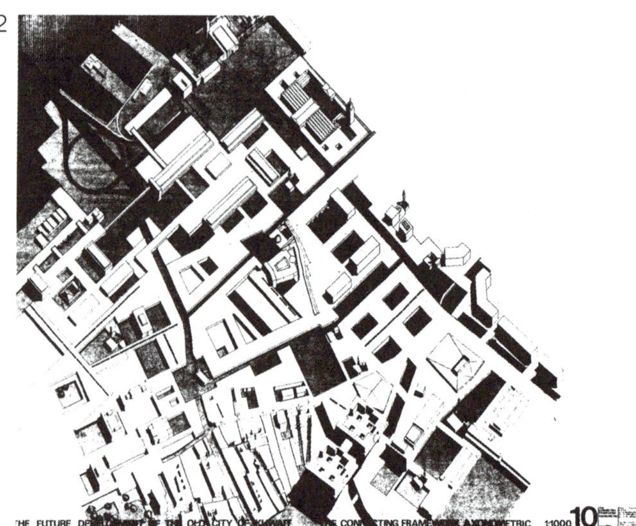

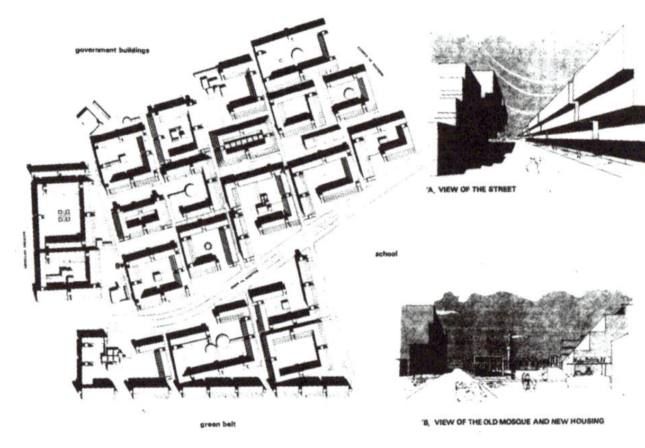

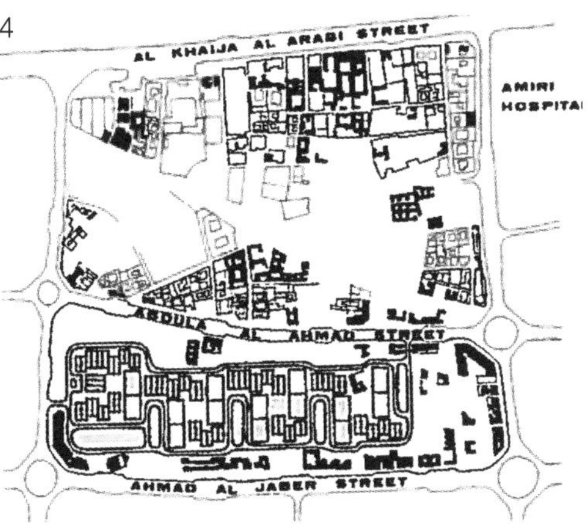

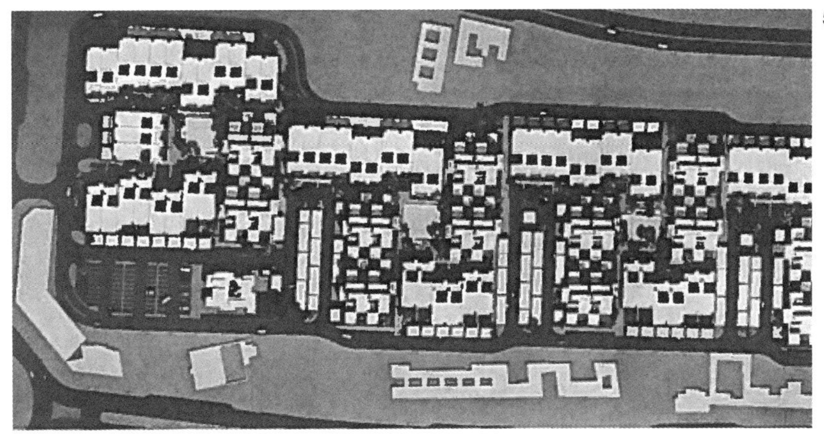

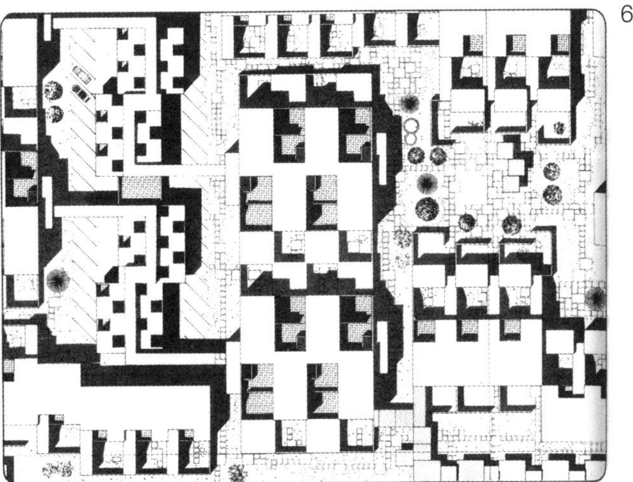

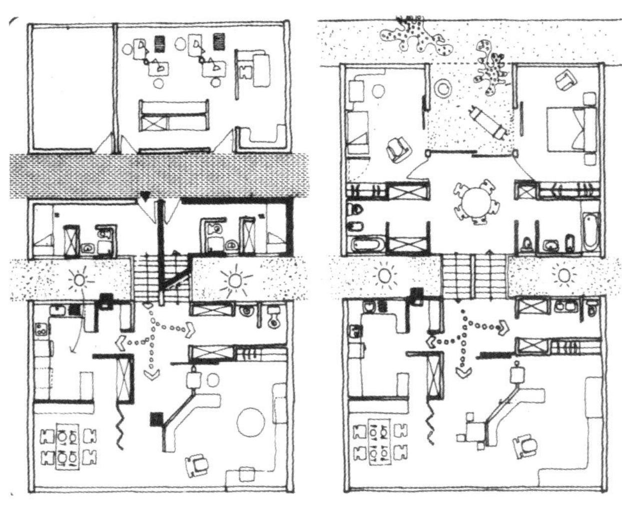

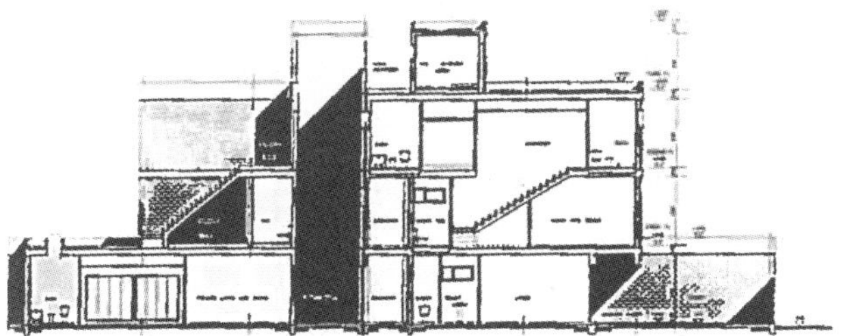

BBPR PROPOSAL:

1. The Connecting Framework Plan
2. The Connecting Framework Axonometric
3. Residential area general plan (Mirqab)

G. CANDILIS' PROPOSAL:

4. Site plan
5. Scale model, top view
6. Detail of the site plan
7. Plan of a two-storey housing unit
8. Section and elevation of a three-storey housing unit

169

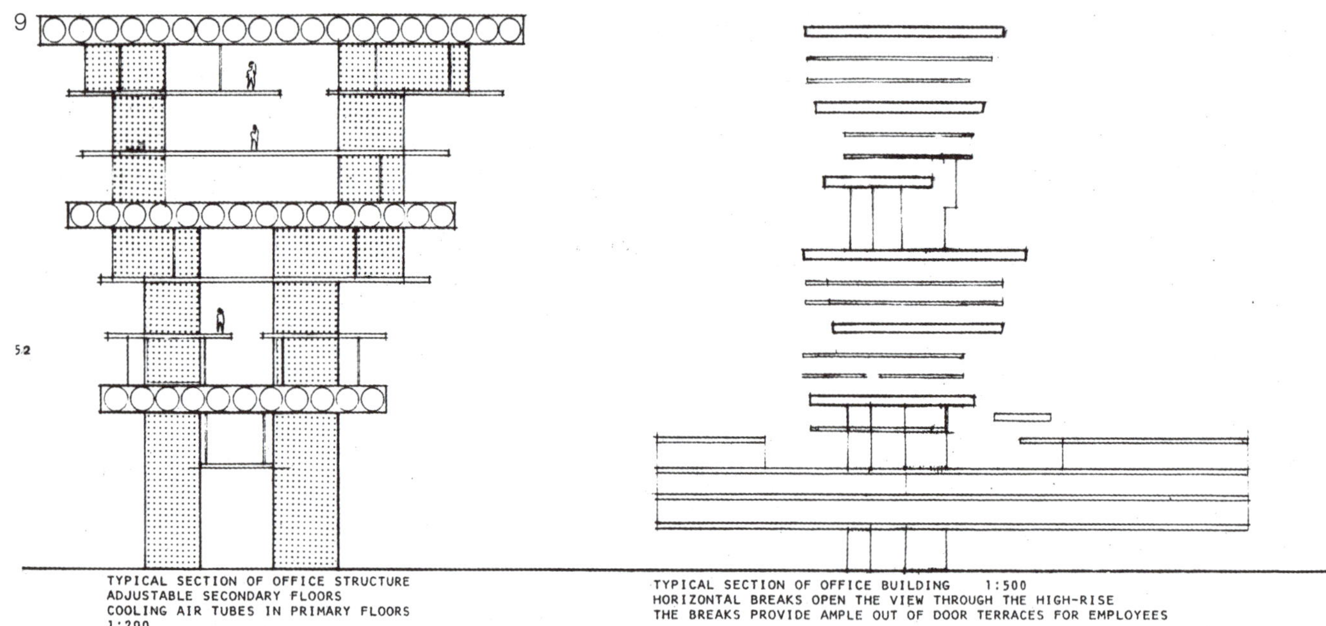

9

5.2

TYPICAL SECTION OF OFFICE STRUCTURE
ADJUSTABLE SECONDARY FLOORS
COOLING AIR TUBES IN PRIMARY FLOORS
1:200

TYPICAL SECTION OF OFFICE BUILDING   1:500
HORIZONTAL BREAKS OPEN THE VIEW THROUGH THE HIGH-RISE
THE BREAKS PROVIDE AMPLE OUT OF DOOR TERRACES FOR EMPLOYEES

12

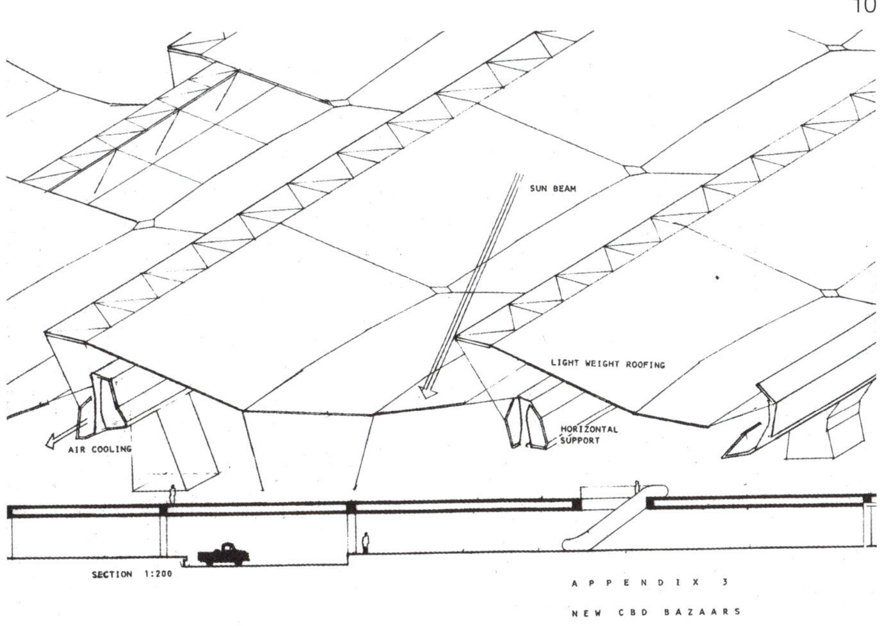

SUN BEAM
LIGHT WEIGHT ROOFING
HORIZONTAL SUPPORT
AIR COOLING
SECTION 1:200
APPENDIX 3
NEW CBD BAZAARS

R. AND R. PIETILÄ'S PROPOSAL:

9. Micro-climatic office building, typical sections
10. New CBD Bazaars, bazaar and market hall
11. Pedestrian movement facilities. scale model

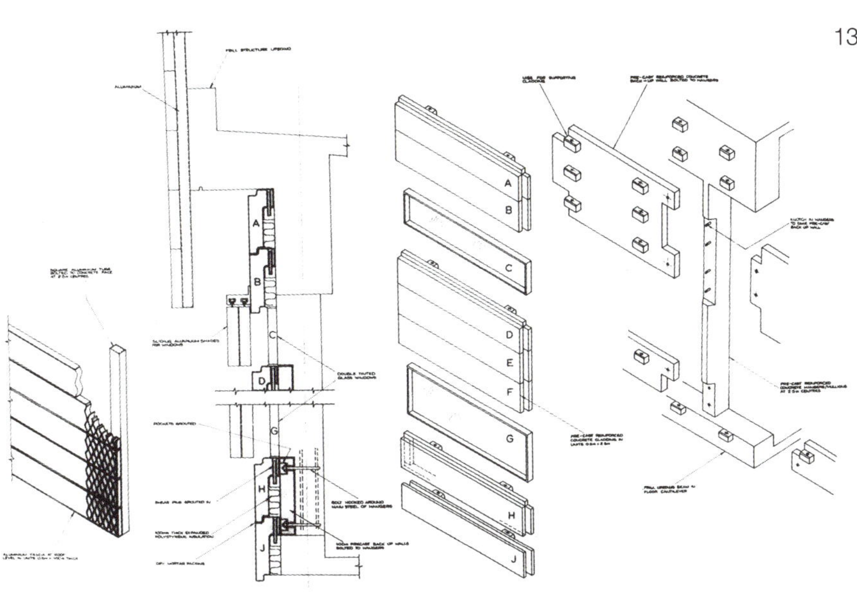

TYPICAL JOINTS IN CLADDING

KUWAIT OLD CITY   MINISTRY BUILDING
CONCRETE CLADDING DETAILS

OVE ARUP & PARTNERS
CONSULTING ENGINEERS
LONDON

SCALES: 1:20
DATE: JUNE 1970
DRAWING NO: 3632/8

A. AND P. SMITHSON'S PROPOSAL:

12. Perspective looking down Galleria Al-Fleij
north towards Al-Fleij mosque, showing place
created by location of ministries, July 1970
13. Ministry Building, concrete cladding
details, by Ove Arup & Partners, June 1970
14. Structural model, structure and skin detail
by Ove Arup & Partners, June 1970
15. Model in relation to the skyline of Kuwait
16. View across Hilali Street from the Kuwait
Institute, November 1970

NATIONAL ASSEMBLY COMPETITION

JIBLA
1971–1972

PARTICIPANTS • Sir Basil Spence, Bonnington & Collins; Studio Nervi; Balkrisna V. Doshi; Mohamed Ramzy Omar; Rifat Chadirji & Ihsan Sherzad (Iraq Consult); Joint Local Kuwaiti Consortium (KEO; NEB; KAC; PACE; GEO); Jørn Utzon
CLIENT • Ministry of Public Works

UNBUILT

During the development of the Second Master Plan, in January 1971 an international competition was launched for the design concept of the National Assembly Building. The competition brief was established by the Advisory Board, which also shortlisted the candidates, while the building programme was mainly drafted by Albini. The scope of the work was extremely detailed for function allocation and adherence to the urban plan, but it had very few constraints on the designers' expression. For this the competition entries showed very diverse approaches. One major aspect they shared was the idea of a building not a rhetorical representation of power, but a public space, partially shared with the citizens.[80]

Spence, Bonnington & Collins proposed a superstructure based on a hexagonal grid, with a permeable ground floor and a lightweight parasol for shading, similar to their previous proposal for the Borough Civic Centre (1964). The honeycomb system, being modular, was not only very flexible in accommodating the complex functional programme, but it also projected solutions for any possible future extension. The main concept of the project was a long, horizontal sequence of spaces punctuated by hanging gardens for climate mitigation.[81]

Doshi's programme instead postulated a direct continuity with the sea. It minimized and subdued the costal vehicular circulation and emphasised the idea of a public piazza with a large platform protruding into the water. With this simple reverse approach, it created the most evocative point of view to appreciate the new Assembly Hall. The latter is generated by a cluster of simple prisms in geometrical aggregation and shares a similar repetitive façade treatment. Only the volume of the two Assembly Halls protruded and manifested themselves as centres of the composition.

Chadirji's idea moved from a visual reflection on the arcades of the cloister in the Grand Mosque of Damascus (Umayyad Mosque). This element, a slender round arch surmounted by plane brickwork, is the key module which gave proportion to the entire complex. Similar to Udson's winning project, Chadirji organised the complex around a central axis, which connected the two main entrances.

The central spine intersected the main courtyard, which was also where the external round volume of the Assembly Hall can be appreciated.

Unfortunately, Ramzy Omar's proposal is not known. Maath Alousi (ex-IQC) mentions the Egyptian architect as part of the jury and not as one of the entries, while the late Pier Luigi Nervi was probably disheartened by the result of the 1968 Kuwait Sport Centre competition and decided to not submit any project at all.

Interestingly enough, a pool of five local firms were invited to compete with major international designers, instead of providing the usual role of supporting partner. This proposal is also not available, but shows how in the early 1970s, the capacity of local firms grew competent to deal with major international projects. The first prize was awarded to Jørn Utzon.

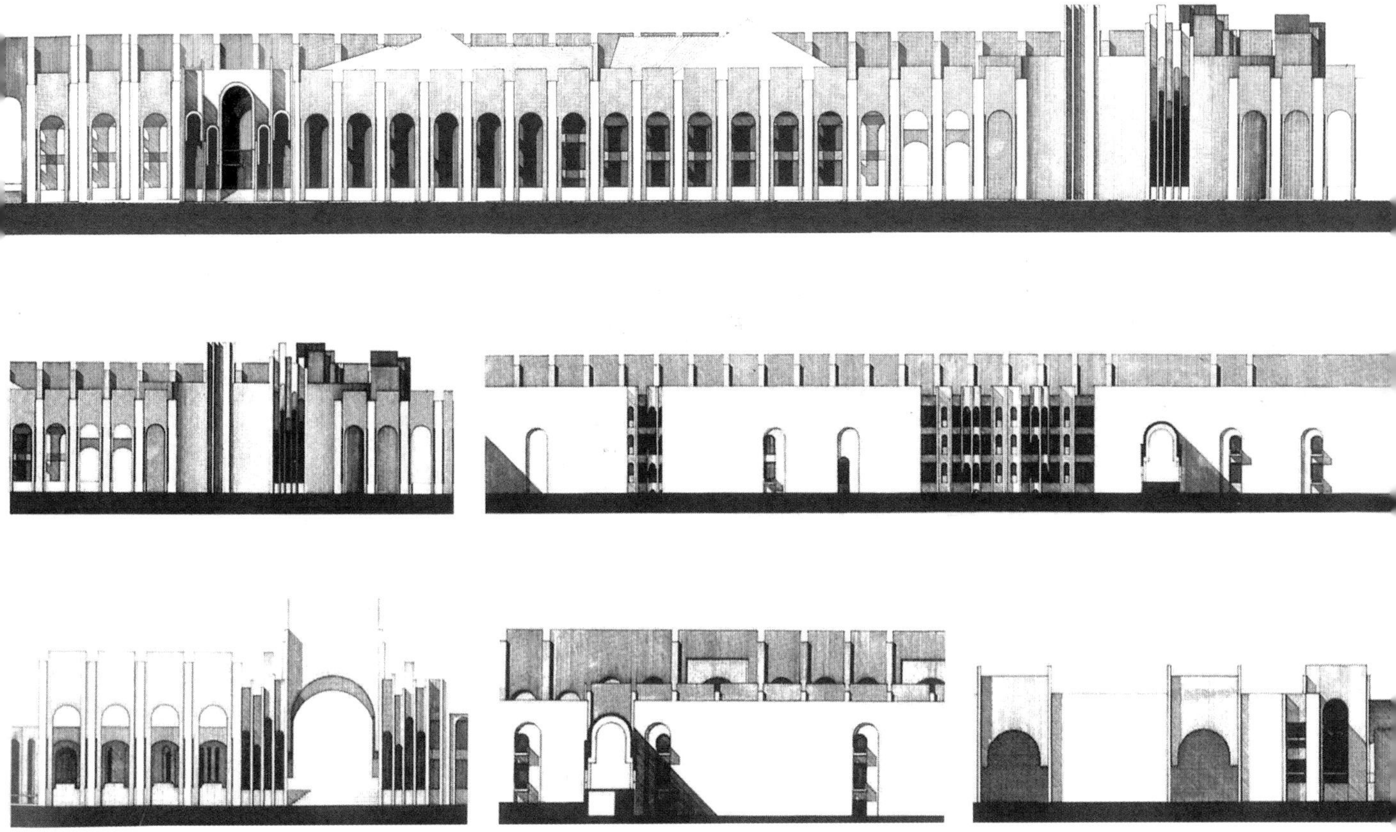

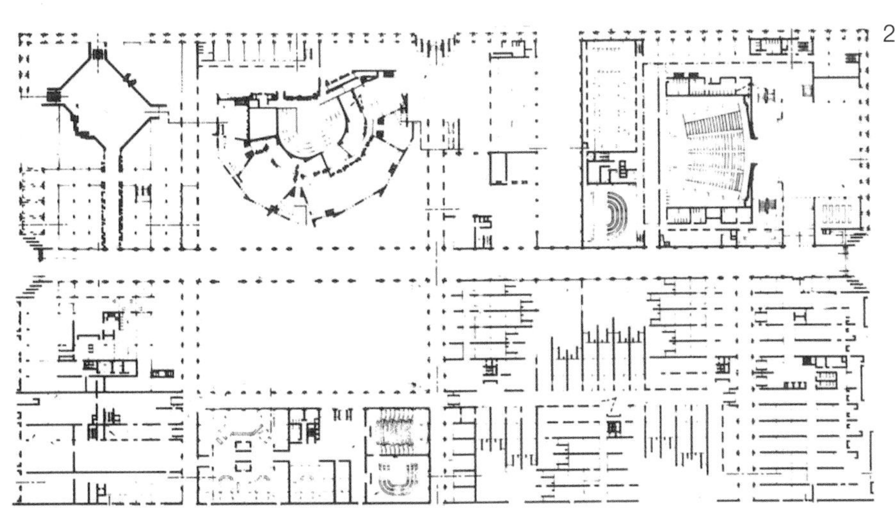

R. CHADIRJI'S PROPOSAL:

1. Elevations
2. Ground floor plan

3

4

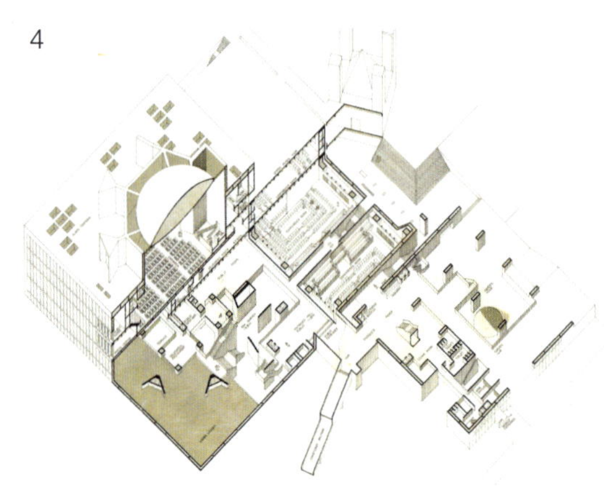

5

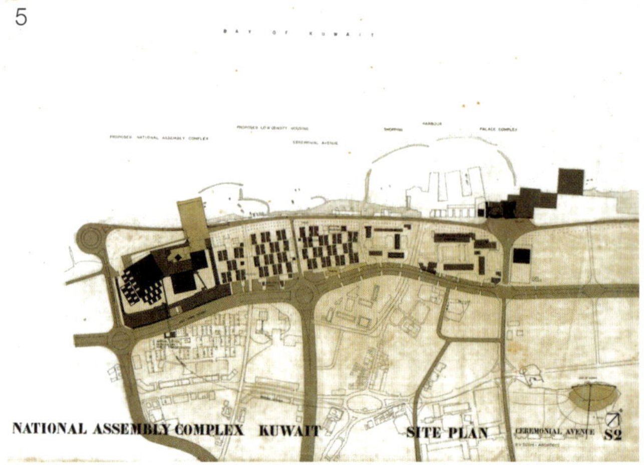

6

7

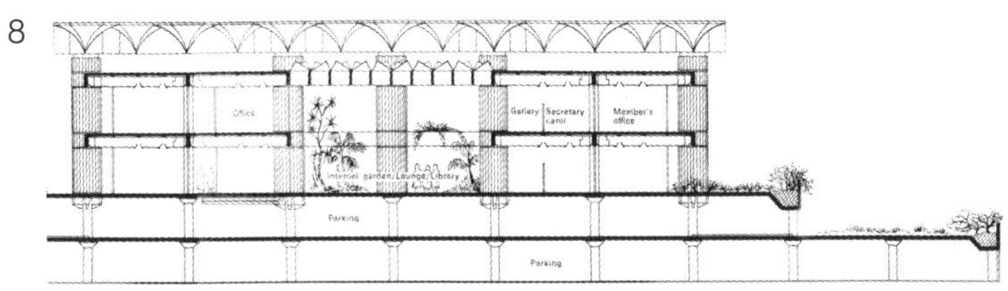

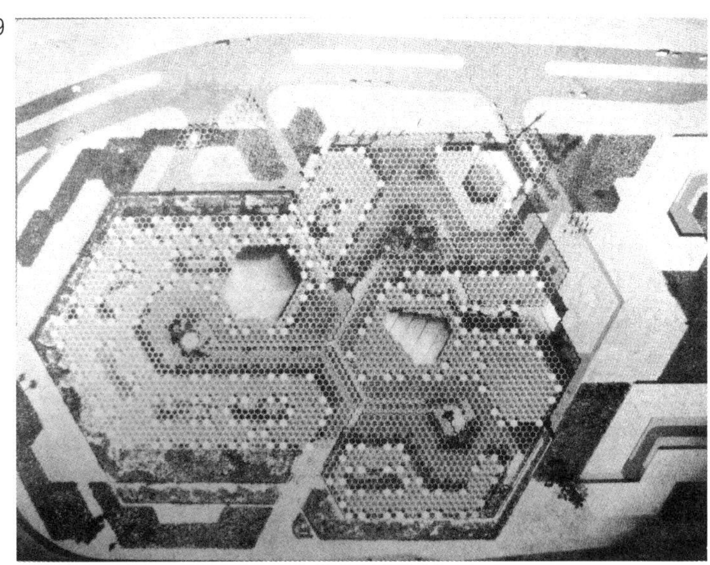

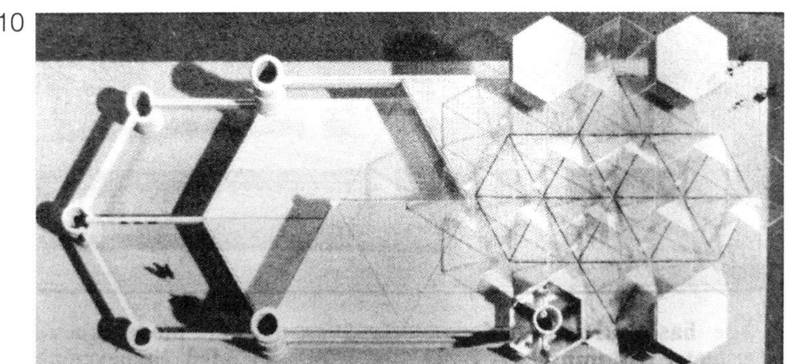

B.V. DOSHI'S PROPOSAL:

3. Scale model
4. Axonometry of the Assembly Hall
5. Site plan
6. Section through the Assembly Hall
7. View from the sea, sketch

SPENCE, BONNINGTON AND COLLINS' PROPOSAL:

8. Section of one pavilion
9. Site view, scale model
10. Detail of the structure, scale model, top view
11. Detail of the structure, scale model, perspective view

KUWAIT NATIONAL ASSEMBLY

JIBLA
1972–1982

DESIGNERS • Jørn Utzon;
Max Walt Ingenieurbüro (structure);
Consultair AG (services)
CLIENT • Ministry of Public Works
CONTRACTOR • Kuwait Prefabricated
Building Co.

IN USE

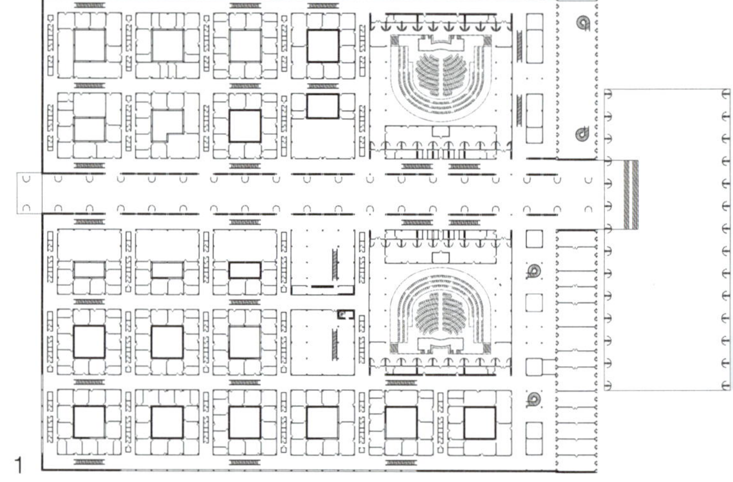

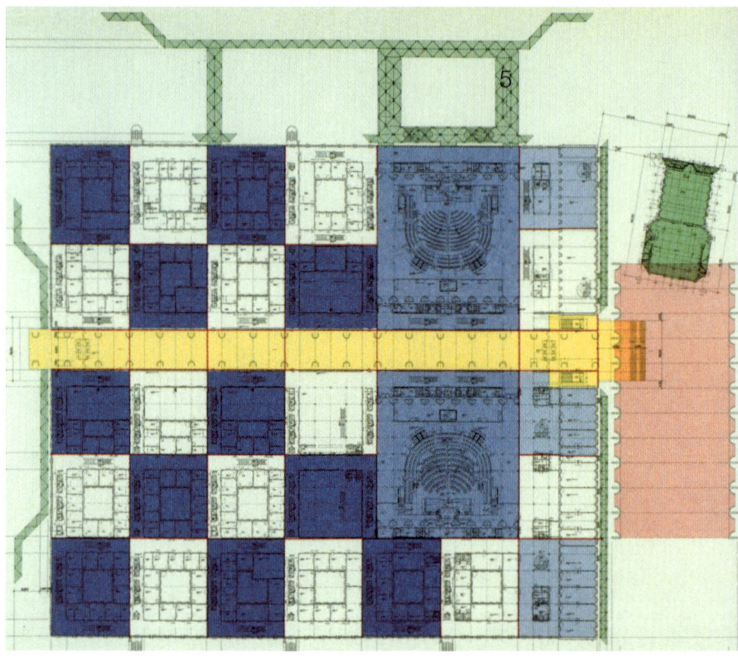

Built between 1972 and 1985 on the seafront, it is one of the most iconic buildings of Kuwait. Its unique silhouette, with waving roof lines and curved concrete canopy softly evoke natural shapes, and at the same time forms a narrative about human construction elements, such as desert tents and sails, two interwoven essences of the country.

The competition project was deeply affected by the designer's previous encounter with Islamic architecture, in particular his trip to Morocco (1949) and later to Iran to design the Melli Bank (1959). On the latter occasion he had the chance to visit the bazaar and the Royal Square in Isfahan, which was to become a strong typological reference for the Assembly.[82]

Three elements define the entire project: the bazaar, the tent, and the covered square.

The first element is a central, covered road that distributes all the different functional spaces. Beside this spine is a cluster of squared spaces organised around courts that resemble a rectified and slightly rigid version of an old Arab city centre.

The tent-roofs emerge from this flat complex/bazaar to cover and to emphasise the most important spaces in the complex: the Assembly Hall and the monumental square open to the sea view. The latter was initially conceived to be a real urban *piazza* accessible to the public, suggesting an openness in the exercise of democracy, but was found not to be viable in the local political environment.[83]

The project was based on a square grid of 20 x 20 m and used prefabricated, exposed, concrete structures composed of few elements and repeated hundreds of times. This approach was found to allow eventual future extensions in harmony with the original design, while the recently adjacent expansion was created as a completely different building.

4

3

1. Ground floor plan
2. Diagram
3. Aerial view, 1985
4. Sketch by the designer

KUWAIT SPORT CLUBS

HAWALLY
MANSOURIYA
KAIFAN
1970–1977

DESIGNERS • Ministry of Public Works, Design Department (lead consultant); Iraq Consult, IQC (architect, structure); TEST (associated architect); PACE (services)
CLIENT • Ministry of Public Works
CONTRACTOR • Unknown

MODIFIED

In 1963, following the completion of Cairo stadium, Mahmoud Riad was commissioned for Kuwait Sport Club facilities, including tennis courts, swimming pool, football stadium, gymnastic arena and basketball courts. The project was never implemented.

After Kuwait being announced as host for the 1980 Asian Cup, the Ministry of Public Works commissioned the Iraqi consultant involved in the construction of the Al-Shaab football stadium in Baghdad.[84]

Following the termination of two years association with PACE, Iraq Consult was to have its first and last major public project in Kuwait. The young but already experienced Maath Alousi, who graduated from AA's Department of Tropical Architecture, led the construction of these large sport facilities including a covered sports hall with a space frame structure and football stadium with a covered seating structure in reinforced concrete, similar in cross-section to that in Baghdad.

Apart from the facilities of three rivals, the Qadsia S.C. (Hawally), Al-Arabi S.C. (Mansouriya) and Kuwait S.C. (Kaifan), a fourth was implemented in Adeliya between 1974–78 to host Kazma S.C. This last complex followed the same design but with no involvement from IQC as it was meant to be the National Olympic Stadium.

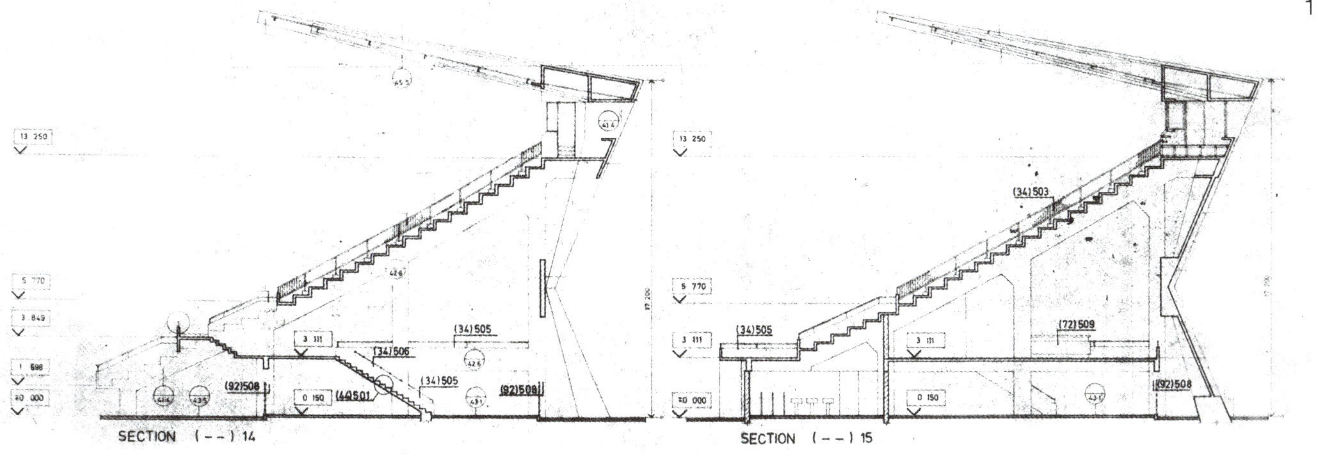
SECTION (--) 14
SECTION (--) 15

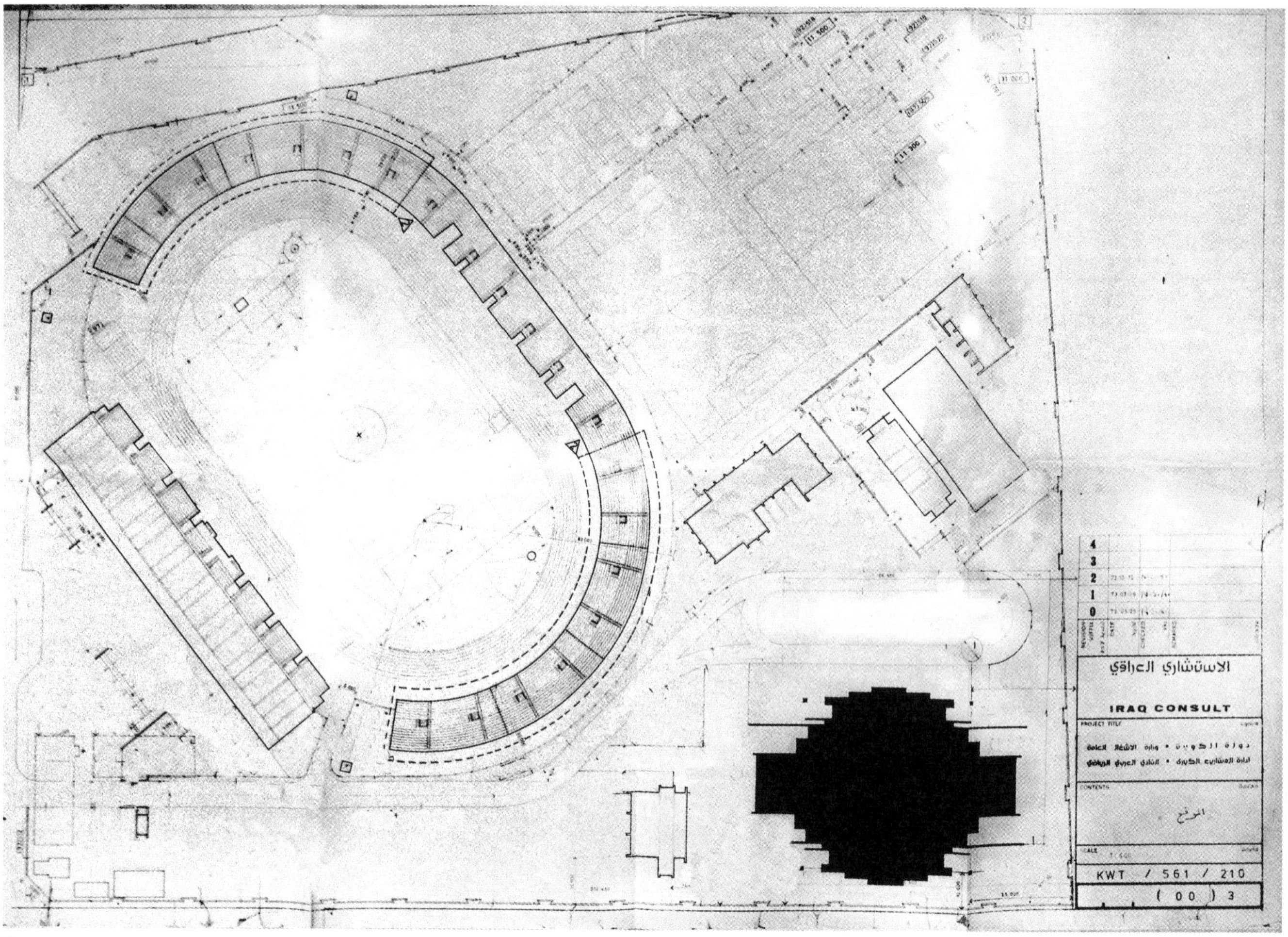

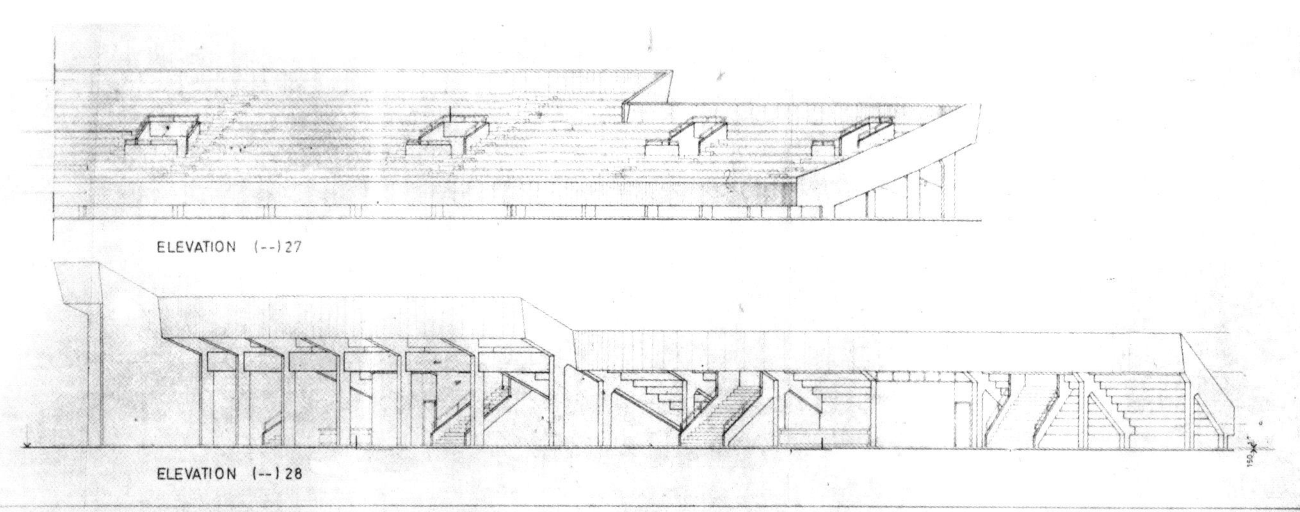

2

ELEVATION (--) 27

ELEVATION (--) 28

3

180

4

5

PREVIOUS PAGES:

1. Sections of the main stand

THESE PAGES:

2. Site plan
3. Elevation of the lower stands
4. Scale model
5. Rear view of the main stand, undated

GULF BANK HEADQUARTERS

MUBARAKIYA (CBD AREA 5)
1969–1974

DESIGNERS • Jean-Robert Delb
(architect); KEG (services)
CLIENT • Gulf Bank
CONTRACTOR • Unknown

IN USE

Jean-Robert Delb was awarded the
Deuxième Prix de Rome in 1957. He
was appointed to design the Gulf Bank
after completion of the well-known *Tour
Europe* in Paris. The same as there, the
concrete pre-moulded elements in the
façade are the main design elements,
together with the ground outdoor
pergola with faceted columns, similar to
the KNPC offices.

Erected in the emerging urban Area
5 of the Central Business District,
where other bank head offices were
also located, the new Gulf Bank
Headquarters was built only few years
later after the completion of its previous
offices in Area 1.

It is among the most recognisable
buildings in the city for its façade
of freestanding concrete elements,
shading the inner glass curtain
façade. With a similar appearance
to the *accropodes* used for marine
construction, these pre-cast concrete
elements control the sun exposure and
give uniformity to the façade. The plan
follows the plot's rectangular geometry,
regular and organised around a central,
open, triple-height hall. It has nine
floors above ground and two in the
basement.

Today, Delb's subtle sculptural pattern
works in opposition to TAC's brutalist
approach in the adjacent Souq Al
Manakh, built four years later.

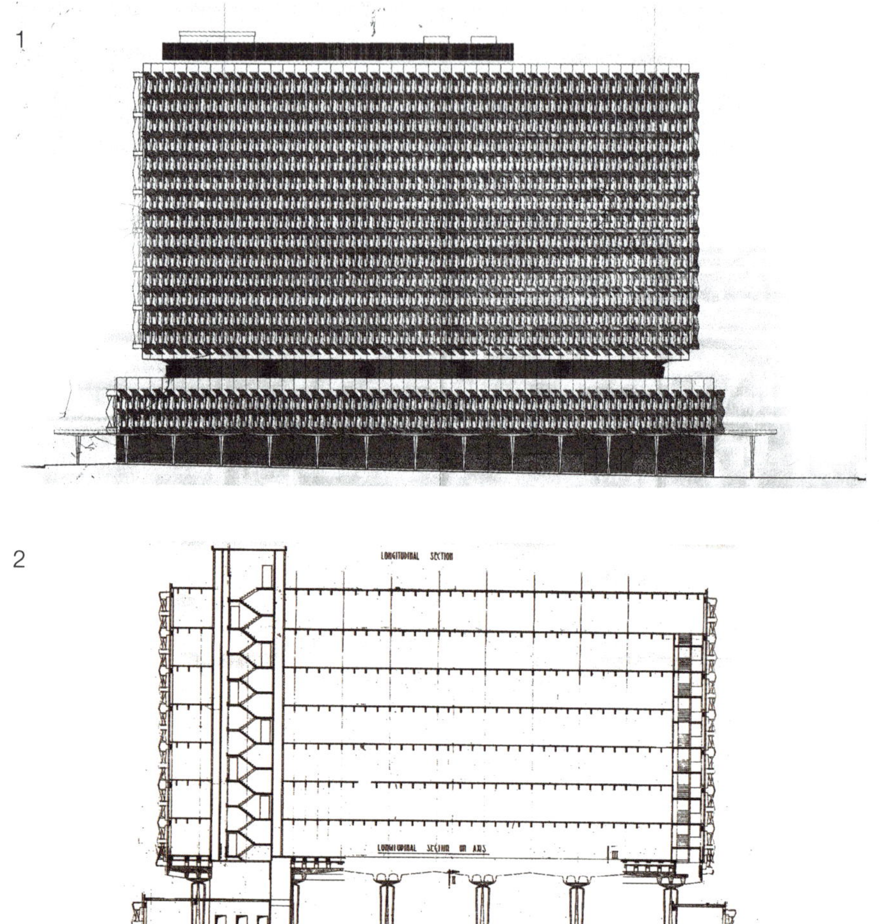

1

2

1. Elevation
2. Section
3. View from Mubarak Al-Kabeer Street
4. Gulf Bank Building and Souq Al-Manakh

SAVINGS & CREDIT BANK MAIN OFFICES

JIBLA
1970–1977

DESIGNERS • Remi Lopez
and Associates (architect);
PACE (second phase architect)
CLIENT • Savings & Credit Bank
CONTRACTOR • Al-Kosaf Co.

MODIFIED

The building was the result of a design competition in 1970. Together with the Ahmadi branch, the construction of the main offices behind the Municipality Complex was concluded by 1975. Later PACE was called in to re-design the elevations, which led to structural adjustments of the façade.

The branch office was located on the ground and mezzanine floors, above which are five typically planned office floors, with the length enlarged in the mid position. The irregular layout became a dominant feature in the building's original façade; however there is no visual record of it. The building had a system composed of big aluminium framed windows with light marble cladding above and red granite at the base. Two years after its completion the building was re-clad. The façade redesign gave a futuristic look to the bank's main offices with matt sheened, bronze aluminium, punched, horizontal fenestrations and reflective shading elements.

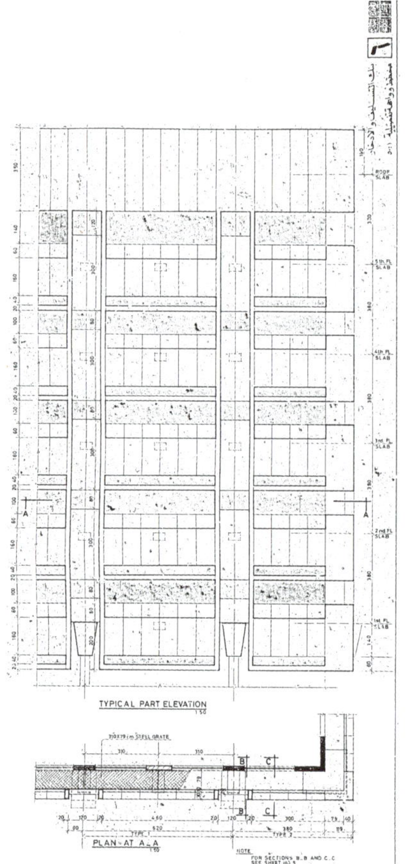

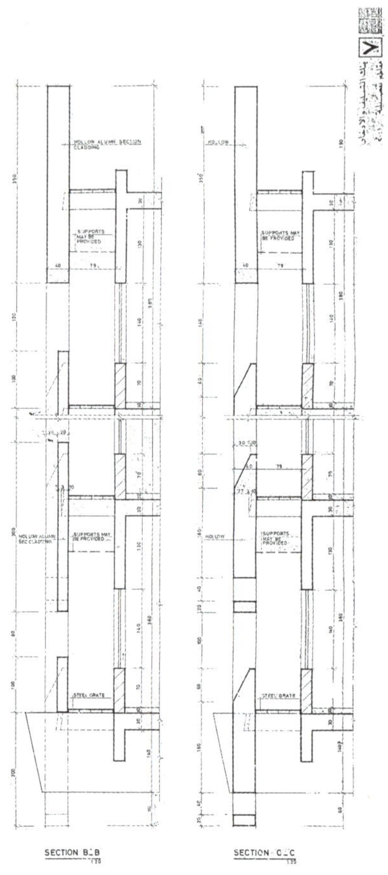

2

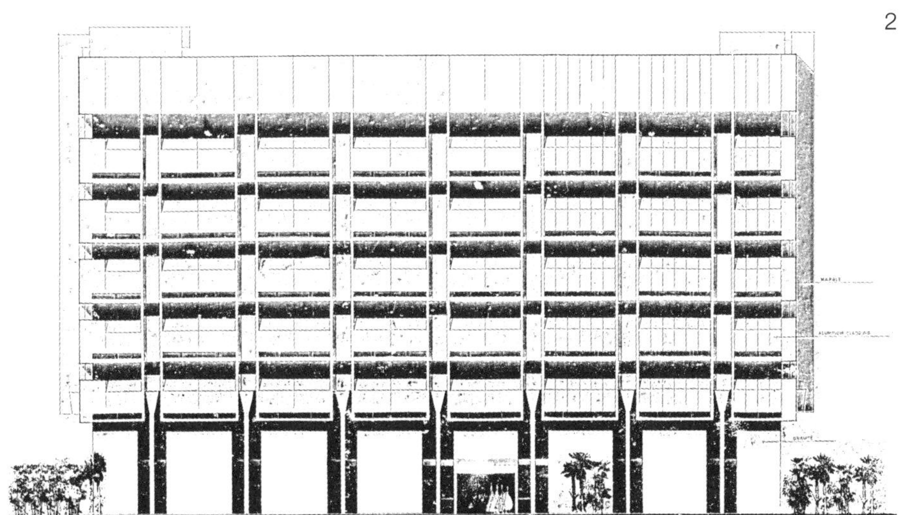

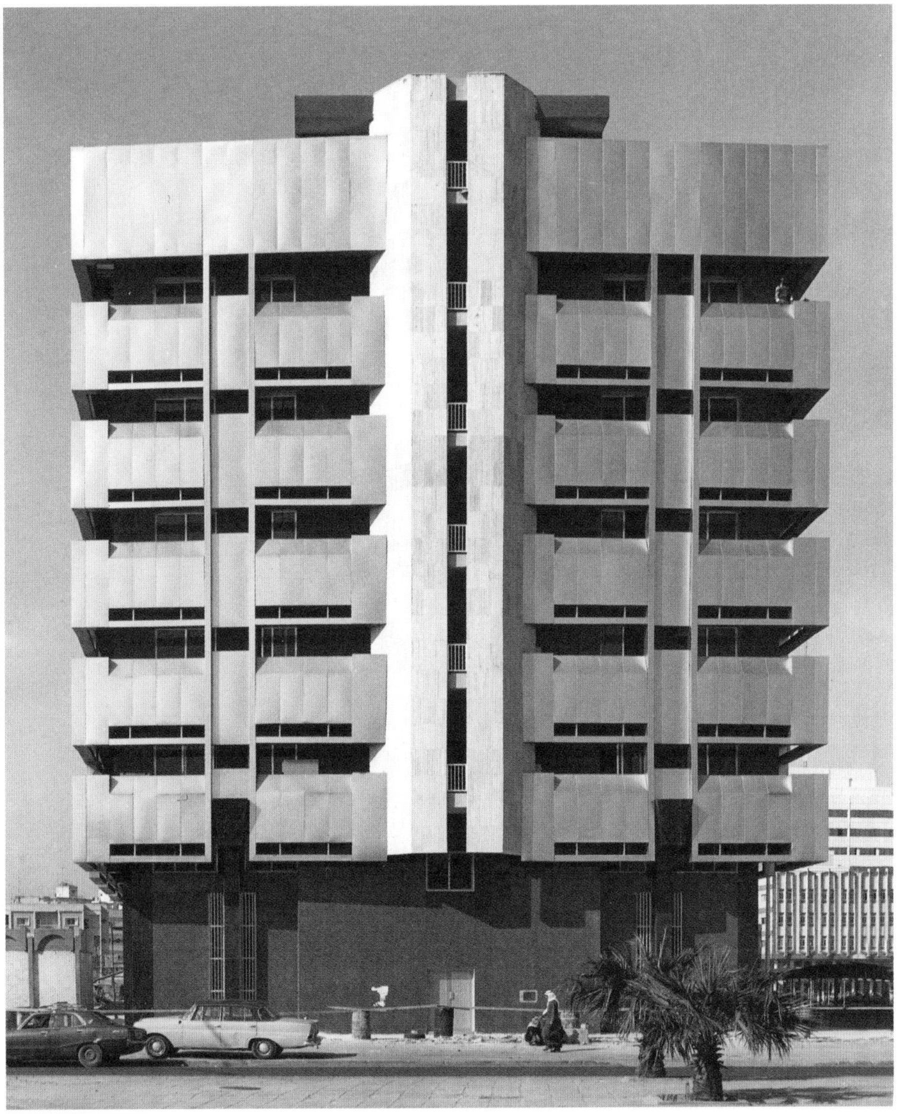

1. Detail of the façade system
2. Main elevation

SALEM AL-MUBARAK STREET

SALMIYA
1970–1982

1

Salem Al-Mubarak Street expresses the manifold problems of uncontrolled development in the district of Salmiya. In 1977, with the Salmiya Local Plan, the area's primary problems are noted as land use shortage and over-population leading to the development of several large-scale building operations as the "Salmiya Concourse" and other mixed-use complexes.[85]

From Souq Al-Salmiya[86] to Sheikha Badriya Mosque,[87] the spine of the district became the main commercial conduit of Kuwait. Commercial galleries, such as Issa Al-Saleh Commercial Galleria[88] and other shopping mall complexes, sporadically of mixed-use, form the majority of linear buildings of low profile, catering to shopping needs and allowing internal and external pedestrian linkage at all levels. The complexes such as Zahra,[89] Anjari,[90] Maryam[91] and Al-Salam[92] were developed after 1977, combining a shopping mall facing Salem Al-Mubarak Street with apartments and other large developments facing towards secondary parallel streets and Gulf Road itself.

These schemes show a common rejection to the traditional Souq typology, catering instead to a more modern, affluent community, whose lifestyle demands more recreational and entertainment facilities as well as modern boutiques.

Housing pressures eventually led to the construction of the Salmiya Outpatients Clinic situated halfway down the main street.[93]

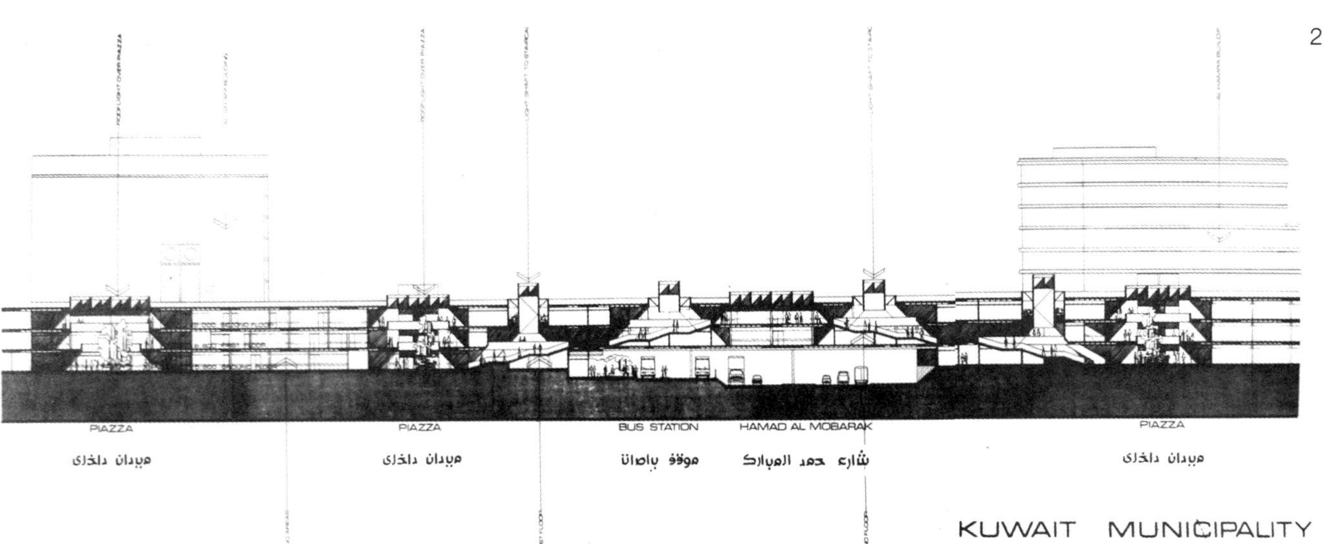

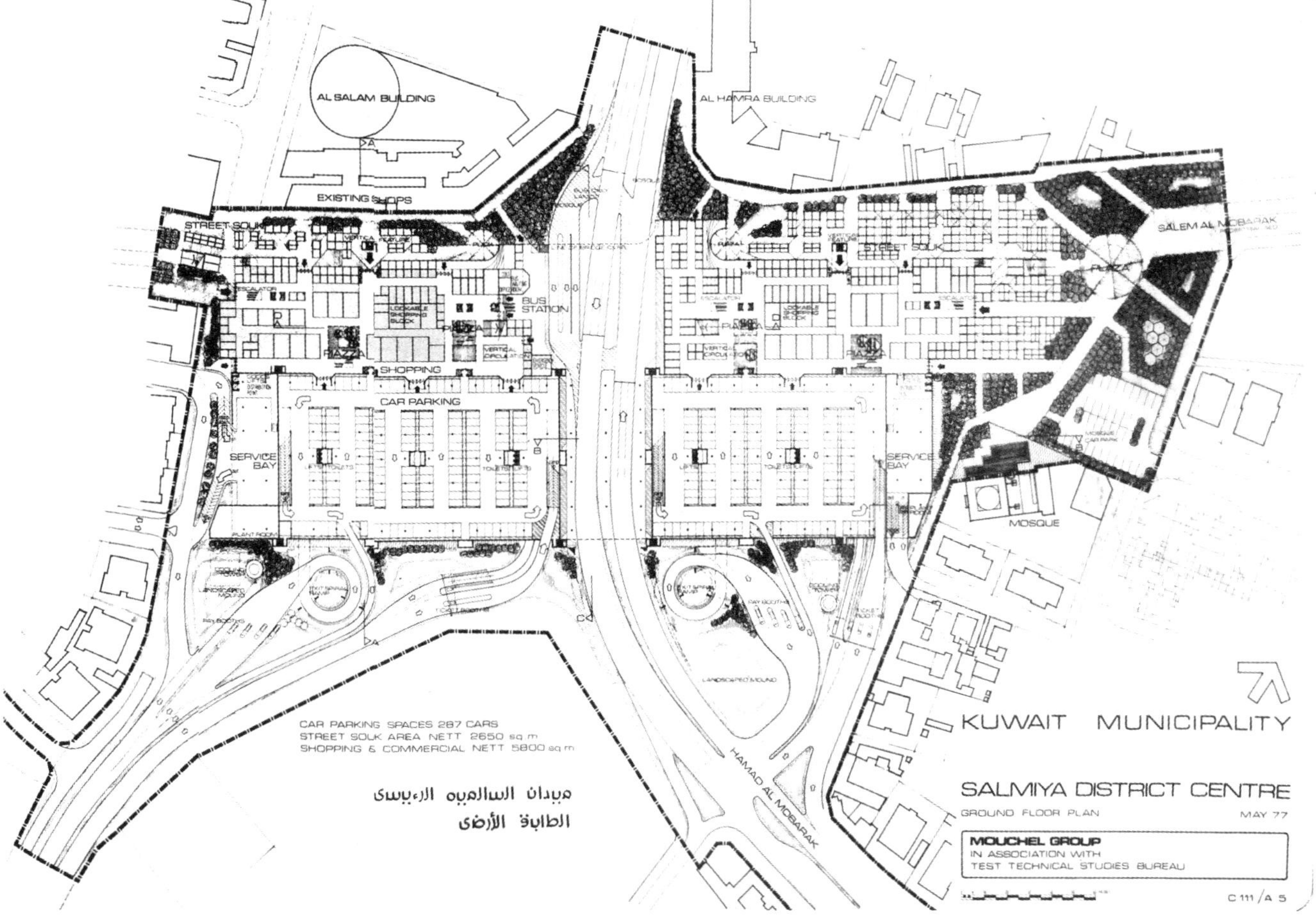

SALMIYA DISTRIC CENTRE MASTER PLAN BY MOUCHEL GROUP LEAD CONSULTANT, 1971-1977:

1. Kuwait Central Transpot Terminal, render by TEST Kuwait

SALMIYA CONCOURSE

2. Section, architecture design by TEST, 1977
3. Ground floor plan, architecture design by TEST, 1977

4

WIMPY

5

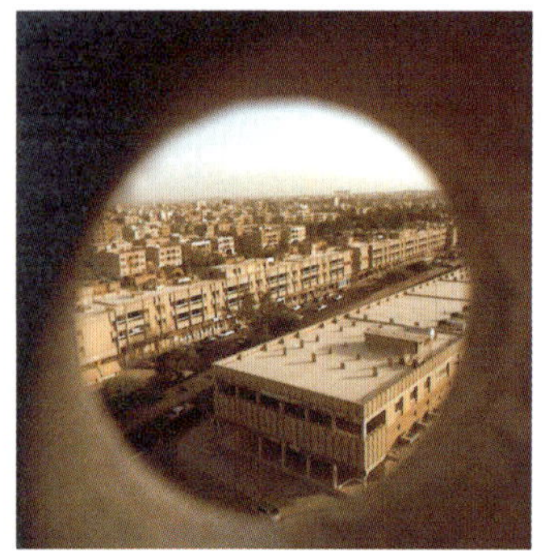

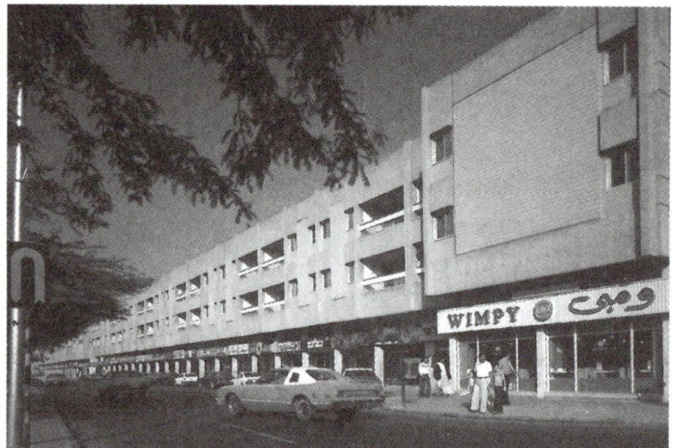

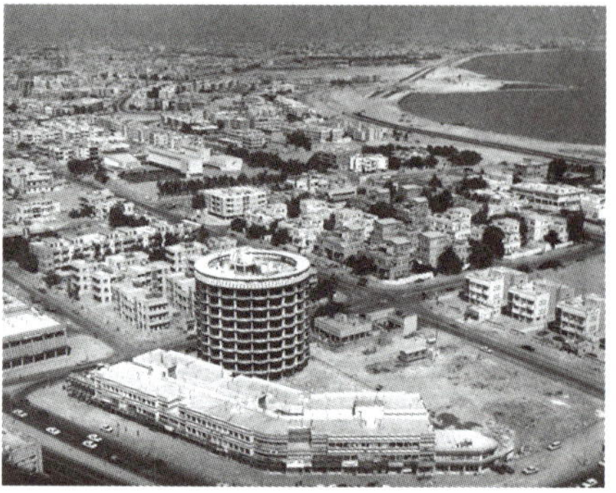

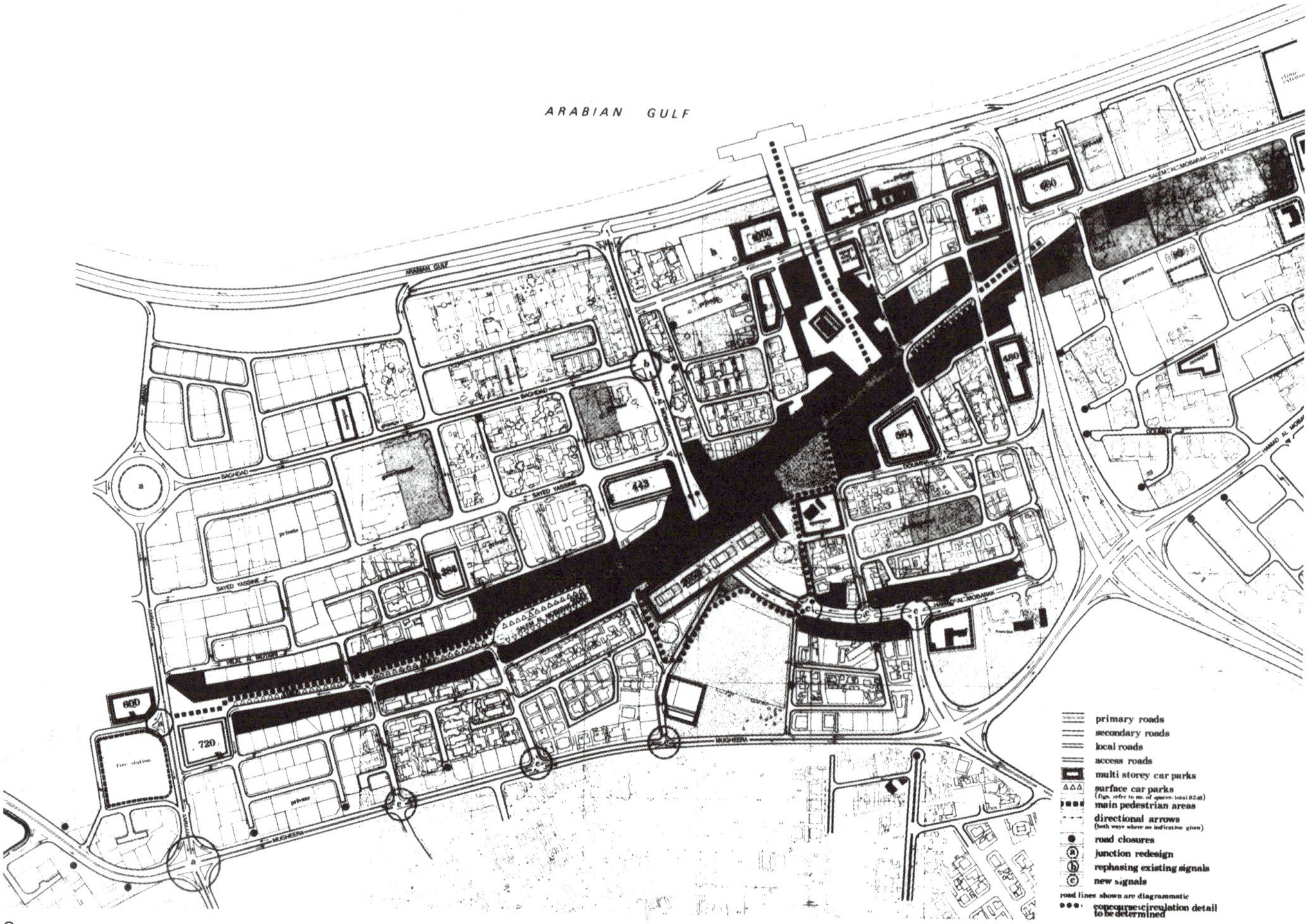
ARABIAN GULF
609
720
443
450
480
661
728
1000
primary roads
secondary roads
local roads
access roads
multi storey car parks
surface car parks
(figs. refer to no. of spaces: total 8246)
main pedestrian areas
directional arrows
(both ways where no indication given)
road closures
junction redesign
rephasing existing signals
new signals
road lines shown are diagrammatic
concourse:circulation detail to be determined

6

7

8

4. General view of Salmiya Souq scheme, 1971
5. Salam Commercial and Residential Complex, 1982 (demolished)
6. Salmiya Distric Centre Masterplan by Mouchel Group, lead consultant, 1971–1977
7. Southern and northern Salmiya Souq, by SSH
8. View of the northern Salmiya Souq built after 1977

Miss Matu

9. Al-Anjari Complex, view of the commercial gallery
10. Issa Al-Saleh Commercial Galleria,1968–1972, by SSH
11. Al-Zahra Complex, 1975–1982, by G. Sultan and KEO
12. Views of Al-Anjari Residential Complex.

13

14

15

AL-ZAHRA COMPLEX,
1975–1982, BY
G. SULTAN AND KEO:

13. Residential tower
entrance
14. Commercial Gallerias
display to the main street
15. Shopping mall interior
view

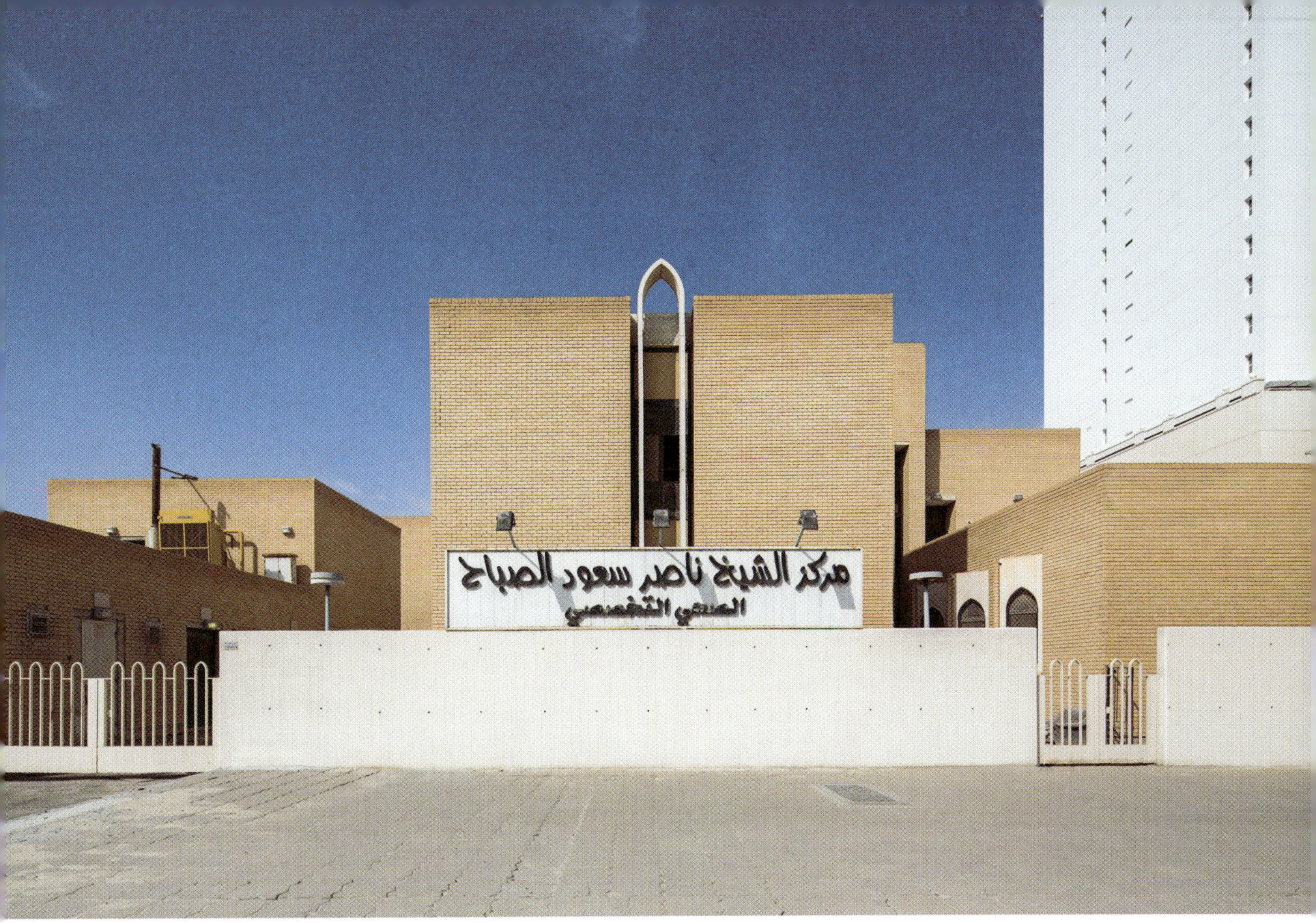

16

17

18

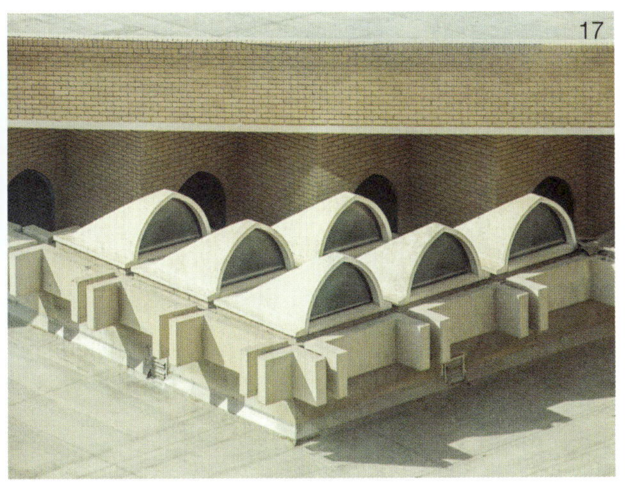

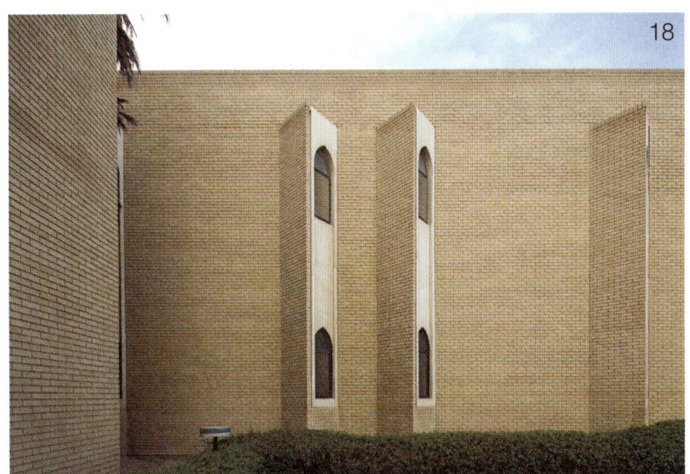

NASSER SAUD AL-SABAH CENTRE (SPECIALISED CLINIC), INAUGURATED IN 1981:

16. View from Salem Al-Mubarak Street
17. Detail of the skylight
18. North-west elevation

NOTES

28. Écochard, Michel, "Museum Architecture: Projects and Recent Achievements", in *Museum*, v. XVII, n. 3, 1964

29. Écochard, Michel, "Museum Architecture: Projects and Recent Achievements", in Museum, Unesco, v. XVII, n. 3, 1964, pp. 146–151

30. Écochard, Micheal, "National Museum, Kuwait", in *Architectural Design*, Apr. 1962, v. 32, p. 209

31. *Report on the Proposed Development of the Waterfront – Kuwait by Scott & Wilson, Kirkpatrick & Partners, London – October 1961.* Reprinted by the Center for Research and Studies on Kuwait, Kuwait 2008

32. Shiber, Saba George – *The Kuwait Urbanization: Documentation, Analysis, Critique,* Kuwait Government Printing Press, Kuwait, 1964, p. 169

33. *Kaysariya* is a set of buildings housing shops, workshops, and sometimes accommodation, organised around a courtyard.

34. The areas of CBD were a proposal of the urban planner Saba George Shiber. The plan was approved in August of 1960 by the Supreme Council, Municipal Council, and Development Board and implemented the following year.

35. First Master Plan.

36. Shiber, Saba George, *The Kuwait Urbanization: Documentation, Analysis, Critique*, Kuwait Government Printing Press, Kuwait, 1964, pp. 165 – 167

37. Ibid.

38. Cf. National Bank of Kuwait (1961) and Commercial Bank of Kuwait Headquarters

39. "Deux projets au Kuwait", in *Al-Mouhandess*, n. 3, Dec. 1964, p. 20

40. "Deux projets au Kuwait", in *Al-Mouhandess*, n. 3, December 1964, p. 20

41. "Lebanese engineering achievements", in *Al-Mouhandess*, 1968, p. 168

42. Dar Al-Handasah, *Company Brochure: Hotels and 5 Touristic Complexes*, undated.

43. The projects were deposited for permit in Kuwait Municipality under these names.

44. Shiber, Saba George, *The Kuwait Urbanization: Documentation, Analysis, Critique*, Kuwait Government Printing Press, Kuwait, 1964, p. 188

45. Cf. *Interbuild*, Jan. 1963

46. Alfred Roth, *The School Buildings of Kuwait*, Report, 1966

47. Sweet, Rod (ed.), *SSH Design. The First 50 Years*, Al-Khat Printing Press, Kuwait, 2011, p. 28

48. Al-Hashimy, M. "Nomad and Nomadism in Kuwait", The General Administration for Planning Affairs, Department of Social Planning, Planning Council, Kuwait, 1976

49. Al-Moosa, A. "Bedouin shanty settlements in Kuwait: A Study in Social Geography", Ph. D. Thesis, SOAS London, 1976

50. Cf. Thurfjell, Jan "Nästan allt om strömming: recepten", Cewe-förlaget, Bjästa, 1994

Thurfjell Consult, or T-Consult, was one of the main consultants of the Swedish renown housing policy named "Million Program" between 1965–74.

51. Al-Hashimy records the environmental concerns of the project as main aims and describes the material condition of pre-fabricated housing units in wood as part of it.

52. Santuccio, Salvatore (ed.), *Luigi Moretti*, Zanichelli, Bologna, 1984

53. *Project brief for Al Rikka Low-Income Rural Housing Scheme*, Savings & Credit Bank, Kuwait, 1966

54. Chadirji, Rifat, *Concepts and Influences: Towards a Regionalized International Architecture*, Routledge & Kegan Paul, London, 1986

55. "Kuwait : Mädchen-Sekundarschule", in *Werk*, 1973, v. 60, n. 11, pp. 1358–1361

56. Cf. *Kuwait First Master Plan Residential Zoning*.

57. The IMS Institute developed during the 1950s and 1960s a skeleton system in pre-stressed reinforced concrete elements – columns and slabs, for the construction of New Belgrade that was later implemented all over the world. The first structure erected in Kuwait was for a residential complex in Beirut St., Hawally (c.1969) published in *Al-Kuwait*, Kuwait, March 4, 1970

58. Cf. "Kuwait Central Bank, Kuwait; Architects: Dissing and Weitling", in *Domus*, Jun. 1979, n. 595, pp. 46–47

59. Thurfjell, Jan "Nästanalltomströmming: recepten." Cewe-förlaget, Bjästa, 1994

60. The other renowned association in the same years is with Rifat Chadirji's Iraq Consult.

61. According to an interview with Charles Haddad this was the first building approved with more than 9 floors in Kuwait City.

62. Another possible reference is to S.O.M.'s Beinecke Library (Yale, 1963) in the concept of a

translucent box. The CBK was in fact used as headquarters for few years and then SOM was appointed to develop the Central Bank Operations Centre in the proximity of Irving's building. The initial idea for this was a translucent marble in the proximity of Irving's building.

63. Portoghesi, Paolo, "Il non finito come alternativa: un'opera inedita di Kenzo Tange, l'ambasciata del Kuwait a Tokyo", in *Controspazio*, Jun.–Jul. 1970, v. 2, n. 6–7, pp. 2–12

64. *Kuwait Al-Youm*, September 29, 1962

65. Bettinotti, Massimo, *KENZO TANGE 1946–1996. Architecture and Urban Design*, Electa, Milan, 1996, pp. 144–149

66. "Kuwait Sports Centre", in *Architectural Design*, 1970, v. 40, n. 3, pp. 134–137

67. Solomita, Pasqualino, "Pier Luigi Nervi: forma e sezione nel tema della cupola", Università degli Studi di Bologna, 2010, Ph.D.

68. "Frei Otto at Work", in *Architectural Design*, Mar. 1971, v. 41, pp. 137–167

69. See Shuwaikh Power and Desalinization Plant.

70. The first example of this type of structure was built in the Swedish city of Örebro in 1958

71. http://www.akdn.org/architecture/pdf/0159_Kuw.pdf

72. http://whc.unesco.org/en/tentativelists/5933/

73. Different models were done for this specific group of water towers, representing several designs of VBB team and the single proposal of Malene Bjørn; after a first selection by a Kuwait delegation, Sune Lindström went to Kuwait to present the three selected ones to the Amir Jaber Al-Ahmed Al-Sabah, who made the final decision.

Bjørn, Malene, *The Light & Air – how it all began in Sweden in 1945*, Translation Eva Lindström, Baltic Books, Sweden, 2013, pp. 23–29

74. The "viewing sphere" was designed in collaboration with Buckminster Fuller, with his signature geodetic domes: aluminium trusses fitted with triangular glass pieces. Some diagrams of this project are conserved at the University Archives and Special Collections, University of Nebraska-Lincoln Libraries.

75. Cf. the report for The Aga Khan Award for Architecture, 1980

76. The local architects were Hamed Shuaib, Ghazi Sultan and others at the Department of Planning at the Municipality.

The Advisory Board was: the Prime Minister, Minister of Public Works Minister of State (in charge of Municipality), Director General of the Planning Board Assistant Director for the technical Affairs and three independent advisors, Dr. Omar Azzam, Prof. Franco Albini, Prof. Sir Leslie Martin.

Buchannan is the author of Second Kuwait Master Plan in late 1968.

77. The Alison and Peter Smithson Archive, Special Collections, Frances Loeb Library, Graduate School of Design, Harvard University.

78. "Proposals for Restructuring Kuwait", in *Architectural Review*, Sep. 1974, v. 156, pp. 178–182

79. "Demonstration Housing" scheme between Abdulla Al-Ahmad St. and Ahmad Al-Jaber St.

See Candilis, G., "Habitat expérimental au Koweït", *Architecture d'Aujourd'hui*, n. 177, 1975

80. Utzon, Jørn; Nisses, Børge, eds., *Jørn Utzon Logbook IV/ Kuwait National Assembly. Prefab*, Edition Blondal, Hellerup, 2008

81. "Kuwait National Assembly Competition; Competition Entry by Sir Basil Spence, Bonnington & Collins" in *Building Design*, n. 137, 1973 Feb., pp. 16–17

82. Utzon, Jørn; Nisses, Børge, eds., *Jørn Utzon Logbook IV/ KuwaitNational Assembly. Prefab*, Edition Blondal, Hellerup 2008, pp. 14–30

83. Vale, Lawrence J., *Architecture, Power and National Identity*, Yale University Press, New Haven, 1992, pp. 271

84. The stadium was developed with Le Corbusier's City of Sport and designed by the Portuguese architect Keil do Amaral between 1958–66. Iraq Consult was awarded the role of local office and site supervisor.

85. Salmiya District Centre (1971–77) designed for Kuwait Municipality by L.G. Mouchel and Partners, Derek Lovejoy and Partners, Hoare Lea and Partners and TEST Technical Studies Bureau.

86. Developed by SSH, c. 1975.

87. Conceived by Saba Abi-Hanna between 1961–68.

88. Designed by Saba Abi-Hanna in 1968–70 for Khaled al-Issa al-Saleh.

89. Designed by Ghazi Sultan and KEO for A. A. Muttawa in 1976 inaugurated in 1982.

90. Unknown author.

91. Unknown author.

92. Famous circular 10 storey-high tower owned by Saud Sahoud Al-Mutairi.

93. Shaikh Saud Nasser Al-Sabah Health Specialist Clinic

SPECIMENS III

Building as cityscape
1971–1979

KUWAIT SHIPPING COMPANY HEADQUARTERS

SHUWAIKH
1969–1973

DESIGNERS • PACE;
KEO (competition entry)
CLIENT • Kuwait Shipping Company
CONTRACTOR • Unknown

UNDER THREAT OF DEMOLITION

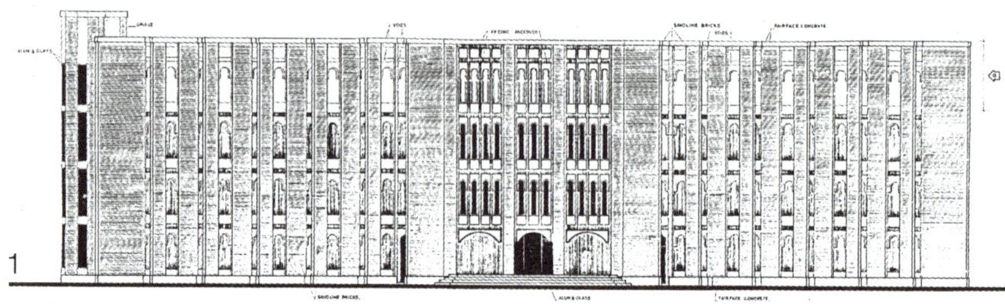

1

With the completion of Mubarak Hassawi residential complexes where the use of reinforced concrete exposed frames filled with Iraqi brick, Pan Arab won the competition for the Kuwait Shipping Co. offices. The Iraqi associated consultants[94] for the initial years of practice were not present on this project, but the culture of shaded façade and expressionist form remained in place.

In the west end of the building, the staircase curls in the brick wall surface exposing the main façades to an accordion of reinforced concrete arched frames. The four-storey building was meant to accommodate a free partitioning scheme to allow flexibility in the office plans. The brief asked for a free exposed ceiling to allow for this flexibility. The basement, open above in the façade plan, is only interrupted by the staircase top core, the fortified edge opening the building span from bottom and top.

The main entrance remains as an example of glorious times, with a cantilevered shade and featuring locally made porcelain tiles in a dark brown colour, although today the building remains abandoned and is expected to be demolished soon.

2

3

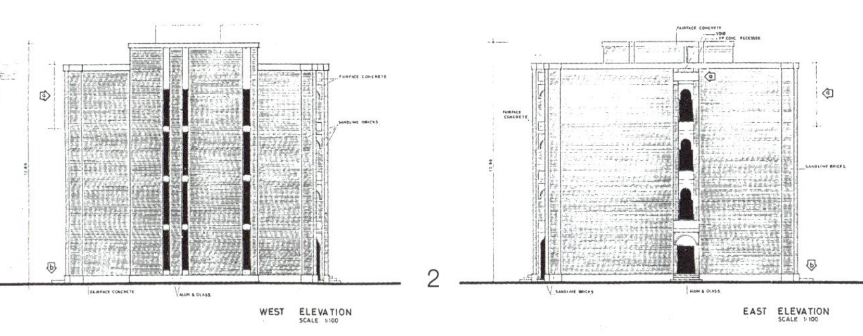

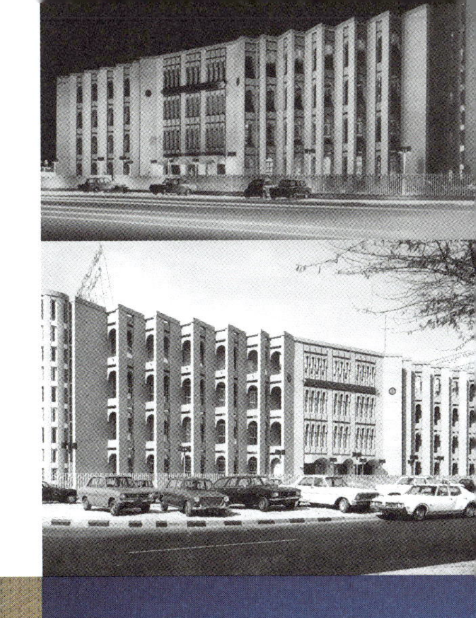

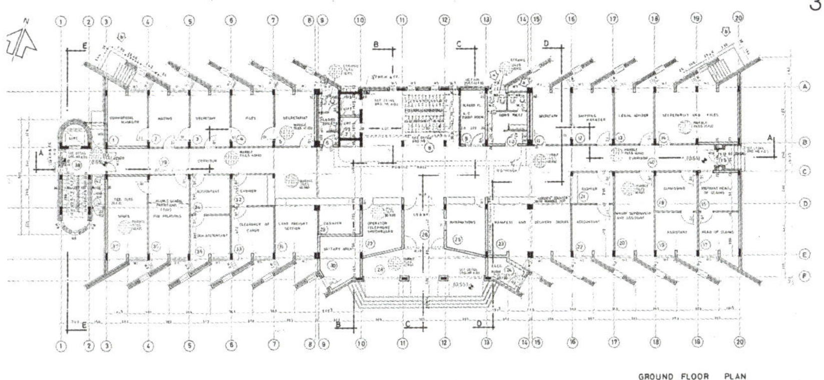

1. South elevation
2. West and east elevations
3. Ground floor plan

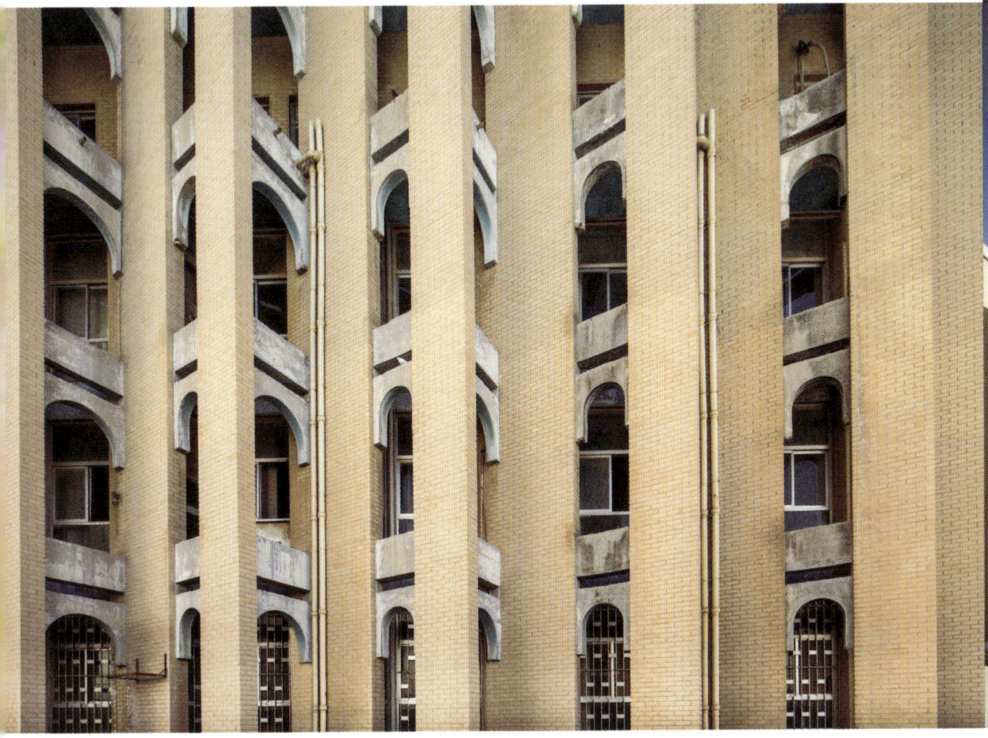

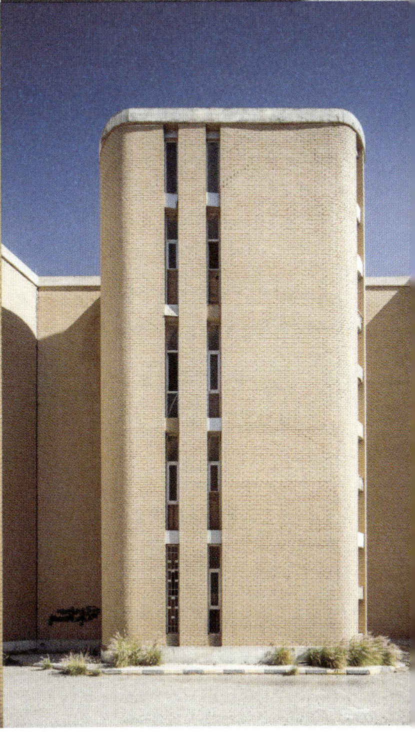

HILTON HOTEL

BNEID AL-GAR, GULF ROAD
1969–1974

DESIGNERS • J. Ritchie Architects;
PACE (extension)
CLIENT • Kuwait Hotel Company
CONTRACTOR • Unknown

PARTIALLY DEMOLISHED / IN USE

Before recent demolitions, the Hilton Hotel was composed of the older main building and tower extension that is now the Safir hotel.

The history of the old building is related to Kuwait's hotel saga of the early 1960s and Shiber's effort to relocate the Governmental Hotel project out of the Green Belt. This latter project, never executed, was designed by Raglam Squire who was also the designer of Hilton Hotels in various locations; Bahrein, Cyprus, Tehran and Jakarta. There is no direct source that attributes the Hilton Kuwait to Squire, even if his involvement seems plausible. However several sources attribute the Hilton Kuwait to J. Ritchie, the firm who worked with Mahmoud Riyad in 1964 for Aswan, Alexandria, and Luxor in Egypt.

The hotel was a horizontal bar building, sitting on a large platform. It hosted rooms on seven floors while the reception, ballroom, restaurant, pool and garage were accommodated in the lower volume. The main elevation and the short sides were enveloped in a metal latticework with hexagonal openings, slightly protruding for sun-protection.

In 1974 the complex was enlarged with a 20-storey tower, increasing the capacity to over 400 rooms. The tower, designed by PACE, survived the demolition works of mid-2000. It is a solid monolith of beige concrete with deep, punched openings. These are diagonally cut to offer not only sun protection, but also a better sea view. It was originally connected to the older building at the ground floor level, through the platform.

1

2

1. South elevation
2. Detail of the façade, shaded balconies
3. View from Mohamad Abdulmohsin Al-Kharafi Street
4. Aerial view showing the original, horizontal volume before demolition, undated, circa 1983

3

4

SHEIKH NASSER PALACE

RAS AL-SALMIYA
1969–1972

DESIGNER • Unknown
CLIENT • Sheikh Nasser Al-Sabah
CONTRACTOR • Unknown

IN USE

In conjunction with the Pearl Al-Marzouq residential development, this pavilion was among the first to be built on the Salmiya shoreline, known as Ras Al-Salmiya.

Rectangular in plan and with three storeys (the third floor is recessed on the roof), the pavilion has on the façades its main display element, a pre-moulded grille adapted to different exposures. Towards the sea, on the north side, a colonnade evolves into big glass fenestrations to the lower external garden framing the bay with Kuwait City skyline. On the opposite side, a formal white *mashrabiah* screen, lifted from the ground and made by prefabricated concrete cast blocks, protects the elevation from the blazing sun, and secludes an internal courtyard.

From both ends, east and west, the access to the lifted floor ground is made by symmetrical ramps covered by a simple canopy allowing car-passengers to alight.

1. South elevation
2. Detail of the façade, ceramic screens
3. Aerial view of Ras Al-Salmiya, 1977

SHEIKHA FATIMA MOHAMED ALI´S MOSQUE

ABDULLAH AL-SALEM
1972–1976

DESIGNERS • Medhat El-Abd; PACE; Ove Arup & Partners
CLIENT • Sheikha Latifa Fahed Al-Salem Al-Sabah
CONTRACTOR • Unknown

IN USE

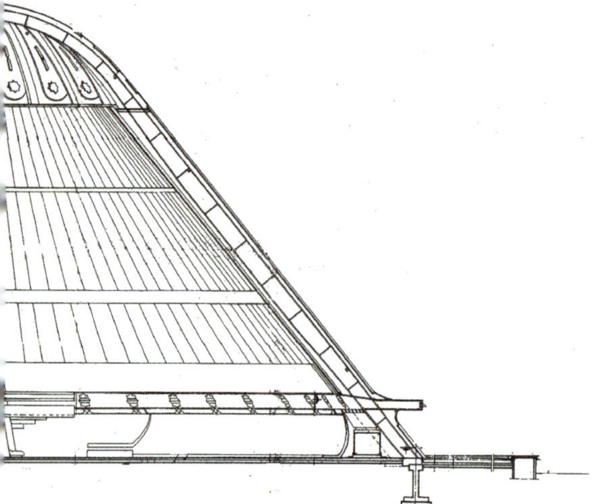

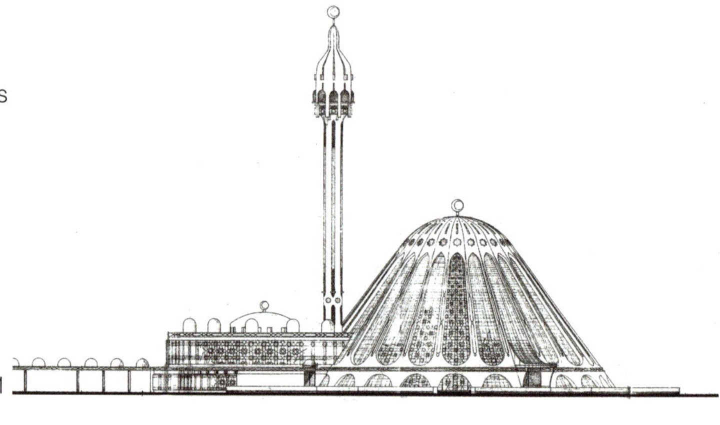

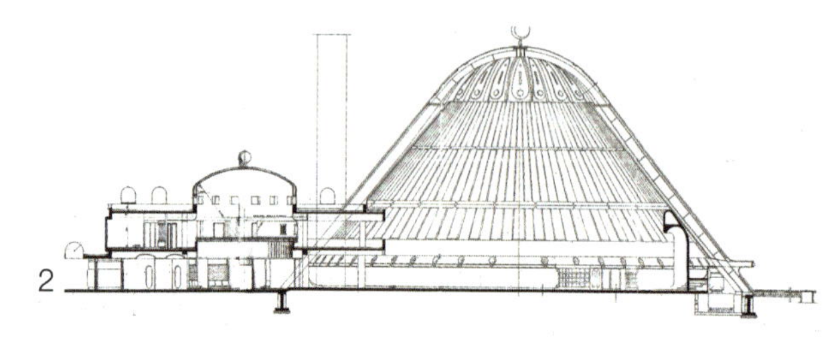

The Fatma Mosque was placed in one of the most prestigious neighbourhoods of the city, Abdullah Al-Salem, and proportioned to host large religious celebrations in the country, prior to the construction of the Grand Mosque.

With capacity for 60,000 worshipers, the Mosque and its surrounding landscape are organised on a central axis orientated to Mecca from its exterior covered access to the main entrance, crossing a central hall and onwards to the prayer room. Attached to the prayer dome another circular room accommodates a library of religious books, the Imam's apartment and a mezzanine, which hosts the women's prayer hall.

The dome interior with its skylight, amplifies the depth of space and emphasises the highest point. The exterior carries a carved surface with modern Islamic motifs.

Built on an exterior arrangement in the form of an octagonal star, the Mosque became a landmark on the city skyline due to its candle-shaped minaret.

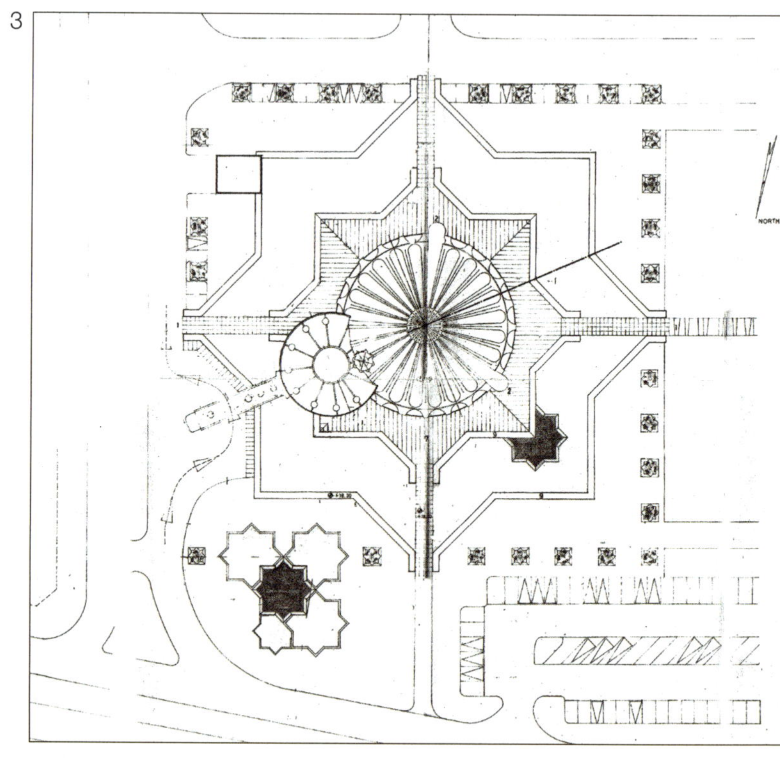

1. North-west elevation
2. Section through the prayer hall
3. Site plan
4. Internal view of the dome
5. Entrance to the prayer hall

UNITED CENTRE HOUSING PROJECT

BNEID AL-GAR
1971–1975

DESIGNER • Georges Candilis architect
CLIENT • United Realty Company;
Kuwait Hotels Company
CONTRACTOR • Musaad Al-Saleh and
Sons Co.

IN USE

This housing project was the first action planned to complete Hilton's plot in Bneid al-Gar, which later led to the demolition of the hotel itself in favour of more residential blocks. The project was developed for a private investor by Candilis while he was involved in the Kuwait City redevelopment plan for the Government. In this latter document the architect refers to Bneid al-Gar as an area with new housing, poorly adapted to climate and with inefficient land use.[95] His proposal is a low and dense group of high-end collective housing blocks, but the only erected is the one facing south-west. The building is a cluster type. It is a reiteration of prims shifted and re-aggregated in apparent scattered order. This configuration is able to cast shadows on itself. The main feature consists in the persistent use of deep balconies all along the south façades. The bronze coloured glass parapets of the balconies strengthen the beige tone given by the brickwork. Despite local skepticism about these verandas, considered of no use in hot climate, the architect conceived them not as outdoor rooms, but as a climate mitigation tool: a second permeable layer which cast shadows and protects the domestic inner spaces. In recent years the majority of them were enclosed to gain living space, nullifying the initial purpose.

1

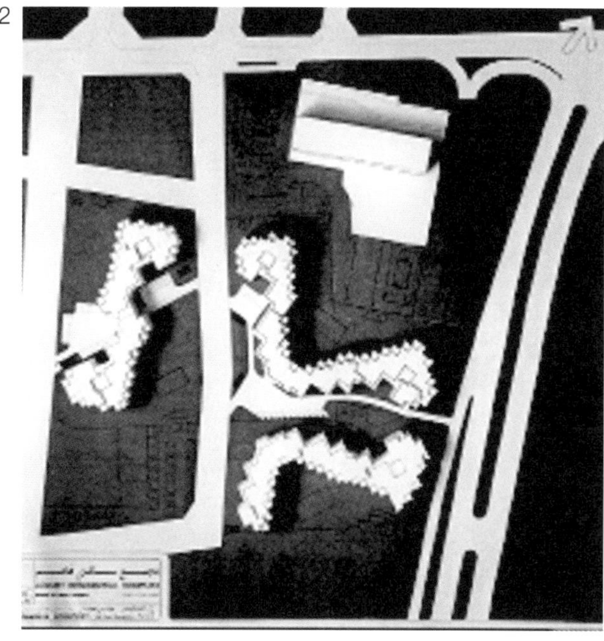

1. View from Gulf Road, 1977
2. Scale model of the original project, showing three distinct housing complexes in relation with the existing Hilton Hotel at the north boundary
3. Details of the balconies, undated

LOULOU'A AL-MARZOUQ

RAS AL-SALMIYA
1968–1971

DESIGNER • Sabah Abi-Hanna
CLIENT • Khalid Al-Marzouq
CONTRACTOR • Unknown

UNDER RENOVATION

1

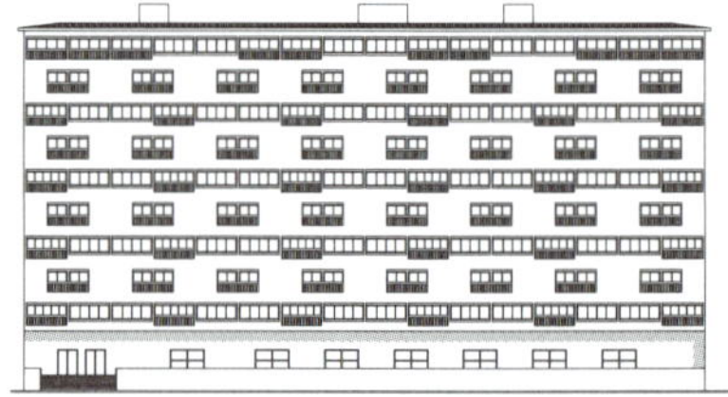

2

3

Also known as Pearl Al-Marzouq, this project demonstrated a different approach to the development of residential blocks in the country. In the late 1960s the regulation limited the height of similar buildings to three storeys if located outside the city centre.[96] The client was Khalid Al-Marzouq, who later became very active in the real estate market, chairing from 1972 the Kuwait Real Estate Co. He found the regulation too restrictive for the economic feasibility of this residential project. The solution did not come from legal disputes, but from the architectural design. The building was planned with split-levels and interposed mechanical floors, doubling, de facto, the entire height. This solution also allowed the construction of different flat typologies, which includes duplexes. All the various typologies were grouped in three linear blocks, arranged in a U-shape plan, offering different sea views and enhancing the cross ventilation. Out of the many outcome of this project, one of the most important is that it triggered the collaboration between Abi-Hanna with the young engineer Salem Al-Marzouq, the client's cousin. The duo were later to found the firm SSH.

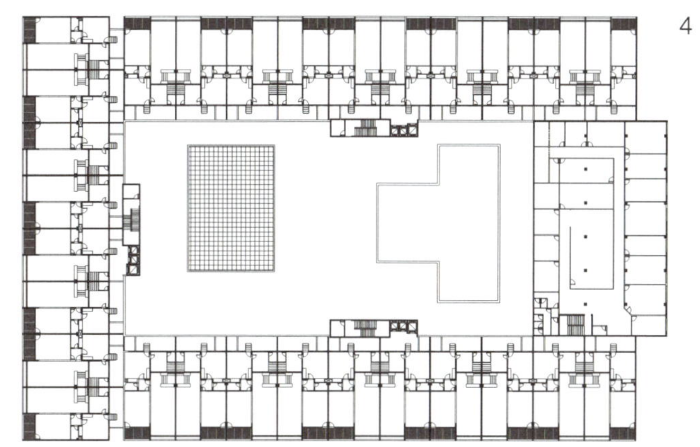

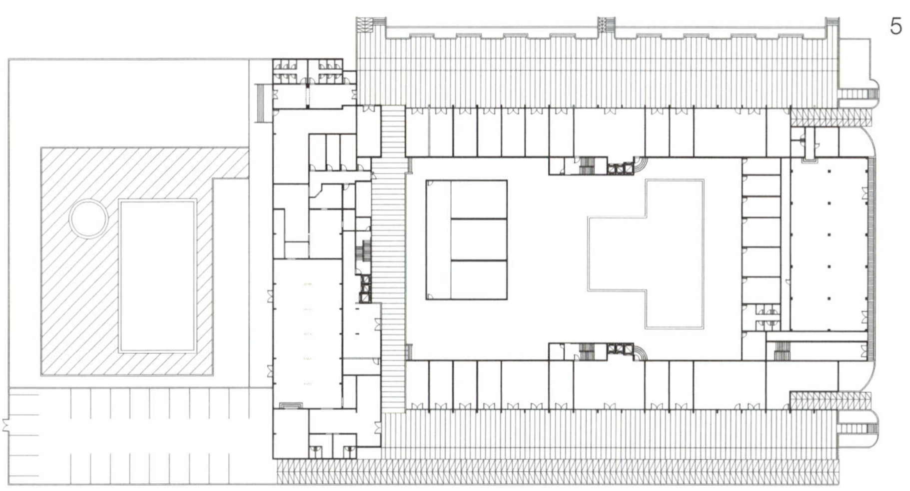

1. South elevation
2. North elevation
3. Aerial view, undated, circa 1973
4. Typical floor plan
5. Ground floor plan
6. View of the east front, 2009

KINDERGARTEN

MANSOURIYA
1971–1972

DESIGNER • Alfred Roth
CLIENT • Ministry of Education;
Ministry of Public Works
CONTRACTOR • Unknown

MODIFIED

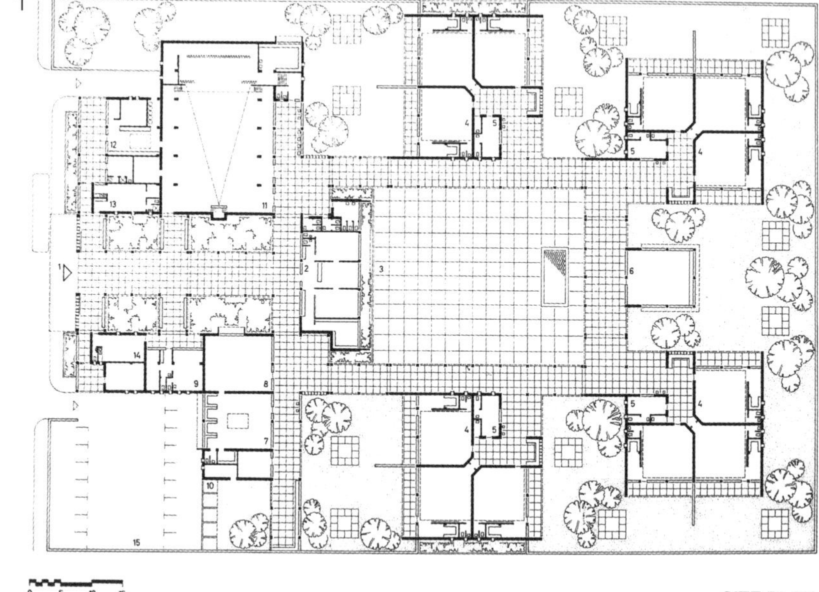

SITE PLAN

1. Main entrance
2. Administration
3. Courtyard
4. Classroom
5. Teachers' room
6. Music room
7. Library
8. Teachers' meeting room
9 Medical room
10. Pet zoo
11. Dining/Assembly hall
12. Kitchen
13. Guard's apartment
14. Helpers' room
15. Car park

Right after the completion of the intermediate school in Rumaithiya, Roth developed the prototype for a kindergarten, to be constructed in a different neighbourhood, close to the city centre. It was based on similar principles but the size and the relationship between spaces were adapted to the pedagogical necessity of children of a very young age. The central courtyard is still the pivotal space, however in this case smaller green yards were added for single class outdoor activities. Therefore the building was a cluster of interconnected pavilions among fenced open spaces.[97] Every pavilion hosts three classroom/changing room units and a teacher's office, making it a fully self-sufficient functional entity. On the opposite end, two separated pavilions control the main entrance and the drop-off area; they host the administration, the library and the assembly hall for indoor group activities. All the pathways and apertures were carefully shaded with projecting roofs. The building is still in use.

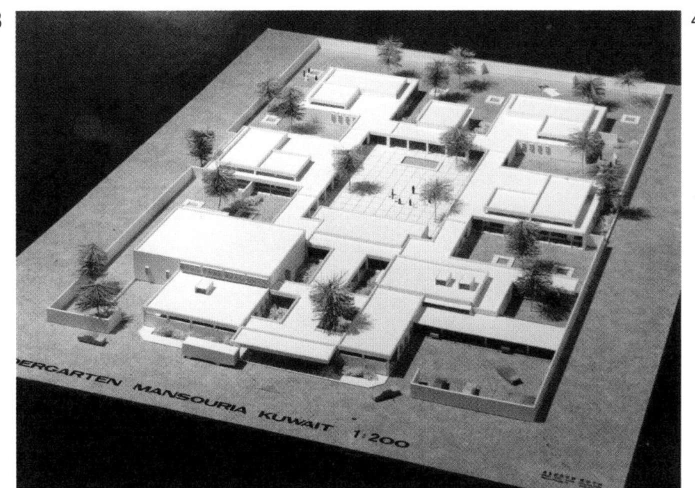

1. Ground floor plan
2. View of one classroom unit, undated, circa 1972
3. View of the courtyard, undated, circa 1972
4. Scale model, 1971
5. Detail of the decorative pattern of the brick wall

SIEF PALACE EXTENSION
MINISTRY OF FOREIGN AFFAIRS

SIEF, GULF ROAD
1973–1983

DESIGNERS • Raili and Reima Pietilä
CLIENT • Ministry of Public Works

MODIFIED

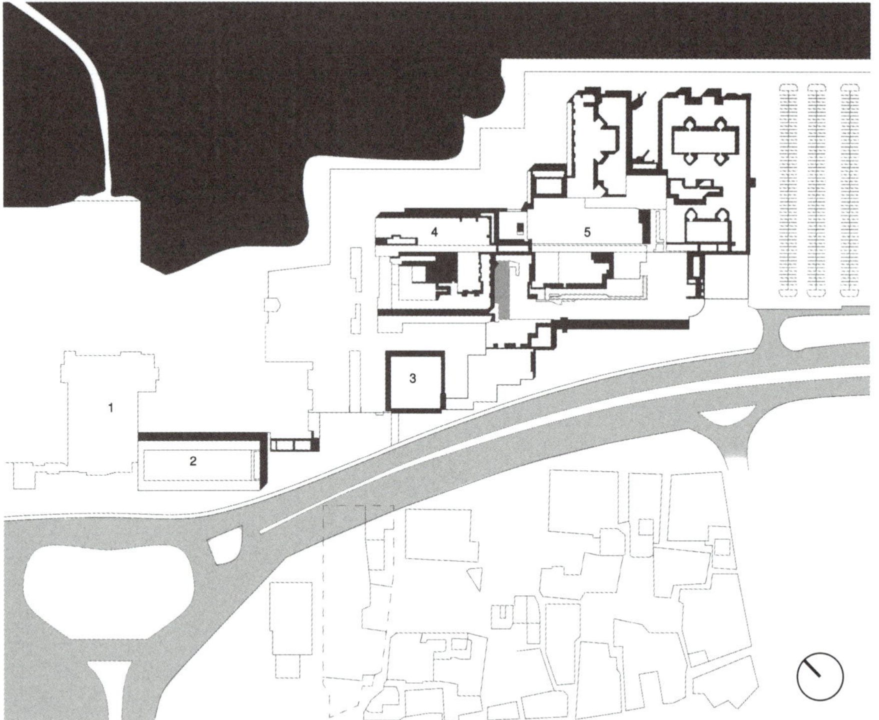

SITE PLAN

1. Reception Hall
2. Sief Palace Extension
3. A/C Centre
4. Council of Ministers
5. Ministry of Foreign Affairs

The design for the Ministry of Foreign Affairs is a consequence of Pietilä's previous involvement in urban studies of Kuwait City. The project started in 1973 as a wider plan to extend the old Sief Palace, the Amir's Reception Hall, in a contiguous area traditionally dedicated to wharves. The new work included the Sief Palace Extension, adjacent to the older structure, the Council of Ministers and, at the eastern end of the plot, the Ministry of Foreign Affairs. The project's theme was the understanding of the *genius loci* and a harmonious coexistence with the pre-existing structure.[98] Consequently, the colour palette and materials were dictated by the old palace. Nevertheless the design is a progressive shift from traditional motifs and appearance to more experimental and abstract expressions, along with the distance between the old structures.

The regular sequence of pointed arches in the extension became a syncopated rhythm of diagonally cut arcades in the Ministry of Foreign Affairs building. This geometry created a screen of sand-lime bricks, framing the inner walls, clad with colourful tiles. In the architect's imagination, this refers to the pattern of a woven partition that divides the nomad's tent.[99]

The project is a composition of juxtaposed boxes that find the architectural expression in the pattern of openings, always shaded by a second skin of arcades or by a sequence of concrete T-shaped eaves. These tri-dimensional elements, protruding or recessed, always create different patterns in casting their shadow on the brick walls. The structural design was conducted by Mikko Vähänen office while the services were done at the Devecon subsidiary. In the recent years, the building was radically transformed. The interior mosaic tiling was clad with black marble while the east elevations were completely altered in shape and material.

3

4

5

6

7

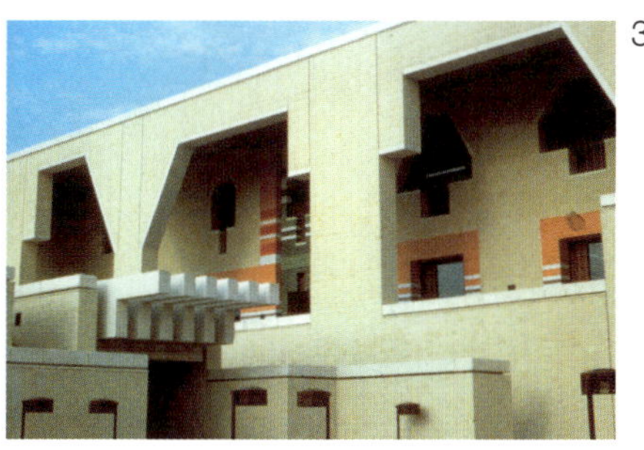

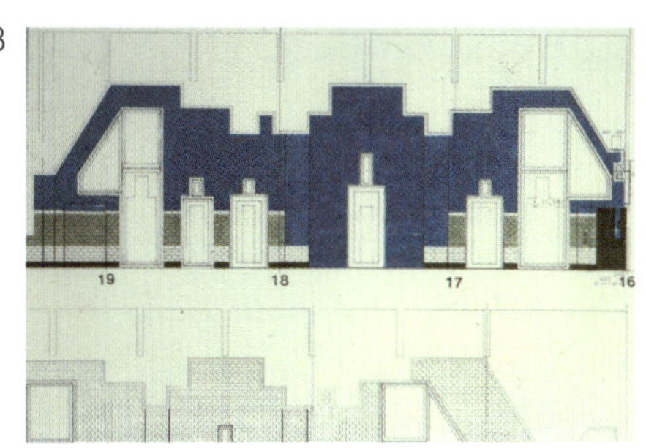

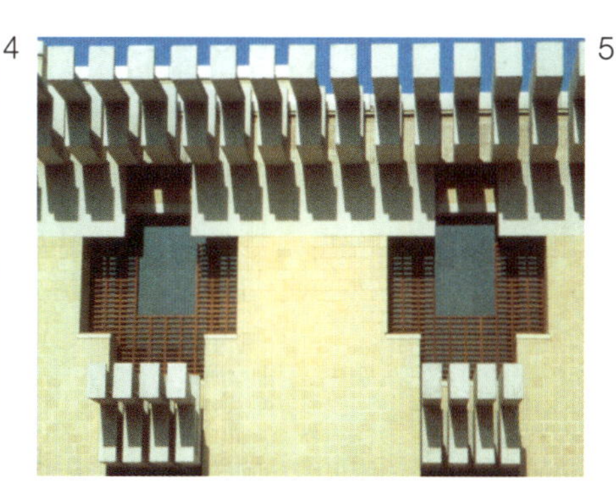

1. Site plan
2. Aerial view, 1985
3. Front façade, close-up, 1985
4. Façade study, coloured drawing
5. Façade, close-up, 1985
6. Drawings, elevations and sections
7. Internal court, detail of the fountain

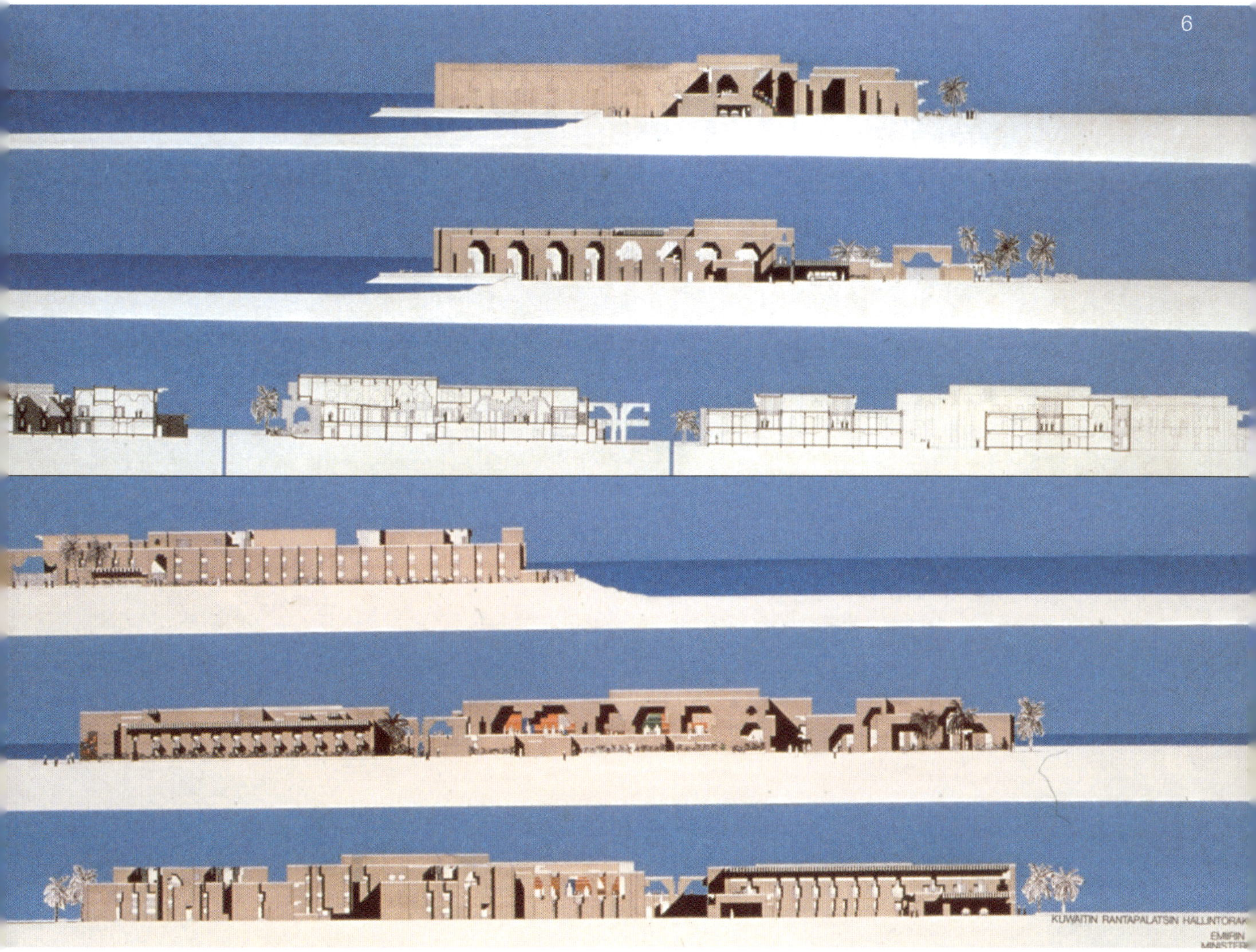

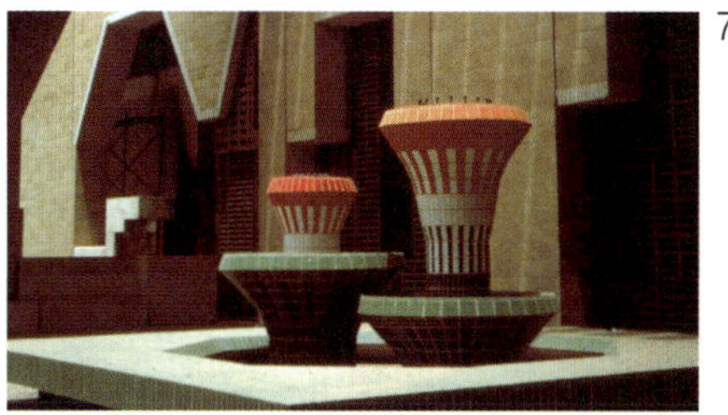

KUWAIT AIRWAYS TOWER

JIBLA
1969–1972

DESIGNER • Dar Al-Handasah
CLIENT • Kuwait Airways
CONTRACTOR • Ahmadiah Contracting
& Trading Co.; Al-Hani Contracting &
Trading Co. (services)

UNDER DEMOLITION

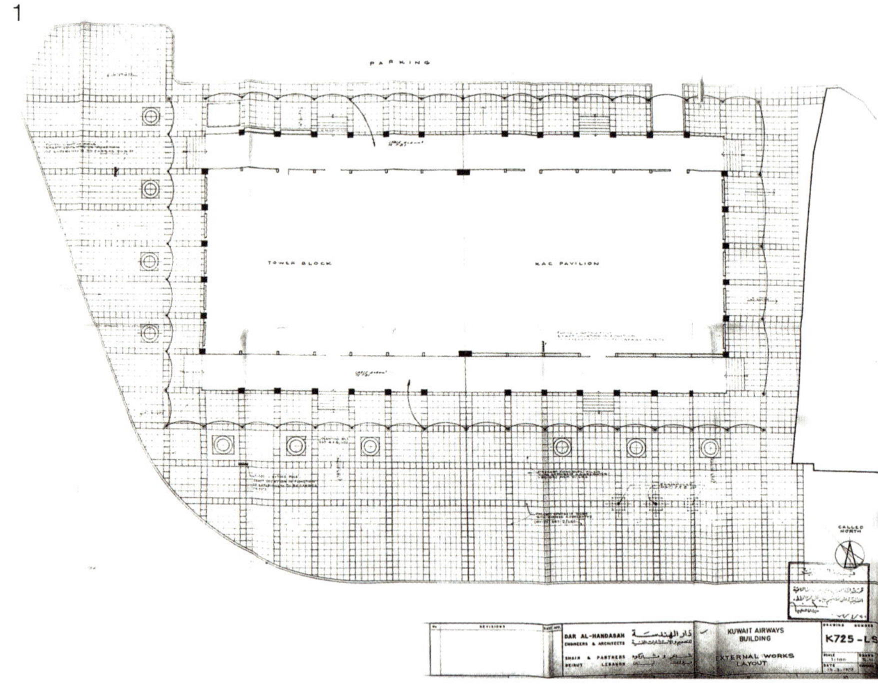

Once the tallest building in the
city, the office tower was seriously
damaged during the 1990 invasion and
consequently restored in the aftermath,
which made it a national symbol of
resistance. Located in the Central
Business District Area 12, reference
to the first proposed scheme can be
found in the Saba Shiber book.[100] In this
model photo dated from 1962 reveals
a similar volume and façade ornament.
No proposal of a high-rise building for
Kuwait is known prior to this except for
John R. Harris' architectural sketches
for the 1961 Waterfront Competition.

The building podium is short and
defined by an incomplete arcade of
columns. The tower façade screen
reveals an interlaced geometry of
vertical elements eventually inspired
in the fenestrations and motifs of
the Ottoman Sultans' residencies.
Natural light is introduced through
these perforations to provide a good
environment for office work and at the
same time affords less distraction from
outside elements. At the corners and
crown, a modern colonnade marks a
break in this pattern: the open-to-view
corners inform the internal hierarchy
of the floor and the two top floors are
reserved for noble rooms and higher
management.

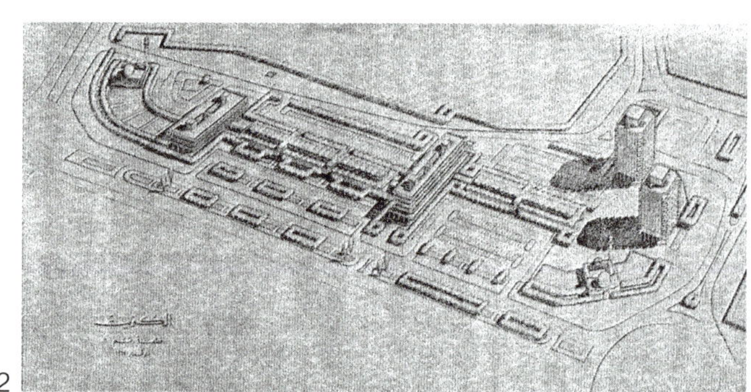

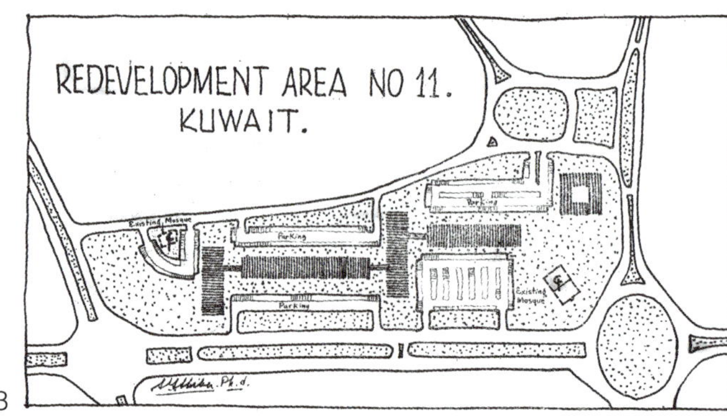

1. Site plan
2. Perspective showing the final design of the redevelopment of Area 11, 1962
3. Preliminary sketch of the plan for Area 11, 1962
4. Building under demolition, 2015
5. Detail of the arcade
6. Façade detail, loop holes

AL-REHAB COMMERCIAL COMPLEX

HAWALLY
1971–1973

DESIGNERS • Sabah Abi-Hanna
(architect); UNETEC (services)
DEVELOPER • United Realty Co.
CONTRACTOR • United Building Co.

IN USE

Eventually, the first housing and commercial complex developed by URC, the unit reflected all the previous motivations for the development of *self-contained* buildings throughout the "Urban Form Studies for the Old City" that had taken place.

Prior to the formation of the National Housing Authority, the rise of state-sponsored funding in the early 1970s inspired new directions towards housing. The demographic growth acknowledged by the Second Master Plan, demanded the increase of capacity in the existing urban areas plus a tentative solution to ending the problems of the shanty areas. Colin Buchanan's team appointed several locations for large re-housing projects. The building name indicates some relation with this programme that might be subject of a tentative framework for it.

With the dominant element facing towards Tunis and Beirut Streets, the white cubic volume comprehends two levels of basement as parking plus 3 levels of shopping mall, one floor of offices and 10 floors catering to middle and high income housing. The structural elements are combined and exposed within a regular and constant grid that allows different façade conditions. The Mall is organised looping around two major triple height halls exposed to natural light through fibreglass skylights. The pedestrian linkage at street level is constructed in white marble.

1. Access to the external commercial gallery
2. General view
3. Interior, detail of the staircase

التجارة
BOOKSHOP
شركة سوق اضواء المضيان المركزي
CRYSTAL LIGHT
اضواء الكريستال

AL-RIHAB
الرحاب
Arena آدينا
الهاجرة صيدلية AL-Hajery Pharmacy
مؤسسة عبد النبي الصراف الكهربائية ABDULNABI AL-SARRAF ELECT. EST. 22630984 226369
سوق إنارة المركزي INARA Central Market Tel: 22667744 Fax:22615915
CLASSIC LIGHT كلاسيك لايت TELEFAX:22 TEL.22

SOUQ AL-KUWAIT

MUBARAKIYA (CBD AREA 8)
1973–1976

DESIGNERS • BBPR (preliminary design); SOM, Paris (architect); SSH (associate architect); Nelson Khoury (structure); Ove Arup & Partners (structure)
CLIENT • Kuwait Muncipality (1973); Kuwait Real Estate Co. (1974–76)
CONTRACTOR • Unknown

IN USE

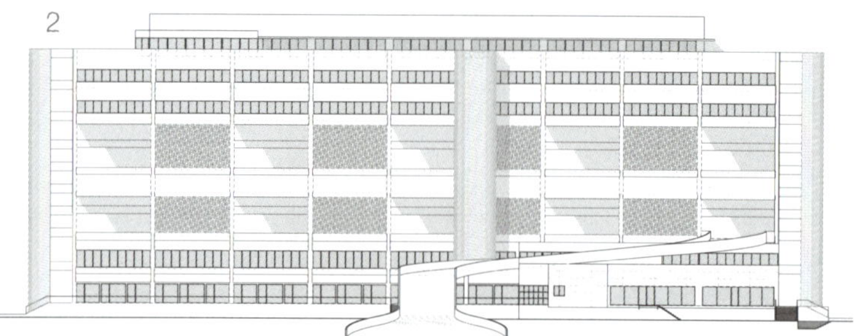

The "Demonstration Building" Initiative eventually resulted in BBPR commissioning of the preliminary development of a mixed-use programme for the CBD Commercial Area 8. In the 1969 entry for "Urban Form Studies for the Old City," the argument for construction of landmark sare as reference points of "volumetric structure."[101] The BBPR study allotted a total height of 60 m, 45 of those dedicated to car parking and 15 for other uses. On the upper levels it was proposed to have internal shaded courtyards. The BBPR study proposed constructing such massive structures around the city for large public accessibility with observation points and communal entertainment areas.

However, in the following year the project was awarded to SSH with SOM as design consultant, following a similar scheme and volume of the prior proposal. This included a shopping mall in the first floors, parking in the intermediate and offices on top, with construction starting in the same year. The building collapsed during construction and Ove Arup was hired to redesign the structure allowing its final completion.

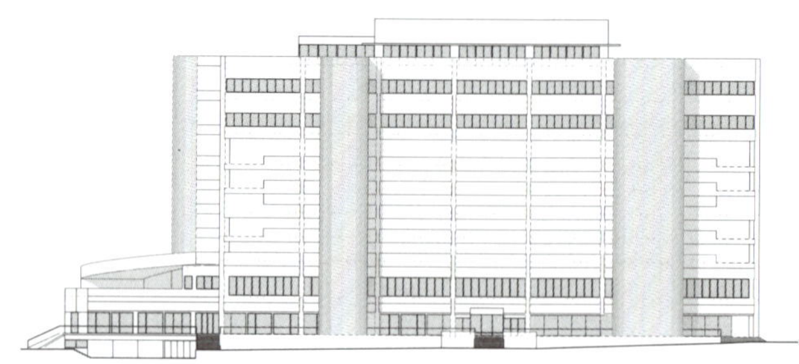

1. BBPR proposal axonometric view, 1973
2. Elevations: south-east, north-east, north-west and south-west
3. Detail of the external staircase
4. View of the commercial gallery
5. Overall view

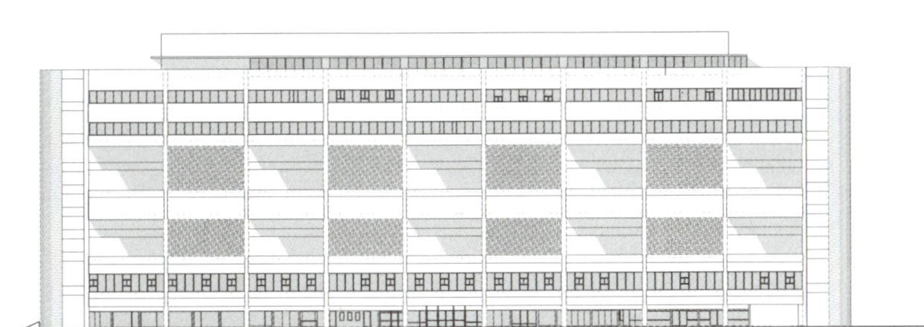

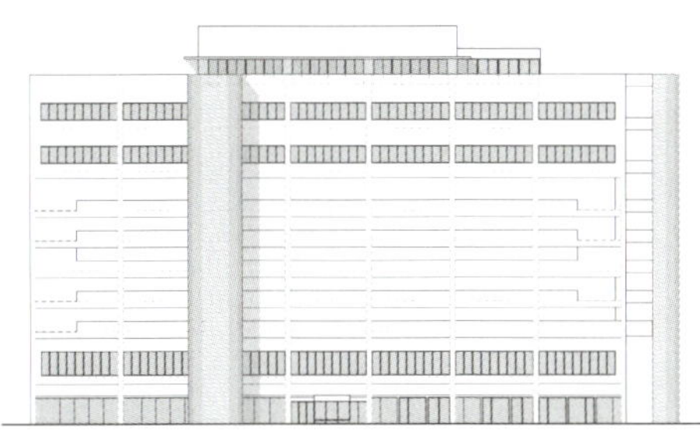

SOUQ AL-KABEER

SALHIYA
1973–1976

DESIGNERS • SOM, Paris (architect);
SSH (associate architect);
Ove Arup & Partners (structure)
CLIENT • Kuwait Real Estate Co.
CONTRACTOR • Unknown

IN USE

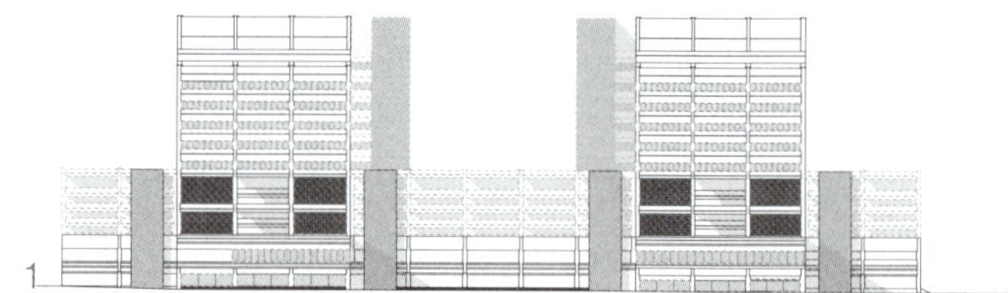

Souq Al-Kabeer was developed in parallel with Souq Al-Kuwait and the Al-Rehab Complex. The role of SOM in the design process is not entirely known. The construction speed and the complex location of the site imposed a simple and efficient structural resolution that resulted in all these buildings sharing a common condition in image and material.

Embedded in the modern urban fabric, the plot has only two access points to the primary road system. The site selection challenges the feasibility of many of the areas left behind the modern frontage for avenues.

The scheme is organised along the plot length with the two main entrances from each side enclosing a loop shopping mall distributed through three floors. The car parking capacity is divided in two underground floors accessed from the Municipality Building side and four intermediate floors above the shopping with entrance and exit through a fly-over ramp. The mirrored plan is defined by lower frontages to the edges and the two central towers, which initially comprised housing units.

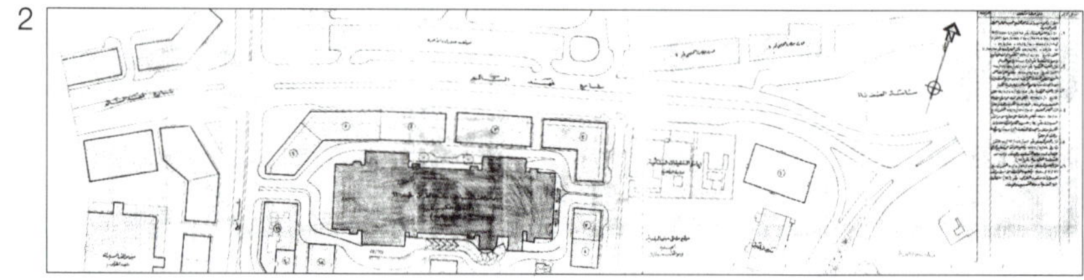

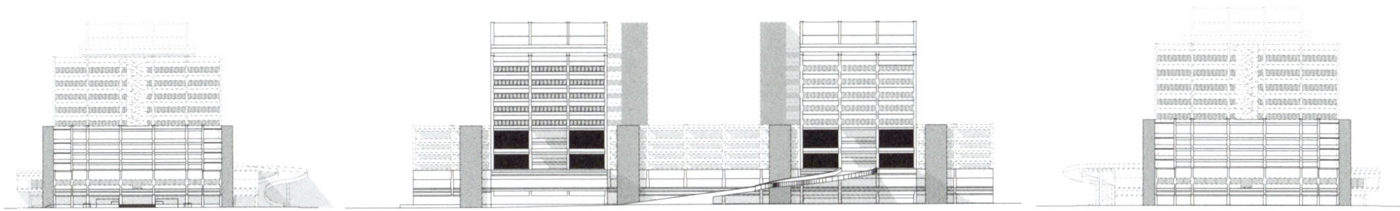

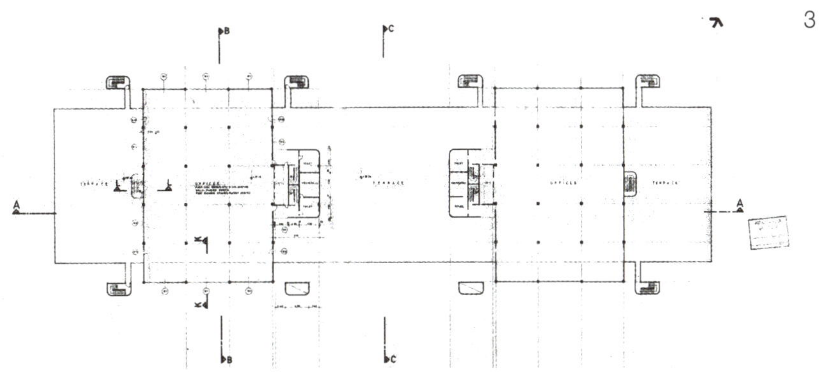

1. Elevations: north, west, south and east
2. Site plan, 1975
3. Typical floor plan, 1975

SOUQ AL-SAFAT

MIRQAB (CBD AREA 9)
1973–1975

DESIGNERS • TAC (architect and lead consultant); PACE (associate architect)
CLIENT • Kuwait Investment Co.
CONTRACTOR • Unknown

IN USE

1

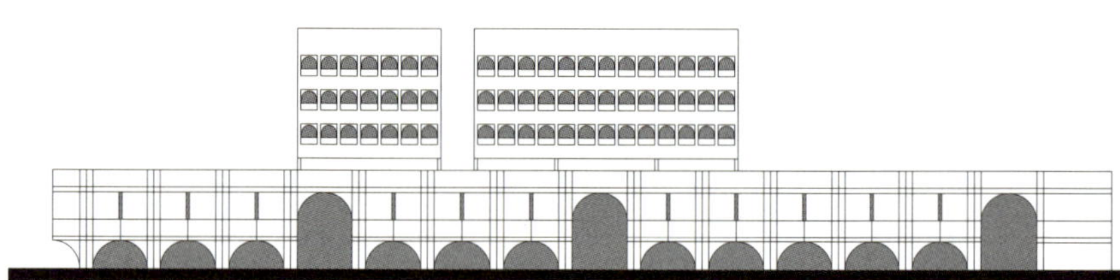

2

Souq Al-Safat remains embedded in the commercially dense Area 9 of the Central Business District. Tendered in conjunction with Souq Al-Manakh, the development comprises a new retail area and offices, with a total of seven storeys plus two underground floors for 1000 parking spaces. The building comprises two volumes; the commercial platform and the offices over it.

At street level, the façade distributes the visitor's flow through spacious arched colonnades connecting the surrounding pedestrian piazza with the inner commercial areas. The higher arches direct pedestrians to the main entrances and to a double-height internal courtyard, with water features, staircases and enclosed balconies. The simplicity of the initial design was meanwhile compromised by a more informal bazaar with the initial 60 retail units tripling in number.

The second volume hosts offices of 3,500 m² over four storeys. Each of the façades is different, changing between several geometric elements within a regular metric.

It was the first of four similar souqs completed by TAC. Its acceptance determined the designer's success in Kuwait and especially in fostering this new typology throughout the second half of the 1970s. Multipurpose buildings catered to supply the needs and expectations of a new cosmopolitan wave in the modern city.

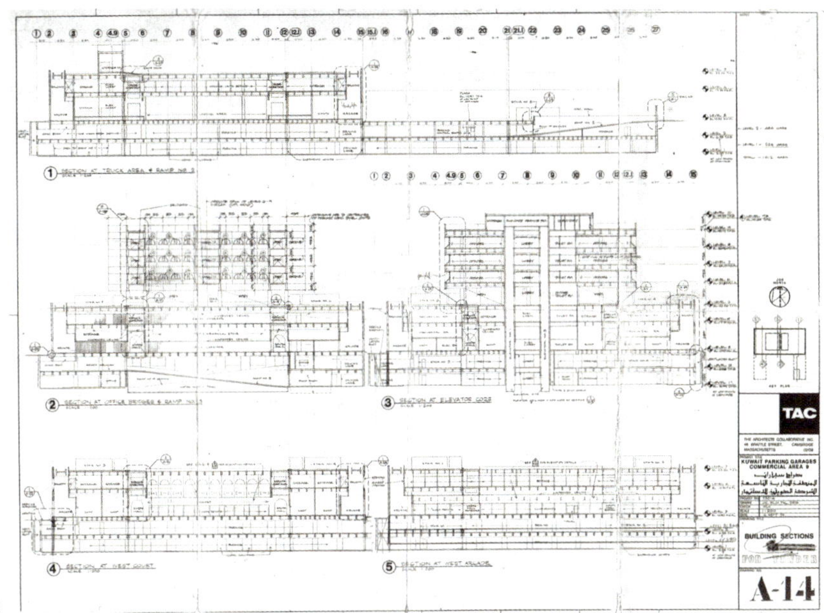

3

4

5

1. Perspective view, 1979
2. South-west elevation
3. Sections, 1979
4. View of the north-east front, 1984
5. Internal court with fountain, 1984

SOUQ AL-MANAKH

MUBARAKIYA (CBD AREA 5)
1973–1975

DESIGNERS • TAC (architect and lead consultant); PACE (associate architect)
CLIENT • Kuwait Investment Co.
CONTRACTOR • Unknown

IN USE

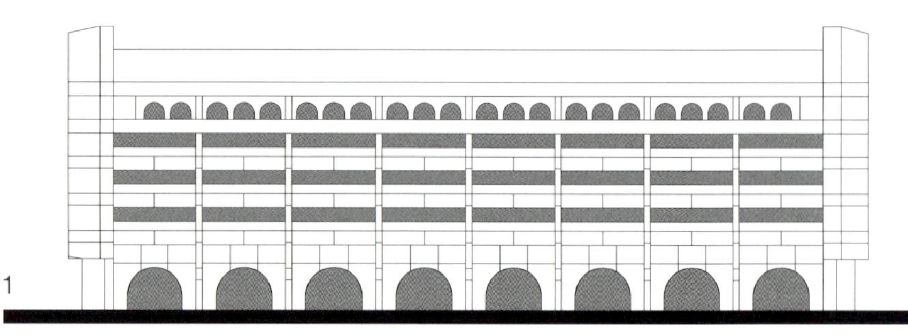

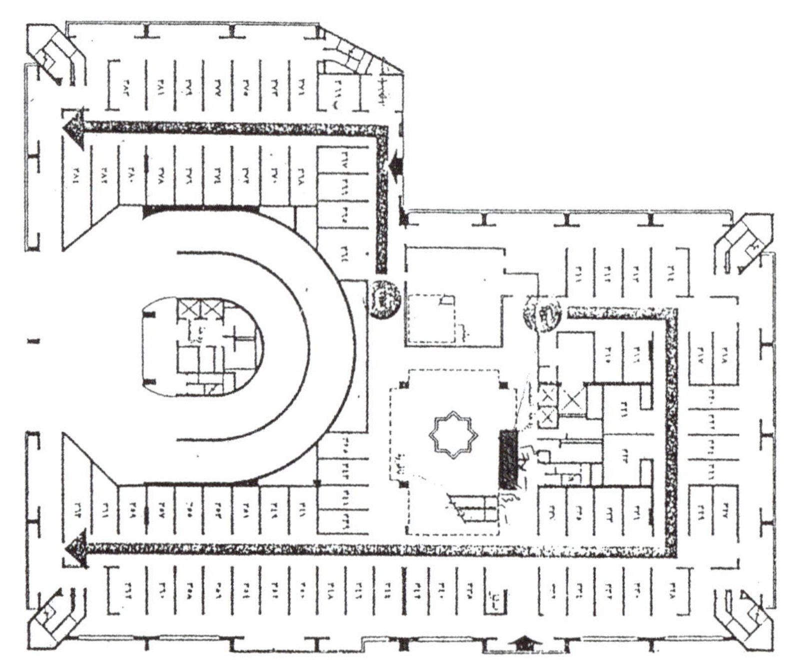

KIC commissioned PACE for the development of the CBD Commercial Areas 9 and 5. The last of these is Souq Al-Manakh where by the summer of 1982 the Kuwait informal stock market stopped trading.[102] The *crash* led to the interruption of some of TAC ongoing projects, and eventually to its bankruptcy.

The site is interlocked between three bank office towers (Gulf Bank, ABK and CBK) and the State Library (former Mubarakiya School). The entrance from Mubarak Al-Kabeer Street provides conditioned access to the underground parking and the entrance from Oman Street to the intermediate floors for public parking. This entrance and exit ramp forms with the central covered court a solid core surrounded by a shopping mall that loops in the two lower floors.

On the top level an office-typical floor cantilevers outside providing the opportunity for an external gallery enclosed by perfect arches in sandblasted concrete. The four most exposed corners of the building are defined by prominent staircase towers that allow various vertical circulation options.

1. North-east elevation
2. Ground floor plan
3. View of the skylight in the central lobby

SOUQ AL-WATANIYA

ABDULLAH AL-SALEM ST.
(CBD AREA 10)
1974–1979

DESIGNERS • TAC (architect);
PACE (associate architect)
CLIENT • National Real Estate Co.
(NREC)
CONTRACTOR • Unknown

IN USE

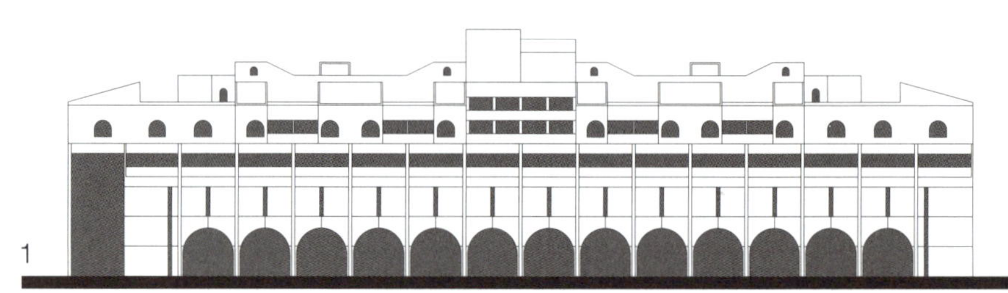

1

2

3

The commission of a complex with a total build area of 67,500 m^2 was first awarded to PACE by NREC together with Souq Al-Watiya. Following the ongoing developments for CBD Areas 5 and 9, TAC was awarded the entire design, pursuing the use of a "self-contained" concrete volume, shaped by arches and small openings, to reactivate the city centre.

From the outside, the building is a compact solid divided into four horizontal bands. Internally the eight floors are divided into a shopping centre on the ground and first floor levels, parking for 1,000 cars in two basements and intermediate levels and courtyard housing on the double roof levels. The high-end duplex apartments with 2 or 3 bedrooms are open to landscaped communal courts with fountains, and covered parking on the same level. These "courtyard houses" on the rooftop echoe the traditional street life of the demolished old town and reveal an interpretation of architectural form, which leads to a recognition of local characteristics.

Today the focus of activity is the shopping area, subdivided into 126 small shops, catering to the low-income expat community, distributed under the arcades and through interior courtyards that were once decorated by plants and fountains lit by skylights. This multifunctional use integral to community needs expanded the urban experience.

1. South elevation
2. Rooftop, outdoor sitting areas
3. View of the south front
4. Interior of one residential unit, 1979
5. Aerial view, showing the residential units
   at the upper level, 1979
6. Rooftop, ambulatory, 1979
7. Plan at the level of the car park
8. Plan at the level of the residential units

4

5

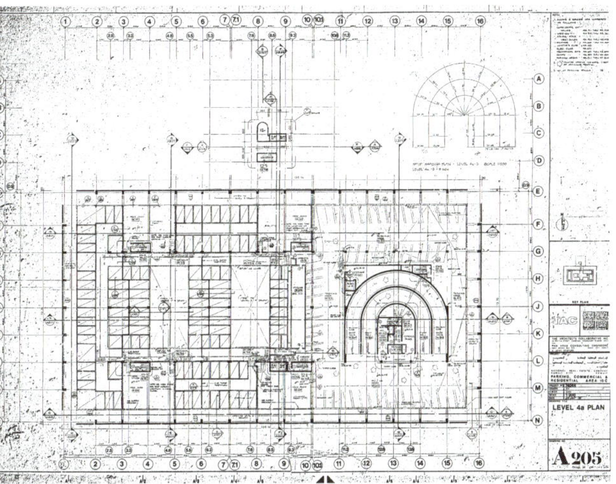

6

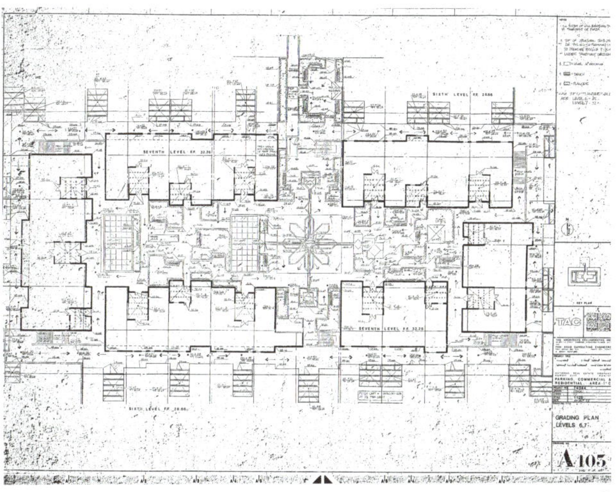

7

8

SOUQ AL-WATIYA

AL-WATIYA
1974–1979

DESIGNERS • TAC (architect); PACE
(associate architect and lead consultant)
DEVELOPER • National Real Estate Co.

UNBUILT

This complex was first commissioned
to PACE and consequently to TAC,
together with Souq Al-Wataniya.
Contrary to the other souq projects,
here the local office had developed
the implementation and all the non-
architectural design. This fact may have
led to the conclusion that the original
design was implemented with some
modifications. However, the known
proposal from TAC and PACE has no
resemblance to any of the elements or
parts actually built later.

In the proposed scheme the arches of
other souqs are not present and the
pre-fabricated concrete units are the
elements defining the building volume
and geometry. The project eventually
undertook similar requirements to
those for Al-Muttaheda and Al-Masseel
souqs, developed by United Real
Estate Company.

The eight-storey complex included
underground parking plus a detached
unit containing six floors above ground
for a total of 1,000 spaces. The commercial area is mainly concentrated in a
two-floor block of adjacent volumes.

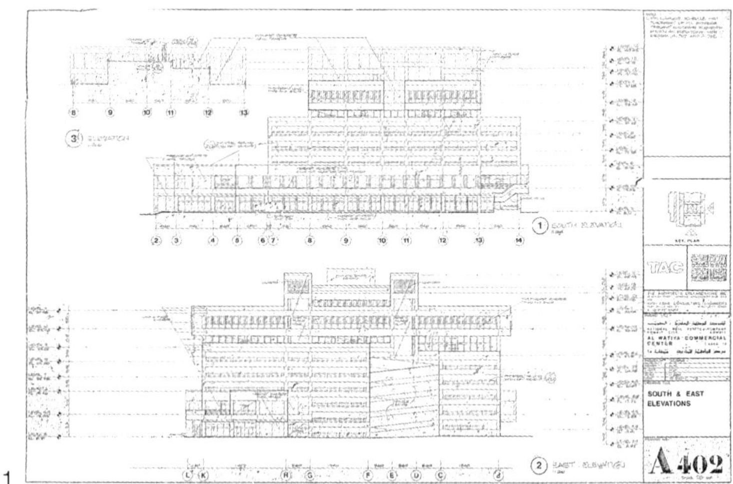

1

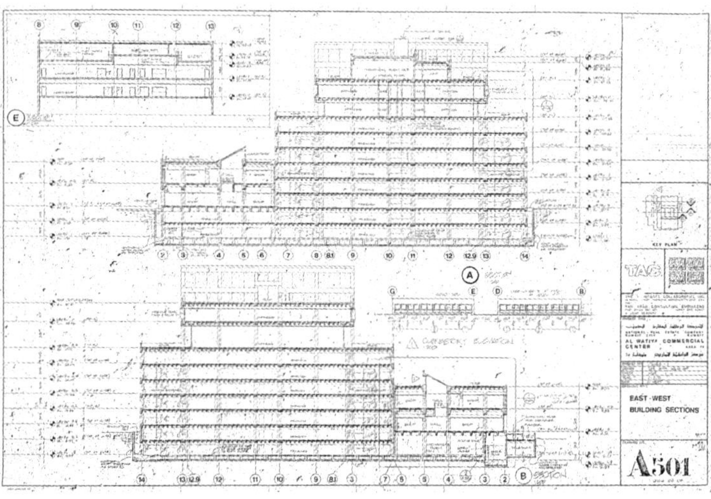

2

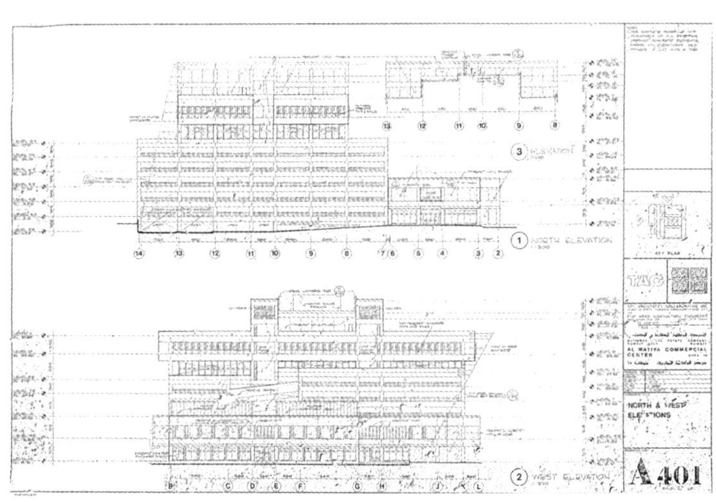

3

1. South and east elevations
2. South-west sections
3. North and west elevations
4. Perspective view in the city context

SOUQ AL-MUTTAHEDA AND AL-MASSEEL

SALHIYA, CBD AREA 10
1973–1979

DESIGNERS • John Bonnington Partnership
(architect); KEO (associated consultant);
Thosti AG of Nuremberg (structure)
CLIENT • United Realty Company
CONTRACTOR • United Prefab Building Co.

IN USE

Two multi-use commercial
developments were commissioned
to John Bonnington Partnership in
association with KEO. The developer
required a completely precast concrete
structural system based on columns
with load-bearing brackets supporting
primary twin lateral beams, which in
turn support T-beam floor panels.[103]
The project was intended to serve as
a laboratory for the establishment of
a new precasting factory for National
Industries.[104]

With 911 parking spaces distributed
along the three intermediate levels, the
Al-Muttaheda Souq is conceived of two
main volumes connected by bridges
in the upper floors where offices are
located.[105] On the ground the gap
between these defines the circulation
allowing the main entrances and the
vertical connection in the central hall
between ground and mezzanine retail
areas.

The precast façade components
create repetitive façade frames, which
emphasise the effects of sunlight and
recessed shadow, more evident when
applied as protective elements for the
upper office floor.

1

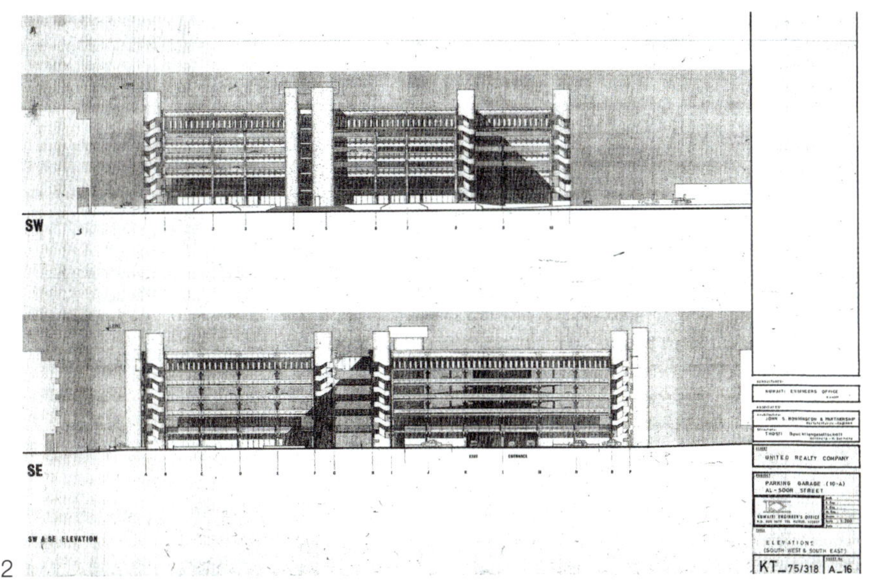

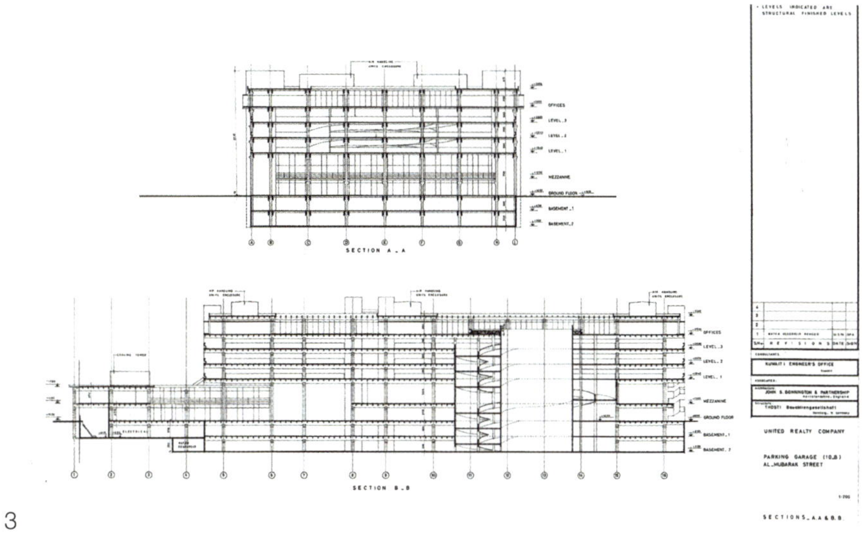

SOUQ AL-MASSEEL:

1. Elevations and internal view
2. Souq Al-Muttaheda, south-west and
south-east elevations
3. Souq Al-Muttaheda, sections
4. Detail of the construction system
5. Sketch by the designer

KBE
Kuwait Bahrain International Exchange

6

7

9

8

البحرينية للصيرفة الدولية
Kuwait Bahrain Internation
KBE

SOUQ AL-MUTTAHEDA:

6. General view
7. Car park floors
8. Roof level, distribution spaces
9. Detail of the parking ramp
10. South-west elevation

HOSPITALS: MUBARAK AL-KABEER, AL-ADAN, AL-JAHRA

JABRIYA, HADIYA, JAHRA
1972–1985

DESIGNERS • AART/ATEA (Leon Forgia, principal); Uniconsult (design competition entry)
CLIENT • Ministry of Public Works
CONTRACTOR • Perini Corporation (Al-Adan), Inter G (Mubarak Al-Kabeer), Atelier Construction Schwartz Hautmont (Farwaniya and Al-Jahra)

MODIFIED / UNDER DEMOLITION

Following the expansion of the city in the 1970s, towards the west and south, a number of hospitals were constructed in proximity to the new neighbourhood units. To optimise the process and meet the time constrains, the design and the construction elements were contracted to a large joint venture of international specialists and companies specialised in medical facilities. The concept was to have an autonomous healthcare facility with dental and outpatient clinic, nurses' dormitories with recreation and dining spaces and a mosque. The result was replicated in several cases around the country for more than a decade. The layout varied accordingly to the plot size or the necessity of a particular medical unit, but most of the prefabricated concrete elements that compose the volumes were recurrent.

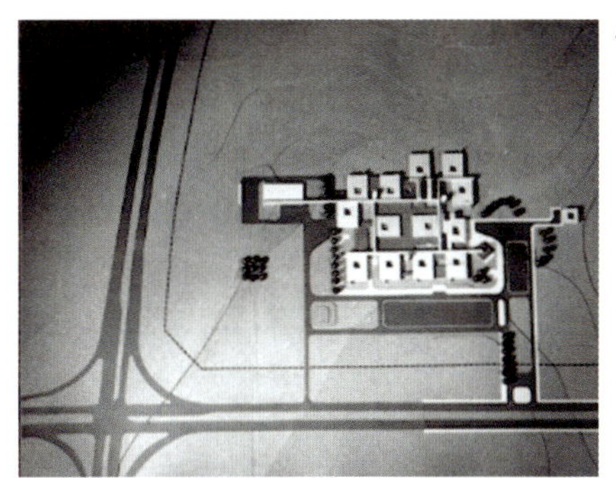

1. Mubarak Al-Kabeer Hospital,
main building, front view
2. Concept for Farwaniya Hospital,
scale model, close-up
3. Scale model, aerial view
4. Scale model, top view
5. Mubarak Al-Kabeer, west elevation
6. Mubarak Al-Kabeer, nurses' dormitories

KUWAIT FUND FOR ARAB ECONOMIC DEVELOPMENT

MIRQAB
1968–1973, 1975–1978

DESIGNERS • TAC (architect and lead consultant), PACE (associate architect)
CLIENT • KFAED
CONTRACTOR • Al-Othman Contracting Co.; Mohammed Abdulmohsen Al-Kharafi & Sons

IN USE

Since its inception in 1961, KFAED's mission was to support other Arab countries in developing their economies and social welfare programmes, anticipating the 1970 UN resolution in favour of underdeveloped states. In 1974 the help was extended beyond the Arab world and, in the same year, the project for the new head office was laid down. It was one of the earliest collaborations between TAC and PACE. It was built on a strategic corner plot, siding Mubarak Al-Kabeer Street and facing key public buildings. It was developed in two phases. The first construction is a rectangular, compact, three-storey-high building on a raised platform. The masses are fragmented in the shape of an inverted ziggurat: sharp lines and small apertures define monotone rhythms in the façades.[106] The outdoor appearance, muted and austere despite its dimensions, is contradicted by the openness of the interior space, which flows fluidly around the central courtyard. A central atrium, which accommodates fountains and flower beds is dramatically emphasised by the indirect light coming from the skylight.

The intentionally quiet horizontality of this volume is challenged by the vertical stretch of the addition, erected few years later. It is a tall massive tower of 18 floors. With the exclusion of the entrance at the bottom and the mechanical floor at the top, the building is a stack of office plans delimited by the two vertical distribution cores at both sides. The most characteristic architectural features are the deep, splayed jambs of the windows, meant to filter the light.

Both projects reflect on the climatic influences on the architectural forms. The major design tool in this regard is the Kuwaiti sun: its intensity, its angle and the strong, dark, shadows generated by it, emphasise the forms and the expression of materials, which are mostly limestone and beige-pigmented sandblasted concrete. The latter was probably used here for the first time in the country.

The two buildings are perfectly aligned, beside each other, facing the main street and the city centre. They share colours, materials and intentions but their substantial difference in size destabilises the composition. Nonetheless they sit on a common platform, a sort of piazza, initially conceived of a vast public area in contrast to the dense city fabric of the souq areas.

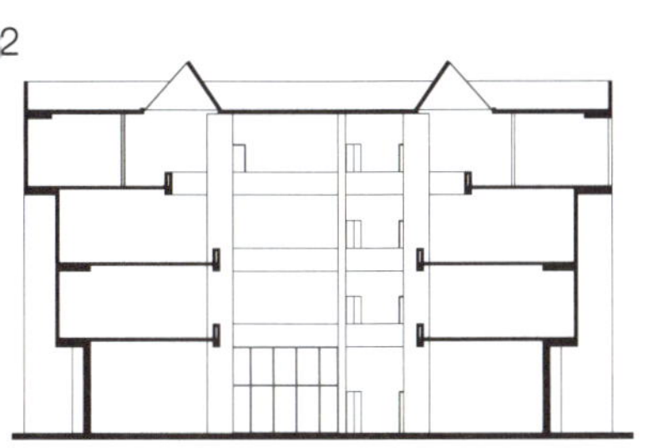

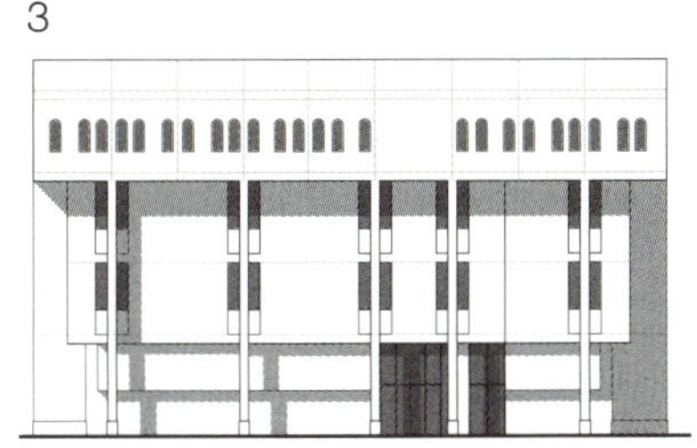

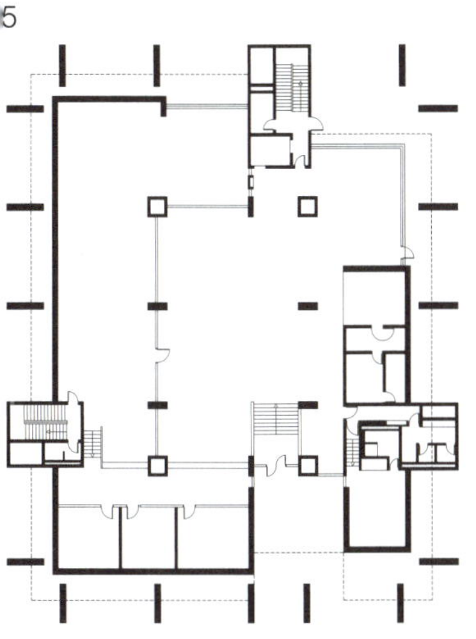

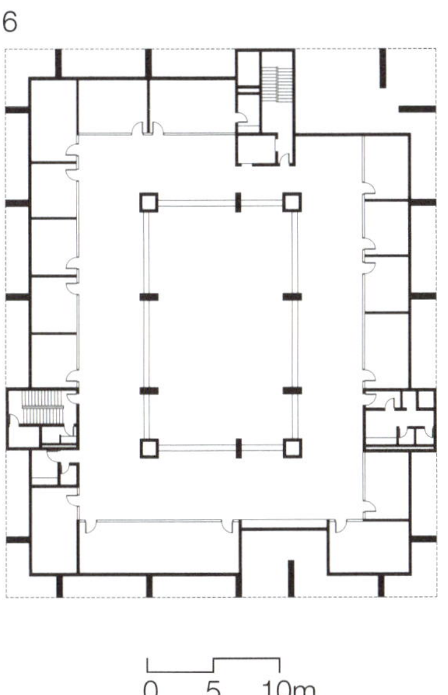

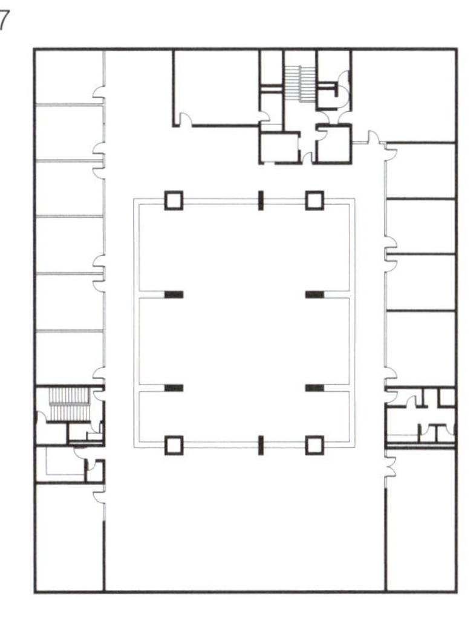

1. General view, undated
2. Section through the main hall
3. South elevation
4. East elevation
5. Ground floor plan
6. Third and fourth floor plan
7. Top floor plan

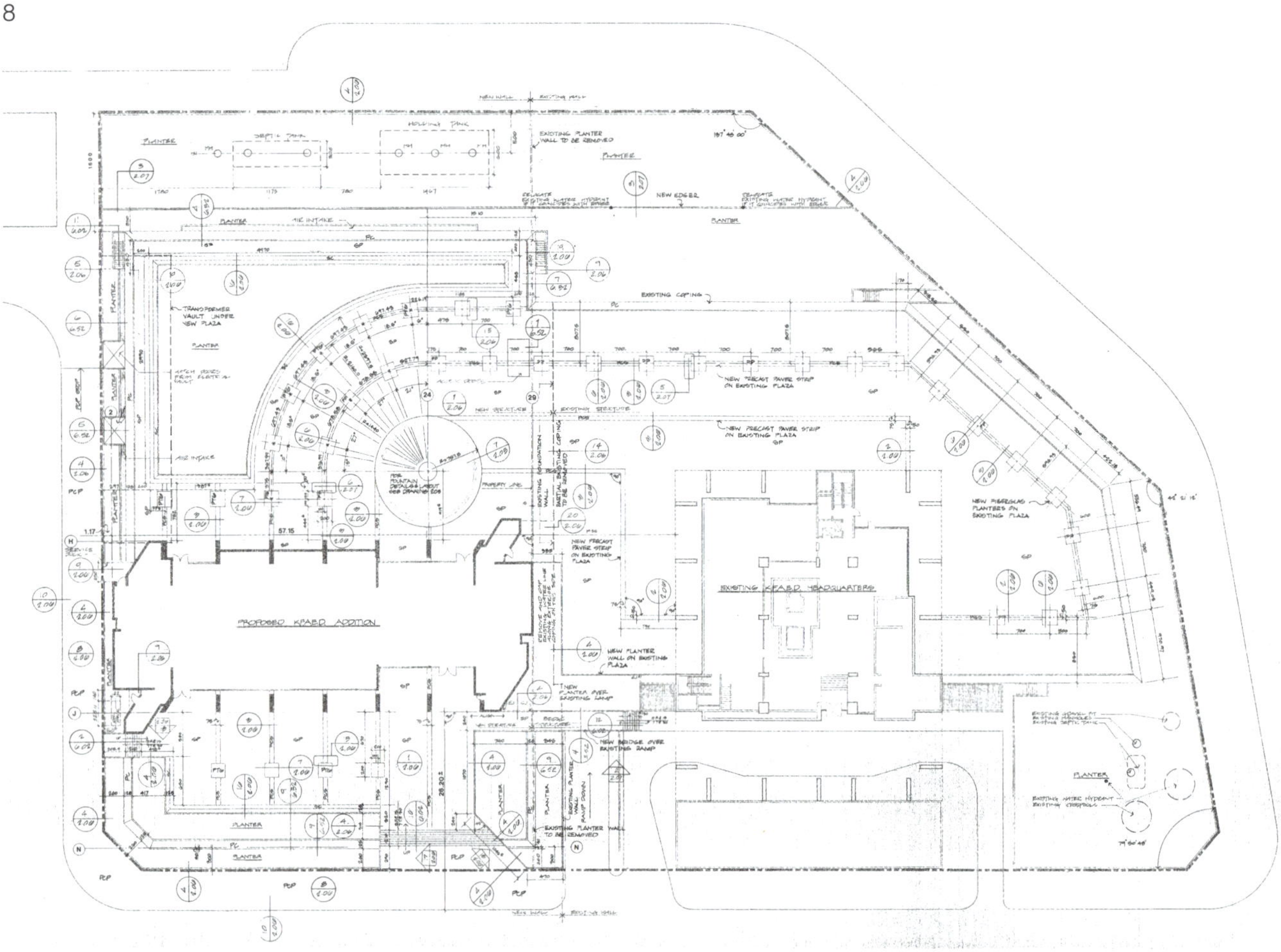

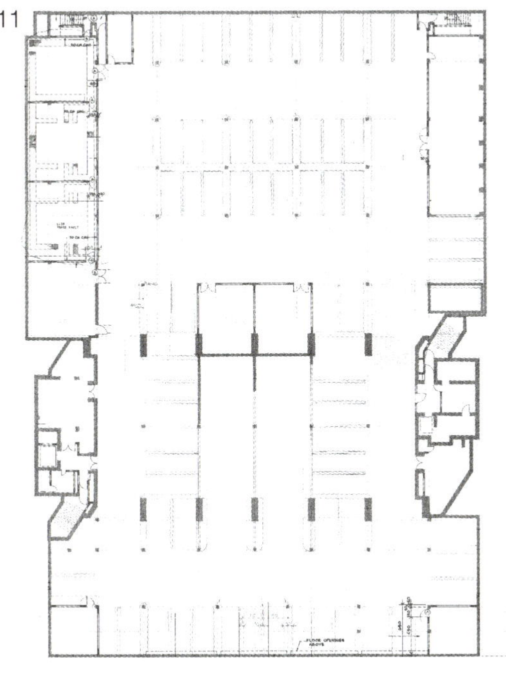

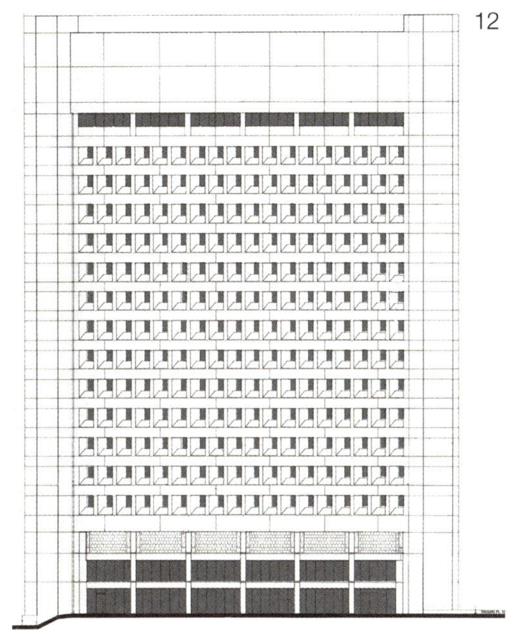

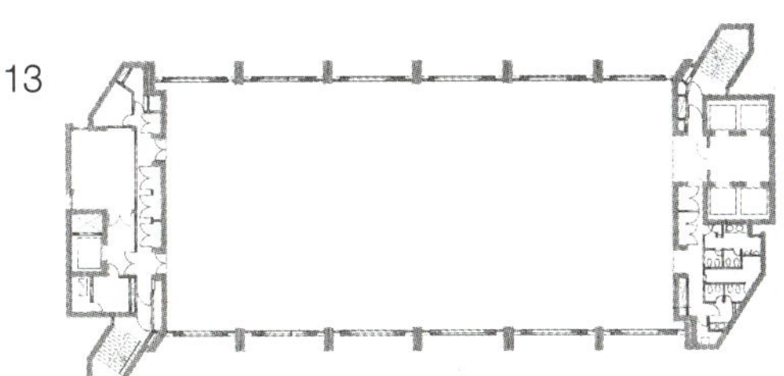

8. Layout plan showing the relation of the two buildings, 1975
9. Aerial view, undated
10. Detail of the façade
11. Tower building, basement, 1975
12. Tower building, elevation, 1975
13. Tower building, typical floor, 1975
14. Tower building, internal view, 1975
15. Scale model, 1975

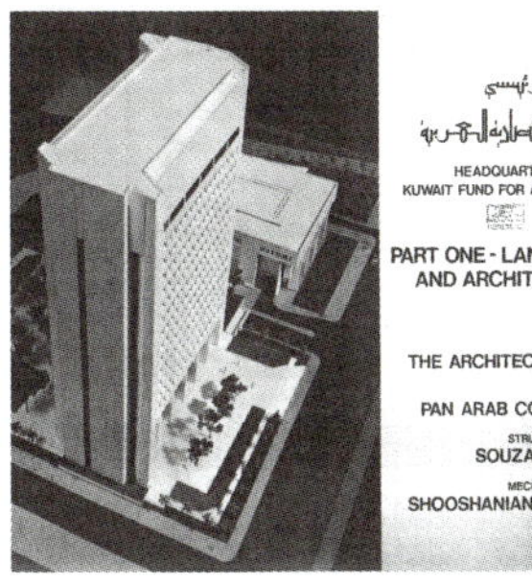

NUGRA COMMERCIAL AND RESIDENTIAL COMPLEX

HAWALLY
1975–1986, 1980–1987

DESIGNER • PACE
CLIENT • Sheikh Jaber Al-Ali Al-Sabah
CONTRACTOR • Arab Centre for Commerce & Real Estate; The Arabian Contracting Co.

IN USE

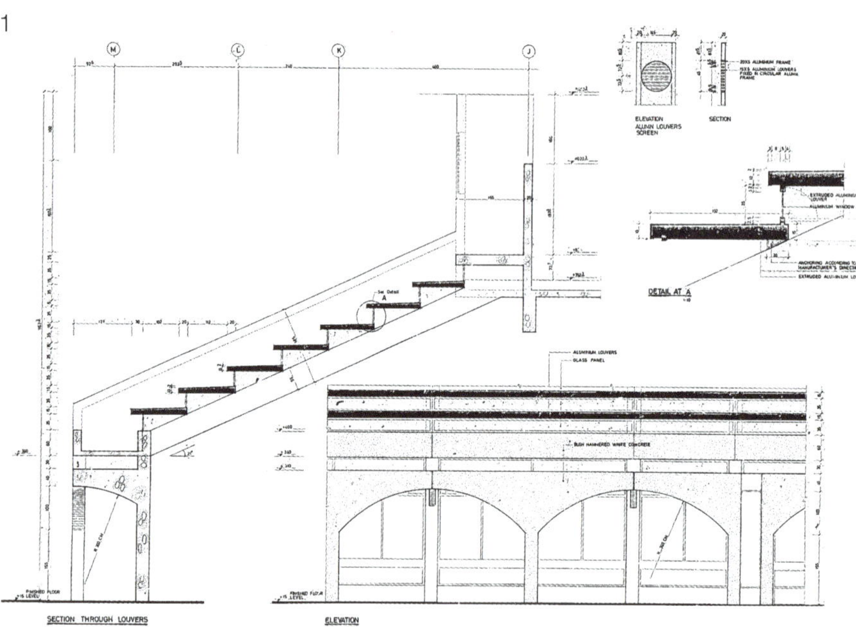

This complex was an opportunity to develop a whole area of the city during the late 1970s assuming the model of residential plus retail on the verge of market speculation. As with other similar complexes in the city (Al-Muthanna and Al-Rehab Complexes), Nugra promised not only housing and high living standards, but also a new lifestyle with all the aesthetic references of a 'futuristic' living.

Built in different stages the scheme can be understood from the air-conditioned pedestrian bridge that connects the commercial southern complex to the mixed-use complex north. The north complex is arranged on an elevated podium above two underground parking floors, a terraced three-storey shopping mall and three blocks (A, B and C). The blocks (A & B) were developed into ten-storey residential towers comprising 180 apartments augmented by a swimming pool and a children's play area in the mezzanine. Block C is devoted to offices distributed over five floors. All these elements are detached allowing airflow and providing access to services and vehicle loading.

The southern element includes an extra mall area with a commercial basement plus two floors and a single office floor above, connected to the street by detached vertical cores.

1. Detail section of the commercial hall, phase I
2. Scale model of phase II
3. View of the connection bridge over Beirut Street, the commercial gallery (phase I) and the residential towers (phase II)
4. View of the commercial gallery (phase I), after completion
5. Interior of the commercial gallery, after completion

4

5

6. Access tower of the commercial complex (phase III)
7. Air-conditioned pedestrian bridge
8. South elevation of the tower (phase III)
9. Commercial complex hall
10. Residential towers, external lobby (phase II)

DASMAN COMPLEX

SHARQ
1975–1979

DESIGNER • KEO with Ghazi Sultan
CLIENT • National Real Estate Co.
CONTRACTOR • Unknown

IN USE

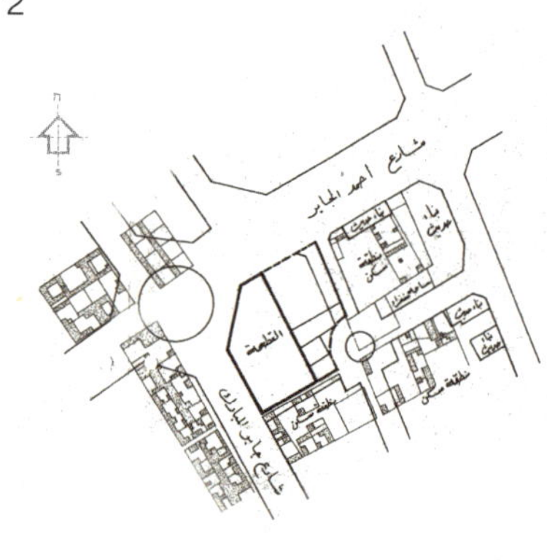

The much competed for site, facing the former Dana Roundabout encompasses a 13-storey building that includes a basement (parking), ground floor, mezzanine, and 10 levels of open-plan office space. The building section is defined by the regulatory capacity enforced before the first revision of the Second Master Plan in 1977.

The L-shaped footprint opens a fountain square lowered from the street level and provides the primary access to the office floors through two solid lift cores clad in white travertine at the base and plain sandstone above. The shopping gallery has main accesses at each end raised from the street and entered via a processional staircase extracted from the sandstone façade. In this way the three commercial floors were provided with different contexts, typologies and accesses. The commercial section is punctuated by large windows, open to the square that promotes multilevel interaction.

The solid façades are only interrupted by the white travertine clad elements on the base of lift cores and the exposed concrete staircases to the back. Along the façade these are the only exceptions in a regular composition where the exposed *béton brut* of these stairs project outside, in front of the white travertine strips cladding the columns and confining the external wall cladding in brown sandstone.

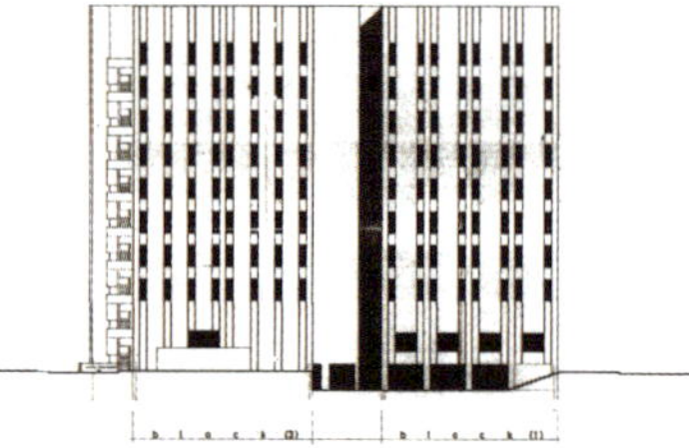

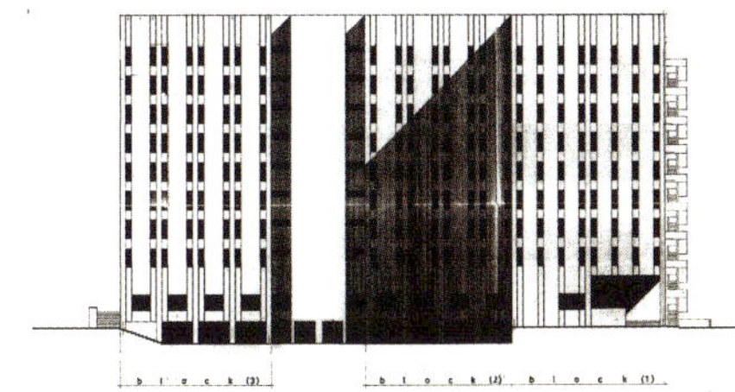

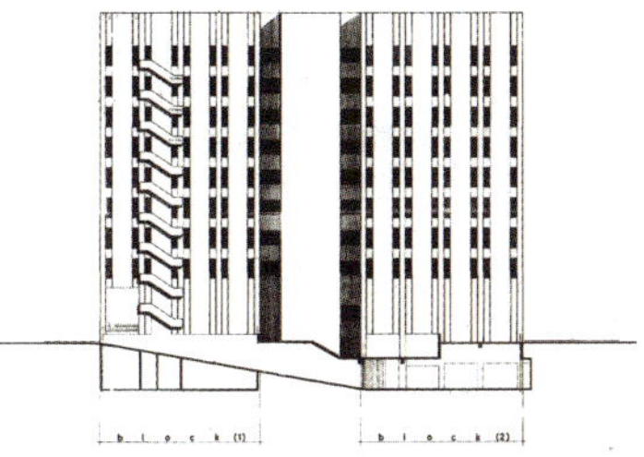

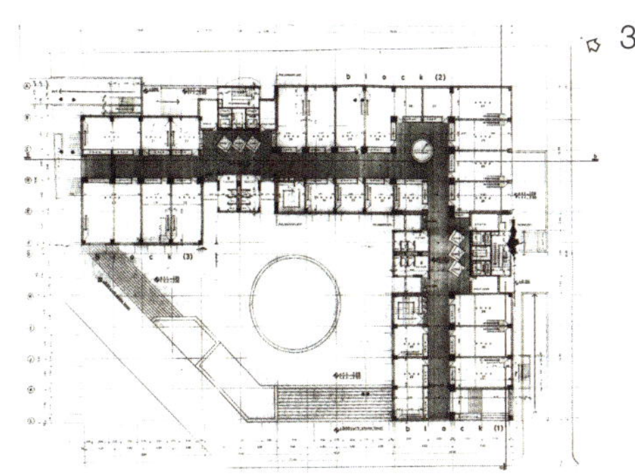

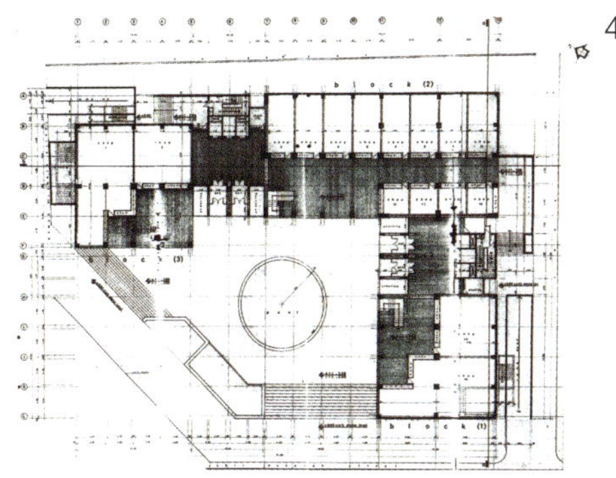

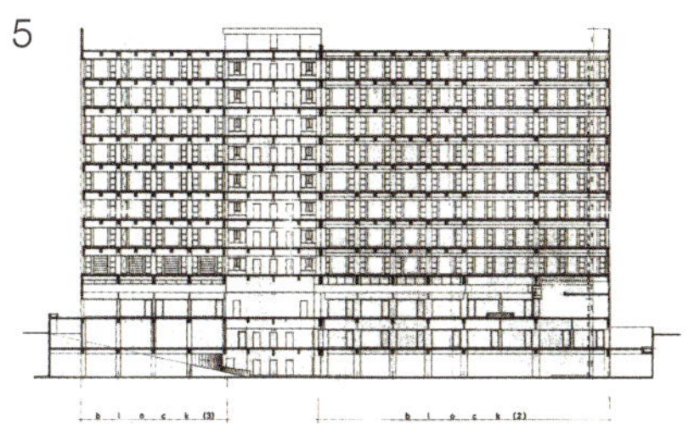

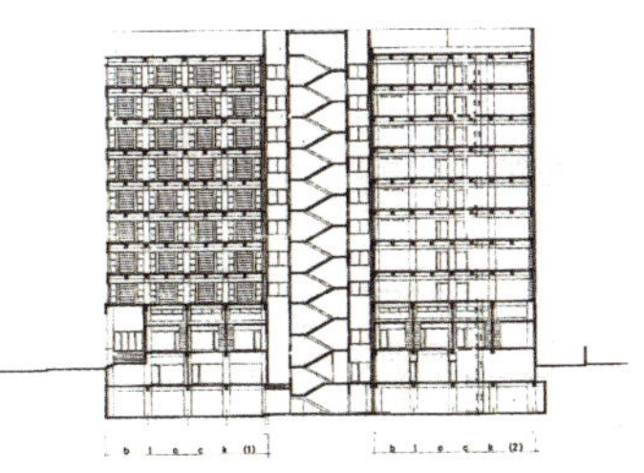

1. Elevations: north-east, north-west, south-west and south-east
2. Site plan, with the pre-existing urban fabric
3. Ground floor plan
4. Mezzanine floor plan
5. Sections

BANKING STUDIES INSTITUTE

MIRQAB (CBD AREA 10)
1976–1979

DESIGNER • TEST (Maath Al-Alousi, principal)
CLIENT • Kuwait Banking Studies Centre
CONTRACTOR • Unknown

MODIFIED

1

This office tower with ten floors occupies a site on the east side of Souq Al-Wataniya, in Area 10 of the Central Business District.

The enclosed and solid façade is accurately "punched" through with arched windows, into the double layer walls, emphasising the visual weight of the building.

Both street façades are similar in the exterior wall material and in the division of wall surfaces into bays divided by vertical piers running the height of the building, except for the last floor with horizontal openings and at ground level, where large apertures allow access to main entry points. Located in the building's centreline with double high vertical openings, the entrances reveal an inner transparent glass skin opposite the outer solid shell.

Following the programme of a professional training centre for bank staff, the typical plan was conceived to allow flexibility in placing the core of stairs, lifts and services in the middle and leaving the remaining area as an open space.

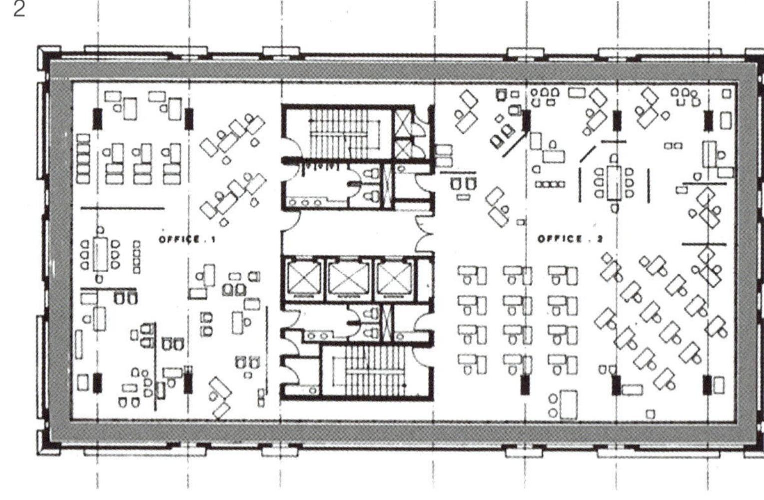

2

1. Perspective view, circa 1976
2. Typical floor plan

JOINT BANKING CENTRE

MUBARAKIYA
1976–1983

DESIGNERS • Skidmore, Owings & Merrill (principal, Roger Radford); PACE (associate architect); Weilinger Associates (structure); Jaros Baum & Bolles (services); Michael McCarthy (SOM interior design)
COMPETITION ENTRIES • Kenzo Tange, Philip Johnson, TAC (PACE) and SOM (PACE)
CLIENT • Industrial Bank of Kuwait; Bank of Kuwait and the Middle East; Kuwait Real Estate Bank
CONTRACTOR • Hang Yang Construction Co.

IN USE

I.M. Pei and Paul Rudolph were the competition jury for the design of the three banks head office buildings on one single plot. The winning entry by SOM, under Gordon Bunshaft's lead, disposed three equal towers of 18 storeys staggered but precisely placed with the glazed curtain facing north (the sea) and the solid vertical circulation exposed to south. With a relatively reduced floor plan in area, the towers are grounded in a geometrically designed green square through a canopy – the banking hall. This urban piece covers the garage and distributes pedestrian and vehicular hierarchies considering different speeds and functions through a system of tree planters and steps. The precast T-slabs provide free floor plans in the offices and when exposed outside subdivide the glass curtain. The complex was internationally acclaimed as the "first world class" office towers in Kuwait with "high interest."[107] Johnson proposed three shapes in different metals: round, triangle and square.

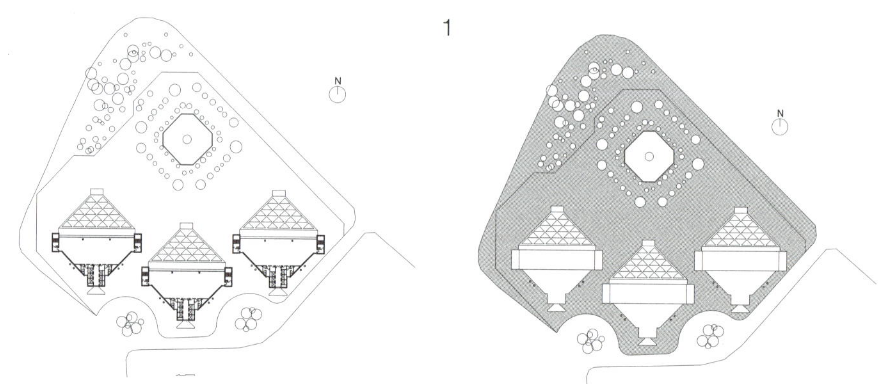

2

3

4

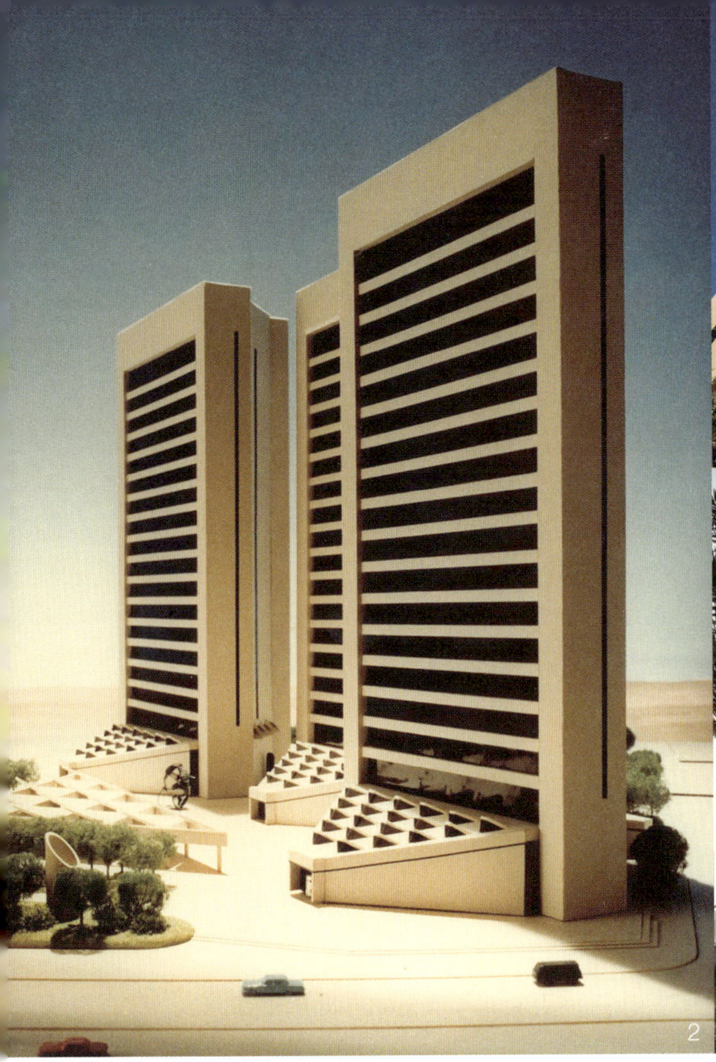

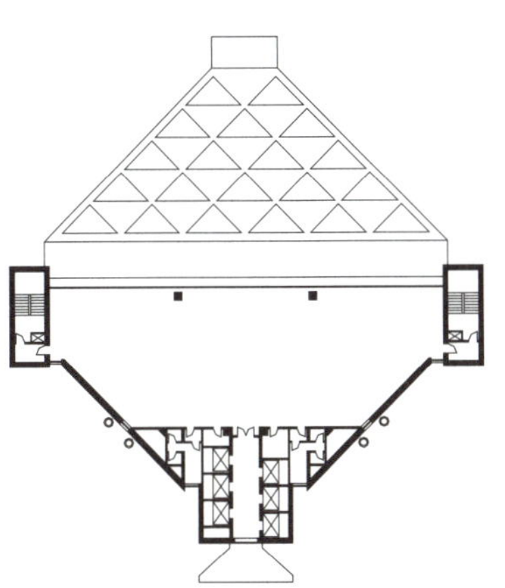

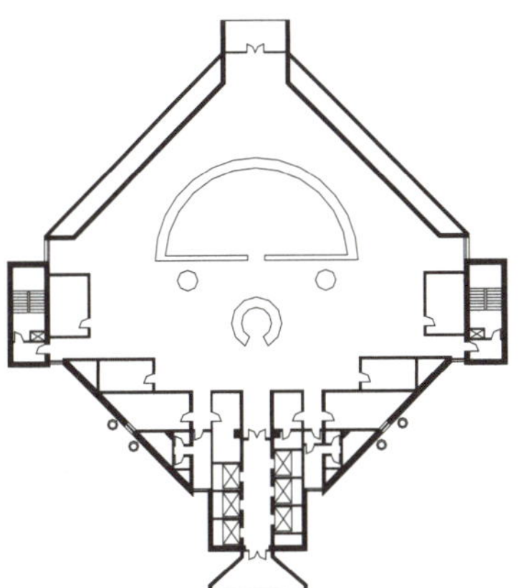

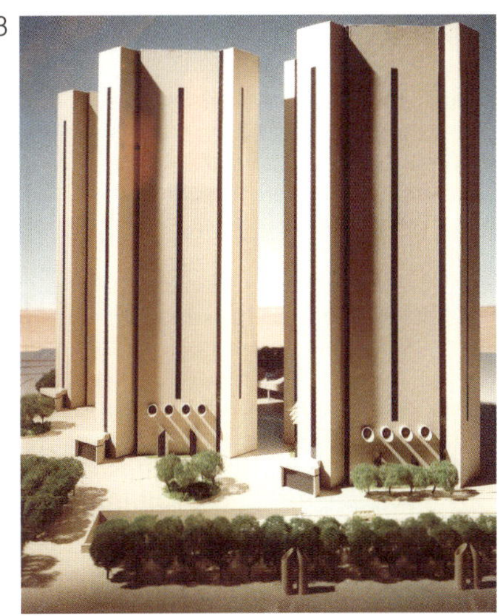

1. Site plan
2. Scale model, side view
3. Scale model, rear elevation
4. Typical floor and ground floor plan

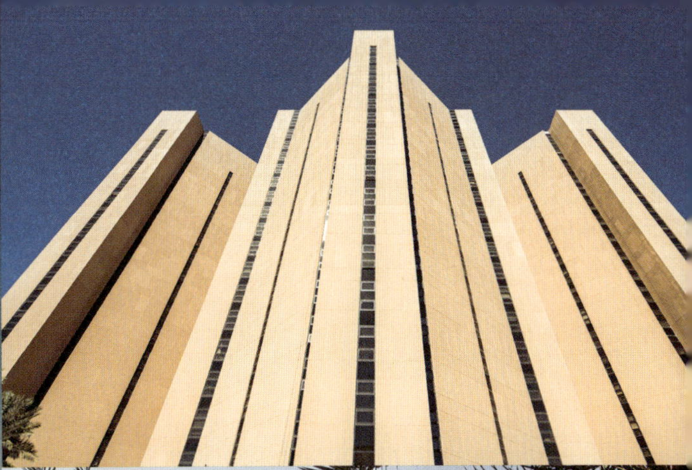

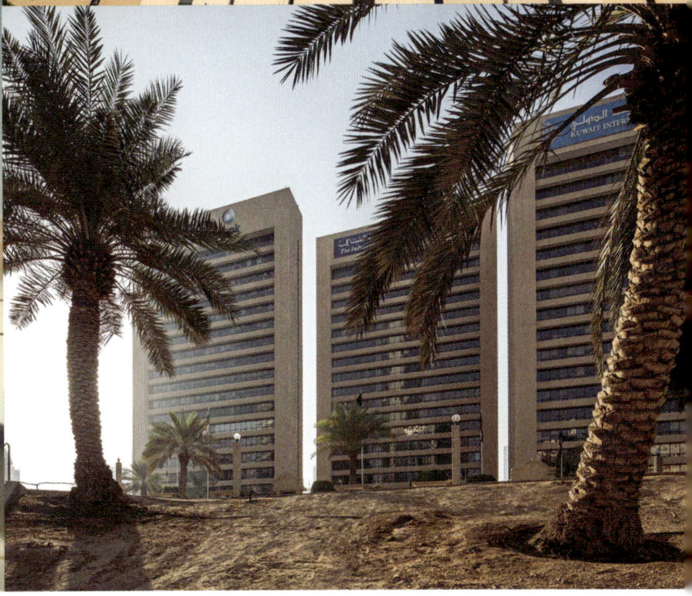

KUWAIT LAW COURTS

JIBLA
1976–1983

DESIGNERS • The Sir Basil Spence
International Partnership (architect);
The Fitzroy Robinson Partnership
(associated architect);
White Young Partners (engineers);
Williams Sale Partnership (services);
White Young Partners (engineers)
CLIENT • Ministry of Justice;
Ministry of Public Works
CONTRACTOR • Al-Hani Construction &
Trading Co.

IN USE

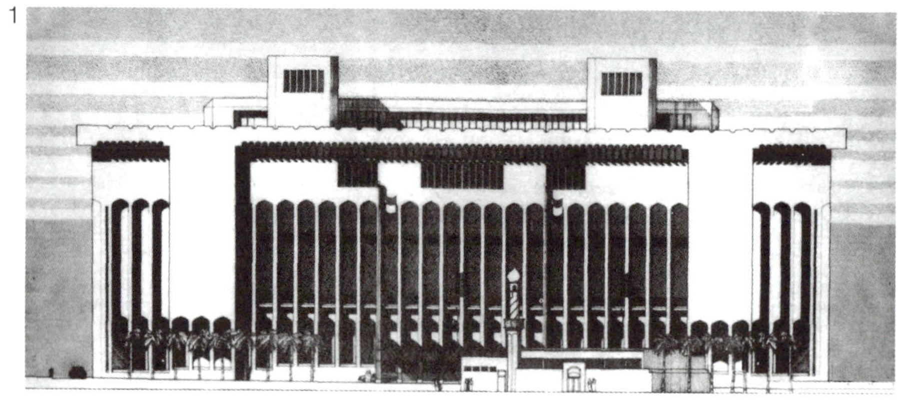

Under the "sunshine and the rule of
law,"[108] ten different façade schemes
were developed after the project was
awarded. A client/designer research
process was entered into, in search
of traditional Islamic architectural
elements, displayed in the referred
article as an architectural lexicon of
large buildings.

Perceived by an international competition the winning proposal was
defined by a nine-floor cubic volume,
surrounded by shaded façade elements
along the perimeter and a central courtyard garden. The peripheral galleries
at the ground connect to a large and
complex system of public lobbies and
waiting areas, including a *diwan* for 320
seats.

The building's 50,000 m² for a total
of 1,500 people features vertical
and horizontal separation of various
functions: 52 courts differentiated by
first instance, cassation and the highest
courts of appeal, plus several offices,
judges' rooms, library and rooms for
lawyers, police and interviews.[109]

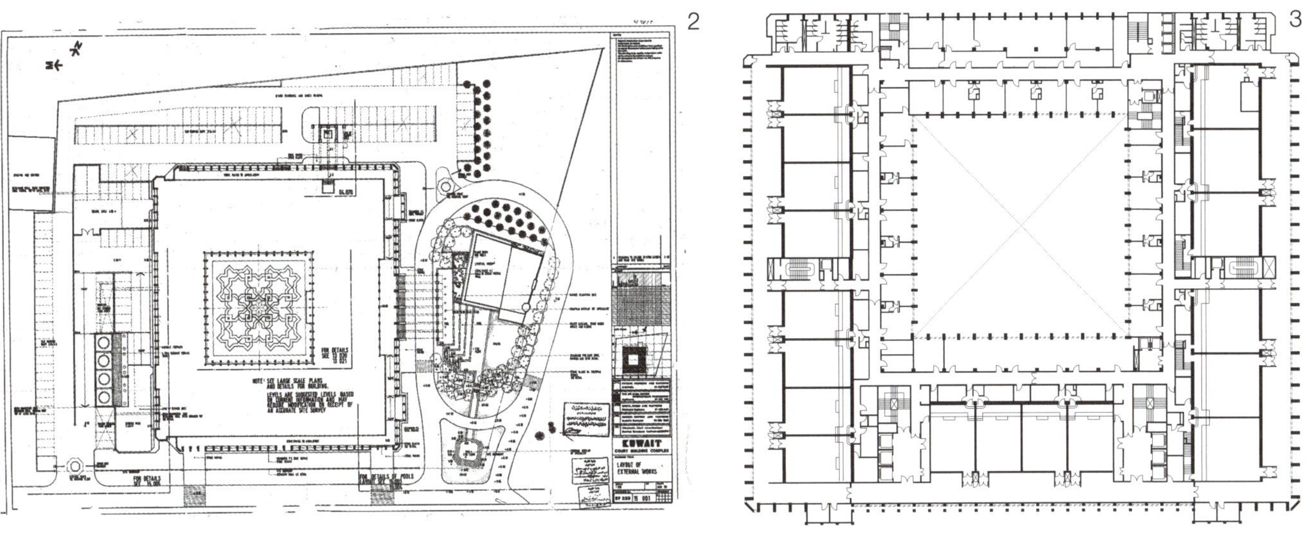

1. North elevation, circa 1976
2. Site plan, with the layout of external works
3. Typical floor plan

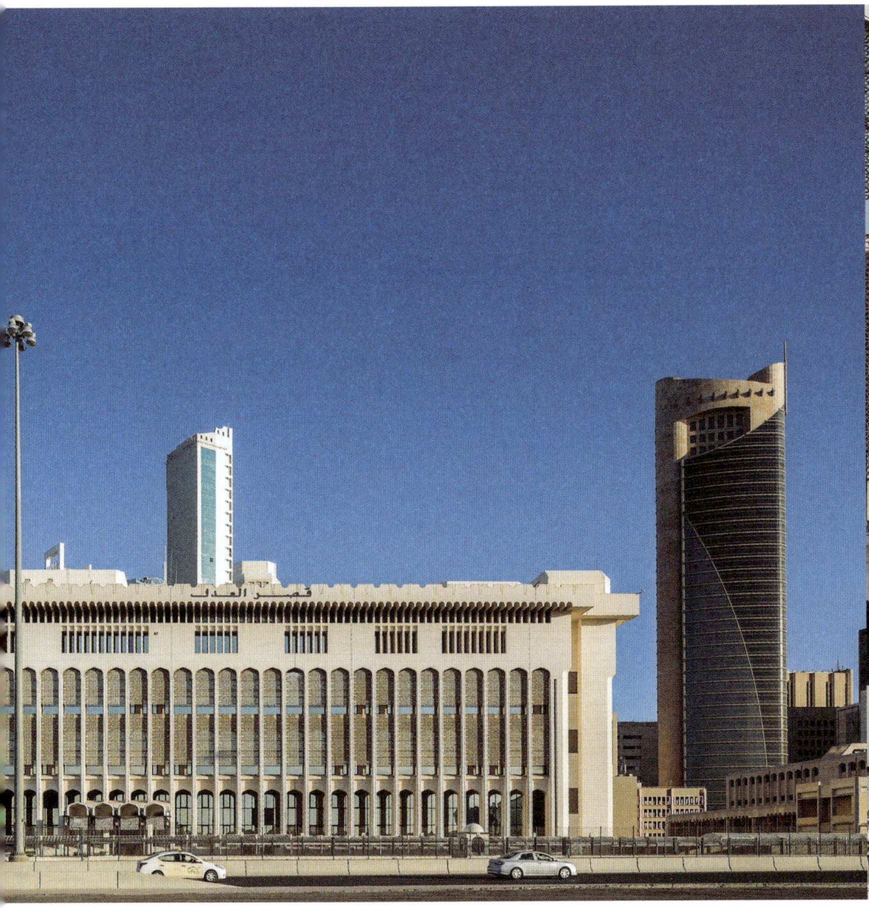

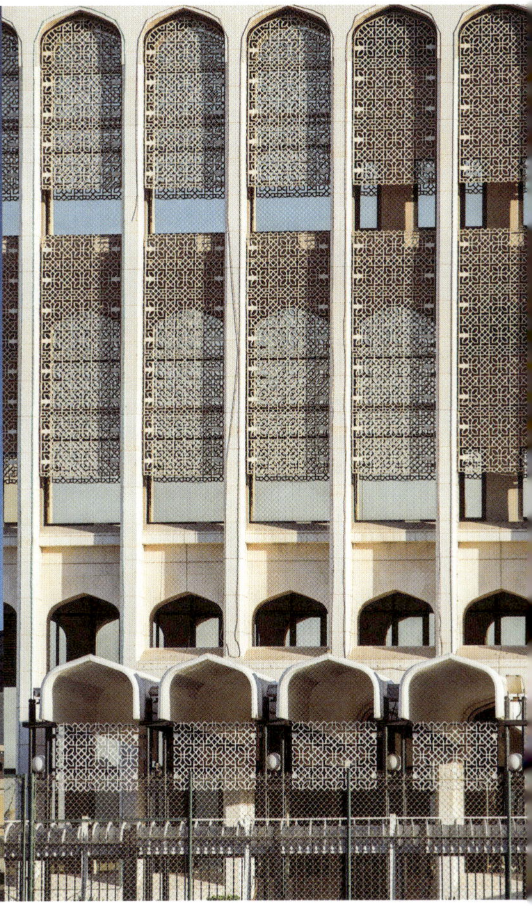

MIDEAST MARKET

MUBARAKIYA (CBD AREA 4)
1976–1978

DESIGNER • Marcel Breuer Associates
CLIENT • Kuwait Municipality

UNBUILT

This new souq, to be implemented in the city's old core in phases, was motivated by the success of the Co-Op supermarkets that were by then diverting traditional shopping patterns from the old Mubarakiya market.

Marcel Breuer, 74 years old by then, retired in 1976, whereupon Marcel Breuer and Associates became Marcel Breuer Associates. Arthur D. Little was asked to address the competitiveness of a fresh produce market in the 1970s with the integration of air conditioning to allow the open display food in a healthy and safe way and designed to sell fish, meat, and vegetables.[110]

In contrast to other projects, programmatically similar, the new approach to the reinvention of the souq was functional and rational. The connection with the past was done through preserving the traditional interaction between consumer and seller. The double high interior in fluid corridors allowed maximum visibility to the customers and gave them the feeling of the street corridor.

1

VEGETABLE MARKET AND MAIN SOUK

1. *Architectural rendering of the Vegetable Market and Main Souq, part of the Mideast Market in Kuwait*
2. *Architectural rendering of the Fish Market, part of the Mideast Market in Kuwait*

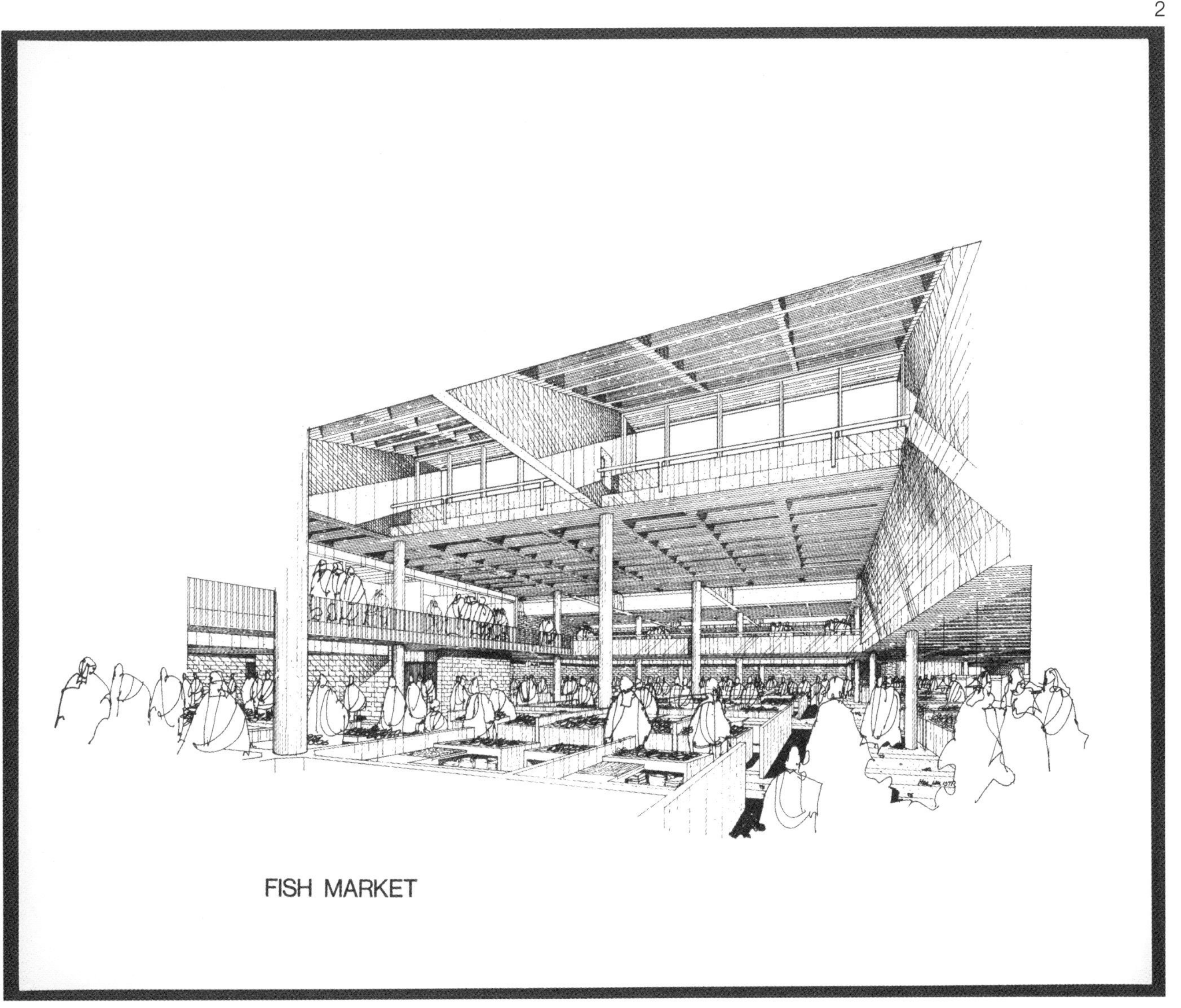

GOLD MARKET

MUBARAKIYA (CBD AREA 4)
1976–1982

DESIGNER • PACE
CLIENT • Kuwait Foreign Trading Contracting & Investment Co.
CONTRACTOR • International Contracting Co. (Ahmadiah Contracting & Trading Co. subsidiary)

IN USE

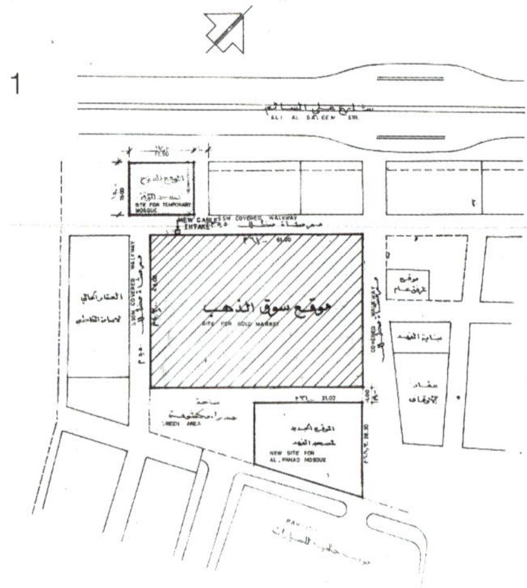

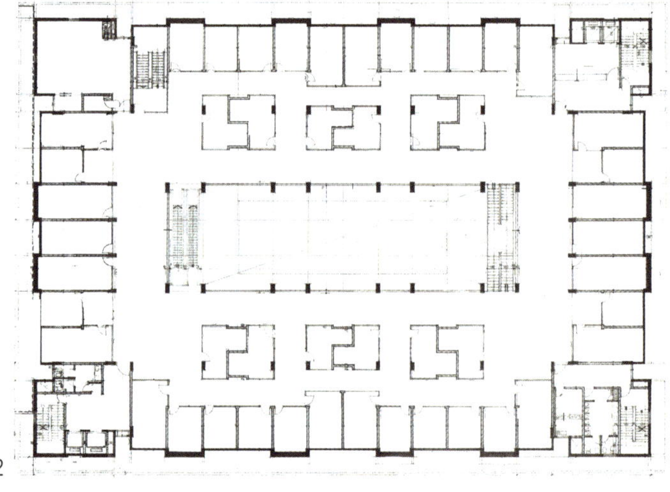

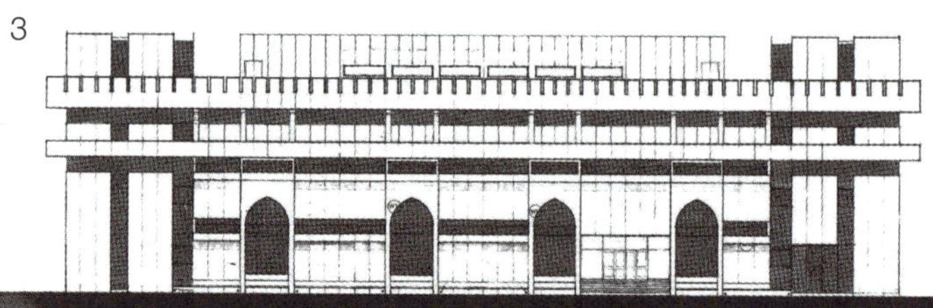

Inserted in the city's old commercial area and facing Mubarakiya School, the new market was developed in conjunction with Al-Fahed Mosque and together they make an urban statement. Both buildings are linked by one point: the crown of the mosque's minaret adjacent to the market façade.

The market is a solid volume of white cement concrete with a bush-hammered finish, and occupies an area of 2,600 m². Elevated from the street level, it uses exterior stairs on all sides to establish a pedestrian relationship with the surrounding urban fabric.

The building façades allude to a fortification with architectural elements recalling battlements at the top, four turrets placed at the angles of the building and the bronze anodised aluminium grid framed by the arches suggests the heavy grating of iron.

The building is 4 storeys high and there is a vault in the basement. Small shops (185 in number) dedicated to jewel manufacturing and gold trading are distributed through three floors open to a central courtyard, naturally illuminated by a skylight. The upper floor is for offices, vaults and laboratories.

1. Site plan, showing the Souq and the Mosque within the urban fabric
2. Typical floor plan
3. South-east elevation
4. Perspective view
5. Sections across the main lobby

4

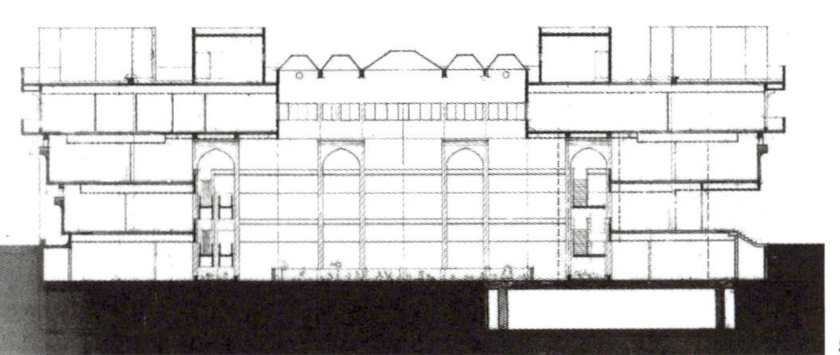

5

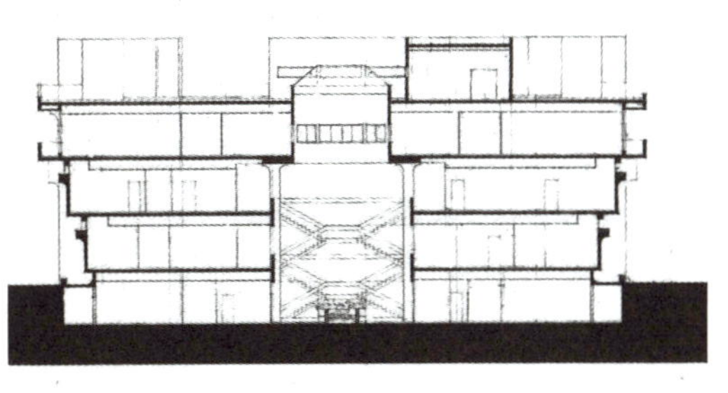

SALHIYA COMMERCIAL PROJECT AND LE MERIDIEN HOTEL

SALHIYA
1975–1980

DESIGNER • Kuwait Engineering Group, Ove Arup & Partners
CLIENT • Salhia Real Estate Co.
CONTRACTOR • Ahmadiah Contracting & Trading Co.

IN USE

Developed in parallel with the Anwar Residential Complex Phase II (1975–76), this project with strong programmatic ambitions was among the first attempts for an high-end package of hotel, shopping mall and offices.

Developed along the full length between the Salhiah area to the west and Al-Muthanna Complex, the linear scheme, approximately 200 m long is wedged between the empty site of Salhiya cemetery and the Fahad Al-Salem Street *backyard*. In the west end, the entrance to the shopping mall is punctuated by five stair and lift doubled cores providing separate access from the underground parking to the three retail floors and offices five storeys above.

From the opposite end a luxury hotel tower clad in anodised aluminium composite panels, fulfilled a promise of unlimited aesthetic facilities. The sixteen-floor dark and opulent volume was originally crowned by a nightclub and swimming pool, covered by a retractable roof.[115]

At KEG the project was conducted by a group of Egyptian architects which during this project's construction period established ASA Consultants, Ahmed Nour (1943–), Seif Heikal (1944–) and Nabil Saleh (1945–).

The hotel is known today as the J.W. Marriot.

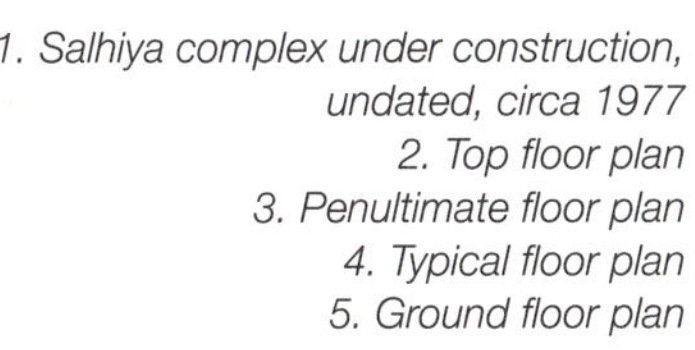

1. Salhiya complex under construction,
   undated, circa 1977
2. Top floor plan
3. Penultimate floor plan
4. Typical floor plan
5. Ground floor plan

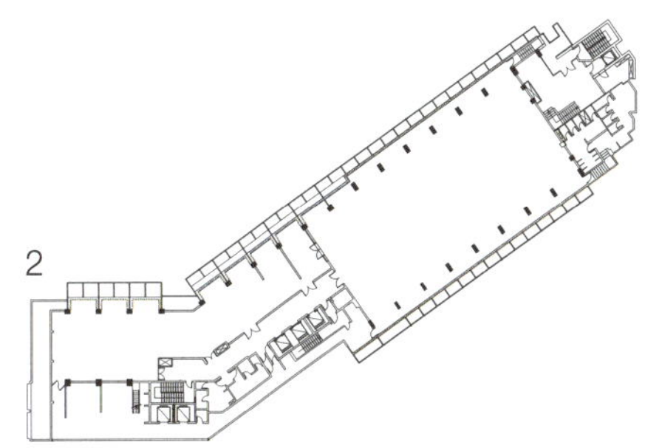

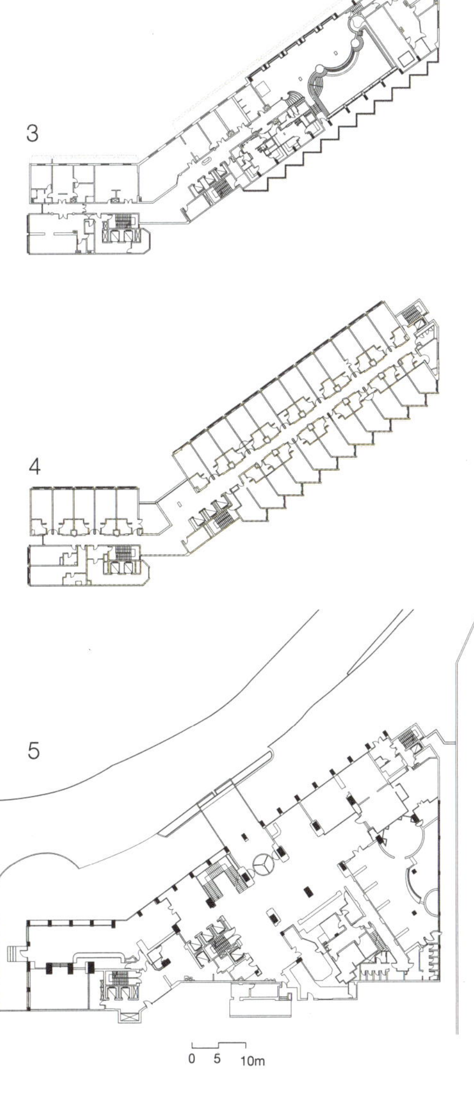

0 5   10m

KUWAIT STATE MOSQUE

ABDULLAH AL-AHMED ST. SIEF
1976–1983

DESIGNERS • Makiya Associates Consultants; Archicentre (local associate)
CLIENT • Ministry of Public Works
CONTRACTOR • United Building Co.

RENOVATED IN 2013

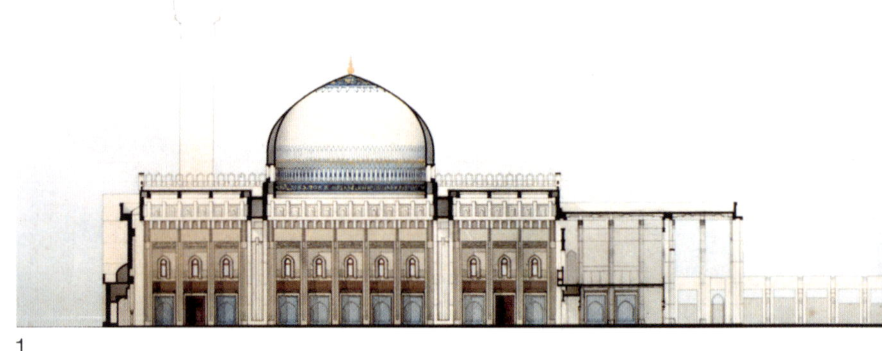

1

Ancient Abbasid tectonic is the basis of the State Mosque project. In Kuwait, Makiya's research of a modern path to local identity,[112] away from the simplistic translation of traditional shapes into decorative elements, results in a solid work, articulated and quietly monumental, which celebrates the Islamic past without overt rhetoric.

The building is in a prime location, across the street from the Amir's office (the Sief Palace). Two major spaces of equal size balance the composition in plan: the *Grand Sahan* (courtyard) and the main prayer hall, covered with a big dome on four massive pillars. The transitional space in between (*Haram*) is a hypostyle hall, which again refers to an early typology of mosques. The northern corner is dedicated to the Amir's entrance and to the ablutions. From the outside, the façade is a repetition of independent modular elements: a series of wall bay units assembled in clear, hierarchical order. Pigmented concrete is the main material, often textured by bush hammering or sandblasting.[113]

The initial concept was not easily realised. Several compromises had to be accepted for technical reasons and ultimately the client was not entirely satisfied with the lack of decoration in the interiors. Consequently the barefaced concrete gave space to a large ornamental mosaic siding.[114]

In the recent years the interiors were renovated with more decorative patterns reinforcing the contrast with the austere outdoor appearance of the building.

2

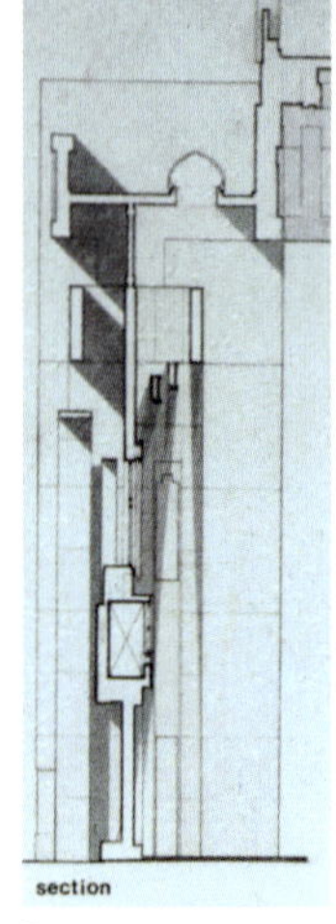

3

4

5

">

1. Sections
2. Detail of the north and south wall bay unit, external elevation
3. Detail of the north and south wall bay unit, section
4. Detail of the north and south wall bay unit, internal elevation
5. View of the prayer hall
6. View of the colonnade
7. Detail of the west elevation
8. Ground floor plan, 1977

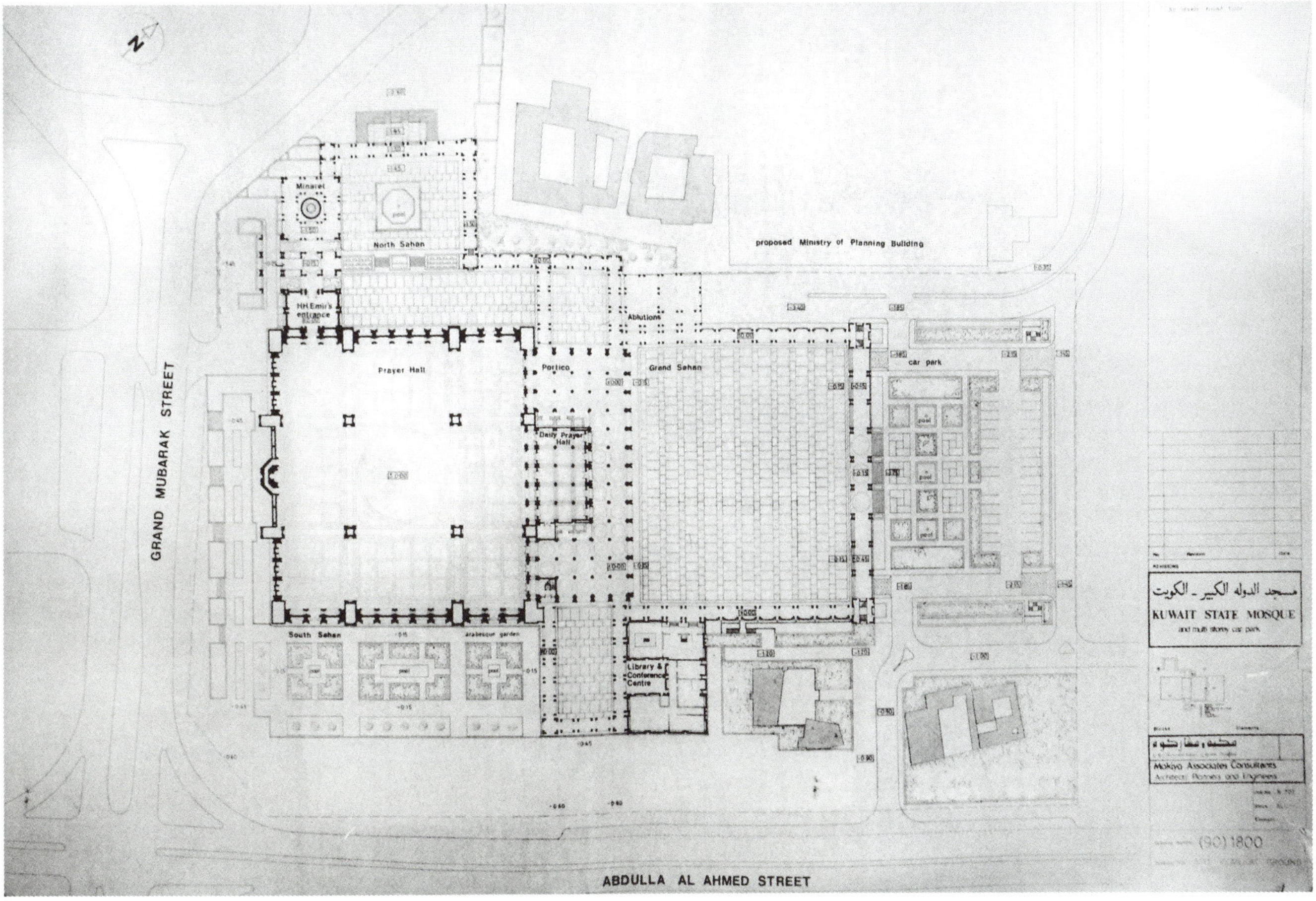

STOCK EXCHANGE

SIEF AREA
ABDULLAH AL-AHMED ST.
1978–1986

DESIGNERS • John S. Bonnington Partnership (architect), KEO (associate architect); Newton Watson (environmental studies)
CLIENT • Ministry of Finance and Economy
CONTRACTOR • Al-Hani Construction & Trading Company

IN USE

1

Middle East Construction magazine called it "the Gulf's first custom-designed stock-market building," a monument to the state's finances, standing in front of the Grand Mosque at the start of the promised, but never yet completed, Abdullah Al-Ahmad Street.[115]

The eight-storey massive volume of the building is clad in granite, grounded by a three-floor podium containing the large open stock market. A free triple height atrium covered by a water garden courtyard and bounded by an L-shaped bank of offices provides space for the remaining functions.

The offices' curtain façade in the intermediate floors overlook this internal garden protected from exposure to the sun. The last two floors designated for executive and principal rooms cover the complete site with a central shading parasol at roof level.

The scheme is inscribed in a 15 x 15 m grid for a total built area of 34,000 m^2 that sits on top of the underground parking.

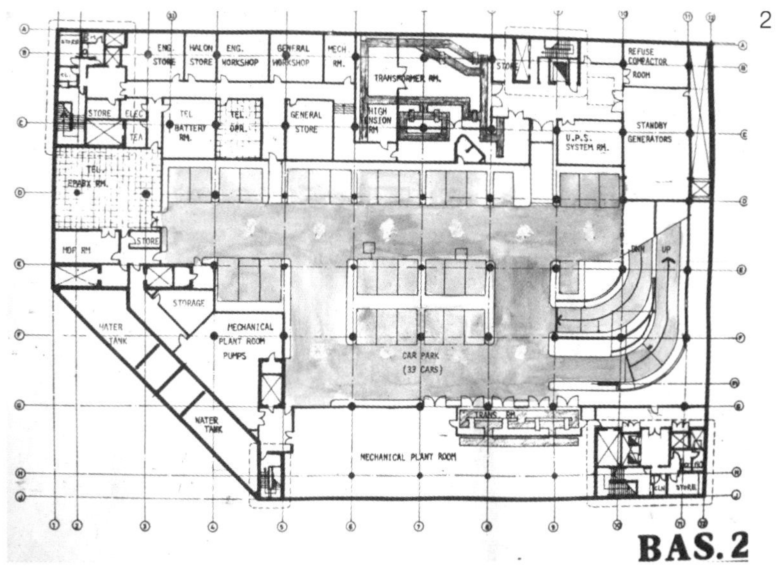

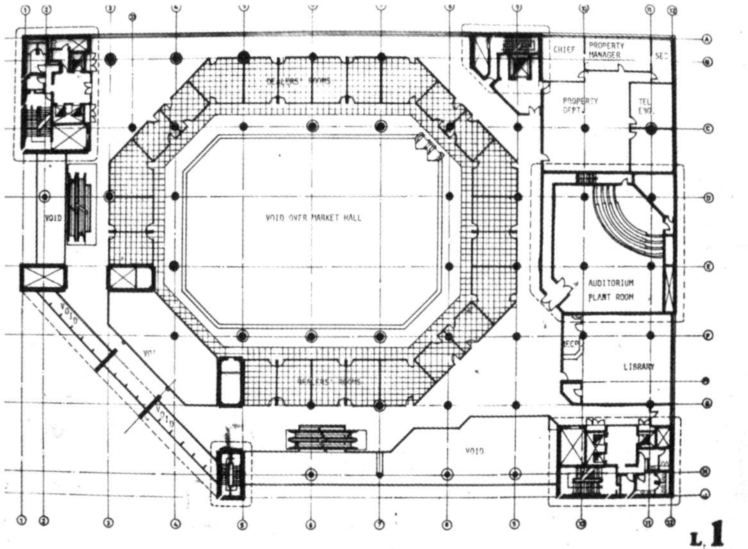

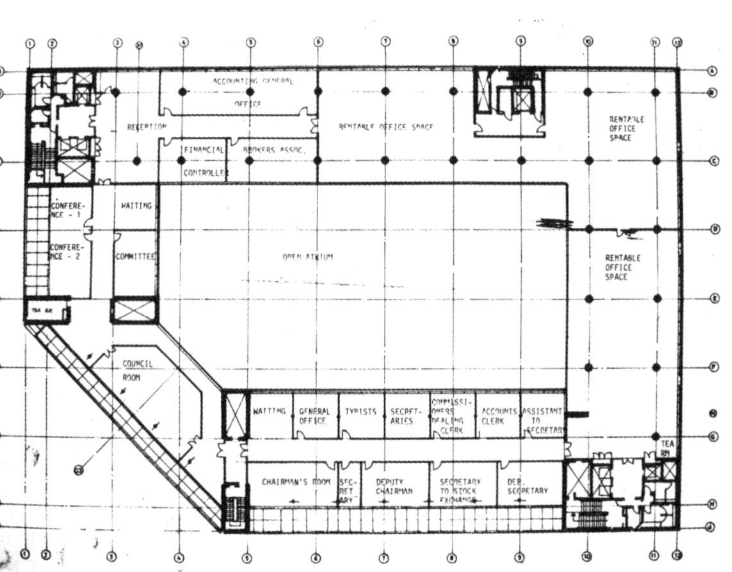

1. Perspective view of the main hall
2. Plan of the basement
3. Plan at level 1
3. Typical office floor plan
5. Scale model, view of the north-east and north-west elevations

IRANIAN EMBASSY

DAIYA DIPLOMATIC NEIGHBOURHOOD
1977–1979

DESIGNERS • Michael Carapetian Associates (architect); Charles T. Haddad and Associates (local associate); Julian Blades (architecture associate); Sam Jampel & Partners (structure); Max Fordham & Partners (services)
CLIENT • Iranian Ministry of Foreign Affairs

UNBUILT

When it was ready for construction the Iranian Islamic Revolution interrupted the works. The building was finally built but the first design proposal was never fully implemented, with the exception to the volumetric scheme and the monumental colonnaded *iwan*.

Michael Carapetian, also known as a photographer, developed the competition entry with the architect and critic Roger Connah. In the following year, with an office already established in Tehran and London, the design was awarded to them.[116]

Despite site constraints and considering the tight geometry, the dependency of one single entrance and the maximum height restriction, the competition entry slices the volume in vertically fluid sections punctuated with the double-T in V-beams for light penetration similar to those of Reima Pietilä's proposal for the "Urban Form Study of the Old City" (1969).

264

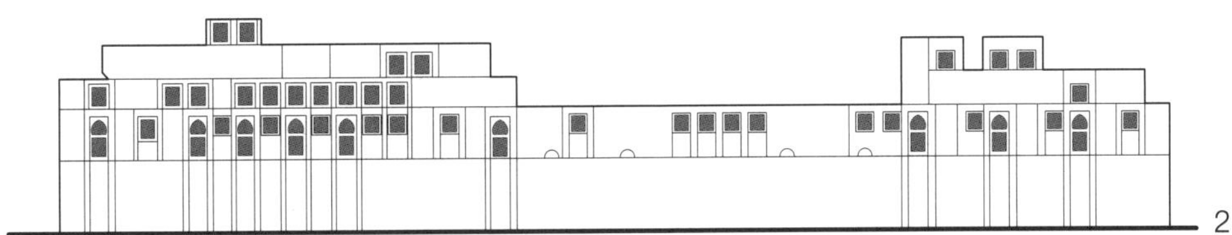

2

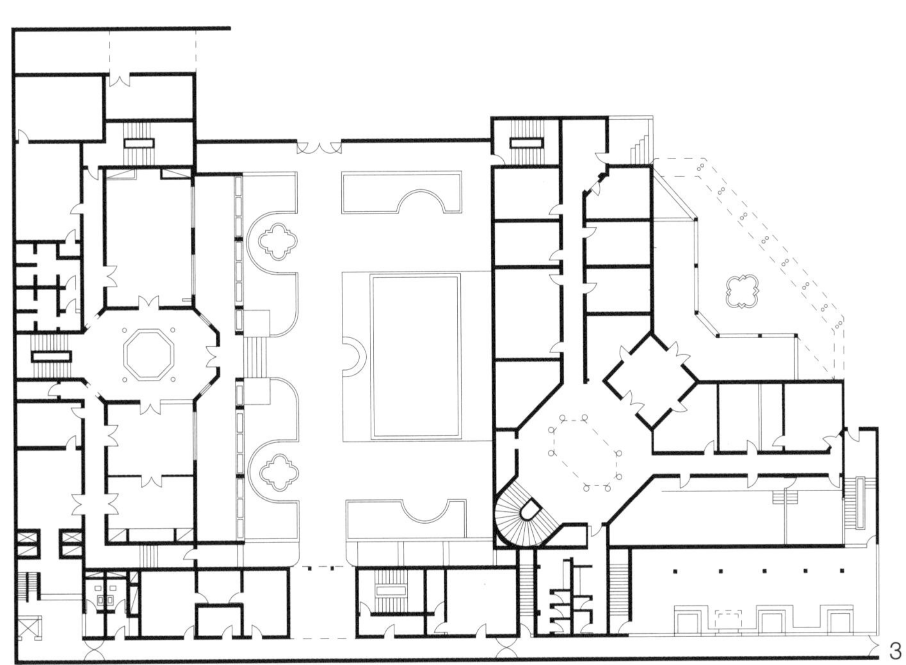

3

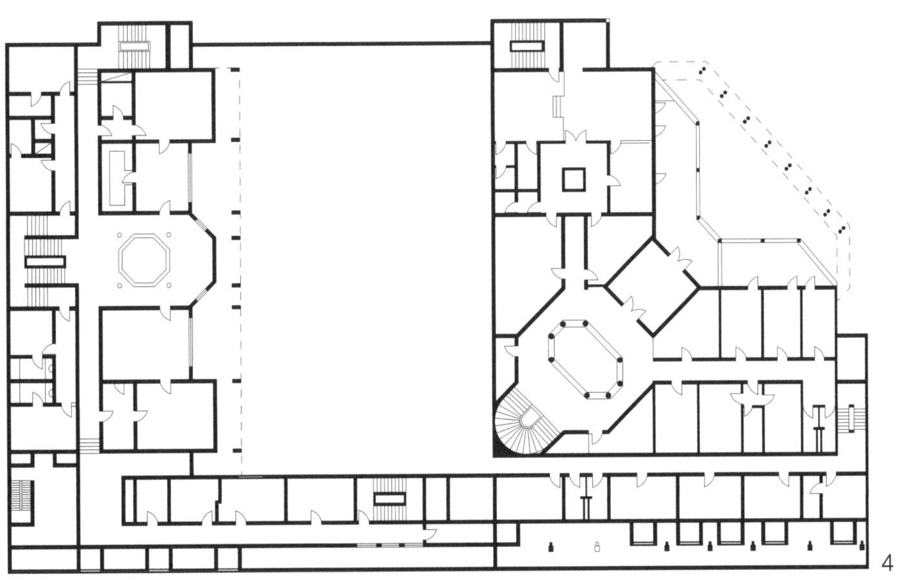

4

KUWAIT NATIONAL THEATRE

JIBLA
1977–1980

DESIGNERS • BBPR (L. Belgiojoso);
INCO (K. Wiśniowski; A. Bohdanowicz,
principal designers);
Denys Lasdun & Partners
CLIENT • Ministry of Public Works

UNBUILT

The National Theatre was initially thought to complete the strip of public buildings facing the Gulf Road, on the opposite side of the Sief Palace, together with National Assembly and the National Museum. The international competition was launched in the late 1970s for a 2,000 seat hall and reception areas, but the project was never realised. The proposals submitted had very different approaches and the results were also very dissimilar. BBPR focused on the acting aspect and developed the design in collaboration with Teatro La Scala of Milan for the scenography and with the (former) Albery Theatre in London for the mechanical aspect associated with stage movement and illumination. INCO and the Polish designers worked primarily on form. They proposed a sculptural element formed by four portions of a sphere with different radii. Each quadrant/shell sheltered a cluster of prisms, home to different functions, including two auditoria, vertical distribution and foyers. The third proposal by Lasdun is a large platform with a wedged crown embracing a series of smaller volumes. Only the fly-tower emerges over the level of the base. The proposal does not go into details, but it is not difficult to imagine this creation with Brutalist concrete surfaces similar to his famous work, the National Theatre on the South Bank, London.

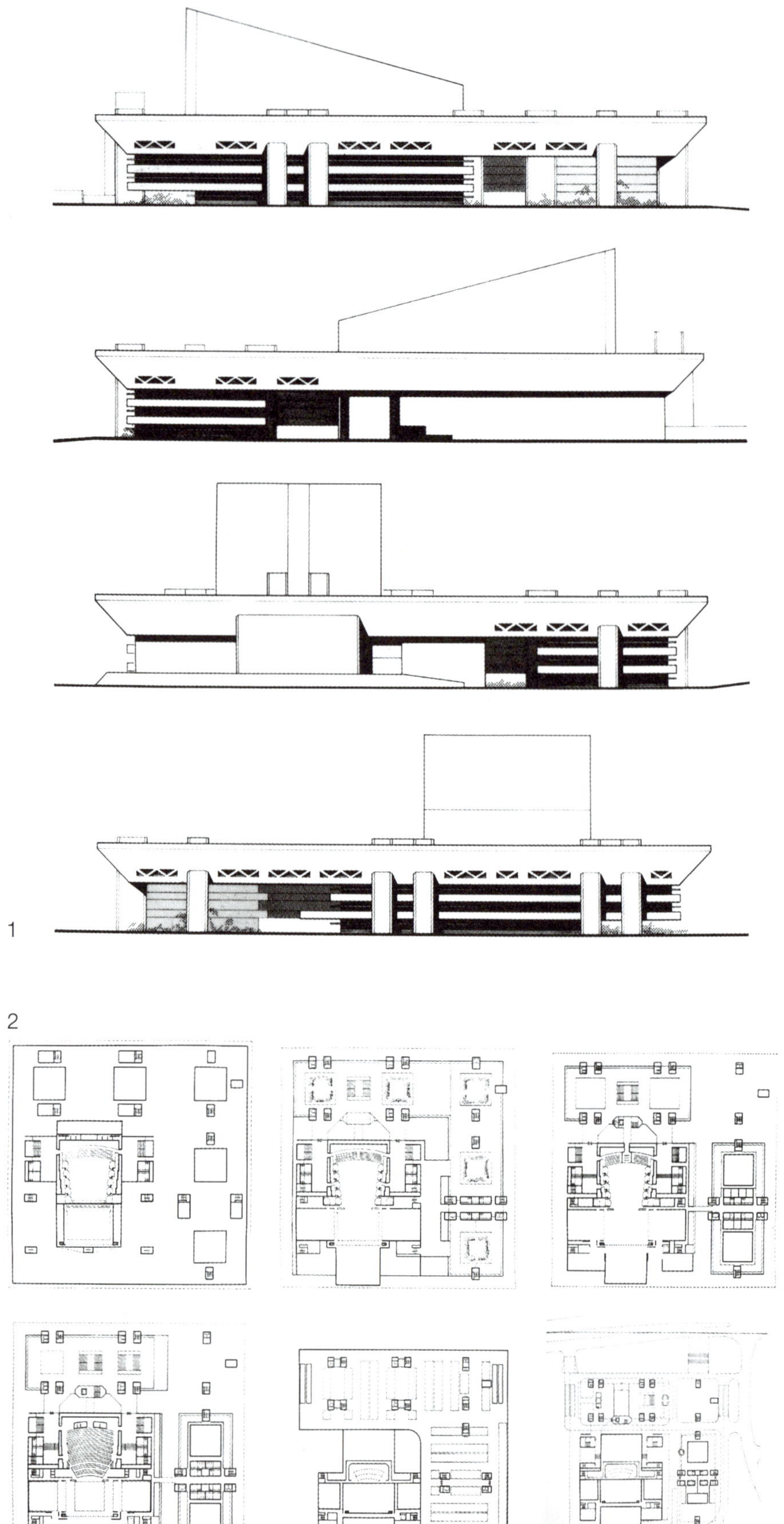

1

2

266

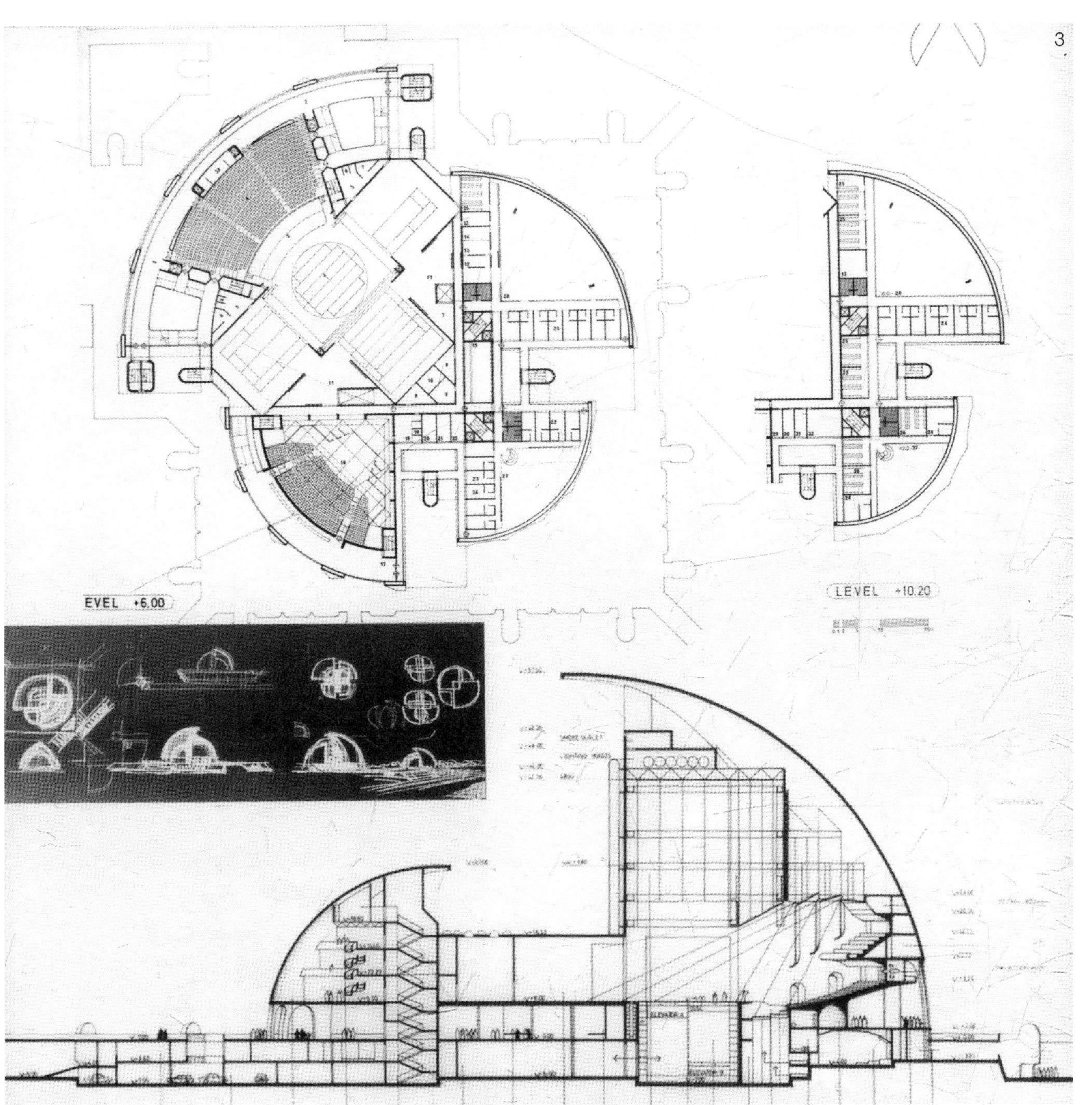

EVEL +6.00
LEVEL +10.20

AL-SABAH HOUSE

MAHBOULA
1978–1984

DESIGNER • Hassan Fathy

IN USE

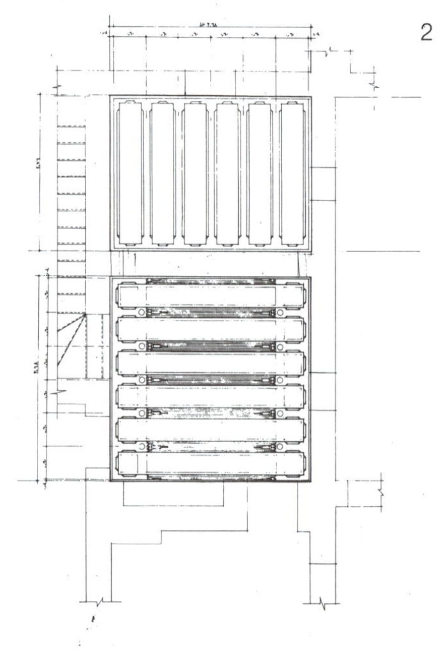

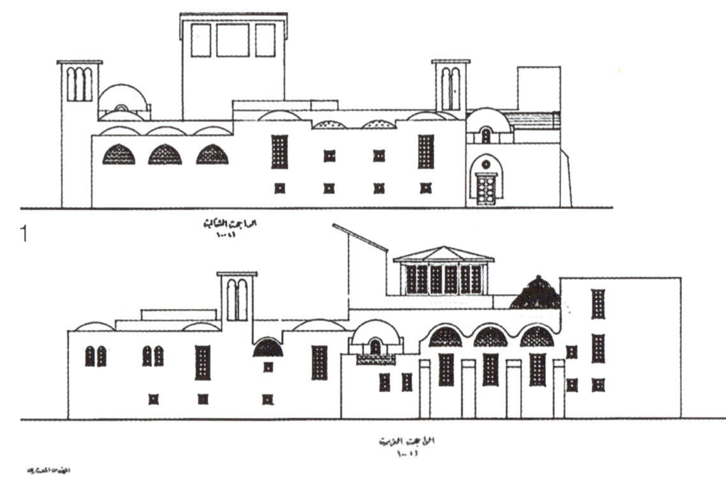

One of Fathy's late works, the large mansion incorporates all the typical characteristics of his architecture: massive brick wall and small controlled apertures, vaults and domes, *malqaf* (wind towers) and passive cooling systems, pergolas and *mashrabiahs* (lattice works). The project's deep investigation of the relationship between public and private space in domestic architecture[117] is more significant, in this case, than the use of vernacular features. The volumetric shift, clearly define the two zones, creating one of the two orthogonal axes of the composition. The house is *introverted* like a *caravanserai*: very few openings interrupt the outer wall, while the interior is rich of porches and open spaces. The plan also has the clarity of the same archetype revolving around three square courtyards, different in sizes according to their proximity to the public area. The transition spaces are arcades overlooking the yards and protecting the inner rooms from the sun. The arches' span of the colonnade is the module that gives proportions to the entire composition.

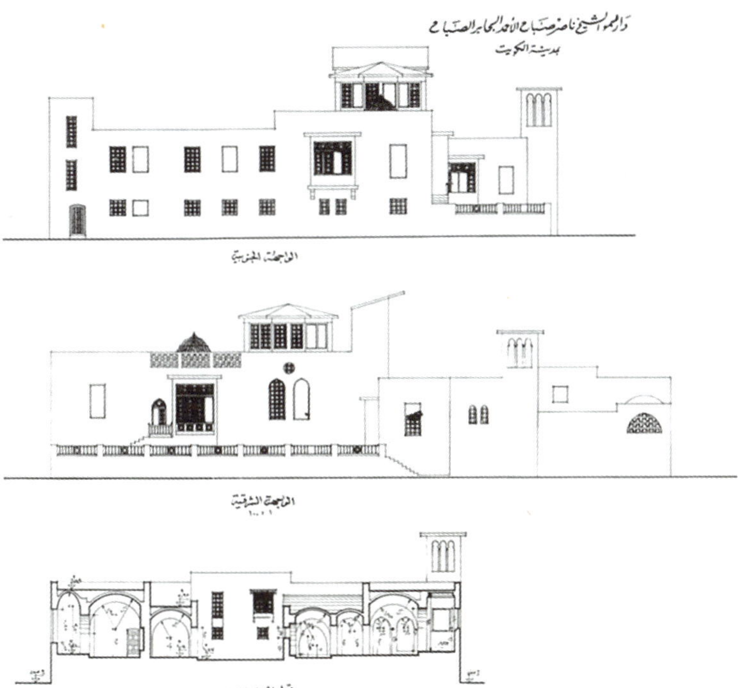

1. North-west and south-west elevations
2. Detail of the ceiling
3. North-east and south-east elevations
4. Ground floor plan
5. Ground floor plan, variation

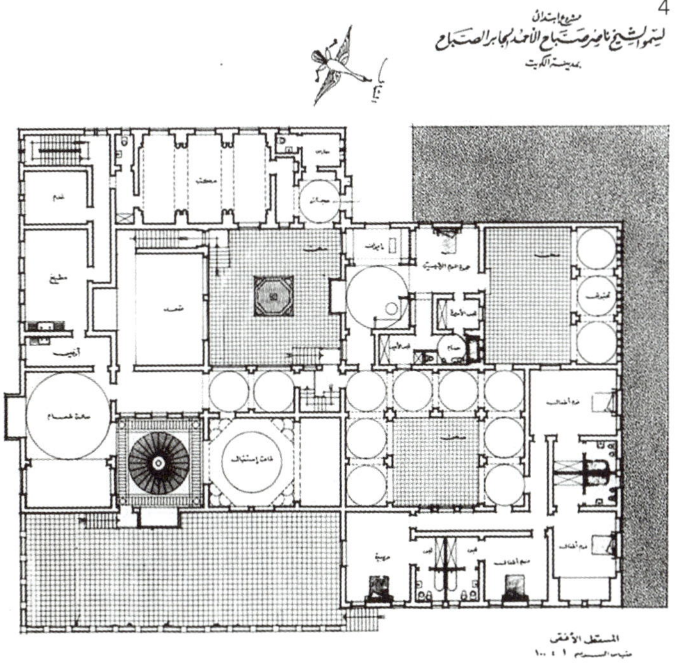

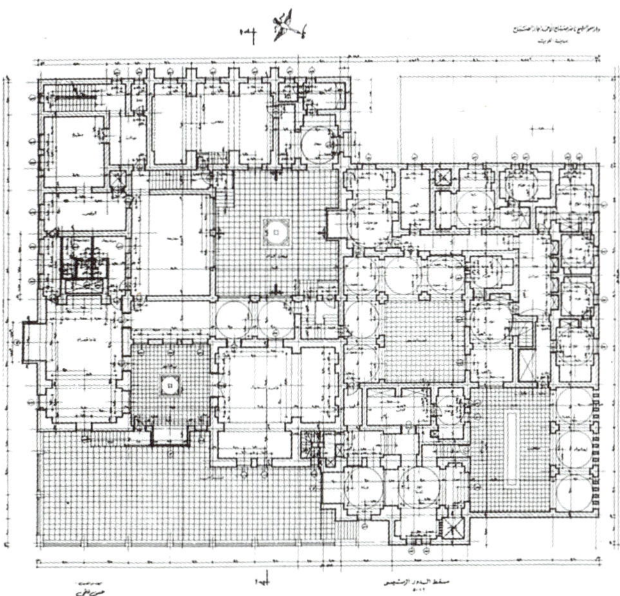

AL-SAWABER HOUSING COMPLEX

SHARQ
1977–1989

DESIGNER • Arthur Erickson Associates
CLIENT • National Housing Authority
CONTRACTOR • Kuwait Singaporean
Trading & Contracting Group

*PARTIALLY BUILT
UNDER THREAT OF DEMOLITION*

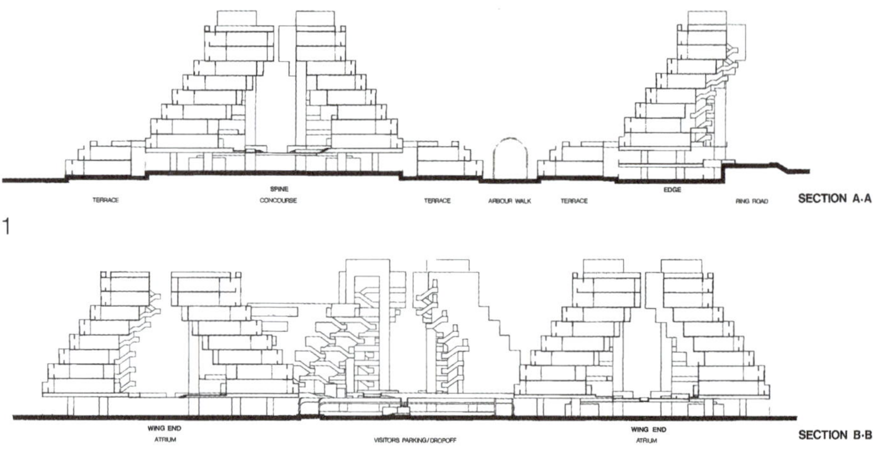

"Winning the numbers game"[118] for housing was the main motivation for Ministry of Housing's recommendation[119] that consequently led to its construction. After several preliminary reports, the project was awarded to a Singaporean-Korean contractor that designed and built 500 of the 900 apartment units initially expected to be built.[120]

The 24.5 ha site was originally divided into nine blocks with average apartment units of 295 m^2. These are distributed in chains of terraced 8-floor-high blocks aligned from east to west, providing large shaded corridors of outdoor common areas connected by an elevated pedestrian structure occasionally accessed by car.

Arthur Erickson's resident engineer described it as an "imaginative design response to the problem of attracting middle income Kuwaiti citizens back into the urban centre."[121]

3

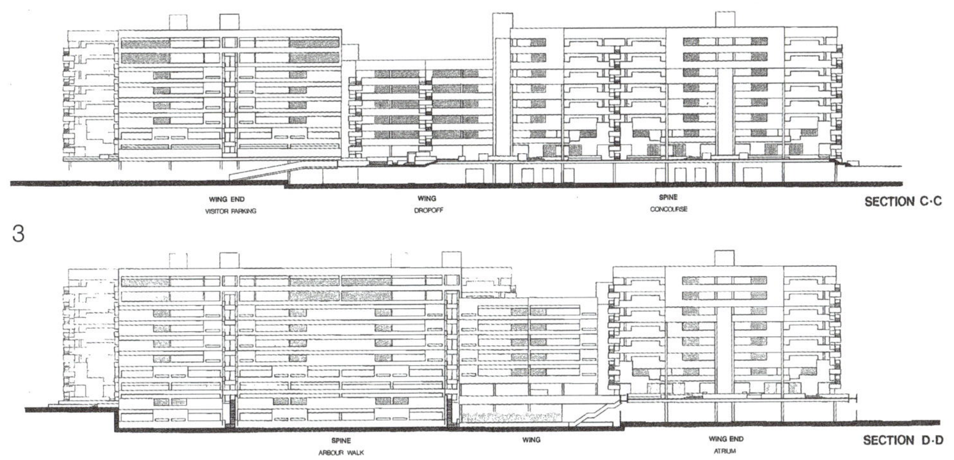

4

1. Cross sections
2. Sketch by the designer
3. Longitudinal sections
4. Scale model, general view

CEMBIT HOUSE

Planning Principles

The following planning principles respond to the specific project site conditions and user requirements. They are the key elements in the approved development concept of Part B, and they have been extended and developed in the course of the work on Part C.

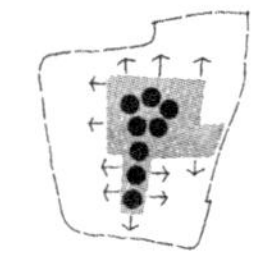

The project gardens are the unifying element and focal point of the community.

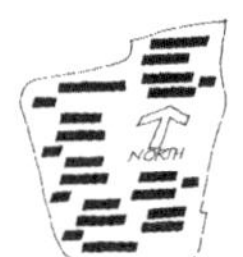

The east-west alignment of residential buildings provides a good climatic orientation for all dwelling units.

Edge buildings provide enclosure for the project garden and protection from outside visual intrusion.

A clear hierarchical organization, from site to neighbourhood cluster to core group to dwelling unit, clarifies the individual's relationship to the whole community.

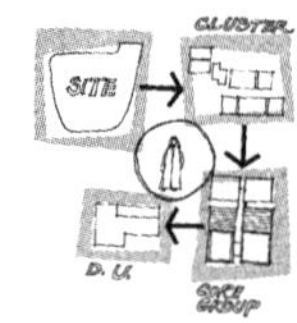

Core groups of up to 20 dwelling units are the basic building blocks of the project.

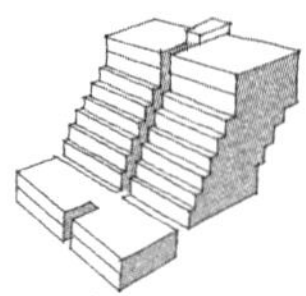

The stepped building form gives the dwelling units the character of hillside villas, and clearly distinguishes the project from existing non-Kuwaiti apartment buildings.

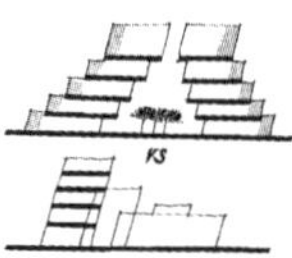

Several different dwelling unit types respond to different conditions in different locations within the building.

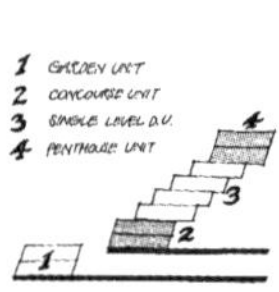

Every dwelling unit has its own private landscaped courtyard, protected from visual intrusion and screened from direct sun.

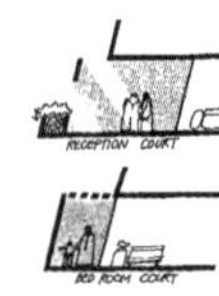

Major rooms have identical internal and external relationships in all dwelling unit types.

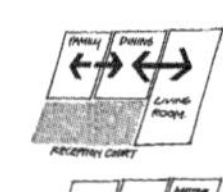

PEDESTRIAN CIRCULATION

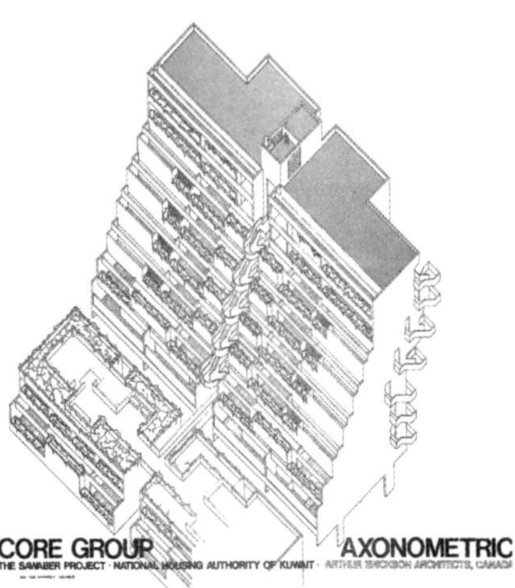

CORE GROUP **AXONOMETRIC**
THE SAWABER PROJECT · NATIONAL HOUSING AUTHORITY OF KUWAIT · ARTHUR ERICKSON ARCHITECTS, CANADA

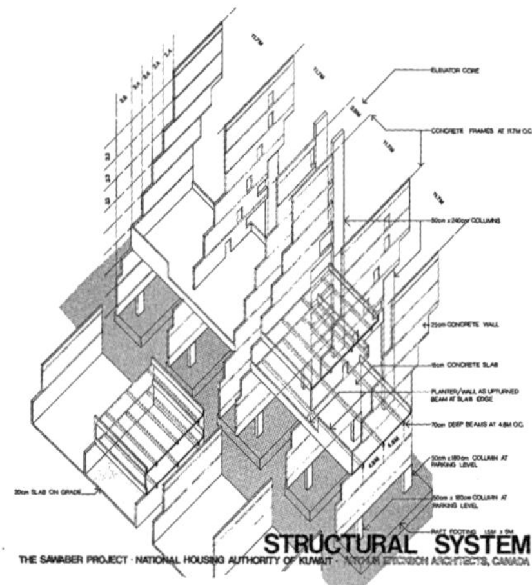

STRUCTURAL SYSTEM
THE SAWABER PROJECT · NATIONAL HOUSING AUTHORITY OF KUWAIT · ARTHUR ERICKSON ARCHITECTS, CANADA

AL-MUTHANNA COMPLEX

FAHAD AL-SALEM STREET
1979–1985

DESIGNER • KEO
CLIENT • Kuwait Finance House (KFH)
CONTRACTOR • Al-Hani Construction &
Trading Co.

IN USE

1

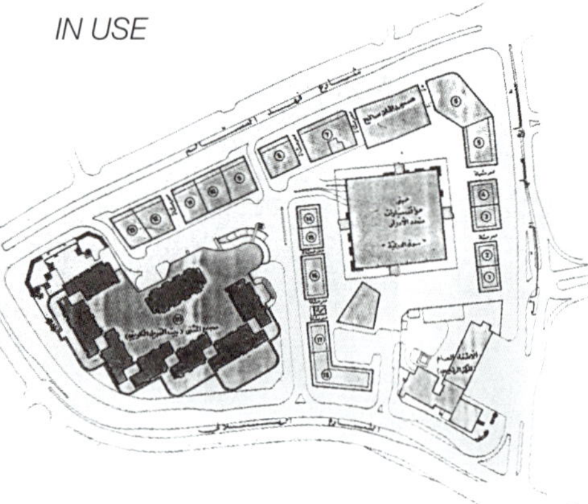

2

With the failure of several state-owned high-rise residential housing schemes, such as Al-Sawaber, the residential units planned by National Housing Authority during the 1970s were converted into private subsidised housing. State-funded investors such as the Kuwait Finance House (1977) took control of the development of schemes on state-owned land.

At almost 150,000 m² this complex was a pioneer in attracting the domestic market to buy private homes. Strongly inspired by the Milano Due mass-housing project, the local advertising campaign had a unique mass appeal that was not repeated.[122]

The seven residential towers with 720 units plus a hotel stand on a commercial podium comprising an indoor mall and a street-level commercial arcade along the perimeter. This last commercial ring resolves the hierarchy of entrances and accesses to the residential towers, shopping mall and underground parking. A corridor giving climatic comfort and public interface follows the legacy of the 1960 street guidance plan for the main avenues.[123] The opportunity for building a curved restaurant on a support in the form of a chalice was provided by the looping of the car park entrance and exit ramps.

1. Scale model, front view and aerial view
2. Site plan
3. Internal view of the commercial gallery
4. Plan of the towers, typical floor

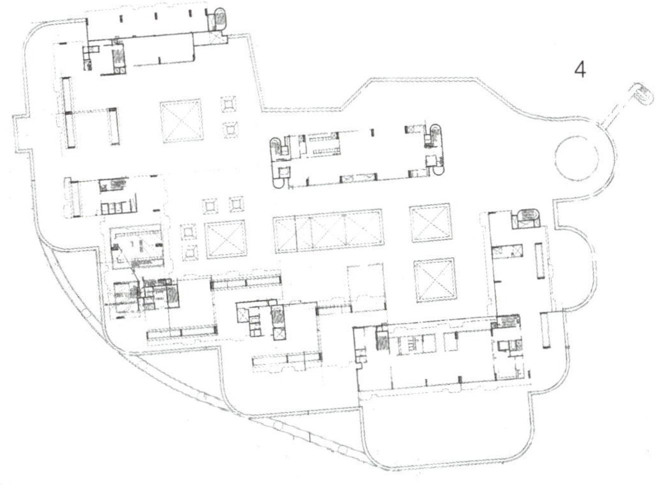

AWQAF COMMERCIAL COMPLEX

MIRQAB
1978–1982

DESIGNERS • Abdul Raouf and Ahmed Mashour
CLIENT • Ministry of Awqaf
CLIENT • Unknown

MODIFIED

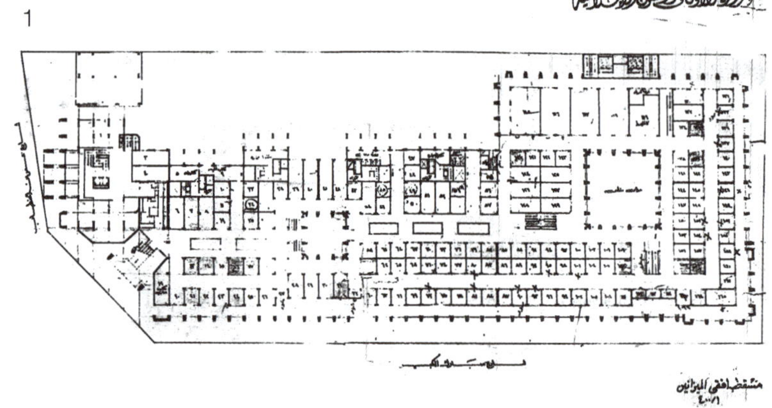

The Ministry of Religious Affairs was engaged in the mission of providing subsidised housing for nationals. As a solution, a building with a commercial podium was expected to financially sustain the residential part of the complex.

The Egyptian architect, son of a prominent practitioner during the early years of town modernisation, developed a long linear scheme elaborated on the colonnade theme and finally implementing the 1969's BBPR proposal for the "Urban Form Study of the Old City," of a residential scheme of inverted terraces providing building shade along the west façade. Stephan Gardiner compared it with the Bologna and Padua arcades.[124]

The lower commercial element is developed along three floors, including offices, plus parking in the basement. The souq-like bar is interrupted by two internal squares with skylight designed to provide restaurant and entertainment facilities. On top, the six towers vary between five and ten floors, never occupied for residential purposes as per the original plan and were later, converted into offices.

During the Invasion the building was seriously damaged and after liberation the white travertine exterior was clad in grey aluminium panelling.

1. Ground floor plan
2. Skylight and internal view

WATERFRONT

SHAAB – SALMIYA
1978–1988

DESIGNERS • Sasaki Associates (lead consultants); Ghazi Sultan (architect); KEO (associate consultant); Geotechnical Engineers Inc.; Normandeau Associates Inc. (oceanographic and sedimentation); Research Planning Institute (marine environment); Joseph W. Stichter (landscape); Charles F. Breuel (recreation)
CLIENT • H.H. the Amir of Kuwait
CONTRACTORS • Ivan Milutinovic-Pim (marine works); various others

IN USE

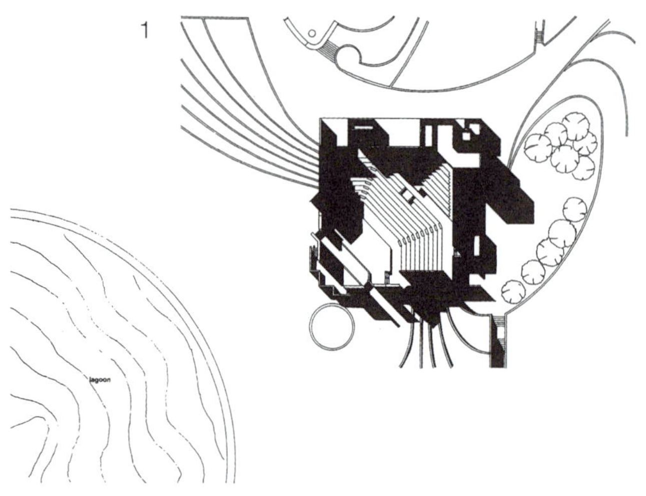

The winning entry of the 1975–76 competition (among five international design firms), led by Sasaki Associates and the Kuwaiti architect Ghazi Sultan for the ambitious Kuwait Waterfront project was finally implemented in 1978. The Master Plan aimed to restore the sea to the city's inhabitants after that access was broken by the highway construction. A continuous strip of 21 km, from Ras Al-Salmiya to Shuwaikh, was segmented into twelve zones distributing the designated "major use areas."[125]

Different points of interest, recreational spaces and other public facilities were implemented along the waterfront: swimming pools and beaches with planted trees, playgrounds for children and water parks, restaurants, plazas and a dhow harbour. The focal 'major area' was, and still is, despite poor maintenance, the artificial Green Island. Between the 2nd and the 3rd Ring Roads, a man-made island was generated with an artificial lake surrounded by sandy beaches, an open amphitheatre, restaurants, and other small entertainment features.

Today it still plays a major role on the waterfront adding to the democratisation of the public space. Along the pedestrian promenade, more structures were subsequently added in a random way since its inception, slightly affecting its physical integrity but reinforcing its social meaning.

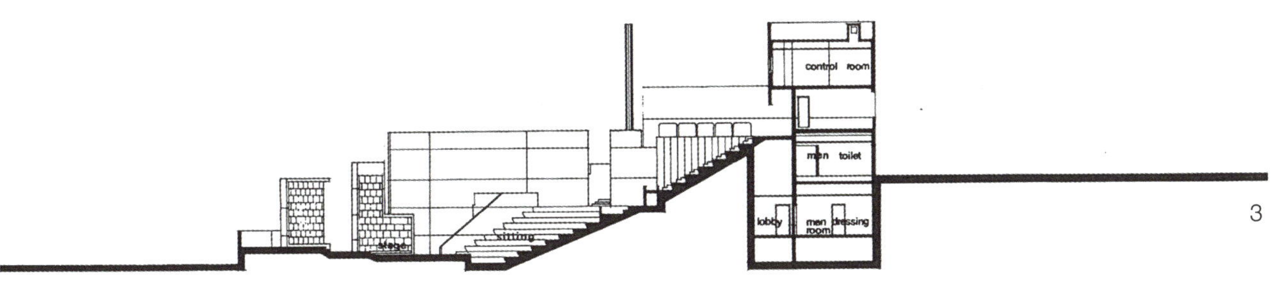

3

4

5

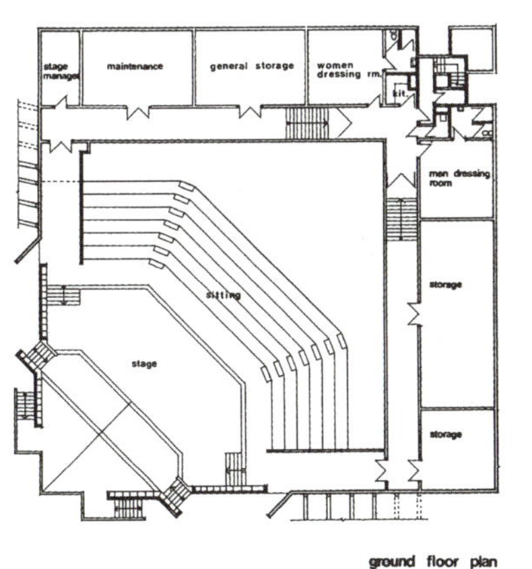

6

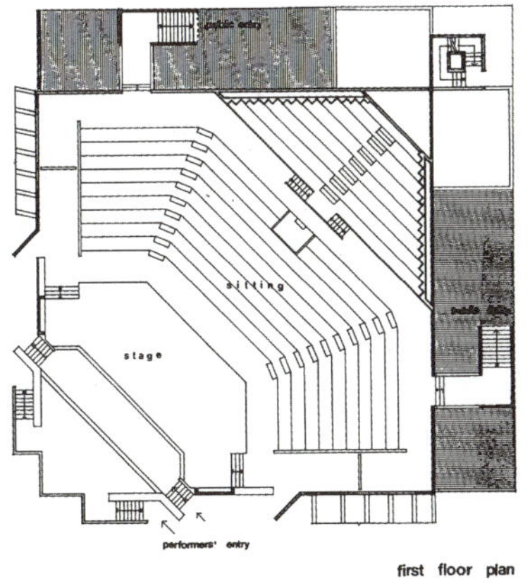

1. Green Island, amphitheatre, site plan
2. Waterfront restaurant (Sultan Restaurant)
3. Green Island, amphitheatre, section
4. Group of lighting elements along the promenade
5. Access stairs to the restaurant upper level
6. Green Island, amphitheatre, ground floor and first floor plans

283

7. Green Island, aerial view: the lagoon, the ziggurat ramp,
the amphitheatre, the geodesic dome, the restaurants,
the children's playground, the observatory

8

11

Sharq Historic Dhow Harbor and Museum
Kuwait Towers Park and Promontory
Renovated Dhow Harbor and Market
Seif Pleasure Dhow Harbor and Plaza
Swimming Beaches
Boat Launch
Green Island Theme Park and Lagoon
National Assembly Plaza
Sea Jet
Shuwaikh Children's Water Park
Swimming Beaches
Fishing
Doha Al Shaab Recreation Complex
Salmiya Island Aquarium Park
Kilometers 1 2 3 4 5 6 7 8 9 10 11 12 13 14 15 16
Miles 1 2 3 4 5 6 7 8 9 10

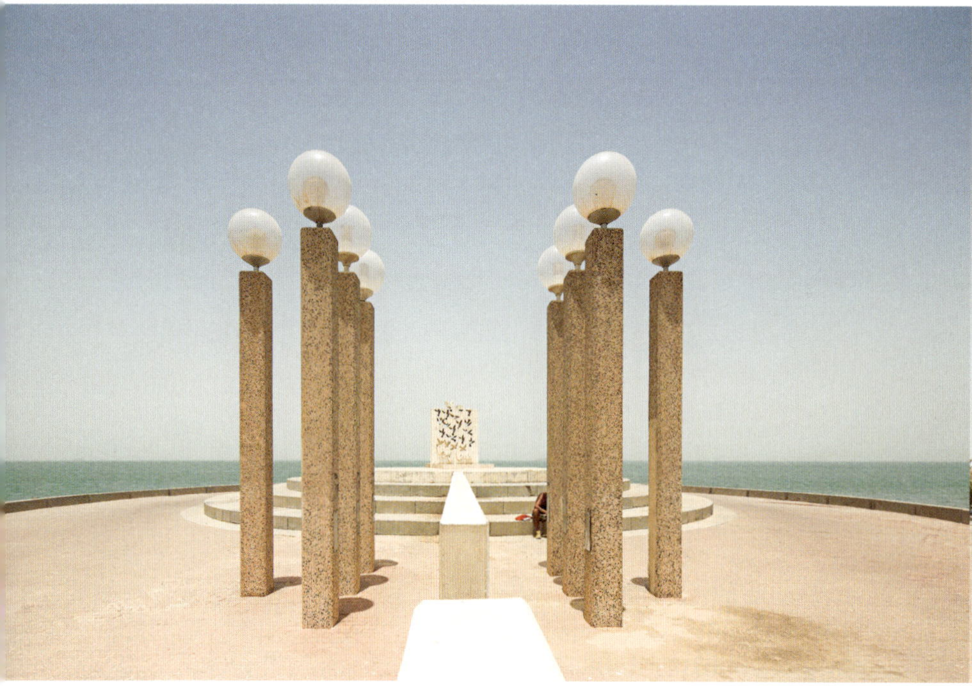

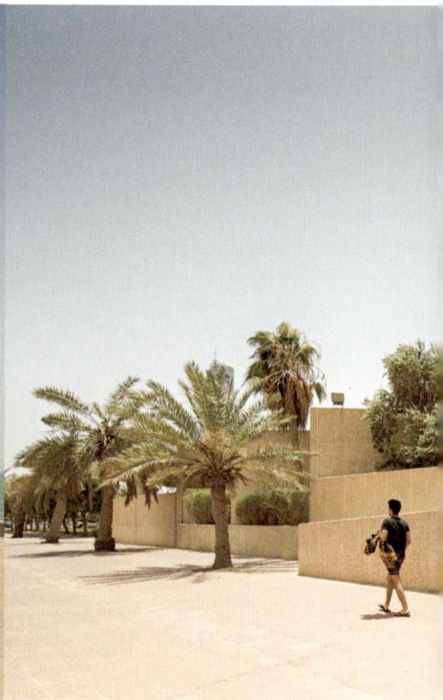

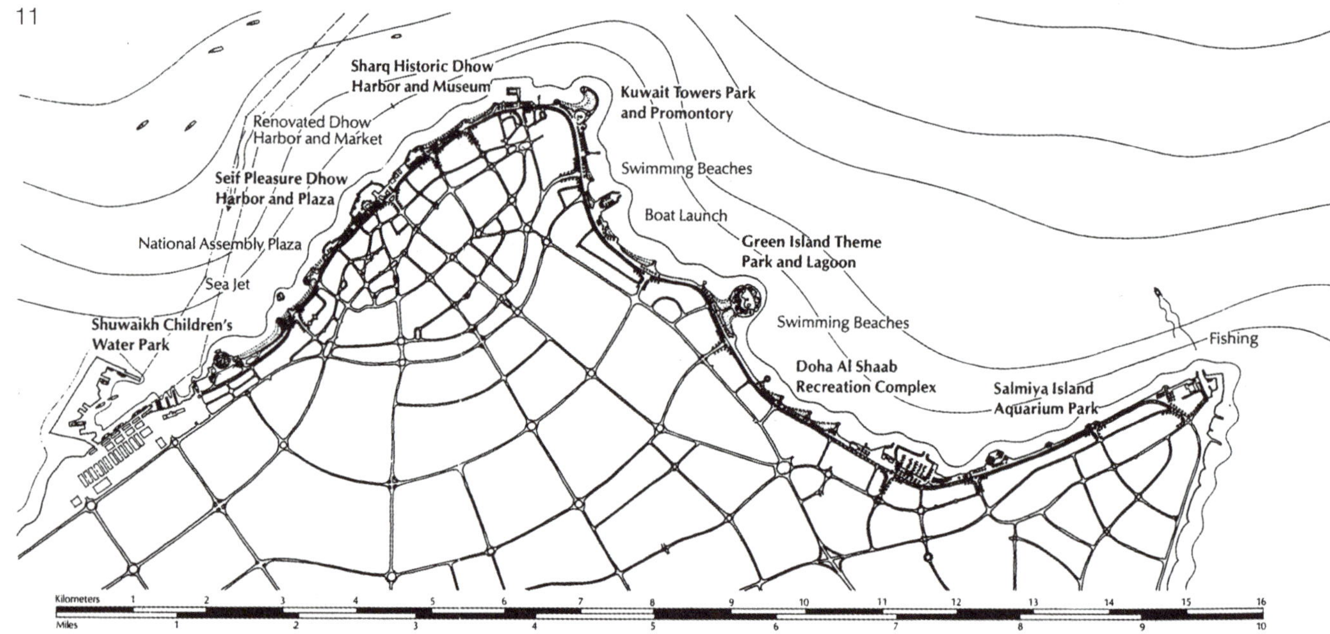

8. Detail of the concrete lighting poles
9. Mediterranean gardens
10. Entrance to the swimming pool compound
11. Site map of the 21 km long waterfront, partially completed in 1988
12. Sketches related to the conceptual plan, dated 1989, based on F. James's evaluation of the implemented project: plantings; built and unbuilt elements behaviour; modular "halas" sketches for the wall "halas" and the "hemi-cyls" shading performance

9

10

12

water containment
"thick" trees ~ "thin" trees
"Sunsets"
...in Kuwait on Thurs.–Friday
winds
Noon
le Places
shade!!!
view open
1,5 m. ht.
Plantings
3–4 m.
"WALL-HALA"
cobbles except "pockets"
one brick wide [all zones]
"HEMI-CYL"
zone 8
Pavement change

287

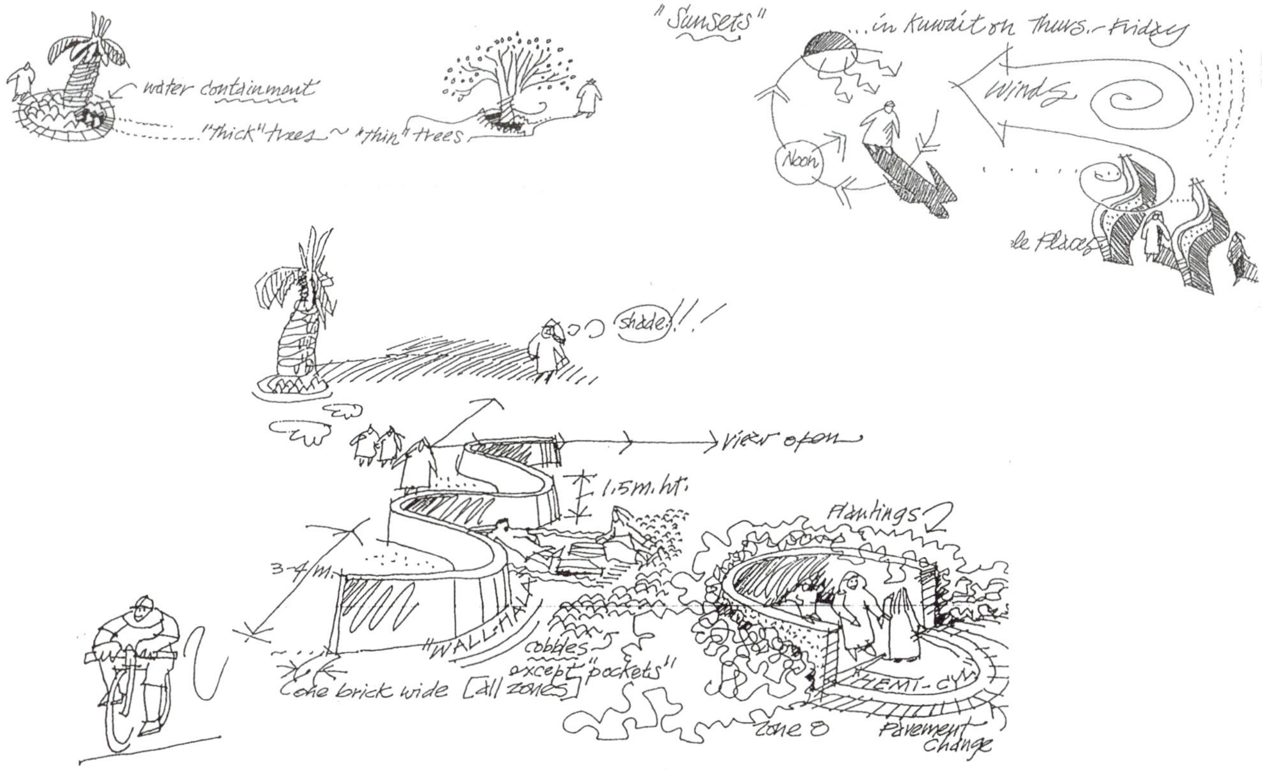

HILTON AREA APARTMENTS

BNEID AL-GAR
1977–1979

DESIGNERS • I.M. Pei & Partners (architect); KEO (lead consultant); Hisham Munir Associates (competition entry)
CLIENT • United Realty Company; Kuwait Hotels Company
CONTRACTOR • Musaad Al-Saleh & Sons Co.

PARTIALLY BUILT / IN USE

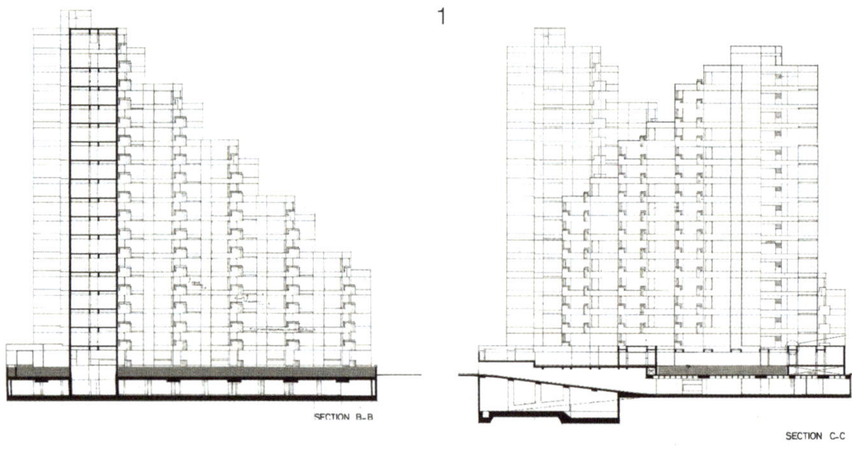

The Candilis proposal for residential blocks in the former Hilton area was never fully implemented. Indeed only one phase, from the initial three, was built. Therefore, a few years later I.M. Pei was commissioned to develop the central portion of this prominent plot, facing the Gulf. He created luxury apartments of different sizes and typologies, including duplexes and penthouses. The building design is based on a geometrical grid that fosters diagonal cuts and characteristic octagonal volumes, where the living rooms are placed. This scheme distances the building from the road, creating two large triangular plazas at the ground floor. It also allows each apartment to be appropriately open to the sea view. The aggregative system is a repetition of similar volumetric units that differ in height. The latter aspect reinforces the diagonal tension of the composition, giving to the complex the distinguishing step-pyramidal shape. In the recent years the area has been under intense construction. Several high towers, with different design features, were erected in proximity, weakening the balance of the initial volumetric configuration.

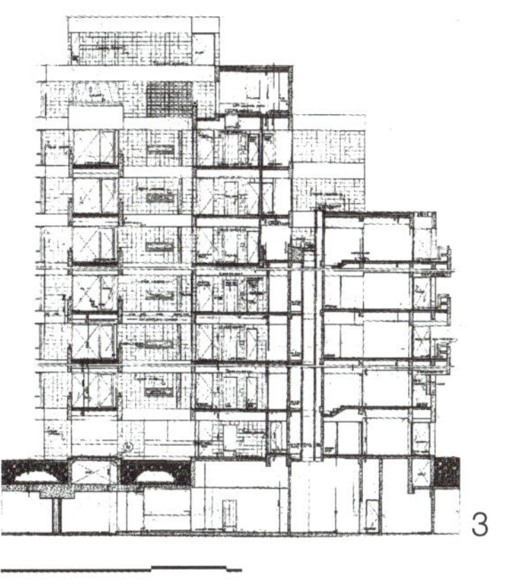

3

1. Sections
2. Site plan
3. Detailed section
4. Ground floor plan with landscape
5. Typical floor plan of a residential unit

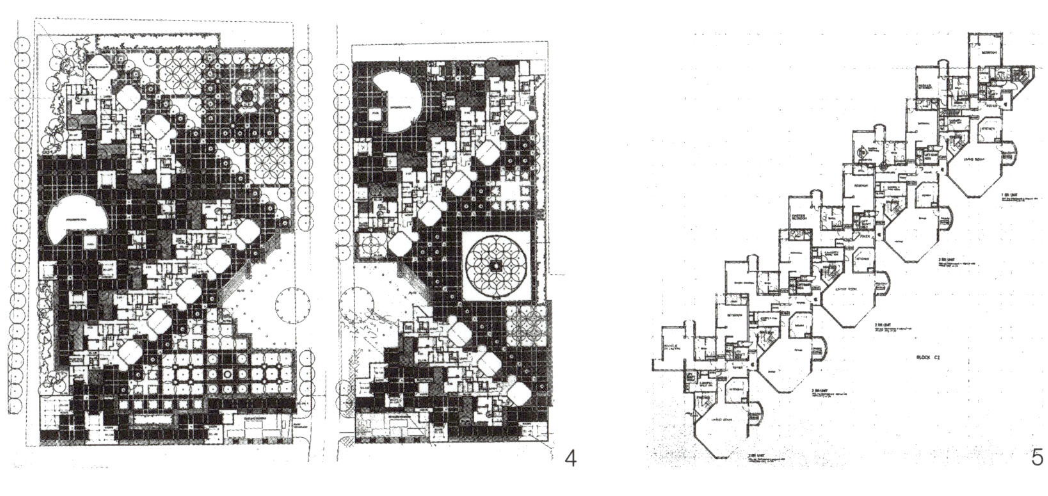

4

5

OFFICE TOWERS

SHARQ
1973–1986

DESIGNERS • PACE; KEO; Arab Consultants

IN USE

The idea of a "street of important civic status" connecting Mubarakiya (the old core) to Sharq (the merchants area) was never consolidated.[126] To this day there is a spatial discontinuity between these two, causing the most critical interruption in the city's fabric. After the 1968 call for "the physical re-planning of Kuwait"[127] and "Urban Form Studies for the Old Town," this area became relevant to the planned development of the city centre. Both urban policies intensified the concern regarding the preservation of the old core and releasing urban expansion towards Sharq. It was thought private investment would negotiate landownership and design guidelines for Yousif Al-Roumi Street and Ahmad Al-Jaber Street. The first towers to be built during the 1970s were seen as an important instrument to promote progress in the absence of planning. This legacy formulates the common approach in the majority of the cases, namely the unfinished project; a tower in a vacant plot that was left as an informal car parking.

The Al-Asmak Tower (Arab Consultants 1976–79) was eventually the first to be erected in Sharq. Following high speculation in the city real estate market[128] this model gained momentum, that is, increasing competition for the tallest tower. In the first four years of 1980s PACE alone conceived Public Institute for Social Security Tower (1973–1979), Imad Tower (1978–1981), Raed Centre Tower (1979–1982) and Behbehani Tower (1978–82), the latter with a 19 floor height. Burgan Bank HQ Tower (1978–1981) with 21 floors was completed in the year before.[129]

PACE, under Bob Khewro[130] was also responsible for Khaleejia Complex (1978–1983) and PAMA Tower[131] (1982–1984) all with 20 floors above ground, only superseded by Sharq Tower (1978–1981) with 23 floors (104 meters high). In 1986 the Al-Awadi Towers and the Jazz Tower were completed.[132]

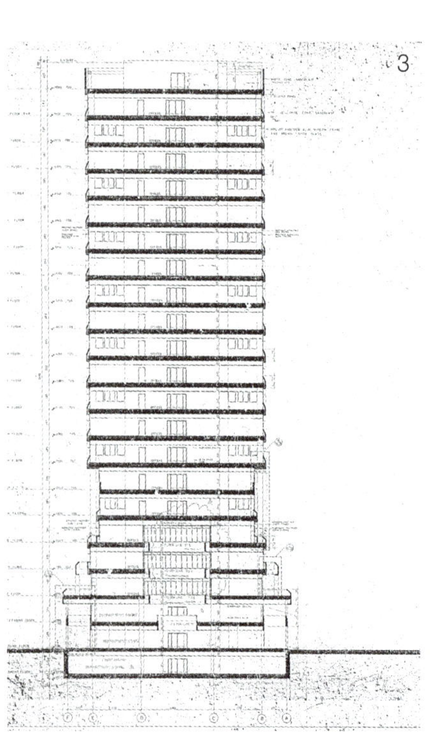

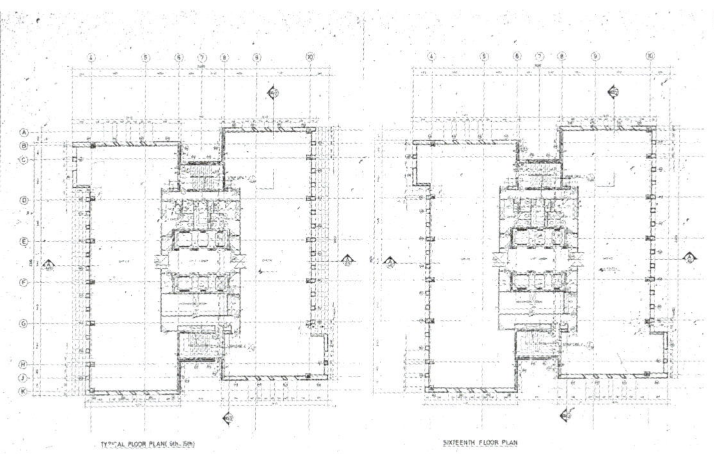

PACE, AL-KHALEEJIA TOWER:

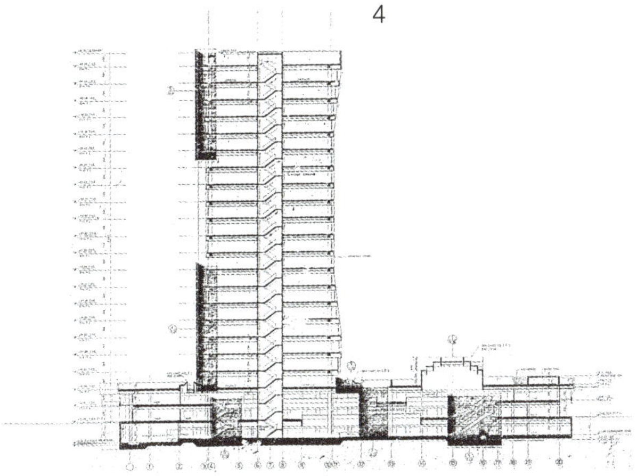

1. Perspective
2. General view, undated
3. Section

PACE, BEHBEHANI TOWER:

4. Section
5. Plans, typical floor and 16th floor
6. General view, undated
7. Internal view of the commercial gallery

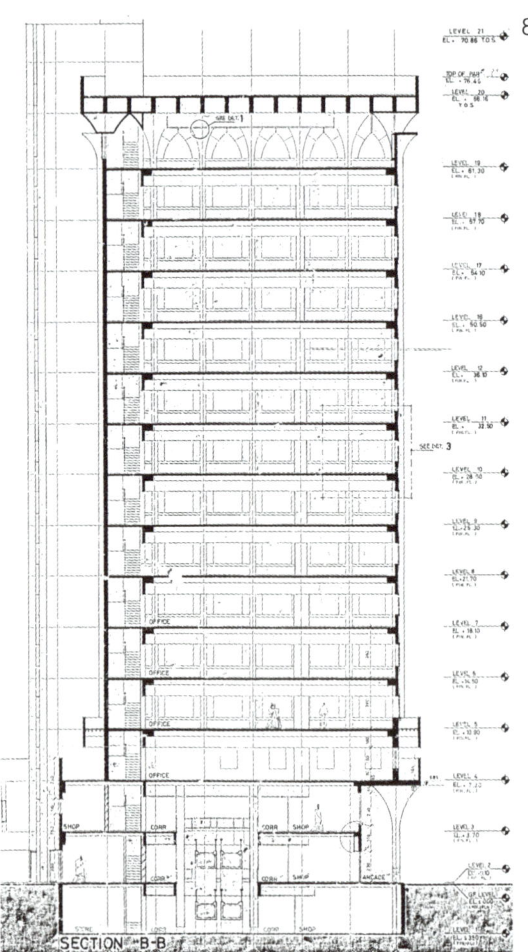

8

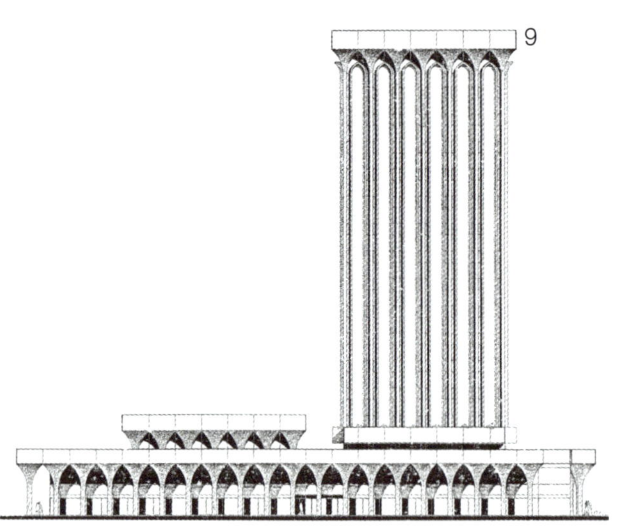

9

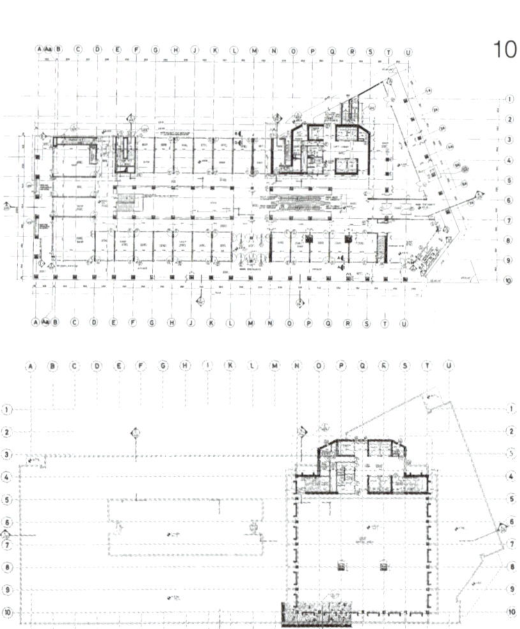

10

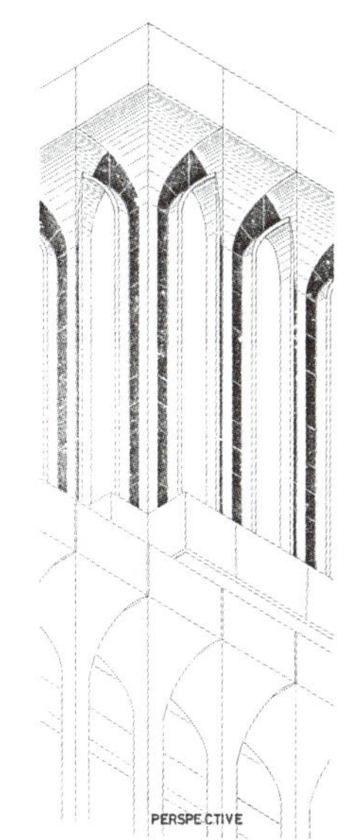

PACE, PUBLIC INSTITUTION FOR SOCIAL SECURITY BUILDING (PFISS):

8. Section of the tower
9. West elevation
10. Ground floor and typical office floor plan
11. Detail of the façade

12

north west elevation

KUWAIT FINANCE HOUSE
بيت التمويل الكويتي

13 14

15

BUS BAR RISER
CABLE TRAY

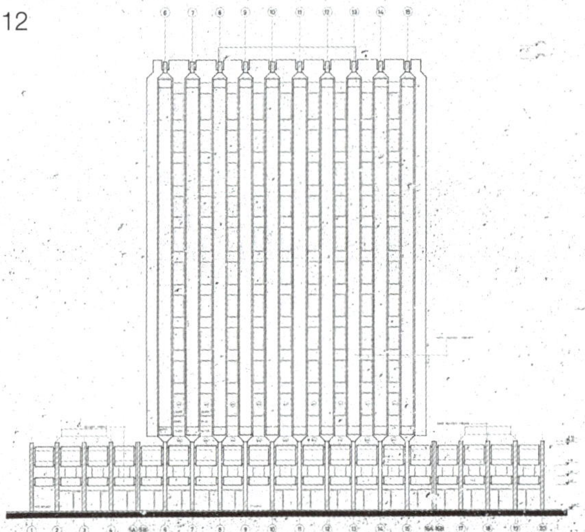

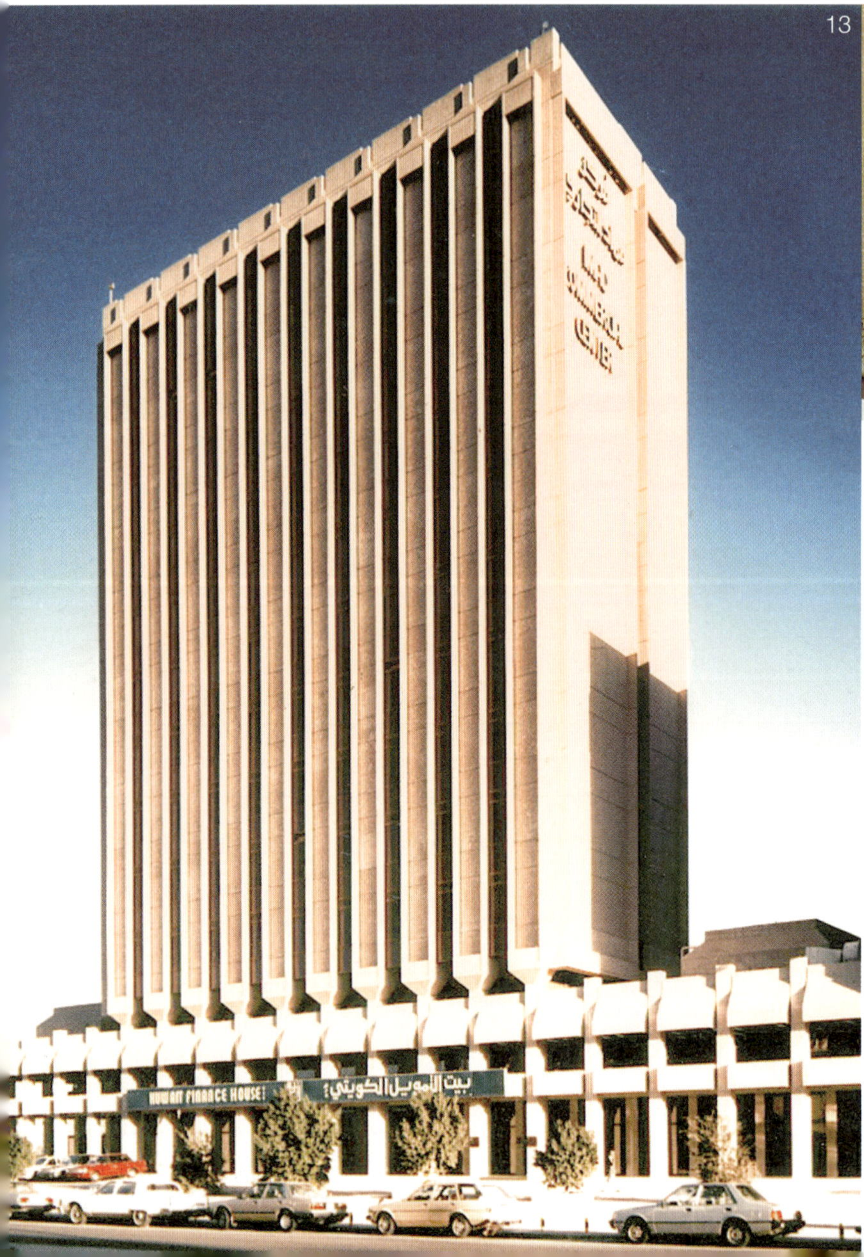

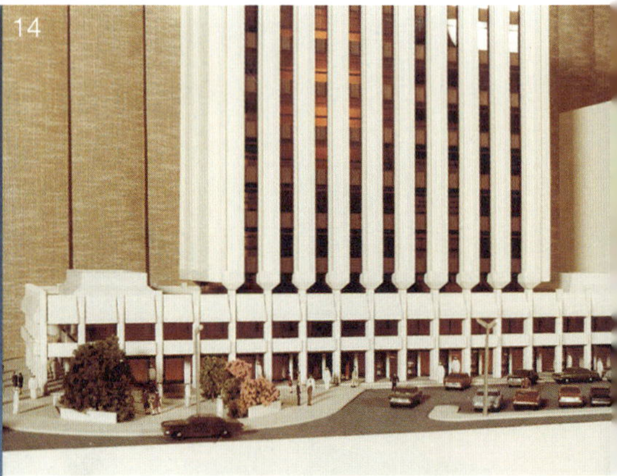

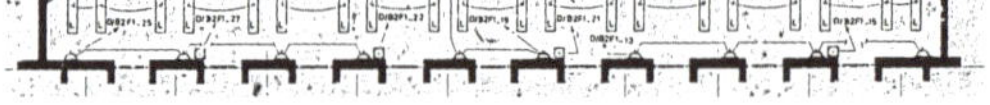

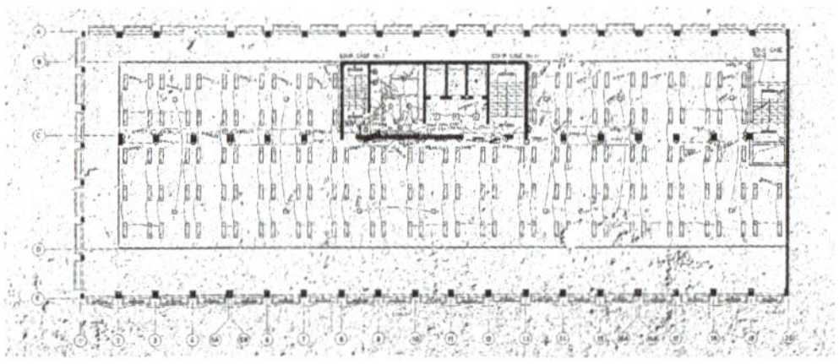

PACE, IMAD COMMERCIAL BUILDNG:

12. Front elevation
13. General view, undated
14. Scale model, detail
15. Typical floor and ground floor plan
16. PACE, Public Authority for Minors Affairs (PAMA)
17. Sharq Tower, west side

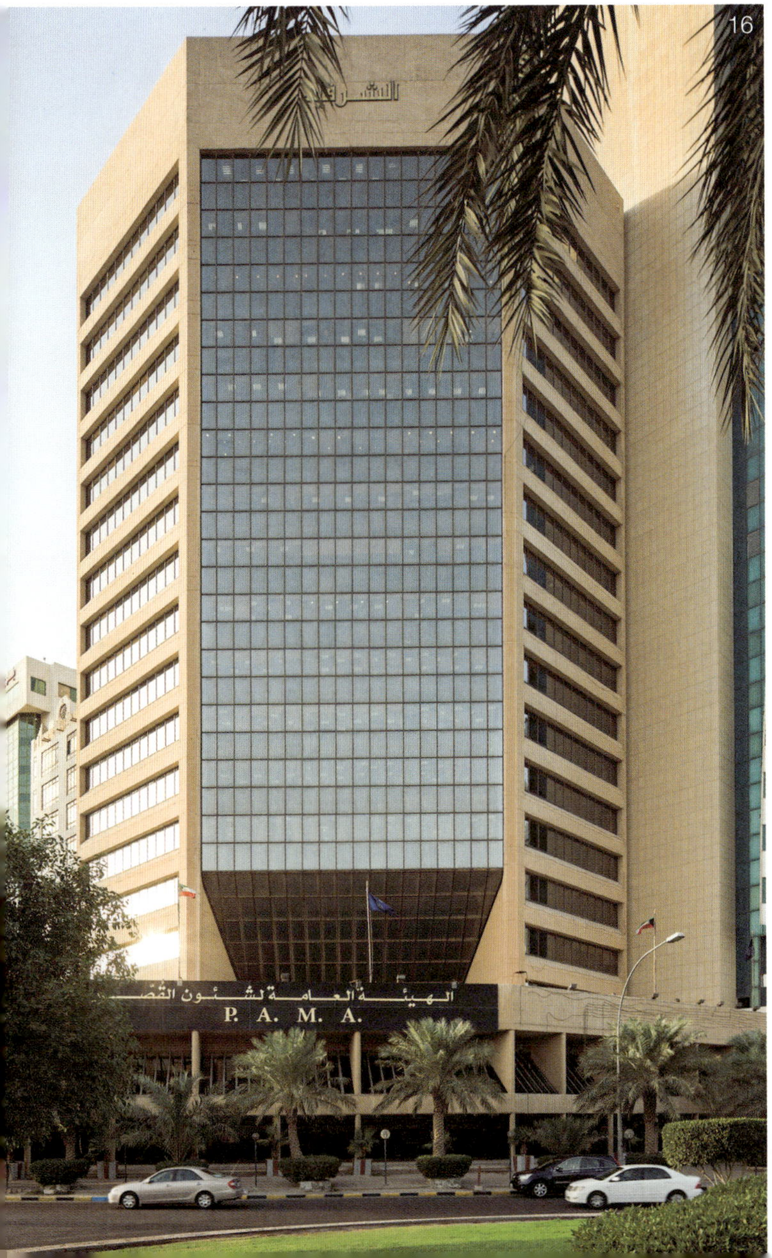

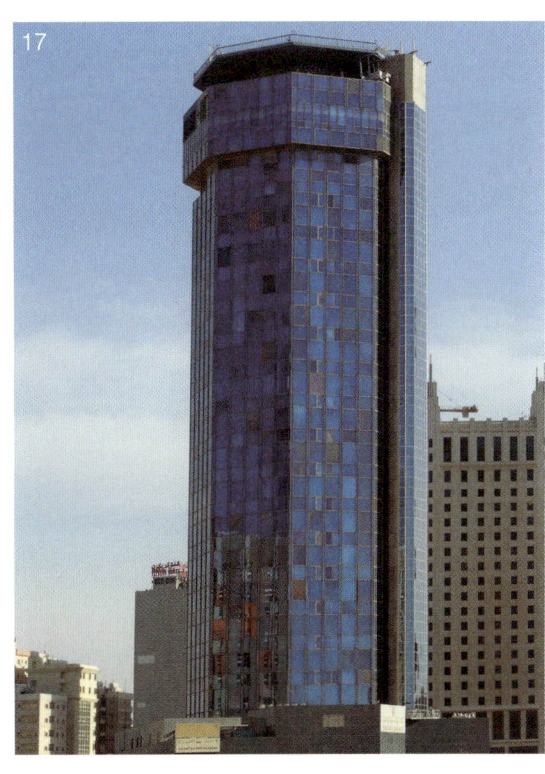

18

19  20

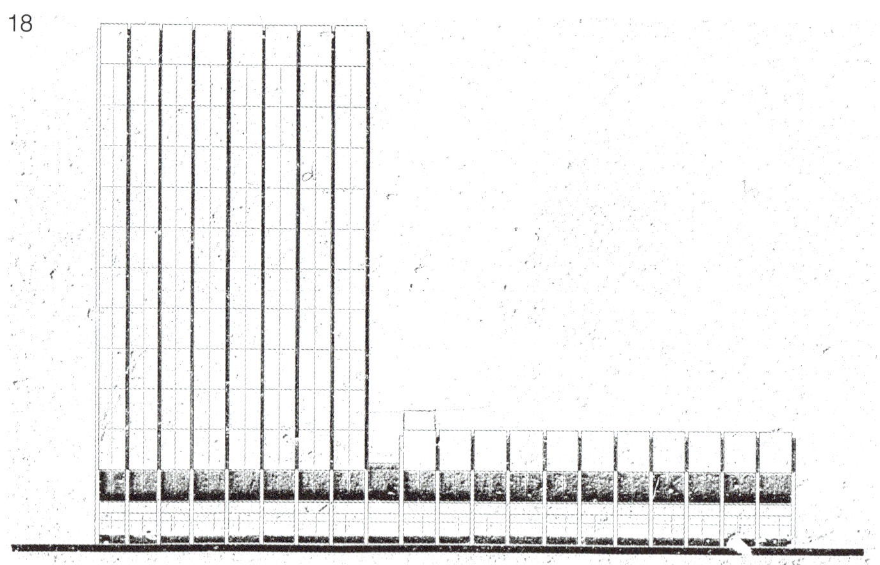

21

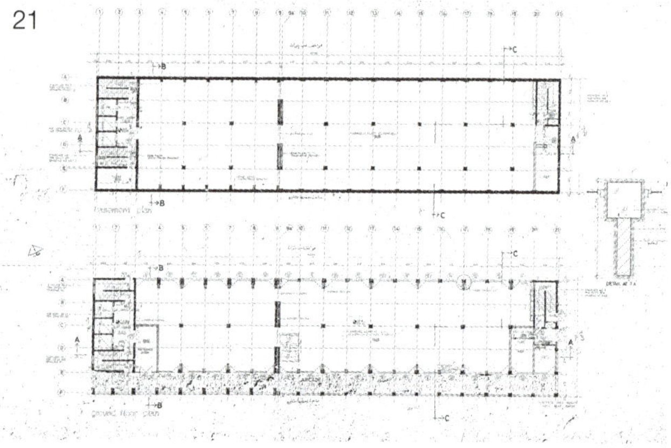

FINTAS TOWN CENTRE

FINTAS
1978

DESIGNER • Arthur Erickson Associates (architect); KEG (lead consultant)
CLIENT • State of Kuwait

UNBUILT

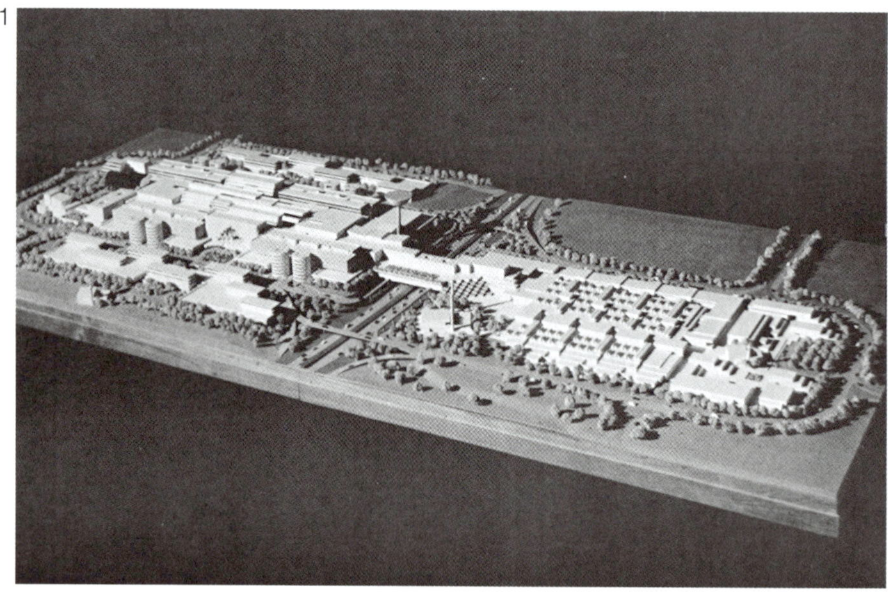

One of the most impactful indicators contained in the Second Master Plan was the idea of releasing the pressure on the metropolitan areas, with the construction of satellite urban centres: Fintas, identified by Buchanan as "Action Plan" in the "Kuwait Costal Corridor," was planned to become the second major centre in the country by 1990. The Canadian firm Erickson, which was by that time finalising the proposal for the Sawaber social housing complex in the city, was asked to revise the Fintas plan initially done by Shankland Cox.

The initial idea was to "internalise everything as much as possible: get rid of the car, put it underground or in parking structures, and centralise the offices and housing into the core of the complex."[133] The Fintas Centre was designed to accommodate any sort of functions for a population of 300,000 inhabitants, with retail and commercial offices, a covered market, a cultural district, clinics, cinemas, sport facilities and recreational areas including a botanical garden. The project was articulated in two main volumes connected by a bridge over a central spinal road. The result was to be a superblock of about 1 hectare with four main gates at the cardinal points.

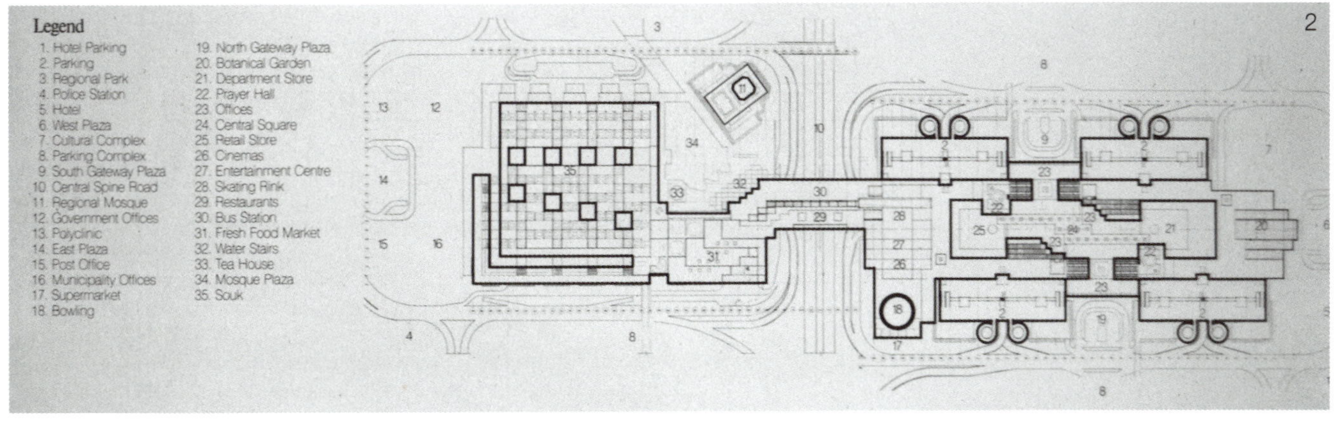

1. Scale model, general view of the Superblock
2. Site plan with function allocation
3. Scale model, overview of Fintas Superblock with residential
area and reserved land for educational use in the foreground

MINISTRIES COMPLEX

MIRQAB
1978–1982

DESIGNERS • Ministry of Public Works, Design Division; Energoprojekt Engineering and Contracting, Sector of Architecture and Construction
CLIENT • Ministry of Public Works
CONTRACTOR • Energoprojekt Engineering and Contracting

UNDER RENOVATION

Following Peter and Alison Smithson's "demonstration building" experience that lasted till 1975,[134] the Ministry of Public Works developed further the conceptual *mat-building* into a real project. In 1978 the Yugoslav contracting firm Energoprojekt that had considerable experience in Kuwait, was also commissioned for this construction.[135]

The complex eventually designed by Adullah Qabazard, the head of the Ministry's design team, has 360,000 m² of offices and underground garages based on a 5 x 5 m regular grid of pre-cast concrete columns and walls. The staircase and cooling external towers are also part of the precast system widely used by IMS systems in the former-Yugoslavia and eventually applied to other buildings in Kuwait.

The ministry complex interconnects eighteen four-storey buildings that sit above two-storey underground parking, all built around a central atrium. The central element initially covered by a lightweight spatial structure is punctuated by elements, such as the central water feature[136] and other fountains clad in colourful tiles borrowed from a Reima Pietilä scheme for the Sief Palace Extension.

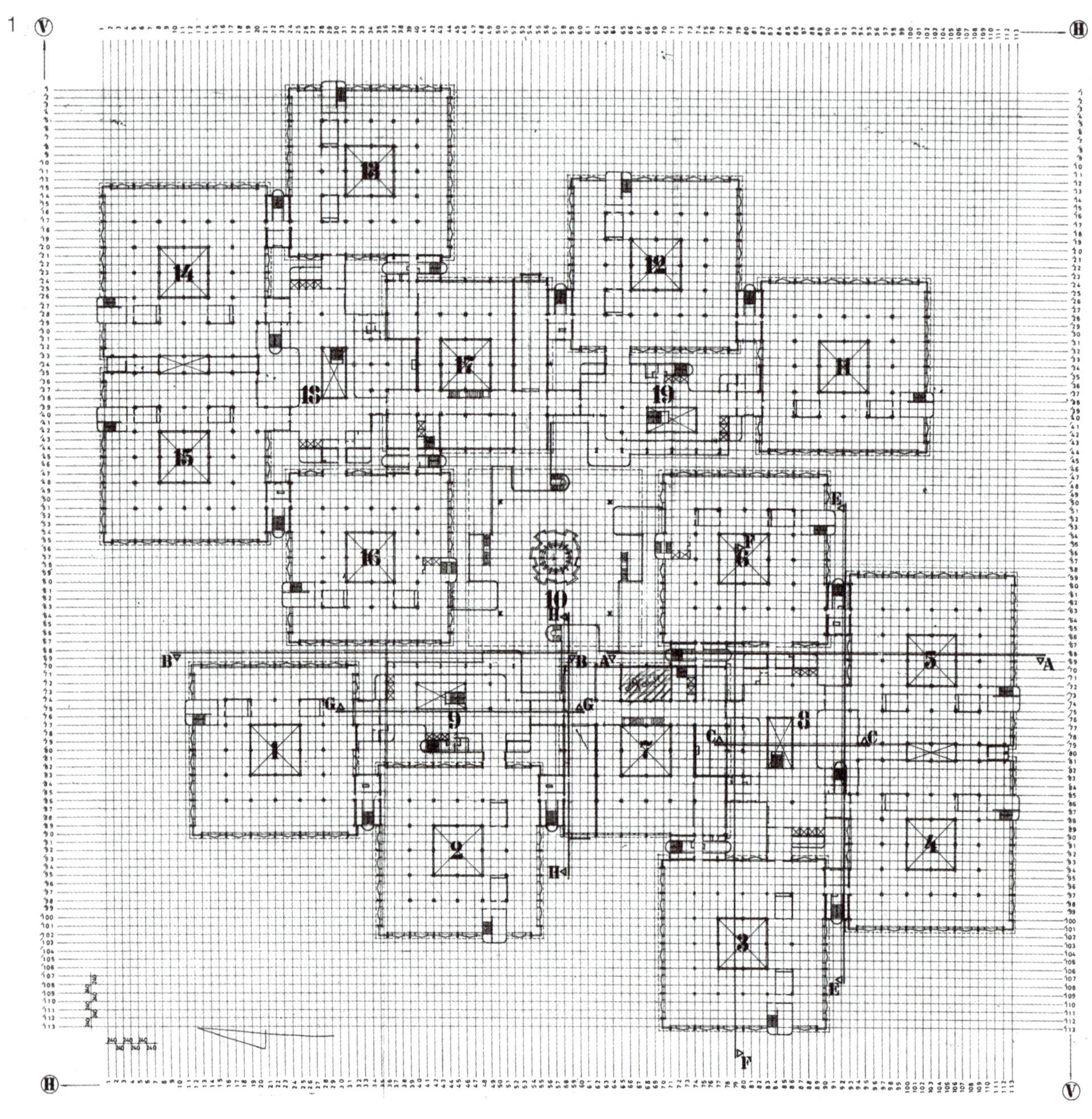

2

3 4

5

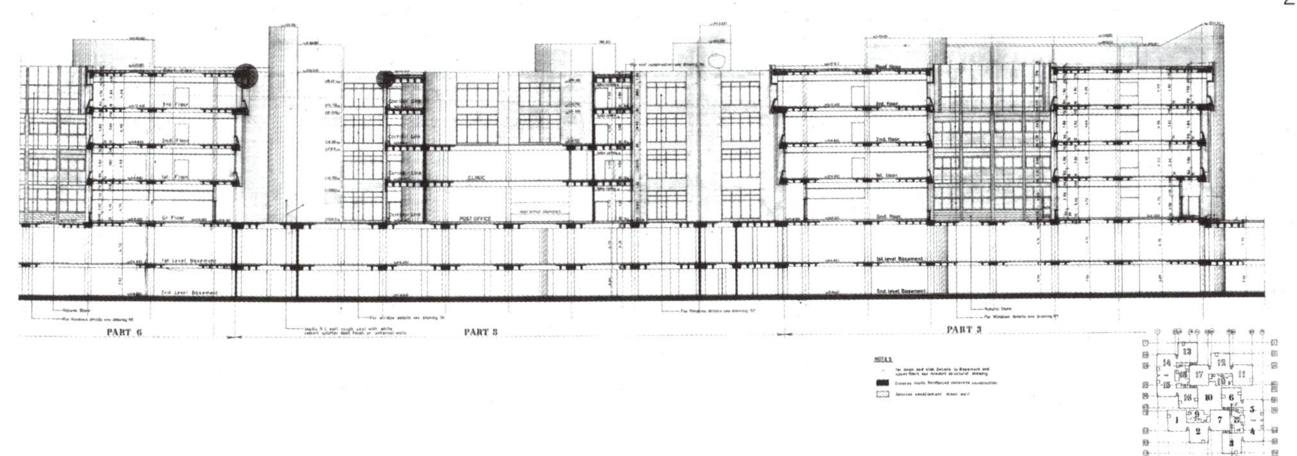

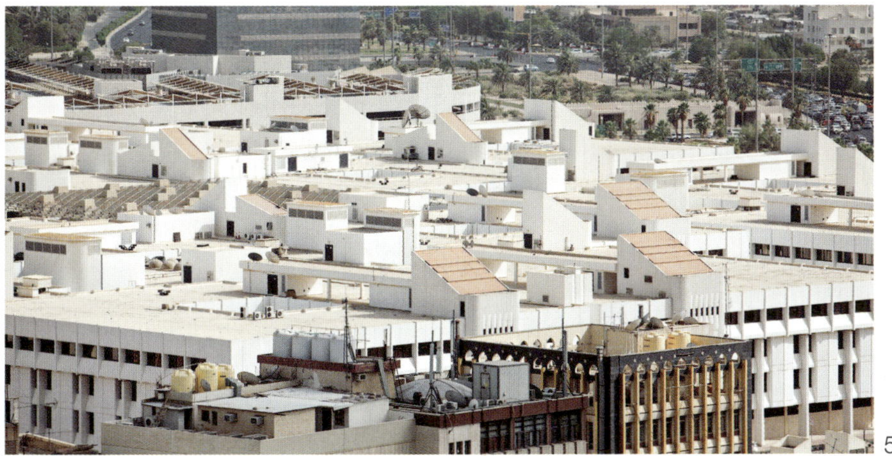

1. Aggregation scheme of the units, first floor plan
2. Longitudinal section
3. View of the main courtyard, 1982
4. Close-up view of the typical staircase element
5. General view of the complex

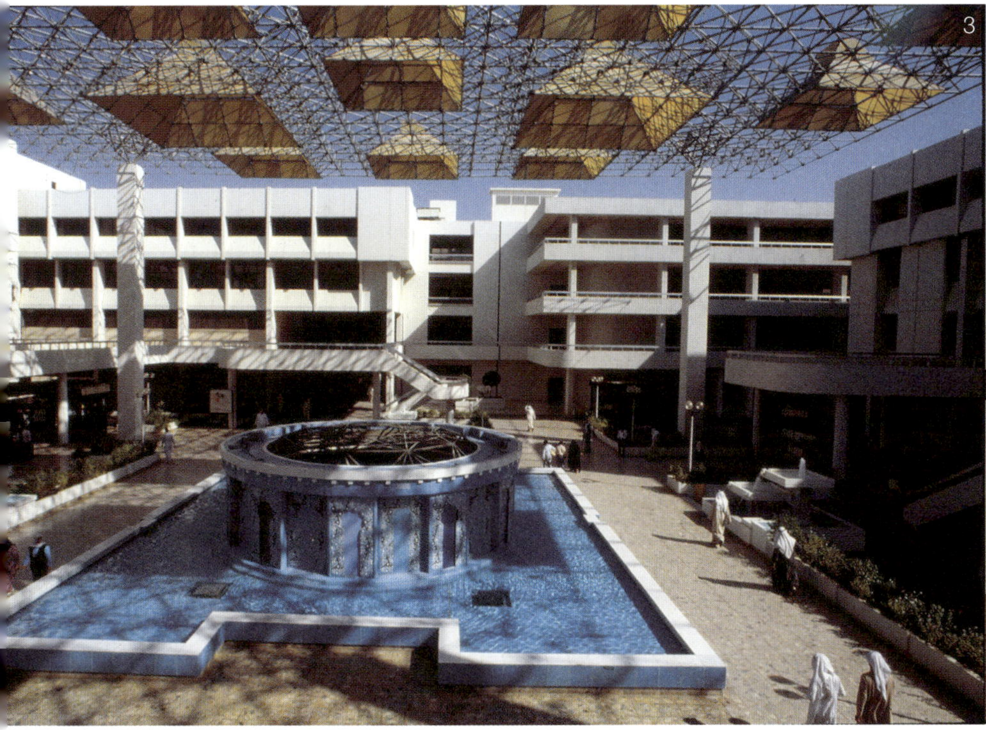

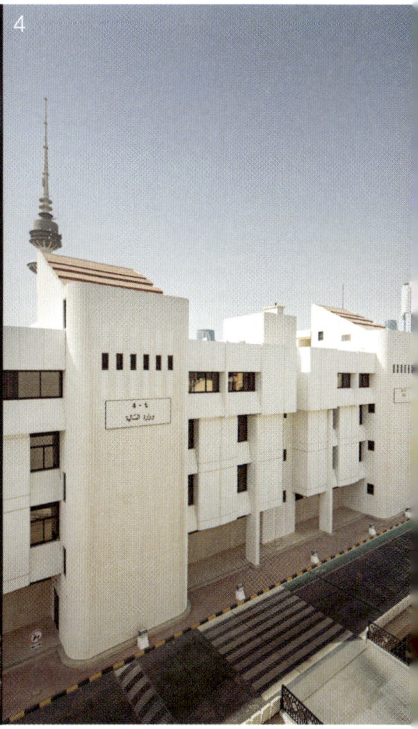

KUWAIT RADIO TELEVISION CENTRE

MIRQAB
1968–1978

DESIGNERS • Bureau d'Etudes Cordonnier (lead); J. Sutour (PTT architect); G. Mélicourt (planner)
CLIENT • Ministry of Public Works
CONTRACTOR • Ballast Nedam Group N.V.; Al-Hani Construction & Trading Co.

IN USE

The first national television broadcast dates back to 1961. At that time Kuwait was among the few countries in the Gulf with a state television programme. Later, in 1976, an Amiri decree established new and broader powers in this regard for the Ministry of Information. This issue led to the construction of a new complex to allocate the numerous technical needs, related to production and broadcasting. It was developed under the supervision of ORTF (Office de Radiodiffusion Télévision Française), which probably suggested the French design team.[137]

The preliminary concept carefully focused around a strict efficiency-oriented programme. It dictated the necessity to gather functions together and around a central core with a tower. In this concentric scheme, the production areas gravitate around the antenna, leaving enough space in the periphery for future growth. Once the forms were defined and proportioned, they were enveloped in a tri-dimensional skin that gives unity to the complex and (potentially) some sort of regionalist hint. This decorative apparatus, wrapped around a humble functional mass, is a reiteration of slender vertical prefabricated elements, which culminate with octahedrons: the negative space in between, create pointed arches. Sutour later proposed the same façade system for other projects in Kuwait, for example, the never built metro stations. The complex is now the Ministry of Information.

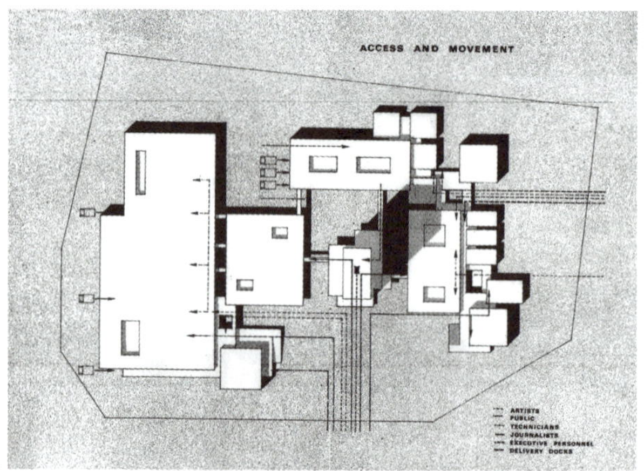

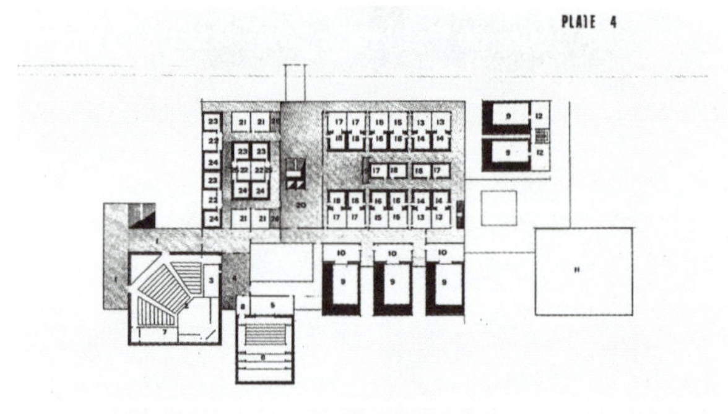

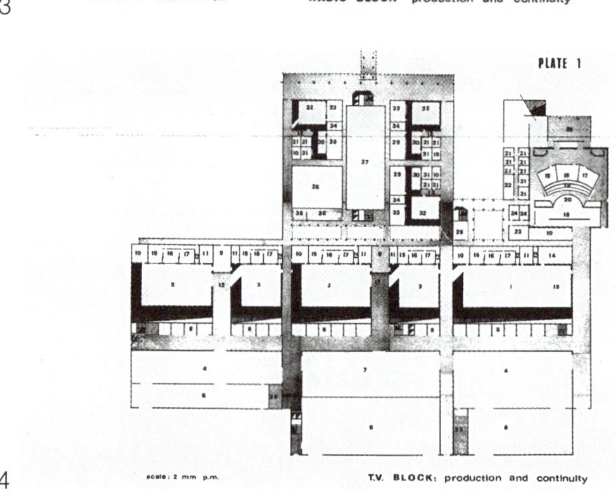

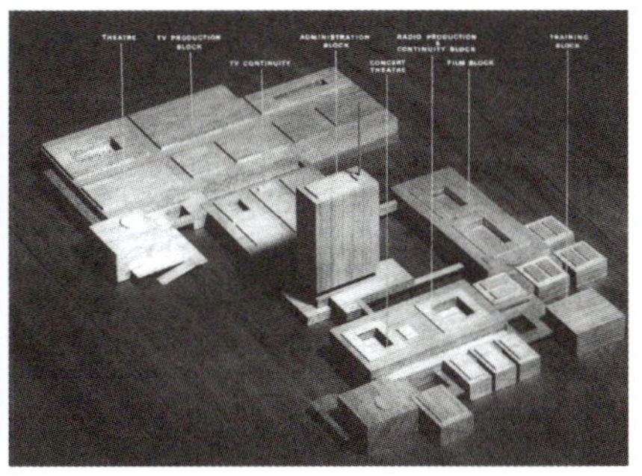

1. General view, circa 1978
2. Site plan, with masses and distribution
3. Plan detail, radio block
4. Plan detail, TV block
5. Scale model with function allocation

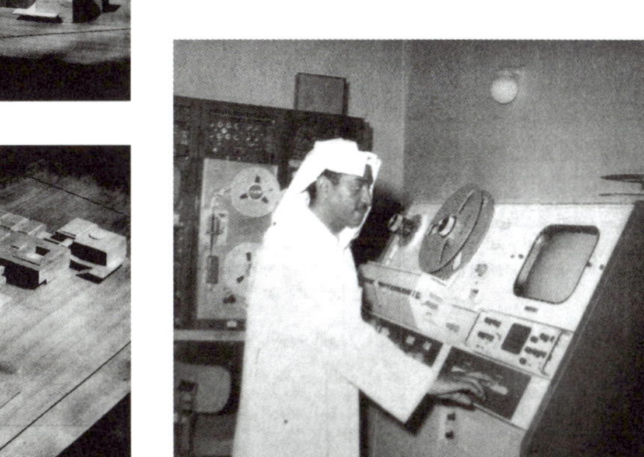

5

KUWAIT INSTITUTE FOR SCIENTIFIC RESEARCH (KISR)

SHUWAIKH
1979–1983

DESIGNERS • TAC; PACE; Arup Kuwait Ltd. (Ove Arup & Partners)
CLIENT • Kuwait Institute for Scientific Research
CONTRACTOR • Ahmadiah Contracting & Trading Co.

MODIFIED

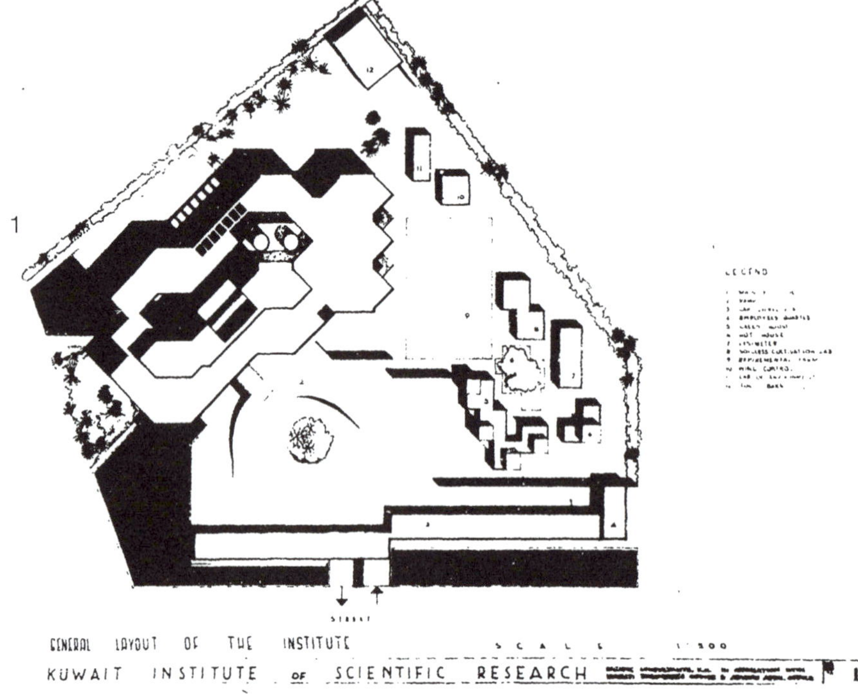

The new institute complex was assigned to PACE in a 22 ha site by the sea shore.

A U-shaped building of three floors opens up to the vehicular entrance, providing a protected arrival experience to the main door. On the ground floor the laboratories, a library, cafeteria and restaurant lead to the entrance garden, distributed along the two wings. Behind the entrance, a 250-seat lecture hall faces the sea. The scholars' offices on the second floor and the administration offices, housed on the third floor, are both connected to the garden by exposed concrete stairs that build the profile of each wings' top elevation.

All exterior masonry surfaces are white cement concrete with a sandblasted finish. A research lagoon and staff housing were also to be part of the scheme.[138] Being designed for a three phased development, the complex was to be consecutively extended up to 1989 with the addition of the Date Palm Tissue Culture Laboratories developed by PACE.

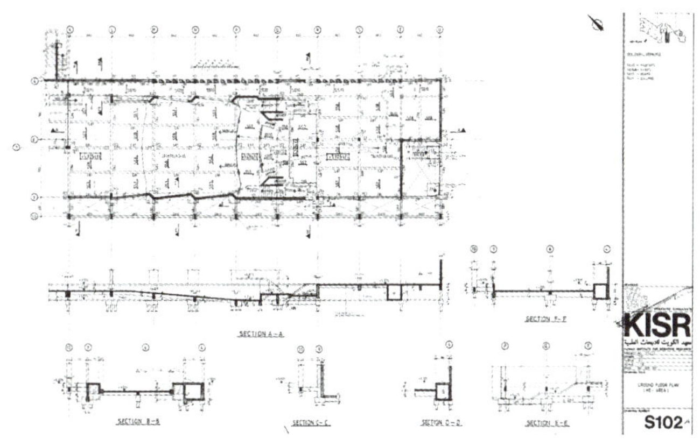

1. Site plan of the first institute by Pacific International Consultants, Asabuki Architects and KEO (1967–70), demolished
2. Entrance of the first institute
3. New institute (second project), view of the administrative support area including auditorium and restaurant
4. New institute, ground floor plan, detail

NOTES

94. Iraq Consult was associated in practice with PACE between 1968 to 1969

95. Candilis, George, *Reflection on the Development of the "City of Kuwait,"* typewritten, undated (c. 1970)

96. Sweet, Rod (ed.), *SSH design. The First 50 years,* 2011, Al-Khat Printing Press, Kuwait, p. 34

97. "Kuwait: Kindergarten," in *Werk*, 1973, v. 60, n. 11, pp. 1358–1361

98. Randall, Janice. "Sief Palace Area Buildings," in *Mimar 16: Architecture in Development*, Hasan-Uddin Khan (ed.), 1985, p. 32

99. Clouten, Neville, "Kuwait: Brilliant Desert Complex by Architects from a Frigid Arctic Climate," in *Architecture: the AIA journal*, Aug. 1983, v. 72, n. 8, p. 144

100. Shiber, George Saba, "The Kuwait Urbanization. Documentation Analysis Critique", Kuwait Government Printing Press, Kuwait, 1964

101. Cfr. BBPR, *The Future Development of the Old City of Kuwait*, Municipal Archive, 1969

102. Kubo, Michael "'Oil-Slick': Middle Eastern Economy and Late-Modern Aesthetics," in *Dis-appearing Non-West Conference*, Columbia, May 2012

103. *Middle East Construction*, Jul. 1979

104. "United Pre-Fab Building Company," in *Building Design*, Jun. 20, 1975

105. "Middle East," in *Architectural Design*, May–Jun. 1979

106. Cf. Gardiner, Stephen, *Kuwait. The Making of a City*, Longman, Harlow 1983, pp. 136–138

107. Salvin, Maeve, "Three Kuwait Banks of High Interest on Single Site by Skidmore, Owings & Merrill," in *Middle East Construction*, Aug. 1985

108. Anthony Blee, resident engineer for Sir Basil Spence International Partnership, interviewed in *Building Design*, Jun. 20, 1980

109. "Kuwait Law Courts," in *Middle East Construction*, Sep. 1980, v. 5, n. 9, pp. 84–85

110. "Covered Market" in *Mideast Markets*, Chase, Jun. 1976, p. 7

111. "Middle East Structures," in *Consulting Engineer*, Jun. 1979, v. 43, n. 6, p. 51

112. Kultermann, Udo, *Contemporary Architecture in the Arab States: Renaissance of a Region*, McGraw-Hill, 1999

113. *Makiya Associates*, company brochure, undated (probably 1986), p. 8

114. Cf. Kanan Makiya interviewed in: Weschler, Lawrence, *Calamities of Exile: Three Nonfiction Novellas*, University of Chicago Press, 1999, pp. 19–22

115. "Kuwait Stock Exchange," in *Middle East Construction*, Sep. 1979, v. 4, n. 9, pp. 67–69

116. Carapetian is famous for the picture at the Economist HQ by Alison and Peter Smithson "The Man on the Economist Plaza." He is co-author and photographer of several architectural publications.

Connah probably came to Kuwait while working for Reima Pietilä in the Sief Palace extension and in 1976 worked on a scheme for a housing complex that was never built.

117. Steele, James, *The Hassan Fathy Collection. A Catalogue of Visual Documents at the Aga Khan Award for Architecture*. Bern, Switzerland, 1989, The Aga Khan Trust for Culture, p. 53

118. Parkyn, Neil, "Winning the Numbers Game," in *Middle East Construction*, Apr. 1982

119. Al-Tehaih, S. "Housing Service in the State of Kuwait," A study submitted to His Highness the Amir, Kuwait Government Press, Kuwait, 1981. Charles Haddad Archive

120. Al-Ragam, Asseel, "The Destruction of Modernist Heritage: The Myth of Al-Sawaber," in *Journal of Architectural Education*, 2011, v. 67, n. 2, pp. 234–252

121. Richard Blagborne, *Sawaber Housing Project*, Kuwait Municipal Archive

122. Milano Due was completed in 1979.

123. Fahad Al-Salem Street was built in the first years of post 1952 urban development with no building regulations or guidelines. After Saba George Shiber arrival in Kuwait, from July 1960 the Municipal Council initiated "architectural control." Cf. Shiber, Saba George, *The Kuwait Urbanization: Documentation, Analysis, Critique*, Kuwait Govt. Printing Press, Kuwait, 1964

124. Gardiner, Stephan, *Kuwait: The Making of the City,* Harlow, Longman, 1983, p. 138

125. Taylor, Brian Brace, "Kuwait City Water Front Development." *Mimar 34, Architecture in Development*, London, Concept Media Ltd., 1990, p. 14

126. Cfr. *Abdulla Al-Ahmed Street Development Project, Sharq Phase II Report,* Kuwait, CRSK Archive

127. Second Kuwait Master Plan

128. Which led to the crash known as the 1982 Souk Al-Manakh crisis.

129. Kuwait Real Estate Development Company originally designed as a commercial office building and at the final stage of construction was converted to the Burgan Bank's Headquarters.

130. Former associate of Hisham Munir between 1974–79 and later chief architect of Archicentre.

131. Today, Public Authority for Minors Affairs, this was initially a commercial tower owned by Salah Al-Sultan.

132. These projects are eventually designed by Arab Consultants.

133. Ericksson, Arthur, "Projects in Kuwait and Saudi Arabia," in *Places of Public Gathering in Islam: Proceedings of Seminar Five* from the Series *Architectural Transformations in the Islamic World*, Amman, Jordan, May 4–7, 1980, The Aga Khan Award for Architecture, Philadelphia, 1980, p. 81

134. *The Alison and Peter Smithson Archive: An Inventory,* Special Collections, Frances Loeb Library, Graduate School of Design, Harvard University

135. Among other projects Energoprojekt participated in the construction of buildings such as the Kuwait Towers and the Waterfront facilities.

136. Following the competition in 1981 the main water fountain of the building was awarded to the local artist Ja'afar Islah.

137. *Kuwait Radio Television Centre*, brochure, Municipal Archive, undated

138. Cf. *Middle East Construction*, Oct. 1982

SPECIMENS IV
Building as programme
1980–1989

COMMERCIAL BANK OF KUWAIT OPERATIONS CENTRE

SHARQ
1979–1986

DESIGNERS • Skidmore Owings & Merrill (architect); PACE (associate consultant)
CLIENT • Commercial Bank of Kuwait
CONTRACTOR • Impresa Castelli & Al-Sayer Co.

IN USE

The CBK building assignment helped to establish SOM as the reference firm for Kuwait banking groups in the late 1970s. The initial client's request was for a new headquarters. Three proposals were developed and submitted, but none implemented; meanwhile the request changed into an operations centre.[139] Despite the programme's reduction, the building shows interesting design aspects. The functional space is a "stone translucent box."[140] The inner volume of glass blocks is protected by a detached second skin: a stone clad layer that shades the offices. Consequently, the façade appears like an abstract geometrical grid. The building is enveloped in a squared mesh, which has different densities on different planes. Each element of the volume is proportioned and defined by the monotonous regularity of this *Cartesian tessellation*. The distance between the two skins helps to break the regularity with the shifted pattern created by the shadows. The same façade system was later proposed for the SOM's unrealised project for the Ahmed Al-Jaber Commercial Complex, on the opposite side of the road, in 1982.

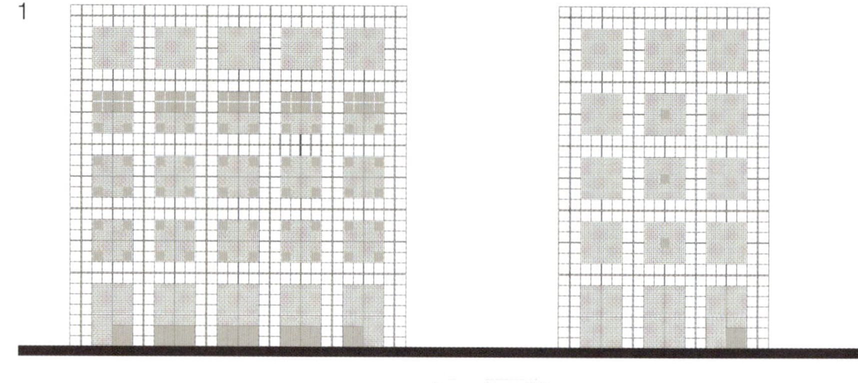

0   5   10m

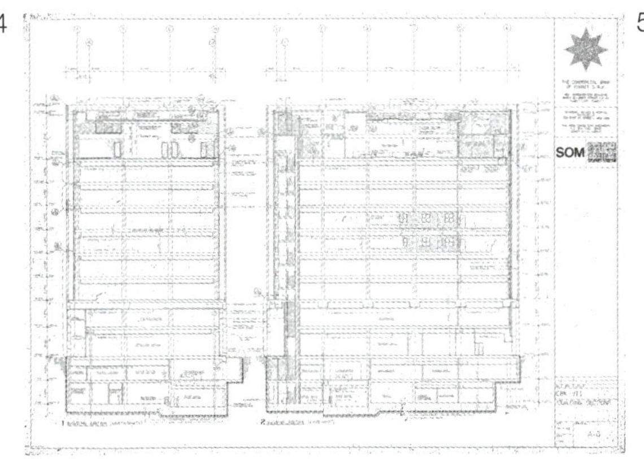

1. Front and side elevations
2. Façade detail
3. View from Ahmed Al-Jaber Street
4. Side view
5. Sections

ALGHANIM INDUSTRIES HEADQUARTERS

SHUWAIKH
1978–1980

DESIGNERS •Perkins & Will (architect); KEO (associate architect)
CLIENT • Alghanim Industries
CONTRACTOR • Unknown

IN USE

The zig-zag façade defines the building as it faces towards Airport Road. The curtain façade prismatic arrangement is walled towards the south and has open aluminium framed glazing facing north. Fully equipped with state-of-the-art computer systems by the early 1980s the building was to house the Alghanim Industries operations centre and corporate offices.

The building, comprising of one single bar, has two floors above-ground that are open plan and punctuated by circular partitions that confine access to restricted areas and interrupt the façade accordion system, allowing for the major entrances to the showroom and management offices area.

The ingenious façade system is clad in travertine stone mechanically fixed, allowing for air circulation. On the opposite side a dark glazed curtain provides natural light horizontally to the offices and functions as a skylight for the basement. The internal elements are carefully detailed such as the full-height interior doors. The flexible partitions show a level of precision not often seen in Kuwait.

1

1. Main elevation, details of the entrance and of the apertures
2. Interiors, office spaces, 1980

ممنوع الوقوف
من هذا الجهة
NO PARKING
THIS SIDE

KOC COMPUTER & TRAINING CENTRE

MINA ABDULLA REFINERY
1979–1983

DESIGNER • Tripe and Wakeham Partnership with Charles Turfat Haddad Associates (CTHA)
COMPETITION ENTRY •
John S. Bonnington Partnership with KEO
CLIENT • Kuwait Oil Company

MODIFIED

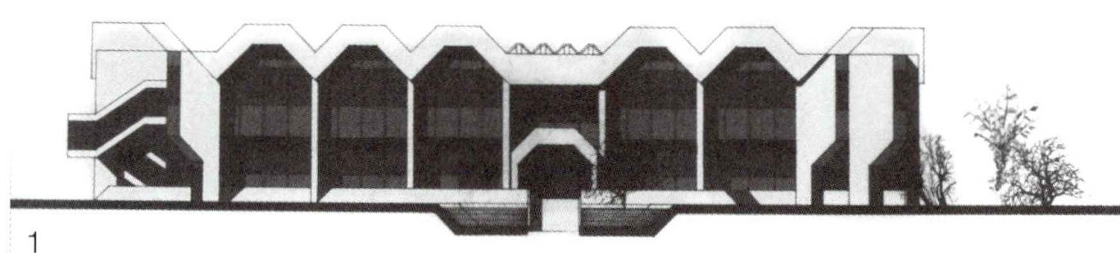

1

2

This complex is referred to as an office mat-building; an integrated office building including facilities for training and a computer centre.[141] The CTHA bid mentions a coherence with the "architectural style of the existing buildings" and the application of "local materials" such as the precast concrete frame and the lime brick partitioning. This mat-building complex of 1,400 m^2 providing training for 450 students and was prepared for an extension towards a maximum populaion of 1,500.

For the computer centre, CTHA presented its bid with Morrison Design Partnership, well-known for similar projects.[142] However the single-storey, long-span, column free scheme of the John S. Bonnington Partnership was eventually built as the winning proposal. With a perimeter zone of cellular offices, made of dismountable partitions and the central zone with open-plan office areas, this bar scheme was considerably more flexible and centralised around the computer machine room. The false ceiling and the continuous raised floor are arguments put forward by A. E. J. Morris for an efficient modern office layout.[143]

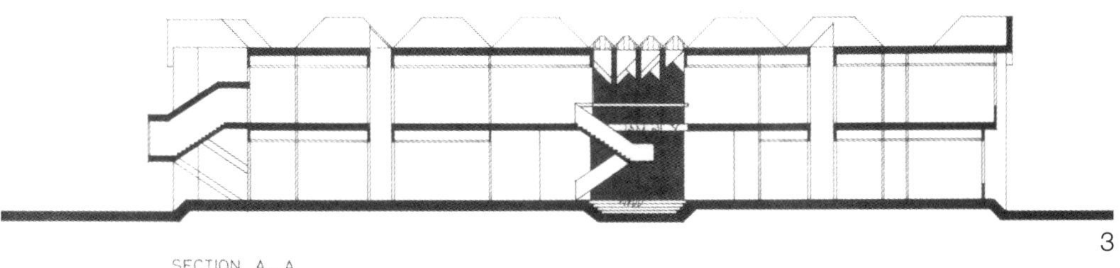

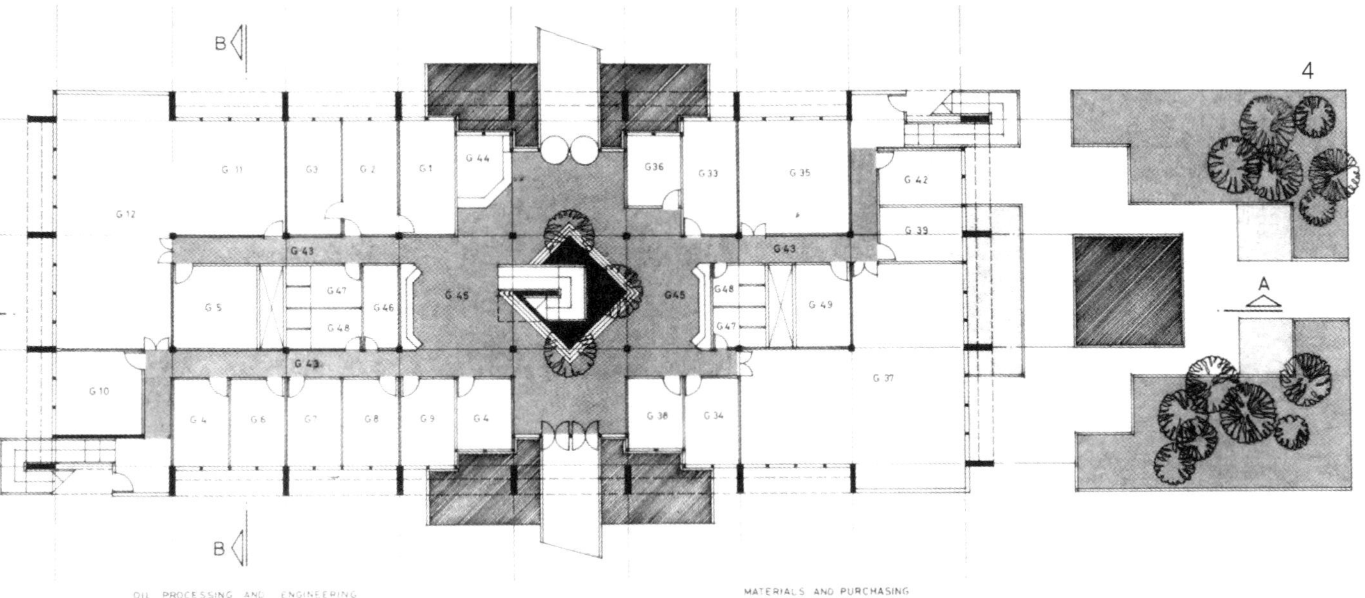

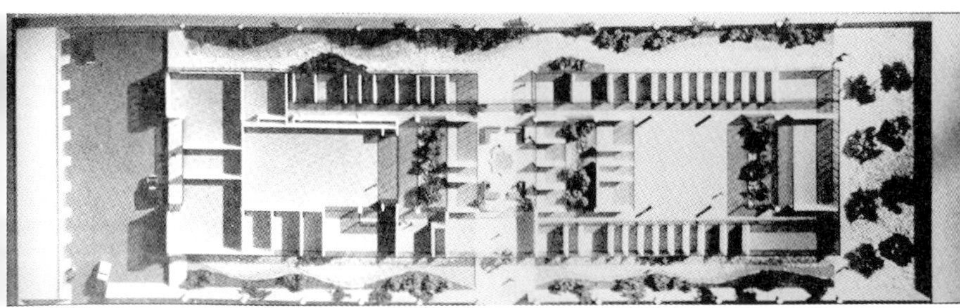

INTEGRATED CENTRE BY CTHA, VERSION C:

1. East elevation
2. Perspective view
3. Longitudinal section
4. Ground floor plan

5

BONNINGTON PARTNERSHIP AND KEO PROPOSAL FOR THE COMPUTER CENTRE BUILDING:

5. Scale model, top view

TRIPE & WAKEHAM PROPOSAL FOR TRAINING CENTRE COMPLEX:

6. Scale model, general views

6

AL-AHLI BANK HEADQUARTERS

SAFAT SQUARE
1979–1988

DESIGNERS: Skidmore, Owings & Merrill (architect); PACE (associate consultant)
CLIENT: Al-Ahli Bank of Kuwait
CONTRACTOR • Mohammed Abdulmohsen Al-Kharafi & Sons Co.

IN USE

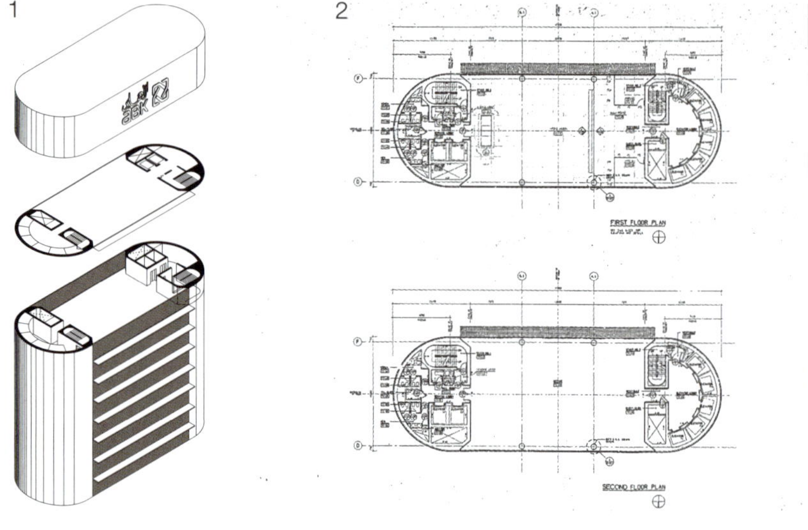

This project refers to the client's choice after three different schemes were proposed. The twenty-storey new Al-Ahli Bank tower, located in Kuwait City's downtown facing the old souq, reveals some design influences from the nearby Joint Banking Centre Towers also from SOM.

The compact building is formed by three solid geometric volumes, coated in the same stone. The tower has a rectangular footprint with round sides and comprises two structural cores at the west and east edges. The other elevations reveal two large glass panes, one of which has a special-linear shading device to protect it from the southern sun.

At ground level, the main entrance is a triangular prism. At the opposite end, the third rectangular volume features a double façade with standard quadrangular cuts into the exterior level providing shadow to the inner fenestration.

The banking hall is naturally illuminated by skylights at the mezzanine level. The interiors are enriched by well-crafted golden and polished bronze details.

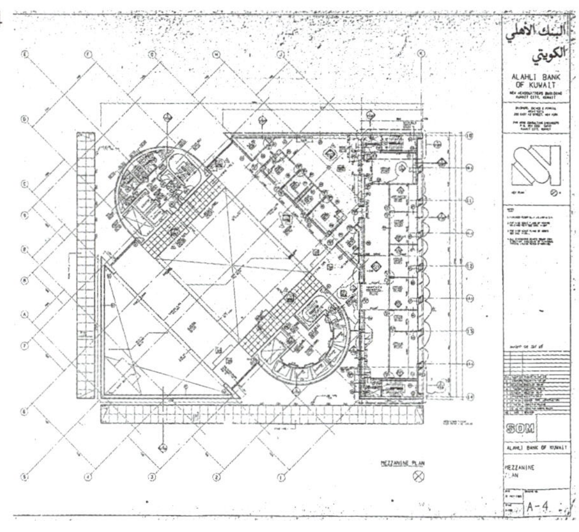

1. Axonometric view
2. Typical office floor plans
3. Scale model, south elevation with light study. Shows a different proposal for the horizontal structures and for the entrance
4. Bank branch, mezzanine floor plan

DERWAZAH ABDULRAZAQ AND SAFAT SQUARE

MUBARAKIYA
1977–1986

DESIGNERS • Devecon Arkitekter (architect);
Devecon Ekono Oy (services); INCO (associate architect)
CLIENT • Kuwait Municipality

MODIFIED

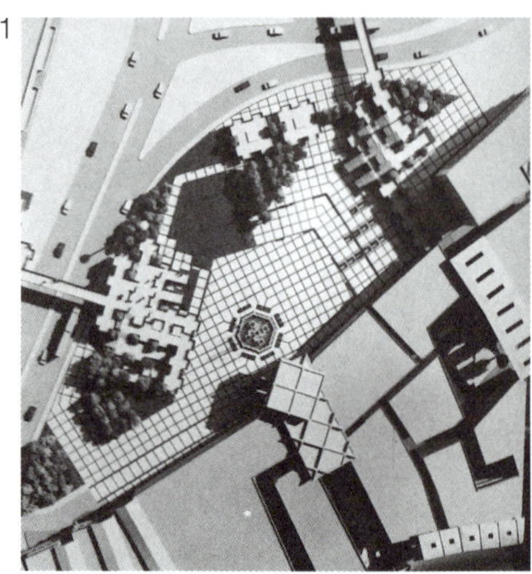

BBPR PROPOSAL FOR SAFAT SQUARE:

1. Scale model, 1977

DEVECON PROPOSAL FOR SAFAT SQUARE:

2. Perspective view, 1981
3. Opening ceremony for Safat Square, 1988
4. Construction detail for ceiling and pavement of
Derwazah Abdulrazaq square under passage

The consecutive detailed urban plans and reports by BBPR interfacing the city old core with a modern transportation infrastructure layer, both current and future, led the Municipality to pursue public space "beautification." Several design consultants were invited to submit proposals for two critical nodes, at the time operating as traffic roundabouts.

The Finnish practice was awarded the first prize for both nodes. First for the Derwazah pedestrian underpass in 1979 and two years later for Safat Square lowered piazza with a monument surrounded by retail units that are screened by Ja'afar Islah's murals. In both schemes, the use of structural elements as ornament was a major aspect in the ceilings under the road.

Once the first of these spaces was completed, it relieved the traffic congestion at the crossroads and extended public space underground at the base of the Joint Banking Centre (1976–83) and Souq Al-Kuwait (1973–76). This underpass remains a major connection between the large housing scheme of Al-Sawaber and the old city.

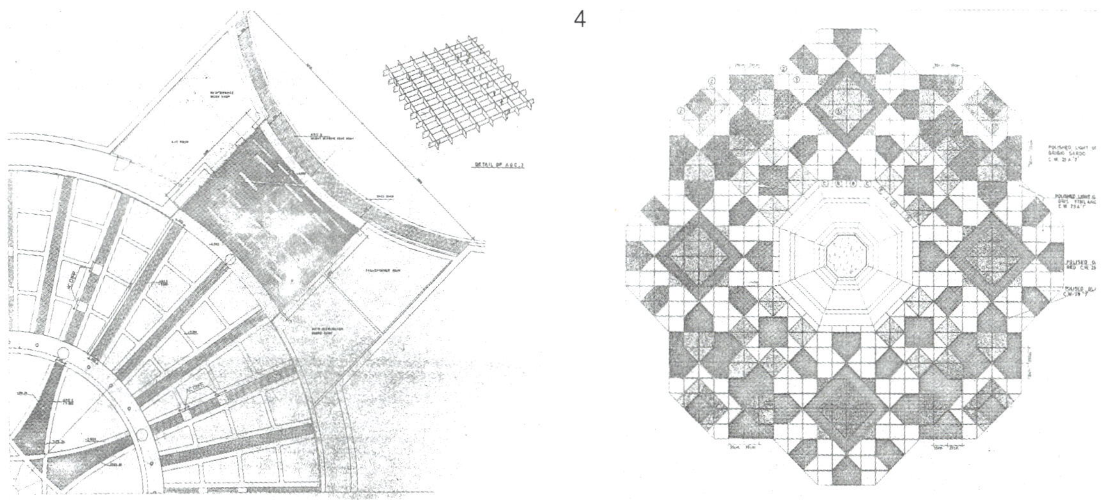

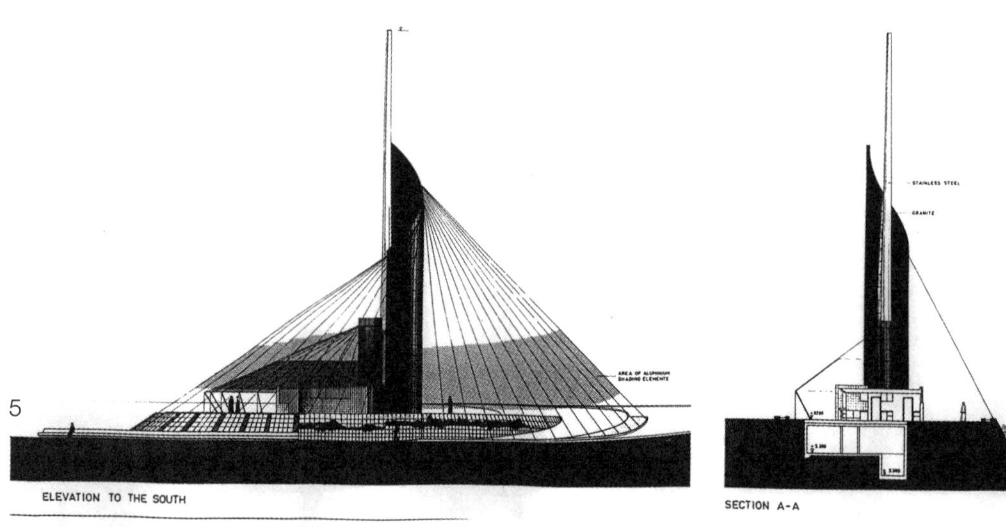

ELEVATION TO THE SOUTH

SECTION A-A

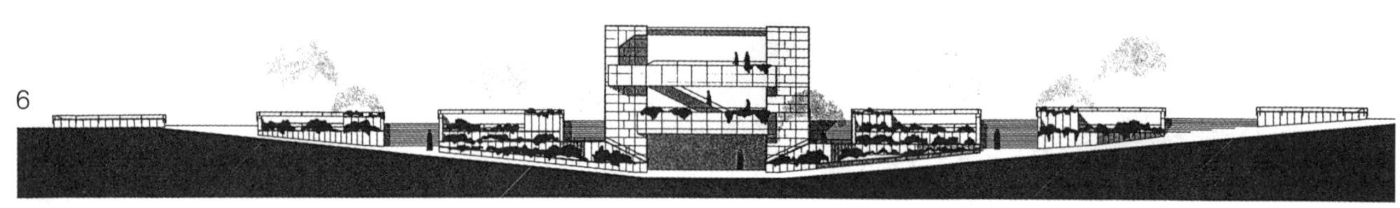

SECTION B-B

SECTION C-C

SECTION D-D

SECTION E-E

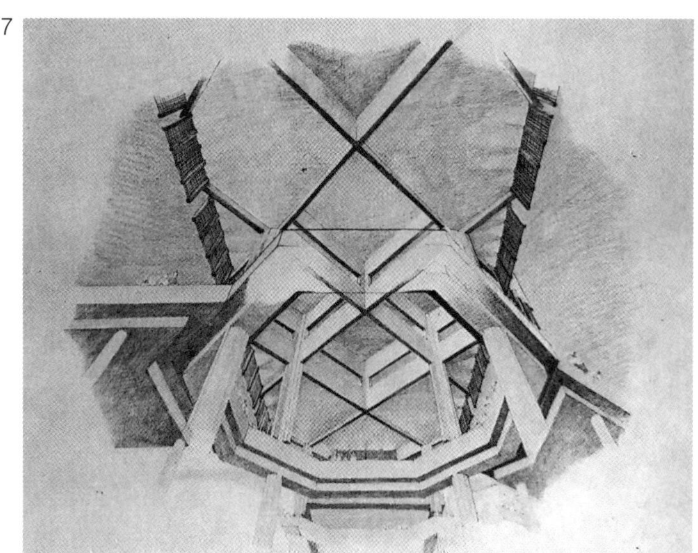

DEVECON PROJECT:

*5. Details of the sculptural element by Ja'afar Islah,
in the centre of the composition*
*6. Sections of the sunken piazza and relative
vertical connections to the street level*
*7. BBPR, perspective views of the covered market
connecting Safat Square with Mubarakiya Souq:
the New Street and Galleries*

CENTRE FOR PHYSICAL MEDICINE AND REHABILITATION

SULAIBIKHAT
1979–1981

DESIGNERS • IMOS (Stanko Kristl, principal)
CLIENT • Ministry of Public Works

UNBUILT

1

A Slovenian architectural corporation specialising in hospitals was asked to develop this centre for 80 inpatient beds as well as outpatient, diagnostics, laboratory and prosthetics services.[144] With the completion of the University Medical Centre in Lujbljana, a group of experts within this institution under Stanko Kristl's guidance became specialists in "medical architecture."[145] The architectural direction of IMOS can be found in Kristl's previous work.

The proposal uses all the site extension maximising the building footprint to respond to a centralised and organic scheme. The implementation of the medical programme generated both form and shape.

The inpatient and ambulatory room units are concentrated in two four-storey capsules with octagonal plans, one of the sides devoted to access, the opposite side to staircases and the remaining to pairs of rooms. The rest of the programme is displayed in stepped levels overlooking big halls filling the angled gaps between long corridors. Considering the material and spatial conditions proposed, one can imagine similarities with Izola Hospital, completed by the designer in 1981, with the use of identical façade cladding and the open spaces for swimming pools.

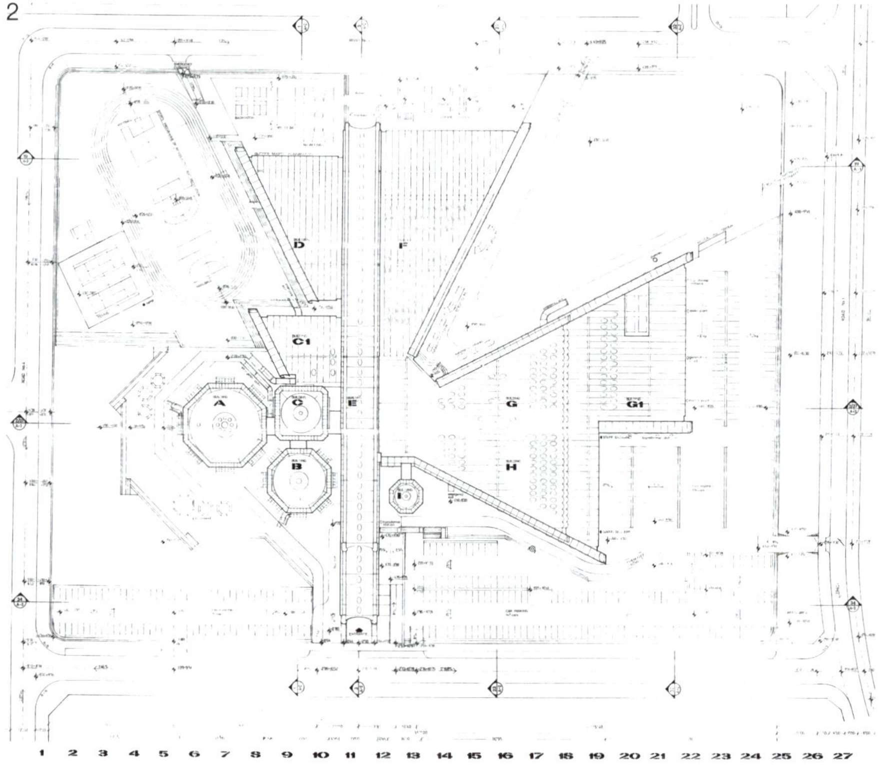

2

1. Perspective
2. Roof level plan
3. Main floor plan
4. Sections

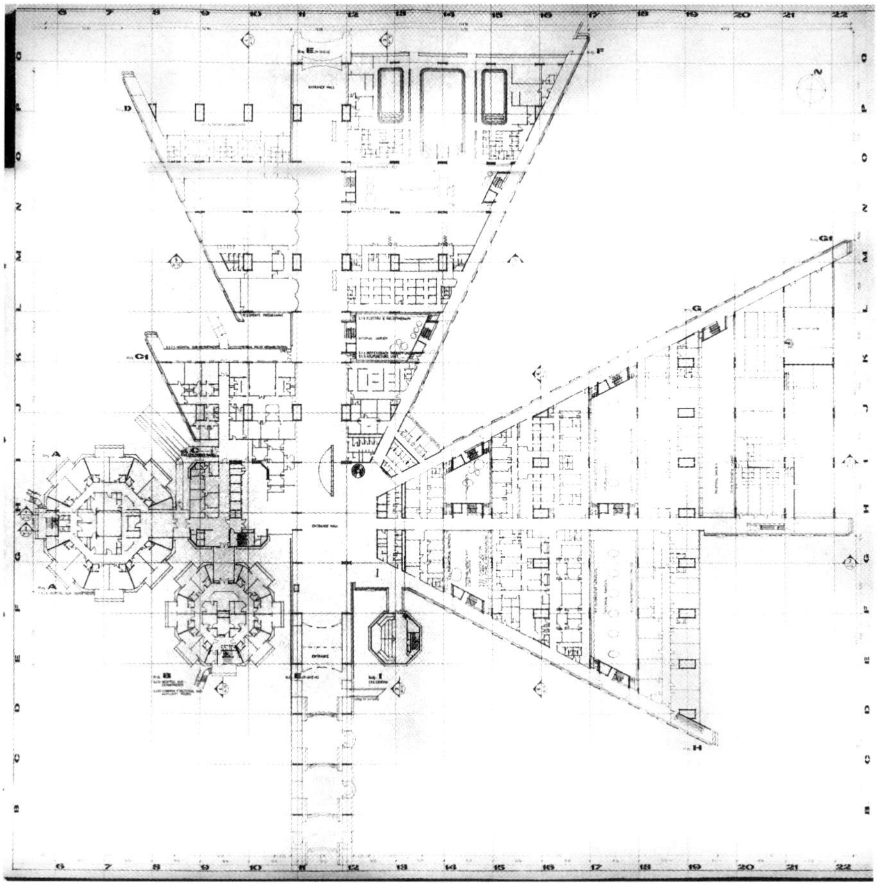

3

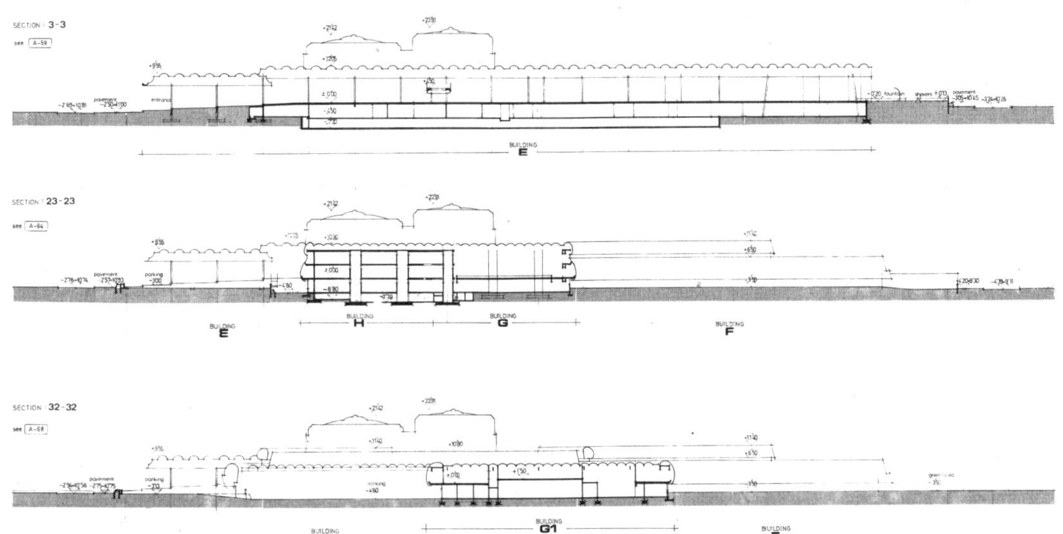

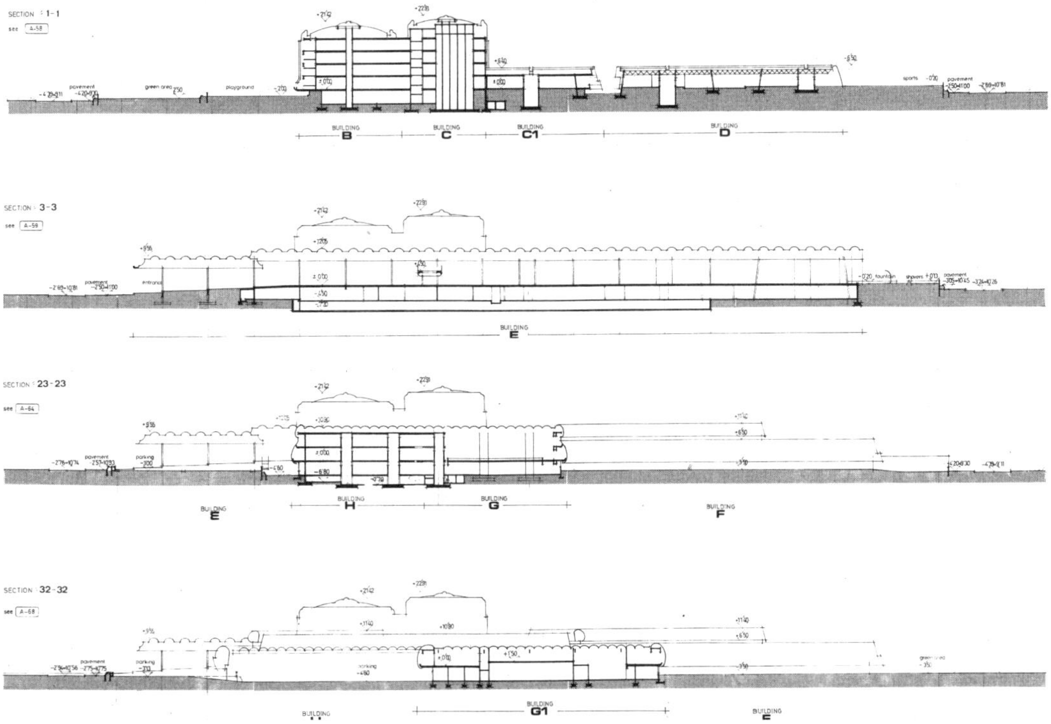

4

UNITED ARAB SHIPPING COMPANY HEADQUARTERS

SHUWAIKH
1980–1984

DESIGNER • PACE (lead consultant)
CLIENT • United Arab Shipping
Company Headquarters (UASC)
CONTRACTOR • Kuwait Singaporean
Trading & Contracting Co.

IN USE

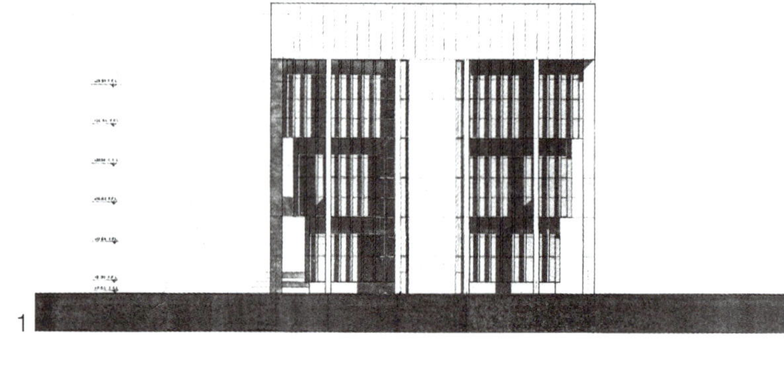

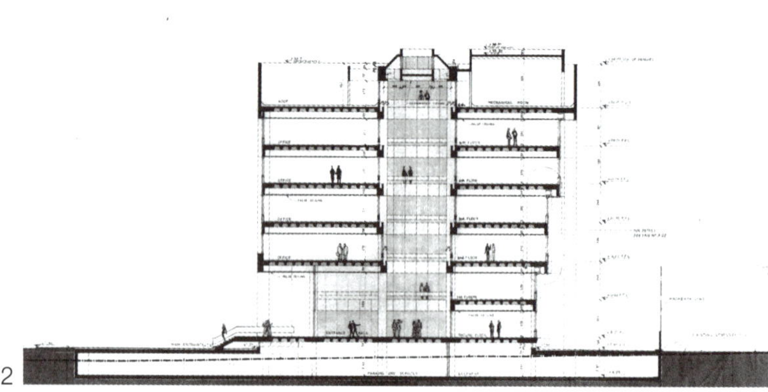

The shipping company was founded in 1976, joining six shareholding states of the Gulf to serve the shipping needs of the region. The headquarters was placed in Kuwait. The context is an industrial area and the building is conveniently aligned with the main road, which leads to the main port.[146]

The building is a variation on the design theme of the inverted step pyramid. Volumetrically it is a basic rectangular prism, tapered at the bottom. Five floors high, with a mechanical room and services hidden on the roof by a tall parapet, the building finds its distinctive spatial quality in its central hollow core from a vertical light well that cuts all the way to the roof. Three solid cores, in the centre of each side, host the vertical distribution and the service pipes, leaving free office spaces at each floor. Externally a white marble exoskeleton surrounds and supports the glass box stacks. In direct contrast with the bright colour of the cladding structure, the glazes are tinted and the metal supports are in bronze anodised aluminium.

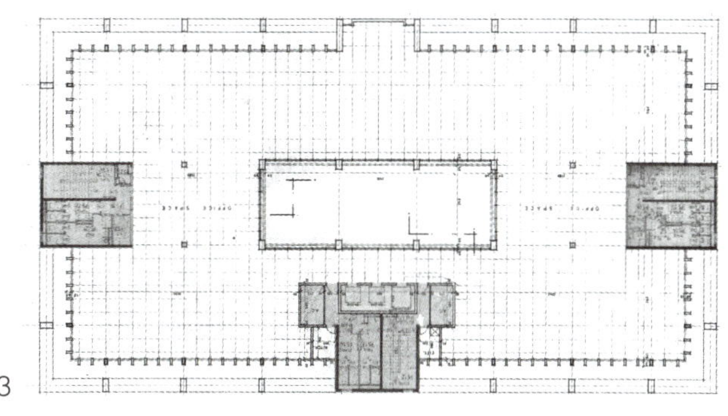

3

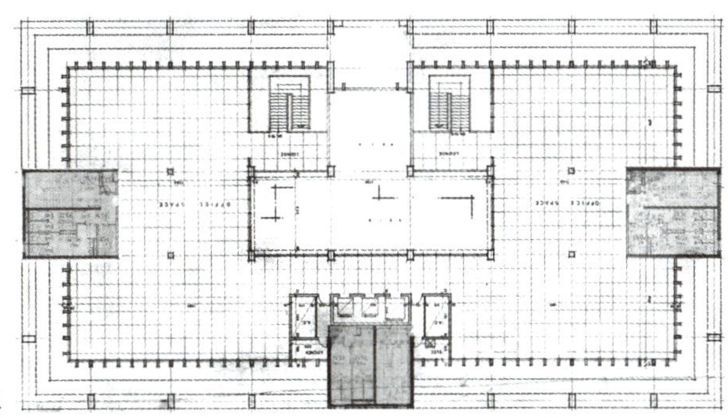

4

5

1. Side elevation
2. Section through the central hall
3. Upper floor plan
4. Ground floor plan
5. Overall view

CONFERENCE CENTRE

BAYAN
1980–1986

DESIGNERS • Stojan Maksimović, Sava Centar Foundation (architect); Archicentre (associated architect); KEO; PACE; SSH (associated architect venture from 1983)
CLIENT • Ministry of Public Works
CONTRACTOR • Ahmadiah Contracting & Trading Co.

MODIFIED

The Kuwait Conference Centre was commissioned through an international competition in the early 1980s with the intention to provide the country with a main convention facility, deep in a lush garden.

It was inaugurated by H.H. the Amir in 1986 and hosted, soon after the opening, the Fifth Islamic Summit Conference. In its rooms the agreement on the International Islamic Court of Justice was promulgated, for settling disputes arising among Islamic States in accordance with Sharia.

The design competition was won by Sava Centar Foundation design team Stojan Maksimović and further developed in Kuwait with Archicentre, but the work was delayed and the Serbian architect never continued its development. The design was implemented, some years later, by three of the major local firms; it is not clear how much of the initial winning scheme was finally translated into reality.[147]

In its final configuration the complex was centred on a flat square pavilion accommodating one auditorium for 2,000 participants and six other minor halls. The back of the main building opened onto a formal geometric garden with shaded walkways, regular tree rows and water features. All around the park, six U-shaped buildings accommodated visiting Heads of State, staff and delegates, a mosque and recreational facilities.

The complex is still in use today, hosting major international political events and summits.

1

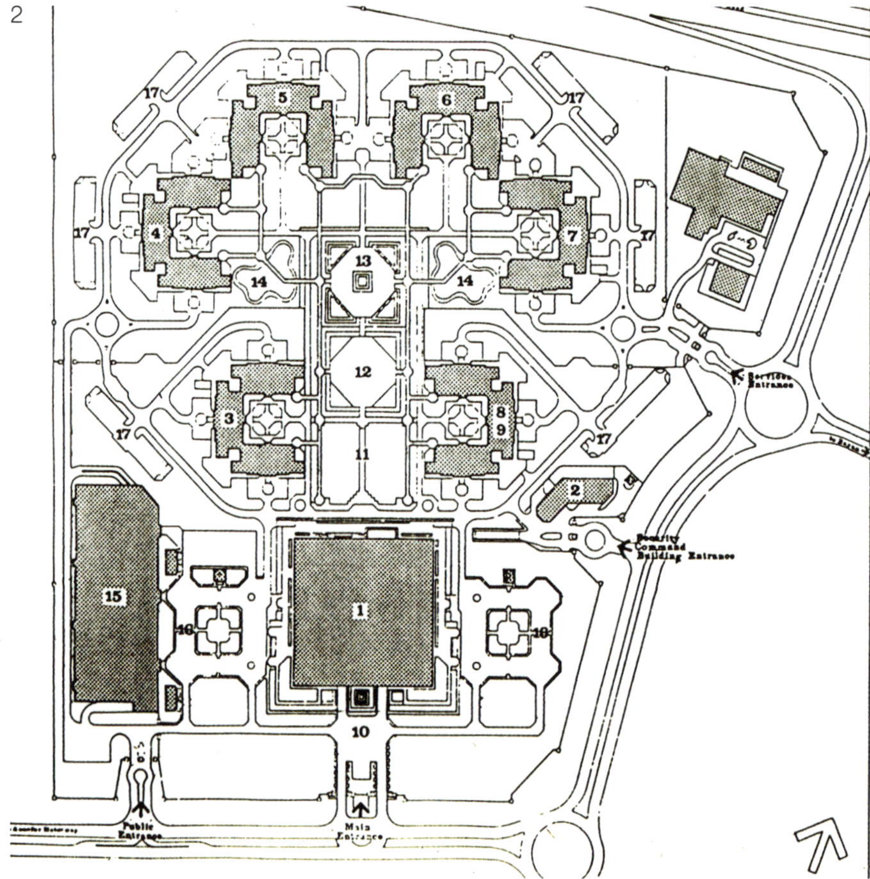

2

3 4

S. MAKSIMOVIĆ PROPOSAL:

1. Perspective view of the entrance of the main pavilion, undated
2. Site plan
3. View of one residence building for guests
4. View of the gardens
5. Scale model, general view of the complex

5

HOTEL INTERCONTINENTAL PROJECT

SALMIYA
1980

DESIGNERS • Alfred Roth (architect);
Arab Consultants (associate consultant)
CLIENT • Al-Mishbah Industrial and
Trading Co.

UNBUILT

In the early 1980s a hotel, with
shop gallery and garage complex,
was commissioned to Roth by the
businessman and developer, Khalid
Al-Essa. The two knew each other
well since Al-Essa was the Minister
of Public Works from 1965 to 1971,
the same period in which Roth's
schools were built. The hotel was to
have been situated on the seafront in
Salmiya, an area that was intended to
be transformed soon into a very busy
commercial district. The reception and
the public and commercial spaces
were located on the ground floor,
in a square platform. On top of this
space the rooms were distributed in a
staggered order. The idea was to have
each of the 220 rooms equally facing
the sea view and exposed to the north,
for better climate control. The project
was completed and submitted to the
municipality for approval, but was never
executed; nonetheless Roth published
it among his most recent work in
1983.[148]

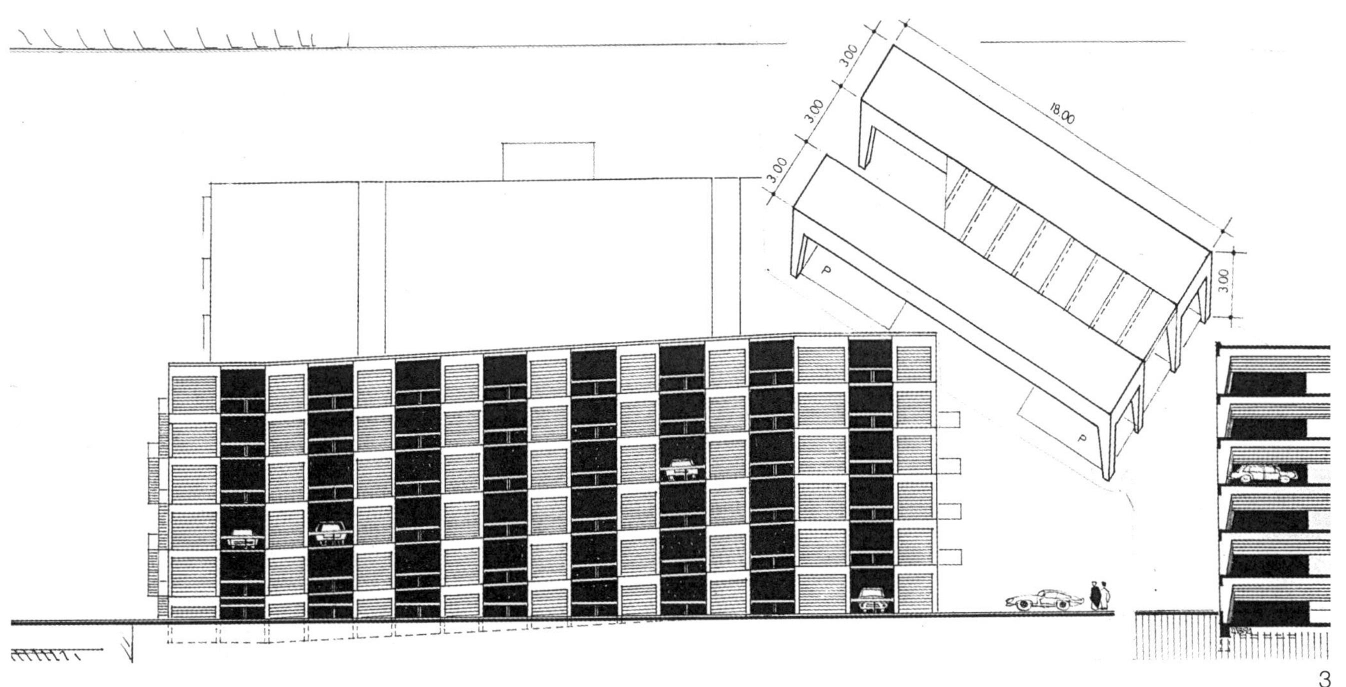

TYPICAL FLOOR PLAN

1. Guest rooms
2. Storage
3. Swimming pool
4. Car park

4

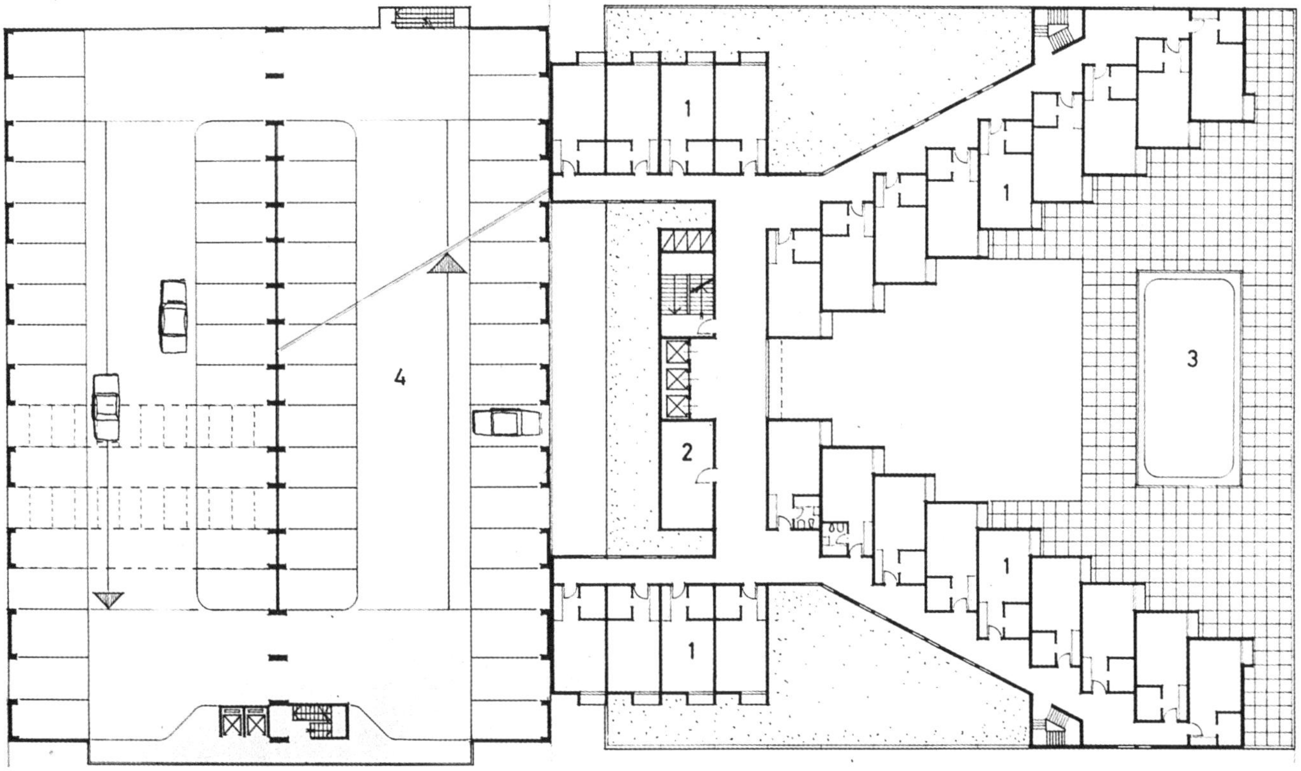

SHEIKH NASSER AL-SABAH MOSQUE

RAS AL-SALMIYA
1980–1981

DESIGNERS • Geteco;
Bureau d'Architecture Henri Montois (architect);
KEG (services)
CLIENT • Kuwait Projects Co. for Contracting
and Buildings (KSCC)
CONTRACTOR • Unknown

IN USE

The mosque was commissioned by
Sheikh Nasser al-Sabah and offered
to the neighbourhood, near his pre-
existing palace. The project combines
two distinct masses: the prayer hall is
a stepped pyramid, while the prism is
the entrance with ablutions, a library, an
Islamic research centre and the Imam's
office. The vertical axis of the slender
minaret marks the connection between
the two bodies.

From a distance the pyramid's horizontal pattern, created with glass-fibre
reinforced concrete bands, works in
intentional contrast with the vertical
rhythm of the travertine fins, which
punctuate the entrance block. The
whole project is about light and the
control of it. The reiterated horizontal
and vertical elements, staggered with
the recessed groves, act as filters for
the sun. The *intrados* of the pyramid
is a tinted glass cladding that works in
resonance with the outdoor membrane,
modulating the light. The structural
design plays an important role in the
definition of the prayer hall.

The pyramidal structure involves four
large hollow beams connected to a
platform, which supports the cupola.
The hollow beams work as chimneys,
while the intake of cooled air is above
the perimeter walls.[149]

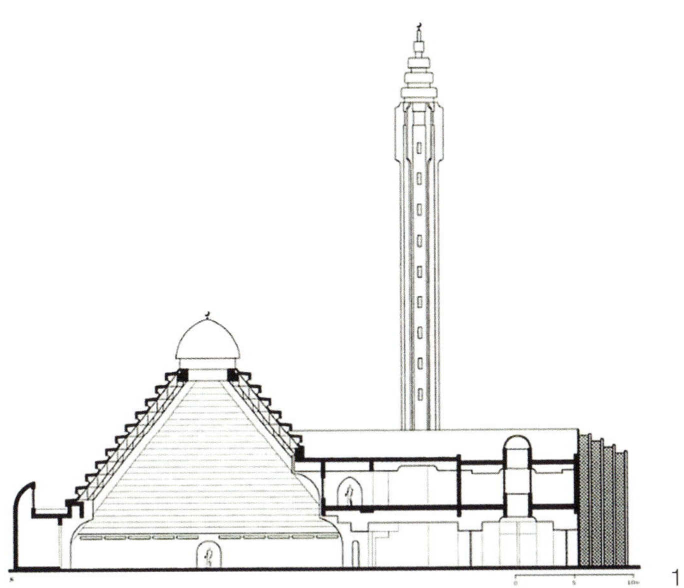

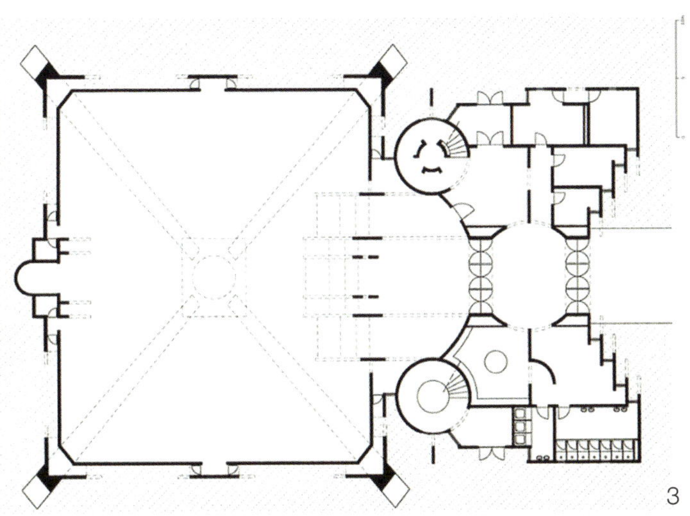

1. Section through the prayer hall
2. Scale model, 1980
3. Ground floor plan

KUWAIT ZOO EXTENSION AND RENOVATION

OMARIYA
1981–1982

DESIGNERS • John S. Bonnington Partnership (architect); KEO (associate architect); Michael Barclay Partnership (structural); Mero Raumstruktur GbmH (space frame)
CLIENT • Ministry of Public Works, Major Projects Department

UNBUILT

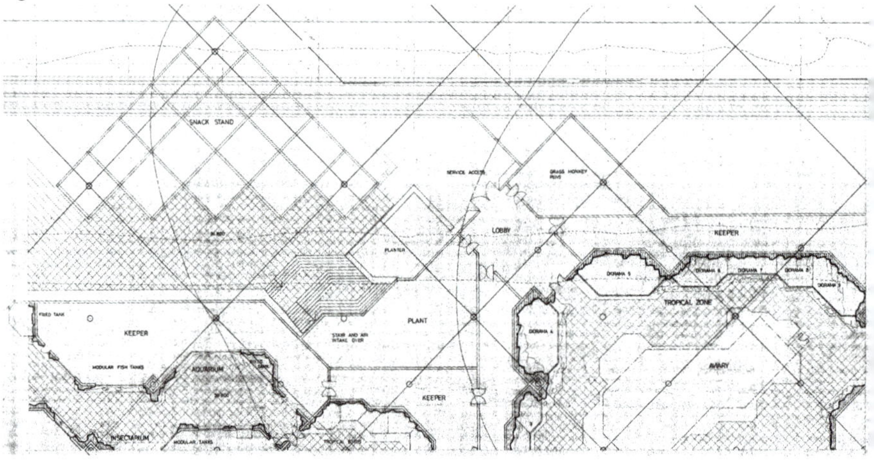

Similar to a previous project in Doha,[150] the main zoo building was intended to be a single podium block in reinforced concrete. Internally it encloses two main areas labelled as flight cages; one for a savannah habitat and the other dedicated to marsh and shore habitats. In between, the Central Garden defines the arrival experience, organising a series of common services and facilities, the interpretative centres for the different continents together with the nocturnal and tropical houses. This central area is edged by two large excavated lagoons, one of those with a cafeteria floating with parasol-style timber roofing, overlooking crocodiles, jaguars and alligators. The opposing lagoon houses monkeys, orang-utangs, baboons and Barbary apes.

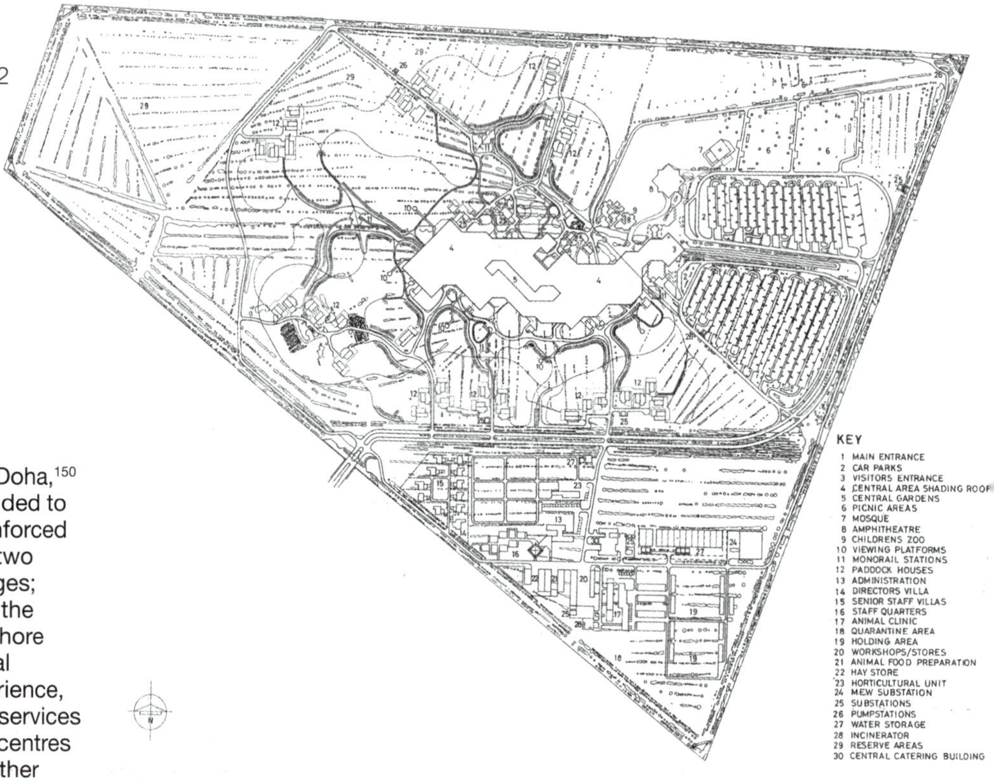

A German-built space frame over the upper level is equipped with two forms of sun shading: timber round the perimeter and specially developed sails of green Tygaflor PTFE-coated glass fibre. In the scheme, the limits were defined by a Safari Park with lions, tigers, buffalos and giraffes and other fauna.

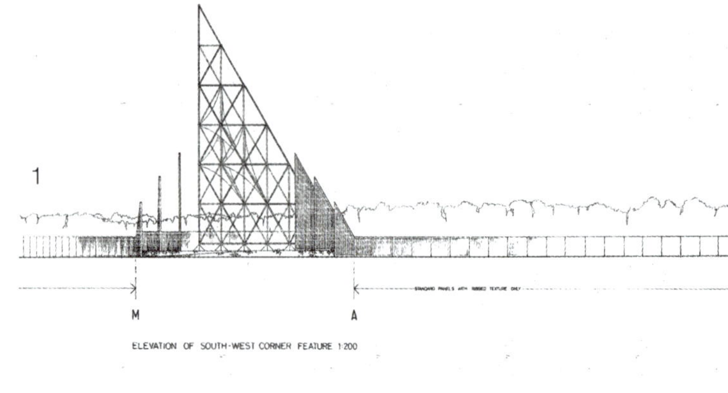

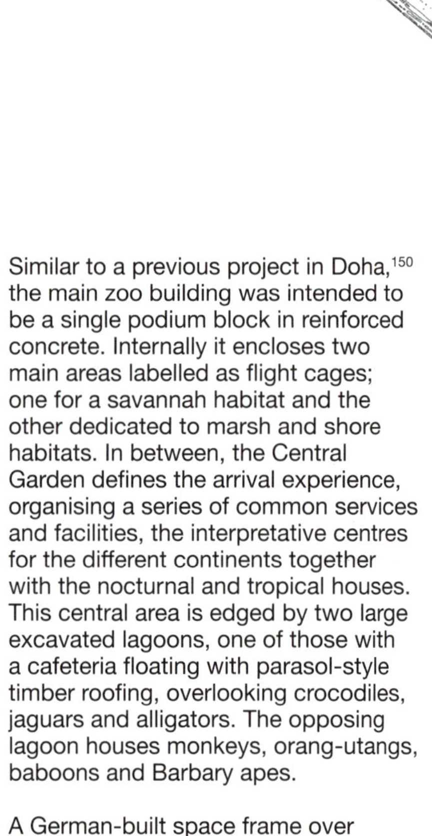

4

5

6

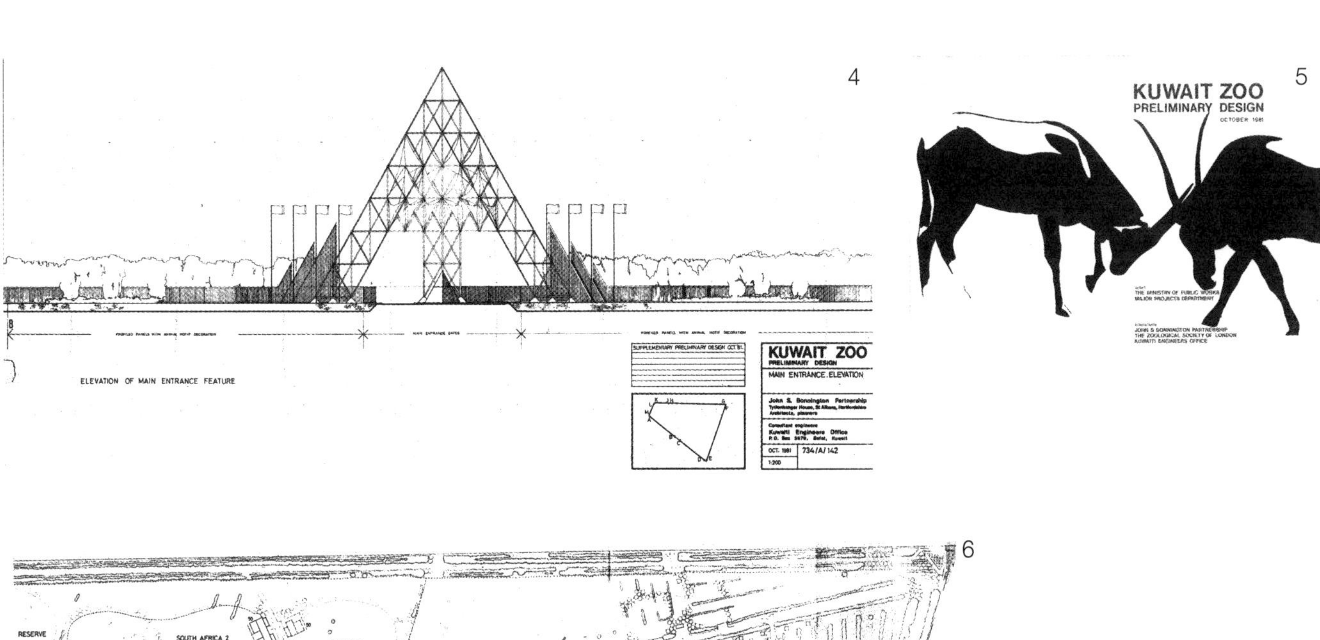

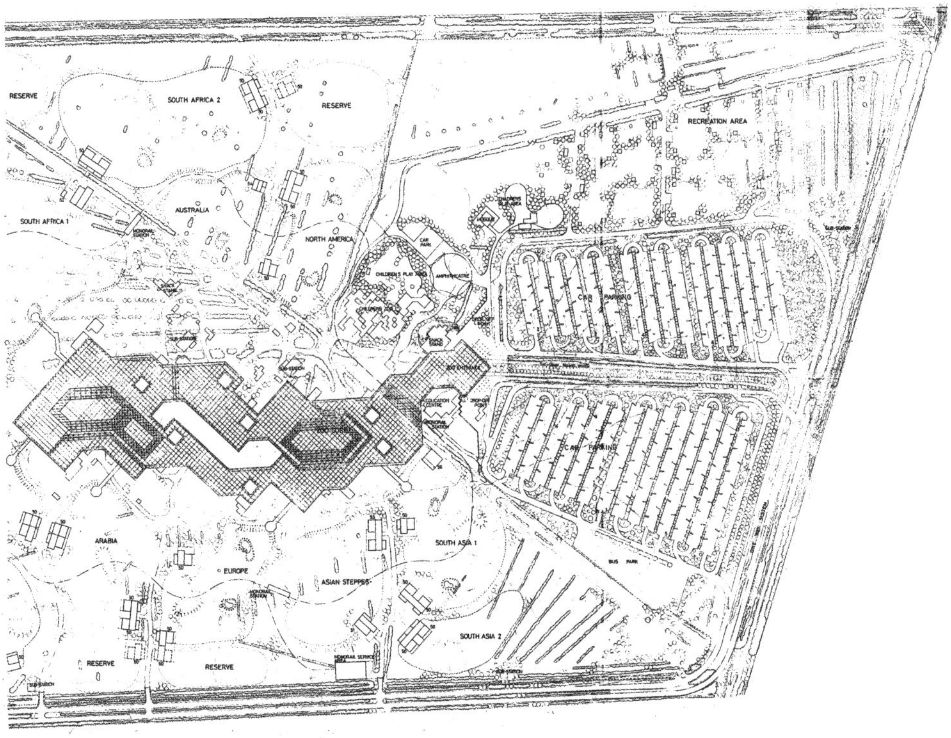

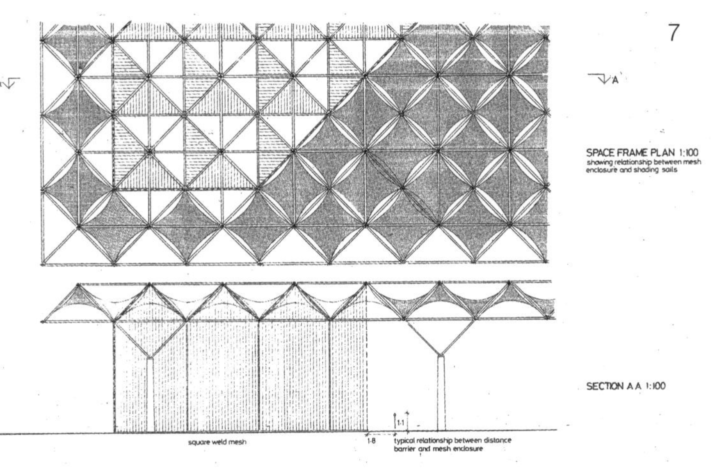

1. Elevation of south-west corner feature
2. Site plan
3. Plan detail
4. Elevation of the main entrance feature
5. Project logo
6. Site plan, detail of the main building
7. Modular building elements

7

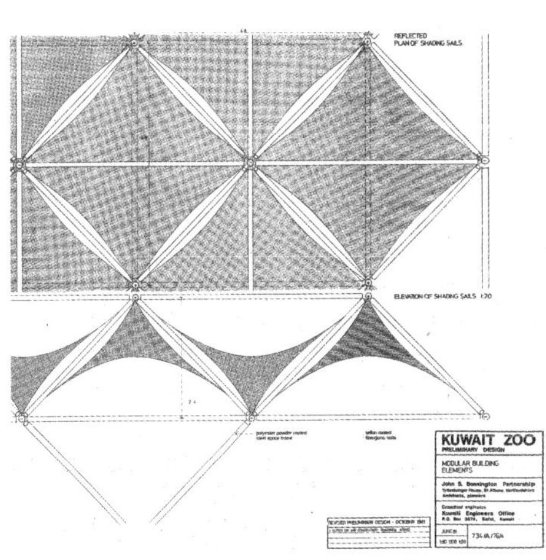

TELECOMMUNICATION CENTRE AND ANTENNA TOWER

MIRQAB
1981–1995

DESIGNER • Electrowatt Engineering Service Ltd. (lead designer); UNETEC (local associate)
CLIENT • Ministry of Public Works
CONTRACTORS • International Contractors Group (Ahmadiah Contracting & Trading Co. subsidiary); Sogea France; Mostostal Zabrze S.A. (steel works)

IN USE

When completed in 1995, the 372 m tall antenna embodied not the most important technical challenge in the country, but also engaged a competition with Kuwait Towers in defining the city skyline and representing a symbol of national unity and re-birth after the 1990 Invasion. The project inception, back in the early 1980s, was developed to strengthen the network capacity of the existing communication complex, built in 1968. The work started in 1987, stopped after only three years, and then resumed after Liberation.[151]

The compound includes the public offices, two main facilities and the antenna. The latter is a slender needle that supports a dish-shaped volume (the visitors' centre/restaurant) and a metal cylinder (the technical head). The structure is a post-tensioned tapering concrete shaft topped by a steel must, calculated to optimise the performance of wind resistance. The concrete ribs are clad with ceramic tiles, diamond patterned and punctuated by the glass glaze of the elevators and the visitors' centre.

During the inauguration, on the 5th anniversary of the end of the war, the antenna was named Liberation Tower.

1
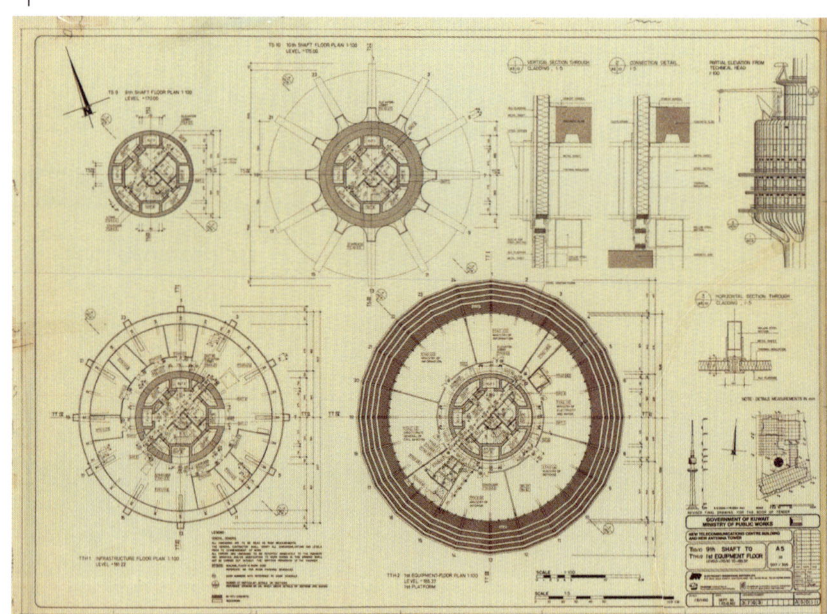

2
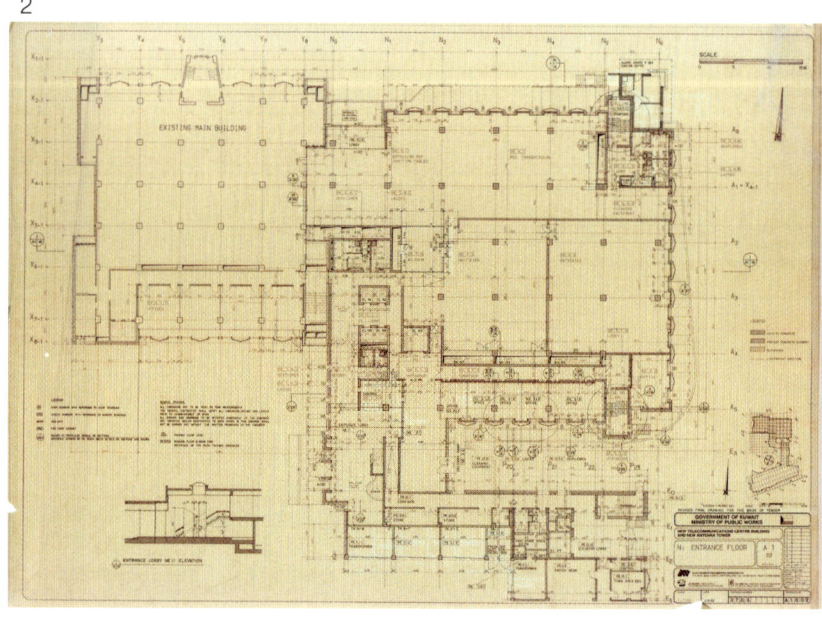

"

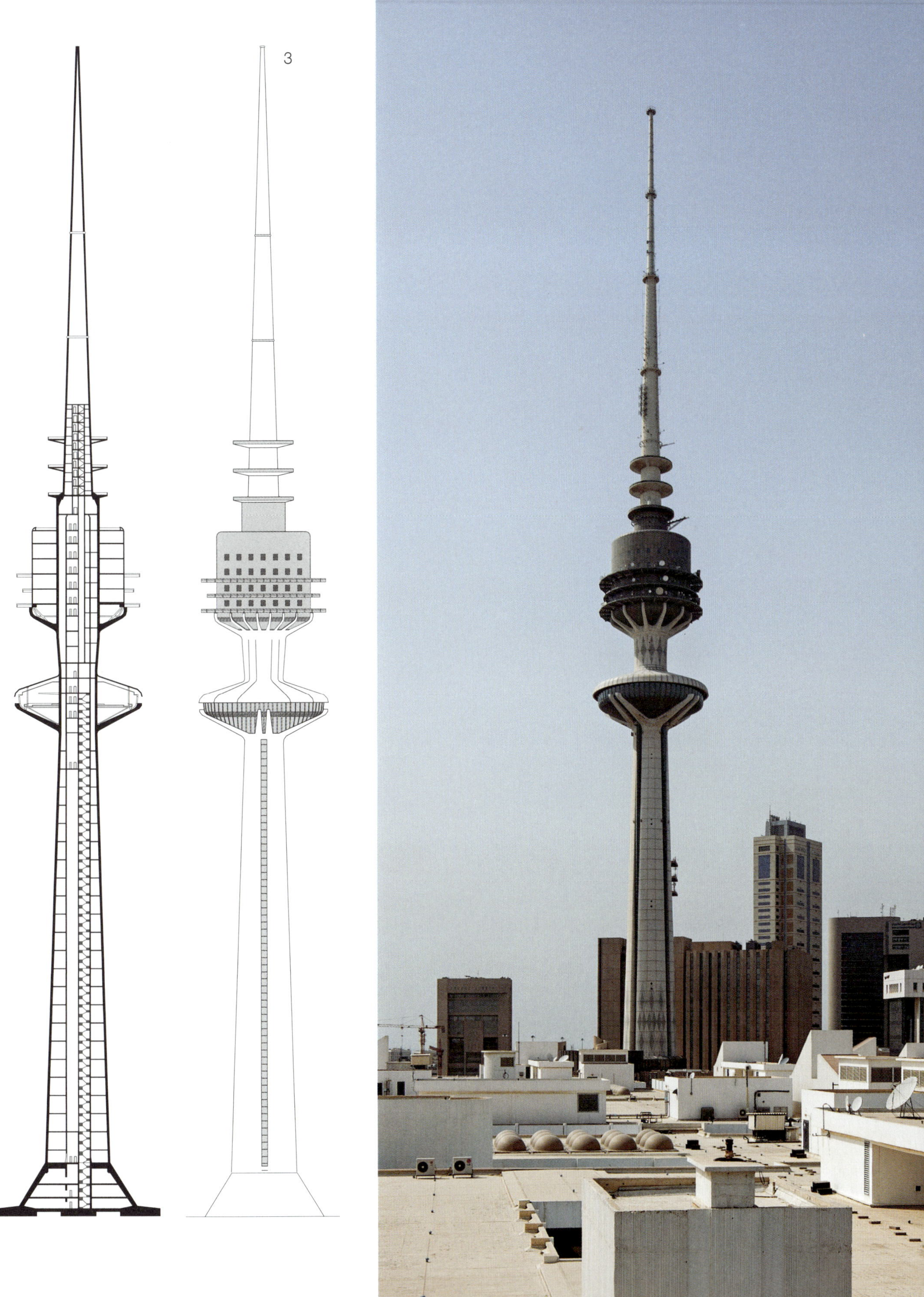
3

MINISTRY OF COMMUNICATION AND TOWERS

SHUWAIKH, KAIFAN
1981

DESIGNER • INCO
CLIENT • Ministry of Transport and Communication
CONTRACTOR • Elektrim, Poland

IN USE

The relationship between this complex and the actual Liberation Tower (former Telecommunication Centre and Antenna Tower) is of major relevance considering the programme and building typology references. Some of the elements were considered for the Ministry of Communication Tower. Located in Kaifan, this was eventually the first of several other replicas of the same prototypical scheme, such as those in Hawally, Salmiya and Al-Jahra. All have the same material condition and share a solid and robust image. In sandblasted, reinforced white concrete the towers are strong, hierarchical and urban references within their different contexts.

The project is mentioned by INCO, KEG and UNETEC as part of their work during the early 1980s. However, the only design claim one can find among these is with an eclectic group of Polish architects who worked for the three offices in those years. Another claim to this complex is by Stojan Maksimović, the designer of the winning entry for Bayan Palace Conference Centre, referring to the design and execution of the Kuwait Post Office facility, which is still active in the complex described here. This element at the base of the tower, facing Airport Road, preserves all the rationality of a building meant to be functional.

وزارة المواصلات
مركز خدمات كينده
MINISTRY OF COMMUNICATION
KINDAH SERVICES CENTER

KUWAIT FOUNDATION FOR THE ADVANCEMENT OF SCIENCES

SHARQ
1982–1986

DESIGNERS • TAC (architect); PACE (associate architect); Arup Consulting Engineers (Ove Arup & Partners)
CLIENT • Kuwait Foundation for the Advancement of Sciences (KFAS)
CONTRACTOR • Ahmadiah Contracting & Trading Co.

IN USE

The KFAS foundation was established by an Amiri decree in 1976 with the mission of supporting scientific research in Kuwait and abroad, with a long-term contribution from Kuwait Shareholding Companies. A few years after its inception, the foundation opened a consultancy for the design of its head office, involving TAC and Arthur Erickson among others.[152] The plot is in a prime location at one end of Ahmed Al-Jaber Street, the vehicular axis at the centre of key developments in the 1970 Master Plan for the amount of unbuilt land available. Until 1977, in fact, the same area was destined to be part of the university, a function which would have been in strong relation with the foundation's mission. Subsequent reviews of the plan re-assigned the area as commercial/high-density residential.[153]

In this context, TAC's preference for solid design delivered an isolated cubic mass with very few contact points with the surroundings. From the main road the building appears like a stronghold in bush-hammered stone with minimal apertures: a series of loopholes and the main arched portal. The other side exposes a more complex spatial concept. One large curtain wall embraces the northern corner revealing the inner hollow core. Orthogonally to this, a deep 45° cut separates the cube in two triangular prisms, adding to the composition a dynamic shift. This diagonal axis identifies the main vertical distribution and also the key structural element, similar to a *concrete gantry*. Eight office floors stretch between the two ends of the *gantry*, receiving mitigated light from the northern glass, through the hollow core and its suspended planters.[154] In between, a long pendulum, hanging from the centre of the structure points down to the main lobby, symbolises the ultimate institutional aim: knowledge.

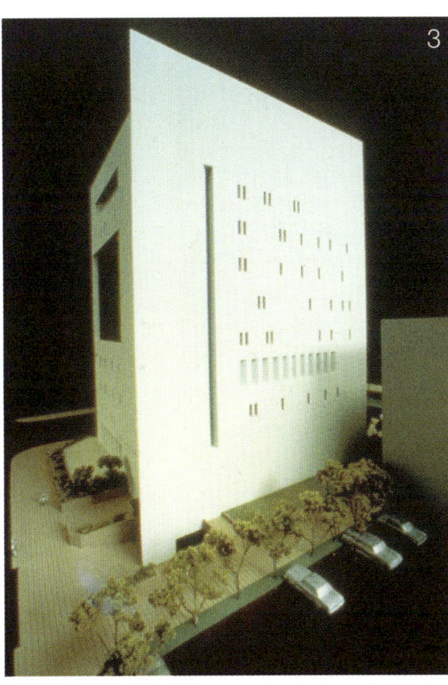

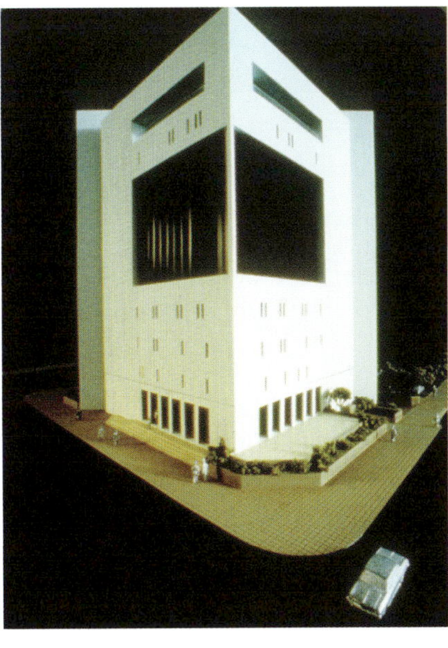

1. View from Ahmed Al-Jaber Street
2. Interior, view of the central hall
3. Scale model, 1984

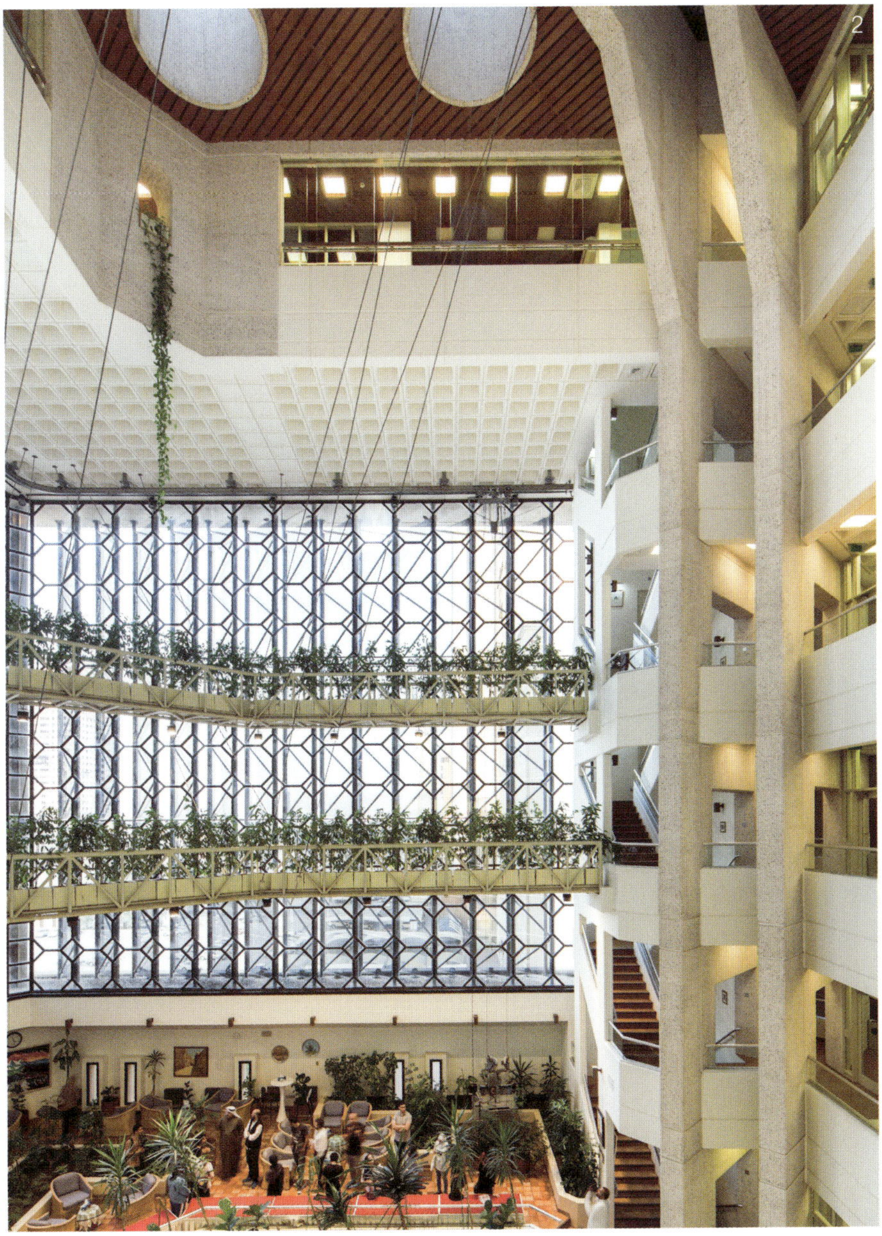
2

3

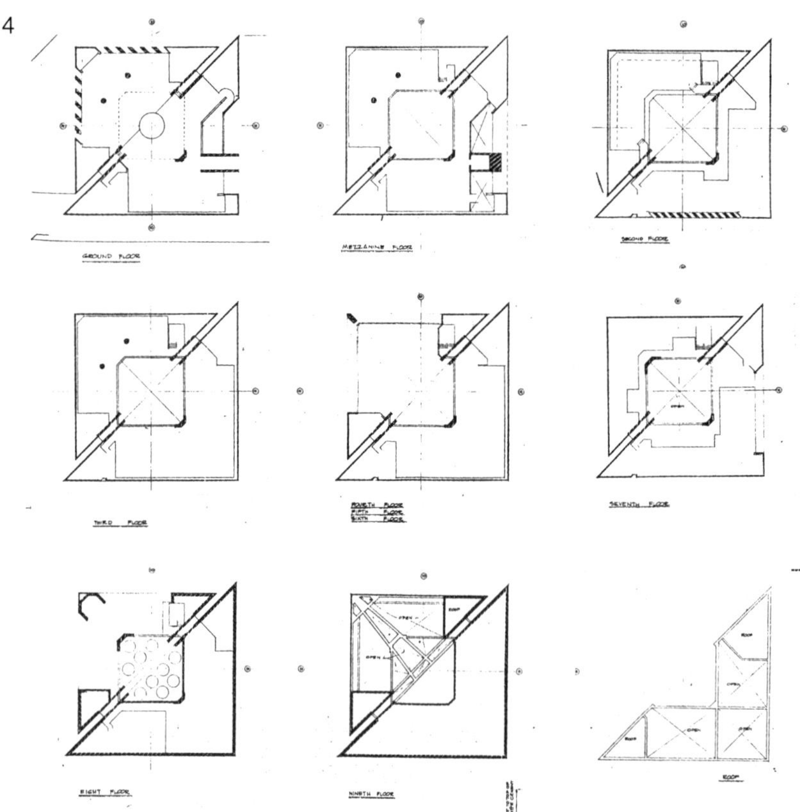

4

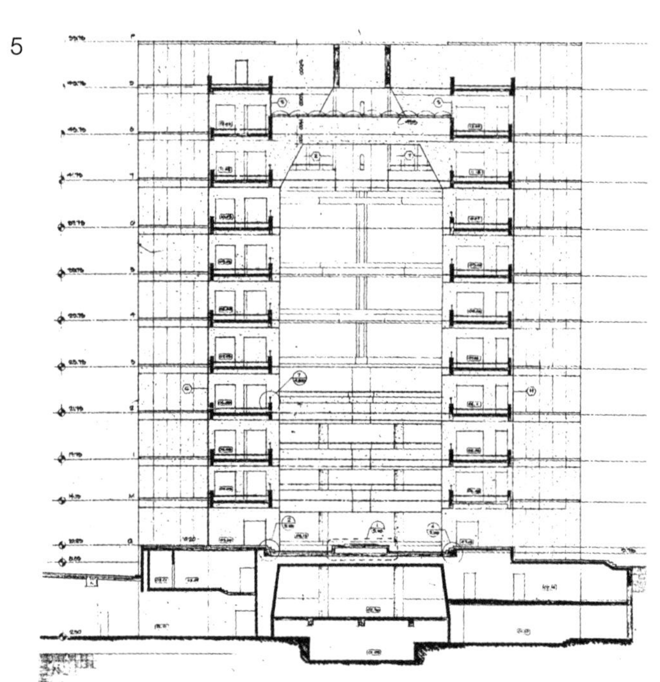

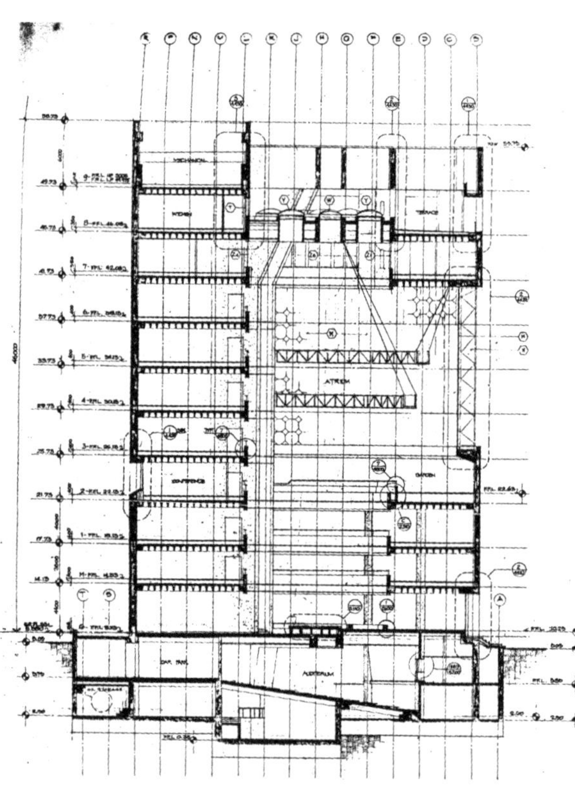

5

4. Plan diagrams
5. Sections

MIRQAB TRANSPORTATION CENTRE

MIRQAB
1977–1984

DESIGNERS • Perkins & Will (plan); WS Atkins with SSH (architect)
CLIENT • Ministry of Public Works, Ministry of Planning, Kuwait Municipality

UNBUILT

In the "Structure Plan Study" for traffic and transportation systems, the Maghreb Motorway extension through the city was proposed.[155] Both this and Mubarak Al-Kabeer Street (Cairo Street) were suggested as a depressed configuration, releasing pressure on the roundabouts, but increasing the road footprint in the area between the two.

The "Mirqab Action Area Plan"[156] would finally dictate the Mirqab Transportation Centre project as the interface of the city motorway loop.[157]

Placed behind the KFAED Headquarters (1974–1981), a superblock composed of nine floors with a parking facility for 5,000 cars was aimed at encouraging drivers to leave their cars on the periphery of the city centre. A monorail system above the surface would distribute pedestrian access to the city centre. In addition, it envisaged sport facilities, a health club, restaurants, a bowling alley, a hall for cultural events and exhibitions and a conference centre.

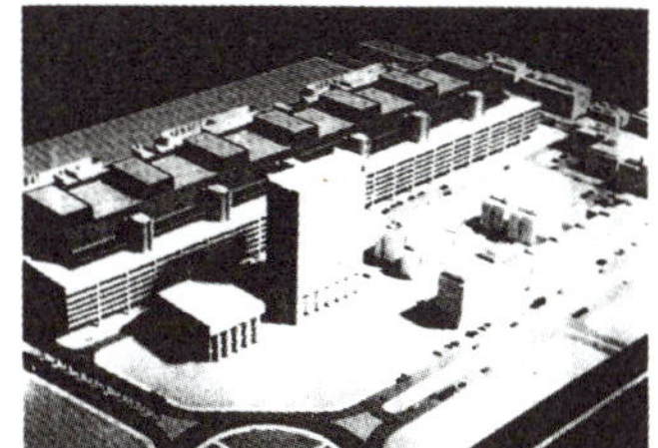

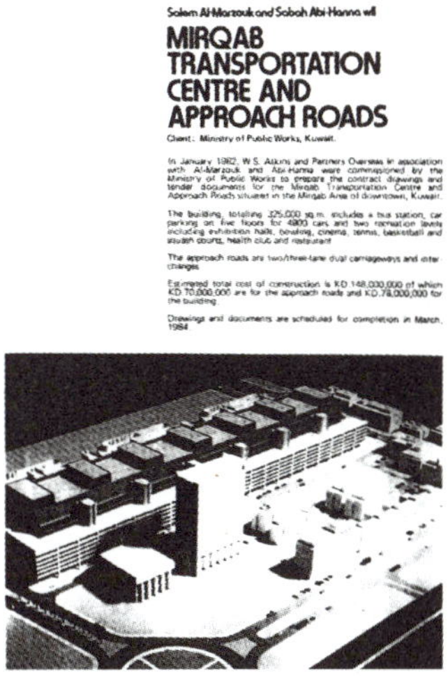

Salem Al-Marzouk and Sabah Abi-Hanna wll

MIRQAB TRANSPORTATION CENTRE AND APPROACH ROADS

Client: Ministry of Public Works, Kuwait.

In January 1982, W.S. Atkins and Partners Overseas in association with Al-Marzouk and Abi-Hanna were commissioned by the Ministry of Public Works to prepare the contract drawings and tender documents for the Mirqab Transportation Centre and Approach Roads situated in the Mirqab Area of downtown, Kuwait.

The building, totalling 325,000 sq.m. includes a bus station, car parking on five floors for 4800 cars, and two recreation levels including exhibition halls, bowling, cinema, tennis, basketball and squash courts, health club and restaurant.

The approach roads are two/three-lane dual carriageways and interchanges.

Estimated total cost of construction is KD 148,000,000 of which KD 70,000,000 are for the approach roads and KD 78,000,000 for the building.

Drawings and documents are scheduled for completion in March, 1984.

6

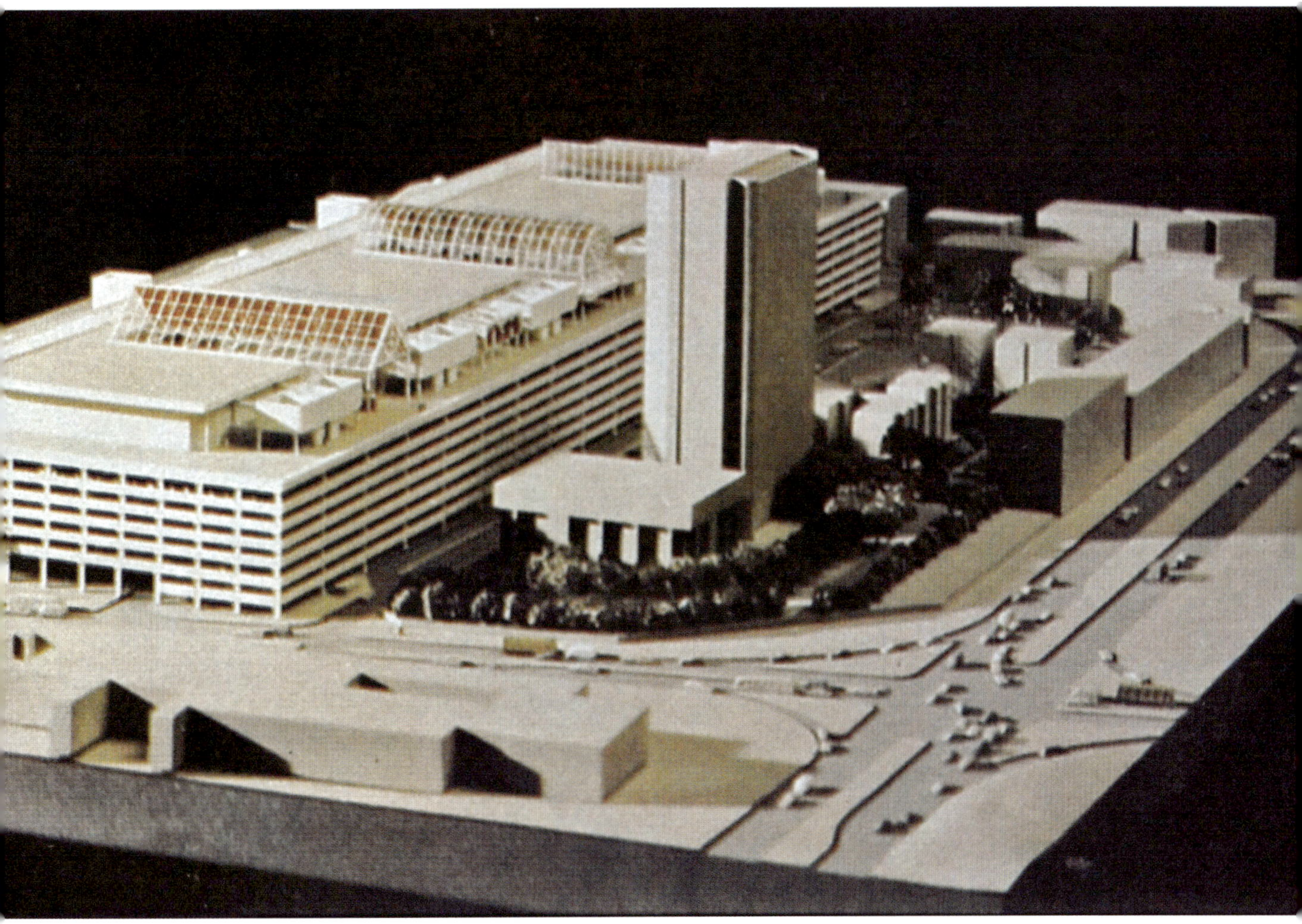

1. J. Suter's proposal for a monorail station in Mirqab, perspective view
2. Proposed monorail in Sharq, circa 1977
3. View of the project site in Mirqab, behind the Kuwait Fund for Arab Economic Development's first building
4. J. Suter's proposal for the monorail interface with Mirqab Transportation Centre, perspective view
5. Proposal for Mirqab Transportation Centre, scale model, 1977–1983
6. SSH and WS Atkins report, tender document for the Ministry of Public Works, Jan. 1982

AL-BALOUSH BUS STATION

SHARQ
1986–1988

DESIGNERS • INCO
(K. Wiśniowski, A. Bohdanowicz, J. Urbanowicz)
CLIENT • Kuwait Public Transportation Company (KPTC)
CONTRACTOR • Musaad Al-Saleh & Sons Co.

IN USE

Together with the Port Authority Headquarters (1984–92) this terminal results from the collaboration between a team of Polish architects and the engineering consultancy established by Mohammed Al-Sanan in 1975. Founded in 1962, KPTC assumed a relevant role in the country's Public Works agenda after the Second Master Plan. Following the construction pressure in Sharq[158] and the failure of the Mirqab Transportation Centre interface, the bus terminal near the Ahmad Al-Jaber Street became a necessity and was subsequently tendered, designed and built.

Echoing the plan of the Kuwait International Airport, the terminal offices and enclosed facilities are organised around the central station hall and external loading gallery. The central element is framed by an arch that defines the façade of the main entrance and the spatial environment of the main hall. The use of anodised black aluminium and limestone reveal the clarity of the building's pure geometry and volume.

3

4

5

1. KPTC Bus Station and company's first head
office in Mirqab, circa 1965
2. Al-Baloush Bus Station Hall
3. KPTC workshops in Shuwaikh, circa 1962
4. Al-Baloush Bus Station, external view from the
drop-off/pick-up area
5. KPTC Bus Station, view of the main entrance

PORT AUTHORITY HEADQUARTERS

SHUWAIKH
1984–1992

DESIGNER • INCO
(K. Wiśniowski, A. Bohdanowicz, J. Urbanowicz)
COMPETITION ENTRY • SSH
with Dino Georgiou Architects
CLIENT • Kuwait Port Authority Company (KPAC)
CONTRACTOR • Unknown

IN USE

An international competition was launched for the Shuwaikh Port Complex, close to Kuwait Shipping Co. headquarters, containing a car park for 3,000 vehicles, administrative department offices, general registration offices, customs' offices, import/export deptartment, goods clearance dept., marine agency, insurance agency, post office, 3 bank branches, duty free zone with shops and cafeteria, a multi-purpose hall and the Marine Museum and Library. The Centre Georges Pompidou, inaugurated in 1977 was a clear reference for the project's client.[159]

The requirement for a very large car-parking surface, three times larger than the remaining programme became the relevant condition in generating the 10-storey height volume. A 9.60 x 9.60 m structural grid through the whole building organises both programmatic dimensions. The exposed concrete façade defines the volume of the car park, while offices and other common areas have a glass curtain framed in aluminium. The whole scheme is resolved by an elevation within a perfectly square street grid. The corners serve the pedestrian access and the square sides are dominated by the cylindrical car park ramps. An internal central atrium enclosed by the offices defines the public areas in the building and distributes the surrounding hierarchies.

1. Ground floor plan
2. South corner entrance
3. Interior, view of the central covered piazza
4. South-east elevation

KUWAIT INSURANCE COMPANY

SHARQ
1983

DESIGNERS • Arthur Erickson Associates (architect); SSH (associate architect)
CLIENT • Kuwait Insurance Co. (KIC)

UNBUILT

The Insurance Company Complex was developed in collaboration with SOM and PACE to accommodate four company headquarters on a platform raised over a shared underground garage. The project's interest lies in not only in the architectural aspects of the solution, but also in the urban implication of the layout. It can be read as a tentative formulation of connective tissue in a part of the city (Sharq) where the buildings were isolated objects, individually served by the front road.

The scheme creates a central piazza protected and shaded by the four corner buildings. The paved walkway in between connects with the surrounding plots and emphasised the permeability of this urban space. In the diagrams, again, the four corner prisms were meant to face the piazza and to share with it the lobbies in a gradual progression from public to private. Based on this layout, Erickson and SSH developed one of the office block for KIC. The main architectural invention is the use of a giant glass *muqarnas* that frames the piazza and makes an invitation towards the building entrance.

This dramatic solution, which of course relies heavily on the powerful tools of regional architectural shapes, also allows a diffused and controlled illumination of the office inside.

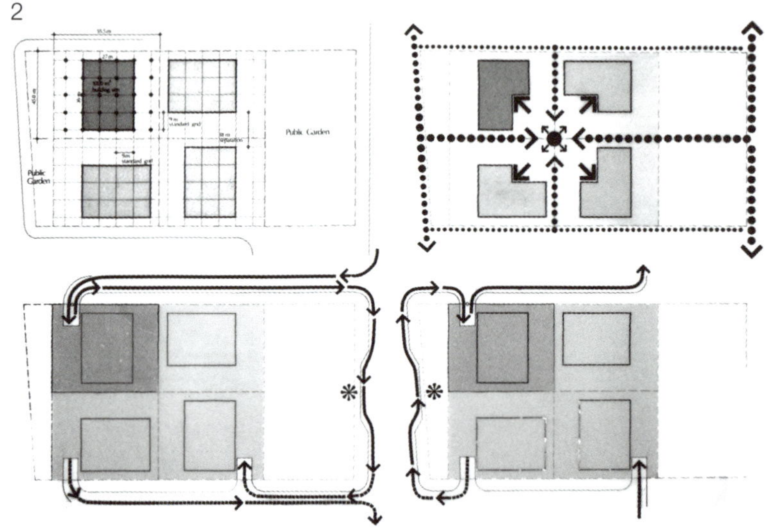

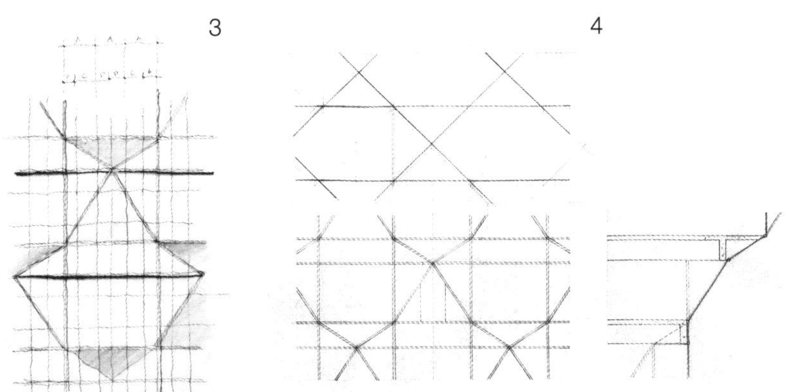

SECTION X-X

SECTION Y-Y

1. KIC Building, perspective view
2. SOM; PACE; SSH and Arthur Erickson Associates, Insurance Companies Complex, urban analyses
3. Façade studies, elevations
4. Façade study, section
5. KIC Building, sections
6. Axonometric view of the structure and sketches

5

6

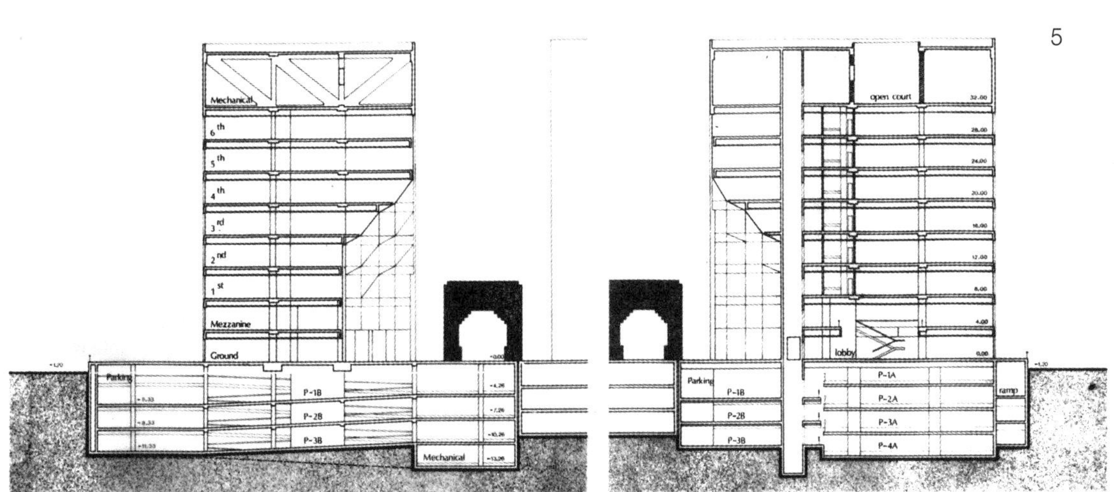

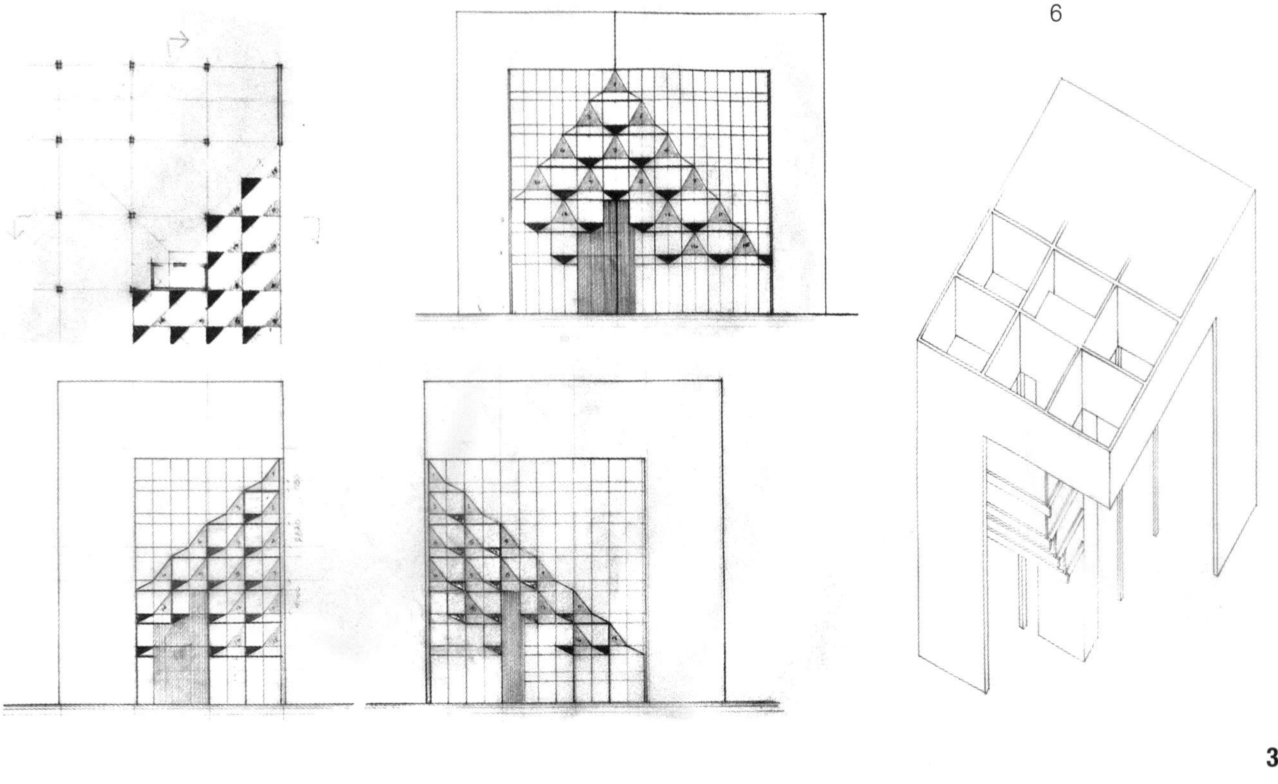

NOTES

139. "Materials in Context," in *Middle East Construction*, Feb. 1982, v. 7, n. 2, p. 51

140. The Michael A. Mc Carthy and SOM LLP Collection at Cornell University Library. Series VII. Architectural Project, Commissions and Built Works. 1964–1998. Part 3

141. CTHA bid for KNPC Administration in Mina Al Ahmadi Tender RMP/BLDG-006, Aug. 1982

142. The East Midlands Electricity Board Computer Centre and the Rolls-Royce Computer Centre

143. A. E. J. Morris is the author of the biography *John R. Harris architects*, Hurtwood, Westerham, 1984

144. Teržan, Vesna, "Arhitektura Je Umetnost Prostora," *Mladina*, v. 16–17, Apr. 22, 2011

145. This definition is labelled below the company name in the project drawings.

146. See Kuwait Fund for Arab Economic Development building designed by PACE with TAC.

147. "Stojan Maksimović. Pismo iz nahanta," in *Arhitekton ArchArt magazine*, Jan.–Feb. 2011, v. 1, n. 3, p. 33

148. "Alfred Roth: Engagement für eine architektonische Kultur: zum 80. Geburtstag," in *Werk, Bauen+Wohnen*, 1983, n. 5 (70), p. 36

149. Binder, George, *Montois Partner: Selected and Current Works*, Images Publishing, Victoria, 2001

150. Qatar Zoo was developed by Bonnington from 1973 and completed in 1986.

151. Cf. Haidar, Mirza; Kuruvilla, Varghese, *Kuwait Liberation Tower. A Profile*, Dar Al-Watan Printing, Kuwait, 1999

152. "Americans in the Arab World," in *Middle East Construction*, Feb. 1982, v. 7, n. 2, p. 51

153. 1977 corresponds to the revision of the Second Master Plan, which reformulates the balance between private and public investment in the city transformation.

154. This transparent green filter and the idea of the green lobby suggest a parallel with the Ford Foundation, built by Kevin Roche in Manhattan 20 years earlier.

155. Cf. *Kuwait Second Master Plan* by Colin Buchanan and Partners, 1970. Structure Plan Study, 1971

156. *Mirqab Action Area Plan*, Perkins & Will International + De Leuw, Catter International Inc., 1977, CSRK Archive

157. In the First Master Plan the Hilali Street Extension connected with Abdullah Al-Ahmed Street to define the internal ring of transport distribution inside the city centre.

158. Several high-rise towers were built in Sharq between 1975 and 1986.

159. Interview with Krzysztof Wiśniowski, Mar. 2014

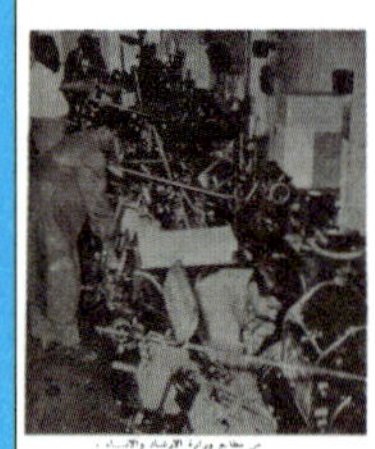

الارشــــاد والأنبـــاء

١٧

دَار الهندســة نزيه طالب

dar al-handasah NAZIH TALEB

تأسست «دار الهندسة نزيه طالب» أصلا في بيروت ١٩٥٦ . تضم حاليا ٧٠ موظفا بينهم ٤٠ مهندسا وعدد وافر من المستشارين في حقول مختلفة . وقد قامت بتصميم مشاريع بلغ قيمتها حوالي ٤٠٠،٠٠٠،٠٠٠ دولار . نفذ منها ما يساوي ٢٠٠،٠٠٠،٠٠٠ دولار بإشرافها .

تعمل المؤسسه في معظم الدول العربية وبعض الدول الافريقية .

"dar al-handasah Nazih Taleb" was founded in Beirut in 1956. At present it has a staff of over 70 full time employees including 40 engineers and technicians, and also consultants in different fields.

dar al-handasah has designed projects of an estimated cost of $400,000,000 out of which projects worth about $200,000,000 have been executed under its supervision.

The firm operates in most Arab countries and in some African countries.

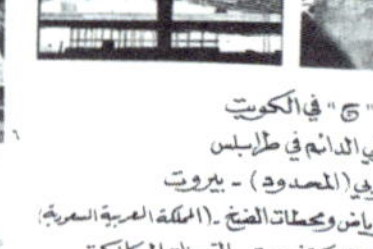

١ ـ محطة كهرباء «G» في الكويت
٢ ـ معرض لبنان الدولي الدائم في طرابلس
٣ ـ بناية البنك العربي (المحدود) ـ بيروت
٤ ـ خطوط انابيب مياه الرياض ومحطات الضخ ـ (المملكة العربية السعودية)
٥ ـ المركز الطبي للجامعة الاميركية في بيروت ـ التجهيزات الميكانيكية
٦ ـ بناية شركة البترول الوطنية الكويتية
٧ ـ جادة فؤاد شهاب في بيروت ـ النفق

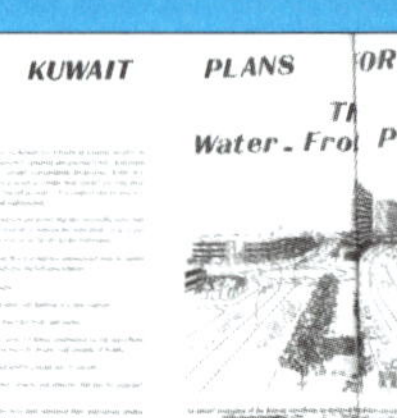

لؤلؤة المرزوق تلفت الانظار
the KUWAITI
No. 825   Saturday, 23rd May, 1964.
Big lift at Shuaiba

ملامح
العام الجامعي الجديد

وهو ما يسمح بوجود ممر تجاري مُغطى, يتوسع لاحقاً إلى ما بعد المبنى حتى يصل إلى ميدان الصفاة.

ومع هذا المبنى الذي يعد بمثابة أول مبنى متعدد الطوابق في الكويت, بدأت أسرة الغانم سلسلة من عمليات التشييد والتطوير.

وزارة الإرشاد والإعلام
شارع مبارك الكبير, ١٩٥٩-١٩٦٢

المصمم • سامي عبد الباقي مع إرنست فان دروب
العميل • وزارة الأشغال العامة
المقاول • شركة الشايع للمقاولات
(المبنى: مستخدم)

يعد المقر الرئيسي الحالي للمجلس الوطني للثقافة والفنون والآداب معلماً حضرياً بارزاً عند مدخل الشريان الرئيسي في المدينة, وهو شارع مبارك الكبير الذي يُفضي إلى قصر السيف.

وقد وضع سيد كريم الخطة المبدئية لتصميم المبنى, على أساس إقامة مبنى من أربعة طوابق يضم مكاتب مع مطبعة. ولكن التحديات التي صادفها, فضلاً عن موقع المبنى عند رقعة تقع في ملتقى طرق, هو ما أدى إلى ضرورة اللجوء إلى مفهوم جديد يركز على الإنسياب الديناميكي كعنصر أساسي لتحديد شكل المبنى. لكن هذه الخطة لم يتسن تطبيقها على الإطلاق, فلم يتم الحفاظ سوى على موقع المبنى, وبعض عناصر التصميم في المبنى الذي بدأ تشييده عام ١٩٥٩ (٥).

يتحدد إيقاع الواجهة, إن اقتربنا من المبنى من جهة الجنوب, من خلال عناصر خرسانية هندسية منتظمة الشكل. وتمنح الشبكة الواقية وصول أشعة الشمس الحارقة, يدعمها انتظام المبنى وخطوطه الأفقية. أما الطابق الأرضي فيتميز ببلاطات زخرفية رسمت بألوان تتسم بالجسارة, وتجمع بين عناصر ترمز للمدينة القديمة والجديدة. أما المدخل الرئيسي فإنه يتحدد من خلال شريط من بلاطات بيضاء يمثل خلفية رأسية تحمل رسوما مجردة تجمع بين أشكال وخطوط هندسية وعناصر تصويرية.

وهناك جداريات من البورسلين بالبهو العام بالمبنى, عليها لوحات مستوحاة من جزيرة فيلكة ومن الحقبة الهلينستية.

وكان المكان يُستخدم قبل ذلك مقراً لوزارة الإرشاد والإعلام, كما أنه كان مقراً لأول مطبعة بالبلاد.

مدرسة البنات الثانوية
الخالدية, ١٩٦٢- ١٩٦٦

المصمم • رامبالد فون شنايتبوفل - راينوال
العميل • وزارة الأشغال العامة
المقاول • شركة AST المحدودة
(المبنى يعمل)

تم توكيل أحد المهندسين المعماريين النمساويين, وكان لديه مكاتب بفرانكفورت, بتنفيذ المشروع. وقد تم ذلك بعد الانتهاء من برنامج بناء المدارس العامة عام ١٩٥٦, وكذلك بعد الانتهاء من مدرسة البنين الثانوية بالشيوخ.

وكان موقع المشروع المقترح وفقاً لشبير هو بنيد القار, أما تاريخه فهو ١٩٥٧. (١) وبناءً على هذا الاقتراح, في عام ١٩٦١, وافقت وزارة التعليم على تحويل المشروع, وكان قد تم إرساء العطاء بالفعل, من بنيد القار إلى الموقع الحالي بالخالدية.

وبعد ذلك تم بناء المدرسة لتستوعب ...افتاة, مع ٣٥٠ مكاناً للإقامة ولهيئة التدريس, وبالمدرسة صالة تسع لـ...١٦ شخص, إلى جانب مركز للموسيقى, ومنطقة منفصلة للرياضة تشمل حمام سباحة, وذلك كجزء من الهدف الأشمل المتمثل في تزويد البلاد بكافة التسهيلات الترفيهية والرياضية. وكان ذلك هو الدافع في فصل البرنامج التدريسي عن الأماكن الرياضية التي يمكن الوصول إليها مباشرة من طريق المطار السريع (٢).

وقد تم تصميم حمام السباحة على شكل خرساني متعرض تعترضه نوافذ قطرية بارتفاع المبنى بأسره, بما يسمح بالإضاءة الطبيعية والتهوية الكاملة للمبنى. وكان هناك مدخل للسباحين في المستوى الأرضي, من خلال صالة الجمنازيوم. أما مدخل

المشاهدين فكان في الطابق الأعلى من خلال سلمين خارجيين. وعلى الرغم من أن التصميم عادة ما يشار إليه على أنه مثال يحتذى به من حيث الاستغلال الأمثل للمناخ (٣), إلا أن الفرد روث قد انتقد في تقرير عام ١٩٦٦ حالة الإهمال فيما يتعلق بالاستغلال المناسب للظروف المناخية. إلا أننا نرى في ذلك التقرير صور لوحدات مدرسية تبرهن على كفاءة استغلال البيئة المحيطة من حيث وجود نظام حماية من العواصف الرملية ومن الشمس, كما نرى طبقات متفاوتة رأسية وأفقية تسمح بانسياب الهواء, مع سطح مزدوج.

ويصل مركز الموسيقى بين وحدات المدرسة وبين الصالة الكبيرة وهناك أماكن تحيط بالمركز وبوحدات المدرسة بما يسمح بسهولة انسياب المرور الذي يربط بين المباني والشرفة الخارجية. ويحدد مركز الموسيقى والصالة مع بهو الاستقبال الخارجي الهيكل الكلي للمبنى الذي يتسم بالتناغم المحوري الكامل.

وكانت المدرسة تضم مباني إدارية وفصول دراسية وصالة لتناول الطعام, فضلاً عن فناء واسع لم يعد موجوداً الآن. وتنفتح الفصول الدراسية على ناحية الشمال. إلا أن باقي عناصر المبنى كلها تطل على جهة الجنوب والشرق, وهي كلها تحظى بحماية من الشمس عن طريق نظم حماية رأسية أو أفقية. وإلى الجنوب الشرقي من ذلك نرى غرف الممرضات, وهي مصممة على شكل غير متعامد حسب اتجاه الشمس.

وهناك تناغم تام بين الألوان في المبنى بأسره, بما يكشف خبرة المصمم في المشاريع المماثلة في ألمانيا, ويكشف كذلك عن خبرته في المعارض المعمارية المماثلة في مدن مثل جراتز وبرلين. ولعل البرنامج الطموح للمدرسة, إلى جانب المساحة الحرة للحرم المحيط به هو الذي دفع إلى تحويل المبنى إلى جامعة عام ١٩٦٦.

مدرسة المباركية
شارع المباركية, ١٩٥٧-١٩٥٨

المصمم • سيد كريم
العميل • وزارة الأشغال العامة
المقاول • مجهول
(ترميم ١، ٢)

تم بناء هذه المدرسة على نفس موقع أول مدرسة في البلاد (١٩١٢), وقد دخلت في النسيج الحضري القديم القائم بالفعل, وأحيت هذه المدرسة الثانوية للبنين الموقع الذي أقيمت به, وقدمت طرازاً جديداً من البناء إلى البلاد.

يرتفع المدخل الرئيسي من ناحية الواجهة الغربية عن الشارع, وهو مغطى بألواح رقيقة للتظليل. أما الطوابق الأعلى فهي كلها طوابق ناتئة مع ألواح أفقية رقيقة, وأخرى رأسية, تحاكي تلك الموجودة في مباني نيان الغانم الحالية, كما تحاكي وزارة الإعلام والإرشاد. وفي الجهة الخلفية, تنفتح الفصول الدراسية على رواق بواجه الفناء الرئيسي. وفي مقابل الواجهة الرئيسية نجد قاعة محاضرات تحيط بالفناء.

وتدريجيا, تحول هذا الموقع ليؤدي عدداً مختلفاً من الاستخدامات بعد أن أغلقت المدرسة أبوابها, فكان على سبيل المثال مقراً للمكتبة المركزية في العام ١٩٧٩, وكان مقراً للمكتبة الوطنية بين عامي ١٩٨٥ و ١، ٢, ويؤدي المبنى في الوقت الحاضر دور متحف تاريخ التعليم.

وعلى الرغم من التعديل الذي تم إدخاله على المساحة الداخلية للمبنى, فإنه يعد أحد الأمثلة القليلة للمباني التي يمكنها التواؤم مع عدد متباين من الاستخدامات, كما أن المبنى يشهد على إمكانية الحفاظ على هياكل المباني في الوقت الحاضر.

السينما
الأحمدي, شرق, حولي, الجهراء, السالميه
١٩٥٤ –١٩٧٣

المصمم • سيدكريم , استشارات العراق , PACE
العميل • شركة السينما الوطنية الكويتية
المقاول • عددين
(تم هدم العديد والباقية في طريقها للهدم)

كانت دور السينما من بين المشروعات التي ورد ذكرها في «مشروع البناء بالكويت» الخاص بالأحمدي. لكن أول سينما

فعلية في تلك المدينة افتتحت في العام ١٩٦٦ تتسع لاف ومئاتين شخص, على حين تأسست شركة السينما الوطنية الكويتية في العام ١٩٥٤. وبعد عام واحد تم افتتاح مسرح سينما الشرقية, وهي دار سينما تتسع لألف شخص, وإن ظل المصمم مجهولاً. وتعد تلك السينما أول دار سينما تقام بمدنية الكويت (٢٣) وفي نفس الفترة نسب العديد من مشاريع دور السينما للمهندس المعماري المصري سيد كريم, ومنها سينما الفردوس و سينما الحمراء, وقد تم تشييدهما في العام ١٩٥٨ من مواد خرسانية, وتقع الإثنتان في المنطقة ذاتها (٢٤). كما أن سينما الأندلس والتي بنيت بعد ذلك بعامين في حولي تتشابه إلى حد كبير مع سينما الفردوس وسينما الحمرا, ولذا فانه يمكن نسبتها إلى المصمم ذاته(٢٥). وتستخدم هذه المباني فكره الواجهة الهندسية المظللة, كما أنها كلها تتشابه من حيث التصميم المعقد للكتل الخرسانية.

وقد فتحت ٢٥ دار سينما أبوابها للجمهور في الكويت في الأعوام التالية, ومنها مسرح سينما الجهراء والتي صممتها PACE بسعة ٥٠٠ زائر , وذلك بالتعاون مع استشارات العراق, وقد تم الانتهاء منها في العام ١٩٧٣. والمبنى عبارة عن كتلة مكعبة منتظمة محاطة بحائط من الطوب مع نوافذ مدعمة بالالومنيوم.

فندق حكومي
الحزام الأخضر, ١٩٥٨

المصمم • راجلان سكواير وشركاه
العميل • مجلس التطوير الكويتي
(لم يتم البناء)

نشأت ضرورة إقامة هذا الفندق مع تكثيف الكويت لمعاملاتها التجارية مع دول العالم. ومن المعروف أن الفنادق كانت موجودة بوسط المدينة منذ الأربعينيات, على الرغم من أن مثل تلك الفنادق لم تكن ملائمة لرجال الأعمال أو للوفود الدبلوماسية التي كانت الكويت تسعى لجذبهم. وبناء على ذلك فقد تم الطلب من الشركة البريطانية الدولية سكواير للقيام بتصميم فندق من الطراز الأول, وهو فندق تدعمه الدولة على نحو مباشر. وكانت الكويت قد كلفت شركة سكواير بإقامة أعمال بناء أخرى بالدولة (مثل عدد من مخافر الشرطة إلى جانب السفارة الأمريكية), لكنه من المرجح أنه قد تم اختيار الشركة لصلتها الوثيقة بفندق الهيلتون, وكانت الشركة قد صممت سلسلة فنادق هيلتون في كل المنامة وطهران.

وقد تمحور الاقتراح الأول للشركة حول طراز الباحة المرصوفة, وهي باحة مربعة الشكل تحيط بحديقة شبة مغطاة, وهو ما أطلقت عليه الشركة اسم "المفهوم التركي القديم". (٣٢) لكن العميل فضل إقامة مبنى يتسم بالملامح الغربية مع ساحات مفتوحة, وطابق أرضي يمكنه أن يكون مكاناً للاستقبال, والمطاعم, والمحلات, وغرف الأعمال, وما إلى ذلك. وكانت النسخة النهائية عبارة عن كتلة مستطيلة ذات شرفات عميقة , تحيط بها عناصر رأسية وذلك بغرض حماية الشرفات من الشمس. (٣٣) وقد حظي التصميم الهيكلي بعناية خاصة, بما يمنع من تأكل الخرسانة.تحت وطأة درجات الحرارة العالية كما أن اللمسات النهائية من رخام وأحجار جيرية, وخشب الساج, والفسيفساء الملونة في حواجز الشرفات, قد حظيت كلها باهتمام بالغ في التصميم. وقد أثنى شحيبر على المبنى واعتبره مثالا للبساطة في مواجهة انتشار نوع من المغالاة والخلط بين الأساليب المعمارية في تصميم مباني المدنية, ومع ذلك فان شحيبر اقترح إقامة المبنى في مكان أخر بحيث لا يتدخل مع ساحة الانتظار بالمدينة والمعروفة باسم الحزام الأخضر. (٣٤)

مستشفى الطب النفسي
الصليبخات, ١٩٥٤_ ١٩٥٨

المصمم • مجهول
العميل • سمو أمير الكويت
المقاول • مجهول
(المبنى يعمل)

يقع هذا المجمع اليوم في الصليبخات, وهو غير متصل بباقي مستشفى الصباح, كما أن المجمع يُعرف باسم مستشفى الطب النفسي السابق. وتعد الإشارات الزمنية إلى المستشفى الأول في هذه المنطقة غير دقيقة, لكنها تجمع على أن المستشفى تم بناؤه في الفترة بين العامين ١٩٥٤ و ١٩٥٨. وتشير المطبوعات المختلفة إلى المستشفى باستخدام عدة أسماء منها مصحة

عينة رقم ١
مبان كبنية تحتية: ١٩٤٩ - ١٩٦٠

مصنع تحليه المياه ومحطة الطاقة A و B
الشويخ، ١٩٥٦ - ١٩٦٢

المصمم • إيوبانك وشركاها لمحدوده (مستشارين اساسيين) المعماريون فار مر اند دارك للهندسة المعمارية، جون تيلور وأبناؤه (الخدمات)
العميل • سمو أمير الكويت
المقاولون • ريتشار كوستين (الشرق الاوسط) المحدودة، الشركة الكويتية النمساوية للهندسة (تم تعديل التصميم)

بعد تدشين صادرات الكويت من النفط الخام بثلاثة اعوام، كلف الأمير عام ١٩٤٦ إيوبانك وشركاه بتصميم مجمع عملاق في ميناء الاحمدي (١) وقد اشتمل نطاق العمل على مشروعين، أحدهما لتوفير مياه صالحة للشرب، وآخر للتزويد بالكهرباء.١٩٥١اعتمد البرنامج مستشار في انشاء ميناء الشويخ.

وقد شمل مشروع إقامة محطة الطاقة ومصنع تحلية المياه وإنشاء عدد من التوربينات ومحطات الضخ والمحولات الكهربائية، فضلا عن إقامة مناطق ادارية.

وقد كان التصميم الهيكلي للمشروع يتكون من أطر حديدية ممتدة النطاق، وهو ما سمح بإنشاء وحدات المشروع بمرونة وسرعة. ولقد ساعدت الحوائط السميكة المبنية من الطوب على العزل الحراري، وعلى تخفيض حدة الضوضاء الناجمة عن مصنع الطاقة. وقد تم اضفاء قدر من الديكور على الواجهات وكذلك على الطابق الأرضي، الذي يحمل بعض البلاطات الزخرفية. ومن الملامح المميزة في محطة التحلية ذلك البرج الذي تم تشييده من طوب العمارة (العراقي)، ليكون العنصر الرئيس بالمجمع كله. و قد تم افتتاح محطة الطاقة الأولى في العام ١٩٥٣.

مدرسة الشويخ الثانوية
الشويخ، ١٩٥١ - ١٩٥٧

المصمم • شركة المقاولات والتجارة (المستشارين الاساسيين)
العميل • وزارة الاشغال العامة، مجلس التعليم
المقاول • شركة المقاولات والتجارة (CAT)، شركة الاحمدية للمقاولات والتجارة (تم تعديل التصميم)

يعد هذا المشروع من أوائل المشاريع العملاقة في الكويت. وكانت هذه المدرسة الثانوية تمثل لسنوات طوال نموذجاً لنظام تعليمي إقليمي يحتذي به. وتقع المدرسة في منطقة إستراتيجية في المنطقة التعليمية وهي جزء من المرحلة الأولى للخطة الرئيسية، وتضم تجهيزات رياضية، ونادي دبلوماسي، وأماكن منفصلة مخصصة لإقامة التلاميذ والأساتذة. وكانت المدرسة تستقطب أشخاصا من كافة أرجاء الشرق الأوسط للدراسة والعمل. وقد قدمت عدة مناهج تعليمية تقنية، ولعل ذلك يرجع إلى المساحة الكبيرة المتاحة للمعامل بالمدرسة.

ويستند تصميم المبنى الرئيسي للنمط الكلاسيكي القائم على محور مركزي متناسق. ويتألف المبنى من طابقين، ومن أجنحة منحنية من طابقين، تفضي إلي المدخل الرئيسي، كما أن كافة واجهات المدرسة محاطة بأروقة. ومن ناحية أخرى فان الأجنحة تتواصل على نحو عمودي لتنقابل في نهاية المبنى، بما يشكل عموداً فقرياً، وتحيط بغناء كبير. ولذا فإن المحور الرئيسي تتحدد معالمه من خلال سلسلة من المباني العالية كقبة المدخل، وقاعة الإجتماعات، وبرج الساعة القريب من الشاطئ.

ولسوء الحظ فان مصمم هذا المبنى يعد مجهولاً. وإن تشابه التصميم العام، وبعض الملامح المعمارية إلى حد كبير مع معهد عبدان للتكنولوجيا، الذي تم تشييده في العام ١٩٣٩، والذي صممه في إيران كل من ويلسون وماسون. وقد كان للشركة نشاط ملموس في الكويت في سنوات الأربعينات، حيث صممت مسجدين بالأحمدي وقصر ضيافة صاحب السمو الأمير، من بين عدد آخر من المشاريع.

وقد تحول المبنى منذ العام ١٩٧٢ ليصبح جامعة الكويت. واستدعى ذلك الدور الجديد إدخال عدد من التعديلات والإضافات على المبنى، وهو ما نتج عنه تغيير التصميم الأصلي.

مدارس حكومية
أماكن متعددة، ١٩٥٢ - ١٩٥٦

المصمم • تريب واكهام - شركة تضامن
العميل • وزارة الأشغال العامة، قسم التربية
المقاول • متنوعين (تم تعديل التصميم)

كان الاضطلاع بتنفيذ برنامج تعليم وطني من الأولويات التي وضعتها الحكومة إبان المراحل الأولى لتحديث البلاد، وعندما كانت مدرسة الشويخ الثانوية قيد الإنشاء، وتحديداً في الفترة من العام ١٩٥٢ إلى العام ١٩٥٦ تم تكليف كلاً من تريب واكهام بتصميم كلية فنية، فضلا عن عدة مدارس إبتدائية ودور حضانة، إضافة إلى تصميم المطبخ المركزي بوزارة التربية بطاقة .... واجبة تقدم للمدارس الحكومية في العام ١٩٥٤.

وقد تم تشييد الكلية الفنية بالشويخ ١٩٥٣-١٩٥٤، مع ديفيد اوكلي ١٩٢٧-٢٠٠٣ ضمن فريق التصميم من مجمع يضم عددا من المباني، منها ٦ مقار لإقامة الطلاب، تستضيف ٢٥٠ طالبا من بين ٧٥٠ طالباً يدرسون بالكلية، فضلا عن ٣ مبان تستخدم كمعامل لتدريس الهندسة الميكانيكية والالكترونية، والفيزياء، والعلوم، والمعادن، والدراسات المتصلة بالسيارات، وذلك إلى جانب ٤ ورش تختص بالإصلاح والصيانة.

وقد تم تشييد المدارس الأولى في مناطق صلاح الدين، والشامية، والصديق، وكانت كل من تلك المدارس تستوعب ٨٠٠ طالباً، فضلاً عن ٣٠ مدرساً مقيماً. أما دور الحضانة في بوابة الجهراء والمقوع، وطارق والمهلب، فكان من المزمع أن تستوعب ١٥ طالبا موزعين بنسبة ١٥ طالباً بكل فصل دراسي.

وقد تم إنشاء المدارس على أساس شبكه من ٣ م مصنوعة من عناصر خرسانية نمطية مدعمة وسابقة التجهيز، للتغلب على مشاكل الزمن و المواد المحلية المتاحة. وفي المرحلة الأولى لم يكن هناك أجهزة تكييف، مما تطلب تصميماً يتلاءم مع متطلبات الحرارة المستعرة. ومن هذا المنطلق فقد كان التظليل والتهوية من النواحي التي حظيت باهتمام بالغ. ولذا فإن عرض المبنى لم يتجاوز سمك حجرة واحدة. وكانت النوافذ تواجه الشمال الشرقي، وقد تم استخدام المشربيات الخرسانية، فضلا عن استخدام الألوان الزاهية التي تحمل صبغة صحراوية. كما تم استخدام الممرات المظللة، و بناء الحوائط والأسقف المعلقة، بما يضمن كفاءة التهوية. أما المواد التي استخدمت في وضع اللمسات النهائية فقد تم اختيارها بناء على قدرتها على التحمل وانخفاض تكلفة صيانتها. نلمس بوضوح استخدام الطوب البغدادي في الحوائط، مع الطوب الرملي أو مع بلاطات زخرفية من السيراميك أحيانا. أما الأرضيات فقد كسيت بطوب محلي الصنع. (١٧)

مستشفى الصليبخات
الصليبخات، ١٩٥٤-١٩٦٤

المصمم • جون آر هاريس - مهندسون معماريون، سعت اند ولسون، كركبترك وشركاهم (البناء)، هور لي وشركاهم (الخدمات)
العميل • وزارة الأشغال العامة
المقاول • شركة كونسوليداتد للمقاولات (CONCO) (تم تعديل التصميم)

تم تنفيذ هذا المستشفى، وهو المستشفى الذي يُطلق عليه كذلك مستشفى النساء، في "المنطقة الصحية" بالصليبخات، وذلك وفقاً لتعريف الخطة الرئيسية. وقد تم تكليف المهندس المعماري البريطاني الشاب جون آر هاريس في العام ١٩٥٢ من جانب مجموعة معامل البحوث الكويتية بتصميم المشروع، وكان ذلك هو أول عمل يقوم به المهندس البريطاني خارج المملكة المتحدة. وقد نتج عن ذلك أن أسس المهندس مكتباً له في الكويت، ولعل ذلك كان أمراً بالغ الأهمية لفهم طبيعة المواد الملائمة للمناخ الحار. وبعد أن فاز المهندس في مسابقة إقامة مستشفى في منطقة الدوحة (١٩٥٢-١٩٥٧)، تم تكليفه بإقامة مستشفى الأمراض الصدرية بالكويت، وقد تم تحويل المستشفى بعد ذلك ليصبح مستشفى الولادة. ويتألف المجمع من أحد عشر جناحاً، وهي أجنحة متصلة ببعضها البعض، وتتباين الأجنحة من حيث عدد الطوابق، وإن كانت كلها تشترك في أنها موازية للشاطئ. وتقع كلها في ثلاثة وحدات, هي الأكثر ارتفاعا, ويتألف كل منها من أربعة طوابق, في الناحية الشمالية مقابل الخليج، وذلك إضافة إلى مركز العلاج الطبيعي والتأهيل، وهو المركز الذي تم هدمه لاحقاً. وكان المركز يتكون من مسطح دائري مميز ومن سطح خرساني متعرج.

وتتكون وحدات المجمع من واجهة خرسانية مسبقة التجهيز، تم بناؤها على نحو فعال من حيث الشكل والوظيفة، وقد تم تغطيتها بطوب رملي محلي الصنع، مع نوافذ رئيسية من الألمنيوم، وتمتد هذه النوافذ من الأرض إلى السقف، مع وجود قنوات مياه خرسانية لصرف المياه(١). وتقع مداخل الزوار على المحور الجنوبي ـ الغربي، وتغطيها مظلات, مشيدة من الخرسانة.

قصر الشيخ جابر العلي
السرة، ١٩٥٥ - ١٩٦٠

المصمم • المعماريون فارمر اند دارك (المسئول جون بارتون)
العميل • الشيخ جابر العلي الصباح
المقاول • شركة المقاولات والتجارة (CAT) (تم تعديل التصميم)

تم تشييد قصر الشيخ جابر العلي في ذات الوقت الذي شيد فيه قصر الامير اكيهتيو في اليابان، وقصر بلان التو في البرازيل. إلا أن هذا القصر لم يعد مستخدماً الآن. والمصدر الوحيد للمعلومات عن هذا القصر هي ما ورد في إحدى المقالات المنشورة بإحدى المجلات. أما الصور المتاحة عن القصر فهي تلك التي نشرها ريجينالد هوجو دي بورج جالاوي. ووفقاً لتلك المعلومات فان القصر قد تم تشييده على موقع يرتفع بمقدار ٧.٥ متر عن المنطقة المحيطة به، وهي منطقة تم استصلاحها وزراعتها على نحو كثيف بعد ان كانت منطقة جرداء(٣).

وتعطي الحديقة التي تشتمل على فناءين، إضافة إلى النافورة وحمام السباحة، نوعا من "الإحساس ببرودة الطقس" لمن يقترب من المدخل الرئيسي للقصر. ومن هذه المنطقة يفضي المدخل إلي شرفة، يقود إلي الصالون الكبير وغرفة ملحقة به، و إلي صالة الطعام. وتقع شرفة كبيرة بطول الدور الأول، وهي شرفة ذات درابزين من خشب الساج، محاطة بزجاج سميك ملون، تفضي إلى أجنحة الضيوف، ويمكن من خلالها رؤية المدنية، و تغطي هذه المساحة بسقف نصف دائري مبني من النحاس.

اما الواجهات المتنوعة الألوان فإنها تتسم بوجود قدر كبير من الفسيفساء والرخام, مما يخلق "إحساسا بالثراء" مع تجنب التفاصيل غير الضرورية، ومع ذلك فان استخدام شبكات من الالومنيوم المعالج مع مصاريع منزلقة من خشب الساج للنوافذ يعطي للزائر إحساسا بالرفاهية.

بناية ثنيان الغانم
بوابة الجهراء، ١٩٥٧-١٩٥٩

المصمم • سيد كريم
العميل • يوسف، أحمد الغانم
المقاول • مجهول (البناء: مستخدم)

شجعت سياسات شراء الأراضي, في إطار الخطة الرئيسية الأولى, القطاع الخاص الناشئ على الاستثمار في تشييد مباني متعددة الاستخدام. وقد أدت ضغوط التطوير على شارع فهد السالم في الخمسينات، فضلا عن هدم السور الثالث بالمدينة، والانتهاء من إنشاء الطريق الدائري الأول، أدى كل ذلك إلى خلق سياق مناسب لإقامة مثل هذا المبنى التجاري السكني. وقد تم تحويله لاحقاً إلى مكانين (٢). وكان موقع ورقعة المنطقة المواجهة لبوابة الجهراء (٣) عند مدخل أول شارع حديث بالمدينة، وهو شارع فهد السالم، هو من المواقع الهامة لإقامة مثل هذا المشروع. وقد تم تصميم المبنى فوق قطعة من الأرض ذات زاوية منفرجة، ليكون بمثابة مبنى كبير الحجم على شكل مربع مع توفير وسائل التظليل والإضاءة الطبيعية والصناعية.

وتُفضي الواجهة الخلفية إلى ممر مع سلم يوزع تدفق الزوار على الطوابق الأربع العليا وعلى الوحدات المختلفة، التي تنتظم في أزواج, و تلتئم حول محور رأسي. وتقع الوحدات وعددها ٤٨ وحدة، على الجزء الناتئ من الواجهة، التي تقع خارج الطابق التجاري الأرضي،

الكويت (٢) إنسان الكويت، (٣) كويت اليوم والغد و (٤) البعد الثقافي (٢٧) وبناء على اقتراح منظمة اليونسكو فقد وقع اختيار إدارة التعليم على التصميم الذي تقدم به ميشيل ايكوشارد من بين ستة مشاريع متنافسة.

وقد كان المشروع الذي وقع عليه الاختيار مشابها لما تم بناؤه بعد ذلك بعشرين عاماً، وان كان ذلك قد تم في إطار مشروع أكثر تعقيداً، فقد استند التصميم إلى أربعة أقسام متكاملة هندسياً، تلتق كلها حول ساحة مربعة الشكل، مع سلسلة من المباني الأصغر حجماً، وساحات مغلقة، وهذه كلها لم تكن جزءاً من الخطة المبدئية المقترحة (٢٨).

والواقع أن الخطة اشتملت على أربعة أجنحة, يتكون كل منها من طابقين، وتتصل بعضها البعض (فضلا عن المرصد) من خلال جسور معلقة. وكان التصميم يسمح للزوار بسهولة الحركة عبر الأجزاء المختلفة وحول الفناء/الحديقة المركزية والتي تم حمايتها من حرارة الطقس من خلال هيكل ثلاثي الأبعاد من عناصر متطابقة رباعية الأسطح. وكان يتخلل الممرات منحدرات تنساب وتتقاطع بشكل سلس، ومنصات, مما يسمح بوجود مناظر متعددة الزوايا للمعروضات وللبر وللحديقة، وذلك من خلال الجسور والنوافذ. و تتكون الواجهة من أطر خرسانية محشوة بالطوب الأحمر.

ولقد تعرض المتحف لتلف بالغ أبان الغزو العراقي ر في العام ١٩٩٠ حيث نهبت محتوياته من التحف. ومنذ ذلك الحين والمتحف لا يؤدي وظائفه على نحو كامل. وقد تم إجراء عدد من التقييمات الفنية، فضلا عن القيام بعمليات تجديد مازالت مستمرة إلى يومنا هذا تحت إشراف المجلس الوطني للثقافة والفنون والآداب بالتعاون مع منظمات الأمم المتحدة المختلفة.

العطاء التنافسي لإقامة الواجهة البحرية
مدينة الكويت، ١٩٦١

المصمم • سكوت ويلسون، كيركباتريك وشركاه مع جون ار هاريس، ماكلين ل هنكوك/مجموعة تخطيط المشاريع المحدودة: رندل، بالمر وترنتون، كود وشركاه. الاستشاريون البحريون المتحدون
العميل • مجلس التنمية الكويتية
(لم يتم البناء)

كان الكورنيش الكبير هو الاسم الذي تم إطلاقه على مشروع إعادة تطوير منطقة المرفأ القديم، التي كانت آنذاك تحفل ببقايا المواد المهدمة من المدينة القديمة. وكانت فكرة الحصول على أرض جديدة عن طريق ردم جزء من البحر لبتسنى بناء واجهة بحرية، كانت مجالا لعطاء تنافسي تم طرحه في العام ١٩٦١.

وكانت الخطة الرئيسية للمشروع التي تم وضعها في العام ١٩٥١ قد حددت عدداً من الجوانب التي ينبغي تطويرها بالمدينة وإن لم يشتمل ذلك على إقامة واجهة بحرية. ومع ذلك فقد بدا أن تخفيف الحمل عن المناطق المزدحمة حول قصر السيف، و تحديد موضع آخر كمرفأ للصيد وأماكن الاصطياد البحري، بدا أن ذلك يمثل أولوية ضرورية وهو ما أدى إلى طرح هذه المنافسة.

وقد شارك في المنافسة التي تم طرحها في العام ١٩٦١ خمس شركات, وإن كانت اثنتان منها فقط أبدتا استعدادها للمشاركة. وكانت إحدى الشركتين, تلك الشركة البريطانية المعروفة باسم سكوت وويلسون, وهي شركة هندسية كان لها باع طويل في مجال تصميم هياكل المركبات.

وقد استفادت الشركة من خبرة سيريل كيركباتريك, الذي عمل لسنوات طوال مديراً لهيئة ميناء لندن. وقد تمثل اقتراح الشركة في إقامة شريط طويل منحني من الأرض المستصلحة يحيط بها طريق دائري يمتد من دسمان إلى ميناء الشويخ. وقد حدد المشروع عدداً مختلفاً من المناطق الوظيفية التي تم تطويرها استناداً إلى مفاهيم ثلاثية الأبعاد. وذلك بالتعاون مع جون هاريس, وذلك قبل عدة سنوات من تعاون الفريق ذاته في تصميم مستشفى النساء. ومن الجدير بالملاحظة هنا, أن تصميمهم استند إلى فكرة إقامة سور بحري متدرج حتى يتسنى رؤية الشاطئ دائما من خلال الممشى البحري، مع توفير المقاعد لتزجية وقت الفراغ (٣٨).

أما العطاء الثاني فقد تقدم به المهندس المعماري الكندي هانكوك، وكان له خبرة طويلة في تصميم المستوطنات

البشرية والطبيعية. وكانت تلك الخبرة العريضة واضحة وجلية في المشروع الذي تقدم به. ويتسم تصميم هانكوك بالمرونة كما أنه يتسم بأنه أكثر انسيابية. ويستند التصميم إلى إقامة بحيرة اصطناعية تواجه قصر السيف (وهو ما تم تنفيذه لاحقاً في أعوام التسعينيات) بالإضافة إلى مرفأ معلق في عمق البحر. وقد فاز المشروع في المنافسة لكن لجنة اختيار الواجهة المائية رأت أنه بالغ البذخ على نحو غير ضروري ' ولذا فقد مر المشروع بمراجعات عدة. وفي عام ١٩٦٤ كان المشروع ما زال حبيس أدراج وزارة الأشغال العام طبقا لما ذكره شحبير.

وعلى الرغم من أن هذا المشروع لم يقدر له البتة أن ينفذ، إلا أن المنافسة التي تم طرحها قد أشارت إلى عدد آخر من مناحي التطوير، مثل إنشاء شارع الخليج، أو إقامة عدد من المباني الوظيفية كالفنادق والموانئ والمباني العامة. الخ. كما أن هذه المنافسة قد مهدت الطريق أمام مشروع الواجهة البحرية في العام ١٩٧٦ والذي تم إنشاؤه بالفعل. وقد نتج عنه إعادة تشكيل العلاقة بين الكويت وساحلها البحري عن نحو عميق.

منطقة الأعمال المركزية
المنطقة ١ والمنطقة ٢
السيف، ١٩٦١ – ١٩٦٥

المصمم • قسم التخطيط بالبلدية. (رئاسة سابا جورج شحبير)
العميل • بلدية الكويت
المقاول • العديد
(تم تعديل التصميم)

كانت المنطقة رقم ١ والمنطقة رقم ٢ هما المنطقتان اللتان تم تطويرهما بعد أن تم تطوير المنطقة رقم ٣ وفي إطار الإرشادات ذاتها. لكن الاهتمام في هاتين المنطقتين تركز على تأسيس علاقة مع المعالم المحيطة من خلال مفهوم ثلاثي الأبعاد ومن خلال التحكم في الطراز المعماري للمباني.

وقد تم إرساء عطاء تصميم المنطقة رقم ١ في أكتوبر ١٩٦٢. وتتألف المنطقة من ثلاثة مباني ارتفاع كل منها طابقين,, ومبنين ارتفاع كل منهما طابقين مع طابق للميزانين, بالإضافة إلى مبنى متعدد الطوابق يستخدم كفندق. وإن تم لاحقا إعادة تصميم المكان ليكون مقراً لمكاتب إدارية. وعلى النقيض من الخطة الأصلية فان المسجدين القائمين تم هدمهما ليتم بناء مسجد أكبر في الميدان المركزي (٣٠).

وتقع قيصرية الأمير إلى جوار المنطقتين ١ و ٢. وكانت هذه المنطقة ذات يوم مقراً لمكاتب التجار المشهورين بالمدينة القديمة. ومع المجموعة الجديدة من المباني وصل إجمالي عدد المكاتب إلى ١٧٠ مكتباً. تم تصميمها حول ميدان عام ووفقاً لطبوغرافيا القيصرية ذاتها(٣١).

وتتميز هذه الكتل المستطيلة، الممتدة في صف واحد، بطابق أول ناتئ به عدد من الفتحات المربعة، على مسافات متساوية. مع المداخل الرئيسية التي تصل إلى ذات ارتفاع الطابقين الذين يتألف منهما المبنى، ويفضي ذلك إلى شارع داخلي. وفي أواخر السبعينيات كان من المزمع أن يشغل بنك الكويت المركزي احد أطراف هذه المنطقة.

وتقع المنطقتان ١ و ٢ بمحاذاة شارع الخليج، وتتمتعان بدور هام في السياق الحضري من خلال إرساء علاقة بين منطقة السوق والبحر.

منطقة الأعمال المركزية
المنطقة رقم ٣
القبلة، ١٩٦١ – ١٩٦٥

المصمم • قسم التخطيط بالبلدية. (رئاسة سابا جوج شحبير)
المصمم • بلدية الكويت
المقاول • العديد
(عدلت بعد الأماكن. الأخرى هدمت)

كانت المنطقة ٣ هي أول منطقة يتم تنفيذها بمنطقة الأعمال المركزية من بين ١١ منطقة تولى سابا جورج شحبير إنشاءها وكان يقوم بدور المنسق في البداية ليتحول في نهاية المطاف إلى مخطط حضري (٣٢). وقد كان التقسيم إلى مناطق، وهي إستراتيجية وضعها شحبير لإنشاء منطقة الأعمال المركزية، بمثابة خطوة رئيسية من خطوات تطوير المدينة، التي اتخذت في

أعقاب عام ١٩٥٢(٣٣). وقد أدت خطة تقسيم المناطق إلى إنشاء مباني وأنماط حضرية جديدة, وإلى تعزيز مشاريع البناء التي تعمل على إقامة نوع جديد من العلاقة بين المشروع العام وتفاصيله.

ولم يتم رسم هذه العلاقات من خلال 'التشريعات العامة الموحدة ' فحسب، وإنما تم كذلك تنظيمها من خلال تلك التشريعات، وهو ما أرسى من القواعد ما يلي: أن تكون المباني بنفس الارتفاع، وأن تدمج المساجد القائمة في التخطيط الحضري، كما أوصى بضرورة أن يكون لكل من المباني أربعة واجهات، وأن تكون متصلة من خلال ممرات مغطاة (٣٤). ومع ذلك فإن تلك القواعد لم تكن كافية لتحقيق التوحد في البناء؛ حيث كانت رقعة واحدة أحيانا، تشتمل على ثلاث قطع من الأرض مملوكة لعدة أشخاص، مما كان يؤدي إلى أن يعمل عليها ثلاث معماريين مختلفين. وقد عقدت البلدية اجتماعات مع المهندسين المعماريين في المراحل المبدئية للمشروع، استناداً إلى فكرة 'الاتفاق، والتعاون، والإرشاد' وهي خطة تستهدف البحث عن أفضل 'معايير جمالية معمارية' (٣٥). وقد كان من المزمع في بادئ الأمر أن تكون هذه البقعة منطقة بنوك، فكان بنك الكويت الوطني، والبنك البريطاني للشرق الأوسط. هما أول ما تم بنائه. وبعد ذلك توسعت المهام فضمت المنطقة غرفة التجارة والصناعة، وشركة نفط الكويت، وشركة الطيران الكويتية، فضلا عن ٢٤ مكتباً للصيارفة واستبدال العملات.

المقر الرئيسي للبنك الوطني
منطقة الأعمال المركزية، منطقة ٣،
١٩٦١–١٩٦٣

المصمم • مجموعة التصميم الإنشائي (انطوني ايرفنج وجوردون براون)
العميل • بنك الكويت الوطني
(تم تعديل التصميم)

كان بنك الكويت الوطني في البداية بمثابة مبادرة من المواطنين، لكن تأسيسه كان بموجب مرسوم أميري صدر عام ١٩٥٢. وقد تم افتتاح أول مكتب للبنك في ساحة الصفاة. لكن سرعان ما دعت الحاجة لإقامة مقر رئيسي للبنك ولعل المبنى كان هو أول مبنى يتم إنشاؤه في منطقة الأعمال المركزية، منطقة ٣، والتي كانت السلطات قد أعادت تخطيطها حديثاً. وقد حصلت إحدى الشركات اللبنانية، وهي مجموعة التصميم الإنشائي، على تكليف بإقامة المبنى، وهي ذات الشركة التي تولت من قبل تصميم مبنى بنك الخليج، ومبنى البنك التجاري. ويتشابه تصميم بنك الكويت الوطني مع هذه البنوك من ناحية استخدام فكرة الكتلة المستطيلة البسيطة مع وجود طابق أرضي فسيح غير ناتئ, ودعامات صلبة. وقد تم التركيز في التصميم على نمط هندسي يهتم بوسائل التظليل، التي تهدف إلى وقاية المكاتب من الحر الشديد. وذلك باستخدام عناصر خرسانية رأسية متكررة, على درجات متفاوتة العمق لخلق نمط إيقاعي منتظم بالمبنى. وفضلا عن ذلك فان الشركة قد أولت عناية متكافئة، كما هي عادتها دائماً، بتصميم المساحات الداخلية، بما يحدد الأسطح ونمط الأثاث بالمبنى.

وما زال هذه المبنى قائما يمارس وظائفه، وإن كانت الشبكة الخارجية التي استهدفت وقاية المكاتب من الشمس قد أزيلت، وتمت تكسية المبنى بطبقة من الحجر التقليدية، الأمر الذي غير تماماً من المظهر الخارجي للمبنى.

بنك الخليج
منطقة الأعمال المركزية، المنطقة رقم ١،
شارع على السالم، ١٩٦١ – ١٩٦٣

المصمم • مجموعة التصميم الإنشائي (انطوني ايرفنج وجوردون براون)
العميل • بنك الخليج
المقاول • مجهول
(تم تعديل التصميم)

تولى المهندسان المعماريان البريطانيان توني إرفاين وجوردون جونز من مجموعة التصميمات الإنشائية تصميم هذا المبنى عام ١٩٦٣. ويتبع التصميم الإرشادات التي وضعها شحبير، فضلا عن تلك الإرشادات الخاصة بإقامة مناطق تجارية في منطقة الأعمال المركزية. ويقع المبنى الذي تؤول ملكيته إلى عدة أطراف, في المنطقة رقم ١، ويشتمل على طابق عادي للمكاتب يرتفع طابقين فوق الأرض، وينقسم إلى ٣ أماكن مستقلة عن بعضها البعض

عينة رقم ٢
مباني كهوية وطنية: ١٩٦١-١٩٧٠

منافسة متحف الكويت الوطني
القبلة، ١٩٦٠

المشاركين • هانز اسبلوند ، زدرافكو بريجوفاك ، ايجناسيو جارديلا ، سيد كريم، الفونسو ريدي ، ميشيل ايكوشار (مع بير لاجوس)
العميل • وزارة التعليم
(لم يتم البناء)

وضع هذا البرنامج الخاص بإقامة متحف وطني سليم عبد الحق من منظمة اليونسكو في العام ١٩٦٠ بناء على طلب من حكومة الكويت [٢٦]. وبناء على ذلك فقد أعلنت وزارة التعليم عن منافسة معمارية دولية دعت فيها المهندسين المعماريين التالية أسماءهم: هانز اسبلوند (استكهولم)، زدرافكو بريجوفاك (اوبتيا)، ايجناسيو جارديلا (ميلان)، سيد كريم (القاهرة)، افونسو ريدي (البرازيل) وميشيل ايكوشار (بيروت، باريس) وقد فاز بهذه الأخير بالمنافسة.

وكان على كل منافس أن يتبع مجموعة من التعليمات الدقيقة كما أن كافة المشاريع كان عليها أن تأخذ في الاعتبار ما يلي: (١) أرض الكويت، (٢) إنسان الكويت، (٣) كويت اليوم والغد، (٤) البعد الثقافي، والذي يشتمل على نواحي تتصل بالإدارة، والمعارض المؤقتة، فضلا عن عدد من قاعات المؤتمرات، ومكتبة، وكافيتريا، (٥) مرصد لعرض الأدوات القديمة المستخدمة في رصد الكواكب Planetarium.

وقد استلهم اسبلوند في مشروعة فكرة الواحة في الصحراء. وفي هذا المشروع نجد أن هناك رقعة شاسعة مساحتها كيلومتر مربع واحد قد تركت خاوية تقريباً، وتلك الرقعة محاطة بصف من الأشجار بما يفضي إلى منطقة مركزية تسمح بوصول الزوار، وهي محاطة بنوافير مياه كما لو كان ذلك للترحيب بالزائرين، في موكب مهيب. وقد لبى المشروع المتطلبات التي وضعتها وزارة التعليم من خلال إقامة ٤ أشكال متداخلة تفضي كلها إلى فناء مفتوح.

أما المهندس المعماري البرازيلي الذي حصل على المركز الثالث في هذه المنافسة، فإنه عرض مشروعاً يتناقض، مع سابقه، حيث وزع برنامج المشروع على الرقعة المتاحة بأسرها، وفي هذا المشروع نجد أن المبنى الرئيسي مع المرصد متصلان ببعضهما البعض من خلال ممرات مغطاة، بما يسمح بعبور العناصر المائية المحيطة بهما. أما باقي المنطقة فتشغلها مباني خدمية مكملة، مع نوافير مياه، وحدائق، وأصص للزهور، وهو ما يؤدي إلى خلق اتصال عميق مع باقي المباني من خلال حوائط زجاجية. أما المدخل إلى القسم الثقافي فيبدو مرتفعاً عن الأرض، بما يسمح بخلق قاعة بعلو ٢٠ متراً وهي تصلح كذلك لأن تكون قاعة للمعارض المؤقتة. أما قاعة المرصد فهي على شكل صدفة، وهي مطمورة جزئياً بما يوحي بأنها تبزغ من تحت الماء. أما بريجوفاك والذي ربح المركز الثاني في المنافسة، فقد قدم مشروعاً يتمحور حول فكرة الأجنحة الأفقية مع عدد كبير من الأفنية والحدائق، وكلها تشكل مربع حول باحة مرصوفة رئيسية مفتوحة. أما المرصد فقد بدا وكأنه قبة في جناح "كويت اليوم والغد".

متحف الكويت الوطني
القبلة، ١٩٦٠-١٩٨٣

المصمم • ميشيل ايكوشار (المعماري) ، اندري دوفيداري (مساهم معماري) ، بيير سادي (مساهم معماري) ، زيجمنت سلطان (مساهم معماري) ، نيكوس شانزيداكس (الهيكل المعماري)
العميل • وزارة الاشغال
المقاول • مجهول
(تحت التجديد)

بعد تأسيس متحف الكويت الوطني في العام ١٩٥٧، وبعد تحقق الاستقلال والسيادة الوطنية، تم الإعلان عن منافسة دولية تدعو لإنشاء متحف جديد على رقعة مساحتها كيلومتر مربع واحد، على أن يشتمل ذلك على مرصد وأربعة أقسام مستقلة هي: (١) أرض

أحدث ما توصلت إليه التكنولوجيا، فيما يمكن تسميته بالطراز الدولي.

أما الواجهات العليا فتتميز بقرميد أزرق بلون البحر، مع فسيفساء ملونة صغيرة الحجم. أما المدخل الرئيسي فيتحدد من خلال قوس حر.

وتعد هذه المباني، إلى جانب وزارة الإرشاد والإعلام، بمثابة رمز لمدينة حديثة جديدة، كما أنها مازالت تعد إلى يومنا هذا معالم حضرية بارزة بالمدينة.

مجمع أنوار الصباح، المرحلة ١ والمرحلة ٢
الصالحية، ١٩٧٥-١٩٨١

المصمم • غازي سلطان مع KEO
العميل • الشركة المتحدة للعقارات
المقاول • شركة مساعد الصالح وأبناءه
(مهدد بالهدم)

أصبح شارع فهد السالم في الستينيات منطقة جاذبة للاستثمار الخاص [٢٨]. كما أنه كان بمثابة نقطة مرجعية تنشير إلى بواكير التحديث بالمدينة، وقد كان أعضاء الأسرة الحاكمة من أوائل المستثمرين بالبلاد. ويعرف هذا المجمع على نحو عام باسم "مجمع الصباح". وقد تم تصميم هذا المجمع التجاري والسكني وفقاً لمعايير سابا شحبير في التصميم [٢٩]. ويتألف المجمع من ثلاثة أبنية تجمع بينها واجهة واحدة، ومساحة تجارية مقنطرة مشتركة تواجه الشارع، كما أن هناك عريشة تصل المبنى بالفناء الخلفي. والمجمع ما زال يُستخدم في أغراض السكني والتجارة إلى الآن وإن اعتراه الكثير من التردي.

وبعد بناء المشروع بخمسة عشرة سنة، طرح الفناء الخلفي للمبنى لمنافسة دولية. وكان المشروع الرابع عبارة عن مجمع من الحجر الرملي. لكن المشروع لم يكتمل و مازال غير مأهول إلى الآن.

قصر السلام
شارع الخليج العربي، ١٩٦١-١٩٦٤

المصمم • مدحت العبد
العميل • الشيخ سعد العبد الله الصباح
المقاول • مجهول
(تحت التجديد)

كان قصر الإستقبال الذي يُقابل الواجهة البحرية، عند نهاية الطريق الدائري الثاني، محاطاً في السابق بحدائق غنّاء، كما أنه كان محاطاً بسور من الطوب لا تعترضه سوى بوابتين من الحديد مع أماكن للحراسة. وتحدد خطة البناء، التي تشير إلى تقابل عمودي للمبنى مع البحر، التنظيم الداخلي ونقاط الدخول.

يتكون قلب القصر من باحة مغلقة، ذات مستويات ثلاثة، على شكل دائرة مركزية تنبثق منها كافة حوائط القصر، ويعلوها سقف مغطى بقبة خرسانية. أما الشكل الخارجي فهو عبارة عن مزيج من أسطح غير شفافة وشبكات ذات زخارف هندسية.

وفي الداخل نرى نافورة مياه بمحاذاة ثريا كبيرة تشير إلى مركز قاعة الاستقبال الرسمية، ويتحدد محيطها بعناصر بيضاوية الشكل ترتفع إلى عنان السطح. ويؤدي المزج بين عناصر البناء المختلفة إلى تحسين الانسياب في المكان، وتشتمل اللمسات النهائية على داخل القصر على استخدام خشب الجوز، والماهوجني في ألواح من رقائق الخشب، والفسيفساء الزجاجية، وبلاط الأرضيات المبني من الحجر والسيراميك، وكذلك الجدران والأسقف المصورة و المزركشة.

الأمراض الصدرية، مستشفى الأمراض العصبية، مستشفى الطب النفسي، ومستشفى الأمراض المعدية، وأحياناً ما يُكتفى بالإشارة إلى موقع المستشفى. لكنه تجدر الإشارة هنا إلى أنه في العام ١٩٥٧ أشارت "الإحصائيات الصحية" الواردة بتقرير وزارة الصحة الكويتية إلى زيادة أعداد الأسرة من ٦١٢ سريراً إلى ١٣٢٢ بالمستشفى. وتصف أقرب إشارة إلى المبنى على أنه مجمع تم تشييده على "طراز المقصورات" بسعة ٢٠٠ سرير، وقد تم توسيعه لاحقاً ليشمل ضعف ذلك العدد [٢٥].

وتشير الكتابات الطبية إلى وجود زيادة كبيرة في الخدمات الصحية والنفسية [٢٦] التي بدأت تقديمها بالمستشفى العام ١٩٧٢، ولعل ذلك قد يشير إلى حدوث توسع في المبنى. ومنذ ذلك الحين وحتى يومنا هذا فإن المجمع يتوزع على جناحين متصلين من خلال ممرات مغطاة للمشاة سواء للاستقبال أو للحالات الطارئة، أو الخدمات الطبية الإكلينيكية، أو التشخيص الوظيفي، أو الطب المعملي، أو العلاج الطبي النووي، أو العلاج الطبيعي، أو الإدارة ومكاتبها، أو الأرشيف أو المكتبة، أو التعليم والتدريب، أو مركز رعاية الطفل، أو مساكن الموظفين.

مستشفى الصباح
الصليبيخات، ١٩٥٨-١٩٨٢

المصمم • مجموعة دورش الإستشارية (التخطيط والخدمات)، سكوت و ويلسون، كيربكباتريك وشركاه KEO
العميل • دولة الكويت
المقاول • (CAT) للمقاولات والتجارة، الشركة العالمية المحدودة (AST)، شركة المقاولون المتحدون (CONCO)
(مهدد للهدم)

تم الانتهاء من وضع الخطة الرئيسية للمستشفى في العام ١٩٥٩ [٣٨] وبعد ذلك تم إضافة عدد من المباني للمستشفى بما في ذلك ثلاث وحدات رئيسية تصل سعتها إلى ٦٠٠ سرير مكرسة للعلاج التخصصي، بما يسمح بعلاج مرضى العيادة الداخلية والحالات الطارئة، مع وجود وحدات منفصلة للأمومة، والجراحة، وطب الأطفال مساكن للممرضات وللأطباء، وأماكن الإقامة للموظفين، فضلا عن كلية للممرضات، ومخزن أدوية طبية. [٣٩]

ولا يعرف على وجه الدقة من اقترح التصميم الهندسي المبدئي، أو كيف تم تنفيذ أغلب العمل الذي استمر حتى فترة الستينات، ولعل الاستثناء في ذلك هو المخزن الذي بناه كل من سكوت وويلسون ن وكيركباتريك وشركاه في الفترة من ١٩٦٣ إلى ١٩٦٥ وكان ذلك جزءاً من التصميم المبدئي الذي تم نشره في العام ١٩٥٩. أما مساكن الممرضات في المبنيين الأول والثاني (وقد تمت إضافة مبنيين آخرين لاحقاً) فإنها كانت كذلك جزءاً من المشروع المبدئي لإسكان الموظفين.

وقد تم توسيع المستشفى لاحقاً ليضم مركزاً لزرع الأعضاء (KEO، ١٩٨٢)، ومباني مركز الكويت للتحكم في السرطان، بما في ذلك مبنى حسين مكي جمعة للجراحة المتخصصة ومبنى الشيخة بدرية الصباح لعلاج الاورام.

مجمع البلدية
شارع عبد الله السالم، ١٩٥٩-١٩٦٢

المصمم • سامي عبد الباقي
العميل • وزارة الأشغال العامة
المقاول • شركة عثمان احمد عثمان (العربيه للمقاولات)
(تم اجراء تعديلات على البناء)

تم إسناد مجمع البلدية الحالي، والذي يعرف اختصاراً باسم البلدية، إلى مهندس معماري عربي وفقاً لتوجيهات الشيخ فهد السالم. [٧]

وما أن انتهى البناء حتى تم استخدام المبنى ليكون كذلك مقراً مؤقتاً لمجلس الأمة الذي استضاف أول جلساته بعد انتخابات ديسمبر ١٩٦٢.

ويتألف المبنى من ثلاثة وحدات متشابهة وإن كانت مستقلة عن بعضها البعض، هي الوحدات A و B و C. وهناك مكان انتظار موحد للوحدات الثلاث، وكانت هذه الوحدات من أوائل المباني التي تم تشييدها من الخرسانة المدعمة بالبلاد، وبدلا من الاعتماد المكثف على استخدام الخرسانة، فيما يطلق عليه العمارة الحديثة [٨]. فإننا نجد أن هذا المبنى يشتمل على واجهة تمثل

وبالنسبة للسقف فهو من الخرسانة المسبقة التجهيز, المضلعة, بحيث يتناغم مع العناصر الرأسية. وقد استهدف المصمم بالدرجة الأولى أن تكون الأسطح الخارجية ناعمة قدر الإمكان, لا سيما من حيث اللمسات النهائية الخارجية, وذلك لمنع البقع التي قد تظهر على المبنى من جراء الغبار, والرمل والمطر. وبعد تحويل المبنى ليكون مؤسسة تعليمية ذات نشاط مختلف, تم طلاء واجهات المبنى بأشكال حبيبية مسبقة الخلط, وهي طبقة يسهل أن يظهر عليها آثار الاتساخ.

المدارس النموذجية
أماكن متعددة، ابتداء من عام ١٩٦٣

المصمم • وزارة الأشغال العامة، عدل التصميم ألفرد روث
العميل • وزارة التعليم، وزارة الأشغال العامة
المقاول • متعددين
(المبنى : تم هدم بعض من المباني وتعديل اخرى)

مع النمو السكاني في بداية الستينيات، زاد عدد الأطفال في سن المدارس. ونتيجة لذلك فقد تولت كل من وزارة التربية والتعليم، ووزارة الأشغال العامة مهمة تطوير تصميم نموذجي للمدارس يتسم بسرعة التنفيذ واقتصادية التشغيل. ويتكون التصميم، وهو على شكل حرف E، من ثلاثة مستويات. ويشتمل كل جناح على ثلاثة فصول، ويضم الجناح أماكن الخدمات والسلالم، في حين يضم مدخل المبنى الاستقبال، والإدارة، وغرف المدرسين، والمعامل، والشرفات. وقد تم تجميع كافة الفضاءات الوظيفية في المركز، حيث تم تصميم شرفات جانبية خرسانية الإطار لتخدم تلك الفضاءات الوظيفية، وتعد تلك سمة أساسية تحدد معالم الواجهات، كما أنها تزود الساحة بالظل.

وقد أثنى الفرد روث في العام ١٩٦٥ على وضوح التصميم وكفاءته العملية، واقترح إدخال بعض التعديلات بهدف تحسين أداء المباني، وذلك من خلال تقليص الفضاءات المكررة وغير اللازمة، وتخفيض ارتفاع السقف، وإعادة تصميم الفصول من خلال إعادة تحديد أبعادها، وإعادة ترتيب مواضعها. كما أنه رأى ضرورة تخفيض عدد المستويات والأجنحة، وضرورة استحداث أماكن راحة جديدة، ومزيد من التظليل. والواقع أنه تم البناء على غرار هذا الطراز في كافة الأحياء السكنية تقريباً، وظلت هذه المدارس مستخدمة حتى الأعوام القليلة الماضية.

مسجد فهد السالم
السالمية، ١٩٦١- ١٩٦٨

المصمم • صباح أبي حنا
العميل • الشيخة بدرية الصباح
المقاول • مجهول

يعد هذا المسجد من أوائل أعمال المهندس المعماري اللبناني الشاب صباح أبي حنا. وقد اعتمد التصميم في جوهره على تفاصيل دقيقة قدمتها العميلة واستلهمتها من رحلاتها إلى مصر (٢١)، وهو ما يتجلى في الكتل الصلبة السميكة، وفي هندسة المنارات. ويتسم المسجد بتصميم عادي شائع، حيث يتكون من مسطح مربع الشكل، وصحن مغطي يفضي إلى المصلى، ومع ذلك، فهو ينطوي على بعض الملامح التي تجعله تصميما فريداً في طرازه، ولا سيما المدخل المدعم بسلسلة من الأقواس التي تمتد للخارج تجاه السور المقابل. وتتكرر هذه العناصر كذلك على الأبواب الجانبية بما يشبه جناح طائر. وهذا النوع من المداخل المؤدية إلى صحن المسجد. فضلا عن الأفاريز المتوجة التي تنتظم حول المبنى بكامله، وحدها تشكل الأشكال الثلاثية الأبعاد التي صممت لكسر الرتابة التي تميز المبنى.

ومن المدهش كذلك ذلك المزج الرائع بين المواد التقليدية في البناء كالحجر الجيري وتركيبات من مواد ليفية حديثة مدعمة، وخاصة في القبة الرئيسية للمصلى.

مشاريع إسكان للدخل المحدود- بالمناطق الريفية
الصليبية (القيروان)، ميناء عبد اللَه (ام الهيمان، على صباح السالم)، ١٩٦٨-١٩٦٩، الفنطاس, الرقة, الوفرة الجديدة، ١٩٦٦-١٩٧٦

المصمم • لويجي موريتي مع المكتب العربي للاستشارات، دار الهندسة، سرفيل للاستشارات، جعفر طوفان مع KEB، كاظم كنان من CAT، بسفك للاستشارات العالمية مع معهد توشيبكاجاكو، كولن بيوكان وشركاه
العميل • بنك الادخار والائتمان
المقاول • مجهول
(البناء : البعض لم يتم بناء واخرى تم التعديل)

عندما بدا البدو، وهم سكان الصحراء الأوائل، في الاستقرار، تم بناء عدد من أماكن السكني المؤقتة لهم. وقد أقيمت تلك الأماكن في أماكن جرداء، كانت تقع عادة إلى جوار أماكن عملهم، أو إلى جوار حقول النفط. وسرعان ما أظهر ذلك ضرورة تدخل الدولة للمساعدة (٦٧).

لقد أدت الهجرة من المناطق الريفية إلى المناطق الحضرية الخالية، إلى جانب التدفق الهائل للوافدين الأجانب، وقد أتوا من مناطق ريفية، إلى ضرورة إقامة مستوطنات ملائمة لطبيعة كل هؤلاء (٦٨).

وانطلاقاً من العام ١٩٦٦، وفي إطار التعاون بين هيئات الإسكان المختلفة، وعدد من مستشاري التخطيط، تم اقتراح عدد من الأماكن التي تصلح كمستوطنات زراعية، عند أطراف المناطق الحضرية. ولا سيما جهة الشمال الغربي (الجهراء)، والجنوب (ميناء عبد اللَه وام الهيمان). لكن هذه المبادرة لم يتم تنفيذها. ومرت عشر سنوات قبل أن يتم تنفيذ مشروعين اثنين على نحو جزئي. وقد تم تنفيذ المشروعين على نحو مشابه لما كان مخططاً من قبل وفي الأماكن ذاتها. وكان أحد هذه المشاريع هو نموذج مدينة زراعية مثالية. وتم تطوير المشروع في إطار رعاية البنك الدولي وبتصميم السويدي يان نورفيل وشركته T للاستشارات. وكان للشركة سمعة طيبة في مجال مشاريع الإسكان الهندسية السابقة التجهيز والمصنوعة من الخشب (٦٩).

وكانت المدينة الزراعية تشابه إلى حد كبير من حيث المفهوم مدينة كيشو كوروكاوا الزراعية بالمملكة العربية السعودية (١٩٦٠-١٩٦١). وكانت المدينة تستند إلى فكرة الرقة الزراعية المستقلة ذاتياً بما يعمل على خلق فرص وظيفية وسكنية في الوقت ذاته. وتم ذلك من خلال استصلاح المناطق الجرداء من الصحراء والتي لا تصلح لاستكشاف المعادن، وكذلك في إطار متابعة تنفيذ قرارات المناطق المحايدة (٧٠).

وفي العام ١٩٦٨ أعلنت دولة الكويت عن منافسة دولية للإسكان الريفي. وحددت كتيب المنافسة منطقتين هامشيتين في الأطراف الشرقية والجنوبية للمدينة. وتم تحديد رقع متماثلة كل منها بمساحة ١٥٠ متر مربع، على أن يتم تجميعها في شكل قرية تسع لـ ٥٠٠٠ فرد. وكان المشروع عبارة عن نمط خطي بسيط يتكون من وحدات، تبلغ مساحة كل منها ٥٠ متر مربع، وتحتوي على غرفتين. وكان ذلك بمثابة حل مقترح ممكن تم طرحه (٧١). وقد وضع لويجي موريتي خطة واضحة تلبي تلك الشروط الصارمة. وقد استند المشروع إلى فكرة إقامة نموذج مستطيل مع تحديد واضح للشوارع والميادين. وقد ركز موريتي في مشروعه على أداء فعال للوحدات من حيث طبيعة المناخ بتلك المناطق. وقد اقترح إقامة عوازل مزدوجة وأسطح منحنى منفصلة عن المباني، وذلك بهدف تسهيل التهوية الطبيعية. وقد تم استخدام العناصر ذاتها لإضافة نوع من التميز المعماري على تلك الصناديق السكنية الجامدة وللأسوار، وذلك بما يسمح بتحديد واضح للمناطق العامة والمناطق الخاصة. ومع ذلك فإن هذا المشروع كذلك لم يتم تنفيذه.

و كان الإستثناء من ذلك هو مشروع الرقة لذوي الدخل المنخفض. وقد تم بناء المشروع في الفترة من ١٩٧١ إلى ١٩٧٣ في إطار مشروع الإسكان الريفي الذي خطط له البلدية في العام ١٩٦٦. وضحت عملية التطوير الكبرى في بناء ٣٣٠٠ وحدة سكنية شبه منفصلة، كل منها من طابقين، مع قدر كبير من استخدام العناصر الخرسانية سابقة التجهيز. وقد تولى المهندس المعماري الأردني جعفر طوقان تصميم المشروع بالتعاون مع المكتب الهندسي الكويتي في العام ١٩٧٦، على أن تكون نسبة ٤٠% من المساحة

مفتوحة للتنمية الزراعية وبذلك يكون المشروع مشابهاً للمشاريع آنفة الذكر. ومشابهاً لمشروع الوفرة الجديدة الذي قدمته دار الهندسة، وهو المشروع الذي تم بناؤه في المنطقة المحايدة السابقة أي عند حدود الكويت الجنوبية في العام ١٩٨٢ (٧٢).

مجمعات الحساوي السكنية
حولي والسالمية، ١٩٦٨ - ١٩٧٣

المصمم • استشارات العراق مع PACE
العميل • مبارك عبد العزيز الحساوي
المقاول • مجهول
(مهدد بالهدم)

كان هذا اكبر مبنى وهو أول مشاريع البناء التي نفذها رفعت شاديرجي بالكويت، بعد انتهائهم من بناء منزل الحمد ١٩٦٧، وكان ذلك ثمرة تعاون استمر عامين بين مكتبه وبين استشارات العراق وشركة التصميم المحلية الناشئة التي تعرف باسم الاستشارات الهندسية العربية PACE.

ويشتمل هذا المجمع المتعدد الاستخدام على مركز تجاري يطل على شارع بيروت، فضلاً عن تسعة مباني سكنية يصل ارتفاع كل منها إلى ستة طوابق. والمبنى يعكس تأثيرات عناصر جمالية ومادية في العمارة الإقليمية الحديثة.

ويظهر التعبير عن العناصر المعمارية من خلال المواد الخام المستخدمة كالواجهة المشيدة من الطوب. إلى جانب استخدام آخر صحيح في مجال تكنولوجيا البناء، وهو ما يعمل على إنتاج صورة بصرية قوية تتألف من أروقة حرة وفتحات صغيرة تم تنظيمها على نحو بالغ الدقة. وفي هذا المجمع نجد بصمات مسجد الجمعة (إيران) والمسجد الأقصى (القدس) وذلك من خلال الطبيعة المادية للمبنى، وكذلك من خلال المغزى العاطفي بما يعكس فكرة وجود المساحات شبه الخاصة والوحدات السكنية (٦). ويلعب الانسياب بين الوحدات السكنية والأروقة التجارية دوراً هاماً في تعزيز الأنشطة الاجتماعية، وفي تعزيز الأواصر الإنسانية. وقد تولى نفس المهندس تشييد مشروع آخر للعميل ذاته في منطقة السالمية. وقد انتهج نفس المبادئ التي سلكها في مشروع حولي وكانت النتيجة متشابهة للغاية، ولاسيما من حيث تصميم الواجهة. ومن الناحية العملية فإننا نجد أن محيط المبنى محاط بسور، بما يؤدي إلى خلق قاعدة تشتمل على أربع مباني سكنية، ولا تضم أي مجمعات تجارية. وبالطابق السفلي نجد ساحات انتظار السيارات عند أحد أركان المكان.

نقابة المهندسين
بنيد القار، ١٩٦٨

المصمم • غازي سلطان (فائز بالجائزة الأولى)، PACE (قيادة المستشارين)، لويجي موريتي مع المكتب العربي للاستشارات (مشاركة في المنافسة)، العراقية للاستشارات (مشاركة في المنافسة)
العميل • نقابة المهندسين الكويتية
المقاول • مجهول
(عطاء تنافسي، تم البناء ولكن مع تغييرات)

طرحت نقابة المهندسين في العام ١٩٦٨ منافسة دولية لإقامة مقرها الرئيسي الجديد المزمع إقامته في شارع الخليج، مقابل السفارة الأمريكية وفندق هيلتون القديم. وكانت رقعة الأرض الخالية تكفي لإقامة المكاتب الإدارية، فضلاً عن نادي يتسع لـ ٩٠٠ عضو ومنتزه.

وقد اقترح موريتي تصميماً يستند إلى إقامة أربعة مباني مستقلة عن بعضها البعض، فضلاً عن حديقة مورقة، على حين يضم مبنى الإدارة المكاتب، ومكتبة دائرية كبيرة. أما النادي فيضم مبنى منحني وصالة واسعة، فضلاً عن مطعم ومنطقة تجارية ترفيهية. لكن هذا المشروع لم يتم تنفيذه. وإن كان من الممكن لنا أن نتخيل شكل هذه المباني الصلبة التي تتسم باستخدام المواد التقليدية التي كانت شائعة آنذاك.

أما مشروع شاديرجي فقد كان مختلفاً تمام الاختلاف عن ذلك. لقد كان المشروع بمثابة رقعة شطرنج من الغرف بعضها داخلي وبعضها في الهواء الطلق بين النباتات والأشجار. ويوحي ارتفاع المبنى بغاية من الأقواس المبنية من الطوب والجدران المنحنية، تفضي إلى ممرات غير متوقعة بين المباني.

استقلال ذاتيا. وأحد هذه الأماكن تمثل المقر الرئيسي للبنك.
ويقع مدخل البنك عند أحد الأطراف التي لا ترتفع كثيراً عن الأرض.
ويعد المدخل هو العنصر الوحيد الذي يعترض نظام الواجهة الذي
يتكرر بانتظام. ويتخذ المدخل المغطى بطبقة من الأحجار مع
المشاريع المماثلة التي وضعها المصمم ذاته (٢٢). وتتحد أجزاء
هذا المبنى الطويل كلها عند الطابق الأول وذلك من خلال تصميم
خرساني مسبق التجهيز ومطلي باللون الأبيض، مع أشكال عربية
في التصميم تتماشى مع المباني الأخرى الموجودة في منطقة
الأعمال المركزية، ولاسيما في المناطق ١ و ٢ و ٣، وذلك بما يركز
على الهوية البصرية المميزة للمبنى.

ويلعب التصميم السداسي الأبعاد مع الشرائط المعدنية المحيطة
به دوراً هاماً في حجب لظى الشمس عن الواجهة الخرسانية
الممتدة. أما الطابق الأرضي فيرتفع عن الشارع بشكل يتجه إلى
الداخل بهدف إقامة صف من الأعمدة، يسمح بوقاية عملاء البنك
من الشمس.

مبنى مكتب شركة البترول الوطنية الكويتية
منطقة الأعمال المركزية، المنطقة رقم ٣
١٩٦٤–١٩٦٥

المصمم • دار الهندسة (برئاسة غسان كلينك)
العميل • شركة البترول الوطنية الكويتية
المقاول • مجهول
(تم التعديل ٢.١٣)

فازت دار الهندسة في العام عام ١٩٦٤ في منافسة دولية لتصميم
مبنيين رئيسيين في منطقة الأعمال الرئيسية، المنطقة رقم
(٣). وكان أحد المبنيين هو غرفة التجارة والصناعة(١) أما الثاني وهو
المبنى المجاور، فكان المقر الرئيسي لشركة البترول الوطنية.

تأسست شركة البترول الوطنية الكويتية في أكتوبر من العام
١٩٦٠. وبعد ذلك بعدة سنوات أنشأت مقرها الرئيسي بالمدينة.
ويتكون المبنى من مكاتب على ثلاثة طوابق. بالإضافة إلى طابق
على السطح العلوي تتم ويه الوظائف الرئيسية بما يفسح المجال
لفضاء مفتوح بالطابق الأرضي كمنطقة استقبال تشتمل على
صالة عرض وقاعة محاضرات صغيرة. وتستند الطبقة الخرسانية
على صف مزدوج من الأعمدة الخارجية، فضلاً عن النواة المركزية
التي ترتكز عليها الدعامات الخرسانية للطوابق الثلاث العليا.
والواقع أن هذا الطراز لم يكن شائعاً في الكويت في ذلك الوقت،
لكنه يسمح بالمرونة الكاملة في التوزيع الداخلي على كافة
مستويات المبنى. كما يسمح بتصميم الواجهة على نحو مستقل
عن تصميم المبنى.

وتتكون الطوابق المرتفعة المتقابلة على نحو هندسي يقي من
قيظ الشمس. وهذه العناصر الفرعية كلها تقع على مقربة من
بعضها البعض، مما يوفر نظام حماية فعالا من لظى الشمس.
وعلى حد قول المصمم، فإن ذلك يعطي المبنى "شخصية شرقية"
[٢]

غرفة التجارة والصناعة
منطقة الأعمال المركزية، المنطقة ٣
١٩٦٤–١٩٦٦

المصمم • دار الهندسة (برئاسة غسان كلينك)
العميل • غرفة التجارة والصناعة
المقاول • مجهول
(تم الهدم)

في ظل الكتيب الإرشادي الذي وضعه شحير، تم الإعلان عن
منافسة دولية فازت بها دار الهندسة، وهي شركة لبنانية ناشئة
يترأسها كمال شعير.

ويقع مبنى الغرفة المتعدد الطوابق في منطقة الأعمال المركزية
رقم ٣. حيث تجمع بين طابق أرضي مفتوح، و مساحة للمكاتب
التي ترتفع عن مستوى الطابق الأرضي. وتضم الواجهة المزخرفة
والصالة نوعاً من التصميم يدمج بين تكنولوجيا البناء الحديثة مع
جماليات الثقافة العربية وطرزها المعمارية.

ويمكن الوصول إلى الطابق الأرضي عبر ممر من الألمنيوم
مطلي بلمسات من الذهب. وهذا الجزء منفصل عن الهيكل
الخرساني الرئيسي. أما الطوابق التي تضم المكاتب فإنها محاطة
بواجهة خرسانية مخرمة مسبقة التجهيز ومزخرفة بقطع

معدنية مطلية بالذهب. و تغطي المبنى الرئيسي مناور هرمية من
الأكريليك تسمح بدخول الضوء الطبيعي إلى الداخل.

كانت هناك قاعة محاضرات تسع لـ ... شخص وكانت تقع في
الطابق السفلي (٤). لكن هذا المبنى أصبح مهجوراً بعد بناء المقر
الرئيسي الجديد عام ١٩٩٩، وذلك على الرغم من الحالة الجيدة التي
كان عليها، وعلى الرغم من موقعه المتميز عند السوق القديم.
وقد تم هدم المبنى عام ٢.١٤ وكان ذلك دافعا لأول مظاهرة عامة
ضد عملية الهدم التي كانت تمس أحد معالم التراث الوطني
المعاصر بالبلاد.

فندق الشيراتون وتوسعاته
بوابة الجهراء، ١٩٦٦–١٩٧٨

المصمم • دار الهندسة (برئاسة سامي حوري، ١٩٦٤–١٩٦٥).
TEST (تقريبا ١٩٧٣، TAC مع PACE (١٩٧٥–١٩٧٨).
العميل • أحمد الفهد، الشركة الشرقية للفنادق
المقاول • CAT للمقاولات والتجارة (١٩٦٤–١٩٦٦).
جمعية هانينج (١٩٧٦، مجموعة الهاني للمقاولات والتجارة
(١٩٧٥–١٩٧٨)
(تم تجديده عام ١٩٩٢)

أخفقت محاولة بناء هذا الفندق المملوك للدولة في أواخر
الخمسينات. ومع ذلك فإن الخطط الحضرية، مثل مشروع الواجهة
البحرية, الذي طرح في العام ١٩٦١، أظهرت أن قطعة الأرض بين دوار
الجهراء، والبحر بإمكانها استيعاب مثل هذا الفندق. وفي العام ذاته
تمكنت أحدى مجموعات الاستثمار المحلية من توقيع عقد بناء
أول فندق شيراتون خارج الولايات المتحدة. وكان المشروع بمثابة
حل جذري للمشكلة المزمنة التي كانت تعاني منها الكويت
والمتصلة بعدم وجود مكان رفيع المستوى للوفود الرسمية
ورجال الأعمال القادمين للكويت.

وقد ضم المبنى المكون من عشرة طوابق ١٤٤ حجرة و ١٢ جناحاً،
بالإضافة إلى الأماكن العامة، والمطاعم، والمحلات، (.٣) وقد تم
تخصيص ستة طوابق تقليدية كغرف للنزلاء، وهي على شكل
مستطيل مع أشكال منشارية تحيط بالجوانب الأربع للمبنى. (٣١)
وقد تم تزيين الأسطح بمشربيات معدنية تعد الملمح المعماري
المتميز في فندق شيراتون الكويت. وقد افتتح صاحب السمو
أمير البلاد المبنى في العام ١٩٦٦. لكن العمل لم يتوقف البتة وذلك
بسبب الحاجة لمساحات إضافية. وقد وصلت هذه العملية إلى
ذروتها عام ١٩٧٦ عندما قدمت شركة TAC الأمريكية مشروع
إقامة مبنى جديد تماماً يوافق تصميم المختلف لي حمام
السباحه والمطعم الذي صممة قبل عده اعوام شركة TEST.
ويتمثل مشروع الشركة الأمريكية في منشور خال من الزخارف,
تتخلله صخور مصقولة مع نوافذ محاطة بإطار برونزي , تفتح
إلى الخارج. و رغم مظهره المتحفظ, قد أدى ذلك إلى خلق خلفية
محايدة مع المبنى الرئيسي على نحو رائع.

وقد تعرض المبنى لتلف كبير أثناء الغزو العراقي ، كما تحطم
بالكامل من الداخل. وبعد التحرير تم تجديد فندق الشيراتون على
نحو كامل، مع الحفاظ قدر الإمكان على المظهر العام الخارجي.

منطقة الأعمال المركزية
المنطقة رقم ٩
مرقاب، ١٩٦١ – ١٩٧٥

المصمم • قسم التخطيط بالبلدية (برئاسة سابا جورج شحبير)
العميل • بلدية الكويت
المقاول • العديد
(تعديل وهدم بعض المباني)

كانت المنطقة ٩ هي أخر المناطق التي تم تنفيذها في ظل
إرشادات سابا جورج شحبير بعد المنطقة ٣ والمنطقتين ٢ و ا.
ولم يتم تخطيط باقي مناطق الأعمال المركزية إلا بعد مرور
عقدين من الزمان. وكما هو الحال في المناطق الأخرى فإن الخطط
الحضرية، والتشريعات القائمة قد تم الانتهاء منها في العام ١٩٦١.
وبعد أن تمت عمليات الهدم والانتهاء من الخدمات الرئيسية
وأعمال الطرق، تم عرض رقع الأراضي المختلفة بالمنطقة للبيع
في مزاد علني يومي ١٩ و ٢٠ يناير ١٩٦٣. وقد تم اللجوء إلى مبادرة
خاصة بغرض تطوير الأراضي والمناطق التجارية بالمنطقة. وقدمت
الخطة توزيعا عقلانيا للمباني ينتظم حول الميادين الرئيسية.
وكان من المزمع تقييد حركة المرور ليقتصر على ساحات الانتظار
وسيارات الأجرة. كما أنه من المزمع الحفاظ على المساجد

القائمة على ما هي عليه، أما الأماكن المغطاة، فكانت أمر لا غنى
عنه لحماية الزوار من لظى الشمس.

كان من بين من بادروا بالتطوير في المنطقة ٩ كلا من محمد
كميخ، وعبد الله جاسم شهاب ومهني عبد الرحمن مهني.
وشركه(٣٦). لكن التأثير الأكبر كان لجمعية تجار القماش،
حيث عملت على تطوير عدد كبير من المحال فيما يعرف لدى
العامة باسم سوق القماش. وبحلول عام ١٩٦٤ كانت المنطقة
هي الأحدث والأكبر من حيث التسوق، فضمت ٤٥٠ محلا للتسوق
(٣٧). وقد حددت هذه المباني على شكل ممرات متصلة ببعضها
البعض الشكل الحضري الجديد، تماماً كما كان الحال بالنسبة
للسوق القديم، مما أدى إلى خلق دافع تجاري، وكذلك إلى خلق
مستقبل واعد للمنطقة برمتها فيما يعرف الآن بالبلوكات (سوق
القماش).

ويتمثل المحور الرئيسي في الخطة في أحد معارض التسوق
المغطاة (رقم ٢) والتي تعد المحور الرئيسي في اتجاه المسجد
القائم هناك, وفضلا عن ذلك فانه يسهل الوصول إلى المباني رقم
ا و ٣ و ٤ و ٥ فهي كلها متصلة كبازار عربي ، تم تصميمه لجلب
طرق التسوق التقليدية في أول سوق حديث مغطى. وقد تم تزيير
المكان بعناصر هندسية، وترتفع المباني ثلاثة طوابق فوق مستوى
الأرض مع طابق سفلي يستخدم كمخزن يمكن الوصول إليه على
نحو مباش، وهو مضاء وبه فتحات تهوية بالسقف. وعلى الطابق
الأرضي نرى سلسلة من محلات النسيج المختلفة تواجه ممراً
مركزيا مرتفعاً. ويعد ذلك بمثابة شارع مغطى مع سقف يصل
ارتفاعه إلى ٧ أمتار ومدعم بدعامات هندسية بديعة التنسيق، وهو
ما أدى إلى خلق نوع من التبادل بين الهياكل الخرسانية والزجاج
الذي تمر منه الإضاءة الطبيعية, ويتبع طابق الميزانين المحل أما
الطابق الأعلى، فهو عادة ما يستخدم كورشة للحياكة.

والى جانب ذلك نجد عناصر أخرى تمزج بين أنماط معمارية
مختلفة، تولى تصميمها صباح أبي حنا نفس الجمعية. (رقم ١١٢).
أما أعلى هيكل بناء (رقم ١١٣) وهو برج KIC, السكني فقد صممته
دار الهندسة. أما أرقام ا ا و ٨ وهي مبان تتشابه من حيث الواجهة
فقد كانت هي أخر المباني التي تم هدمها إضافة إلى مبنى وزارة
الدفاع السابق. وفي وسط الميدان الرئيسي نجد مبنين متشابهين،
وقد تم تنفيذهما لاحقا باستخدام الواجهات الخرسانية التي تغطي
فتحاتها عناصر لتظليل الواجهة.

معهد ذوي الاحتياجات الخاصة
حولي، ١٩٦٣ – ١٩٦٩

المصمم • بارتلت، وجراي المعماريون، نوريس وشركاه
(مهندسين)
العميل • وزارة الأشغال العامة، وزارة التعليم
المقاول • انزجيزريك للهندسة والمقاولات
(تم تعديل التصميم)

تم تكليف شركة معمارية من نوتنجهام بتطوير رقعة تمتد إلى
٨ هكتار، وقد جاء ذلك بعد تعمير شرق حولي بعد عدد من مشاريع
الإسكان لذوي الدخل المحدود، وبعد أن تم إنشاء شارع القاهرة إبان
فترة الخمسينات. وكان من المزمع أن يسع المشروع لـ ٦٤ طفلا
من الجنسين، فضلا عن ٤٠ مكان للإقامة للمبيت ، وكان هناك
فصل صارم بين الجنسين. كما كانت هناك أماكن لتدريب وتأهيل
الصم والمكفوفين، والأطفال ذوي الإعاقة الذهنية.

ووفقاً للمصادر المتاحة المكتوبة، فقد كان التركيز على الفصل
بين الجنسين، فضلا عن تهيئة بيئة" مواتية للتعليم المريح"
(٦٦). ولعل ذلك كان أهم الشروط التي تلائم تحفيز الأطفال الذين
يعانون من إعاقة بدنية أو ذهنية.

وتوجد بهذا المبنى الشامل أماكن مظللة، كما أنه يستفيد من
الاستغلال الجيد للطاقة الشمسية. أما المكان الخارجي، ومناطق
الألعاب والشرفات الداخلية فهي كلها أماكن مظللة بعناية ولما
كانت هذه المناطق تقع داخل أفنية، فإنها كانت كذلك تخضع
لحماية من الرمل والغبار. وقد استخدمت الكوات المغطاة على
نحو رأسي، بشكل دقيق، وتم بناء مركزين للاستفادة من الطاقة
الشمسية. كما تمت الاستفادة من خبرة قسم الهندسة
المدنية بجامعة نوتنجهام التقنية لاختبار زاوية سقوط أشعة
الشمس وما يترتب عليها من الظلال، بما يتناسب مع الظروف
المناخية بالكويت.

سفارة وقنصلية دولة الكويت
طوكيو (اليابان)، ١٩٦٨-١٩٧٠

المصمم • كنزو – تانج + URTEC
العميل • دولة الكويت
المقاول • مجهول
(مهدد بالهدم)

تم تعيين تانج لتصميم سفارة الكويت في طوكيو، في نفس العام الذي تم فيه تكليفه بإنجاز المركز الرياضي والمطار. ويضم مبنى السفارة المكاتب الدبلوماسية ومقر إقامة السفير. ولم يحاول المشروع أن يحاكي الهوية الوطنية الكويتية، سواء من حيث الشكل أو من حيث مواد البناء، لكنه يعد تكرارا للأنماط المعمارية التي يتم استخدامها غالبا في المدن اليابانية: فهي تتمثل في وحدات رأسية لتوائم طبيعة البيئة اليابانية التي تتميز بالكثافة السكانية(١٤). ويعد المبنى نموذجاً مصغراً من مركز شيزوكا (١٩٦٧)، أو من مركز ياماناشي (١٩٦٦) من حيث أنه لم يستلهم أي طراز معماري عربي.

والسفارة، مثل هذين المركزين المشار إليهما، تتسم بوجود أسس رأسية، مع مركزي توزيع محوريين ترتكز عليهما سلسلة من الأحجام المعلقة والمبعثرة هنا وهناك. ويستفيد التصميم كله من فكرة الفضاء السلبي، من حيث أن الفراغ هو الأداة التي تنتظم حولها المباني. ويمكننا أن نرى الغموض المكاني كذلك داخل المبنى، حيث تتماهي الأماكن العامة مع الخاصة بشكل لافت.

مطار الكويت الدولي
الفروانية، ١٩٦٧ – ١٩٨١

المصمم • باسفيك العالمية للاستشارات (قيادة المستشارين)، كنزو تانج +URTEC (معماري)، KEO (هندسة)
العميل • دولة الكويت
المقاول • مجموعة بلست نيدم NV وشركة سولكو للمقاولات LLC (مقاول عام)، انريكو رومنيولي سبا، شركة الهاني للمقاولات والتجارة، هجنز و كاسل، برونورك هيت نرسمار، ايدو الدولية المحدودة، FMC تعاونية، تعاونية سنتراي، شركة مسون للهندسة المحدودة
(تم تعديل التصميم)

في العام ١٩٦٢ وقع الاختيار على المقاول البريطاني السير فردريك سنو وشركائه لبناء المطار الجديد (٣)، ولكن تم إيقاف العمل للمشروع فيما بعد، كما تم إلغاء العقد، مما أدى إلى اللجوء للتحكيم الدولي. وقد أدت هذه الإشكالية إلى أن أسند المشروع إلى مجموعة المستشارين اليابانيين التي اقترحت اسم كنزو تانج كمهندس معماري رئيسي لبناء مبنى المطار.

وبناء على طلب العميل، اتخذ التصميم شكل طائرة. ومن وجهة نظر المعماري الياباني كذلك، فإن المبنى قد تم تصميمه ليكون معلماً بصرياً بارزاً في رقعة صحراوية جرداء بعيدة عن مركز العمران (٤). ويوحي التصميم الفخم بظلال طائرات متحركة، أما السقف الذي المكسو بالحديد الصلب، وكذا الجدران، فهي أشبه بهيكل الطائرة، مما يدفع من بداخل المطار للشعور بأنه داخل تجربة طيران حقيقية.

ويحدد الهيكل المتناغم، والمكون من مستويين متصلين ببعضهما البعض بشكل واضح، المنطقتين المختلفتين المتصلتين بمرحلتي الإقلاع والهبوط. وقد تم وضع الخطة المبدئية بما يسمح بالتوسع المستقبلي عند الأجنحة، لاستقبال عدد أكبر من المسافرين، كما يسمح بإقامة أماكن انتظار. وقد تم إجراء تطوير شامل للمطار في التسعينات، دون الالتزام بخطة التوسع الأصلية. لكن ذلك سمح بإضفاء تعديل كبير على المحور الطولي للمبنى، ما أدى بالتالي إلى تعديل المداخل الأخرى كذلك. وقد نتج عن كل ذلك وجود مواد وأشكال في المبنى تتناقض مع التصميم الأصلي.

مركز الكويت الرياضي
صباح السالم، ١٩٦٨

المصمم • كنزو تانج + URTEC مع فراي أوتو، ستوديو نبري، فيلكس كندلا مع اميلو بريد بنرو، لويد، مورغان، وجونز
العميل • وزارة التخطيط في الكويت
(عرض تنافسي، لم يتم البناء)

كانت المنافسة الدولية التي تمت في العام ١٩٦٨ لإنشاء ثلاثة ملاعب رياضية، هي من أولى النتائج التي تمخض عنها تعيين كل من مارتين، وألبيني وعزام بمجلس التخطيط. ولكل من الشركات المدعوة للمناقصة باع طويل في تصميم الملاعب الاولمبية. ويتضمن كتيب المناقصة الموجز وصفا لمجمع رياضي عملاق مع متطلبات تفصيلية محددة تتمثل في إقامة ملعب لكرة القدم لا تقل سعته عن ٤٠,٠٠٠ متفرج، وحمام سباحة أولمبي، وقاعة متعددة الأغراض، وعدد من ملاعب التدريب، مع مواقف سيارات كبيرة فضلا عن أماكن للاستقبال(١٠).

وقد تمثل المقترح الذي عرضه نبري في شكل خطة محكمة غير مرنة تضم الملعب الرئيسي في المركز، في حين تقع المباني الأخرى في المحيط المجاور للملعب. ويولي المقترح أهمية خاصة لتوزيع مواقف السيارات والمشاة، وتشتمل المناطق الداخلية على ممرات مسقوفة وأماكن انتظار واسعة. وقد استخدم نبري خبرته الواسعة في الخرسانة المسلحة في تصميم الساحة الرئيسية، وقدم بذلك نظاماً جديداً لفضاء الملاعب (نظام شركة فيكرز المحدودة) بغية إنشاء قبة شفافة يصل قطرها إلى ٣٠٠ متراً(١١). ويعتبر لويدز ومورغان وجونز من شركة المجموعة الهندسية ويلسون وموريس وكرين وأندرسون أن القبة التي شيدت في العام ١٩٦٥ عملاً رائعاً، وأن المبنى يعد أكبر ملعب محدب في العالم في ذلك الوقت. وقد بنى المصممون، على نحو يماثل المشروع الذي أقاموه في مدينة هيوستن، مشروعهم عبر من خلال طبقة منخفضة تدعم القبة المضلعة. ويتشابه المقترح الذي قدمه كاديلا مع مشروع الشركة الأمريكية من حيث المسطح الحر ومن حيث التجميع الفضفاض للمباني، وإن كان كاديلا قد فضل استخدام خرسانة على شكل صدفة مدعمة بأضلع خارجية من الحديد الصلب، وهو ما يناظر ما أقامه في قصر الرياضة الذي استضاف الألعاب الاولمبية الصيفية في مدينة المكسيك في العام ١٩٦٨. أما مشروع تانج، فقد ركز على الساحات المفتوحة المظللة جزئيا، دون أن تتأثر من التعقيدات التي تسببها أنظمة تكييف الهواء، وقد سارت خطتة على نحو متتابع. وكانت قائمة على محور رئيسي يتوزع على كافة المباني. ولم يكن كذلك العمود الفقري المحوري هو همزة الوصل فحسب، بل كان يمثل كذلك المساحة الخضراء المعشوشبة. وعندما طرح هذا المشروع انضم فراي لحل القضايا الإشكالية المتصلة بأجهزة التظليل. وفي العام ذاته كان المهندس الألماني إكسبو ٦٧ والذي استضاف الألعاب الأولمبية في ميونخ في العام ١٩٧٢. وقد افترح إقامة مشروع مماثل في الكويت. ويضم التصميم هياكل ذات غشاء مشدود على شكل ثلاثة أقواس متعاقبة. وكان هذا الأسلوب جديداً نسبياً في ذلك الوقت، وقد أعطى للمشروع برمته وزناً أخف وجاذبية معاصرة. وتكمن الميزة العملية في هذا الحل في أنه يعتمد كثيراً على أنظمة التكييف، وقد حظي لذلك باستقبال جيد من جانب لجنة التحكيم، وحصل على الجائزة الأولى. لكنه لسوء الحظ لم يتم تطبيق أي من هذه المشاريع.

أبراج المياه
عدة أماكن، ١٩٦٥-١٩٧٦

المصمم • VBB (فاتنبجنا دسبيران)
العميل • وزارة الكهرباء والمياه
المقاول • متعددين
(البناء مستخدم)

بعد أن حدثت التطورات الأولى في مجال تحلية المياه، أصبحت عملية توزيع المياه يتم من خلال إقامة عدد من الأبراج ذات الهياكل الفولاذية في مختلف أرجاء المدينة القديمة (١٤). ومع النمو الحضري الكبير في البلاد، ضعفت فعالية هذا النظام، في مواجهة عدد من التحديات منها تكنولوجيا التشييد، وضرورة سرعة الإنشاء لتلبية احتياجات الضغط المائي. وقد أصبحت أبراج المياه، إلى جانب أبراج الكويت، تشكل جانباً من جوانب إرساء نظام حديث لتوزيع المياه.

وكانت أهم معالم التصميم التي اضطلع بها مكتب VBB مع المهندس المعماري الرئيسي سون لندستروم وفريقه تتركز حول التحدي الهيكلي للارتفاع الشاهق لتلك الأبراج. وقد تولى ذلك الفريق تشييد ٣١ برجاً من أبراج المياه. وكما هو الحال في أوريبرو، فإنه تم الاعتماد على فكرة القمة المخروطية المقلوبة، وقد تم تشييدها من خلال عناصر سابقة التجميع على الأرض، ليتم بعد ذلك وضعها أعلى البرج. أما البرج ذاته فيتم بناؤه من الخرسانة المدعمة التي تصنع في الموقع ذاته.

ولازال بناء مثل هذه التصميم النموذجي مستمرا حتى اليوم، بما يدعم من دوره في رسم خط الأفق في صورة المدينة وفي البلاد بأسرها.

أبراج الكويت
دسمان، شارع الخليج، ١٩٦٥-١٩٧٧

المصمم • VBB AB فاتنبجنادسبيران (مصمم ومهندس، برئاسة سون لند ستروم) بنزرون وبيورن للتصميم-مالين بيورن (مشاركة)، فولر وسدوا المحدودة (الواجهة)
العميل • وزارة الكهرباء والمياه
المقاول • انرجوبرويكت للهندسة والتصميم (اتحاد المهندسين)
(تحت التجديد)

حصلت أبراج الكويت على جائزة الأغاخان الأولى في مجال العمارة في العام ١٩٨٠ (٩). وتم إدراجها على القائمة المحتملة لمواقع التراث العالمي، التي تضعها منظمة اليونسكو (١٠). وتعد خزانات المياه وأبراج المراقبة هذه أكثر ما يعبر عن التحديث بالبلاد في يومنا هذا.

وقد وقع اختيار سمو الأمير على هذا المشروع من بين عدد من المشاريع الأخرى. والمشروع عبارة عن هيكل متكامل من ثلاثة أبراج. اثنان منها على شكل كرة تم تنفيذها بمحيط دائري مع قاعدة خضراء في الأراضي التي تم استصلاحها على شاطئ البحر (III). ويتفاوت ارتفاع الأبراج، كما أنها تؤدي وظائف متباينة. ويصل أعلى هذه الأبراج إلى ١٨٥ متراً وبه مكرس لتخزين المياه، وبه بعض الأماكن العامة مثل المطعم. كما أن الشرفة العليا تسمح برؤية المدينة برمتها، بل ورؤية البحر والصحراء كذلك، حيث أن تلك الشرفة يمكنها أن تدور حول نفسها بزاوية ٣٦٠ درجة كل نصف ساعة. ويمكن للزوار أن يصلوا إلى المكان من خلال قاعدة البرج بمستوى سطح البحر، كما يمكنهم أن يصعدوا السلالم أو المنحدرات بمساعدة درابزينات أنيقة التصميم. أمام البرج الثاني فيعلوه كرة واحدة، ولا يؤدي سوى وظيفة واحدة تتمثل في تخزين المياه. و ويشبه البرج الثالث الإبرة، وهو أصغر الأبراج، كما أنه مجرد بناء معماري به نظام إضاءة يستهدف إضاءة البرجين الآخرين. وتجمل الأشكال البيضاوية ٤١,٠٠٠ قطعة من فولاذ مطلي بالمينا.

تحمل أبراج الكويت بصمات إسلامية تستوحي شكل المنارة والقباب المكسوة بالبلاطات الخزفية، لكنها تجمع مع ذلك أحدث ما توصلت إليه تكنولوجيا البناء خلال القرن العشرين (١٣).

أربعة "دراسات حضرية للمدنية القديمة"
مدينة الكويت، ١٩٧٩

المصمم • ألبسون وبيتر سمبثسون، رنما و ريلي نيتيلا، كانديليس، يوستش وودز (جورج كندلس المسئول)، BBPR
العميل • بلدية الكويت
(لم يتم البناء)

تمت دعوة أربع مجموعات من المعماريين للاضطلاع "بإعداد دراسات حضرية للمدنية القديمة"، وذلك بالتنسيق المباشر مع المهندسين المعماريين المحليين، ومع المجلس الاستشاري، وكذلك مع فريق كولين بوكانان (٣٤)وقد أصبح هذا النوع من الحوار منذ ذلك الحين الطريقة المثلى لتطوير المدنية في ظل حالة عدم التأكد المتصلة بتملك وتطوير أراضي الكويت. وكان المعماريون الذين تمت دعوتهم على دراية بحالة انعدام الكفاءة الخاصة بإجراءات التخطيط المعمارية، وذلك في ظل معدل نمو مرتفع و إن كان يتم في ظل حالة من سوء التنظيم الإداري. ولقد بدأت BBPR تحليلاً تفصيلياً لقلب المدنية القديمة آخذة في الاعتبار إعادة ترتيب المباني السكنية القائمة، فضلاً عن تحديد صور وأنماط حركة المرور بين المشاة والسيارات، وذلك انطلاقاً من السور الثاني بالمدنية إلى الواجهة البحرية. وقد تمثل مشروع الواجهة البحرية في إقامة ست جزر مع جسر للسيارات و "جسر

وفي عام ١٩٧١ أسند تصميم المشروع لغازي سلطان، بالتعاون مع PACE و KEO للقيام بالمزيد من التطوير. وقد تم إلغاء فكرة إقامة المنتزه، كما تم تقليص المشروع من الناحية الوظيفية. وكانت المحصلة النهائية مبنيين على شكل كتلتين مستطيلتين، يصل بينهما سلم صغير. أما الإطار الخرساني فكان بادياً للعيان، يبرز لون الطوب الأبيض. ويبدو السطح المائل من عناصر البناء، غير المألوفة في المنطقة، وقد أضاف ذلك نوعاً من الديناميكية على مبنى يتسم بالجمود إلى حد ما.

المدرسة المتوسطة للبنات
الرميثية، ١٩٦٧- ١٩٧٠.

المصمم • العرد روث
العميل • وزارة التربية ووزارة الأشغال العامة
المقاول • مجهول
(تم تغيير التصميم)

في العام ١٩٦٥، أوكلت منظمة اليونسكو للألفرد روث القيام بتقييم واقع المباني المدرسية في الكويت. وقد أدى المسح المبدئي إلى المزيد من التعاون مع وزارة التربية بهدف تطوير أنواع محددة من المدارس بما يتناسب مع الضرورة الملحة لتحديث المباني التعليمية. وكان أول ما تم الاتفاق عليه هو بناء مدرسة ثانوية للبنات تكون نموذجا للمدارس في ضاحية الرميثية الجديدة. وقد بنى روث فكرته من خلال التأمل في دور المدرسة في المجتمع، وموقع المدرسة كنقطة مركزية في الضاحية، إلى جانب المسجد والمركز الإداري.

صمم روث مبنى يبدو مغلقاً على نفسه، أي على شكل فناء مدرسي تدور حوله كافة الأنشطة التعليمية والترفيهية. وكان هذا الفراغ المركزي بالمدرسة بمثابة المركز الرئيسي الذي تنطلق منه باقي الأنشطة. كما كان بمثابة أداة التحكم الرئيسية في المناخ. والواقع أن المدرسة في البداية لم تكن مكيفة الهواء. ولذا فقد كان الحل الوحيد الممكن هو اللجوء إلى التهوية الطبيعية التي تبدأ من الساحة وتتجه للخارج عبر قنوات تم شقها بين المباني الخرسانية والدعامات الأفقية الرئيسية. [١٥] ولما كانت المدرسة قد صممت لتكون نموذجاً فقد تم تصميمها في البداية على غرار المباني الجاهزة. لكن التكنولوجيا اللازمة لذلك لم تكن متاحة في الكويت في ذلك الوقت، ولذا تم اللجوء إلى فكرة إقامة المبنى في الموقع ذاته ومن ثم تكسية واجهتها بالحجر الجيري. والواقع أن هذا التصميم لم يتم يطبقه في مواقع أخرى كما كانت الفكرة المبدئية. بل تم إدخال عناصر أخرى. ومنها ساحة المدرسة عندما شرع في بناء العديد من المدارس الأخرى في الأعوام التالية.

ثمان وحدات للمخابز آلية
أماكن متعددة، ابتداء من عام ١٩٦١

المصمم • مجهول
العميل • شركة مطاحن الدقيق الكويتية (KFMC)
المقاول • رينتشارد كوستين (الشرق الأوسط) المحدودة وآخرون
(المبنى مستحدم)

تم اقامة نظام متكامل لإنتاج الدقيق وتخزينه، ليتم بعد ذلك خبز وتغليف الخبز، وقد تم تنفيذ هذا النظام على مدى عدة سنوات عبر المدينة بأسرها. وفي العام ١٩٦٥ بدأت الوحدة المركزية للدقيق عملية الانتاج في ميناء الشويخ. كما تم تنفيذ ثمان وحدات لمخابز آلية مجاورة [٢] لإنتاج الخبز.

وقد تم اختيار المواد المستخدمة في تشييد تلك الوحدات بعناية فائقة نظراً للظروف المناخية التي كان يتم في ظلها الانتاج والتخزين. وكان على المجمع أن يتواءم مع الوظائف العملية المتصلة بآلية الطحن الحديثة للقمح. والمتصلة كذلك بعملية التعبئة والتخزين. كما كان على المشروع كذلك أن يتواءم مع المعدات الحديثة الخاصة بشحن الإنتاج عبر عربات النقل لتتم عملية التسليم.

وكانت النقطة المرجعية الرئيسية بالمشروع هي صومعة التخزين التي يصل ارتفاعها إلى ثمانية أمتار. وكان للصومعة شكل مميز وسط المباني السكنية المجاورة. و تهيمن الصومعة المغطاة بالطوب على صالة كبيرة للتعبئة قبل الإنتقال لمنطقة التحميل. وهناك منفذ تجزئة صغير لخدمة أغراض توزيع الخبز محليا. وقد أقيمت الصالة على شكل إطار خرساني جاهز يضم فواصل مبطنة بالطوب المصقول. وهو ما يعكس نمط البناء الذي أصبح شائعا في الكويت إبان تلك السنوات.

مبنى سكن الطالبات - كلية التربية
كيفان، ١٩٧٩-١٩٨١.

المصمم • إرزجو بروجكت للهندسة والمقاولات، قسم العمارة والانشاءت
العميل • جامعة الكويت.
المقاول • إرجو بروجكت للهندسة والمقاولات
(المبنى مستخدم)

يتألف هذا المجمع على نحو رئيسي من مبنى سكني مع برج مركزي يضم ثلاث ممرات، ويتكون من ستة طوابق، بعدد إجمالي مقداره ٣٠٠ غرفة، وذلك فضلا عن طابق أرضي مع أماكن خدمة مشتركة. ويتألف "البرج" من واجهات خرسانية في الأعلى مع طبقات خرسانية رأسية مغطاة بستائر زجاجية. وتعد تلك هي العناصر المعمارية الرئيسية بالمبنى. ولذا فإن المبنى يتألف من ثلاثة كتل رئيسية منفصلة عن بعضها البعض: صالة رياضية، المطبخ الرئيسي وصوبة زجاجية للنباتات.

وعلى الرغم من أننا لم نتمكن من تحديد تاريخ إنشاء وتشييد هذا المبنى على وجه الدقة. إلا أنه من المعروف أن هذا المشروع قد تم تطويره بالتزامن مع برج وزارة الاتصالات. وإن كان الدكتور بيتر بيروفيتش، وهو مهندس معماري يعمل بإنرجو بروجكت يشير إلى أن المشروع تم بناؤه في الفترة من ١٩٦٧ إلى ١٩٦٨. كما أن المشروع اعتمد أساساً على الحوائط الخرسانية المدعمة وفق نظام IMS، كما اعتمد على فكرة الواجهات المدعمة بالألواح كذلك [٣٨]. ولعل ذلك هو ما يحدد الشكل النهائي للمبنى على نحو يبرز بوضوح تقسيمات الواجهة. والواقع أن الواجهة مجزأة إلى وحدات منتظمة، وتشتمل على وحدات تظليل، مع نافذة واحدة محاطة بإطار من الألمنيوم.

بنك الكويت المركزي
منطقة الأعمال المركزية، المنطقة ٢، ١٩٦٦-١٩٧٦

المصمم • آرني ياكوبسن، ديسنج ووتيلنج.
العميل • وزارة الأشغال العامة
المقاول • شركة الهاني للتجارة والمقاولات
(تم تعديل التصميم)

تم تكليف آرني ياكوبسون بتصميم بنك الكويت المركزي، وذلك بعد أن فاز بمسابقة تصميم بنك الدنمارك المركزي في العام ١٩٦١. وقد كان هذه المشروع من أواخر المشاريع التي صممها ياكوبسون كما أن تشييد بنك الكويت المركزي تم بعد وفاته (١٩٧٣- ١٩٧٦)، حيث تولى الإشراف على التنفيذ كل من هانز ديسنج و أوتو ويتلنج.

ويقع بنك الكويت المركزي في المنطقة ٢ من منطقة الأعمال المركزية، ويتألف المبنى من كتلتين رئيسيتين وإن كانتا متداخلتين مع بعضهما البعض. ويلعب المبنى المنخفض الارتفاع دور المنصة التي يستند إليها المبنى الأكثر ارتفاعا، وقد تم تشييدها من طوب رمادي. وتحدد تلك المنصة محيط البناء، فيما يعتقد أن في ذلك إشارة إلى سور المدينة القديمة. أما المبنى الثاني فهو مربع الشكل، ناتئ عن المنصة، ويصل ارتفاعه إلى خمسة طوابق.

ويعمل الغطاء الألمنيوم للفتحات في الواجهة الزجاجية على تظليلها، بما يحمي المبنى من لظى الشمس. أما في الداخل فان المكاتب تتوزع حول فناء رئيسي. وكما هو الحال في بنك الدنمارك، فإن المحور الرئيسي بالمكان يتمثل في سلم مسلط عليه ضوء اصطناعي. والواقع أنه لم يبق سوى بضعة عناصر قليلة من التصميم الأصلي الذي وضعه آرني ياكوبسون، وتحدد تلك العناصر من خلال المدخل الرئيسي والقبة الذهبية. وبعد ٩ سنوات فحسب من انتهاء البناء، تم تغيير التصميم وذلك للوصول إلى تصميم يقترب من الهدف الأصلي، وهو تشييد مبنى أقرب لطراز العمارة الإسلامية.

البنك الأهلي
المباركية، المركز التجاري منطقة ٥، ١٩٦٨- ١٩٧٤.

المصمم • نورفيلي للإستشارات مع PACE
العميل • البنك الأهلي - الكويت
المقاول • شركة الاحمدية للمقاولات والتجارة
(تم هدم المبنى)

كان مكتب جانبواري نورفيلي الدولي للاستشارات TConsult، وهو من رواد بناء المشاريع السكنية مستقبلة التجهيز. من أوائل من تعاونوا مع PACE(١٩). وقد تم تطوير المشروع في لحظة فارقة مر بها تطوير قلب المدينة القديمة. وقد أدت هذه المبادرة إلى إطلاق عدد من مشاريع التطوير المستقبلية لمنطقة تحولت فيما بعد إلى المركز المالي للمدينة بعد عدة سنوات.

وكانت النية تتمثل في إقامة أعلى مبنى في المدينة، وهو مبنى يتألف من ١٠ طوابق [٢٠]. وكان يمكن أن يكون للمبنى تأثير أكبر. لكن وتيرة البناء كانت بطيئة للغاية بالنسبة للمباني المناظرة والتي تم بناؤها خلال السنوات ذاتها. و تبلغ مساحة المبنى ١.٨٠٠ متر مربع، ويضم طابقين أرضيين للانتظار. وتتشابه خطة المبنى العامة مع غيرها من الخطط المشابهة من حيث الطوابق الأرضية المفتوحة التي تضم المكاتب، مع واجهة ممتدة في الطوابق العليا. على حين يقع الفرع الرئيسي للمبنى في الطابق الأرضي ذاته، وكذلك في طابق الميزانين، الذي يليه والطابق الأول.

أما العنصر الأدنى من البناء فانه ينفصل عن الشارع من خلال منصة مرتفعة من الرخام الأسود. تحدد الرقعة الهندسية للمكان، فضلا عن حدوده. أما البرج، والسلم المتصل به، فقد كان مغطى بواجهة مفتوحة مزودة بشرائح من الالومنيوم.

بنك الكويت التجاري، المكتب الرئيسي
المباركية، المركز التجاري منطقة ٥، ١٩٦٨- ١٩٧١.

المصمم • مجموعة التصميم الإنشائية (انطوني ارفن و دوردن براون)، KEO
العميل • بنك الكويت التجاري
المقاول • مجهول
(تم تغيير التصميم)

عندما تم تكليف فريق توني إرفنح بتنفيذ هذا المشروع. كان الفريق يعد مرجعاً في مجال تصميم المقار الرئيسية للبنوك، حيث قام الفريق بتصميم المقار الرئيسية لبنك الكويت الوطني ولبنك الخليج. وقد كان المهندس الرئيسي في هذين المشروعين هو بريان براوتون الذي انضم لغازي سلطان عام ١٩٦٥ لتأسيس قسم الهندسة المعمارية بشركة نفط الكويت KEO.

وقد سار بنك الكويت التجاري على ذات المنوال الذي سار عليه تصميم البنك الأهلي من حيث تجاوز الارتفاع الذي كان مسموحاً به من قبل وفقاً لإرشادات المنطقة ٥ لمنطقة الأعمال المركزية. وقد وصل ارتفاع مقر البنك التجاري إلى عشرة طوابق. وأصبح بالتالي من المعالم الرأسية البارزة في المنطقة.

ويشترك البنك التجاري مع البنك الأهلي من حيث التصميم ومن حيث تخصيص طابقين للفرع الرئيسي. وهناك في الطابق السفلي مكان مخصص كخزائن آمنة للمودعين. كما أن المكاتب الموجودة بالطوابق محاطة بواجهة زجاجية مظللة بشبكة من الالومنيوم [٢٩]. أما الطبقة الثالثة للواجهة فتعبر عن طراز معماري يستلهم عددا متباينا من الإشكال والمواد ويعد لذلك تفسيراً معاصراً لفكرة المشربيه التقليدية. وقد أدى ذلك إلى بعض التعقيد في عملية الصيانة وهو ما أدى في نهاية المطاف إلى استبدال تلك الملامح الخارجية فحلت محلها طبقة من الحجر. وذلك ما حدث كذلك بالنسبة للبنك التجاري الذي تم تغطية طبقة من الجرانيت الرمادي مع زجاج عاكس وهو ما أثر على ما كان يتميز به من تكامل جمالي في بادئ الأمر. كما أن ذلك جعل من العسير تمييز المبنى بسهولة.

التي تعد العنصر الرئيسي في تصميم الواجهة، إلى جانب العريشة الخارجية الارضية التي تحملها أعمدة متعددة الأوجه، تشابه تلك في مكاتب شركة البترول الوطنية الكويتية KNPC.

وقد تم التشييد في المنطقة الحضرية رقم ٥ من منطقة الأعمال المركزية، وهي المنطقة التي تعج بمقار البنوك الأخرى، وقد تم تشييد المقر الجديد لبنك الخليج بعد عدة سنوات من الانتهاء من إقامة مقره القديم في المنطقة رقم ١.

ويعد المبنى من بين المباني التي يسهل تمييزها في المدينة وذلك من خلال العناصر الخرسانية الحرة بالواجهة التي تظلل واجهة من ستار زجاجي بالداخل. ويتشابه ذلك مع أسلوب الاكروبود (طبقة واحدة من مادة اصطناعية مدعمة) الذي يستخدم في الإنشاءات البحرية. وتتحكم هذه العناصر من الخرسانة مسبقة التجهيز في قيظ الشمس، كما تضفي على الواجهة نوعاً من وحدة الشكل. وتنتهج الخطة تصميماً هندسياً مستطيلاً، وهو تصميم منتظم يتمحور حور صالة مركزية مفتوحة يصل إرتفاعها إلى ثلاثة طوابق. ويضم المبنى تسعة طوابق فوق الأرض وطابقين سفليين.

ويمثل هذا النمط من التصميم الراقي لجان روبير دلب، نوعاً من التناقض مع الأسلوب الوحشي، الذي انتهجته شركة TAC في بناء سوق المناخ المجاور، الذي تم بناؤه بعد ذلك بأربعة أعوام.

المقر الرئيسي لبنك الائتمان والادخار
القبلة، ١٩٧٠-١٩٧٧

المصمم • ريمي لوبيز وشركاءه (معماري).
PACE (مصممين المرحلة الثانية)
العميل • بنك الائتمان والإدخار
المقاول • شركة الكوساف
(تم تعديل التصميم)

جاء اختيار تصميم هذا المبنى في منافسة تمت في العام ١٩٧٠. وإلى جانب فرع البنك بالأحمدي، فانه تم الانتهاء من تشييد المقر الرئيسي للبنك خلف مجمع البلدية في العام ١٩٧٥. وقد طلب من شركة PACE إجراء بعد التعديلات على التصميم، وهو ما أدى في نهاية المطاف إلى إدخال تعديلات هيكلية على الواجهة.

كان مكان إجراء المعاملات المصرفية يقع في الطابقين الأرضي والميزانين، وفوق ذلك نجد خمسة طوابق لمكاتب، تنتهج ذات التخطيط التقليدي مع زيادة عرض المكان في المنتصف. وقد أصبح هذا التصميم غير المنتظم هو الملمح المهيمن على الواجهة الأصلية للمبنى، وإن كان لا يوجد سجل بصري يدل على ذلك. وهناك نوافذ كبيرة ذات إطار من الالومنيوم بالمبنى مع طبقة خفيفة من الرخام بالأعلى وجرانيت أحمر اللون عند القاعدة. وبعد عامين من بدء المشروع تم تكسية المبنى بطبقة جديدة. وقد أدى إعادة تصميم الواجهة إلى إضفاء لمسة مستقبلية على المبنى، حيث استخدمت ألوان هادئة، و مواد كالبرونز والالمنيوم, وصممت النوافذ بشكل أفقي, فضلا عن عناصر تظليل عاكسة.

شارع سالم المبارك
السالمية، ١٩٧٠-١٩٨٢

المصمم • متعدد
العميل • متعدد

يعد شارع سالم المبارك تعبيرا جليا عن المشاكل المتعددة التي تنشأ نتيجة عدم وجود ضوابط واضحة تحكم تطوير منطقة السالمية. وفي العام ١٩٧٧, في إطار خطة السالمية المحلية تحددت المشاكل الجوهرية الرئيسية في صورة نقص في استخدام الاراضي ، مع زيادة في السكان ، وهو ما أدى في نهاية المطاف إلى تطوير عدد من الإنشاءات العملاقة كساحة السالمية Salmiya Concourse وعدد آخر من المجمعات المتعددة الاستخدامات (٤٦).

وكان العمود الفقري للمنطقة الممتدة من سوق السالمية (٤٧) حتى مسجد الشيخة بدرية (٤٨) قد أصبح بمثابة القلب التجاري للكويت. وهنا تم انشاء مجمعات كمعرض عيسى الصالح التجاري (٤٩) فضلا عن عدد آخر من مجمعات تضم مراكز تسوق، و مجمعات متعددة الاستخدام, وإن كانت أغلب المباني التي تم بناؤها في هذه المنطقة تتسم بأنها طولية الشكل, وغير مميزة من الناحية المعمارية ، وهي مباني تم تشييدها لتلبية الحاجة للتسوق ، مع السماح للمشاة في الوقت ذاته بالوصول

إلى تلك المجمعات سواء من خلال مستويات خارجية أو داخلية. وهناك مجمعات مثل مجمع زهرة (٥٠) والعنجري (٥١) ومريم (٥٢) والسلام (٥٣) وهي كلها مجمعات تم تطويرها في العام ١٩٧٧. وكلها مراكز تسوق تواجه شارع سالم المبارك، كما أنها تضم شققاً سكنية فضلا عن مشاريع أخرى تم تطويرها بمحاذاة بعض الشوارع الجانبية، وشارع الخليج ذاته.

وتظهر هذه المشاريع نوعا من الرفض للمفهوم التقليدي للسوق، بما يركز على تلبية احتياجات مجتمع معاصر يتسم بأنه أكثر رفاهية من حيث نمط الحياة، كما أن هذه المشاريع تميل لأن تكون ترفيهية بما تضمه من أماكن للتسلية فضلا عن البوتيكات الحديثة.

وقد أدى هذا الضغط على المشاريع الاسكانية في المنطقة في نهاية المطاف إلى إقامة مستوصف السالمية (٥٤) الذي يقع في منتصف الشارع الرئيسي بالمنطقة.

عينة رقم ٣
مبان كمشهد للمدينة: ١٩٦١-١٩٧٠.

المقر الرئيسي لشركة الشحن الكويتية
الشويخ، ١٩٦٩ – ١٩٧٣

المصمم • PACE
شارك في العطاء التنافسي KEO
العميل • شركة الشحن الكويتية
المقاول • مجهول
(مهدد بالهدم)

مع الانتهاء من تشييد مجمعات مبارك الحساوي السكنية، وهي المشروعات التي تم فيها استخدام الأطر الخرسانية والطوب العراقي، ربحت الشركة العربية المنافسة على إقامة مكاتب شركة الشحن الكويتية. ولم تكن مجموعة المستشارين العراقية (٦١) حاضرة في السنوات الأولى من عمر المشروع، لكن بصمتها من حيث الشرفات المظللة ومنهجها التعبيري كان حاضرا في المكان.

وهناك سلم في الطرف الغربي من المبنى، ينحني في مواجهة مسطح السور الحجري مما يكشف عن الواجهات الرئيسية على شكل أكورديون من الأطر الخرسانية المقوسة. ويتسم المبنى المكون من أربعة طوابق بنظام من الحواجز الحرة بين أقسامه، يعطي قدراً كبيراً من المرونة بالنسبة للمكاتب. وكان كتيب المنافسة قد ذكر أن يتم ذلك من خلال إقامة سقف حر, أما الطابق السفلي فيعترضه هيكل السلم، على حين تعمل الحافة المدعمة للمبنى على إقامة ما يشبه فضاء يمتد من أسفل إلى أعلى.
أما المدخل الرئيسي فيظل بمثابة تذكار لأيام المجد الخوالي , وتعلوه مظلة. وقد تم بناؤه باستخدام البورسلين المحلى بلون بني داكن وذلك على الرغم من أن هذا المدخل لا يستخدم اليوم ومن المتوقع أن يتم هدمه قريباً.

فندق هيلتون
بنيد القار، شارع الخليج، ١٩٦٩ – ١٩٧٤

المصمم • ج. ريتشي معماريون، PACE
العميل • شركة الفنادق الكويتية، هيلتون
المقاول • مجهول
(تم هدم جزء من الفندق وجزء اخر بعمل)

كان فندق الهيلتون يتألف – قبل أعمال الهدم الأخيرة – من المبنى القديم الرئيسي مع برج أصبح الآن هو فندق سفير.

ويرتبط تاريخ المبنى القديم بملحمة بناء الفنادق في الكويت والتي بدأت مع بواكير الستينات، وكذلك مع الجهد الذي بذله شحيبر لبعيد بناء الفندق الذي تمتلكه الحكومة خارج نطاق الحزام الأخضر. لكن هذا المشروع المشار إليه لم يتسن له البتة أن يشيد. وهو مشروع كان قد صممه راجلام سكواير، وهو ذات المصمم الذي تولى تصميم سلسلة فنادق هيلتون في عدد من الأماكن كالبحرين وقبرص وطهران وجاكارتا. ولا يوجد أي مصدر ينسب

هلتون الكويت إلى سكواير، وإن كانت بصماته تبدو واضحة في المكان.

ويتألف المشروع من مبنى أفقي مستطيل، يستند إلى منصة كبيرة ويضم المبنى غرفا فندقية تتوزع على سبعة طوابق. أما الاستقبال، وصالة الحفلات، والمطعم، وحمام السباحة ومرآب السيارات، فهي كلها في الطابق الأرضي. وقد تمت إحاطة الواجهة الرئيسية والجوانب القصيرة نسبيا، بشبكة معدنية كالمشربية، تشتمل على فتحات سداسية الأبعاد، نائثة بعض الشيء للحماية من لظى الشمس.

وقد تم توسعة المجمع في العام ١٩٧٤ ليشمل برجا بارتفاع ٢٠ طابقا، مما أدى إلى رفع الطاقة الاستيعابية للفندق لتصل إلى ما يزيد عن ٤٠٠ غرفة وقد صمم PACE هذا البرج الذي ظل على حاله بعد أعمال الهدم التي طالت الفندق في منتصف العام ٢٠٠٠. ويتألف البرج من مبنى خرساني لونه بيج، به فتحات عميقة غير نائثة. وقد تم شق تلك الفتحات على نحو مائل، ليس لتوفير الحماية من الشمس فحسب، وإنما لإتاحة رؤية أفضل للبحر كذلك، وقد كان هذا البرج متصلا في الأصل بالمبنى القديم للفندق عند مستوى الطابق الأرضي من خلال المنصة.

قصر الشيخ ناصر
رأس السالمية، ١٩٦٩ – ١٩٧٢

المصمم • مجهول
العميل • الشيخ ناصر الصباح
المقاول • مجهول
(البناء مستخدم)

تم بالتزامن مع إنشاء مجمع لؤلؤة المرزوق تشييد هذا القصر ليكون من أوائل القصور التي تم بناؤها على شاطئ السالمية، وهي المنطقة المعروفة باسم رأس السالمية.

القصر مستطيل الشكل، ويتألف من ثلاثة طوابق أعلاها لا يبدو بارزا بنفس مستوى الطابقين الاخرين. وتظهر أهم العناصر المعمارية للقصر في الواجهة، ولا سيما في تلك الفتحات المحاطة بشبكات معدنية سابقة التجهيز، تبدو بأشكال مختلفة. ويواجه البحر من الناحية الشمالية صف من الأعمدة، يضم مجموعة من النوافذ الزجاجية. كما أن هناك حديقة بمحاذاة الخليج المجاور، حيث تبدو في الأفق المباني الأخرى البارزة بالمدينة.

في الجانب المقابل, توجد مشربية ترتفع عن الأرض، وقد تم بناؤها من وحدات خرسانية مسبقة التجهيز، وتلعب هذه المشربية دورا هاما في الحماية من لظى الشمس، كما أنها تحيط بفناء داخلي.

يمكننا الوصول إلى الطابق الأرضي من الناحيتين الشرقية والغربية، الذي يرتفع قليلا إلى أعلى، من خلال منحدرات متناظرة، مغطاة بمظلة بسيطة التصميم تسمح للزوار بالترجل من سياراتهم بسلاسة.

مسجد الشيخة فاطمة محمد علي
عبد الله السالم، ١٩٧٢-١٩٧٦

المصمم • مدحت العيد، PACE . اوفا اروب وشركاءه
العميل • الشيخة لطيفة فهد السالم الصباح
المقاول • مجهول
(البناء مستخدم)

تم تشييد مسجد الشيخة فاطمة في أحد أرقى الضواحي بالمدينة، وهي ضاحية عبد الله السالم. وكان المسجد مقرا للاحتفالات الكبيرة التي تشهدها البلاد قبل تشييد المسجد الكبير.

ويسع المسجد ١.....، مصلي، وقد تم تصميم المحور المحيط به على شكل محور أفقي يواجه مدينة مكة. وهناك مكان مغطى يمكن من خلاله الوصول للمسجد من خلال المدخل الرئيسي، بما يسمح بالوصول إلى الصحن ومكان الصلاة. وتحت القبة التي تطل على ساحة الصلاة نجد غرفة مستديرة هي مقر للمكتبة التي تضم مختلف أنواع الكتب الدينية. فضلا عن سكن الإمام وطابق الميزانين، الذي يضم مكان الصلاة المخصص للنساء.

ويلعب داخل القبة دور المنور الخاص بها، دورا هاما في زيادة الإحساس بعمق المكان، فضلا عن زيادة الإحساس بالسمو

عرض للمشاة'. وقد استلهم كل ذلك تلك الرسومات المبدئية التي وضعها جون أر هاريس عام ١٩٦١ في المنافسة التي أقيمت لهذا الغرض. وقد اقترحت مجموعة كانديليس إحياء تلك الفكرة من خلال إقامة وحدات 'مستوطنات بشرية' وقد تمثل الحل في إقامة شبكة مثالية بطول ٨ أمتار وعرض ٦ أمتار. وهذه الشبكة تهدف لتنظيم العلاقة بين العناصر القائمة بالفعل والوحدات المزمع إنشاؤها. وقد كان إنشاء هذه الشبكة له ما يبرره من حيث أنها تتمتع بالتوفير الاقتصادي والمرونة من حيث تسهيل تخطيط الوحدات الكبيرة الحجم. وفضلاً عن الشبكة المقترحة، والتي تتحدد معالمها من خلال المساجد القائمة بالفعل، فقد اقترح سميثسونز إنشاء مدينة منخفضة الارتفاع (٣٥) عند البحر وقد تم اقتراح إقامة نظام معقد من الأسطح المظللة والمباني المحمية. وذلك بغرض إعادة بناء 'بيئة المدينة القديمة'. وفي هذا التصميم يأخذ الميدان والحزام الأخضر دوراً محورياً في حل مشكلة التكدس المروري. وقد اقترحت ريما بيتيلا مشروعين عمليقين يتمثل أولهما في إقامة نظام مروري يأخذ في الاعتبار توسع المدينة، أما الثاني فيتمثل في إقامة نسيج عضوي جديد للمدينة.

أربعة مناطق نموذجية
مدينة الكويت، ١٩٦٩ – ١٩٧٢

المصمم • السون وينتر سمبتسون، ريما ورللي بيتيلا
جورج كانديليس – معماري (كانديليس، يوستش، وودس)، BBPR
العميل • بلدية الكويت
(لم يتم البناء)

استهدفت 'المناطق النموذجية' التي تمخضت عن الدراسات التي أجريت في العام ١٩٦٩ إقامة 'شكل حضري في المدينة القديمة' وذلك بغرض 'إحياء مبادئ العمارة من خلال إقامة مباني فعلية وفقاً لحجم الطلب المتوفر'. (٣٦)

وكانت الدراسات الأولية في الخطة الرئيسة الثانية هي إطار العمل الأساسي، فيما يتصل بالدراسات السابقة التي وضعتها مجموعة مختلفة من المعماريين. وقد اقترح ألسون وينتر سمبتسون مشروع ضخم لمكاتب حكومية في المرقاب مع تنظيم ذلك البرنامج مع حركة المرور الخاصة به في الوقت ذاته. أما شركة BBPR التي تولت دراسة حجم حركة المشاة في المدينة القديمة بالتفصيل، فقد اقترحت خطة لتقسيم المنطقة برمتها إلى مناطق محددة، مع الأخذ في الاعتبار الحفاظ على المباني القائمة. أما فريق كانديليس وجوستش وووود والذي تم اختياره للاضطلاع بتطوير الأماكن غير المأهولة، فقد اقترح إقامة ثلاثة أنماط سكنية متباينة بحيث يتم دمجها في شكل كتل عمرانية عملاقة في النهاية، وتضم هذه الكتل شققاً سكنية، ومنازل صغيرة الحجم، ووحدات مخصصة للخدم، وفي كل ذلك كان شكل المعيشة المحلي، فضلاً عن طرق الحياة اليومية من النواحي التي أوليت عناية كبيرة إلى درجة أصبحت معها تجربة المستوطنة البشرية المزمع إقامتها نوعاً من التجديد العقلي. (٣٧)

أما ريما بيتيلا فقد أعدت مقترحاً يتسم بالتفصيل الدقيق بهدف إحياء وتوسيع قصر السيف الخاص بأمير البلاد. ولا يأتي عدد كبير من الكتاب على ذكر مسابقة مجلس الأمة التي أجريت في العام ١٩٧٢ أو المنطقة النموذجية الخامسة، التي تمت وفقاً لذات الكتيب الذي تم إعداده لإقامة المناطق الأربع النموذجية وحسب اختيار المكان كما ورد بالخطة الرئيسة الثانية.

عطاء تنافسي لمبنى مجلس الأمة
القبلة، ١٩٧١–١٩٧٢

المشاركون • السير بازل سبنس، بونجتون وكولينز،
ستوديو نرفي، بالكرينسا ف. دوشي، محمد رمزي عمر،
رفعت شاديرجي وإحسان شرزاد (عراق للاستشارات)،
تحالف كويتي محلي مشترك (KEO ،NEB ،KAC ،PACE GEGI)
يورن أوتزون
العميل • وزارة الأشغال العامة
(لم يتم البناء)

عند وضع الخطة الرئيسة الثانية، وتحديداً في يناير ١٩٧١ تم طرح منافسة دولية لإقامة مبنى مجلس الأمة. وقد وضع المجلس الاستشاري كتيب المنافسة. كما أن المجلس ذاته كان هو المنوط بوضع قائمة بالمرشحين المحتملين لتصميم المشروع. على حين تولى ألبيني على نحو رئيس وضع مسودة لبرنامج البناء. كان إطار العمل بالغ التفصيل سواء بالنسبة لتخصيص الوظائف.

أو بالنسبة للالتزام بالخطة الموضوعة. وإن كان إطار العمل لم يضع سوى بعض القيود المحدودة بالنسبة للتصميم ذاته، ولذا فقد أثمرت المنافسة عدداً بالغ التباين من المشاريع. لكن كل تلك المشاريع اشتركت في شيء واحد وهو وإقامة مبنى لا يعكس تمثيلا للسلطة، وإنما يقدم مكاناً به قدر من المشاركة مع المواطنين. (٣٩)

وقد اقترح سبنس وروبجتون وكولينز إقامة هيكل عملاق سداسي الأبعاد، مع طابق أرضي فسيح. فضلاً عن مظلة خفيفة للتظليل، وهو ما يتشابه مع أحد مشاريعهم السابقة والمعروف بمركز بورو المدني في العام ١٩٦٤ (٣٩). وهذا النظام السداسي الذي يشبه قرص العسل كان بالغ المرونة من حيث توفير مقر لهيكل وظيفي معقد، فضلا عن كونه بمثابة حل متاح لأي عمليات توسيع مستقبلية. ويستند المفهوم على فكرة بناء أماكن طولية أفقية تتخللها حدائق معلقة وذلك لتخفيف حدة الطقس. (٤٠).

أما مشروع دوشي، فقد اقترح بدلا من ذلك، إقامة تصميم يوحي بالتواصل مع البحر. فقد عمد إلى تخفيض الالتفاف الدائري المتاح للمركبات على الساحل. مع التركيز على فكرة الساحة العامة التي تمتد بمساحة كبيرة إلى البحر. مع هذا التصميم البسيط، يمكننا أن نرى ما قصده المصمم من وراء بناء مجلس الأمة. لقد سعى المصمم هنا إلى إقامة مجموعة من أشكال هرمية من خلال التجميع الهندسي للواجهات ذات الأشكال المتكررة، وهو نمط لا تشذ عنه سوى القاعتين الرئيسيتين اللتان تعدان بمثابة قلب المبنى.

أما مشروع شاديرجي فقد انطلق من فكرة الانعكاس البصري للأروقة كما هو الحال في المسجد الكبير بدمشق والذي يعود للعصر الأموي. وهذا العنصر الذي يتكون من أقواس رشيقة تتوجها طبقة من الآجر، يعد النموذج الرئيسي الذي يمنح المبنى كله نوعاً من التناسق في النسب المستخدمة. وكما هو الحال في مشروع أودزون، وهو المشروع الذي فاز في المنافسة. ينتظم المبنى حول محور رئيسي يصل المدخلين الرئيسيين. وهذا المحور المركزي يتقاطع مع الساحة الرئيسية، بما يتيح التمعن في المبنى بأسره بغهم وتقدير.

ولسوء الحظ، فإننا لا نعرف شيئاً عن مشروع رمزي عمر.(مماس الوسي كان يعمل مع IQC يصرح بان المصمم المصري لم يدخل المنافسة بل كان من هيئة التحكيم بها)، كما أن بير لويجي نرفي ربما قد يكون أصيب بقدر من الإحباط بعد نتائج المنافسة التي طرحت عام ١٩٦٨ لإقامة مركز الكويت الرياضي. وقرر ألا يقدم أي مشاريع. ومن المثير هنا أن نعلم أن مجموعة من خمس شركات محلية قد دُعيت للتنافس مع المصممين الدوليين، بدلاً من قيامها بدورها المعتاد في دعم ومشاركة أحد أولئك المصممين. لكن ذلك يشي بحجم التطور الذي وصلت إليه الشركات المحلية في السبعينات، بما كان يتيح لها التعامل مع مثل هذا النوع من المشاريع الدولية. وقد حصل يورن أودزون على الجائزة الأولى في هذه المنافسة.

مجلس الأمة
القبلة، ١٩٧٢–١٩٨٢

المصمم • يورن أوتزون، ماكس فالت انجنوربيرو (اساس البناء)، كونسلتير AG (للخدمات البناء)
العميل • وزارة الأشغال العامة
المقاول • الشركة الكويتي للمباني الجاهزة
(البناء مستخدم)

تم بناء مجلس الأمة على الواجهة البحرية في الفترة من ١٩٧٢ إلى ١٩٨٥. ويعد المبنى من أبرز المعالم المعمارية بالكويت. يبدو المبنى فريدا من صورته الجانبية، تعلوه مظلة متموجة من الخرسانة منحنية الشكل, بما يوحي بعلاقة حميمة مع أشكال الطبيعة. كما يستدعي حكاية الاستيطان البشري في الصحراء والخيام، وأشرعة السفن، وهما يُشكلان عناصرين متضافرين في نسيج البلاد.

وقد تأثر المشروع إلى حد كبير بخبرة المصمم السابقة بالعمارة الإسلامية، لا سيما إبان رحلته إلى المغرب (١٩٤٩)، والى إيران حيث صمم البنك الملي (بنك الشعب) عام ١٩٥٩. وفي تلك الزيارة أتيحت له الفرصة لزيارة البازار والميدان الملكي في أصفهان، وهو ما أثر تأثيرا بالغا على تصميمه لمجلس الأمة(٤٦).

والواقع أن هناك ثلاثة عناصر تحدد شكل المشروع برمته: البازار، الخيمة، والميدان المغطي. و يلعب أول تلك العناصر دوراً محورياً, وهو عبارة عن طريق مسقوف, يوزع كافة المساحات الوظيفية بالمبنى. والى جانب هذا العمود الفقري نجد مجموعة من المساحات المربعة الشكل، تنتظم حول باحات, تشابه تلك الموجودة بوسط المدينة العربية، وان كانت أكثر منها جموداً.

أما السطح المستوحى من الخيام فيبزغ من هذا المجمع المسطح/البازار، لتغطية المكان، ولإبراز أهم مساحة بالمجمع، وهي قاعة الإجتماعات في مجلس الأمة، وينفتح ذلك على واجهة بحرية وميدان ضخم. وكان من المزمع أن يكون الميدان عبارة عن ساحة حضرية مفتوحة للجمهور، تعكس فكرة الممارسة الديمقراطية المنفتحة، ولكن البعض وجد أن ذلك غير قابل للتطبيق, في ظل البيئة السياسية المحلية (٤٧).

ويستند المشروع إلى شبكة مربعة مقاسها ٢٠.×٢. مترا، وهي سابقة التجهيز، ومصنوعة من هياكل خرسانية تحتوي على عناصر محدودة تتكرر مئات المرات. ويسمح هذا الأسلوب بإمكانية التوسع المستقبلي, متناغما مع التصميم الأصلي، لكن التوسع المجاور يومي بتصميم مختلف كلية مع التصميم الأصل مما أدى إلى خلق مبنى جديد تماما, مستقل عن المبنى الأصلي.

الأندية الرياضية الكويتية
حولي، المنصورية، كيفان، ١٩٧٠-١٩٧٧

المصمم • قسم التصميم بوزارة الأشغال العامة (رئاسه الاستشاريين)، العراق للاستشارات (اساس البناء)، TEST (مساهمي في البناء)، PACE (خدمات البناء)
العميل • وزارة الأشغال العامة
المقاول • مجهول
(تم تعديل التصميم)

بعد الانتهاء من إقامة استاد القاهرة عامة ١٩٦٣، تم تكليف محمود رياض بإقامة مجموعة من الأندية الرياضية بالكويت، بما في ذلك ملاعب تنس، وحمامات سباحة، وملاعب كرة قدم، وصالة جمانزيوم، وملاعب كرة سلة. لكن هذا المشروع لم يتم تنفيذه على الإطلاق.

وبعد أن تم إعلان الكويت منظماً لكأس آسيا في العام ١٩٨٠، أوكلت وزارة الأشغال العامة بالكويت المشروع لاستشارات العراق، وهي الشركة التي تولت تنفيذ ملعب الشعب لكرة القدم ببغداد. (٢٧)

وبعد أن أنهت الشركة العراقية تعاونها الذي استمر لمدة عامين مع شركة PACE، فإنه كان عليها أن تضطلع بالقيام بإنشاء أول وأخر مشروع رئيسي عام لها بالكويت. وقد تولى المهندس الشاب معاذ الألوسي، وكان قد اكتسب قدراً من الخبرة آنذاك، تنفيذ هذا المشروع. وكان معاذ قد حصل على درجة جامعية في الهندسة المعمارية للمناطق الاستوائية. واشتمل المشروع علي إقامة صالات رياضية مغطاة، وملعب كرة قدم مغطي مع مقاعد مريحة للجمهور، كما أن هيكله مدعم بالخرسانة، على غرار نظيرة في بغداد.

وعلي الرغم من وجود ثلاث نوادي متنافسة هما, نادي القدسية الرياضي (حولي), نادي العربي الرياضي (منصورية), نادي الكويت الرياضي (كيفان), تم انشاء نادي كاظمة الرياضي الرابع في العدلية بين ١٩٧٤-١٩٧٨ . بنفس مواصفات الاندية السابقة علي الرغم عدم مشاركة الشركة العراقية للاستشارات في التنفيذ . والغرض من بناء ليكون استديو الالمبي الوطني .

المقر الرئيسي لبنك الخليج
المباركية، منطقة الأعمال المركزية، المنطقة٥، ١٩٦٩-١٩٧٤

المصمم • جان – روبير دلب(معماري)، KEG (الخدمات البناء)
العميل • بنك الخليج
المقاول • مجهول
(البناء مستخدم)

حصل جان – روبير دلب على الجائزة الثانية لروما في العام ١٩٥٧. وقد تم تكليفه بتصميم بنك الخليج، بعد تشييده لبرج أوربا الشهير في باريس. وكما هو الحال في برج باريس، فإنه تم الاعتماد في تصميم بنك الخليج على العناصر السابقة التجهيز

سوق الكويت

المباركية، منطقة الأعمال المركزية،
المنطقة ٨، ١٩٧٣–١٩٧٦

المصمم • BBPR (أول المصممين)، SOM (معماري)،
SSH (مساهمين في الانشاء)، نلسون خوري (البناء).
اوف ارب وشركاهم (البناء)، بلدية الكويت للدراسات المدنية.
شركة BBPR) ١٩٧٣)
العميل • بلدية الكويت ١٩٧٣.
شركة العقارات الكويتية (١٩٧٤–١٩٧٦)
المقاول • مجهول
(البناء مستخدم)

في إطار مبادرة "المبنى النموذجي"، كلفت بلدية الكويت شركة
BBRP بتطوير برنامج الإستخدام المتعدد للمنطقة التجارية
رقم ٨ بمنطقة الأعمال المركزية. وفي إطار "دراسات الصورة
الحضرية للمدينة القديمة" التي تمت في العام ١٩٦٩، تم النظر في
إقامة "هياكل بناء" تعد بمثابة معالم (٧) مرجعية. وقد خصصت
دراسة الشركة المكلفة من قبل بلدية الكويت مبنى يصل إرتفاعه
٦٠م. على أن يخصص ٤٥م منها لانتظار السيارات، و٥م لأغراض
أخرى. وكان من المقترح إقامة باحات داخلية مظللة في الطوابق
العليا. وقد اقترحت الدراسة تشييد هياكل بناء ضخمة حول
المدينة يكون من السهل على الجمهور الوصول اليها، مع نقاط
مراقبة ومناطق للترفيه.

ومع ذلك فانه في السنة التالية تم تكليف شركتي SSH و SOM
أن يقوما بدور الإستشاري على أن يتم اتباع المشروع المبدئي الذي
تم وضعه من قبل، بنفس الحجم والتصميم. ويشتمل ذلك
على مركز تجاري في الطوابق الأولى، مع أماكن انتظار في الطوابق
الوسطى، ومكاتب في الأدوار العليا على أن يتم التشييد في العام
ذاته. لكن المبنى انهار اثناء التشييد وتم اللجوء الى شركة أوف
ارب لإعادة تصميم المبنى ليتسنى الإنتهاء من تنفيذه.

السوق الكبير

الصالحية، ١٩٧٣–١٩٧٦

المصمم • SOM: بارنس (معماري)، SSH (مساهم معماري)،
اوف ارب وشركاهم (البناء)
العميل • شركة عقارات الكويت
المقاول • مجهول
(البناء مستخدم)

تم إنشاء السوق الكبير في ذات الوقت الذي تم فيه إنشاء سوق
الكويت ومجمع الرحاب السكني، ولا يعرف على وجه الدقة دور
SOM في عملية التصميم. وقد تطلب المشروع من حيث
سرعته ومن حيث موقعه ضرورة وجود هيكل بسيط وفعال
للبناء، وهو ما تمخض عنه أن تشترك مباني المجمع في الشكل
ومواد البناء.

ويمكن الوصول الى هذه الرقعة الحضرية الحديثة من خلال
مدخلين فقط على الطريق الرئيسي. وقد مثل اختيار الموقع آنذاك
تحدياً بالنسبة للمناطق الأخرى على الطرق المجاورة. وذلك لان
تلك المناطق لم تتمتع بالدرجة ذاتها من التطور الحضري.

وقد تم تنظيم المشروع حول الرقعة المخصصة له في النسيج
الحضري، بحيث يكون له مدخلين رئيسين من كل جانب مما
يؤدي الى وجود مركز تسوق موزع على ثلاثة طوابق. أما سعة
المرآب الخاص بانتظار السيارات فتتوزع على طابقين أرضيين
يمكن الوصول إليهما من مبنى جانب مبنى البلدية. كما أن هناك
أربعة طوابق تعلو مركز التسوق مع مدخل ومخرج من خلال
قنطرة منحدرة. وتنعكس خطة المبنى من خلال الأرض المجاورة
للبناء، ومن خلال برجين مركزيين كانا يضمان في البداية وحدات
سكنية.

سوق الصفاة

مرقاب، منطقة الأعمال المركزية، المنطقة ٩،
١٩٧٣–١٩٧٥

المصمم • TAC (البناء ورئاسة الاستشاريين)
PACE (مساهمين في البناء)
العميل • شركة الكويت للإستثمار
المقاول • مجهول
(البناء مستخدم)

يقع مجمع سوق الصفاة في المنطقة ٩. وهي منطقة من مناطق
الأعمال المركزية التي تعج بالنشاط التجاري. وقد تم الإعلان عن
عطاء تنافسي لإقامة المجمع في ذات الوقت الذي تم فيه طرح
عطاء سوق المناخ. وكان المشروع يشتمل على إقامة منطقة
تجارية جديدة وعدد من المكاتب بارتفاع إجمالي سبعة طوابق
مع طابقين سفليين يسعان لـ...١ مكان انتظار. ويتألف المبنى من
كتلتين هما المنصة التجارية والمكاتب التي تعلوها.
وتحدد الواجهة التي تقع على مستوى الشارع شكل تدفق الزوار
من خلال صفوف من الأعمدة المقوسة التي تصل ساحة المنشأة
المجاورة مع المناطق التجارية الداخلية. وتوجه الأقواس العليا
المنشأة إلى المداخل الرئيسية وكذلك إلى فناء داخلي رحب. مزدوج
الإرتفاع. يشتمل على نوافير مياه صغيرة، وسلالم وشرفات. وقد
ضم التصميم المبدئي البسيط بازاراً يسع مبدئياً لـ ٦٠ وحدة بيع
بالتجزئة، لكن ذلك العدد تضاعف ثلاثة مرات فيما بعد.

أما الكتلة الثانية فتضم المكاتب و تصل مساحتها إلى ٣٠..٣ متر
مربع موزعة على أربعة طوابق. ويختلف شكل الواجهة بكل طابق.
فهناك تفاوت من حيث العناصر المعمارية وإن كان ذلك يتم على
نحو متناغم.

وكان هذا المجمع هو أول الأسواق المتشابهة التي أنجزتها
TAC ويشير ذلك إلى نجاح المصمم في الكويت، ولا سيما فيما
يتصل بتعزيز هذا النمط المعماري الجديد إبان النصف الثاني من
سنوات السبعينات. وقد استهدفت المباني المتعددة الأغراض
تلبية احتياجات وتطلعات النزعة الكوزموبوليتانية الجديدة التي
عمت المدينة الحديثة.

سوق المناخ

المباركية، منطقة الأعمال المركزية،
المنطقة ٥، ١٩٧٣–١٩٧٥

المصمم • TAC (البناء ورئاسة الاستشاريين).
PACE (مساهم في البناء)
العميل • شركة الإستثمار الكويتية
المقاول • مجهول
(البناء مستخدم)

أوكلت شركة الاستثمار الكويتية لشركة PACE مهمة تطوير
المنطقتين التجاريتين ٩ و ٥ ضمن منطقة الأعمال المركزية.
وكان آخر تلك الأعمال هو سوق المناخ، الذي كان بمثابة السوق
المالي غير الرسمي بالكويت، والذي توقف عن العمل في صيف
العام ١٩٨٢(٦). وقد أدى "الانهيار" إلى إعاقة شركة TAC عن تنفيذ
بعض مشاريعها، وهو ما أدى في النهاية إلى إفلاسها.

ويتوسط موقع سوق المناخ أبراج ثلاثة لبنوك هي: (بنك الخليج.
بنك الكويت الوطني، وبنك الكويت التجاري) و المكتبة الحكومية
العامة (مدرسة المباركية سابقاً). ويفضي المدخل من ناحية شارع
مبارك الكبير إلى ساحة الانتظار. أما المدخل من ناحية شارع عمان
فيفضي إلى الأدوار الوسطى من ساحة الانتظار العامة. ويشكل هذا
المدخل، فضلا عن المخرج المنحدر، مع الفناء المركزي المغطى.
نواة صلبة محاطة بمجمع تجاري يتداخل مع الطابقين الأرضيين
كذلك.

ويقع في المستوى الأخير طابق للمكاتب التقليدية. وهو ناتئ إلى
الخارج بما يفضي الى ممر خارجي محاط بأقواس من الخرسانة
الخشنة. أما اركان المبنى الأربعة الأكثر انفتاحا، فتحدها
أبراج سلم حلزوني تسمح بوجود عدد من الخيارات المتاحة
للحركة الرأسية المتباينة.

سوق الوطنية

منطقة الأعمال المركزية، المنطقة ٥،
شارع عبد الله السالم، ١٩٧٤ – ١٩٧٩

المصمم • TAC (معماري) PACE (مساهمين في البناء)
العميل • شركة الكويت للإستثمار
المقاول • مجهول
(البناء: مستخدم)

تم تخصيص مساحة ٦٧٥.. متر مربع لإقامة مجمع سوق
الوطنية. وقد تم تكليف PACE في البداية بتصميم المشروع،
بالإضافة إلى سوق الوطية. ولكن نتيجة لعمليات التطوير
المستمرة التي شهدتها المنطقتين ٥ و ٩ بمنطقة الأعمال
المركزية، فان المشروع برمته قد تم اسناده لـ TAC. وقد
انتهجت الشركة استخدام فكرة الخرسانة "المكثفة بذاتها" في
إقامة المبنى من حيث الأقواس والفتحات الصغيرة، وذلك لإعادة
إحياء وسط المدينة.

والمبنى من الخارج عن هيكل صلب مضغوط ينقسم إلى
أربعة قطاعات افقية. أما من الداخل فان المبنى يضم ثمانية
طوابق تم تقسيمه إلى مركز تسوق يقع في الطابقين الأرضي
والأول مع مساحة تسع لـ...١ سيارة في طابقين سفليين. و تضم
باقي الطوابق منازل تتوسطها أفنية. وتتألف منازل الدوبلكس
الفاخرة من غرفتين أو ثلاث غرف، وهي كلها تنفتح على ساحات
ونوافير مياه. كما أن هناك ساحة انتظار مغطاة على نفس
المستوى. وهذه "المنازل ذات الأفنية" على السطح تعكس حياة
الشارع التقليدية التي كانت سائدة في المدينة القديمة التي تم
هدمها كما تكشف عن صورة معمارية مميزة تعكس السمات
المحلية للبلاد.
وتعد منطقة التسوق هي مركز الأنشطة في يومنا هذا، وقد
تم تقسيمها إلى ١٢٦ محلا صغيراً، بما يلائم احتياجات الوافدين
محدودي الدخل. وقد تم توزيع هذه المحال على أروقة وأفنية
داخلية كانت ذات يوم مزدانة بالنباتات ونوافير المياه وفتحات
الإضاءة. وقد أدى هذه الاستخدام الوظيفي المتعدد إلى تلبية
احتياجات فئة هامة من فئات المجتمع، فضلا عن أن ذلك قد أدى
إلى توسيع مفهوم التجربة الحضرية.

سوق الوطية

الوطية، ١٩٧٤–١٩٧٩

المصمم • TAC (معماري).
PACE (مساهم في التصميم و رئاسة الاستشاريين)
العميل • شركة العقارات الوطنية
(لم يتم البناء)

تم تكليف PACE في بادئ الأمر لتصميم المشروع، ولكن ذلك
تغير لاحقا حيث تم إسناد المشروع لـ TAC بالإضافة إلى سوق
الوطنية. وعلى خلاف مشاريع الأسواق الأخرى، فإن المكتب المحلي
بالسوق هو الذي تولى التنفيذ وكافة الأعمال غير المعمارية. وقد
تقضي هذه الحقيقة إلى أن نستنتج أن التصميم الأصلي قد تم
تنفيذه بعد إدخال عدد من التعديلات. لكن الواقع أن المشروع الذي
اقترحته كلا من TAC و PACE لم يكن يتشابه مع أي من العناصر
أو الأجزاء التي تم بناؤها بالفعل.

في المشروع المقترح لم يكن للأقواس وجود على خلاف الأسواق
الأخرى، أما الخرسانة مسبقة التجهيز فتعد هي العنصر الحاكم في
تحديد كتلة المبنى وهندسته.

وقد أضحى المشروع في نهاية المطاف مشابهاً من حيث
متطلباته مع أسواق من قبيل السوق المتحدة وسوق المسيل
وهما المشروعان اللذان نفذتهما شركة العقارات المتحدة. وقد
اشتمل المشروع على ثمانية طوابق مع ساحة انتظار أرضية، فضلا
عن وحدة منفصلة تحتوي على ستة طوابق ترتفع فوق الأرض
وتسع لـ...١ سيارة. أما المنطقة التجارية فتتركز في مبنى مجاور
مكون من طابقين.

وقد تم تصميم الجزء الخارجي ليكون على شكل نجمة ثمانية الأبعاد. وقد أصبح المسجد معلماً من معالم المدينة البارزة بسبب منارته التي شيدت على شكل شمعة.

مشروع الإسكان
بنيد القار، ١٩٧١–١٩٧٥

المصمم • المعماري جورج كانديليس
العميل • شركة العقارات المتحدة. شركة الفنادق الكويتية
المقاول • شركة مساعد الصالح وأبناءه
(البناء مستخدم)

كان هذا المشروع الإسكاني هو أول مشروع تم التخطيط له لإكمال خطة بناء فندق هيلتون في بنيد القار. وهو الذي أدى في النهاية إلى هدم الفندق ذاته لصالح إقامة المزيد من الوحدات السكنية. وقد قام المهندس المعماري كانديليس بتصميم هذا المشروع لصالح مستثمر خاص. وكان قد شارك في خطة إعادة تطوير مدينة الكويت لصالح الحكومة الكويتية. ويشير المصمم في هذه الوثيقة إلى أن منطقة بنيد القار كمنطقة عمرانية جديدة. وأن كانت لا تتوافق على نحو جيد مع المناخ. كما أنها منطقة لا تتسم بالكفاءة في استخدام الأراضي المتاحة. وقد تمثل مشروعه في إقامة مجموعات سكنية متراصة ومنخفضة الارتفاع ومرتفعة التكاليف. لكن هذا المشروع لم يكتمل منه سوى الجزء المواجه للجنوب الغربي. وتتخذ هذه المباني شكلا عنقوديا. وهي عبارة عن وحدات مكررة منتظمة على شكل مكعبات غير منتظمة. ويسمح هذا التصميم بإلقاء الظلال على المباني ذاتها. ويتألف الملمح الرئيسي لهذه الوحدات من تكرار استخدام الشرفات العميقة بطول الواجهات الجنوبية. وتعزز الحواجز الزجاجية ذات اللون البرونزي للشرفات من ظلال اللون البيج. وهو لون الطابوق المستخدم. وعلى الرغم من عدم اقتناع السكان المحليين بهذا التصميم للشرفات التي تعد عديمة الجدوى في المناخ الحار. إلا أن المصمم ينظر إلى هذه الشرفات على أنها غرف خارجية. وإنما على أنها أداة للتخفيف من وطأة المناخ. أي على أنها طبقة ثانية تلقى ظلالا لحماية المسكن من الداخل من قسوة الطقس. وقد تم في الأعوام الأخيرة إدخال معظم هذه الشرفات إلى المساحة الداخلية للوحدة لزيادة مساحتها. وهو ما أدى إلى انتفاء الهدف الأصلي لهذه الشرفات.

لولوة المرزوق
رأس السالمية، ١٩٦٨ – ١٩٧١

المصمم • صباح أبي حنا
العميل • خالد المرزوق
المقاول • مجهول
(تحت التجديد)

يمثل هذا المشروع الذي يعرف باسم لؤلؤة المرزوق اتجاهاً جديداً في تطوير المجمعات السكنية في البلاد. والواقع أنه وفقا للتشريعات التي كانت سارية خلال نهاية فترة الستينيات من القرن الماضي. لم تكن المباني تتجاوز الطوابق الثلاثة في حال وقوعها خارج وسط المدينة. (٢٠) وكان العميل هو خالد المرزوق الذي نشط لاحقاً في سوق العقارات. حيث ترأس ابتداء من العام ١٩٧٢ شركة عقارات الكويت. فقد رأى المرزوق أن التشريع المشار إليه بالغ الصرامة فيما يتعلق بالجدوى الاقتصادية لهذا المشروع السكني. لكن الحل لهذه المشكلة لم يكن من خلال النزاع القانوني. بل من خلال التصميم المعماري للمبنى الذي تمثل في بناء مستويات منفصلة عن بعضها البعض. وضم عدة طوابق مما ضاعف. من الناحية الفعلية. من الارتفاع الكلي للمبنى. وقد مكن هذا الحل أيضاً من إقامة عدة أنواع من الوحدات. وفق نظام الطابقين للوحدة (دوبلكس). وقد تم ضم كافة أنواع الطوابق في ثلاثة مباني تم تنظيمها على شكل حرف لا. بطريقة يمكن من خلالها رؤية البحر من عدة زوايا. كما يساعد في عملية التهوية الشاملة. ولعل إحدى أهم النتائج التي تمخضت عن هذا المشروع هو ذلك التعاون الذي توطد بين صباح أبي حنا والمهندس الشاب سالم المرزوق. ابن عم العميل. اللذين أسسا فيما بعد شركة سالم المرزوق وصباح أبي حنا.

روضة أطفال
المنصورية، ١٩٧١–١٩٧٢

المصمم • ألفرد روث
العميل • وزارة التعليم. وزارة الأشغال العامة
(تم تعديل التصميم)

فور الانتهاء من بناء المدرسة المتوسطة في الرميثية، قام روث بتطوير نموذج لروضة أطفال. ليتم بناؤها في حي مختلف بالقرب من مركز المدينة. واستندت روضة الأطفال إلى المبادئ ذاتها. وإن تم إدخال تعديلات على الحجم. وعلى العلاقة بين المبنى والفضاءات المختلفة الخاصة به. وذلك بما يتواءم مع الاحتياجات التربوية لصغار السن من الأطفال. وقد ظلت الساحة المركزية هي الفضاء المحوري. وإن تم إضافة ساحة خضراء صغيرة لتكون مكاناً للأنشطة الفصل الخارجية. ولذا فإن المبنى يعد تجمعاً لساحات متصلة ببعضها البعض كفضاء مفتوح محاط بسياج. وكل ساحة تضم ثلاثة فصول أو وحدات لتغيير الملابس. ومكتب للمعلمات. بما يجعل منها وحدة وظيفية مستقلة بذاتها. وعلى الجانب المقابل. تم بناء ساحتين منفصلتين للتحكم في المدخل الرئيسي وفي منطقة إنزال الأطفال قبل دخولهم للروضة. وتتحكم الساحات كذلك في مبنى الإدارة. والمكتبة. وصالة الطوابير المخصصة للأنشطة الداخلية. وقد تمت تغطية كافة الممرات والفتحات بعناية من خلال أسطح حماية. ومازال المبنى مستخدما حتى يومنا هذا.

وزارة الخارجية
منطقة قصر السيف، شارع الخليج، ١٩٧٣–١٩٨٣

المصمم • رايلي و ريما بيتيلا
العميل • وزارة الأشغال العامة
(تم تعديل التصميم)

يشكل تصميم مبنى وزارة الخارجية استكمالا لمجموعة مشاريع تولى تنفيذها كلا من رايلي وريما بيتيلا في مدينة الكويت. وقد بدأ المشروع عام ١٩٧٣ في إطار خطة أوسع لتوسيع قصر السيف القديم. وقاعة استقبالات الأمير. وذلك في منطقة متاخمة. عادة ما كانت تخصص لأرصفة تحميل وتفريغ السفن. وقد شملت الأعمال الجديدة توسعة قصر السيف. بالقرب من المبنى القديم، ومجلس الوزراء. في الرقعة الشرقية من المكان، و وزارة الخارجية. وتستند فكرة المشروع إلى استلهام عبقرية الموقع. ومراعاة التعايش مع المباني القائمة بالفعل، (٤٨) ولذا فان مجموع الألوان والمواد التي تم استخدامها قد تحددت بلون القصر القديم. ومع ذلك فان التصميم يعد تحولا تدريبيا متطورا عن الموضوعات و الشكل التقليدي. بما يسمح بنوع من التعبير التجريدي التجريبي على خلاف المباني القائمة.

هكذا تحول التتابع المنتظم للأقواس المدببة في المبنى الجديد (التوسعة). إلى إيقاع مختلف. يتألف من عقود في أروقة مائلة الزوايا. في مبنى وزارة الخارجية. وتعمل هذه الهندسة على لوحة من الحجر الجيري تحدد الجدران الداخلية المغطاة ببلاطات ذات ألوان زاهية. لعلها مستوحاة في مخيلة المصمم من الألوان التي كانت تستخدم في نسيج الحواجز الفاصلة في خيام البدو الرحل (٤٩). ويتألف المبنى من وحدات متقابلة تجد تعبيرها المعماري في شكل الفتحات. وهي دائما فتحات مغطاة بسلسلة العقود من أو من خلال صفوف من الطنف على شكل حرف T. وتعمل هذه العناصر ثلاثية الأبعاد. سواء كانت ناتئة أو غير ناتئة. على خلق أنماط متباينة من الظلال المنعكسة على الجدران.

شيد المبنى مكتب ميكو فهانن، أما خدمات المبنى تم من خلال إحدى فروع شركتهم دفهكن. وقد أدخل تغيير جذري على شكل المبنى في الأعوام القليلة الماضية. فتم تغطية الفسيفساء الداخلية بطبقة من الرخام الأسود. بينما تم تغيير الواجهات الشرقية تغييرا تاما من حيث الشكل والمادة الخام المستخدمة في البناء.

برج شركة الخطوط الجوية الكويتية
القبلة، ١٩٦٩–١٩٧٢

المصمم • دار الهندسة
العميل • الخطوط الجوية الكويتية
المقاول • شركة الأحمدية للتجارة والمقاولات، شركة الهاني للتجارة والمقاولات (خدمات)
(تحت طائلة الهدم)

كان هذا المبنى ذات يوم هو المبنى الأكثر ارتفاعاً في المدينة. وهو يضم مكاتب إدارية. لكن هذا البرج تعرض لتلف كبير أثناء الغزو. خلال العام ١٩٩. فقد كان رمزاً وطنياً للمقاومة. وتم ترميمه فيما بعد. ويقع البرج في منطقة الأعمال المركزية CBD (٤) رقم ١٢. وترجع أول إشارة الى المشروع المقترح في كتاب سابا شبحير(٥). الذي تظهر به صورة فوتوغرافية ترجع إلي العام ١٩٦٢. وتبين نفس الحجم والزخارف المعمارية على الواجهة. لم يكن هناك إى اقتراح بإقامة مبنى شاهق الارتفاع في الكويت قبل هذا المبنى، سوى ذلك التصميم الذي قدمه المهندس المعماري ري جون و هاريس عام ١٩٦١ في مسابقة لتصميم الواجهة البحرية.

يستند المبنى إلى قاعدة منخفضة الارتفاع. تتحدد من خلال ممرات غير مكتملة من الأعمدة. وتكشف واجهة البرج عن أنماط هندسية متداخلة من عناصر رأسية، مستلهمة من الزخارف و من تصميم النوافذ الخاصة بقصور السلاطين العثمانيين. ويمر الضوء الطبيعي من خلال تلك الكوات بما يسمح بتزويد المكاتب بيئياً أفضل. كما أن ذلك لا يشتت الانتباه كثيراً بما يقع خارج المبنى. وعلى الاركان يوجد صف من الأعمدة الحديثة الطراز التي تمثل تنافرا مع النمط المعماري العثماني. أما الأركان المنفتحة. فتفضي إلى هيكل متدرج داخلي يبدأ من الطابق الأرضي. وبالنسبة لأعلى طابقين بالبرج. فقد تم حجزهما لعلية القوم وللإدارة العليا.

مجمع الرحاب التجاري
حولي، ١٩٧١–١٩٧٣

المصمم • صباح أبي حنا (المعماري). UNETEC (الخدمات)
العميل • شركة العقارات المتحدة
المقاول • شركة البناء المتحدة
(البناء مستخدم)

صممت شركة العقارات المتحدة أول مشروعاتها الإسكانية والتجارية. ويعكس المجمع جميع الأفكار السابقة المتصلة بإقامة مجموعة مبان متكاملة في إطار " الدراسة الحضرية للمدينة القديمة ".

وقد أدى التمويل الذي وفرته الدولة في بداية السبعينات. وقبل إنشاء الهيئة الوطنية للإسكان. إلى ظهور اتجاهات جديدة في البناء. وقد تطلبت الزيادة السكانية. التي أقرت بها الخطة الرئيسية الثانية. زيادة سعة المناطق السكنية في المناطق الحضرية القائمة. فضلا عن ضرورة توفير حلول لمشاكل المناطق العشوائية. وقد استقر فريق كولين بوكانان على عدد من المناطق لإنشاء مشاريع إسكان عملاقة. ولعل اسم هذا المشروع يشير إلى نوع من العلاقة بالمشروع الذي يعد إطارا مبدئيا قد يخضع للتوسع في المستقبل.

وتواجه الكتلة الرئيسية بهذا المجمع شارعي تونس وبيروت. والمبنى عبارة عن مكعب أبيض اللون يضم طابقين سفليين كساحات انتظار. فضلا عن ثلاثة طوابق مخصصة للمراكز التجارية. وطابق للمكاتب. وعشرة طوابق مخصصة للإسكان ذوي الدخل المتوسط والمرتفع. وتسمح العناصر الهيكلية بالمبنى بوجود عدد متباين من الشرفات. وقد وضع تصميم المجمع التجاري ليكون ملتفاً حول صالتين رئيسيتين. ترتفع كل منهما الثلاثة طوابق. معرضتين لضوء الشمس من خلال منور زجاجي من مادة الفبر. وقد تم بناء مدخل للمشاة على مستوى الشارع. وهو مدخل من الرخام الأبيض.

وقد تم تطوير هذه المكان بطول المنطقة التي تقع بين الصالحية إلى الغرب من مجمع المثنى. ويصل طول المشروع إلى حوالي ٢٠٠ متر، ويمتد من المكان غير المأهول الذي يقع إلى جوار مقبرة الصالحية، و"المنطقة الخلفية " من شارع فهد السالم. ومن الناحية الغربية نجد أن المدخل إلي مركز التسوق يتميز بوجود سلم ومصعد بما يسمح بالوصول إلى المكان من ساحة الانتظار التي تقع تحت الأرض إلى الطوابق التجارية الثلاث وإلى المكاتب التي تقع إلى الأعلى من ذلك بخمس طوابق.

وعلى الناحية المقابلة نجد فندقا رفيع الطراز يرتفع كبرج من الألمنيوم المعالج، مما يضفي قدراً كبيراً من الجمال على المكان. وهذا الفندق الذي يصل ارتفاعه إلى ستة عشر طابقاً كان يعلوه في البدء ملهى ليلي، وحمام سباحة مغطى بسقف يمكن التحكم به (٣٠).

مجموعة الكويت الهندسية استعانة بي مجموعة معماريين مصريين واقامة في ذلك الوقت شركة استشارات معمارية ASA احمد نور (١٩٤٣)، سيف هيكل (١٩٤٤)، نبيل صالح (١٩٤٥) تغير اسم الفندق الي جي دبيلو ماريوت.

مسجد الدولة الكبير
السيف، شارع عبدالله الاحمد، ١٩٨٣-١٩٧٦

المصمم • مكية وشركاؤه -- المستشارون. اركبسنتر (مشارك محلي)
العميل • وزارة الأشغال العامة
المقاول • الشركة المتحدة للبناء
(تم تجديده في العام ٢٠١٣)

بني هذا المسجد على الطراز المعماري العباسي. فقد سعى مكية للبحث عن طريقة جديدة تلائم الهوية المحلية (١٧) بعيداً عن محاكاة الأشكال التقليدية والعناصر الزخرفية، فكانت المحصلة مبنى ضخم يتسم بمعالم واضحة، تحتفي بالتاريخ الإسلامي، من دون مغالاة.

ويقع المسجد في منطقة بالغة الأهمية، فهو على الشارع المقابل لمكتب الأمير مباشرة (قصر السيف). ويتألف المبنى من فضاءين متساويين في الحجم بما يؤدي إلى إحداث توازن في مستوى المبنى، ويتألف الفضاء الأول من الصحن الكبير وصالة الصلاة الرئيسية التي تغطيها قبة كبيرة تستند إلى أربعة أعمدة ضخمة. أما الفضاء بين المبنيين وهو الحرم، فهو عبارة عن صالة مسقوفة ترتكز على صف من الأعمدة على غرار المساجد التقليدية. وأما الركن الشمالي، فإنه مخصص كمدخل للأمير، وللوضوء. وتبدو الواجهة من الخارج على أنها تكرار لعناصر مستقلة عن بعضها البعض، وتبدو هناك سلسلة من الأسوار تنتهج نهجاً متدرجاً واضحاً للعيان، والمادة الرئيسية للبناء هي الخرسانة، وإن كانت هذه المادة قد تم صقلها من خلال المطارق أو أدوات معالجة الرمال(١٨).

والواقع أن التصميم المبدئي لم يتحول بسهولة إلى واقع، فلقد تم إجراء العديد من التعديلات لأسباب تقنية، لكن العميل لم يكن راضياً تماماً في نهاية المطاف بسبب خلو المسجد من الداخل من الزخرفة، ولعل ذلك هو السبب في إدخال مساحات كبيرة من الزخرفة بالفسيفساء على الجدران الداخلية للمسجد. (١٩) وقد تم مؤخرا تجديد المسجد من الداخل باستخدام أنماط متعددة من الزخرفة، عزز التناقض بين الداخل والشكل الخارجي المتواضع للمسجد.

البورصة
السيف، شارع عبدالله الاحمد، ١٩٨٦-١٩٧٨

المصمم • جون اس بونجتون -- شركة تضامن (المعمار)، KEO (تعاون في الانشاء)، نيونن واطسون(دراسات البيئة)
العميل • وزارة المالية
المقاول • شركة الهاني للتجارة والمقاولات
(البناء مستخدم)

أطلقت مجلة ميدل ايست كونستركشن على مبنى البورصة لقب "أول مبنى لبورصة خليجية يأخذ في الاعتبار عند تصميمه احتياجات العملاء "ويرمز المبنى لمالية الدولة، ويقف شامخاً مقابل المسجد الكبير مع بداية شارع عبدالله الأحمد، وهو الشارع الذي كان من المزمع انشاؤه و لم يتم حتى الآن. (٤٢).

سوق الشرق الأوسط
المباركية، منطقة الاعمال المركزية، منطقة ٤ ١٩٧٦ – ١٩٧٨

المصمم • مارسل برور وشركاه
العميل • بلدية الكويت
(لم بنم البناء)

جاءت فكرة هذا السوق الجديد، الذي كان من المزمع إقامته على مراحل في قلب المدينة القديم، من النجاح الذي حققته الجمعيات التعاونية، التي أصبحت قادرة على تحويل نمط الشراء من سوق المباركية القديم.

وقد تولى مارسل برور، وكان قد تقاعد في العام ١٩٧٦ عن عمر يناهز ٧٤ عاما، تصميم المشروع مع شركاه، والواقع أنه في سنوات السبعينات طلب من آرثر دي ليتل أن يجد وسيلة لإقامة سوق للمنتجات الطازجة في سنوات السبعينات، على أن يشمل التصميم وجود مكيفات هواء بما يسمح بعرض الطعام في مكان مفتوح وبطريقة صحية وآمنة (٢١). وقد تم تصميم المكان لبيع الأسماك، واللحوم والخضروات.

وعلى النقيض من المشاريع الأخرى التي تتشابه في الغرض، فإن الأسلوب الجديد الذي تم انتهاجه في إعادة ابتكار مفهوم السوق الوظيفي كان مميزاً. وقد تم توطيد العلاقة مع الماضي من خلال تقديم نوع من التفاعل بين المستهلك والبائع. ويسمح ارتفاع المبنى الداخلي مع الممرات المتاحة للمستهلك برؤية كاملة للمنتجات، كما أن ذلك يعطي للمستهلك إيحاء بأنه يتحول في أروقة أحد الأسواق الموجودة بالشارع.

سوق الذهب
المباركية، منطقة الاعمال المركزية،منطقة ٤، ١٩٧٦ – ١٩٨٢

المصمم • PACE
العميل • شركة الكويت للتجارة الخارجية والاستثمار
المقاول • شركة المقاولات الدولية (شركة الاحمدية للتجارة والمقاولات)
(البناء مستخدم)

تم إقامة السوق الجديد في المنطقة التجارية القديمة بالمدينة بمواجهة مدرسة المباركية. و شيد جنباً إلى جنب مع مسجد الفهد، وهما يشكلان معاً تعبيراً حضرياً موحداً، ويتصل المبنيان من خلال نقطة واحدة بحيث تطل منارة المسجد على واجهة السوق.

ويتألف المبنى من كتلة صلبة من خرسانة أسمنتية مخشنة بيضاء، ويشغل المبنى مساحة ٦٠٠ متر مربع. ويرتفع عن مستوى الشارع، ولذا فهناك سلالم خارجية من كافة النواحي بما يسمح بسلاسة وصول المشاة من النسيج الحضري المجاور.
تذكرنا الواجهات بقلعة حصينة، وتوجد عناصر معمارية تشبه أبراج الرماية في زوايا المبنى الأربع. و تتألف الأقواس من البرونز والألومنيوم وتشترك في حمل شبكة الحاجز الحديدي الثقيل. ويتكون المبنى من أربعة طوابق وهناك قبو في الطابق السفلي ويوجد ١٨٥ محلا صغيرا مخصصة لصياغة الذهب والإتجار فيه، وهي كلها موزعة على طوابق ثلاثة، تنفتح على فناء رئيسي مضاء على نحو طبيعي، من خلال مناور تسمح بدخول الضوء. أما الطابق العلوي فهو مخصص للمكاتب و الأقبية والمعامل.

مشروع الصالحية التجاري وفندق الميريديان
الصالحية، ١٩٧٥-١٩٨٠

المصمم • مجموعة الكويت الهندسية، أوف أروب وشركاه
العميل • شركة الصالحية العقارية
المقاول • شركة الأحمدية للمقاولات والتجارة
(البناء مستخدم)

تم تطوير هذا المشروع بالتزامن مع المرحلة الثانية من تطوير مجمع أنوار السكني (١٩٧٥ ١٩٧٦). ويعد المشروع بالغ الطموح من حيث أنه يعد من أوائل المشاريع التي استهدفت إقامة مبنى يشتمل على فندق متميز، ويضم في نفس الوقت مركزا للتسوق ومكاتب.

مقر البنوك المشترك
المباركية، ١٩٧٦ – ١٩٨٣

المصمم • سكيدمور، اوينجز، وميريل (برئاسة روجر ردفورد)، PACE (مساهمون في الانشاء)، ويلندجر وشركاه (الانشاء). بروت بوم و بوليص (خدمات البناء). مايكل مكارثي (SOM مصمم داخلي)
شارك في المنافسة على اقامة المشروع • كنزو تانخ فيليب جونسون (PACE) TAC و(PACE) SOM
العميل • بنك الكويت الصناعي، بنك الكويت والشرق الاوسط، بنك الكويت العقاري
المقاول • مجهول
(البناء مستخدم)

كان كل من أي. ام. باي وبول رودولف عضوين في لجنة التحكيم الخاصة بتصميم المقرات الرئيسية للبنوك الثلاث في مكان واحد. وقد فاز بالتصميم شركة SOM تحت إدارة جوردون بونشافت، واقترح المشروع إقامة ثلاثة أبراج متساوية الارتفاع من ١٨ طابقاً، كل منها مبنى عملاق مذهل، وإن كان متناعماً بحيث تواجه واجهته الزجاجية الشمال (البحر)، على حين يمتد الجانب الرأسي الصلب من البناء، الخاص بتوزيع الحركة، تجاه الجنوب، مع وجود مساحة صغيرة نسبياً للطابق الأرضي. وترتفع الأبراج علي نحو هندسي من خلال مساحة خضراء مربعة تعلوها مظلة، وهي صالة المعاملات المصرفية. وتغطي المساحة الأرضية المرآب وأماكن سير المشاه والسيارات من خلال نظام متدرج، يحتوي على بعض الأشجار والسلالم. وتزود ألواح البناء المسبقة التجهيز، وهي على شكل حرف T، طوابق حرة تصلح كمكاتب، أما من الخارج فإنها تبدو كفواصل للستائر الزجاجية. وقد أثنى الجميع على المجمع وذلك باعتباره "أول طراز عالمي "لأبراج مكتبية في الكويت وهو ما يثير "الكثير من الاهتمام "(٨) بالمبنى. وفيما يتعلق بالمشاريع الأخرى، فإننا نرى أن التصميم الذي اقترحه جونسون يتكون من ثلاثة أشكال مختلفة من المعدن وهي على هيئة شكل كروي، وهرمي، ومكعب.

مجمع محاكم الكويت
القبلة ١٩٧٦ – ١٩٨٣

المصمم • السير باريل سبنس، شركة تضامن دولية (معمار)، شركة تضامن فينزروي روبنسون(تعاونية للمعمار)، وايت يونج شركاء (مهندسون)، ويلمز سال وشركاه (خدمات البناء). وايت يونج شركاء (مهندسون)
العميل • وزارة العدل، وزارة الأشغال العامة
المقاول • شركة الهاني للمقاولات والتجارة
(البناء مستخدم)

تحت شعار "الشمس المشرقة وحكم القانون "(١٣) تم تطوير عشر واجهات بناء بعد التفويض بإقامة المشروع. وقد تم اللجوء في عملية بحث قام بها العميل أو المصمم وذلك بغية الوصول إلى العناصر المعمارية الإسلامية التقليدية الملائمة. وقد وصفت تلك العناصر على أنها بمثابة معجم معماري للمباني الكبيرة الحجم.

ومن خلال منافسة دولية كان المشروع الفائز عبارة عن مبنى مكعب الشكل يتألف من تسعة طوابق ومحاط بواجهة مظللة بطول محيط المبنى، فضلا عن وجود حديقة في وسط باحة مركزية. وتتصل الأروقة الجانبية الأرضية بمحيط المبنى بنظام ضخم ومعقد من الأبهاء العامة ومناطق الانتظار، بما في ذلك "ديوان" يتسع لـ ٣٢٠ شخصا.

وتصل مساحة المبني إلي ٥٠٠٠٠ م٢ ويتسع لـ١٥٠٠٠ شخص، و يقوم بالفصل بين الوظائف المختلفة، رأسيا وأفقيا، فهناك ٥٢ قاعة محكمة تختلف باختلاف درجة التقاضي، فهناك قاعات محاكم الدرجة الأولى والاستئناف و محكمة النقض (١٤)، فضلا عن عدد من المكاتب، وغرف القضاة، ومكتبة وغرف للمحامين، وللشرطة، ولإجراء المقابلات.

سوق المتحدة والمسيل
الصالحية، منطقة الأعمال المركزية،
منطقة ١،٠، ١٩٧٣ – ١٩٧٩

المصمم • جون بونجتون وشركاء (معماري)،
KEO (مساهمين استشاريين)، ثوستي AG من بوغمبرج
العميل • شركة العقارات المتحدة
المقاول • شركة المباني الجاهزة
(البناء مستخدم)

تم توكيل شركة تضامن جون بونجتون، بالتعاون مع KEO
لإقامة مشروعين تجاريين متعددي الاستخدام. وقد طلب
العميل أن يكون المشروع عبارة عن نظام خرساني سابق التجهيز
بالكامل يستند إلى أعمدة تعلوها أقواس تدعم صفين من
العوارض الجانبية المزدوجة، والتي تدعم بدورها العوارض الأرضية
على شكل حرف T (٢٢). وكان المشروع المزمع بمثابة مبنى
اختباري استعداداً لإقامة مصنع جديد سابق التجهيز للصناعات
الوطنية (٢٣).

ويشتمل سوق المتحدة على ٩١١ مكان انتظار (٢٤) موزعة على
ثلاثة مستويات وسط. والمشروع عبارة عن مبنيين رئيسيين
يتصلان عن طريق عدد من الجسور في الطوابق العليا حيث تقع
المكاتب. والفجوة بين المكاتب في الطابق الأرضي هي التي تحدد
الانسياب عند المداخل الرئيسية والصالة الرئيسية حيث مناطق
بيع التجزئة.

وتعمل مكونات الواجهة سابقة التجهيز على خلق نوع من الأطر
المتكررة، التي تحدد معالم ضوء الشمس والظلال، و تبدو أكثر
وضوحاً عندما يتم استخدام عناصر الوقاية من الشمس في
الطابق المخصص للمكاتب.

مستشفيات مبارك الكبير، العدان، الجهراء
الجابرية، هدية، الجهراء، ١٩٧٢–١٩٨٥

المصمم • AART\ATEA (ليون فورجيا الرئيس)،
Uniconsult (الشارك المنافسة)
العميل • وزارة الأشغال العامة
المقاول • شركة بيريني (العدان)، Inter G (مبارك الكبير)،
استوديو الهندسة شوارتز اومو (الفروانية والجهراء)
(تم تغيير خطة البناء وهدم جزء)

مع توسع مدينة الكويت في السبعينيات غرباً وجنوباً، تم إقامة
عدد من المستشفيات على مقربة من مراكز الأحياء الجديدة.
وحتى يتحقق الاستخدام الأمثل لعملية البناء، ولتلبية القيود
الزمنية على التصميم والبناء، تم التعاقد مع شركة مساهمة
دولية تضم عدداً من الخبراء والشركات المتخصصة في الإنشاءات
الطبية. وكانت الفكرة هنا تدور حول إقامة وحدة رعاية صحية
مستقلة ذاتياً مع عيادة للأسنان، وعيادة خارجية للمرضى، فضلاً
عن مكان لإقامة الممرضات، وأماكن للترفيه والطعام ومسجد.
وقد تم تكرار المشروع في العديد من الحالات بمختلف أرجاء
الدولة لمدة عقد كامل. وقد اختلف التصميم في كل حالة تبعاً
لاختلاف رقعة الأرض المخصصة، أو تبعاً للحاجة لإقامة وحدة
طبية معينة، ولكن أغلب عناصر الخرسانة سابقة التجهيز التي
استخدمت في إقامة المباني لم تتغير من مستشفى لآخر.

الصندوق الكويتي للتنمية الاقتصادية العربية
المرقاب، ١٩٦٨، ١٩٧٤ – ١٩٨١

المصمم • TAC (رئاسة الاستشاريين ومعماريون)،
PACE (مساهمين البناء)
العميل • الصندوق الكويتي للتنمية الاقتصادية العربية
المقاول • محمد عبد المحسن الخرافي وأولاده، شركة العثمان
للمقاولات
(البناء مستخدم)

تمثلت رسالة الصندوق الكويتي للتنمية الاقتصادية العربية منذ
تأسيسه في العام ١٩٦١م، في مساعدة الدول العربية الأخرى على
تحقيق التقدم الاقتصادي والرخاء الاجتماعي. وقد أتى تأسيس
الصندوق في إطار توقع صدور قرار من الأمم المتحدة لمصلحة
الدول النامية. وفي العام ١٩٧٤م، توسعت مساعدة الصندوق
لتشمل دولاً غير عربية. وفي العام ذاته، تم وضع حجر الأساس
للمقر الرئيسي الجديد للمشروع. وقد كان المشروع أحد بواكير

التعاون بين المصممين TAC و PACE، وأقيم في منطقة
إستراتيجية بمحاذاة شارع مبارك الكبير، وفي مواجهة مجموعة
من المباني العامة الرئيسية. تم تطوير المشروع على مرحلتين،
تمثلت أولاهما في شكل مستطيل في حيز صغير، يتألف من
ثلاثة طوابق على قاعدة مرتفعة. والمبنى على هيئة هرم متدرج
مقلوب، فهناك خطوط حادة وفتحات صغيرة تحدد تحدد الإيقاع الرتيب
للواجهات (٢٣). أما المنظر الخارجي الذي لا يميزه شيء ويتسم
بالتقشف على الرغم من أبعاده الكبيرة، فهو يتناقض مع انفتاح
الفضاء الداخلي الذي ينساب على نحو سلس نحو الفناء المركزي.
وهناك فسحة مركزية تضم عدداً من نوافير المياه وأحواض
الزهور، يتعزز جمالها من خلال الإضاءة غير المباشرة التي تأتي من
منور في السقف.

ولقد تعمد المصمم إضفاء صبغة أفقية ساكنة على المبنى
برمته، وإن كان ذلك قد تغير مع إضافة برج طويل، منذ بضعة
أعوام، يتكون من ١٨ طابقا. وباستثناء المدخل، والطابق العلوي
الذي يضم غرفة الآلات، فإن المبنى يضم سلسلة من المكاتب
الإدارية تتحدد بالارتفاع الرأسي على جانبي المبنيين الرئيسيين.
ولعل من أهم الملامح المعمارية المميزة للمبنى، هي النوافذ
الفسيحة في المبنى، ذات الضلف المنبسطة، والتي تهدف إلى
ترشيح الضوء إلى داخله.

ويعكس كلا المشروعين التأثير المناخي على التصميم المعماري،
وتتمثل أداة التصميم الرئيسية هنا في شمس الكويت بشدتها
وكثافتها والظلال القائمة التي تنتج عنها، وهو ما نجده في
الأشكال والتعبيرات المختلفة للمواد المستخدمة والتي تتشكل
في أغلبها من الحجر الجيري والخرسانة الرملية ذات الطلاء البيج
اللون، ولعل هذه المادة الأخيرة قد استخدمت للمرة الأولى في
الكويت في هذا المبنى.

وفي تناغم رائع يقع المبنيان جنباً إلي جنب في محاذاة الشارع
الرئيسي ووسط المدينة. ويتقاسم المبنيان الألوان والمواد
والتصميم، لكن الفرق الجوهري بينهما يكمن في الحجم الذي
يسبب قدراً من الاختلال في التناغم. ومع ذلك فإن المبنيين
يستندان إلى القاعدة ذاتها، وهي عبارة عن ساحة شاسعة منها
في البداية أن تكون ساحة عامة شاسعة في مقابل منطقة السوق
التي تعج بالحركة.

مجمع النقرة التجاري والسكني
حولي، ١٩٧٥ – ١٩٨٦ و ١٩٨٠ – ١٩٨٧

المصمم • PACE
العميل • الشيخ جابر العلي الصباح،
المركز العربي للتجارة والعقارات
المقاول • المركز العربي للتجارة والعقارات
(البناء مستخدم)

أتاح هذا المجمع الفرصة لتطوير منطقة بأسرها من المدينة إبان
فترة السبعينات، وفقاً لنموذج يستند إلى إقامة منطقة سكنية
وتجارية في الوقت ذاته. وقد تم ذلك في فترة شهد فيها سوق
العقارات قدراً كبيراً من المضاربات، وكما هو الحال بالنسبة
للمجمعات الأخرى بالمدينة، كمجمعي المثنى والرحاب، فإن
مجمع النقرة لم يستهدف إقامة مساكن على مستوى رفيع
فحسب، بل استهدف التأسيس لأسلوب حياة جديد مع الكثير
من الملامح الجمالية المعمارية التي تشير إلى نمط الحياة
المستقبلي.

ولما كان المشروع قد تم بناؤه على عدة مراحل، فإنه يمكن أن
ندرك طبيعته انطلاقا من جسر المشاة المكيف الهواء الذي يصل
المجمع التجاري الجنوبي بالمجمع الشمالي المتعدد الاستخدامات.
ويستند المجمع الشمالي في تصميمه إلى منصة مرتفعة فوق
طابقين يقعان تحت الأرض مخصصان كساحات انتظار، كما أن
هناك مركز تسوق مكون من ثلاثة طوابق وثلاث أبنية هي A و B
و C. وقد تم تطوير الأبنية الثلاث لتصبح أبراجا سكنية من عشرة
طوابق وتضم ١٨ شقة سكنية، وحمام سباحة ومناطق ألعاب
أطفال في الطابق السفلي. أما المبنى C فإنه مكرس للمكاتب
التي تتوزع على خمسة طوابق. وكافة هذه العناصر منفصلة عن
بعضها البعض بما يسمح بتدفق الهواء، كما يسمح للمشاة
بالوصول إلى المكان، وللعربات من تفريغ حمولتها.

ويشتمل المبنى الجنوبي على منطقة تسوق إضافية مع طابق
تجاري أرضي، فضلاً عن طابقين و طابق آخر، مخصص كله
للمكاتب، ويتصل كل ذلك بالشارع من خلال مخارج رأسية
منفصلة عن بعضها البعض.

مجمع دسمان
شرق، ١٩٧٥-١٩٧٩

المصمم • KEO مع غازي سلطان
العميل • شركة العقارات الكويتية
المقاول • مجهول
(البناء مستخدم)

كان هناك تنافس كبير للحصول على هذا الموقع الذي يواجه دوار
الدانة القديم. ويضم المجمع ١٣ طابقا تشمل على طابق سفلي
(ساحة انتظار)، وطابق أرضي و طابق يقع بين الطابقين السفلي
والأرضي، وذلك فضلا عن ١٠ طوابق بمساحات معدة لمكاتب. أما
المبنى ذاته فقد تم تحديده بناء على التشريعات التي دخلت التنفيذ
قبل أن يتم إجراء تعديل على الخطة الرئيسية الثانية عام ١٩٧٧.
ويأخذ المبنى من أسفل شكل حرف L وينفتح على مربع يضم
نافورة مياه. وهذا الجزء يقع في مستوى أكثر انخفاضاً من مستوى
الشارع، كما أنه يعد منفذ الوصول الرئيسي للمكاتب الموجودة
بالطوابق المختلفة وذلك من خلال مصعدين يمران خلال كتلتين
يكسوهما غطاء من الحجر الجيري الأبيض المعرق عند القاعدة
والحجر الرملي في الجزء الأعلى. أما مداخل مركز التسوق الرئيسية
فنجدها عند كل طرف من أطراف المبني وهي ترتفع عن مستوى
الشارع، ويمكن الوصول إليها من خلال سلم يشغل جانبا من
الواجهة المكسوة بالحجر الرملي. وهكذا فإن الطوابق التجارية
الثلاث تختلف عن بعضها البعض من حيث السياق والنوع وطريق
الوصول. وهناك نوافذ كبيرة الحجم تنفتح على الداخل في الجزء
التجاري من المبنى، بما يؤدي إلى وجود نوع من التواصل المتعدد
المستويات.

ولا تعترض الواجهات الصلبة سوى بعض العناصر التي يكسوها
الحجر الجيري المعرق، عند قاعدة المصعد. إضافة إلى السلم
الخرساني في طرف المبنى. ولعل تلك العناصر على جانب الواجهة
هي الاستثناءات الوحيدة في الهيكل العام للمبنى الذي تظهر
فيه السلالم من الخرسانة الخشنة. مقابل الحجر الجيري الأبيض
المعرق الذي يغطي الأعمدة. أما الحائط الخارجي للمبنى فيقتصر
على طبقة من الحجر الرملي البني اللون.

مركز الدراسات المصرفية
المرقاب، منطقة الأعمال المركزية، منطقة ١،٠
١٩٧٩ – ١٩٧٦

المصمم • TEST (رئاسة معاذ الألوسي)
العميل • مركز الدراسات المصرفية
المقاول • مجهول
(تم تعديل التصميم)

يتألف هذا البرج من المكاتب من عشرة طوابق، و يشغل رقعة على
الجانب الشرقي من سوق الوطنية في المنطقة رقم ١،٠ من منطقة
الأعمال المركزية.

وتتخلل واجهة المبنى الصلبة نوافذ مقوسة في الحوائط
المزدوجة. مما يزيد من العمق البصري للمبنى. وتتشابه الواجهتان
المطلتان على الشارع من حيث المواد المستخدمة في الحائط
الخارجي، ومن حيث التقسيم الهندسي بواسطة دعامات، و
يمتد بطول المبنى بأسره، ما عدا الطابق الأخير الذي نجد به فتحات
أفقية، وكذلك الحال بالنسبة للطابق الأرضي الذي تسمح فيه
الفتحات الكبيرة من الوصول إلى نقاط الدخول الرئيسية. وتقضي
المداخل الواقعة وسط المبنى إلي هيكل زجاجي شفاف على نحو
يتناقض مع الطبقة الصلبة الخارجية.

ولما كان المبنى مخصص لتقديم برامج تدريبية لموظفي البنوك،
فقد كانت الخطة التقليدية بالغة المرونة فيما يتصل بالكتلة
الرئيسية للسلالم والمصاعد، والخدمات، وقد تم وضعها جميعاً
في مركز المبنى، بما يسمح بفضاء مفتوح في باقي المبنى.

وقد تم تنفيذ عدد من الأماكن المتباينة مثل أماكن اللهو
التسلية، فضلا عن حمامات السباحة واستزراع الأشجار على
الشاطئ، وساحات لعب للأطفال، ومنتزهات مائية، ومطاعم،
وساحات، ومرفأ لليوم/السفن الصغيرة. وكانت المنطقة
الرئيسية المحورية ولا تزال تتمثل في الجزيرة الاصطناعية
الخضراء، وإن كانت لا تحظى بصيانة كافية في الوقت الراهن. كما
تم بناء جزيرة اصطناعية بين الطريق الدائري الثاني والطريق الدائري
الثالث، و زودت ببحيرة اصطناعية، تحيط بها شواطئ رملية، مع
مسرح مكشوف، وعدد من المطاعم، وأماكن التسلية.

ومازالت الواجهة البحرية تلعب حتى اليوم دوراً هاماً من حيث
أنها تتيح استخدام شاطئ البحر للجميع. وعلى ممشى الواجهة
البحرية، تم إضافة عدد من المباني، على نحو عشوائي، بما أثر
إلى حد ما على التكامل الطبيعي للمكان، وإن كان قد أضفى على
المكان نوعاً من البعد الاجتماعي.

شقق منطقة الهيلتون
بنيد القار، ١٩٧٧ – ١٩٧٩

المصمم • أي إم باي وشركاه (معماري) , KEO
(قيادة الاستشاريين) هشام منير في المنافسة
العميل • شركة العقارات المتحدة، شركة الفنادق الكويتية
المقاول • شركة مساعد الصالح وأولاده
(تم بناء جزء \البناء مستخدم)

الواقع أنه لم يتم تنفيذ كامل مشروع كانديليس الخاص بإنشاء
وحدات سكنية في منطقة فندق هيلتون، إذ من بين المراحل
الثلاث المبدئية منه لم يتم تنفيذ سوى مرحلة واحدة. ولذا فبعد
مضي بضعة أعوام، تم تكليف أي إم باي بتطوير الجزء الرئيسي من
هذا المشروع المهم ولجزء المواجهة الخليج في هذه المنطقة.
وقام المصمم بتصميم وحدات سكنية فاخرة من مختلف
الأحجام والأنواع، منها شقق ذات طابقين (دوبلكس) وشقق فوق
السطوح (بنتهاوس). ويستند التصميم المعماري إلى شبكة
هندسية قائمة على شقوق مائلة ووحدات مثمنة الشكل، حيث
توجد غرف المعيشة. وهذا التصميم يجعل المبنى بمنأى عن
الطريق العام ويشكل ساحتين شاسعتين على شكل مثلث في
الطابق السفلى. كما يسمح التصميم كذلك بانفتاح كل شقة
على نحو مناسب على الواجهة البحرية. والنظام في مجمله
تكرارا للوحدات الهندسية المتشابهة التي تختلف من حيث
الارتفاع، وهذا البعد هو ما يعمل على زيادة الشد المائل، مما يمنح
المجمع شكلاً هرمياً متدرجاً مميزاً. ولقد شهدت هذه المنطقة
في السنوات الأخيرة نشاطا معماريا مكثفا، فظهرت عدة أبراج
سكنية عالية، ذات تصاميم متباينة على مقربة من المبنى، مما
أدى إلى إضعاف التوازن الأصلي في التصميم المبدئي.

أبراج مكاتب
شرق، ١٩٧٣-١٩٨٦

المصمم • PACE و KEO والمستشارون العرب

لم تتبلور على الاطلاق فكرة وجود "شارع ذو مكانة هامة" يربط
المباركية (قلب المدينة القديم) بشرق (منطقة التجار) (١٥). وحتى
يومنا هذا نرى ذلك الانفصال المكاني بين المنطقتين، وهو ما
يعمل على وجود نوع من التمزق في نسيج المدينة، وبعد الدعوة
التي أطلقت فيما بعد عام ١٩٦٨ بشأن "إعادة تخطيط الكويت" (١٦)
وبشأن "إجراء "دراسات حضرية للمدينة القديمة". أصبحت هذه
المنطقة منطقة ملائمة لإجراء التطوير المخطط لمركز المدينة،
وقد أماطت السياسات الحضرية عن بعض المخاوف تجاه الحفاظ
على قلب المدينة القديمة عند التوسع صوب المناطق الحضرية
بشرق. وكان الاعتقاد آنذاك أن الاستثمار الخاص سوف يدرس
الخطوط العامة المتعلقة بالتصميم وملكية الأرض في كل من
شارع يوسف الرومي وشارع أحمد الجابر وقد كان ينظر للأبراج الأولى
التي تم بناؤها في السبعينات على أنها أداة لتعزيز التقدم في ظل
غياب التخطيط المعماري. لكن في أغلب الحالات لم يستكمل
المشروع، وآل الأمر إلى نفس النتيجة: برج في رقعة أرض فارغة،
ينتهي به الأمر إلى يصبح ساحة انتظار سيارات غير رسمية.

كان برج الأسماك (المستشارون العرب، ١٩٧٦ – ١٩٧٩) في نهاية
المطاف أول برج يتم تشييده في منطقة شرق. وبعد عدد من
المضاربات العالية في سوق العقارات بالمدينة (١٧)، اكتسب
المشروع زخماً كبيراً في التنافس على إقامة أعلى برج بالمنطقة.
وفي سنوات الثمانينيات الأربع الأولى أقامت شركة PACE وحدها
برج عماد (١٩٧٩ ـ ١٩٨٣) وبرج مركز الرائد (١٩٧٩ ـ ١٩٨٢) وبرج

بهباني (١٩٧٨ ـ ١٩٨٢)، ويتكون هذا البرج الأخير من ١٩ طابقاً. وفي
العام التالي تم الانتهاء من إقامة البرج الذي يضم المقر الرئيسي
لبنك برقان (١٩٧٨ ـ ١٩٨٣)، وهو برج يصل ارتفاعه إلى ٢١ طابقاً.

وفي ظل إدارة بوب كيورو (١٩)، اضطلعت PACE ببناء المعهد
العام للأمن الإجتماعي (١٩٨٠-١٩٨٣) و برج الخليجية (١٩٨١ ـ ١٩٨٤)
وبرج باما، ولم يتجاوز تلك الأبراج من حيث الارتفاع سوى برج شرق
(١٩٨١ ـ ١٩٨٣) الذي يضم ٢٣ طابقاً (بإرتفاع ١٠٤ متراً). وفي العام ١٩٨٦
تم الانتهاء من برجي العوضي وجاز (٢١).

مركز مدينة الفنطاس
الفنطاس، ١٩٧٨

المصمم • آرثر اريكسون وشركاه (معماري) ,
KEG (قيادة الاستشاريين)
العميل • دولة الكويت
(لم يتم البناء)

تتمثل أحد الأهداف الجوهرية التي تمخضت عن الخطة الرئيسية
الثانية في تخفيف الضغط على المناطق الحضرية الرئيسية، من
خلال بناء مراكز حضرية على أطراف المدينة. ويرى بوكانان أن
الفنطاس تعد بمثابة "خطة عمل "في "ممر الكويت الساحلي".
وقد تم تصميم مركز مدينة الفنطاس لتكون ثاني أكبر مركز
في الدولة بحلول العام ١٩٩٠. وقد طلب من الشركة الكندية آرثر
اريكسون بمراجعة الخطة المبدئية لمركز الفنطاس وهي الخطة
التي وضعها شانكلاند كوكس. وكانت الشركة الكندية آنذاك
على وشك الانتهاء من طرح مشروع مجمع الصوابر للإسكان
الاجتماعي بالمدينة.

وتدور الفكرة المبدئية حول "جعل كل شيء يتم على نحو داخلي
قدر المستطاع: ليتم التخلص من السيارات، بوضعها تحت الأرض،
أو في المرآب، وليتم إقامة المكاتب والمساكن على نحو مركزي
في قلب المجمع"(٣٨) وقد تم تصميم مركز الفنطاس ليخدم
من الناحية الوظيفية ٣.٠٠٠ شخص، بحيث يضم مكاتب تجارية،
ومكاتب تجزئة، وسوقاً مغطي، ومنطقة ثقافية، وعيادات، ودور
سينما، وملاعب رياضية، ومناطق ترفيهية تضم حديقة نباتية،
وقد تم النظر في إقامة المشروع على هيئة كتلتين رئيسيتين
يصل بينهما جسر يمر فوق الطريق الرئيسي، ونتج عن ذلك كتلة
من المباني تصل مساحتها إلى فدان, مع أربعة بوابات رئيسية عند
الجهات الأصلية الأربع للمكان.

مجمع الوزارات
المرقاب، ١٩٧٨ – ١٩٨٢

المصمم • وزارة الاشغال العامة، قسم التصميم،
انبرجوبروجكت للهندسة المعمارية والبناء، قسم التصميم
والمعمار
العميل • وزارة الأشغال العامة
المقاول • انبرجوبروجكت الهندسة والمعمار
(تم تعديل جزء كبير)

بعد تجربة بيتر واليسون سمثسون في "المبنى النموذجي "والتي
استمرت إلى العام ١٩٧٥ (٥٦) واصلت وزارة الاشغال العامة تطوير
المفهوم ليتحول إلى واقع حقيقي، وفي العام ١٩٧٨ تم توكيل
شركة المقاولات اليوغوسلافية انيرجو بروجكت بإقامة المشروع
، وكان للشركة آنذاك خبرة كبيرة بالكويت (٥٧).

لكن تصميم المشروع آل في آخر الأمر إلى رئيس فريق التصميم
بالوزارة وهو عبدالله قبازرد. وتصل مساحة المشروع إلى ٣٦,٠٠٠
متر مربع، وتضم مكاتب وساحات انتظار سيارات سفلية استنادا
إلى شبكة مكونة من ٥ × ٥ م، وهي شبكة من الأعمدة الخرسانة
والجدران المسبقة التجهيز. كما أن السلم وأبراج التهوية الخارجية
هي كذلك جزء من النظام السابق التجهيز، وهو نظام شائع
الاستخدام في يوغوسلافيا السابقة، وقد تم تطبيق الأسلوب ذاته
فيما بعد في عدد من مباني الكويت.

ويضم مجمع الوزارات ١٨ مبنى يصل ارتفاع كل منها إلى أربع طوابق
تعلو ساحة انتظار سفلية من طابقين, بنيت وكلها حول صالة
دخول مركزية غير مسقوفة. ويغطي العنصر الرئيسي بالمبنى
هيكل خفيف الوزن, تتخلله عناصر أخرى كنوافير المياه (٥٨) التي
تكسوها بلاطات بأشكال زخرفية تم اقتباسها من مشروع ريما
باتيلا الخاص لتوسعة قصر السيف (١٩٧٣ – ١٩٨٣).

مركز راديو وتلفزيون الكويت
المرقاب، ١٩٦٨-١٩٧٨

المصمم • مكتب دراسات كوردوبيه (قيادة) ,
جاك سوتور (معماري للاتصالات) , جي ميلكور (التخطيط)
العميل • وزارة الأشغال العامة
المقاول • مجموعة بالاست نيدم NV , شركة الهاني للتجارة
والمقاولات
(البناء مستخدم)

يعود أول بث تلفزيوني إلى العام ١٩٦١، وفي ذلك الوقت كانت الكويت
من بين الدول القليلة بالخليج التي لديها برنامج تلفزيون حكومي.
وقد صدر بعد ذلك، وتحديداً في العام ١٩٧٦، مرسوم أميري بإنشاء
هيئة أوسع تضم الراديو والتلفزيون، وهي وزارة الإعلام. وقد أدى
ذلك إلى إقامة مجمع جديد ليضم التخصصات التقنية المتعددة
والتي تتصل بعملية الإنتاج والبث. وقد تم تطوير ذلك تحت إشراف
مكتب الراديو والتلفزيون الفرنسي ORTF، ولعل المكتب هو الذي
اقترح فريق التصميم الفرنسي للمجمع. (٢٩)

وقد تركز المفهوم المبدئي على برامج عالية الفعالية، وذلك من
خلال تجميع الوظائف حول مركز رئيسي مع برج اتصالات. وتقع
منطقة الانتاج، في هذا المشروع المركزي، حول اللاقط الهوائي
اللاسلكي، بما يسمح بوجود مساحة كافية في أطراف المبنى
تسمح بالتوسع المستقبلي. وما أن تم تحديد أماكن ونسب
كل مكان، حتى تم إنشاء المجمع وفق مفهوم الأبعاد الثلاثية
الذي يضفي نوعاً من الوحدة على المجمع، كما أن ذلك قد يشير
إلى بعض الملامح الإقليمية. وهذا الديكور البسيط حول الكتل
الوظيفية يتمثل في عدد متكرر من العناصر الرأسية النحيلة
سابقة التجهيز تصل إلى ذروتها في شكل مجسم ثماني الأسطح.
ويشكل الفضاء السالب حول تلك الأسطح أقواس مدببة. وقد
اقترح سوتور فيما بعد نفس نظام الواجهة في مشروعات أخرى
بالكويت مثل محطة المترو التي لم يتم بناءها على سبيل المثال.

معهد الكويت للبحث العلمي KISR
ميناء الشويخ، ١٩٧٩-١٩٨٣

المصمم • PACE , TAC ,
اروب كويت المحدودة (أوف اريب وشركاهم)
العميل • معهد الكويت للبحث العلمي
المقاول • شركة الاحمدية للتجارة والمقاولات
(تم تعديل التصميم)

تم تكليف PACE بإقامة مجمع المعهد الجديد والذي يقع على
مساحة ٢٢ هكتاراً على ساحل البحر. وقد كان التصميم على
شكل حرف U لمبنى يضم ثلاثة طوابق منفتح على مدخل
للسيارات، بما يسمح بوصول آمن إلى الباب الرئيسي. وتقع المعامل
في الطابق الأرضي وكذلك المكتبة والكافيتريا والمطعم، وهو ما
يفضي إلى حديقة تمتد بطول جناحي المبنى، وتقع خلف المدخل
قاعة محاضرات تسع لـ ٢٥٠ شخصاً، وهي تواجه البحر. أما مكاتب
الباحثين فتقع في الطابق الثاني، على حين تقع المكاتب الإدارية في
الطابق الثالث، وهي كلها متصلة بالحديقة من خلال سلم خرساني
يحدد ارتفاع كل جناح من جناحي المبنى.

وكافة أسطح المبنى الخارجية من الاسمنت المسلح الأبيض
مع لمسة من الحجر الرملي، وكان من المزمع كذلك إقامة
بحيرة أبحاث اصطناعية مع مقار لسكن الباحثين(٦٥). ولما كان
المشروع قد نفذ بناؤه على مراحل ثلاث، فإنه خضع
لتوسعة في العام ١٩٨٩ مع إضافة معامل زراعة الأنسجة الخاصة
بالنخيل وهي المعامل التي صممتها PACE.

يضم المبنى الضخم ثمانية طوابق وهو مبني من الجرانيت، ويرتكز على منصة مكونة من ثلاثة طوابق، تضم سوق أسهم كبير مفتوح، وهناك ساحة مرتفعة بها حديقة داخلية وعناصر مائية، تحدها مجموعة من المكاتب على شكل حرف L، بما يوفر مساحة تتم فيها مزاولة باقي الأنشطة الوظيفية.

وتطل واجهة المكاتب في الطوابق الوسطى على الحديقة الداخلية مما يحميها من التعرض للشمس. أما الطابقين العلويين فقد تم تصميمهما ليضما المكاتب التنفيذية والمكاتب الرئيسة. وهما يغطيان المكان برمته بمظلة مركزية على مستوى السطح. وقد تم تصميم المبنى على شكل شبكات كل منها عبارة عن ١٥ م × ١٥ م بمساحة اجمالية قدرها ٣٤,... متر مربع تقع فوق مكان انتظار للسيارات أسفل المبنى.

السفارة الإيرانية
الحي الدبلوماسي بالدعية، ١٩٧٧-١٩٧٩

المصمم • مايكل كاريتيان وشركاه (معماري)، شارل حداد وشركاه (شريك محلي)، جوليان بلادس (المهندسون الانشائيون) سام جامبل وشركاه (معماري)، مكس فورده وشركاه (خدمات البناء)

العميل • وزارة الخارجية الإيرانية

(البناء لم يتم)

عندما أصبح هذا المشروع جاهزا للبناء، قامت الثورة الإسلامية في إيران بإعاقة التنفيذ. وقد تم بناء المشروع في نهاية المطاف لكن التصميم المبدئي لم يتم تنفيذه على نحو كامل على الاطلاق، باستثناء الهيكل الرئيسي والإيوان الكبير ذي الأعمدة. وقد أعد المعماري مايكل كاريتيان، وهو مصور معروف كذلك، العطاء التنافسي للمشروع بالتعاون مع المهندس المعماري والناقد روجر كونا. وفي العام التالي أسند المشروع لهما، وكان لهما آنذاك مكتبين أحدهما في لندن والآخر في طهران. (٤٣)

وعلى الرغم من ما فرضه الموقع، ووجود القيود الهندسية، والاعتماد على مدخل واحد فضلاً عن القيود المفروضة على الحد الأقصى للارتفاع، فإن بنود المنافسة أوصت بتجزئة المبنى إلى عدة شرائح رأسية انسيابية على شكل حرف T مزدوج مع اللجوء إلى عوارض على شكل حرف V للسماح بمرور الضوء. وفي ذلك نجد تشابهاً مع المشروع الذي اقترحته ريما بيتيلا بشأن "دراسة الصورة الحضرية للمدنية القديمة " (١٩٦٩).

المسرح الوطني الكويتي
قبلة ، ١٩٧٧ - ١٩٨٠

المصمم • BBRR (المدير لودي بلجيويسو)، INCO (فسنوسكي، بوجدا نوفيتش، المصممين المعتمدين)، دانيز لادسون وشركاه

العميل • وزارة الأشغال العامة

(لم يتم البناء)

تم التفكير في إقامة المسرح الوطني استكمالاً لمجموعة المباني الحكومية التي تواجه شارع الخليج، على الطرف المقابل لقصر السيف، إلى جانب مجلس الأمة، والمتحف الوطني. وقد تم طرح منافسة دوليه في أواخر السبعينيات بغرض إقامة قاعة تسع لـ ٢... شخص، فضلاً عن مناطق ترفيهية، لكن هذا المشروع لم يتسن انجازه على الإطلاق. وكان لكل مشروع من المشاريع المقدمة منهجاً مختلفاً، كما أن النتائج كذلك كانت بالغة الاختلاف. لقد ركز المشروع الذي طرحته شركة BBPR على الجانب الوظيفي، كما أن الشركة تولت إجراء التصميم بالتعاون مع مسرح لاسكالا في ميلانو وذلك بالنسبة لتصميم المشاهد المسرحية، وبالتعاون مع مسرح ألبري (السابق) بلندن, فيما يتعلق بالنواحي الميكانيكية المتصلة بخشبة المسرح والإضاءة. أما شركة INCO ومجموعة المصممين البولنديين فقد ركزوا على الشكل، فكان اقتراح بإقامة عنصر من عناصر النحت، كروي الشكل, يتألف من أربعة جوانب, متعدد الأقطار. و يشتمل كل ربع من هذه الأرباع على مجموعة من المباني الهرمية التي تؤدي وظائف مختلفة، بما في ذلك قاعتين للاستماع وعدد من الدهاليز ذات التصميم الرأسي, والأبهاء. أما العطاء الثالث فقد اقترحه لادسون، وهو عبارة عن قاعدة عملاقة عليها شكل تاج يحيط بعدد من المباني الأصغر حجماً. ولا يرتفع فوق القاعدة سوى برج معلق. ولا يدخل هذا المشروع في التفاصيل، ولكنه ليس من العسير علينا أن نتخيل أن مثل هذا المشروع من الخرسانة الجرداء كان سوف يبدو على غرار ما قام به المهندس المعماري بروتاليست من قبل في تصميم مبنى المسرح الوطني الملكي في ساوث بانك, في لندن.

دار الصباح
المهبولة، ١٩٧٨-١٩٨٤

المصمم • حسن فتحي

العميل • خاص

(البناء مستخدم)

هذا القصر الكبير الذي يعد أحد أواخر أعمال المهندس حسن فتحي يضم كافة السمات التقليدية لتصميماته المعمارية: الحوائط اللبنية الضخمة التي تشتمل على فتحات صغيرة يمكن التحكم بها، والكوات والقباب، وأبراج الرياح (البادگير أو الملقف)، وأنظمة التبريد، والعرائش والمشربيات. ما يميز المبنى هو الإلمام الكامل بالعلاقة بين الفضاء العام والفضاء الخاص في مجال المعمار المحلي. وذلك أمر واضح للعيان إن قارناه بغيره من الملامح. كما أن التحول في الحجم بين الفضاء العام والخاص محدد بوضوح، وهو ما يشكل في نهاية المطاف هيكلاً من محورين متعامدين. وهذا المبنى يشبه الخان المعزول، فلا يوجد به سوى عدد محدود للغاية من الفتحات التي تسمح بالوصول إلى السور الخارجي. أما الفناء الداخلي، فإنه ثرى بالشرفات والفضاءات المشرعة. ويحمل التصميم بصمات الخطة الأصلية التي تتمحور حول ثلاث باحات مربعة الشكل، وإن كانت مختلفة الحجم على حسب قربها من المنطقة العامة المتاحة للجمهور. والفضاءات سواء منها العام أو الخاص تتصل بأروقة تطل على الحدائق، كما أنها تحمي الغرف الداخلية من سعير الشمس. وتحدد الأقواس شبه المستديرة النسب المختلفة للتصميم.

مجمع مساكن الصوابر
شرق، ١٩٧٧ - ١٩٨٩

المصمم • أرثر اريكسون وشركاه

العميل • الهيئة الوطنية للإسكان

المقاول • مجهول

(تم بناء جزء / مهدد بالهدم)

كان " الفوز في لعبة أرقام " (٩) الإسكان هو الدافع الرئيسي لوزارة الإسكان (١٠) من إقامة هذا المشروع. وقد فاز مقاول من سنغافورة – كوريا بتصميم وبناء المشروع وذلك بعد الاطلاع على عدد من التقارير المبدئية. وقد تم بناء ٥٠ وحدة سكنية من بين ٩٠٠ وحدة , التي كان من المزمع بناؤها(١١١)

وقد تم تقسيم الموقع الذي يتكون من ٢٤.٥ هكتاراً في بادئ الأمر إلى تسعة أبنية، يصل متوسط مساحة الشقة السكنية بها إلى ٢٩٥ م٢. وقد تم توزيع تلك الوحدات على شكل سلاسل بحيث يتكون كل مبنى من كتل سكنية متلاصقة، ترتفع إلى ثمانية طوابق ذات شرفات، وتمتد من الشرق إلى الغرب، مما يؤدي إلى تكوين ممرات مظللة من المناطق العامة التي تتصل ببعضها البعض، من خلال هيكل مرتفع للمشاة يمكن الوصول اليه أحيانا عن طريق السيارة.

ويصف آرثر اريكسون، وهو الذي تولى التصميم، هذا المشروع كما يلي: "إنه تصميم إبداعي يسهم في إيجاد حل لمشكلة إسكان المواطنين الكويتيين، متوسطي الدخل، عن طريق جذبهم من جديد للمركز الحضري".

مجمع المثنى
شارع فهد السالم، ١٩٧٩ - ١٩٨٥

المصمم • KEO

العميل • بيت التمويل الكويتي (KFH)

المقاول • شركة الهاني للتجارة والمقاولات

(البناء مستخدم)

مع فشل عدد من مشاريع الاسكان متعددة الطوابق المملوكة للدولة مثل مشروع الصوابر، تم تحويل الوحدات السكنية التي كانت هيئة الإسكان الوطنية تزمع اقامتها خلال السبعينات، لتصبح مشاريع إسكان خاص مدعم، وقد اضطلع المستثمرون الذين كانوا يحصلون على دعم من الدولة، كبيت التمويل الكويتي (١٩٧٩) بتطوير تلك المشاريع على أرض مملوكة للدولة.

وهذا المجمع الذي تصل مساحته لما يناهز ١٥٠,... متر مربع، كان من المشاريع الرائدة التي عملت على جذب السوق المحلي نحو شراء عقارات خاصة. وقد استلهم هذا المشروع فكرته من مشروع الاسكان الكبير بميلانو والذي يعرف باسم مشروع ديو. وقد حظيت الحملة الإعلانية المحلية لترويج المشروع بإقبال واسع.

وتشتمل الوحدات السكنية السبع بالمجمع على ٧٢٠ وحدة، فضلا فندق يرتكز على منصة تجارية تضم مجمع تسوق داخلي ومجموعة من المحال التجارية بمستوى الشارع. وهذا الطابق الدائري من المحال التجارية يحل مشكلة المداخل. كما يمكن من خلاله الوصول إلى الأبراج السكنية، ومحال التسوق. وكذلك ساحة انتظار السيارات. وقد تم بناء ممر مكيف. كما أن الأماكن المتاحة للجمهور بالمبنى قد تم تصميمها على ضوء خطة تنظيم الشوارع الرئيسية التي وضعت عام ١٩٦. (٤١) و قد أتيحت فرصة إقامة مقطع منحني الشكل يستند إلى دعامة تماثل الكأس، وذلك من خلال استغلال المداخل والمخارج المنحدرة لموقف السيارات.

مجمع الأوقاف التجاري
المرقاب، ١٩٧٨ - ١٩٨٢

المصمم • عبدالرؤوف وأحمد مشهور

العميل • وزارة الأوقاف

المقاول • مجهول

(تم تعديل التصميم)

اضطلعت وزارة الأوقاف بمهمة إقامة مساكن مدعمة للمواطنين. وقد تم في هذا الاطار اقتراح اقامة مجمع يمول فيه المركز التجاري الجزء السكني من المجمع.

وقد قام مهندس معماري مصري وهو ابن احد المهندسين المعماريين الذين اضطلعوا بتطوير المدنية في بواكير عهدها، قام بتطوير مشروع طويل الشكل يستند إلى أعمدة وهو التصور الذي أدى إلى تنفيذ مقترح BBPR المقدم في العام ١٩٦٩، الخاص بـ " الدراسة الحضرية للمدنية القديمة ".

ويتيح المشروع السكني طراز معماري يسمح بتظليل المبنى بواسطة شرفات متجهة إلى الداخل، في الواجهة الغربية من المبنى. وقد قارن ستيفان جاردينز هذا المشروع بالمشاريع المناظرة له في بولونيا وبادوا (٥٥).

يتكون الجزء التجاري السفلي بالمبنى من ثلاثة طوابق، تضم مكاتب، فضلا عن ساحة انتظار سيارات بالطابق السفلي. ويتخلل صف المحلات، الذي يشبه السوق مساحتين داخلتين بكل منهما منور، تصلحان تستخدما للمطاعم وللترفيه. أما الست أبراج للمبنى فإنها تتفاوت بين مباني يصل ارتفاعها إلى خمسة طوابق، وأخرى يصل ارتفاعها إلى عشرة طوابق. لكن هذه الأبراج لم تكن في أي وقت من الأوقات محلا للسكن كما كان مقررا في الخطة الأصلية. وتم تحويلها إلى مكاتب في وقت لاحق. وقد تعرض المبنى لتلف بالغ إبان فترة اجتياح الكويت، وبعد التحرير تم تغطية الجزء الخارجي للمبنى وكان من الحجر الجيري الأبيض المعرق، بألواح الالومنيوم الرمادي اللون.

الواجهة البحرية
شعب - سالمية، ١٩٧٨ - ١٩٨٨

المصمم • سيساكي وشركاه (رئاسة الاستشاريين) ، غازي سلطان (معماري)، KEO (استشارات مشتركة) ، جيوتكنكل للهندسة المحدودة، نوميدو المتحدة المحدودة (علوم المحيطات والترسيب)، معهد البحث والتخطيط (البنية البحرية) جوزيف، دبلو ستختطور (المناطر الطبيعية) ، شارلز إف بروول (الترفية)

العميل • صاحب السمو أمير البلاد

المقاول • اعان ملوتنفتش - بم (الاعمال البحرية)، ومشاركين اخرين

(البناء مستخدم)

فاز فريق ساسكس وشركاه تحت قيادة المهندس المعماري الكويتي غازي سلطان في العام ١٩٧٥-٧٦ للتصميم بالمركز الأول في المنافسة التي جرت لتصميم الواجهة المائية. على خمس شركات انترناشيونال للتصميم.

وقد تم تنفيذ هذا المشروع الطموح في نهاية المطاف في العام ١٩٧٨. وقد استهدفت الخطة الرئيسية للمشروع استصلاح المنطقة المطلة على شاطئ البحر ليستفيد من ذلك سكان المدينة، بعد أن أعاق تشييد طريق سريع رؤية الشاطئ. وتتألف الواجهة البحرية من شريط متصل بطول ٢١ كيلومترا يمتد من رأس السالمية حتى الشويخ. وقد تم تقسيم الشريط إلى ١٢ منطقة وهي في مجملها تحدد " مناطق الاستخدام الرئيسية بالمشروع (١٦).

الموجودة بالفعل في رسم خط الأفق الذي يحدد شكل المدينة، كما أنه كان رمزاً للوحدة الوطنية، والميلاد الجديد للبلاد بعد الاحتياج العراقي في العام ١٩٩٠.

وكانت بداية المشروع في الثمانينيات حيث استهدف تقوية طاقة شبكة الاتصالات والتي تم بناؤها في العام ١٩٦٨، وقد بدأ العمل بالمشروع في العام ١٩٨٢، لكنه توقف بعد ذلك بثلاث سنوات ليتم استكماله بعد التحرير [٢٧].

ويشتمل المجمع على المكاتب العامة، وعلى مبنيين رئيسيين وبرج هوائي لاسلكي، وعبارة عن شكل يشبه الإبرة الرشيقة التي تدعم هيكل على شكل صحن استقبال فضائي (مركز الزوار ومطعم) بالإضافة إلى اسطوانة معدنية (الرأس التقنية). والهيكل عبارة عن بناء من الخرسانة المسلحة، يوجد على قمته صاري من الصلب المقوى، تم اختياره بهدف الوصول إلى الحد الأمثل لمقاومة الريح، وتحيط بلاطات من السيراميك بالأضلع الخرسانية، عليها تصميمات تأخذ أشكال المعينات، وتتخللها المصاعد الزجاجية ومركز الزوار.

وقد أطلق على برج الهوائي اللاسلكي اسم برج التحرير عند الافتتاح الرسمي الذي صادف الذكرى الخامسة لنهاية الحرب.

وزارة الاتصالات والبرج التابع لها
الشويخ، كيفان، ١٩٨١

المصمم • INCO
العميل • وزارة النقل والمواصلات
المقاول • لكثرم. بولاند
(البناء مستخدم)

هناك علاقة وطيدة بين هذا المجمع وبرج التحرير الحالي (الذي كان يعرف سابقاً باسم مركز الاتصالات والهوائي)، وتأتى هذه العلاقة من خلال الوظائف و الطبوغرافية الخاصة بكل من المبنيين. وقد تم استلهام بعض العناصر عند بناء برج الاتصالات. يقع المبنى في كيفان ويعد نموذجاً لذات الطراز المعماري الذي تكرر لاحقاً في حولي، والسالمية والجهراء. وتشترك كل تلك المباني في طبيعة مواد البناء والصورة الصلبة الراسخة التي توحي بها. وتم بناء الأبراج من الحجر الجيري المدعم بعناصر خرسانية، ولذا فإن الأبراج تتسم بأنها صلبة ومتعددة الطبقات، فضلا عن أنها تتناغم مع البيئة الحضرية التي تقع بها.

وقد أتى كل من INCO و KEG و UNETEC على ذكر المشروع على أنه جزء من إسهامها في أوائل الثمانينات، ومع ذلك فإن بصمات المجموعة البولندية هي ما نراه واضحاً على تلك الأبراج. وكانت هذه المجموعة قد عملت مع ثلاثة مكاتب معمارية بالبلاد إبان تلك السنوات. كما أن ستوجان مكسيموفيتش، الذي صمم قاعة مؤتمرات قصر بيان، يشير كذلك إلي إسهامه في التصميم ضمن مبنى بريد الكويت، الذي مازال يمارس وظيفته أسفل البرج، مواجهاً طريق المطار، وهو ما يؤدي إلى الحفاظ على شكل معماري وظيفي متميز.

مؤسسة الكويت للتقدم العلمي
شرق، ١٩٨٢-١٩٨٦

المصمم • TAC (معماري)، PACE (مساهم في المعمار)، مجموعة Arup الاستشارية (اوفا ارب وشركاه)
العميل • مؤسسة الكويت للتقدم العلمي (KFAS)
المقاول • شركة الاحمدية للتجارة والمقاولات
(البناء مستخدم)

تم تأسيس مؤسسة الكويت للتقدم العلمي بمرسوم أميري صدر في العام ١٩٧٦، بهدف تعزيز البحث العلمي بالكويت والخارج. وتنتمي المؤسسة بمساهمة طويلة الأمد من الشركات المساهمة الكويتية. وبعد سنوات قليلة من بدء عمل المؤسسة، أعلنت عن فتح باب الاستشارات لتصميم مقرها الرئيسي. وقد شارك في ذلك عدد من الشركات الاستشارية مثل TAC و آرثر اريكسون وغير ذلك من الشركات المعمارية [٢٤]. ويحتل الموقع مكانا متميزا على شارع أحمد الجابر، وهو محور لعدد من أعمال التطوير التي تمت في العام ١٩٧٠ على أراضي متاحة للبناء. والواقع أن هذه المنطقة كانت مخصصة حتى العام ١٩٧٧ لإقامة جامعة وهو ما كان سيمثل من الناحية الوظيفية، علاقة وثيقة الصلة بمهمة المؤسسة. لكن الخطة المبدئية تم تعديلها بغرض إقامة منطقة تجارية وسكنية تعج بالحركة [٢٥].

مسجد الشيخ ناصر الصباح
رأس السالمية، ١٩٨٠ - ١٩٨١

المصمم • جنكو، مكتب المعماري هنري منتوا (معماري).
KEG (خدمات البناء)
العميل • شركة مشاريع الكويت KSCC
المقاول • مجهول
(البناء مستخدم)

شيد المسجد بتكليف من الشيخ ناصر الصباح الذي وهبه لسكان المنطقة القريبة من قصره المجاور. ويتألف المبنى من كتلتين متميزتين عن بعضهما البعض: أولاهما مكان الصلاة، وهو على هيئة هرم متدرج، أما الكتلة الثانية، فيضم مدخل الوضوء، ومكتبة ومركز للبحوث الإسلامية، فضلا عن مكتب إمام المسجد. ويؤلف بين المكانين محور رأسي لمنارة طويلة.

والنمط الأفقي للهرم المبني من ألياف زجاجية مدعمة بطبقات من الخرسانة يبدو من بعد على أنه يتناقض، وبشكل متعمد، مع إيقاع الحجر الجيري الذي يشبه الزعانف، والذي يسلط الضوء أكثر على مكان المدخل. ويتمحور المشروع كله حول فكرة الضوء، وطريقة التحكم فيه. وتعمل عناصر البناء الأفقية والرأسية المتكررة والتي تشبه الحقول الغناء، دوراً بارزاً في التخفيف من حدة الشمس. ويتكون باطن البناء الهرمي من كسوة زجاجية ملونة متناغمة مع الطبقة الخارجية للمبنى على نحو يسمح بالتحكم في الضوء. ويلعب التصميم الهيكلي دوراً مهما في تحديد مكان قاعة الصلاة. ويشتمل الهيكل الهرمي على أربع حزم مجوفة كبيرة تتصل بمنصة تدعم قبة المسجد. وتؤدي الحزم المجوفة دور المداخن، في حين تقع أماكن تبريد الهواء أعلى الحوائط المقوسة. [٨]

توسعة وتجديد حديقة الحيوان بالكويت
العمرية، ١٩٨١-١٩٨٢

المصمم • جون اس بونتجتون وشركاه (معماري)، KEO (مساهم في المعمار). مايكل باركلاي وشركاه (الهندسة الانشائية)، مارو راومستركتور GbmH (صمم اطار المكان)
العميل • وزارة الأشغال العامة، قسم المشاريع الرئيسية
(البناء لم يتم)

كان الهدف من إقامة المبنى الرئيسي لحديقة الحيوان، وهو يشابه المشروع السابق بمنطقة الدوحة (٥٩) يتمثل في اقامة كتلة واحدة مدعمة بالخرسانة، ومن الداخل يشتمل المبنى على منطقتين إحداهما مستوطنة سافانا والأخرى مكرسة للأهوار والشاطئ. و تحدد الحديقة المركزية بينهما تجربة وصول الجمهور، و قد تم تنظيمها لتقديم عدد من الخدمات، كما تضم عددا من المراكز لنباتات القارات المختلفة وللحياة الليلة فضلا عن النباتات الاستوائية. وتحيط بالمنطقة المركزية بحيرتين اصطناعيتين كبيرتين، تضم إحداهما كافتيريا عائمة تعلوها مظلة خشبية، وتطل هذه البحيرة على أماكن التماسيح والفهود أما البحيرة المقابلة فإنها تطل على القرود والأورانج أوتان والبابون وغيرها من أصناف القرود.

وقد صممت شركة ألمانية إطارا فوق المستوى الأعلى للمكان، مزود بشكلين من أشكال المظلات، إحداهما من الخشب حول القطر، أما الثانية فهي عبارة عن أشرعة تم تطويرها من مادة زجاجية خضراء، وفي إطار هذه المشروع رسمت حدود المكان بمنتزه سفاري للأسود والنمور والجاموس والزراف وغير ذلك من أشكال الحياة البرية.

مركز الاتصالات وبرج الهوائي اللاسلكي
المرقاب، ١٩٨١ - ١٩٩٥

المصمم • شركة الكترو واط للخدمات الهندسية المحدودة (رئاسة المصممين)، UNETEC (تعاون محلي)
العميل • وزارة الأشغال العامة
المقاولون • مجموعة المقاولون الدوليون (مساندة من شركة الاحمدية للتجارة والمقاولات). Sogea France، شركة موستوستال زبجا (الحدادة)
(البناء مستخدم)

عندما تم بناء برج الهوائي اللاسلكي في العام ١٩٩٥ بارتفاع ٣٧٢ متراً، لم يقتصر الأمر على مواجهة بعض أهم التحديات التقنية العامة في البلاد، لكنه دخل كذلك في منافسة مع الأبراج

الزجاجية ويدعمها. ويلاحظ أن زجاج المبنى ملون، كما أن الدعامات المعدنية مصنوعة من الألمونيوم المطلي بالبرونز المؤكسد، في تناقض واضح مع اللون اللامع لهيكل المبنى.

مركز المؤتمرات
بيان، ١٩٨٠-١٩٨٦

المصمم • ستويان ماكسيموفيتش (مؤسسة مركز سافا، معماري). اركيسنتر (مساهم في المعمار | PACE, KEO,SSH (مؤسسة المعمار من ١٩٨٣)
العميل • وزارة الأشغال العامة
المقاول • شركة الحمدية للتجارة والمقاولات
(تم تعديل التصميم)

تم إجراء منافسة دولية في أوائل الثمانينيات بهدف إقامة مركز الكويت للمؤتمرات، وكان الهدف تزويد البلاد بمركز رئيسي للاجتماعات تحيط به حديقة غناء. وقد افتتح سمو أمير البلاد المبنى في العام ١٩٨٦، وبعد الافتتاح بفترة وجيزة استضاف المركز مؤتمر القمة الإسلامي الخامس. وفي قاعات هذا المركز تم توقيع الاتفاقية الخاصة بمحكمة العدل الإسلامية الدولية، وذلك بهدف تسوية المنازعات التي قد تنشأ بين الدول الإسلامية وفقا لأحكام الشريعة.

وقد فاز بالمركز الأول فريق تصميم مؤسسة مركز سافا في المسابقة وتعاون مركز سافا في الكويت بعد ذلك مع اركيسنتر، لكنه تم تأجيل العمل في المشروع، كما أن المهندس المعماري الصربي لم يلتزم بخطة المشروع. وقد تم تنفيذ المشروع بعد عدة أعوام وتولى ذلك ثلاث شركات محلية، ولذا فإن مقدار ما تم ترجمته من المشروع الأصلي على أرض الواقع ليس معروفا. [٣٦]

يتمحور المشروع في شكله النهائي حول قاعدة مربعة تضم قاعة إجتماعات تسع لـ ٢٠٠٠ شخص، فضلا عن ست قاعات جانبية أخرى. ويطل ظهر المبنى الرئيسي على حديقة، ذات تنسيق هندسي وممرات ظليلة بين صفوف من الأشجار ونوافير للمياه. وحول المتنزه توجد ستة مباني على شكل حرف U وهي مباني مخصصة لرؤساء الحكومات والدول الزائرين، وللوفود الرسمية. كما أن هناك مسجداً وساحة تسلية ومازال المركز يستخدم إلى يومنا هذا، حيث يستضيف العديد من الأحداث والقمم السياسية الدولية.

مشروع فندق انتركونتنتال
السالمية، ١٩٨٠

المصمم • ألفرد روث (معماري).
الاستشاريون العرب (مساهم في الاستشارات)
العميل • شركة المسباح للصناعة والتجارة
(لم يتم البناء)

في أوائل الثمانينيات قام رجل الأعمال والمطور خالد الحسا بتكليف ألفرد روث بإقامة فندق يشتمل على مركز للتسوق، ومرآب للسيارات. وكان الاثنان على معرفة بعضهما البعض منذ أن كان الحسا وزيراً للأشغال العاملة في الفترة من ١٩٦٥ إلى ١٩٧١، وهي الفترة ذاتها التي تولى فيها روث إقامة مجموعة من المدارس بالبلاد. وكان من المفترض أن يتم إقامة الفندق على الواجهة البحرية بالسالمية، وهي منطقة كانت النية تتجه لتحويلها سريعاً إلى منطقة تعج بالنشاط التجاري. وكان الاستقبال والأماكن العامة والتجارية تقع كلها في الطابق الأرضي، على مسطح مربع الشكل. وفوق ذلك المسطح كانت الغرف تتوزع على نحو مبعثر. وكان الهدف من ذلك أن يكون لكل غرفة من غرف الفندق وعددها ٢٢٠ غرفة نفس الرؤية البحرية، كما أنها جميعاً تقع في الناحية الشمالية، بما يسمح بتحكم أفضل في درجة الحرارة. وقد اكتمل المشروع، وتم تقديمه للبلدية للموافقة عليه. إلا أنه لم ينفذ مطلقاً. ومع ذلك فقد نشر روث بيانات المشروع، على أنه من أحدث الأعمال التي أنجزها خلال العام ١٩٨٣[٣٥].

عينة رقم ٤
مباني كمعايير وظيفية:
١٩٨٠-١٩٨٩

البنك التجاري الكويتي، مركز عمليات
شرق، ١٩٧٩ - ١٩٨٤

المصمم • SOM (معماري)، PACE (التعاون الاستشاري)
العميل • البنك التجاري الكويتي
المقاول • مجهول
(البناء مستخدم)

تم إسناد تنفيذ البنك التجاري الكويتي إلى دار التصميم SOM، كمرجعية لتصميم المجموعات المصرفية في أواخر السبعينيات. وقد تمثل الطلب المبدئي للعميل في إقامة مقر رئيسي جديد للبنك. وبناء على ذلك فقد تم طرح ثلاثة مقترحات، وان لم يتم تنفيذ أي منها. كما أن طلب العميل تحول لاحقاً من تصميم مقر رئيسي إلى تصميم مركز للعمليات (٦). وعلى الرغم من تقليص حجم البرنامج المبدئي، فإن المبنى انطوى على تصميم مثيرة للاهتمام، فالمساحة التي تستخدم للعمليات والوظائف المختلفة في البنك تتخذ شكل "صندوق صخري شفاف" (٧)، وتتم حماية النواة الداخلية المكونة من مباني زجاجية من خلال طبقة ثانية منفصلة تتألف من طبقة مكسوة بالطابوق تعمل على تظليل المباني، ولذا فان الواجهة تبدو وكأنها شبكة من الأشكال الهندسية التجريدية. ويحاط المبنى بشبكة مربعة الشكل ذات كثافة تتباين بتباين المستويات المختلفة للمبنى.

ويتناسب كل عنصر من عناصر المبنى مع باقي العناصر، كما أن هناك انتظام رتيب يظهر للعيان من خلال الفسيفساء الإحدائي للمبنى. وتساعد المسافة بين طبقتي المبنى في كسر حالة الرتابة أو الانتظام في التصميم، وذلك من خلال النمط المتغير الذي تخلقه الظلال. وقد طرحت دار SOM فكرة إقامة الواجهة ذاتها في مجمع أحمد الجابر التجاري الذي كان مزمعاً إقامته على الجانب المقابل من الطريق (١٩٨٢) وإن كان ذلك المشروع لم يتسن تشييده.

المقر الرئيسي لمجمع الغانم الصناعي
الشويخ، ١٩٧٨-١٩٨٠

المصمم • بركين وويل (معماري)، KEO (تعاون معماري)
العميل • شركة الغانم للصناعات
المقاول • مجهول
(البناء مستخدم)

تحدد الواجهة المتعرجة على طريق المطار شكل المبنى. تميل هذه الواجهة المنشورية صوب الجنوب، كما أن بها إطار من الألمنيوم يحمل ألواحا من الزجاج، و يواجه الشمال. وقد تم تزويد المبنى بنظام حاسب آلي متطور للغاية وذلك منذ بناء المبنى في أوائل الثمانينات. ويضم المبنى مركز العمليات الصناعية بشركة الغانم فضلاً عن المكاتب الإدارية.

يتكون المبنى من كتلة واحدة مستطيلة، تضم طابقين عبارة عن سطح منفتح مع وجود حواجز داخلية دائرية، تقيد الوصول إلى الأماكن التي يحظر الدخول فيها، كما أنها تتقاطع مع الواجهة، وهي على شكل أوكرديون، مما يسمح بالوصول إلى صالات العرض وإلى المنطقة التي تضم المكاتب الإدارية.

يتميز نظام الواجهة بالإبداع، وتكسوها طبقة من الحجر الجيري المعرق الذي تم تثبيته على نحو ميكانيكي، بحيث يسمح بمرور الهواء، وعلى الجانب المواجه نرى واجهة زجاجية داكنة، بما يسمح بالمرور الأفقي للضوء إلى المكاتب، كما أن هناك منور يسمح بوصول الضوء إلى الطابق السفلي. أما العناصر الداخلية بالمبنى فتتسم بالعناية الفائقة بالتفاصيل، ومن أمثلة ذلك، تلك الأبواب الداخلية المرتفعة، والتقسيم المرن للمكان الذي يشي بقدر كبير من الدقة التي لا نراها كثيراً في مثل هذه المباني بالكويت.

مركز شركة النفط الكويتية KOC للحاسب الآلي والتدريب
مصفاة ميناء عبد الله، ١٩٧٩-١٩٨٣

المصمم • شركة تضامن من تزايب ووكهام مع شارلز تروفات حداد (CTHA)
شارك في العطاء التنافسي • جون اس بونتجتون وشركاه مع KEO
العميل • شركة النفط الكويتية
(تم تعديل التصميم)

يشار إلى هذا المجمع على أنه مبنى متكامل من المكاتب، وهو يضم أماكن للتدريب فضلا عن مركز للحاسب الآلي (٦٢). ويشير مقترح شارلز تروفات حداد CTHA إلى فكرة "طراز معماري للمباني الحديثة" كما يشير كذلك إلى استخدام "المواد المحلية" "كالأطر الخرسانية المسبقة التجهيز والحجر الجيري". ومساحة المبنى ٤٠ ألف متر مربع، وهو يقدم برامج تدريب لـ ٤٥٠ طالباً. كما أن هناك إمكانية للتوسع بما يسمح بتدريب ٥٠٠ طالب.

أما بالنسبة لمركز الحاسب الآلي، فان مشروع تشارلز تروفات حداد قد تم بالتعاون مع شركة تصميم موريسون، وهي شركة لها باع طويل في عدد من المشاريع المماثلة (٦٣). لكن ما تم بناؤه في نهاية المطاف هو ذلك المشروع الذي اقترحه جون اس بونتجتون. ويتألف هذا المشروع من منطقة حدودية تحتوي على مكاتب، تحددها حواجز قابلة للفك والتركيب، فضلا عن منطقة مركزية تتألف من مناطق مكاتب مفتوحة. ويعد هذا المشروع أكثر مرونة، كما أنه يتمحور حول غرفة الحاسب الآلي. وقد اقترح ابي.جي موريس استخدام فكرة السقف المعلق مع وجود طابق يرتفع تدريجياً وذلك بهدف الوصول إلى تصميم مكتبي فعال حديث (٦٤).

المقر الرئيسي للبنك الأهلي
ميدان الصفاة، ١٩٧٩ - ١٩٨٨

المصمم • سكيدرمور، أونجز، وميريل (معماري)، PACE (مساهم استشاري)
العميل • البنك الأهلي -- الكويت
المقاول • مجهول
(البناء مستخدم)

يعكس المشروع اختيار العميل من بين ثلاثة مشاريع مقترحة تم طرحها. ويتألف المقر الرئيسي الجديد للبنك الأهلي من ٢٠ طابقاً، ويقع في وسط مدينة الكويت ويواجه السوق القديم، ويكشف بعض التشابه في التصميم المعماري مع مركز البنك المجاور، وهو التصميم الذي اقترحه كذلك سكيدمور، أونجس وميريل. ويتكون المبنى من ثلاث كتل هندسية صلبة مغطاة بنفس النوع من الحجارة. ويأخذ البرج شكل المستطيل مع جوانب مستديرة. ويضم هيكلين رئيسيين على الجانبين الغربي والشرقي. وتكشف الجوانب الأخرى من المبنى عن لوحين زجاجيين كبيرين، أحدهما يشتمل على جهاز تظليل خاص من ناحية الجنوب لحماية المبنى من الشمس.

يأخذ المدخل الرئيسي على المستوى الأرضي شكل مثلث منشوري، أما من الناحية المقابلة، فإن الكتلة المستطيلة الثالثة تكشف عن واجهة مزدوجة مع فتحات مربعة الشكل بتظليل المدخل.

وهناك إضاءة طبيعية بصالة البنك من خلال مناور بالميزانين. وقد تم زخرفة الأماكن الداخلية للبنك من خلال استخدام تفاصيل برونزية مطلية بالذهب ومشغولة بعناية فائقة.

دوازة عبد الرزاق وميدان الصفاة
المباركية، ١٩٧٧ - ١٩٨٦

المصمم • دبغكون أركتكتر (معماري)، شركة دبغكون ايكونو (خدمات البناء)، INCO (مشاركة في البناء)
العميل • بلدية الكويت
المقاول • مجهول
(تم تعديل التصميم)

اضطلعت بلدية الكويت بعملية "تجميل" الأماكن العامة، وكانت البلدية مدفوعة في ذلك بتلك الخطط الحضرية المتتالية والتفصيلية، وكذلك بالتقارير التي رفعتها BBPR والتي تحدد طبيعة العلاقة بين قلب المدينة القديم والبنية التحتية الحديثة للمواصلات. وقد تمت دعوة عدد من الاستشاريين لتقديم مقترحاتهم فيما يتعلق بنقطتي عبور هامتين كانتا آنذاك تمثلان دورانين للمرور.

وقد فاز في مشروع نقطتي العبور شركتين من فنلندا. كان أول المشاريع يتصل إقامة ممر سفلي للدوارة في العام ١٩٧٩، وبعد ذلك بعامين تم إقامة المشروع الثاني الخاص بساحة في ميدان الصفاة مع نصب تذكاري، محاط بوحدات لتجارة التجزئة، مع رسوم جدارية للفنان جعفر إصلاح. وكان استخدام العناصر المعمارية الزخرفية من الملامح البارزة ولاسيما في الأسقف التي تقع أسفل الطرق.

وما أن تم الانتهاء من أولى تلك المشاريع، حتى تم تخفيض التكدس المروري عند تقاطع الطرق. كما أن ذلك أدى إلى زيادة رقعة المساحة العامة تحت الأرض عند قاعدة المركز المشترك للبنوك (١٩٧٦ ـ ١٩٨٣) وسوق الكويت (١٩٧٣ـ ١٩٧٦). ومازال هذا الممر السفلي يعد إلى اليوم همزة وصل رئيسية بين مشروع الصوابر الإسكاني الكبير وقلب المدينة القديم.

مركز العلاج الطبيعي والتأهيل
الصليبيخات، ١٩٧٩ - ١٩٨١

المصمم • IMOS (ستانكو كريستل، المسؤول)
العميل • وزارة الأشغال العامة
(لم يتم البناء)

تم إسناد تصميم هذا المبنى لشركة معمارية من سلوفينيا، وهي شركة متخصصة في المستشفيات. وكان من المزمع أن يسع المركز لـ ٨٠ مريضا مقيماً، فضلا عن عيادة خارجية، وأقسام للتشخيص، ومعمل وأقسام للأطراف الصناعية والجراحة التبديلية (٤٤). ومع انجاز المركز الطبي بجامعة لوبليانا، أصبح لدى هذه الشركة المعمارية فريق متخصص في "الهندسة المعمارية الطبية" (٤٥) وهو فريق تحت قيادة ستانكو كريستل. والواقع أنه يمكننا أن نجد التوجهات المعمارية لـ IMOS في الأعمال السابقة التي أنجزها كريستل.

ويعتمد مشروع الصليبيخات على الاستخدام الفعال للموقع، بحيث تصل مساحة المبنى إلى الحد الأقصى، الذي يتماشى مع مشروع مركزي عضوي، فيكون تنفيذ البرنامج الطبي المزمع هو ما يملي شكل ووظيفة المبنى.

وتتركز غرف المرضى الداخليين، والغرف الخاصة بالتدرب على المشي، في مبنيين مثمنين، كل منهما يتألف من أربعة طوابق، وأحد جوانب المبنى مكرس كنقطة وصول. أما الجانب المقابل فهو للسلالم، و باقي المبنى مخصص للغرف. وقد صمم باقي المبنى على مستويات متدرجة تطل على صالات كبيرة، تشغل الزوايا بين الممرات الطويلة. وفي ظل الظروف المادية والمكانية المتاحة، فانه يمكننا أن نرى نوعاً من التشابه بين هذا المشروع، وبين مستشفى ايزولا وهي المستشفى التي أنجزها المصمم ذاته في العام ١٩٨١، باستخدام فكرة الواجهات المتطابقة في تكسيتها، والمساحات المفتوحة في بناء حمامات للسباحة.

مقر شركة الملاحة العربية المتحدة
الشويخ، ١٩٨٠

المصمم • PACE (رئاسية الاستشاريين)
العميل • مقر شركة الملاحة العربية المتحدة UASC

تم تأسيس هذه الشركة في العام ١٩٧٦، وهي شركة مساهمة تضم دول الخليج الست، وتهدف إلى تقديم خدمات الملاحة التي تحتاجها المنطقة، وكانت الكويت مقرها الرئيسي. ويقع المبنى في منطقة صناعية، كما أنه يطل على شارع رئيسي يفضي إلى ميناء المدينة الرئيسي.

ويعد المبنى تنويعاً لفكرة الهرم المتدرج المعكوس (٢٢)، فهو على شكل مستطيل يتناقص تدريجياً عند المستوى الأدنى. ويتألف المبنى من خمسة طوابق مع غرفة آلات وخدمات على السطح، يحجبها عن العيان حائط مرتفع. ولعل ما يميز المبنى هو قلبه المركزي الرأسي المجوف الذي ينفذ منه الضوء من الأرض وحتى السطح. وهناك ثلاث دعامات أساسية في مركز كل جانب من جوانب المبنى، تعمل على التوزيع الرأسي ودور المساندة للأماكن الخدمية بما يؤدي إلى وجود مساحات للمكاتب في كل طابق. أما من الخارج، فهناك هيكل من الرخام يحيط بالمباني

وفي هذا السياق فقد استقر رأي TAC على القيام بتصميم يستند إلى كتلة مكعبة الشكل مع وجود عدد محدود للغاية من نقاط الاتصال بالبيئة المحيطة. ويبدو المبنى من الطريق الرئيسي وكأنه قلعة بنيت من الحجارة المخشنة، بأقل عدد ممكن من الفتحات التي تبدو كسلسلة من الكوات، إضافة إلى المدخل الرئيسي المقوس. أما الجانب المقابل فيكشف عن مفهوم أكثر تعقيداً للمكان، حيث نرى سوراً يحيط بالواجهة الشمالية، مما يتيح رؤية القلب المجوف الداخلي. ويشطر المكعب، بشكل عمودي، شق عميق بزاوية مقدارها 45 درجة، مما ينتج عنه مثلثين، ويضفي ذلك على التصميم نوعاً من الديناميكية. ويحدد هذا المحور العمودي التوزيع الرأسي للمبنى، فضلاً عن العناصر الهيكلية الرئيسية، كالمسند الخرساني. وهناك ثمانية طوابق من المكاتب تمتد بين (المسندين) الخرسانيين، بما يسمح بتخفيف حدة الضوء الآتي من الزجاج الشمالي ومن خلال الأسطح المعلقة. وفي مركز المبنى، يشير بندول ساعة معلق إلى البهو الرئيسي في الجانب السفلي، وهو ما يرمز إلى الهدف النهائي للمؤسسة المتمثل في المعرفة.

مركز مواصلات المرقاب
المرقاب، 1977 – 1984

المصمم • بركينز ووبلز (تخطيط).
W.S. Atkins مع SSH (معماري)
العميل • وزارة الأشغال العامة، وزارة التخطيط، بلدية الكويت
(لم يتم البناء)

تم اقتراح توسيع طريق المغرب السريع عبر المدينة في اطار دراسة الخطة الهيكلية «الخاصة بأنظمة المرور والمواصلات (31) وقد تم اقتراح ذلك، فضلاً عن شارع مبارك الكبير (شارع القاهرة) كحل لمشكلة تكدس المرور بهدف تخفيف الضغط المروري على الدوران مع السماح بزيادة اتساع رقعة الطرق في المنطقة بين الطريقين المذكورين.

وقد حددت خطة عمل منطقة المرقاب (32) إقامة مشروع مركز مواصلات ليكون نقطة التقاء لطرق المدينة. (33) ويقع المشروع خلف المقر الرئيسي للصندوق الكويتي KFAED (1974 ـ 1981). وهو عبارة عن كتلة ضخمة تتكون من تسعة طوابق مع مساحة انتظار تسمح بوجود ...5 سيارة بهدف تشجيع السائق على ترك سيارته عند أطراف مركز المدينة. و كان من المزمع إقامة نظام قطار كهربائي فوق السطح لنقل المشاة، بما يسمح لهم بالوصول إلى وسط المدينة. وفضلاً عن ذلك كان من المزمع إقامة ملاعب رياضية ونادي صحي، ومطاعم، وصالة بولنج، وصالة للأنشطة الثقافية ومعارض ومركز للمؤتمرات.

محطة باصات البلوش
شرق، 1986 – 1988

المصمم • INCO (كريستوف فشنوفسكي، أنجايه بوهداناوفيش، يان اوربانوفيتش)
العميل • شركة المواصلات العامة الكويتية KPTC
المقاول • شركة مساعد الصالح وأولاده
(البناء مستخدم)

تعاون فريق من المهندسين البولنديين مع شركة الاستشارات الهندسية التي أسسها محمد السنان في العام 1975 في إقامة هذه المحطة، وكان الفريق قد أقام ذلك المقر الرئيسي لهيئة الميناء (1984 – 1992).

وقد تم تأسيس شركة المواصلات العامة الكويتية في العام 1962 للاضطلاع بدورها في إطار خطة الأشغال العامة بالبلاد وذلك بعد أن تم إعداد الخطة الرئيسية الثانية. وبعد ازدياد ضغط البناء على منطقة شرق (44)، ومع إخفاق مشروع مركز مواصلات المرقاب، أصبحت هناك ضرورة لإقامة محطة للباصات قرب شارع أحمد الجابر، وقد تم لذلك إعداد عطاء تنافسي نتج عنه تصميم وبناء المحطة.

وعلى غرار مبنى مطار الكويت، فإنه تم تنظيم مكاتب المحطة وأماكن الخدمات المغلقة حول صالة المحطة المركزية، ومحيط تحميل الركاب المجاور لها. وهناك قوس يحيط بالعنصر الرئيسي بالمحطة وهو الذي يحدد واجهة المدخل الرئيسي والبيئة المكانية للصالة الرئيسية. ويكشف استخدام الالومنيوم الأسود والحجر الجيري في البناء عن مدى حجم المبنى وكتلته الهندسية المتميزة.

المقر الرئيسي لهيئة الميناء
الشويخ، 1984-1992

المصمم • INCO (كريستوف فشنوفسكي، أنجايه بوهداناوفيش، يان اوربانوفيتش)
شارك في العطاء التنافسي • SSH مع دينو جيورجبو للهندسة المعمارية
العميل • شركة هيئة ميناء الكويت (KPAC)
المقاول • مجهول
(البناء مستخدم)

تم الاعلان عن منافسة دولية لإنشاء مجمع ميناء الشويخ القريب من المقر الرئيسي لشركة الكويت للشحن. وشملت تلك المنافسة إقامة ساحة انتظار سيارات تسع لـ ...3 سيارة، ومكاتب إدارية، ومكاتب تسجيل عامة، ومكاتب للجمارك، وقسم للاستيراد والتصدير، وقسم للتخليص على البضائع، وهيئة ملاحية، وهيئة تأمين، ومكتب بريد وثلاثة أفرع لبنوك، ومنطقة حرة لا تخضع للجمارك مع محلات وكافتيريا، وصلة متعددة الأغراض، ومتحف بحري، ومكتبة. وقد استلهم المشروع فكرته من مركز جورج بومبيدو الذي كان قد تم افتتاحه عام 1977 (45). وقد دعت الحاجة إلى إقامة مساحة كبيرة لانتظار السيارات تتجاوز بثلاث أضعاف ما كان مخططا بالبرنامج، وهو ما دعي إلى إقامة مبنى بارتفاع عشرة طوابق. وهناك شبكة بطول المبنى كله بطول 9.6 م وعرض 9.6 م، هي التي تتحكم في تنظيم المبنى. وتحدد الواجهة الخرسانية للمبنى حجم ساحة انتظار السيارات، على حين تكسو ألواح من الزجاج ذات أطر من الالمنيوم واجهات المكاتب. وهناك شبكة مربعة الشكل يتمحور حولها المشروع كله على نحو متناغم حيث تهيمن الجوانب المربعة الشكل على ساحة انتظار السيارات، و يستطيع المشاه الوصول إليها من الأركان، أما السيارات فتستخدم فتحات أسطوانية منحدرة. وتربط المناطق العامة ساحة داخلية مركزية تحيط بها المكاتب، تلك الأماكن العامة هي التي تحدد الأشكال الوظيفية من حولها.

شركة التامين الكويتية
شرق، 1983

المصمم • ارثر اريكسون وشركاه (معماري).
SSH (مساهم معماري)
العميل • شركة التامين الكويتية (KIC)
(لم يتم البناء)

تم تصميم مجمع شركة التامين بالتعاون مع PACE – SOM لتكون مقراً رئيسياً لأربع أفرع، ترتكز على قاعدة مشتركة، وتقع أعلى مرآب مشترك للسيارات. ولا تكمن أهمية المشروع في الجوانب المعمارية للمشروع، بل كذلك في المضامين الحضرية للتصميم ذاته. ويمكن قراءة المشروع على انه صياغة مبدئية لحلقة وصل بأحد جوانب المدينة (شرق) حيث كانت المباني تتسم بأنها منفصلة عن بعضها البعض، وكل ما يجمع بينهما هو الطريق المقابل.

وقد استهدف المشروع إقامة ساحة رئيسية تحيط بها وتظللها الأركان الأربعة للمباني، على حين يعمل الممشى المعبد الذي يخترق الساحة على وصلها بالأماكن المحيطة، كما يؤكد على أهمية هذا الفضاء الحضري. وكانت الأركان الأربعة في الرسومات الهندسية تقابل الساحة وتتقاسم معها الردهات الممتدة وذلك في إطار انسياب سلس من الأماكن العامة إلى الخاصة.

وقد تولى اريكسون و SSH تطوير أحد مباني مكاتب شركة التامين الكويتية استناداً إلى هذا التصميم. ولعل الابتكار المعماري الرئيسي في التصميم هو ما تمثل في استخدام مقرنص زجاجي عملاق يحيط بالساحة وكأنه يدعو الزائر إلى مدخل المبنى.

وكان هذا الحل الإبداعي، الذي يستمد إلهامه من الأنماط المعمارية المحلية يسمح كذلك بالتحكم في الإضاءة، وفي توزيعها على المكاتب الداخلية.

Canon

BIOGRAPHICAL NOTES
Designers, planners and builders who shaped Kuwait's environment

Between 1949–52, Guy Lagneau (1915–1996), Michel Weill (1914–2001), and Jean Dimitrijevic (1926–2010) established a practice of architecture and urbanism in Paris. The first two were assistants of the Atelier Auguste Perret at École Nationale Supérieure des Beaux-Arts since 1942 and met Dimitrijevic when he joined as student in 1947 (in 1959 a Master's degree in Planning from MIT). The academic agency, as they were called, collaborated with the master Auguste Perret for the Le Havre reconstruction project (1946–49), declared as a World Heritage site by UNESCO. In 1952 the Atelier Lagneau/Weill/Dimitrijevic (LWD) et Associes, known also as AS ATEA+SETAP (Architectes Associes Atelier d'Études Architecturales et Societé pour l'Étude Techinique d'Amènagements Planifiés), was established. During the first years they kept working at Le Havre, in projects such as the School Paul Bert d'Aplemont (1952–55) and the Musée-Maison de la culture du Havre (1952–61) where they collaborated with Jean Prouvé to build a glass and louvered enclosure. The Hôtel de France in Guinea Conakry (1952–54) where Jean Prouvé's systems were also used and the interiors by Charlotte Perriand (1903–99) while she was working on the "cuisine-bar" for le Corbusier's "L'unité d'habitation de Marseille" (1947–52) was the first work overseas. The successful team of Hôtel de France presented in 1958 at the "Salon Des Arts Ménagers" in Paris, the Sahara house, an aluminium frame house prototype for extreme climate conditions. Under Dimitrijevic the firm was responsible for town planning all over Africa, from Abidjan (1959–61) in the Ivory Coast to Cansado (1959–63) in Mauritania and Edéa in Cameroon where aluminium was mass produced for 600 schools all over the country, designed by the firm. During the 1960s the firm took over several sites for tourism development in the coastal towns of France, Spain, Yugoslavia and Portugal, the "Résidence de vacances des Marines de Cogolin" (1971) and Vilamoura Master Plan (1965) being some of the better known. From 1972 seven new associates joined, among those Renzo Moro (1933–), a graduate in Architecture from ETH where he probably met Dr. Omar Azzam and Alfred Roth, together with Dimirijevic, Samir Farah (1943–) and Léon Forgia (1930–) became the new directors, upon a new designation of AART (Atelier d'Architecture, Recherche, Technologie) ATEA International Groupement d'Interêt Économique, that was to last up to 1985. Forgia was another graduate and instructor at École Nationale Supérieure des Beaux-Arts, who graduated in 1964 and assistant of the Atelier Guillaume Gillet, (1912–87) who served as a UNESCO consultant all over the Middle East. Among the first commissions were the detailing of Le Corbusier's Gymnasium for Baghdad under the responsibility of Zina Allawi, a former collaborator with Iraq Consult (IQC), the mall "Les Quatre Temps" at La Défense, Paris (1972–85) led by the old LWD group, the EDF-GDF tower at Cergy-Pontoise (Val-d'Oise) (1971–76) under Renzo Moro and a series of commissions for hospitals in Kuwait (Mubarak Al-Kabeer, Al-Adan, Al-Jahra, Al-Farwaniya) that started in 1973 and continued through to the 1980s. The Kuwait work was led by Forgia and the young Farah. In 1978 the firm was commissioned for several master plans in Iraq (Baghdad, Kerbala, Mossoul) that were interrupted by the war. Upon Lagneau and Weill's retirement the remaining team remained together until 1985–87, with Farah taking over the hospitals, it being this his expertise and was responsible for several hospital commissions in Kuwait, such as the Al-Bahar Eye Centre (1988–90) completed by UNETEC, the Military Hospital (1989), the Saud Al-Babtain Centre for Burns & Plastic Surgery (1989) and the Adult Psychiatric Hospital (1987–91) completed in 2002 by Gulf Consult. The company still operates today under AART Farah Architectes Associes from Samir Farah and AS (Architectes Associes) ARTEO, established by Moro in 1987 and since 1997 under Léon Forgia's daughter and son-in-law, Anne Forgia and Didier Leneveu.

Source: Exhbition catalogue for "Guy Lagneau, Michel Weill, Jean Dimitrijevic: une autre pratique de l'architecture" by Joseph Abram for l'École Nationale Supérieure d'Architecture de Nancy, March 1999

Fonds Dimitrijevic, Jean (1926–2010). 424 Ifa, Fiche descriptive: http://archiwebture.citechaillot.fr/fonds/FRAPN02_DIMJE

AART Farah Architectes Associes, online company profile: http://www.aart.fr/index_fr.html

"Concurso Internacional de Ideas Maspalomas i Costa Canaria 1961 El paisaje como argumento, lo natural como base Paisajes, ENSBA, ATEA+SETAP, Concurso" PhD thesis by Iván Álvarez León for the Departament d'Urbanisme i Ordenació del Territori Universitat Politècnica de Catalunya Barcelona, 2013

ABDUL RAOUF AND AHMED MANSOUR

Stephan Gardiner in his book "Kuwait: The Making of the City," (1983) makes reference to the architectural venture between Abdul Raouf and Ahmed Mansour, son of Hassan Mansour, a long collaborator of Mahmoud Riad (1905–79) in projects such as the Arab League Headquarters (1955–59), The Nile Hotel (1955–56), and The Socialist Union Building (1959) – all in Cairo – and the Kuwait Sport Club (1963). Hassan Mansour remained in Kuwait after 1967 and eventually established a small firm in which his son Ahmed may have practiced and directed.

Source: Gardiner, Stephan, Kuwait: The Making of the City, Harlow, Longman, 1983, p. 138

Riad Architecture, Generation One online platform with description and credits of Mahmoud Riad's (1905–79) practice and projects: http://www.riadarchitecture.com/#!_riad-generation01

AHMAD ALI AL-DUAIJ

Ahmad Ali Al-Duaij (1938–) Bachelor of Economics from University College of North Staffordshire, Keele, UK (1962) and Post Graduate degree from Oxford University (1964). After his Bachelor's he returned to Kuwait to serve in the Ministry of Foreign Affairs but soon became Secretary at the Planning Board (1962–63). After a diploma from Oxford, he became the Director General of Kuwait Real Estate Investment Consortium (1964–75) where he made his career of Managing Director and Chairman after 1975. Meanwhile Al-Duaij sustained in parallel a public career as Director-General of the Planning Board of Kuwait and several other positions many in Sanaa, Yemen where he was Chairman of the Yemeni-Kuwait Real Estate Development Co. After 1975 Al-Duaij was a revered personality for future generations for his role as Head of the Government Scholarship Committee and Member of the Board of Kuwait University.

Source: de Gruyter, Walter, Who's Who in the Arab World 2007–2008, Publitec Publications, Beirut 2007

AHMADIAH CONTRACTING & TRADING CO.

Established in 1954 by Abdul Latif Mohsen Faisal Al-Thuwaini and Tony Najib Najjar. Among the major projects completed by the company in Kuwait were the first Al-Ahli Bank HQ (1968–74) and Kuwait Airways (1969–72), the Salhiya Commercial Project and Le Meridien Hotel (1975–80), the Kuwait Institute for Scientific Research (1979–83), Kuwait Foundation for the Advancement of Sciences (1982–86) and the Kuwait Conference Centre in Bayan (1980–86).

Source: Bricault, G. C. Bricault (ed.), Major Companies of the Arab World 1990/91, Springer Science & Business Media, 2012

ALBINI, FRANCO

Franco Albini (1905–77), a graduate of the Polytechnic University of Milan (1929) commenced his practice at Studio Ponti and Lancia with Giovanni Ponti (1891–1979) in 1930 for a short period. During these years he collaborated with Giuseppe Pagano, Ignazio Gardella, Edoardo Persico, Raffaello Giolli, Giancarlo Palanti, Giovanni Romano and Renato Camus among others exhibiting at Milano Triennale and at the Fiera di Milano untill 1940. However, the most relevant works were done alone, such as the now-iconic "Albini Desk" (1928) still being manufactured by Knoll, the Room for a Man, VI Triennale (1936) and the Living Room for a Villa, VII Triennale (1940). The competition for "Palazzo Della Civiltà Italiana" at E42, Rome, 1937, with Gardella among others, the IACP housing proposal for a neighbourhood in San Siro, Milan (1936–38) and the proposal for the AR Plan (1945) in collaboration with Gardella and BBPR group were fundamental to his expression and experimental ideas of space and organisation. After WWII Albini became extremely interested in material and the culture of construction technology, the idea of the "artigianato razionalizzato" (Albini, Marco) which led him to pursue research into the *vernacular*. However the research initiated with the Casa dei Ragazzi in Cervinia was only developed after establishing a practice with Franca Helg (1920–1989), Albini Studio, and the completion of some of IACP housing units with Gardella (1950–52). Professor in Venice (1949–54; 1955–64) and later in Milan, Albini was an active member in the Italian chapter of CIAM and part of the CIAM summer school in Venice (1952) with Rogers (BBPR) and Gardella. The most famous works with Helg are the museum works in Genoa, the Palazzo Bianco (1950–62), Palazzo Rosso (1952–61) and the Museo del Tesoro di San Lorenzo (1952–56); the building Magazzini Rinascente, Rome (1957–61), the interiors of the Olivetti Showroom in Paris (1959), the Hilton Hotel in Rome (1962–63), San Agostino Museum in Genoa (1963–64) and the Milan Metro Stations (1962–64). In 1968 he was among the international experts invited to join the Advisory Board for the "Urban Form Studies for the Old Town" (1968–69) where he met again Leslie Martin (1908–2000) whom he knew from the CIAM congresses but had also worked in Portugal for the Calouste Gulbenkian Museum (1959–69) in Lisbon as ICOM international experts between 1958–63. In 1965 Albini's son, graduated in Architecture from Milan went for training with Martin in Cambridge. Albini and Martin were to work in Saudi Arabia after the Kuwait project.

Piva, Antonio; Prina, Vittorio, *Franco Albini 1905–1977*, Electa, Milan 1998

Montaner, Josep Maria, *Después del movimiento Moderno. Arquitectura de la Segunda Mitad del Siglo XX*, Ed. Gustavo Gili, Barcelona, 1993, p. 105

França, José-Augusto, *História da Arte Ocidental*, 1780–*1980*, Livros Horizonte, Lisboa,1987, p. 283

AL HANI CONSTRUCTION & TRADING COMPANY

Abdel Mohsin Al-Qattan (1929–) had a Bachelor's degree in Business Administration at the American University of Beirut (1951) and Honorary Doctorate from Birzeit University (1999). He lived in Jordan and Kuwait where he began a career as educator, later as public servant at the Ministry of Electricity and Water in Kuwait (1959). During the construction of Power Station C and the development of the main distribution services, designed by Dar Al-Handasah, Mr. Al-Qattan assumed a relevant role in leading the operation as the client's representative. By 1961 the power station was inaugurated and two years later Al-Hani Construction & Trading Company was officially established, specialising in electrical works. His personal involvement in business and finance along with Mr. Al-Qattan's eventual position as Palestinian Representative at the Arab Fund for Economic and Social Development (Kuwait), led to the first commissions in Beirut, the Arab Bank of Lebanon (1967–69), designed at Dar Al-Handasah, the British Bank of the Middle East central headquarters by Pierre El Khoury, completed in 1966, and Bank Sabbagh (1964–70) by Alfred Roth and Alvar Aalto. By the late 1960s the firm was operating in Jordan and Saudi Arabia with important commissions in Kuwait including Kuwait's Central Bank (1966–76) and Kuwait Airways Headquarters Tower (1971–72), while Mr. Al-Qattan became the president of the Palestinian National Council in 1968. The company emerged later as lead contractor in the Sheraton Hotel extension (1979) and was commissioned for relevant roles in the construction of Kuwait Airport (1978), Radio Television Centre (1978), Kuwait Law Courts (1983) and Kuwait Stock Exchange (1986).

Source: "Al-Hani" Group and Al-Qattan Foundation, corporate profile: http://www.alhani.com/services-civil. aspx; http://www.qattanfoundation.org/en/abdel-mohsin-al-qattan-en

Fischbach, Michael R.; Mattar, Philip, *Encyclopaedia of the Palestinians, Facts on File Library of World History*, Infobase Publishing, 2005

ARAB CONSULTANTS BUREAU

Ahmad Kamal Abdel-Fattah graduated in Architecture and Planning from Ain Shams University in Cairo where he taught and established with Khaled Al-Majeel the practice, Arab Consultants Bureau (ABC) in 1974. The major commissions in the first ten years were the Al-Asmak Tower (1976–79) in Sharq and the Al-Awadi Towers, the Jazz Tower completed in 1986 in Ahmed Al-Jaber Street, the Carlton Hotel in Jibla (1976–77), the Coastal Strip Development Project competition (1985–88) and the Al-Hajri Commercial Tower in Mirqab, which was only completed after the Invasion in 1996. The company is still operating to this day.

Source: Arab Consultants online platform profile: http://www.arabconsultants.com.kw

Aga Khan Seminar on Cairo, Cairo, 12–15 November 1984: http://archnet.org/system/publications/contents/5966/original/DPC2720.pdf?1384795923

ARAB CONSULTING OFFICE (KUWAIT)

An engineering and architectural practice and subsidiary of the Egyptian mother company established in Kuwait by George Habib El-Hag and Michel Habib El-Hag. Following major project commissions in Saudi Arabia, the Egyptian firm was awarded a contract by the Società Appalti e Bonifiche, that was in charge of the new Kuwait International Air Terminal (1967–81) runways and taxiways, designed by Sir Frederick Snow & Partners Ltd. (1962). The problems during construction obliged the Italian contracting firm to review the full design with Arab Consulting, which also took charge of the construction supervision of the project from 1965. In the same year with the establishment of the Savings & Credit Bank, large low-income housing schemes were released for tender. The local branch was now among the established companies and eventually was recommended by the Italian contractors to associate with Luigi Moretti for two large low-income housing schemes in Sulaibiya and Mina Abdullah (1968). With Moretti working in Kuwait the firm participated in another design competition for the Kuwait Society of Engineers in 1968.

ARCHICENTRE

Akram Ogaily (1945–), a Bachelor in Architecture from the University of Baghdad (1967), established a practice in Baghdad in 1970, "Archicentre." In 1973 the firm was eventually awarded some projects in Kuwait but it was only in 1978 that it was locally founded with Jassim Qabazard, with a background in road engineering studies at Ohio State University, and former head of the Construction Section of the Road and Drainage Dept. at the Ministry of Public Works (1973–77). The first major commission was the Bayan Conference Centre (1980–86) in association with the Bosnian architect Stojan Maksimović. In 1982 the team was awarded the first prize in the competition for the Amiri Diwan, the Crown Prince & Prime Ministers' Offices. The scope of such commissions changed the office structure dramatically with the incorporation of several architects from former Czechoslovakia such as Václav Bašta in 1981, Radim Bohacek in 1983, Michal Hron in 1985, and about 12 architects from ex-Yugoslavia. In 1984 Qabazard's brother, the architect Abdullah Mohammed Qabazard, a graduate of Arizona University and former Head of the Design Division at the Ministry of Public Works (MPW), directed projects such as the Ministries Complex (1982) and the Ice Skating Rink (1979). During the 1980s Archicentre was one of the four main architectural consultants in the country working on the development of Adbullah Al-Jaber Street and led to a venture between the four. However with the 1990 Invasion the firm was dissolved and succeeded by Jassim Qabazard Engineering Consultant (JQEC) and Abdullah Qabazard Architecture Consultants (AQAC) firms established in 1992.

Source: Interview with Ala Hason, architect at Archicentre between 1981–83

Jassim Qabazard Engineering Consultant (JQEC) online profile: http://www.jqec.com/overview.html?2

Abdullah Qabazard Architecture Consultants (AQAC) online profile: http://www.qqsons.com/about.html#

ARTHUR ERICKSON ARCHITECTS

Arthur Charles Erickson (1924–2009) graduated in Architecture from McGill University in Montreal, Canada in 1950, following studies in economics, history and Japanese after being commissioned in the army during WWII in Japan and Malaya. After receiving a scholarship to travel through Europe from McGill, Erickson commenced an academic career and established a venture with Geoffrey Massey (1924–), a graduate from GSD Harvard (1948) that became a partnership in 1963 after winning the first prize for the Simon Fraser University Campus in Burnaby, Canada. Upon completion of this project in 1965 the firm's reputation was rewarded with a wide range of commissions for Montreal's Expo '67, including the pavilions for Canada and the thematic Man in the Community, Man and his Health. The firm was also awarded with the Canadian pavilion for Expo '70 in Osaka. In 1972 the partnership was dissolved and Erickson established his own Arthur Erickson Architects with immediate commissions for the Museum of Anthropology at the University of British Columbia (1972), Vancouver's Robson Square complex (1973) as well as his first projects in the Middle East, including Sawaber Housing Scheme (1976–77) and Fintas Centre (1979) in Kuwait. With commissions for California Plaza in Los Angeles (1980) and the Canadian Embassy in Washington (1983) Erickson opened a new branch in Los Angeles and maintained his work in Kuwait, Saudi Arabia, the UAE and Iraq, including the Military Academy in Mishref (1985) and the competition entries for the Kuwait Foundation for the Advancement of Sciences (1979) and the Kuwait Insurance Company's (1983) respective head offices. In 1992 the company closed all its operations and declared bankruptcy.

Source: Arthur Charles Erickson Collection at the Canadian Centre for Architecture (CCA), online platform: http://www.cca.qc.ca/en/collection/434-arthur-erickson-archive

Martin, Sandra, Arthur Erickson Obituary: "The Greatest Architect We Have Ever Produced," in *Friday's Globe and Mail*, Thursday, 21 May, 2009, Toronto, Canada

ASPLUND, HANS

Hans Karl Otto Asplund (1921–1994), son of Gunnar Asplund, was an architect and professor graduated from the Royal Institute of Technology in Stockholm (1947) who the same year won the first prize in the competition for Eslöv Civic Hall (1947–57) with the "Diagonal Balans" (diagonal balance) scheme. During the following years while developing his first project Hans worked for the UN Architectural Office in New York (1947–48), for the "Kooperativa Förbundets Arkitektkontor" (1948–50) and for the "Nordiska Kompaniet" (1951–63) where he developed furniture and designed and supervised a new entrance for the department store in Stockholm. During this period the most relevant achievements of Hans' practice were being credited for coining the term "new brutalism", used to describe the Bengt Edman and Lennart Holm house in Uppsala (1950), and the invitation to submit a proposal for the new Kuwait National Museum (1960). He looked at Modernism with a critical eye and had a well-educated circle of friends, including the Greek linguist and architect Michael

Ventris, Oliver Cox and Graeme Shankland. In 1964 he initiated his career as Professor of Architecture at Lund University that lasted till 1987. He was a regular participant in Dioxiadis' meetings from Delos Nine onwards. In 1980 he published the "Farväl till Funktionalismen!" (1980) as a counter-manifesto to his father's "Acceptera" (1931), the revolutionary Functionalist manifesto published 50 years earlier.

Source: Asplund, Hans, "Farväl till Funktionalismen!," Atlantis, Lund, 1980

Asplund, Gunnar; Gahn, Wolter; Markelius, Sven; Paulsson, Gregor; Sundahl, Eskil; Ahren, Uno, "Acceptera," in *Modern Swedish Design: Three Founding Texts*, The Museum of Modern Art, New York, 2008, p. 338

Fezer, Jesko, "Brutalismus: Architektur gestern. Brutalistische Architektur, Euphorischer Sozialwohnungsbau, Gewalt gegen Architektur im genannten Kontext", seminar presentation, Wissenschaftsakademie, Berlin, Nov. 17, 2000

ASSOCIATED MARITIME CONSULTANTS (AMC)

Established in Southampton, UK in the early 1900s AMC worked in the Gulf for different oil companies in protecting and surveying underwater habitats. As consulting marine offshore and dredging engineers and surveyors they were eventually awarded the first sea-loading line laying project in Kuwait by KOC in 1946. The company remained operating in Kuwait through its work in Shuwaikh Port until 1974.

BALLAST NEDAM GROUEP N.V.

The Amsterdamsche Ballast Maatschappij, under the direction of Charles de Vilder, initiated its operations in the North Sea canal in 1877 through dredging of sand as "ballast." Ballast evolved from a sand supplier to a construction firm, and from 1928 onwards, also operated as a concrete manufacturer. The firm established its reputation within the Netherlands with the construction of the "Afsluitdijk," Closure-dike (1932) and the Velser tunnels (1957) and further expand its operations in the Middle East. In parallel H.F. Boersma established a contracting firm in Den Haag, Netherlands (1899), which accomplished the construction of Vredespaleis (1913) that today houses the International Court of Justice. In 1917 Boersma established the Ned. Aannemingsmaatschappij N.V. and rapidly expanded its operations to Indonesia. In the following years the firm was responsible for the construction of the Nederlandse Handels Maatschappij, the well-known Bazel building in Amsterdam (Karel de Bazel,1919–26). In 1969 both companies merged into the Ballast Nedam Grouep which secured contracts for the Kuwait Air Terminal (1969–78) and for King Fahd Road in Riyadh, Saudi Arabia.

Source: Ballast Nedam online platform profile: http://www.ballast-nedam.com/

Peter Bartlett (FRIBA), with a degree in Architecture from the Nottingham School of Architecture, where he became professor, established the local practice Bartlett & Gray Architects. The first referenced projects are a factory extension in Gotham, Nottinghamshire (1958), the popular Zermatt Bungalow in West Bridgford (1959) and the School for the Handicapped in Chesterfield (1957–59). The firm developed a specific material condition, the brick faced façade fill within a steel framed partition, that was explored throughout the practice's works, the exceptions being the Tesco Department Store of Long Eaton (1963–65) and the Institute for the Physically Handicapped (1963–69) in Kuwait, where the concrete elements in situ and precast were the main material condition. As architect for the Diocese of Nottingham, Bartlett was able to develop during the 1960s a body of work entirely dedicated to the Catholic Church having the firm designing several schools, churches and chapels such as St. Martin's School (1962–56), St. Bernadette School (1962), and St. Patrick's College (1963), popularly known as the honeycomb school. During the 1970s, by then having specialised in health centres and hospitals, the company went through new partnerships and eventually was transferred into one of its former senior partner's practice, that of Richard Ward.

Source: Pevsner, Nikolaus; Williamson, Elizabeth Derbyshire, *Volume 8 of Buildings of England, Nikolaus Pevsner architectural guides*, Yale University Press, 1978

BASIL SPENCE & PARTNERS (SIR BASIL SPENCE, BONNINGTON & COLLINS)

Sir Basil Urwin Spence (1907–76) graduated from the Edinburgh College of Art (ECA) (1929) where he was introduced to the work of Walter Gropius (1883–69) and Erich Mendelsohn (1887–53) as visiting lecturers. After his studies Spence moved to London and worked for Sir Edwin Lutyens (1869–1944) specialising in furniture and garden design for the Viceroy House in New Delhi. While in London he studied at the Bartlett School of Architecture under Professor Albert Richardson. In 1931 he obtained his diploma, awarded with the RIBA silver medal and the Rowand Anderson medal that led to his collaboration with Rowand Anderson, Balfour Paul, & Partners where he became a junior partner in 1935. However in parallel with his old friend, William Kininmonth they established a practice and among the first commissions was Kininmonth's own house at 46a, Dick Place (1933), which brought exposure to both. With more prizes and ARIBA admission he secured a teaching position at the ECA. In 1938 Spence won the competition for the Scottish School of Art & Industry at Kilsyth and two other commissions, the Empire Exhibition held in Glasgow and the later acclaimed Scottish Pavilion, which he designed in collaboration with the Exhibition's organiser, Thomas

Tait. Following armed service during WWII, Spence was appointed chief architect of the *Britain Can Make It* exhibition at the V&A Museum. In 1946 he established Basil Spence & Partners with Bruce Robertson, Andrew Renton, who became a partner in 1949, John Hardie Glover and Peter Scott Ferguson were taken into partnership in 1951. Spence's contribution to the Festival of Britain was marked by the Exhibition of Industrial Power in Glasgow and the design of the Sea & Ships Pavilion. In the same year he eventually won the polemic competition for design the new Coventry Cathedral (1951–62) despite disputed design entries, such as those of Peter and Alison Smithson. Throughout the 1960s from three offices, London, Edinburgh and Glasgow, Basil Spence & Partners were able to build some 50 university buildings in Scotland and England, including three major campuses at Nottingham, Southampton and Sussex, as well as airports, law courts and embassies. During this period the offices operated independently and in 1963, the operations in London were split into two firms: Sir Basil Spence OM RA, with his son-in-law and project manager for Kuwait Law Courts, Anthony Blee and a new office that was opened at Fitzroy Square as Sir Basil Spence, Bonnington & Collins. John (Jack) Bonnington and Gordon Collins had been taken into partnership, based at the Fitzroy Square office. This last firm was to be the one invited for the Kuwait National Assembly competition (1971–72).

Source: RIBA Journal, v. 81, n. 5–8, Royal Institute of British Architects, 1974

"Basil Urwin Spence," *Dictionary of Scottish Architects*, online platform. Architect biograph: http://www. scottisharchitects.org.uk/architect_full.php?id=203352

BBPR

Lodovico Barbiano di Belgiojoso (1909–2004), Ernesto Nathan Rogers (1909–1969), Enrico Peressutti (1908–1976) and Gian Luigi Banfi (1910–1945) all graduated in Architecture from the Polytechnic University of Milan in 1932, with Prof. Gaetano Moretti (1860–1938) and established a common practice in the same year. At school they established relations with Franco Albini (1905–77), Gio Ponti (1891–1979) and Ignazio Gardella (1905–1999). BBPR approach reflected the single member's interest for architectural history, such as the studies of Camillo Boito (1826–1914) for Beljoioso, visible also in the projects for Kuwait (1968–90) or the *continuity* between Classicism and Modernity for Rogers. During the Interwar period and after the design of several pavilions for important exhibitions, the most famous works by the group were the Colonia Elioterapica Legnano (1937–39), the Solar Therapy Institute mentioned by Alfred Roth in *The New Architecture* (1940) and the Palazzo delle Poste, Telegrafi e Te.Ti. at E42 in Rome (1939–42), which received critical acclaim, especially from Gio Ponti. During the 1930s the firm became also known for their planning ventures,

significantly the large plan for Valle d'Aosta (1936–37) under Adriano Olivetti. The regime in Italy at the time, along with its racial laws brought an end to this period forcing Rogers into exile, Belgiojoso and Banfi were imprisoned at the Mauthausen concentration camp where Banfi died. The remaining three decided to continue the work of BBPR after the war, from there on as a professional corporate providing a wide range of services following the Anglo-Saxon model of practice open to new partners, associates and collaborations. The proposed AR Plan, (reconstruction of Milan 1945), with the collaboration of Franco Albini and Ignazio Gardella, among others was the first of these. The practice evolved from there over years with the most recognised work being the Milanese icon, Torre Velasca (1957–60). The individual establishment of Rogers as a critic, editor and educator; the problematic adventures of Peressutti as a professor in Princeton (1952–59) and Belgiojoso's contribution to Kuwait's urban development and his perseverance as an individual practitioner after Rogers' death, keeping faith with the group's ideals.

Sources: Bullene, Richard S., "Architetto-cittadino Ernesto Nathan Rogers," University of Pennsylvania, 1994. Master's thesis

Bertelli, Guya; Ghilotti, Marco, *Lodovico Barbiano di Belgiojoso. Architetto 1909–2004. La ricerca di un'Italia "altra"*, Skira, Milano, 2013

BJØRN & BJØRN DESIGN MALENE BJØRN

Malene Bjørn (1914–) a graduate from the Danish School of Design before WWII established immediately a practice with her husband, architect and designer Acton Bjørn, with most of their work being related to interior design for private houses. After the war the firm Bjørn & Bjørn, was to collaborate with VBB in different projects as interior designers. Among these collaborations were the interiors of the Swedish Intercontinental Airlines (SILA), two Boeing Stratocruiser aircraft for Denmark and Sweden (1945), that finally were bought by BOAC, and later for Scandinavian Airlines System (SAS), 17 Douglas DC-6B aircrafts (1946) doing the flights on the polar route since 1954 from Copenhagen to Los Angeles. A popular flight among the Hollywood celebrities and film industry people which became an important exposure not only for SAS but for Malene's work also, in 1958 it made the cover of Life Magazine with the famous SAS hostess Brigitta Lindman. In 1955 Malene started collaborating more closely with Sune Lindstrom as main designer, first for the Swedish Embassy in New Delhi (1955–1956) and then the Wenner-Gren Centre (1959–1961), the tallest steel frame structured building in Europe upon completion. Later she collaborated with VBB in the Abraj Al-Kuwait (1965–77) having a major role in the tower's form and shape concept as well as interior design. The project led to Malene's nomination for the first Aga Khan Award for Architecture in 1980 together with the VBB team.

Bjørn, Malene, *The Light & Airy – How It All Began in 1945*, Baltic Books, Växjö, 2013

BREGOVAC, ZDRAVKO

Zdravko Bregovac (1924–98) graduated in Architecture from the Technical Faculty of the University of Zagreb having studied and worked with Zdenko Strižić (1902–90) a former student and collaborator of Hans Poelzig. After graduation, Bregovac first collaborated with Vjenceslav Richter (1917–2002), who introduced him to the artists Ivan Picelj and Aleksandar Srnec, with whom they founded the EXAT 51 Group (1950–56), collaborating on numerous Yugoslav pavilions in Europe and America. In 1956, Ritcher and Bregovac were awarded first prize for the competition of the Museum of the City of Belgrade (1954) and Aleppo (1956) in Syria. In 1959 Bregovac moved permanently to Opatija where he developed a body of work in hospitality and tourism. The invitation to participate in the Kuwait National Museum competition in 1960 offered the architect an opportunity to apply independently his earlier experience in national representation and museum design. Bregovac's significant works include numerous hotels on the Adriatic Coast like Helios (1960), the Ambasador (1966), and Barbara (1970), as well as number of tourism complexes. Bregovac served as professor at the Technical Faculty of Zagreb and Faculty of Tourism and Hospitality Management in Opatija.

Source: Nikšić Olujić, Ivana, *Zdravko Bregovac: Architects Archives*, Croatian Academy of Arts and Sciences, Zagreb, 2015

Stanišić, Ardea, "Il Museo Civico di Fiume gli dedica una Retrospettiva. Zdravko Bregovac, Figura «mitica» nell'architettura del Dopoguerra," in *La Voce del Popolo*, Rijeka, Dec. 13, 2007

BRIAN COLQUHOUN AND PARTNERS, CONSULTING ENGINEERS

Cecil Brian Hugh Colquhoun (1902–77), civil engineer from London's King's College. He was responsible for the rehabilitation of war production factories in the UK, Director-General of Aircraft Production Factories and advisor to the International Bank for Reconstruction and Development. The company was incorporated in 1944. In 1958 he completed the rehabilitation of Kuwait Airport Terminal and Strip and in 1960 the design for Abadan and Tehran Airports began under P. Rushton, ex Royal Air Force and graduate from King's College, London who joined the company in 1950. In Kuwait the firm was responsible for several infrastructural design works during the 1970s and 1980s including the ring roads and other road interfaces.

Source: The Papers of Brian Colquhoun, 1925–1977, Churchill Archives Centre, Cambridge, UK

Henri Montois (1920–2009) graduated in Architecture from Saint Luc School of Architecture (1943) with Robert Courtois with whom he established a practice in 1947 that lasted until 1959. From 1980 he worked under the name of Bureau d'Architecture Henri Montois. The first major commissions for Montois-Courtois were the Trois Suisses factory in Tournai, where they also designed a furniture line, and the A. De Backer factory in Brussels, both in 1957. International recognition came in the following year with a commission for the Le Pavillon des Transports for the Brussels World's Fair. The project won recognition from the American Institute of Architects' R. S. Reynolds Prize. During the following years the practice led Brussels' modernisation with several high-rise buildings, including the Fina HQ, CFE HQ (1974) and the well-known Blue Tower (1976). In parallel he worked on commissions for hospitals and university buildings all over Belgium, such as the Faculty of Medicine at UCL and Hôpital Saint-Luc (1967–1976) and the Citadel Hospital in Liege (1978). In 1980 the commission for Sheikh Nasser Al-Sabah Mosque (1980–81) became one of the few projects outside the firm's country and initiated a new period in the office of multiple collaborations with different consultants and individuals.

Source: Binder, Georges, *Montois Partners: Selected and Current Works*, Images Publishing, 2001

CANDELA, FÉLIX

Félix Candela (1910–1997) graduated in Architecture from ETSAM Madrid (1935) after a first attempt to pursue further his interests in advanced structural engineering in Germany, he returned to fight in the Spanish Civil War (1936–1939) and upon Franco's victory he was exiled to Mexico. There, Candela established a construction company and became famous for his thin shell concrete structures. After a first attempt in 1949 with an experimental reinforced concrete hyperbolic paraboloid shell, Candela completed the Cosmic Ray Pavilion (1950–51) at the National Autonomous University of Mexico in collaboration with Jorge Gonzáles Reyna. The project brought great exposure and in the following years Candela would be awarded commissions everywhere in Mexico, from the restaurant in Xochimilco (1957) to the Church of La Virgen Milagrosa (1953–55) in Mexico City. Between 1961–62 he taught at the Graduate School of Design, Harvard University and in 1968 the Sports Palace was ready for the Olympic Games in Mexico City. The conclusion led to the invitation from the Kuwait Planning Board to join Nervi, Tange, Otto and Jones in the competition for Kuwait Sports Centre (1968–69), which he developed with Emilio Pérez Piñero.

Source: Candela, Félix; Pérez Piñero, Emilio, *Letters Candela-Pérez Piñero-Candela, 1968*, Cornell Archive, USA

Georges (Gheorghios) Candilis (1913–1995) graduated from the Polytechnic in Athens (1931–36) where he was unable to meet Constantinos Doxiadis (1913–1975), but did however meet Le Corbusier (1887–1965) at CIAM IV (1933, Athens). Later in 1943 the Swiss architect appointed Candilis for the leadership of ASCORAL, a group that undertook conceptual studies of housing, prefabrication, standardisation and town planning during WWII aiming at post-war reconstruction. Following the liberation of Athens, Candilis joined Le Corbusier's office where he became one of the main collaborators with key roles in projects such as the Unité d'Habitation in Marseille (1945–52) as the project architect for construction with Shadrach Woods (1923–73) under ATBAT. In 1951 both moved to ATBAT-Afrique, first in Tangiers, and from 1952 in Casablanca, Morocco until the company closed two years later. During this period they met Michel Écochard, Director of Morocco Planning Department at the time, with whom they presented at the ninth CIAM congress (1953) as the Gamma group of the well-known Nid d'Abeille (1952–53) housing scheme in Casablanca that gave them international exposure. Peter Smithson recognised its foundational relevance for Team X. Back to Paris the two colleagues met Aljoša Josić (1921–2011) at ATBAT Paris and the three established the group that became known as Candilis-Josic-Woods partnership with the engineers Paul Dony, Henri Piot and Guy Brunache. After winning the first prize for the national competition for large-scale housing, Opération Million, the group built tens of thousands of dwellings including the well-known complex of Le Mirail in Toulouse (1960–64). The practice kept always its research interests alive and being related to the Le Corbusier tradition, were part of Team X till its end. Giving Josić the role for the visualisation of the ideas within the office, Woods was the theoretician that elaborated working methods and the responsibility for the design of Frankfurt-Römerberg (1963) and the Berlin Free University (together with Manfred Schiedhelm, 1963–73). Within the group, Candilis was the official representative and negotiator, permanently in touch with builders and politicians. From 1967 onwards with Woods' departure to the US to teach first at Yale (1967) and then at the Harvard Graduate School of Design (1968–73) the office eventually became less of a partnership and during the proposal for Kuwait's "Urban Form Studies for the Old City" (1969) they eventually terminated the practice. Candilis remained the one to take over the Kuwait proposals submitted in 1969 followed by other projects in Kuwait, establishing a practice on his own with several commissions in the Middle East ranging from dwellings to schools and vacation houses.

Source: Joedicke, Jürgen, *Candilis, Josic y Woods. Una década de Arquitectura y Urbanismo*, Editorial Gustavo Gili, Barcelona, 1968

Charles Toufic Haddad (1934–), graduated from American University of Beirut with a second class Bachelor's degree in Architectural Engineering (1956), Master's in City Planning from Yale University (1961) and MIT SPUTS Fellow (1970) and commenced his practice in Kuwait after 1956 at the Division of Planning Projects Kuwait, for the Municipality, first at the Roads Department and from 1964 as the Head of Division and a member of the counterpart team on the Physical Development Plan for the State of Kuwait. Between 1960–62 Haddad was a planner at the New Haven City Plan Department. From 1964 he was Executive Director for the Residential-Commercial Survey for the State of Kuwait and principal designer in charge of various residential neighbourhoods for Kuwait Municipality till 1972. Haddad is co-author of "Housing for Kuwait University Graduates" a survey report for Kuwait Prime Minister in 1969 and Kuwait Municipality "Rules and Regulations for the Subdivision of Residential Land". In 1968 Haddad was one of the PACE founding members and between 1972–78 the director of PACE International Corporation in Cambridge, Massachusetts, US. In 1978 he left PACE and one year later established his own practice Charles T. Haddad and Associates (CTHA), today known as The Associated Engineering Partnership (TAEP), which he still managing to this date.

Source: Charles Haddad résumé, interview in Kuwait, Mar. 2014

CHARLES T. HADDAD AND ASSOCIATES, ENGINEERS AND PLANNERS (CTHA)

Charles Toufic Haddad (1934–) holding a Bachelor's in Architectural Engineering from the American University of Beirut (1956), a Master's in City Planning from Yale University (1961) and MIT SPUTS Fellow (1970), worked for 20 years at the Division of Planning Projects Kuwait Municipality and one of the founding partners of PACE (1968–). Upon his withdrawal from PACE in 1978, Haddad established Charles T. Haddad and Associates in 1979. During the first four years the firm conducted various projects for KNPC's Mena Abdullah Refinery and for the Shuaiba Refinery, including administration offices, control rooms, warehouses, fire-fighting stations and other facility buildings such as the KOC Computer & Training Centre (1979–83) in collaboration with Tripe and Wakeham Partnership. In the following years the firm developed various industrial plants in Kuwait and Saudi Arabia with assures services of licensing, MEP and structural design for several buildings in Kuwait including shopping arcades in Ibn Khaldoun Street and was eventually commissioned for the development known as the Silver Towers, a complex of tridental twin towers overlooking Dasman Palace. One of the early collaborators with the office was Frederick V. Cowen, a graduate from Northeastern University (1962) and the one responsible for the structural design of the GSD Harvard Gund Hall building (John Andrews, Anderson and Baldwin, 1967–71). In the late 1980s upon partial acquisition the firm was named The Associated Engineering Partnership (TAEP).

Source: Charles Haddad résumé, interview in Kuwait, Mar. 2014

COODE & PARTNERS

John Coode (1816–1892) coming from a background in law, initiated his career as a civil engineer at James Meadows Rendel (Rendel, Palmer & Tritton) in Plymouth. In 1844 he established his practice in London specialising in railways. In 1847 after a short commission with the Santander-Madrid railway he was commissioned by Rendel as Resident Engineer in Portland Harbour, with work that lasted till 1872. Between 1856–59 Coode got his first commission overseas as Engineer-in-Chief for the construction of Table Bay Harbour in Durban, South Africa where he developed an extensive body of work. In 1873 with the commission for the Harbour of Colombo in Ceylon (Sri Lanka) the practice became of world renown with commissions all over Asia, as well as Australia and New Zealand. In 1880 he was awarded with important work in Portugal for a series of floating basins and docks in Lisbon and for the construction of the artificial harbour in Leixoes, Porto. In 1884 he was nominated a member of the International Commission of the Suez Canal, work he carried out till his death. William Mathews (1844–1922) started his practice with Coode in Australia and about 1885 becomes a partner with the firm Sir John Coode, Son & Matthews. In 1912 Maurice Fitzmaurice (1861–1924) the famous engineer and inventor joined the firm becoming partner in charge. After the death of Mathews the firm was renamed Coode, Fitzmaurice, Wilson, and Mitchell and later with Alec George Vaughan-Lee (1869–1960) as partner, Coode, Wilson, Mitchell and Vaughan-Lee were to develop impressive work in the Middle East, such as the Gezira Irrigation Scheme, including the construction of the Sennar and Mohammed Ali Barrage Dams on the Nile in Egypt, a flood relief scheme on the River Euphrates and the Kut Barrage on the River Tigris in Iraq. Upon Vaughan-Lee's retirement in 1956 the company became Goode and Partners, expert in dams, irrigation and rivers studies, public transportation, ports and harbours with major work in Africa, the Middle East and the Far East.

Source: Allinson, Ken, *London's Contemporary Architecture*, Routledge, 2007

James Meadows Rendel Obituary, 1857, *Grace's Guide to British Industrial History*, web platform

Skempton, A. W., *A Biographical Dictionary of Civil Engineers in Great Britain and Ireland: 1500–1830*, Thomas Telford, 2002

William Mathews Obituary, 1923, *Grace's Guide to British Industrial History*, web platform

Maurice Fitzmaurice Obituary, 1925, *Grace's Guide to British Industrial History*, web platform

The Wenatchee Daily World, Tuesday, Mar. 8, 1910

The Engineer, Aug. 5, 1892

The Engineer, Nov. 21, 1924

COLIN BUCHANAN AND PARTNERS

Colin Buchanan (1907–2001) Bachelor in Engineering from Imperial College, London (1929), joined the Public Works Department in Sudan, working on highway planning and bridges untill 1933. From 1936 he worked for the Ministry of Transport. During WWII he served in Egypt. From 1946 to 1960 he was at the Ministry of Town and Country Planning in London where he met Leslie Martin (1908–2000). After working in different inspection departments of the Ministry he qualified as an architect. In 1958 Buchanan published the *Mixed Blessing: The Motor in Britain*, in which he accepted that people had a right to want to own a car. In 1960 The Minister of Transport commissioned a report on UK towns traffic and hired Buchanan as Urban Planning Adviser to the Ministry. The well-known report was published in 1963 *Traffic in Towns. The Buchanan Report* of 1963 became the reference in UK for planning. Following this success Buchanan formed the consultancy Colin Buchanan and Partners, and was appointed to the new Chair of Transport at Imperial College. One of the first major commissions was the Kuwait Second Master Plan (1967–83). In parallel to Kuwait, Buchanan established the Roskill Commission into London's third airport. In 1974 he was appointed the first Director of the new School of Advanced Urban Studies at the University of Bristol. He retired in 1984. From 1980 to 1985 he was President of the Council for the Protection of Rural England.

Source: Professor Sir Colin Buchanan Obituary, *The Telegraph*, Dec. 10, 2001

Sir Colin Buchanan's Obituary by Neil Parkyn, *The Guardian,* Dec. 10, 2001

CONSOLIDATED CONTRACTORS CO. (CONCO)

Hasib J. Sabbagh (1920–2010) and his cousin Said Tawfiq Khoury (1923–2014), both graduates in Civil Engineering from the American University of Beirut in the early 1940s, established in Haifa a contracting firm in 1943. In 1948 both left Palestine and re-established the contracting company, the Consolidated Contractors Group of Companies (CCC Group) in 1950 with four other contractors for the construction of Tripoli Airport. The first commissions included major works for the Iraq Petroleum Company in Syria and Iraq under the American Bechtel Group. The company rapidly became a major contractor with subsidiaries all over Middle East, including The Consolidated Contractors Co.

established in 1952 to operate in Kuwait and Bahrain. After 1976 the company was based in Athens, Greece, remaining in operation to this day.

Source: Said Khoury, *2006 Honorary Degree Recipient*, American University of Beirut online platform: http://www.aub.edu.lb/doctorates/recipients/2006/Pages/khoury-profile.aspx

Hasib J. Sabbagh, *Honorary Doctorate Recipient 2003*, American University of Beirut online platform: https://www.aub.edu.lb/DOCTORATES/RECIPIENTS/2003/Pages/hassib-profile.aspx

Bricault, G. C., *Gulf Consult profile, Major Companies of the Arab World 1991/92*, Springer Science & Business Media, 2012

CONTRACTING AND TRADING CO. (CAT GROUP)

Established in Haifa in 1936 by Emile Bustani (1907–1963), civil engineer at AUB (1928), student at MIT (1933) and a prior employee of the Iraq Petroleum Company. In 1948 the company was displaced from Palestine to Lebanon and working mainly on urban regeneration of the post-independent Beirut (1943). The previous experience of Bustani in Iraq was fundamental to develop work in the oil industry. The political career of its founder made CAT's business prosperous in the public sector, gaining commissions from the State of Kuwait and others in the region. During the political crisis of 1956 the company consolidated strong ties with the Egyptian president, Gamal Abdel Nasser. In parallel contracts were signed all over the region, for example, Shuwaikh Secondary School (1957), Sheikh Jaber Al-Ali's Palace in Surra (1955–1960) and Sabah Hospital, (1960).

Source: Bustani, Emile, *March Arabesque*, Robert Hale Limited, London, 1961

Bustani, Emile, *Doubts and Dynamite: The Middle East Today*, Shenval Press, London, 1958

Mardelli, Bassil A., *Middle East Perspectives: Personal Recollections (1947–1967)*, iUniverse, 2010

BUREAU D'ÉTUDES CORDONNIER

Born into a family with a strong architectural tradition that included Jean-Baptiste Cordonnier (1820–1902), Louis-Marie Cordonnier (1854–1940), Louis-Stanislas Cordonnier (1984–1960); Joseph G. Cordonnier, an acoustic engineer graduate from the l'École Supérieure d'Électricité in Paris, established the Bureau d'Études Cordonnier. J. G. Cordonnier became the most notable French expert in radio and television acoustics, being responsible not only for several studios for the French television (1950–) but also the theatre José Bernardo Alzedo in Lima, Peru (1962), the Iraq Radio Television Centre in Baghdad (1964) and the Kuwait Radio Television Centre (1968). He was also a financial and feasibility advisor for the French Television Foreign Affairs' Service. The studies for Iraq and Kuwait were part of a diplomatic and economic approach to these countries.

Source: *Documents diplomatiques français: 1968. (2 juillet - 31 décembre)*, edited by Ministère Des Affaires Étrangères, Peter Lang, 2010

Cordonnier, Joseph G., *Problèmes économiques de la télévision française: servitudes techniques, possibilités commerciales, perspectives financières*, Dunod, 1950

Etudes du Bureau d'Études Cordonnier pour le centre de radiodiffusion de la ville de Bagdad: plan de masse, plans et coupes schématiques, 1964 et n.d. Cité de l'Architecture et du Patrimoine, Paris

DAR AL-HANDASAH

Kamal A. Shair (1930–2008), with a Bachelor's from the American University of Beirut (1947), a Master's from the University of Michigan (1949) and a PhD from Yale University in Chemical Engineering (1955), where he eventually met with Philip Johnson, Paul Rudolph, Josef Albers, Robert Damora and Hamilton P. Smith, partner of Marcel Breuer between 1954–68. He returned to Lebanon, applying for an assistant professorship of engineering at AUB where he initiated his academic career in 1956. In the same year Shair established with four other professors the Dar Al-Handasah engineering consultancy. In the following year, Sheikh Jaber Al-Ali Al-Sabah commissioned Dar Al-Handasah to design the Power Station C (1957–62) in Kuwait, a 15 million dollar work. In 1959 three of these partners departed, Khalil Maalouf, Samir Thabet, Victor Andraos to establish the Associated Consulting Engineers (ACE). Left with Nazih Taleb as partner Shair diversified the scope of services into architecture and road infrastructure and was awarded first prize for Strand Commercial Centre in Hamra Street (1962–63) and for the Arab Bank (1967), both in Beirut and several other buildings in Kuwait, including KNPC and the Chamber of Commerce Offices, the Sheraton Hotel and the Ministries of Commerce & Industry and Education, all completed by 1965. In Saudi Arabia ARAMCO commissioned several schools (1967) and in Jordan, they were commissioned to create the Amman Central Bank (1967). All these were developed by the Dar Al-Handasah team of senior architects; Robert Wakim (1931–), Ghassan Klink and Sami Khoury. They all became partners of Shair in 1969 with the departure of Nazih Taleb. The split created two new companies: Shair & Partners and Nazih Taleb & Associates. In 1972 Robert Wakim established the Department of Planning and the company expanded internationally, acquiring Perkins+Will (Chicago) in 1986 and Penspen (London) in 1990. In Kuwait, apart from the 1957 Power Station and the CBD Area 3 buildings, the firm was responsible for the design of the Al-Mulla Residential Building (1964), Khaled Al-Issa Department Store (1964); Ministry of Commerce & Industry (1965); Ministry of Education (1965), the Sheraton Hotel (1965), the Salt, Chlorine and Caustic Soda Plant 1966, Al-Wafrah New Town for National Housing Authority (1976–78), the Shuwaikh Master Plan (1983–84), Bubiyan Island Resort (1989–90) and several planning studies for Subiya New Town.

Source: Kamal, Shair, *Out of the Middle East: The Emergence of an Arab Global Business*, I.B.Tauris, 2006

Ghosn, Rania, "Le secteur privé dans l'urbanisme des pays en voie de developpement", in *Villes et Territoires du Moyen-Orient*, 2005, p. 42

Taleb, Nazih, "Se souvient," written for the 40th Anniversary of Dar Al-Handasah, Jun. 1996

DELB, JEAN-ROBERT

Jean-Robert Delb (1925–) graduated from l'École Nationale Supérieure des Beaux-Arts de Paris (1948–53) in Architecture with Ngô Viết Thụ (1927–2000) and Roger Taillibert (1926–), under the Atelier Lemaresquier and was awarded with the *Deuxième Grand Prix de Rome* in 1957. Delb began a career marked by a reflection on urban issues, particularly through the study of Parisian neighbourhoods and new towns or cities in the mountains. In 1963 he established with André Bertrand a practice in architecture and urbanism, which developed several proposals for ski resorts in the Rhône-Alpes area. However none of these proposals were completed and in 1966 a new partnership was formed, named Delb, Chesnau, Verola & Lalande. The first significant project was the Tour Europe in Paris completed in 1969 and followed by other high-rise buildings such as the Tour Atlantique (1970), Tour Franklin (1972), Tour Bourcy (1974) and Tour Winterthur (1974). The success of the Tour Europe was eventually to lead to the commission of the Gulf Bank's new headquarters (1969–74) in Kuwait, developed without affiliation with Michel Chesnau and Jean Verola. Apart from the pre-fabricated concrete screen façade towers and offices building, Delb was commissioned in 1979 for the renovation of the Théâtre du Châtelet in Paris.

Source: Academy of Architecture / Cité de l'Architecture et du Patrimoine / Architectural Archives of the twentieth century

"Renouveau du théâtre du Chatelet," *L'Impartial*, Nov. 11 1980, p. 21

DENYS LASDUN & PARTNERS

Denys Louis Lasdun (1914–2001) graduated from the Architectural Association in London in 1936 and started his practice, working for Wells Coates (1895–1958) between 1935–37 and after that with Berthold Lubetkin (1901–1990) at Tecton until 1948 where he worked with Ove Arup (1895–1988) and Lindsay Drake (1909–80), becoming partner after 1946. With the closure of Tecton in 1949, Lasdun and Drake established a venture and eventually a partnership with Fry & Drew for the next 10 years. During this period Drake & Lasdun were involved with Maxwell Fry (1899–1987) and Jane Drew's (1911–96) work in the Middle East, including the Ahmadi Hospital (1949–60) in Kuwait. In 1951 through Leslie Martin (1908–2000), the LCC commissioned both architects for the Hallfield primary school in London (1951–55). In 1959, upon the retirement of Drake, Lasdun established the firm Denys Lasdun & Partners and completed a block of duplex flats in St. James's Place in London (1958), an important project in building Lasdun's reputation as an architect and led to consequent commissions for the Royal College of Physicians (1959–64), School of Oriental and African Studies (1970–73) and the National Theatre (1967–76) in London. Ultimately the last of these buildings was the most famous work of the architect and led to wide recognition, being knighted in 1976, and awarded the RIBA gold medal for architecture in 1977. In the same year Lasdun was invited for the Kuwait National Theatre competition being one of the finalists. During this period he accomplished the completion of the European Investment Bank in Luxemburg (1974–80). After 1978 the firm was named; Denys Lasdun, Redhouse and Softley.

Source: Curtis, William J.R., *Denys Lasdun: architecture, city, landscape*, Phaidon, 1999

DESIGN CONSTRUCTION GROUP

Anthony Irving (FRIBA) and Gordon Brown Jones established in Beirut an architectural and planning practice that became well-known in the region for bank head offices. Through design competition the firm earned the first commissions in Kuwait and Dubai, for the National Bank and Gulf Bank in 1961 (concluded 1963), and for the First National City Bank of New York in 1964 (concluded 1967), respectively. Upon the completion of these projects, the company managed from Beirut identical building programmes in Abu Dhabi and Saudi Arabia. Among the collaborators was the first Australasian female architect and professor Helen Tippett (1933–2004), Dean of Victoria Architecture School (1980–83), who was a noted figure at the office in those days, being project manager for the Commercial Bank of Kuwait's head offices (1968–71). The 1970s saw collaboration with Michael Rice for the awarded project of the National Museum Doha (1972–75) and the completion of the Qatar National Bank (1977) and Qatar Monetary Agency (1977). In the middle of these projects the company's production back office was displaced from Beirut to Athens due to the war. During this time Anthony Irving transferred the know-how of the "Banks HQ Building" to Herbert Fitzroy Robinson (1914–2005), former partner of Sir Basil Spence, being associated with Fitzroy Robinson & Partners (or Partnership) in several buildings of the kind in Abu Dhabi.

Source: Helen Tippett (1933–2004) Obituary, by John Gray published in the *Cross Section NZIA News*, May 2004.

DEREK LOVEJOY AND PARTNERS

Derek Alfred Walter (1925–2000), landscape architect and a graduate from Harvard Graduate School of Design in 1956 established the practice that soon became Derek Lovejoy & Partners, with

G. M. Langley-Smith, J. M. Graham, D. Simpson and J. M. Whalley. The practice was established in Croydon when Lovejoy became the president of the landscape institute in UK (1971). That exposure brought work from all over Europe and US but also in the Middle East where they were assigned for the Salmiya District Centre and eventually presented a proposal for the Waterfront in 1976. By 1981 the firm was operating with offices in Christchurch, Dorset, Westminster, Manchester, Crawley and Paris. Lovejoy retired in 1988.

Source: Blackwood Murray, David , "Derek Lovejoy," obituary, in *Architects' Journal*, Nov. 16, 2000

DEVECON ARKITEKTER

Following the success of the team led by Heikki Castrén (1929–80), a graduate of the Helsinki University of Technology (1956), in the Toronto Town Hall competition (1958–65), the idea of exporting planning and architectural expertise outside Finland became an opportunity. In 1972 Castrén established Arkkitehtitoimisto CJN Oy (CJN) and joined a series of other discipline related companies under the umbrella of the project management company Devecon Oil Ekono Oy, established in 1971 with the purpose of offering design services all over the OPEC countries. Under the project manager Prof. Pentti Murolen (1934–), also a graduate of Helsinki University of Technology (1961) and faculty of the Building Department, Devecon was able to secure its first projects. The first contracts were signed for Pha Rung Shipyard in Vietnam (1971–73), Annaba and Setif Hospitals in Algeria (1975), Jahra District Centre in Kuwait (1975–77), with Matti Koskimies and Reijo Jallinoja (1941–) as main designers; and the Tripoli Transportation Master Plan (1977) and Ras Jedir-Sahratah Motorway (1975), both in Libya. During the following three decades the company developed a wide range of projects in the Middle East (Kuwait, Saudi Arabia, Syria), Africa (Libya, Algeria, Ethiopia) and Asia (Sri Lanka, Vietnam, Turkmenistan). The Architecture Department Devecon Arkitekter, achieved successful awards in Kuwait winning two competitions for the urban connections of Derwazah Abdul Razaq (1979–86) with Hannu Hermusen and Safat Square (1981–86) under Yki Sahlstedt. Between 1984–85 the firm was commissioned to implement the cast-in-situ terrazzo works.

Source: Murolen, Pentti, "Ihmistä ei voi suunnitella, kiveä voi! Raportti Suomalaisesta ja kansainvälisestä liikennesuunnittelusta," en."Man cannot plan – stone can!," published by B&M Architects, Helsinki, 2012

Leonard, Barry (ed.), *Technology-transfer to the Middle East*, Diane Publishing, 1984

DINO GEORGIOU & PARTNERS (DRGF ARCHITECTS)

Dino Georgiou & Partners (DRGF Architects) was established in 1980 by Dino Georgio who was later joined by his partners,

Ruxandra Georgiou and Florin Grigore in 1989. Since that time, in Kuwait they developed work with Tamdeen, CRC, Al-Tameer, Projacs, Alargan and KCMCC. The firm have collaborated locally with SSH, Gulf Consult and Soor Engineering Bureau.

Source: Dino Georgiou & Partners online profile: http://www.drgf.gr/profile

DISSING + WEITLING

The former collaborators and partners of Arne Jacobsen, Hans Dissing (1926–1998) and Otto Weitling (1930–) established in 1971 Dissing + Weitling to continue Jacobsen's work upon his death. Some of these projects include the Central Bank of Kuwait (1966–76), the National Bank of Denmark (1961–1978), the City Hall of Mainz (1970–74) in Germany and the Danish Embassy in London (1969–1977). The first projects commissioned were the IBM Computer Centre in Hamburg (1972) and the Kunstsammlung Nordrhein-Westfalen Museum (1975–86) in Düsseldorf, Germany.

Source: de Corral, Félix Solaguren-Beascoa, *"Arne Jacobsen: approach to his Complete Works,"* Arkitektens Forlag, 2001

DORSCH CONSULT INGENIEURGESELLSCHAFT MBH

Franz Xaver Dorsch (1899–1986), civil engineer, established the Reg. Baumeister Xaver Dorsch, Ingenieurbüro, Wiesbaden in 1951, converted one year later into Dorsch Consult. A former colleague of the architect Albert Speer (1905–1981), he was appointed in 1944 to lead the Organisation Todt (OT), and was in charge of major construction projects, also directing the move of all German industrial facilities into "concrete factories" and the construction of underground aircraft hangars for the Luftwaffe, a pet project of his. Within the Reich he was also the general commissioner for construction industry matters, being responsible for all building projects in the final year of the war. The company got its first work outside Germany in the post Suez crisis Middle East, as a World Bank listed consultant, which included Low-Income Housing Schemes and Sabah Hospital (1959–62) in Kuwait. In 1974 the contracts in Saudi Arabia and Egypt increased in scale and the Baghdad Metro project and Hijaz Railway line construction led to the establishment of an Abu Dhabi branch in 1987. The company still operates in Kuwait under Dorsch Group (since 2006), and is one of the lead consultants for the new airport terminal under development.

Source: Kokott, Juliane; Scholch, Rainer "Dorsch Consult Ingenieurgesellschaft mbH v. Council and Commission. Case T-184/95," in *The American Journal of International Law*, v. 93, n. 3, Jul. 1999, pp. 685–690

DOSHI, BALKRISHNA V.

Balkrishna Vithaldas Doshi (1927–) graduated from J. J. School of Art, Mumbai (1950)

and initiated his practice in Le Corbusier's office, first in Paris (1951–1954) and later in Ahmedabad and Chandigarh (1954–57). The international fellowship of the Graham Foundation was to lead Doshi to pursue his studies and interest in the education of architecture. After a first teaching experience at Washington University, St. Louis, US (1958–61), Doshi's academic career was developed at the University of Pennsylvania, Philadelphia (1962–88). This was instrumental in the establishment of Ahmedabad School of Architecture and the Centre for Environment Planning and Technology in 1962, where Doshi was the founder and dean till 1972, when he established the School of Planning, also in Ahmedabad, where he was dean till 1981. He subsequently became dean emeritus for the Centre for Environment Planning and Technology. In 1978 Doshi founded the Visual Arts Centre followed by the Kanoria Centre for Arts (1984) and Husain-Doshi Gufa (1994) all in Ahmedabad. In parallel Doshi established an architectural practice in Ahmedabad, Vastu-Shilpa refered to as a consultant office, firm, foundation and centre for studies. Doshi's practice developed mostly city planning and low-income housing schemes. Between 1967–71 he was a regular attendant in the Team X meetings and from 1972 he occupied different positions in different related council and boards of the Indian Government. After serving on the jury of the Aga Khan Award for Architecture in 1991, he was recipient of this prize in 1995 for the Aranya Community Housing in Indore, India.

Source: Aga Khan Award for Architecture

Sharp, Dennis, *The Illustrated Encyclopedia of Architects and Architecture*, Quatro Publishing, New York, 1991, p. 45

Steele, James, *Complete Architecture of Balkrishna Doshi*, Thames and Hudson, London, 1998

DOXIADIS ASSOCIATES (DA)

Constantinos Apostolou Doxiadis (1913–1975) held degree in Architectural Engineering from the Polytechnic in Athens (1935) and a doctorate in Master of Town Planning from Charlottenburg University in Berlin during the Nazi Summer Olympics (1936). Back in Athens, Doxiadis took charge of town planning for the Greater Athens Area. During the war (1940–1945) he moved into the Department of Regional and Town Planning, Ministry of Public Works, and was one of the leaders of the National Resistance Group Hephaestus. Following Liberation Doxiadis became deeply involved in foreign affairs policy, collecting aid for the country's reconstruction and occupied different high-ranking positions in the government, becoming the Minister-Coordinator of the Greek Recovery Programme and Under-secretary of the Ministry of Coordination (1948–51). In 1951 established Doxiadis Associates with a small group of architects and planners with whom he had worked before. Two years later he was commissioned to design in conjunction with UN

consultant Michel Écochard (1905–85)
a refugee housing project near Karachi,
Pakistan. In the following years the firm
developed urban design and planning for
almost every country in the region and was
most famous for his schemes for Riyadh and
Iraq. In 1958 Doxiadis founded the Athens
Technological Organization and in 1963 the
Athens Centre of Ekistics, expanding his
academic career outside Greece. The rapid
growth of the firm led to the establishment
of DA International Co. Ltd., Consultants
on Development and Ekistics in 1963, by
then operating in 40 different countries.
Debilitated by a terminal disease Doxiadis'
competition entry for Kuwait was the last
project of Doxiadis Associates before his
death.

Source: Doxiadis Archive, Benaki Museum, Athens, Greece

ÉCOCHARD, MICHEL

After his studies on archaeology, architecture
and urban planning at the École Nationale
Supérieure des Beaux-Arts in Paris (1929),
he served at the French National Archaeological Research Institute in Syria. Écochard
(1905–1985) initiated his practice with the
restoration of Azzem Palace (1930), the
French Institute director's residence (1936)
and the National Museum (1940) all in
Damascus, together with a new museum
for Antioch, Turkey (1931). With Claude Le
Coeur he worked on several archaeological
sites and was involved in the Damascus
Master Plan, being in 1938 assigned to lead
the Syrian Planning Department. During
these years he was assigned to several
other projects such as the extension of the
French High Commissioner's residence
in Beirut (1933) where he re-established
contact with Antoine Tabet. In 1942 he
submitted a first study on Beirut Urban
Development with a second revision in 1943.
It was a relevant document that showed the
conscientiousness of historical and building
preservation, while defining the new road
network and zoning plan. These plans were
never approved although they generated
a strong impact in the First Master Plan
(1950–52) by Ernest Egli and Rodolphe
Meyer. After the war he joined Le Corbusier
and others on an official visit to US (1946–
47) and soon after he became a member
of the CIAM and was commissioned as UN
consultant to design in conjunction with
Constantinos Doxiadis (1913–1975) refugee
housing near Karachi, Pakistan (1953) and
was commissioned by the UN for a housing
study in Pakistan and also appointed
as Director of the Morocco Planning
Department. There, in close collaboration
with George Candilis and Shadrach
Woods he developed a comprehensive
body of work on housing, presented at
CIAM 9 (1953) under the Gamma group.
Soon Écochard became one of the most
requested UN experts being commissioned
for the Universities of Karachi (1958),
Abidjan (1962–1978) and Yaoundé (1963),
the Master Plan of Conakry (1959) and Dakar

(1963) and a body of work for Iran. During
1950s Écochard developed a substantial
amount of work in Lebanon with different
local architects, including the Master Plans
for Saida, Byblos and Jounieh (1956–61).
He also worked as a consultant in Beirut's
development plan after Fouad Chehab
ascended to power with the nomination
of Joseph Shader as Minister of Finance
and Planning in 1958. During this period
Écochard eventually met Dr. Sami Abdel-
Baki and had his first contact with Kuwait,
from where he joined the competition for the
National Museum, later awarded with the
first prize. In 1967 he became director of the
Degree in Urbanism at the École Nationale
Supérieure des Beaux-Arts in Paris (1967),
continuing to work on the National Museum
in Kuwait up to its completion in 1982, as
well as in Syria with Samir Abdulac, the
acting Secretary-General of ICOMOS.

Source: Casciato, Maristella; Avermaete, Tom, *Chandigarh
Casablanca: How Architects, Experts, Politicians,
International Agencies, and Citizens Negotiate Modern
Planning*, Park Books, 2015

ELECTROWATT ENGINEERING SERVICE LTD.

In 1895 the power supply industry financing
company, Elektrobank (Bank für Elektrische
Unternehmungen) was established in Zurich
following the progressive introduction of
electrification and the need for financing
construction and operation. The main
investors in the bank were from the early
years the AEG Bank Group (Allgemeine
Elektricitäts-Gesellschaft) and the Schweizerische Kreditanstalt (SKA), later the Credit
Suisse. Among the first hydropower plants
financed by the company in Germany and
Switzerland are Rheinfelden (1898), on
the border between the two and a pioneer
producing electricity by waterpower, Augst-
Wyhlen (1912) and Laufenburg (1914). On
the outbreak of WWI the German company
withdrew its support but Credit Suisse
holding company still owned 42 percent of
Elektrowatt as of 1991. In the postwar years
the company rapidly developed a number of
new facilities and took over existing facilities
in Spain, France, England, Belgium, Austria,
and Hungary, leading to the establishment
of the EWI Ingenieurplanungsabteilung,
a construction technical department,
in 1920. From 1946 onwards, renamed
Elektro-Watt Elektrische und Industrielle
Unternehmungen AG. In 1964 as Elektrowatt
Ingenieurunternehmungen AG (EWI) the
company becomes a major world supplier
of design services with subsidiaries in
Germany and UK developing planning
studies and projects all over Europe, Asia
Africa and South America. In Switzerland
the company increased its investment in
atomic power, specifically the construction
of the country's largest atomic power plant
at Leibstadt. During the late 1970s and
1980s the company increased its presence
in the Middle East region with projects such
as dams and hydro-electric power plants of
Atatürk (1983–90) and Karakaya (1981–87) in

Turkey and the atypical Telecommunication
Centre and Antenna Tower in Kuwait (1981–
95) along with the diversification of project
typologies with the commission for the new
Zurich Stock Exchange, the world's first fully
automated trading, clearing and settlement
system (1995), along with the refurbishment
of the runways and tarmac areas at John
F. Kennedy International Airport in New
York. During the 1990s the company was
dissolved due to successive divisions and
acquisitions.

Source: *International Directory of Company Histories*, v. 6,
St. James Press, 1992

Meyer, Herbert, *A History of Electricity and
Magnetism*, Massachusetts Institute of Technology, 1971

Gugler, Adolf, "Elektrowatt: Accepting the Challenge of the
Future," in *Swiss Quality Products*, Autumn 1989

ENERGOPROJEKT ENGINEERING AND CONTRACTING

Energoprojekt was established in 1951
in Belgrade as a working unit for design
engineering and construction of hydro
and thermal power generators and
water management, emerging from the
national company for power distribution
Elektroistok. The national reconstruction
programmes after WWII strengthened the
design department of Elektroistok, which
transformed into the new company, under
the guidance of figures such as the architect
Milica Šterić (1914–1998). During the 1950s
under Šterić the architectural department
of the construction unit developed several
power stations and thermal plants all
over the country. In 1957 Šterić was sent
for six months to the Van den Broek and
Bakema office in the Netherlands, where
she had her first contact with the Middle
East. The first years of 1960s two other
important practitioners were integrated with
the group, Zoran Bojović and Dragoljub
Bakić. The emergence of Tito in the new
socialist Federal Republic of Yugoslavia
gave rise to Energoprojekt's growth outside,
mainly among the *non-aligned* countries.
Among other projects, Iraq and Kuwait
were eventually the first countries to award
commissions in the Gulf region to the
company. In 1964 Dragoljub Bakić was sent
to Kuwait to prepare the design package for
the Institute for the Physically Handicapped
(1963–69), among other projects such as
the resort of Mina Abdullah (Umm-Elhiman,
Um Qasaba) for KOC in 1965 that was
never realised, the Professors' Dormitories,
the Olympic Swimming Pool in Adeliya
(1968–) and the eventual commission for the
design of the Students' Housing Complex
in Kaifan (1967–1978). Energoprojekt was
to become established in Kuwait for a
long time with its architects renowned for
their capability to design and build large
and complex structures in a short period
of time. Among these projects were the
several power sub-stations throughout
Kuwait, the Abraj Al-Kuwait (1965–77), the
Ministries Complex (1978–82) and the Safat

Tower, completed after the Invasion. The company was also involved in low-income housing implementation, mainly in providing schools and clinic units in large re-housing schemes, such as Jahra's Popular Housing Programmes (1971–74) along with Khaitan and Omariya.

Source: Zindović, Milena (ed.), *Women in Architecture. Contemporary Architecture in Serbia since 1900,* Centre for Architecture, Belgrade, 2014

Bakić, Ljiljana, *Anatomija B&B Arhitekture,* Krug Commerce, Belgrade, 2012

EWBANK & PARTNERS LTD.

C.H.P. Ewbank, ex-military and chief-engineer from Edmundsons, founded Ewbank & Partners Limited in 1946. Operating from Brighton, had the UK electricity supply industry as its main clients. The company became a major consultant in power generation, transmission and distribution, desalination and telecommunications. In 1983 it was converted to Ewbank Preece Engineering Consultants and in 1994 became part of Mott MacDonald Group. The first work overseas came with the British-Iranian Oil Company followed by a KOC commission to develop a combined power generating and water desalination plant at Mina Al-Ahmadi (1951) and was later appointed by the Amir of Kuwait for a similar plant in Kuwait City together with electricity and water distribution systems. For their work in Kuwait Ewbank & Partners collaborated with the architects Farmer & Dark. The main project engineers in this country were Deryck Smart and Jean Louis de Neve.

Source: Mott MacDonald Group, company profile 2014

Roberts, Gwilym, *Chelsea to Cairo: 'Taylor-made' Water Through Eleven Reigns and in Six Continents. A History of John Taylor & Sons and Their Predecessors,* London, Thomas Telford, 2006

FARMER & DARK ARCHITECTS

The practice was established in 1934 by Frank Quentery Farmer (1879–1955) and Bernard Frankland Dark (d. 1972). Well-known in Great Britain for projects such as the Bowater-Scott Paper Mill (Kent, 1959), the Central Clinic and the Head Offices for People Corporation (1962, Dorset), the IBM UK Laboratories Limited (1964, Winchester), the Six Schools in Leicestershire County (1960s), the Riverwalk House (London, 1966), the Gulbenkian Theatre and Cinema (University of Kent, 1969), the Countesthorpe School (Leicestershire, 1971), the Telephone Exchange (1978, Oxford) and the Queen Elizabeth II Law Courts (Liverpool, 1984). During the post-war the practice was well connected with the electrical industry and specialised in power station design. Commissioned during the late 1940s for several power plants in the UK, the firm was known by being called in at the last moment to tidy up and make industrial facilities more presentable. That is the case with Cliff Quay (Ipswich, 1950), Brunswick Wharf (London, 1952), West Ham B (London, 1952), Coal-Fired Power Plants and Bowater Industries' Ltd. factory (Cheshire, 1957). Overseas, commissions in Kuwait such as the Power and Water Desalination Plant in Mina Al-Ahmadi (1948) and Shuwaikh (1951– 61), the Naief Avenue (1960) and Sheikh Jaber Al-Ali's Palace in Surra (1955–1960) diversified the firm's production. Also to be noted the late commission for the Kuwait Embassy and Ambassador's official residence in London (1977).

Source: Farmer & Dark, Architects, "Historical Notes Sent to the Survey of London," Feb. 13 ,1987, in Tom Eaton, "Brunswick Wharf Power Station", Feb. 9, 1987

Pollard, Richard; Pevsner, Nikolaus; Sharples, Joseph, *Lancashire: Liverpool and the Southwest,* Yale University Press, 2006

Brooks, Alan; Pevsner, Nikolaus, *Worcestershire,* Yale University Press, 2007

Pevsner, Nikolaus; Williamson, Elizabeth. *Derbyshire,* Yale University Press, 1978

Glendinning, Miles, *Modern Architect: The Life and Times of Robert Matthew,* RIBA Publishing, 2008

FREDERICK SNOW & PARTNERS

Sir Frederick Snow (1899–1976) of Sir Frederick Snow and Partners was a graduate in Civil Engineering who joined the Royal Artillery in WWI and later served in the Royal Engineers. He started his practice right after WWI and among his most notable achievements were the design of the Foundations for Unilever House and South Africa House, both in London and completed in 1933. In 1943 the firm expanded with major works for the aviation industry, including the overall design of Gatwick Airport, completed in the 1950s. In 1958 he was commissioned for the new Kuwait International Air Terminal, runways, taxiways and facilities. During the implementation of the runways, major problems arose and the firm was held responsible after Kuwaiti Government's claim to the International Court (1975–84). In 1965 the name of the firm changed to Frederick S. Snow and Partners. Following the International Court decision on the Kuwait Airport case, the Associated Consulting Engineers (ACE) of Beirut, owned by the former partners of Kamal Shair at Dar Al-Handasah, acquired control of the firm in 1989.

Source: England and Wales / 01 March 1984 / England and Wales, House of Lords / Minister of Public Works of the Government of the State of Kuwait v. Sir Frederick Snow & Partners, 1984 A.C. 426, online: ICLR http://cases.iclr.co.uk/Subscr/Search.aspx

FITZROY ROBINSON PARTNERSHIP

Herbert Fitzroy Robinson (1914–2005) was a graduate from Bartlett School of Architecture under Prof. Albert Richardson (1880–1964), the mentor of Basil Urwin Spence (1907–76) and established his own practice in 1956, Fitzroy Robinson & Partners. During the 1960s the firm consolidated its reputation for bank offices and branch designs including the regional bullion centres for the Bank of England in Birmingham, Manchester and Newcastle. In 1972 he collaborated with Sir Basil Spence International Partnership, upon John S. Bonnington and Gordon Collins' participation in the Kuwait National Assembly design competition (1971–72) under Sir Basil Spence, Bonnington & Collins. Upon Spence's death in 1976, Fitzroy Robinson & Partners assisted Anthony Blee in many of the projects in which Sir Basil Spence was involved, including the Kuwait Law Courts (1976–83). This encouraged the firms' expansion into the Middle East with the development of several bank headquarters buildings in the UAE from 1977 onwards, in association with the former Design Construction Group (DGC) partner Anthony Irving. The practice continues today as Aukett Fitzroy Robinson.

Source: "Herbert Fitzroy Robinson, 1914–2005," obituary, in *Architects Journal.* http://www.architectsjournal.co.uk/news/obituary-herbert-fitzroy-robinson-1914-2005/583145.article

FULLER & SADAO INC.

Shoji Sadao (1927–), a graduate of Cornell University, established in 1964 Fuller & Sadao Inc. with his professor Richard Buckminster Fuller (1895–1983), the renowned inventor and visionary. The first commission was the geodesic dome for the US Pavilion at EXPO 67 (1964–67) in Montreal, following a series of patent applications for geodesic domes' constructive and components systems. In the same year the firm proposed the Tensegrity Dome for Israel and the Geodesic Dwelling Units for General Electric. In 1966 the Japanese Nippon TV Network Co. commissioned the firm to undertake a design feasibility study for a 3.7 km high observation tower and in 1968 the firm was commissioned to design and detail the proposed spheres of Abraj Al-Kuwait (1965–76) as the main tower of a system. While working on the Kuwait water tower, the firm developed the Triton City scheme for Tokyo bay.

Source: Sadao, Shoji, *Buckminster Fuller and Isamu Noguchi: Best of Friends,* Five Continents Editions, 2011

Fuller, R. Buckminster, *Critical Path,* St. Martins Press, 1981

GARDELLA, IGNAZIO

Ignazio Gardella (1905–1999), obtained a degree in Civil Engineering from the Polytechnic University of Milan (1928) and a PhD in Architecture from Venice University Institute of Architecture (1949) where he taught as professor until 1975. He developed strong friendships with Luchino Visconti, Giovanni Romano, Franco Albini and all the future BBPR (1932–) partners. After a first visit to Germany in 1929, he began his own practice. With its first commissions in Milan the new practice was awarded with two projects in Alexandria, Egypt, the Anti-Tuberculosis Dispensary (1934–38) and the Provincial Hygiene and Prophylactic Laboratory (1937–39). In 1936 he participated to the VI Trienniale di Milano with Franco Albini, Camus and Romano, and collaborated to the magazine *Casabella*. He entered with Albini in the competition for a hostel in the E-42 district of Rome. In 1939, with Giuseppe Pagano he visited Gunnar Asplund, Sven Markelius and Alvar Aalto. An active member in the post-war reconstruction enterprise he was involved in the Movement for Architectural Studies (MSA) as president. In 1947 he founded Azucena and in 1952, together with Rogers and Albini organised the CIAM Summer School in Venice. A recipient of the Olivetti Prize for Architecture in 1955, he continued working in Alexandria and in 1960 was invited to enter the Kuwait National Museum competition but declined to submit a proposal. In the coming decades he produced some of his more relevant work and during the 1980s worked with Aldo Rossi at the Teatro Carlo Felice in Genova (1981–90) and taught at Harvard (1986). In 1993 he was awarded honorary citizenship of Alexandria, Egypt and in 1996 received the Leone d'Oro for his career at the Bienniale di Venezia.

Bescós, Rafael; Maggiore, Carlo Alberto, *Ignazio Gardella 1905–1999. Arquitectura a traves de un siglo*, Electa Espana, Madrid, 1999

Casamonti, Marco, *Ignazio Gardella Architetto. Costruire la modernità*, Electa, Milano, 2006

GHAZI SULTAN

Ghazi Sultan (1941–2007), after a child-hood in Mumbai, graduated in Architecture from the Carnegie Institute of Technology, Pittsburgh, USA during the early 1960s, with a strong relationship with William S. Huff, professor of the Basic Design Studio and a former graduate of H.f.G. in Ulm. During those years, urban renewal became a major content of the Carnegie Technical degree, besides a Bauhaus-oriented inspiration and an architecture largely independent from the past. The studio works of Ghazi varied from military facilities to the display of artwork. After a short passage through Kuwait where he implemented KEO's department of architecture in 1965, he returned back to school to attend his Master's in Urban Design, recently created by Sert after the famous Urban Design Conferences (1956–65) at the Graduate School of Design. From 1967 with Jerzy Soltan, the degree content moved closer to Team X's agenda and among his professors were Jaqueline Tyrwhitt, Hideo Sasaki, Shadrach William Woods and eventually Macklin Hancock, who had worked in Kuwait since 1961. He returned to Kuwait in 1968 and was actively participating in the Urban Form Studies for the Old City as Assistant Director for Technical Affairs in the Municipality. In parallel he experimented with his design capabilities in the Kuwait Society of Engineers head office competition, which won the first prize. One year later Ghazi co-founded with his sister Najat the first art gallery in Kuwait and in the following years he occupied different high-ranking positions in the country's planning authorities. As an architect he developed his own practice over the 1970s and 1980s in parallel with KEO. Relevant achievements are the Four Houses project, nominated for the Aga Khan Award for Architecture, the Anwar Al-Sabah Complex, the Dasman Complex and the 14 km long scheme for the Waterfront Competition (1976), built in 1988.

Source: "The Sultan Art Gallery", in *The Kuwaiti*, 1971

Khouri, Kristine, "Mapping Arab Art through the Sultan Gallery", in *The ArteEast Quarterly*, Spring 2014

100 Years of Student Work, An Exhibit of Work from the School of Architecture (1905–2005), The Carnegie Mellon University Archives

Mumford, Eric Paul, *Defining Urban Design: CIAM Architects and the Formation of a Discipline 1937–69*, Yale University Press, 2009

Sert, Josep Luis; Mostafavi, Mohsen, *The Writings of Josep Lluís Sert*, Yale University Press, 2015

GULF ENGINEERING OFFICE (GEO)

In 1967 the engineers Hamad Thunayan Alghanim and Mohamed Tawil formed the Gulf Engineering Office. The actual Gulf Consult gained recognition in the local production of architecture with the incorporation of Ryszard Daczkowski and Edward Lach, both graduated in the mid-1960s from the former Hans Poelzig's Breslau School (Wrocław Polytechnic) and later joined by Jan Matkowski and Mieszko Niedźwiecki. Ryszard Daczkowski, former faculty of History of Urbanism at Wrocław was to lead the firm's design for the multi-storey parking garage and mall, Souk Dawaliya (1978) an important element of the Action 1 plans of Kuwait's Second Master Plan, which included several similar typologies designed by TAC, SOM and the John S. Bonnington Partnership. During the 1980s the firm achieved the completion of the prominent high-rise build of Al-Qibla Tower (1989) and became specialised in hospitals with notable collaborations with AART Farah Architectes Associes (former LWD, AART/ATEA) with Samir Farah for the Adult Psychiatric Hospital (1987–2002) and with the world renowned Llewelyn-Davies Weeks Associates from Richard Llewellyn-Davies (1912–1981) for the Thunayan Al-Ghanim Gastroenterology Centre (1987).

Source: Gulf Consult, company online platform: http://gckuwait.com/history

Bricault, G. C., *Gulf Consult profile, Major Companies of the Arab World 1991/92*, Springer Science & Business Media, 2012

Hawrylak, Jadwiga Grabowska, "Residential and Commercial Team at Pl. Grunwald in Wrocław," in *Architecture*, 1973, n. 10

Wiśniowski, Błażej, "Krzysztof Wiśniowski, Anna Wiśniowska, Magdalena Wiśniowska, Jan Wiśniowski: 1969–2006," Muzeum Architektury we Wrocławiu, Wrocław, 2006

HAMID SHUAIB

Hamid Shuaib (1932–1994) graduated in Architecture from the Oxford Polytechnic in 1958; after an internship in London he returned to Kuwait to serve as assistant architect in the Ministry of Public Works. In 1962 he started his Master's degree in Civic Design at the University of Liverpool with Prof. H. Myles Wright (chair between 1954–75) who continued the strong legacy of Gordon Stephenson (chair between 1948–53) and William Holford (1936–47). Upon the completion of his degree in 1964, Myles Wright was instrumental in recommending Shuaib for a job with Leslie Martin (1908–2000) at the London County Council. The LCC was still then the biggest planning corporation in the world. In 1965 Shuaib returned to Kuwait as Assistant Director for Technical Affairs of the Municipality, becoming, upon completion of the Kuwait's Second Master Plan (1972), the Assistant Director General of the Municipality. After 1973 Shuaib was to hold the position of Municipality Chief Architect up to 1984, accumulating in parallel, different top positions in the country's planning hierarchy and civic society, such as founder member of the Kuwait Science Club, President of the Kuwait Environment Protection Society and of the Arab Union Federation and Chairman of the Planning Committee, Member of the Royal Institute of British Architects (RIBA) and of the Royal Town Planning Institute since 1978. In 1968 Shuaib was one of the founders of the Pan Arab Consulting Engineers (PACE) and co-founder of the Kuwait Society of Engineers.

Source: Gardiner, Stephen, *Kuwait the Making of a City*, Longman Group Limited, Essex, 1983

Gedeon, Charles G., *Who's Who in the Arab World 2007–2008*, Publitec Publications, Beirut, 2007

HASSAN FATHY

Hassan Fathy (1900–1989) completed his studies at Cairo University in 1925, where he met Mahmoud Riad (1905–1979) for the first time, and earned a scholarship to graduate at the École Nationale Supérieure des Beaux-Arts in Paris where he eventually met Michel Écochard (1905–1985), Raymond Lopez (1904–1966) and Louis Skidmore (1897–1962). In 1930 he initiated his academic career as professor at the School of Fine Arts in Cairo and joined Mahmoud Riad at the Cairo Municipal Affairs Department. In 1940 he was commissioned by the Royal Agricultural Society to design an experimental farm and in 1945 commenced the construction of New Gourna in Bahtim, Egypt, a project that continued until 1968. Between 1949–52 he served as Director of the School Buildings Department at the Ministry of Education and from 1953 become the head of the Architectural Department at the School of Fine Arts in Cairo. From 1957 to 1961 he joined Doxiadis Associates in Athens after being recruited by Constantinos A. Doxiadis (1913–1975). The latter had just secured a commission in Iraq for a five-year plan to create new village settlements in former desert areas. Fathy led the plan for the villages of Greater Mussayib, south of Baghdad reapplying the knowledge of New Gourna and recalibrating it for mass-production. His input in this project strongly affected the narratives of Doxiadis and also Jaqueline Tyrwhitt (1905–83). In 1960 he was engaged in Doxiadis' most ambitious project of all, the City of the Future, also shared with Saba George Shiber (1923–1968) in Kuwait, which led to Fathy's return to Egypt upon Gamal Abdel Nasser's call. From 1961 he established a practice in Egypt that served Nasser's revolutionary government and its Pan-Arabist ideology through his quest of an Egyptian/Arab cultural identity. In 1973 Fathy published *Architecture for the Poor: An Experiment in Rural Egypt* and in 1980 he received the first Chairman's Award by the Aga Khan Award for Architecture.

Source: Fathy, Hassan, "Beyond the Human Scale [Interview]," in *AAQ: Architectural Association Quarterly*, n. 6, 1974, pp. 53–57

Fathy, Hassan, *Architecture for the Poor: An Experiment in Rural Egypt*, University of Chicago Press, Chicago, 1973

Pyla, Panayiota, "Hassan Fathy Revisited: Postwar Discourses on Science, Development, and Vernacular Architecture," in *Journal of Architectural Education*, n. 60, 2007, pp. 28–39

Hassan Fathy, ArchNet, http://www.archnet.org/library/parties/one-party.jsp?party_id=1

Goldschmidt, Arthur, *Biographical Dictionary of Modern Egypt*, Lynne Rienner Publishers, 2000

HISHAM MUNIR AND ASSOCIATES

Hisham Munir (1930–), Bachelor's degree in Architectural Engineering from the American University of Beirut and University of Texas, Austin, and M.Arch. from the University of Southern California Los Angeles (1956), he established, in association with Medhat Ali Madhloom, the Hisham Munir and Associates practice after returning back to Iraq in 1957. As head of the Technical Section 3 of the Ministry of Public Works in Baghdad he oversaw some of the key governmental works such as the Civic Centre (W. M. Dudok, 1957) and the University (TAC, 1957). Among the first professors of the Baghdad Faculty of Architecture, he was active in establishing the post-graduate programme and in 1966 presented at the Iraq Engineers' Scientific Conference an article entitled "Environment and Urban Design." As local consultant the firm was involved in many of TAC works in Iraq including the University of Baghdad, the University of Mosul Master Plan (1966), and the Sheraton Hotels in Baghdad and Basra (1981). Following official roles in the Civic Centre and University the firm developed new plans for the Civic Centre (1971) and the Medical City (1973–77). In the mid 1970s the firm was especially active with the accomplishment of the Iraqi Reinsurance Company (1976) and the Agricultural Complex (1975) in Baghdad and the competition entry for the Anwar Al-Sabah Complex in Kuwait (1976). Following Ahmed Hassan Al-Bakr's fall from power and up to the end to Iran-Iraq war, the firm served the regime's vision, being in charge of several projects including the collaboration with Roger Butler & Burgan Associates and Whiting Associates for the development of the Medical City up to completion in 1983, the Ministries of Higher Education, Oil, Interior and Trade head office towers, the Social Security and the Mayor's Office in Baghdad. This period culminated with the collaboration with Khalid Al-Rahaal and Marcello D'Olivo for the Unknown Soldier Monument and the Kuwait Embassy building (1979–84). The departure of several key collaborators in the office such as Sami al-Bader (who left to Kuwait to establish there the local branch of TEST), Bob Khewro (left in 1980 for PACE) and Hisham N. Ashkouri (left in 1986) together with the fall of the regime led eventually to the closure of the firm that today operates from the USA under the Munir Group.

Source: Kultermann, Udo, *Contemporary Architecture in the Arab States*, McGraw-Hill Publishers, 1999

Munir Group online platform profile: http://www. hishammunirarch.com/

HOARE, LEA AND PARTNERS

Henry Lea (1839–1912), engineer and expert in civil, mechanical and electrical disciplines established a consultancy in Birmingham in 1862. In 1882 the firm supervised the implementation of electrical lighting systems in Birmingham Town Hall and public street lighting for Chelsea, London. In the following years the firm pioneered electrical and mechanical design in the UK in the fields of building ventilation and lighting systems including the registration of several patents. In 1902 Lea designed and implemented an air conditioning system with humidity and temperature control at the new Royal Victoria Hospital in Belfast. In 1912 Lea's son took control up to his death in 1939 when Donald Lea led the company to the merger with Edwin S. Hoare (1887–1957) from Bristol. In 1945 Hoare, Lea and Partners opened a branch in London with their first commissions in India. During the 1950s and 1960s the firm developed expertise on large planning multidisciplinary team projects, being involved in the design of university campuses, large schools, hospitals, defence works and a wide range of commercial and industrial projects. By then the firm had opened offices in Nigeria and all over North Africa and gained a hold in the Middle East region with projects such as the Salmiya District Centre (1971–77) in Kuwait and the Al-Ain Hospital (Al-Jimi) in the UAE (1978). The firm is still operating all over the world to this day with a strong presence in the region with offices in Abu Dhabi and Qatar.

Source: company profile in *Hoare Lea 150 years*, http://anniversary.hoarelea.com/

IMOS MEDICAL ARCHITECTURE

With the construction of the Clinical Centre Ljubljana (University Medical Centre) in Slovenia (1967–76), a group of experts involved in the projects established a consultancy, IMOS Medical Architecture, led by Stanko Kristl (1932–) who became an acclaimed architect in ex-Yugoslavia after the completion of the Elementary School Dr. France Preseren in Kranj (1968), and the Kindergarten unit in Vetrnica, Slovenia (1973). Kristl was a graduate from the Ljubljana Department of Architecture of the Technical Faculty (1959) under Prof. Edvard Ravnikar (1907–93). The first major commission for the Clinical Centre was succeed by the General Hospital in Izola (1972–88). Later several other projects were commissioned to IMOS but never realised, such as the Clinical Centre of Faculty of Medicine and a clinic in Novi Sad (1976–82), a centre for physical medicine and rehabilitation in Kuwait (1979–81) and part of a project for the Medical Centre in Sombor (1976–81). In 1980 Kristl was appointed Associate Professor in the field of Social and Residential Buildings, in 1981 he was Doctor of Architectural Sciences, and in 1982 began teaching at the Faculty of Architecture, Civil Engineering and Geodesy, University of Ljubljana. In 1986 he was elected to a full professorship and he taught until 1993. From 1996 to 2007 he lectured at the Department of Landscape Architecture at the Biotechnical Faculty in Ljubljana.

Source: Teržan, Vesna, "Povojna generacija slovenskih modernistov: Stanko Kristl", in *Mladina*, n. 16–17, Apr. 22, 2011

Interview: Stanko Kristl by Ana Gruden Andrejak, Tadej Glažar for *Oris-Magazine for Architecture and Culture*, n.16, www.oris.hr

Kristl, Stanko Biogaphy (sl.) in SASA – Slovenian Academy of Sciences and Arts online platform: http://www.sazu.si/o-sazu/clani/stanko-kristl.html

I.M. PEI & PARTNERS

Ieoh Ming Pei (1917–) graduated in Engineering from the Massachusetts Institute of Technology (MIT) in 1939 and later received a Master's in Architecture from Harvard Graduate School of Design in 1946 where he stayed on as assistant professor until 1948, joining the firm of William Zeckendorf (1905–76) in New York City, as director of the recently created architectural division. Working for a real-estate developer allowed Pei to lead a series of projects in Denver, Montreal and Chicago (the Hyde Park Redevelopment, 1959). Throughout his collaboration with Zeckendorf, Pei established his own practice in 1955 as I.M. Pei & Associates with Henry N. Cobb (1926–) and Eason H. Leonard (1920–03), renamed I.M. Pei & Partners in 1966 and finally Pei, Cobb, Freed and Partners in 1989. In 1956 the incorporation of Araldo A. Cossutta (1925–) who became partner from

1963–73 was fundamental for some of the most acclaimed projects of the firm, such as the Denver Sheraton (1960), University Gardens Apartments (1961) in Chicago and the Cecil and Ida Green Center for Earth Sciences (1964), the Christian Science Center (1968–74) and the Hancock Tower (1968–75) in Boston. In 1977 the firm was commissioned to work on the Hilton Area Apartments, previously developed in 1971 by G. Candilis (1913–95). In 1983 I.M. Pei was awarded the Pritzker Prize and new commissions such as the Grand Louvre extension in Paris (1989) initiated a new era in the firm, which culminated with the success of the Museum of Islamic Art in Doha (2008–12).

INDUSTRIAL & ENGINEERING CONSULTING OFFICE (INCO)

Mohammed Abdullah Al-Sanan graduated in Engineering and in 1975 established the Industrial & Engineering Consulting Office (INCO). During the first years the firm specialised in infrastructural and services design. After being awarded the Al-Qurain (1982–88) and Sabah Al-Salem (1977–82) housing projects by NHA and a successful entry for the Kuwait National Theatre Competition in a joint effort with Victor Shiber Consult. The latter was an architectural practice established in Kuwait since the 1960s under Saba George Shiber's brother. INCO performed as a reputable architectural practice in Kuwait throughout the 1980s. A significant contribution to their reputation was the incorporation of two Polish architects, Krzysztof Wiśniowski and Andrzej Bohdanowicz, both graduates of Wrocław Polytechnic (the former Hans Poelzig's Breslau School) in the mid-1960s and former professors in Planning, Urbanism and History. Both architects were strongly influenced by Prof. Jadwiga Grabowska-Hawrylak (1920–), the author of the Manhattan Project in Wrocław and among the first female architects in Poland. The two were later joined by Leopold Chyczewski who led INCO to a series of architectural achievements such as the Port Authority Headquarters (1984–92) and the Baloush Bus Terminal (1986–88).

Source: Stanek, Łukasz, "Mobilities of Architecture in the Global Cold War: From Socialist Poland To Kuwait And Back," in *International Journal of Islamic Architecture*, v. 4 n. 2, 2015

Krzysztof Wiśniowski interview, 03 March 2014

IRAQ CONSULT (IQC)

A practice established in 1952, under the name of Chadirji, Sherzad and Abdulla Ihsan Kamil, by the architect Rifat Chadirji (1926–), head of Baghdad Building Department from 1954 and a graduate of Hammersmith School of Arts and Crafts, London (1952), by Abdullah Ihsan Kamil, a graduate of Liverpool University (1943) and Professor of Faculty of Architecture in Baghdad and by Ihsan Sherzad, a graduate in Structural Engineering from Baghdad (1946) with a Master's from the University of Michigan (1950), Professor of Structures at Baghdad University, who later completed Bachelor's in Law from Baghdad University (1962) and a PhD from University of California (1987). Sherzad was also an active Kurdish politician and on several occasions a member of the Iraqi government. During the first years the firm based its scope on supervision, commissioning large urban scale operations such as the City of Sports (Le Corbusier, 1957), the Al-Shaab Stadium (Kiel do Amaral, 1961–66), the Calouste Gulbenkian Museum of Modern Art (1958–62), the Civic Centre (W. M. Dudok, 1957) and the University of Baghdad (TAC, 1957). In parallel the partnership, mainly through Chadirji, collected its first commissions for an apartment building (1953), for three monuments in Baghdad, of which only the Monument to the Unknown Soldier (1959) was built, a few private houses, such as the F. Alousi Residence (1961–63), A.S. Azzawi's Residence (1963), the M. Othman Residence (1965) along with different design competitions for the Chamber of Commerce (1964), the Sewage Administration Building (1964), Ministry of Municipal and Rural Affairs (1965), Iraq Scientific Academy (1965) and the Awqaf (1965). Before 1965 the partnership was in charge of the design and construction of some of the most famous works, such as the National Insurance Company in Mosul, the Tobacco Monopoly Administration and the Rafidain Bank branch in Baghdad, all completed by 1967. In 1965 upon the completion of the Iraq Consult Bureau and the appointment for new major works the name Iraq Consult (IQC) was finally established. The first opportunity abroad came from the Kuwaiti Ambassador in Baghdad for his villa in Kuwait, completed in 1967, after which IQC started a collaboration with the recently established Kuwaiti firm Pan Arab Consulting Engineers (PACE). Those were very productive years with interesting competition entries for the Kuwait Society of Engineers (1968), Presidential Palace of Baghdad (1968), London Central Mosque (1969), the Bahrain's Chamber of Commerce (1969), the National Bank of Abu Dhabi (1970). In the same period the firm completed the Central Post, Telegraph and Telephone Administration HQ (1971) and Rafidain Bank in Baghdad (1969) and the first projects in Kuwait and Bahrain. At the office, collaborators like Maath Alousi (1961–74) and Saad Al-Zubaidi (1965–73), were motivated to develop further their studies at the Tropical Studies Department of AA in London. Meanwhile the relationship with PACE was not to last and after 1970 the firm was commissioned directly by the Kuwaiti Ministry of Public Works for several sport complexes and invited for the Kuwait National Assembly Competition (1972). The firm finally expanded abroad and by the mid-1970s established offices all over the Gulf States, with important works in UAE such as the competition for the Municipality of Dubai Administration Offices (1974), the ADNOC Administration Offices, Dubai (1975), the Council of Ministries Buildings in Abu Dhabi (1978), the Abu Dhabi National Theatre (1975) and the Al-Ain Public Library (1978). In Iraq the relationship with the government became more politicised in the competition for the Headquarters Complex for the Regional Command Council of the Ba'ath Party (1975), the first building initiative of Saddam Hussein and the Ministries Council of Iraq in Baghdad (1975). At the time of closure in 1978, following Chadirji's arrest, the firm had many offices in the Gulf region, which were eventually absorbed into their former partners' new firms.

Source: Rifat Chadirji interview, *Bespoke Magazine*, 2009
Rifat Chadirji interview, *The New York Times*, 2003

Chadirji, Rifat, *Concepts and Influences: Towards a Regionalized International Architecture*, KPI, London 1986

Calouste Gunbenkian Archieve, Lisbon

Sharara, Balqis; Chadirji, Rifat, *A Wall between Two Darknesses*, Dar al-Saqi, London & Beirut, 2004

Bazarov, Konstantin, *Rifat Chadirji. Contemporary Architects 163*, St. James Press, Chicago, 1987

JACOBSEN, ARNE

Arne Jacobsen (1902–71), graduated in Architecture from the Royal Danish Academy of Fine Arts (1927) after a short experience as an apprentice mason. Following an incredible student record and being well-travelled around Europe, he started practicing with Copenhagen Municipality's chief architect and in 1929, together with Flemming Lassen won the competition of The House of the Future promoted by the Association of Danish Architects. In 1930 he established his own practice and won the competition for the Klampenborg seaside resort (1930–37) where Jacobsen designed almost all the possible elements, from the lifeguard towers to the employees' uniforms. The practice developed an extensive body of outstanding work, including the SAS Royal Hotel of Copenhagen (1958–1960). During WWII, while exiled in Sweden, Jacobsen turned his hand to product design, becoming well-known as a designer who made prototypes for furniture, textiles, wallpapers, silverware etc. Among his most famous designs are the chairs; the Ant (1952–1953), the Swan (1958), the Egg (1957–1958), the 3107 Series (1955) and his tableware Cylinda-Line (1967). In 1956 Jacobsen began an academic career at the Royal Danish Academy of Fine Arts where he taught until 1965. During the 1960s Jacobsen's most notable work was St. Catherine's College, Oxford (1960–1964) where the interest to control all the elements of a building resembles a life time ambition for the *Gesamtkustwerk* (the total work of art). In 1961 the commission for the National Bank of Denmark paved the way to one of his last projects, the Central Bank of Kuwait (1966–76).

Source: de Corral, Félix Solaguren-Beascoa, *Arne Jacobsen: Approach to his Complete Works*, Arkitektens Forlag, 2001

Faber, Tobias, *Arne Jacobsen*, G. Hatje, 1964

JAFAR TUKAN

Jafar Tukan (1938–2014) was awarded a Degree in Architecture from the American University in Beirut (1955–60). After a brief passage serving the Jordanian Ministry of Public Works as a design architect, Tukan joined Dar Al-Handasah in Beirut (1961–68) and was eventually involved in different stages of the KNPC Head Offices in Kuwait City (1965) under the architect and sculptor Ghassan Klink's lead and at the Amman Central Bank (1967) under Robert Wakim's (1931–) lead. In 1968, he established a private practice in Beirut with several commissions in the same year for Lebanon, UAE and Kuwait, where he teamed up with KEB (Kuwait Engineering Bureau) for the Low-Income Housing Scheme of Riqqa (1971–76) and developed other residential and office units such as the Ibn Khaldoun Street Residences. In 1973 he joined George R. Rais, the former partner of Assem Salaam and Theo Kaanan and co-author of the Pan Am Building (1955), Cinema Hamra (1958) in Beirut, to form Rais and Tukan Architects, developing until 1976 large governmental projects in Saudi Arabia, Jordan and the UAE. After 1976 Tukan became the sole partner of Jafar Tukan and Partners Architects and Engineers, which was relocated in Amman.

Source: Hiari, Sandra, "Jafar Tukan: Remembering an Architectural Giant," in *Venture Business Intelligence Monthly (Venture Magazine)*, Nov. 26, 2014. http://www.venturemagazine.me/2014/11/jafar-tukan-remembering-architectural-giant/

Consolidate Consultants Group online platform: http://www.group-cc.com/en/content/architect-jafar-tukan-leaves-mark-consolidated-consultants-group

JOHN R. HARRIS ARCHITECTS

John and Jill Harris established the practice in 1950, both having graduated from the AA London, with Stuart Aston who became a partner in 1973.They rapidly gained a reputation in the Gulf with the commission for the Kuwait Building Research Laboratories in 1951, supported by George Atkinson's Building Research Station (BRS) in Garston. The team included Bill Allen, Chief Architect (and Deputy Head, Physics) who worked with Scott & Wilson and Leslie Martin on the Royal Festival Hall and later was Principal of the Architectural Association School in London (1961–66). At the same time the firm won the first prize at RIBA's international competition for the State Hospital in Doha, Qatar. The latter defined the firm's specialisation in healthcare buildings in an international contex. This led to the commission for Sulaibikhat Hospital (1954–64) and further collaboration with Fry & Drew for Ahmadi Hospital (1955–60). The consistency of work in the following years established the firm's base in the region for more than 40 years. Some of the most relevant works are in Dubai: the hospitals, the World Trade Centre and First Master Plan.

Source: Morris, A.E.J., *John R. Harris Architects*, Hurtwood Press Ltd, London, 1984

JOHN S. BONNINGTON PARTNERSHIP (SIR BASIL SPENCE, BONNINGTON & COLLINS)

John Smith Bonnington (1929–) graduated in Architecture from the University of Leeds, under Basil Spence (1907–76) in 1955. Bonnington received his first practice experience in the USA straight after completing his degree and in 1956, together with his wife Esme Bonnington (1928–) at Basil Spence and Partners' offices at Fitzroy Square, London, where they worked on the new Coventry Cathedral (1951–62). From 1963 the office started working independently under Bonnington, also known as Jack, which had just completed the Ferrum House in Harpenden, with Gordon Collins. The new practice was first named Sir Basil Spence, Bonnington & Collins and upon invitation for advice on Kuwait University's planning in 1969, Bonnington visited the country and initiated a long and successful professional relationship with the region. The Kuwait National Assembly Competition (1971–72) was eventually one of the last projects under this umbrella. In 1973 the new firm, John S. Bonnington Partnership was chosen to design Souq Al-Muttaheda and Al-Masseel (1973–79) in Kuwait in parallel with several commissions in Doha including the zoo. The success in the Gulf culminated with the Stock Exchange Market (1978–86) and the Extension of Kuwaiti Zoo (1981). During the 1970s the company developed great competence in planning, being awarded international projects such as the Vale do Lobo resort in Portugal for Richard Costain (1971–77).

Source: *MEC. Middle East Construction*, v. 9, New World Publishers Limited, 1984

RIBA Journal, v. 81, n. 5–8, Royal Institute of British Architects, 1974

"Basil Urwin Spence" in *Dictionary of Scottish Architects*, online platform. Architect biograph: http://www.scottisharchitects.org.uk/architect_full.php?id=203352

JOHNSON, PHILIP

Philip Johnson (1906–2005) started his studies in Philosophy and History at Harvard University that were interrupted by extensive trips to Europe, where in 1928 he met Ludwig Mies van der Rohe (1886–69) who eventually inspired Johnson to move his career towards art and architecture. In 1932 Johnson established the department of Architecture and Design at the Museum of Modern Art and co-curated "The International Style: Architecture Since 1922" exhibition in the same year. He was influential in arranging Le Corbusier's first visit to US in 1935 and in the immigration of Mies and Marcel Breuer to the US during WWII. After some politically active years where he attended a Hitler rally in Potsdam, Berlin, the so-called *Sommerkurs für Ausländer* in 1938, he enrolled in the Graduate School of Design at Harvard University in 1942 graduating a year later. In 1949 Johnson designed a residence for himself, the now famous Glass House in Connecticut. In 1955 he joined Mies as the New York associate for the design of the Seagram Building, completed in 1958. Between 1967 and 1989 he established with John Burgee a design practice that was responsible for numerous buildings, including the competition for the Joint Banking Centre (1976) in Kuwait and the Madrid office towers "Puerta de Europa" awarded by the Kuwait Investment Office in 1989 and completed by 1996. Johnson was awarded with the Pritzker Prize in 1979.

Source: Schulze, Franz, *Philip Johnson: a Biography*, A. A. Knopf, New York, 1994

Saint, Andrew. "Philip Johnson: Flamboyant Postmodern Architect Whose Career Was Marred by a Flirtation with Nazism," obituary, *The Guardian*, Jan. 29, 2005

Applebaum, Anne, "Remembering Philip Johnson," obituary, *The Guardian*, Jan. 29, 2005

JOHN TAYLOR & SONS

Founded by John Taylor and his two sons in 1869 upon the collapse of The Chelsea Water Company (1722). As a leading specialist in Water and Public Health Engineering, the firm rapidly acquired an international reputation and, for a century and a quarter, was responsible for many major projects in both the UK and overseas. Among the projects in the Middle East, the firm developed in Kuwait the Water Distribution Network, pipelines, reservoirs, water towers, lorry-filling stations and pumping stations in the city's early modernisation (1951–58), as well as the Kuwait Effluent Utilisation Project (1978), the Shuwaikh Water Distribution Complex (1980–88) and Al-Zour water storage (1987). While working in Al-Zour the firm, by then with a staff of some 500, merged with Freeman Fox & Partners to form the Acer Group, which is now known as Hyder Consulting PLC.

Source: Roberts, Gwilym, *Chelsea to Cairo: 'Taylor-made' Water Through Eleven Reigns and in Six Continents. A history of John Taylor & Sons and Their Predecessors*, London, Thomas Telford, 2006

KUWAIT ARCHITECTURAL CONSULTANTS (KAC)

Kuwait Architectural Consultants (KAC) is an architectural and engineering practice operating since the late 1960s in Kuwait under engineer Sabah Affas. Apart from the reference in the local joint venture invitation for the Kuwait National Assembly design competition, it is worth mentioning two other chief designers, Nicolae N. Enisteanu (1942–) between 1980–82 and Ismail I. Rifaat (1935–) from 1984–86. The first graduated from Bucharest (1967) and received a Master's in Architecture from Rice University, USA (1974). He taught in both schools and before was working in Kuwait for KEO (1976–80) with relevant roles in Salhiya and Al-Muthanna Complexes. He joined the Institute for Studies and Hydropower (ISPH) and the National Center for Tourism in Romania. The second is a Bachelor's in Architecture from Alexandria, Egypt (1957) and a Master in Architecture and Urban Planning (1961) and PhD from ETH Zurich (1965), where he met Alfred Roth and Omar Azzam who eventually recommended his incorporation with SSH in 1984.

Source: *Dicţionar al arhitecturii româneşti moderne (sec. XIX, XX, XXI)*, Uniunea Arhitecţilor din România, 2014

Nicolae Enisteanu profile, *Prosopography Who Is Who*, 36th Annual. Conference on World Affairs, University of Colorado at Boulder, Apr. 3–8, 1983

Ismail I. Rifaat's online profile as Sir Architects' principal: http://www.sirarchitects.com/

KUWAIT AUSTRIAN ENGINEERING CO. (OVERSEAS AST CO. LLC)

Eduard Ast (1869–1945) established Eduard Ast & Co. in 1898, a pioneering contractor in the use of reinforced concrete in Austria. In 1903 he founded with the architect Josef Hoffmann (1870–1956) and the artist Koloman Moser (1868–1918) the Wiener Werkstätte. The group's store, designed by a prominent architect was built by Ast, who eventually became a shareholder of the Werkstätte. In the "Kunstschau Wien 1908" exhibition, co-founded by Bertold Löffler (1884–1960) and Gustav Klimt (1862–1918), the architect and Ast were responsible for the exhibition space and the contractor then bought the Klimt's famous *Danaë* painting from this exhibition. In 1909 Ast commissioned Hoffmann to design his family house in Vienna (Haus Ast 1909–11). The house hosted illustrious residents in the coming years such as the composer Gustav Mahler, the architect Walter Gropius, and eventually the writer Franz Werfel. The villa was at this time a spiritual and cultural centre of Vienna. As Ed Ast & Co, GmbH with a base in Graz, the company built in Austria and Germany various buildings including schools and hospitals, however on the outset of WWII was forced to export his know-how and technology into new markets such as the emerging Gulf countries. Among the first commissions in the region were the Water Distillation Plant and Power Station in Shuwaikh (1951–61), under the local establishment Kuwait Austrian Engineering Co., and several other projects including the Warehouse of Al-Sabah Hospital (1963–65) under Overseas AST Co. LLC. The latter was a branch established in 1959 for the construction of the Dubai Harbour in the UAE, where it became a major contractor for infrastructural work to the present time. In Austria it is today succeded by A.S.T. Baugesellschaft.

Source: Mrazek, Wilhelm; Boltenstern, Erich, "Josef Hoffmann's House for Carl Moll Renovated," in *Ancient and Modern Art. Austrian Magazine for Art, Crafts and Home Decor*, n. 19, 1947, p. 24

Overseas AST online platform profile: http://www.overseas-ast.com/profile.php

Shepherd & Derom Galleries, NY, catalogue for *The Pipes Of Pan And The Kneeling Youth. A painting by Bertold Löffler, a sculpture by George Minne*, Apr. 24–Jun. 28, 2008

Wehdorn, Manfred; Georgeacopol-Winischofer, Ute, *Baudenkmäler der Technik und Industrie in Österreich: Wien, Niederösterreich, Burgenland*, Böhlau Verlag, Wien, 1984

KUWAIT ENGINEERING BUREAU (KEB)

Established in 1966 by Hisham H. Al-Issa and Adnan F. Halawa. Several collaborations were developed with TAC, Rendel, Plamer & Tritton and Colin Buchanan & Partners. In 1990 the firm's principals were M. F. Guncon and W. A. Khalaf.

Source: Bricault, G. C. (ed.), *Major Companies of the Arab World 1990/91*, Springer Science & Business Media, 2012

KUWAIT ENGINEERING GROUP (KEG)

This engineering, architectural and planning practice was established by Othman Saud Al-Rashed in 1971, with a strong connection with Kamal Shair's circles (Dar Al-Handasah). During late 1970s and throughout the 1980s KEG developed several master plan works for Kuwait in collaboration with Dar Al-Handasah and several western consultants including the Fintas Centre Eastern Block development (1985–87) and the Subiya New Town as the local consultant after 1984. Following the success of the Salhiya Commercial Project and Le Meridien Hotel (1976–82) as lead consultants and the incorporation in 1978 of Edward Lach and Wojciech Jarząbek (1950–), both graduates from Wrocław Polytechnic, the company emerged as a major architecture consultant in the late 1980s in Kuwait: the Al-Othman Residential and Commercial Centre in Hawally (1989–94) and the Audit Bureau HQ (1982–96) are the best known works.

Source: Stanek, Łukasz, "Mobilities of Architecture in the Global Cold War: from Socialist Poland To Kuwait and Back," in *International Journal of Islamic Architecture*, v. 4, n. 2, 2015

Bricault, G. C. (ed.), *Major Companies of the Arab World 1990/91*, Springer Science & Business Media, 2012

Wilgocki, Michael, "Architect Wojciech Jarząbek vs. the World," in Gazeta pl. Wrocław, Jan. 19, 2013 (original in polish)

KUWAIT ENGINEERS OFFICE (KEO)

Founded by Faisal and Abdul Aziz Sultan in 1964, the engineering firm integrated an architectural department in the following year under the architect Ghazi Sultan and Brian Broughton, former chief architect of Construction Consultants Kuwait (Richard Costain Middle East Ltd.) and Design Construction Group in Kuwait (Anthony Irving and Gordon Brown Jones). The CBK Head Offices (1968–71) in Mubarakiya were eventually part of this transition. However during the first years of practice, the firm was able to secure projects such as the Kuwait Institute for Scientific Research (1967–70) and the new Kuwait International Air Terminal (1967–81) acting as local counterpart for Pacific International Consultants. During the prosperous 1970s the firm developed an intense relationship with the work of Ghazi Sultan. Both KEO and Ghazi Sultan, in his own right, have produced a quantity of mixed-use buildings such as Anwar Al-Sabah Complex (1975–77), Zahra Complex (1976–80), Bibi Complex (1975–79), Dasman Complex (1975–79) and the Waterfront project (1977–88), in collaboration with Sasaki Associates. In these years the firm established strong collaborations with BBPR for planning matters and John S. Bonnington Partnership for buildings design, with examples such as the Souqs Al-Muttaheda and Al-Masseel (1973–1979), the Stock Exchange Market (1978–86) and the Kuwait Zoo Extension and Renovation (1981–82), the last one never implemented.

Source: Brian Broughton (FRIBA, Canterbury School of Architecture) résumé, Chichester, West Sussex, United Kingdom, 2010

LLOYD, MORGAN & JONES

Lloyd & Morgan was established in 1945 in Houston. Hermon F. Lloyd was a stage actor and a radio personality who graduated in Architecture from Rice University (1941), and after a short experience at Harvin C. Moore partnership he established the firm with William B. Morgan. Arthur E. Jones graduated in 1947 from the same university and joined the firm immediately. In 1961 Jones joined as partner forming the firm Lloyd, Morgan & Jones. The firm developed several high-rise buildings in the city such as the American General Building completed in 1965. The Astrodome, inaugurated as the Harris County Domed Stadium, was completed in the same year with Praeger, Kavanagh & Waterbury, engineering consultants from New York, and became one of the most well-known structures of the kind worldwide. This project was the motivation for the invitation to the design competition of the Kuwait Sports Centre (1968–69). Before the incorporation of Benjamin E. Brewer Jr. in 1976 followed by the death of Moore (1974), the firm became known for the various buildings in the Greenway Plaza in Houston.

Source: Koush, Ben, "The Modern Mr. Jones: A Legendary Houston Architect Shares His Tall Building Portfolio", in *Rice Design Alliance*, n. 72, Fall 2007

Arthur E. Jones Architectural Records, MS 535, Woodson Research Center, Fondren Library, Rice University

MAATH AL-ALOUSI

Maath Al-Alousi (1938–) is a graduate in Architecture from METU, Ankara, Turkey (1957–61) with the architecture historian İnci Aslanoğlu, after completing a first year at the Agriculture College in Baghdad. During his degree work at METU Al-Alousi's strong influences were those of Prof. Abdullah Kuran (1927–02) and the respect for the "inherited architecture" and the context; the work of Louis Kahn (1901–74) taught at the department and the work of Turgut Cansever

(1921–09) who gained attention from the students following the METU Campus International Design Competition in 1959. The interest for the large scale and the sense of architectural heritage was pursued from the very beginning by Alousi who joined Rifat Chadiriji (1926–) at Chadirji, Sherzad and Abdulla Ihsan Kamil, the future Iraq Consult (IQC). During this period Alousi worked with Chadirji in the preliminary stages of the Iraqi Insurance Building in Mosul (1966), the Tobacco Monopoly Building of Jamhouria Street (1967), the Rafidain Bank of Rasheed Street (1967) and many private residences. By then his only experience on site was in the supervision of the Sha'ab Stadium (1959–66), designed by the Portuguese architect Keil do Amaral (1910–75) and the development of Kuwait Sport Clubs projects (1970–74) a few years later. Additionally Alousi was integrated into the Design Department at the Ministry of Housing where he was able to interact with Doxiadis' proposal for Sadr City (Baghdad West) and eventually being responsible for the design of its civic centre and schools. Upon this accomplishment Alousi was awarded a scholarship in Educational Buildings by the Iraqi Ministry at the AA London, Department of Tropical Studies. He completed these studies in 1964 under the strong influence of Prof. Otto Koenigsberger (1908–99). After the establishment of IQC in 1965, Alousi was responsible for the design studio and production drawing studio. He began his first works abroad in Kuwait with the Al-Hamad Villa (1964–67), then followed by the Hassawi Residential Complexes (1968–70) in association with PACE and by the Kuwait Sport Clubs (1970–74). Alousi was then IQC senior architect in charge for all the operations abroad, including Bahrain and the UAE. In 1974 he left IQC and established Technical Studies Bureau (TEST) office in Beirut with three other partners. After TEST's split in 1980, the Alousi Associates Technical Studies Bureau TEST-Baghdad continues Alousi's practice, still being responsible for the Ministry of Planning Head Offices (1980–82) in Kuwait and commissioned for two large mass-housing projects in Baghdad: the Haifa Street Development (1980–84) and the rehabilitation of Doxiadis' project for Sadr City (1982–83).

Source: Kultermann, Udo, *Contemporary Architecture in the Arab States,* McGraw-Hill Publishers, 1999

Maath Al-Alousi interview, Aug. 12, 2015

MAHMOUD RIAD

Mahmoud Riad (1905–1979), graduated from Cairo University (1927) and later from Liverpool University in Civic Design (1931) with William Holford as professor. Riad moved to the US, after have worked in Jerusalem, to join for the well established firm, Shreve, Lamb & Harmon who carried out the construction of the Empire State Building in New York (1929–31). In Jerusalem, Riad was fundamental as a site architect in the construction of the YMCA

complex, which included the teaching, conference and sports facilities, such as the football stadium. Once the building was completed in 1933, Riad returned to Cairo and established his practice. At the same time he began his service at the Ministry of Public Works and after Nasser's rise to power he became the Director General in the Cairo Municipality (1952–69). He was responsible for the major building enterprises and continued his work from King Farouk's era, Nasser's and through to Sadat's time. Among these buildings, the most famous are the Arab League Headquarters (1955), the Nile Hilton, and the Social Union Building (1959) in association with General Mohamed Ramzy Omar. During this period Riad supervised major architectural projects envisioned by Nasser such as Nasr City (1956–58) and Cairo Stadium (1955–60). The experience in the stadium with the German engineer, Werner March brought Riad to international exposure and to his first foreign commission: the Kuwait Sport Clubs (1963) that was never realised. In 1965 he returned to Kuwait, now as the United Arab Republic (UAR) expert, together with Dr. Omar Azzam, the UN representative, to provide a report on the Kuwait Development Plan that would lead to the appointment of Colin Buchanan for the Second Master Plan. Riad remained in Kuwait until his death, as consultant for the Ministry of Housing & Public Affairs. During this period he collaborated with Reima Pietilä (1923–93), Colin Buchanan (1907–01), and Kenzo Tange (1913–05). Some of his collaborators made important careers as architects not only in Egypt but also abroad, such as Hassan Mansour in Kuwait.

Source: *Profile Mahmoud Riad,* Cairo Observer, Jul. 9, 2013, http://tmblr.co/ZHzWbxpFMpC8

MAKIYA ASSOCIATES CONSULTANTS

Mohamed Saleh Aziz Makiya (1914–2015) received his Bachelor's degree from the Liverpool School of Architecture (1941) and a diploma in Civic Planning (1942) under Prof. William Holford (1907–75). Eventually, he was to enjoy the mentoring of James Mollison Wilson (1887–1965) who was a good friend of his uncle. In 1946 he completed his PhD at the King's College in Cambridge and after returning to Baghdad established Makiya Associates. At the same time Makiya was both architect and town planner for the Directorate General of the Municipalities (1947–53) and was a determining factor in awarding Doxiadis' commissions in Iraq. In 1956 he was awarded with a travel scholarship to the US and in 1959 co-founded the Department of Architecture at the College of Engineering, Baghdad University. He remained the Head of Department until 1968. During the following years the office openend branches all over the region, Bahrain (1967), Muscat (1971), Doha (1975), Kuwait (1977), UAE (1975) and London (1974). Among the most relevant projects were the plans for

city preservation in Muscat (1972–76) and Hatta (UAE), Isa Town in Bahrain (1973–77), the Kuwait State Mosque (1977–81). He also collaborated with Akram Ogaily and Jassim Qabazard's practice (Archicentre) on several other projects, including the Arab Organisation Headquarters in Kuwait (1982–90), and a wide range of projects in Iraq and the UAE with special mention of the Khulafa Central Mosque extension in Baghdad, completed in 1965. In 1969 Makiya published a comprehensive survey of Baghdad Architecture under the auspices of the Gulbenkian Foundation.

Source: Dabrowska, Karen, Mohamed Makiya, obituary, *The Guardian,* Aug. 27, 2015

de Gruyter, Walter, *Who's Who in the Arab World 2007–2008,* Publitec Publications, 2007

Kultermann, Udo, *Contemporary Architecture in the Arab States,* McGraw-Hill Publishers, 1999

Makiya Associates CV for the Arab Organisation Headquarters project, 1986

MAKSIMOVIĆ, STOJAN

Stojan Maksimović (1934–) graduated in Architecture and Planning from the Belgrade Faculty of Architecture (1956) and served until 1970 at the Town Planning Institute of Belgrade where he was co-designer, with Branislav Jovin, for the well-known Town Hall in Novi Beograd (1961–71). During this period Maksimović became the institute representative in the reconstruction venture led by the United Nations for Skopje (1965), which included Kenzo Tange (Japan), Arata Isozaki (Japan), Doxiades Associates (Greece), Adolf Ciborowski (Poland), Van den Broek and Bakema (The Netherlands), Luigi Piccinato (Italy), Maurice Rotival (USA) and Janko Konstantinov (JUG), who had previously worked with Alvar Aalto and Victor Gruen, and Blagoja Kolev (1930–). Both the ex-Yugoslav architects joined Maksimović in Kuwait after 1982. From 1970–82 Maksimović conducted several projects at the Directorate for the Construction and Reconstruction of the City of Belgrade, such as the internationally acclaimed conference centre Sava Centar (1976–79) and attended the Munich Faculty of Architecture for specialisation with Prof. Josef Wiedemann. The Sava Centar led to the invitation for the Kuwait Conference Centre design competition (1980–86). After winning the first prize Maksimović was convinced to establish a practice outside the institutional umbrella, the SMMA Associates, that operated in Kuwait from 82 to 87 in association with Archicentre. The collaboration didn't succeeded and later Maksimović joined TAC and moved to the US.

Source: Jelovac, Bojan, "Šteta je što Slavija nije centar" intreview to Stojan Maksimović, Blic online, Sarajevo, May 4, 2007. http://www.blic.rs/Vesti/Beograd/5072/Steta-je-sto-Slavija--nije-centar

MARCEL BREUER ASSOCIATES (MARCEL BREUER AND ASSOCIATES)

Marcel Breuer Associates is the name of the firm after Breuer's retirement from practice in 1976. Beforehand it was Marcel Breuer and Associates established between 1946–56 by Marcel Breuer (1902–81) in New York. The Mideast Market proposal for Kuwait (Fish, Meat, and Vegetable Markets) was probably one of the last projects overseen by Breuer himself. He graduated in Architecture from the Magyar Királyi Föreáliskola in Pécs, Hungary (1920) and joined the Bauhaus in 1921 where he received his degree in 1924. After a short stay in Paris where Breuer met Le Corbusier, he returned to the Bauhaus upon Walter Gropius' invitation to teach and to design the interiors of the school building. Breuer's first practice was established in Berlin in 1928, focusing on housing prefabrication and reinforced concrete. With WWII looming, Breuer joined the GSD at Harvard in 1937 as a professor and established a partnership with Walter Gropius in the US, that lasted until 1941. Under Marcel Breuer and Associates the most famous projects were the UNESCO Headquarters in Paris, (1949–1975), in collaboration with Pier Luigi Nervi and Bernard Zehrfuss, and the Whitney Museum of American Art, in New York City (1963–66).

Source: The Marcel Breuer Papers, 1920–86, in the Archives of American Art online platform. http://www.aaa.si.edu/collections/marcel-breuer-papers

MARTIN, LESLIE

Leslie Martin (1908–2000) graduated in Architecture from Manchester (1930), after receiving the RIBA silver medal in 1929. He immediately started his teaching career at the same university and four years later, as he finalised his PhD, he became the head of the new Architectural School at Hull University (1934). These were active years of involvement in the reformist movement that led to the MARS manifesto of 1938. Martin and his wife, as well as William Holford were called to La Sarraz in 1936 by Maxwell Fry (1899–87), to turn the UK group into pro-active critics of current trends. During this period Martin built relations with Walter Gropius, Fry, a partner by then, Wells Coates (1895–58), Henry Moore (1898–86), Berthold Lubetkin (1901–90) and his group, Tecton (1932–50) and with the young Denys Lasdun (1914–2001). The 1938 MARS' Plan for London was to change Martin's scale of operations and by 1939 Martin was appointed Principal Assistant Architect to the LMS Railway, involved in designing emergency wartime buildings during WWII and later post-war reconstruction works. Such a role was to lead to the position of Deputy Architect at the London County Council (1948) and later Chief-Architect (1953). In 1948 he was appointed to the design team, with Peter Moro and Edwin Williams, of the Royal Festival Hall (1948–51). The building's success brought to London Le Corbusier, Walter Gropius,

and Frank Lloyd Wright. In 1956 Martin became the first Chair of Architecture at Cambridge. He held the position up to his retirement in 1972. In Cambridge, from 1956 Martin established an architectural practice with his wife Sadie Speight collaborating at different times with Colin St. John Wilson, Trevor Dannatt and Patrick Hodgkinson. In 1958, as ICOM international experts, Martin joined Franco Albini (1905–77) in Lisbon, Portugal for the Calouste Gulbenkian Museum (1959–69). A working relationship that Martin was to continue as designer from 1978–83 with the completion of the Center for Modern Art. In 1967 Martin established the Centre for Land Use and Built Form Studies in Cambridge and in the following year was among the international experts invited to join an Advisory Board in Kuwait for the "Urban Form Studies for the Old Town" (1968–69) where he met again Albini. Throughout the 1970s and 1980s Martin was still building in Oxford and Cambridge as well as preparing several proposals for Saudi Arabia, that were eventually never realised.

Sources: "Architect Who Cut His Teeth on the Royal Festival Hall and left a Modernist Mark on Oxford and Cambridge," obituary, *The Telegraph*, Aug. 1, 2000

Holland, Jessica; Jackson Iain, *The Architecture of Edwin Maxwell Fry and Jane Drew: Twentieth Century Architecture, Pioneer Modernism and the Tropics*, Ashgate Publishing, 2014

Sharr,Adam; Thornton, Stephen, *Demolishing Whitehall: Leslie Martin, Harold Wilson and the Architecture of White Heat*, Ashgate Publishing Ltd., 2013

Leslie Martin, obituary, *The Guardian*, Aug. 2, 2000

Sharr, Adam, *Reading Architecture and Culture: Researching Buildings, Spaces, and Documents*, Routledge, 2012

MEDHAT EL-ABD

Medhat Mohamed El-Abd (1938–), B.Sc. in Architectural Engineering (1959), was one of the first graduates from the Department of Architecture at Ain Shams University in Cairo. He established the design section of El-Abed Egyptian Cooperative Contracting Co., his parents' contracting company, until 1965. Following the successful venture in Kuwait for the construction of the Al-Salam Palace (1961–65), Medhat initiated an international practice as consultant engineer and contractor throughout the Gulf up to 1973, when he founded the Al-Mohandes Engineering Office in Cairo and diverted his activities into health and tourism with the construction of a specialist hospital in Cairo (1974) and several hotels and resorts. During the practice's active time in the Gulf, the projects for the Kuwaiti authorities are the most notable, such as the design for Sheikha Fatima Mohamed Ali's Mosque (1972–76) and Kuwait Embassy in Beirut (1972–79). In Egypt during the 1980s Medhat eventually designed the head office of the Taxation Authority and one of the prominent high-rise apartment buildings in Zamalek, with 31 floors, today converted into a hotel.

Source: de Gruyter, Walter, *Who's Who in the Arab World 2007–2008*, Publitec Publications, Beirut, 2007

MÉLICOURT, GUY

Guy Mélicourt, a graduate in Architecture from l'École Nationale Supérieure des Beaux-Arts in Paris, under Atelier Lemaresquier in 1933, became "Architecte des Bâtiments Civils et des Palais Nationaux" in 1960, following his first commission in 1958 for the renovation of the French Embassy in Madrid. During the post-WWII reconstruction effort in France, Mélicourt was responsible for the renovation of the town centre of Bourges, Royan sectors 18-C and D, for Cannes waterfront and marina, with Georges Mass, P. A. Chauveau, P. Bigot and F. Roy. In 1962 Mélicourt was nominated by the Prime Minister Georges Jean Raymond Pompidou (1911–74) to work on Avignon. The relationship with Pompidou was important for Mélicourt to be appointed to several governmental programmes, which also included commissions abroad such as the Kuwait Radio Television Centre in 1968.

Source: "La Résidence de France," Mar. *28, 2014* online platform: http://www.ambafrance-es.org/La-Residence-de-France

Delaunay, Jean-Marc; *Des palais en Espagne: l'Ecole des hautes études hispaniques et la Casa de Velázquez au cœur des relations franco-espagnoles du XXe siècle (1898–1979)*, Casa de Velázquez, 1994

Dufourmont, Sabrina, "Jean-Marie Nunez. The Berruyers aspire to decent housing," in *L'Express*, Jan. 4, 2007

Laurent, Xavier, *Grandeur et misère du patrimoine, d'André Malraux à Jacques Duhamel (1959–1973)*, Librairie Droz, 2003

Troulay, Marcel, "La bibliothèque de la Casa Velàzquez," in *Bulletin des Bibliothèques de France*, n. 2, 1974 online: http://bbf.enssib.fr/consulter/bbf-1974-02-0053-001

MICHAEL CARAPETIAN ASSOCIATES

Michael Carapetian (1938–) graduated from the Architectural Association (AA) of London in the early 1960s under Alison Smithson. His interest in photography led Carapetian to work with Henk Snoek and to publish *British Buildings 1960–64* with Kenneth Frampton and Douglas Stephen as the architectural photographer in 1965. During the survey he produced the well-known photograph *The Man on the Economist Plaza,* picturing the Economist Building in London by Alison and Peter Smithson (1964). In 1966 Carapetian photographed another famous portfolio on Pierre Chareau's La Maison de Verre (1927), which was later acquired by MoMA, New York. In 1967 he established his architectural practice in London and few years later in Tehran, Iran where the firm developed the majority of its production for about ten years. During this period the practice collaborated with several well-known architects such as Kenneth Frampton (1930–), Julian Blades, Roger Connah (1950–) and Elia Zenghelis (1937–). From 1976 to 1979 Michael Carapetian Associates developed work in Kuwait including the Iranian Embassy (1977–79). Carapetian taught at the Architectural Association of London, University of Southern California, Columbia University in New York and IUAV in Venice. In

1987 he was co-author of the book *Helsinki Jugendstil Architecture, 1895–1915*.

Source: Douglas, Stephen; Frampton, Kenneth; Carapetian, Michael, *British Buildings, 1960–1964*, Adam & Charles Black, 1965

Moorhouse, Jonathan; Carapetian, Michael; Ahtola-Moorhouse, Leena, *Helsinki Jugendstil Architecture, 1895–1915*, Otava, 1987

MOHAMED RAMZY OMAR

General Ramzy Omar was an Egyptian architect and author of the first proposal for the London Mosque eventually initiated in 1954, in association with Richardson and McLaughlin. During this period Ramzy developed the Villa Hamdy Wassef (1957) in Cairo. Leslie Martin (1908–2000), meanwhile, as chief-architect in charge at the London County Council considered the London Mosque building inadequate for its context and construction was interrupted in 1959. Ten years later a new design competition was launched, with the participation of Rifat Chadirji (IQC). During the 1950s and 1960s General Ramzy developed a series of well-known buildings in Cairo in association with Ali Nassar including the Sheraton Hotel in Giza (1960), the Social Union Building (1959) with Dr. Mahmoud Riad and the Ministry of Foreign Affairs Building (1960–93).

Sources: *Al-Ahram*, n. 436, Cairo, Jul. 1–7, 1999

The Ogden Standard-Examiner, Mar. 2, 1963, p. 8

Beaulieu, Jill; Roberts, Mary, *Orientalism's Interlocutors: Painting, Architecture, Photography*, Duke University Press, 2002

Isenstadt, Sandy; Rizvi, Kishwar, *Modernism and the Middle East: Architecture and Politics in the Twentieth Century*, University of Washington Press, 2011

MORETTI, LUIGI

Luigi Walter Moretti (1906–1973) graduated from the School of Architecture in Rome, and established a practice while he was still a student with his father's colleague Enrico Vallini. In 1933 Moretti was appointed Director of the Technical Department of the Opera Nazionale Balilla. During these years he participated in major architectural competitions promoted by the Fascist regime: the Palazzo del Littorio (1934 and 1937) and the E42 quarter's Piazza Imperiale (1937), while Franco Albini and Ignazio Gardella were competing for the Hostel. After the war he moved to Milan where he worked among the other well-known practitioners such as Albini, Gardella and the BBPR group. He also founded the magazine *Spazio* (1950–53) in Rome, which had a little success among architects. However, he consolidated relations with some dominant figures in the artistic scene, such as Michel Tapié, and developed an interest in mathematics, formal logic and scientific disciplines leading to the establishment of the National Institute for Mathematical and Operational Planning Research (1957). Through IRMOU Moretti developed studies around parametric architecture, formalised and presented in 1960 on the occasion of the XII Triennale in Milan. In 1960 Moretti began the design of the residential district INCIS at Decima, Rome (1960–1965), and the Montréal Stock Exchange Tower, Canada (1960–64) with Pier Luigi Nervi. However, his most famous work was as consultant to the Società Generale Immobiliare in the USA, developing the Watergate residential quarters (1963–71) in Washington. The international exposure assisted by an substantial record of career prizes and awards, together with the raised awareness in the Arab oil countries of Italian construction groups by the end of the 1960s, opened up possibilities to pursue work in countries such as Algeria, Libya. In Kuwait Moretti was to pursue the realisation of hotels, commercial centres, large housing schemes, school complexes and ventures such as the design competition for the Kuwait Society of Engineers head offices (1968).

Source: Bucci, Federico; Mulazzani, Marco, *Luigi Moretti: Works and Writings*, Princeton Architectural Press, 2002

Santuccio, Salvatore, *Luigi Moretti*, Zanichelli, 1986

L.G. MOUCHEL AND PARTNERS

Louis Gustave Mouchel (1852–1908), a naval officer, trained as an engineer at the École des Mines de Paris. He was later admitted at École Royale Des Ponts et Chaussées where he became a road engineer. In 1875 he moved to Wales and formed the Cardiff Washed Coal & Fuel Company. In 1897 Mouchel became the representative agent for François Hennebique's reinforced concrete technique in the UK and established L.G. Mounchel & Partners, an engineering consultancy specialised in design proofing for the French company. The first contracts were related to harbour and railway infrastructure. Among the most well-known projects was the first reinforced concrete bridge in the UK, a skew bridge at Chewton Glen in Hampshire (1901) and the Michelin Building in London (1910). During the 1930s the company became widely known due to projects such as Battersea Power Station in London (1931) and the Earls Court Exhibition Centre (Earls Court One,1935), which when built, was one of the largest reinforced buildings in the world. In 1978 the first contract awarded and implemented in Kuwait was for the First Ring Road.

Source: L.G. Mouchel, obituary, *The Engineer, Jun. 6, 1908*

Powers, Alan, *Britain*, Reaktion Books, 2007

"Louis Gustave Mouchel," in *Engineering Times*, http://www.engineering-timelines.com/who/Mouchel_LG/mouchelLouisGustave.asp

NATIONAL ENGINEERING BUREAU (NEB)

National Engineering Bureau (Consultant Engineers) was established in Egypt (1976), operating in Kuwait and the UAE from the early 1980s. The company's performance in Kuwait is unclear as well as its actual conditions in the UAE, as there were two firms with the same name and scope of work, one in Abu Dhabi and the other in Dubai. The last is the well-known leading consultancy, operating in Dubai since 1984 and under the leadership of the structural designer Engineer Jamil Jadallah (Managing Director 1976) and the Lebanese architect Elias Daniel (AUB, 1973).

OMAR AZZAM

Omar Abdulrahman Azzam (1930–), son of the popular Azzam Pasha (1893–1976), an Egyptian diplomat and the first Secretary-General of the Arab League (1945–52), obtained his doctorate from ETH Zurich in 1960 under the subject of The Development of Urban and Rural Housing in Egypt. From 1960 he served in different capacities as UN consultant for planning, based in Jeddah. During this period Azzam developed with David Hiram Corm and Mohamed Scharabi studies for Jeddah's Civic Centre. However his major work was to be the plan and housing scheme for the new city of Jubail. In 1963, following Sayed Karim (in 1952) and Jac Thijasse (in 1962) he initiated a series of missions in Kuwait with Mahmoud Riad (1905–1979) as UN consultant for planning and building programmes. Together they evaluated the future Sport Club facilities, the First Master Plan implementation and the CBD zoning plans, among others. In 1964 Azzam hosted the famous American Muslim, Malcolm X on his way to Mecca. In 1965 Azzam and Riad were requested to consult on the Development Plan that had then been elaborated on by the Kuwait Municipality. In 1966 he organised the international competition for the Riyadh Conference Centre with UIA. The competition awarded the construction of the three first schemes, by Otto, Gutbrod and Buro Happold with Trevor Dannatt. In the following year Azzam, as UN consultant, was requested by the Kuwait Government to establish an Advisory Board to oversee the implementation of the "Urban Form Studies for the Old Town" (1968–69). His relationship with Leslie Martin and Franco Albini was later developed through invitations for design competitions to each in Saudi Arabia during the 1970s. the resulting projects were eventually awarded, but never built. Later Azzam recommended his son Khaled Azzam for an internship with Leslie Martin (1979–80).

Source: Azzam, Omar, *The Development of Urban and Rural Housing in Egypt*, Swiss Federal Institute of Technology, Zurich, Ed. Truninger, 1960

Addis, Bill; Walker, Derek, *Happold: The Confidence to Build*, Taylor & Francis, 2005, p. 88

Shepard, Ray, *On Malcolm X's Autobiography of Malcolm X*, Houghton Mifflin Harcourt, 2007

DeCaro, Louis A., *On the Side of My People: A Religious Life of Malcolm X*, NYU Press, 1996

Azzam, Omar; Buchanan, Colin; Thijasse, Jac, "Policies to be Adopted for a Master Plan of Greater Kuwait," report to the Municipality of Kuwait, 1965

Osman Ahmed Osman (1917–1999), graduated in Civil Engineering from the University of Cairo (1940). In the following year he established Osman Ahmed Osman, Engineers & Contractors, which rapidly grew in Egypt and during the 1950s secured contracts all over the Arab world, especially in Saudi Arabia, Kuwait, Libya, Iraq and the UAE. In 1956, Gamal Abdel Nasser awarded Osman's company the contract for Aswan Dam, designed by VBB and in 1959 he was awarded the construction of the Kuwait Municipal Complex (1959–62), which became the National Assembly, after Kuwait Independence in 1961. In the same year the Egyptian President nationalised Osman's company, which became The Arab Contractors (Osman A. Osman & Co.). The company remains in operation to this day with branches all over the Middle East region.

OTTO, FREI

Frei Otto (1925–2015) began his studies in Architecture at the Technical University Berlin in 1943, but because of the war he graduated only in 1952. During his travel scholarship (1950–51) he visited the works of Frank Lloyd Wright, Fred N. Severud, Erich Mendelsohn, Eero Saarinen, Ludwig Mies van der Rohe, Richard Neutra, Charles and Ray Eames and eventually met some of them. During this period he also took courses in Sociology and Urban Planning at the University of Virginia, Charlottesville. Otto's doctorate dissertation *The Suspended Roof, Form and Structure*, at the Technical University of Berlin (1954) initiated an interest of a life-long career. With his practice established, Otto developed an intensive research on lightweight structures that were developed alongside his teaching career. In Germany he taught in Berlin (1952–63), in Ulm at the Hochschule für Gestaltung (1958), in Stuttgart (1964–91), and in Karlsruhe (1995). In the US he was visiting professor at Washington University in St. Louis, Yale University, University of California at Berkeley, the Massachusetts Institute of Technology and Harvard University. Between 1961 and1962 Otto established the Biology and Building Research Group at the Technical University of Berlin and published the first volume of *Tensile Structures: Design, Structure and Calculation of Buildings of Cables, Nets and Membranes* (the second volume was published in 1966). In 1967 Otto was commissioned for the German Pavilion at the Expo 67 in Montréal, Canada. The following year the commission for the Munich Olympic Stadium (1968–72) and the invitation in partnership with Kenzo Tange for the Kuwait Sports Centre Competition (1968–69) was the opportunity to establish the studio Warmbronn with Ewald Bubner. The firm developed numerous collaborations all over the world and particularly in Saudi Arabia for the Intercontinental Hotel and

Conference Centre in Mecca (1968–74), with Rolf Gutbrod, nominated for the first Aga Khan Award for Architecture in 1980. Warmbronn also designed the temporary sun shades for the Hajj in Mecca (1971), the Diplomatic Club Heart Tent in Riyadh with Buro Happold (1980) and the Tuwaiq Palace (1985), again with Buro Happold, that won the Aga Khan Award in 1998. In 2015 Otto won the Pritzker Laureate. It is also worth mentioning the famous umbrellas for Pink Floyd's 1977 concert tour of the US and the Aviary in the Munich Zoo (1979–80,) once again with Buro Happold.

Source: Drew, Philip, *Frei Otto: Form and Structure,* Westview Press, 1976

OVE ARUP & PARTNERS

Ove Nyquist Arup (1895–1988) graduated in Civil Engineering from the Royal Danish Technical College in Copenhagen (1922) after a Bachelor's in Philosophy and Mathematics (1916). He started work in Hamburg at Christiani and Nielsen, a Danish firm specialised in reinforced concrete and a pioneer in implementing François Hennebique's technique under water. In the following year he moved to the firm's office in London and in 1925 was promoted to the post of chief-designer. In 1933 he joined J.L. Kier & Co. and collaborated with Berthold Lubetkin's (1901–90) Tecton Group (Denys Lasdun, Godfrey Samuel, and Lindsay Drake from 1932–50), which included the Highpoint I Apartment Building (1933–35) and the London Zoo Penguin Pool in Regent's Park (1933–34). In 1935 he joined the MARS Group (CIAM group for UK) and in 1938 established with his cousin Arne, Arup & Arup Ltd. that assisted Tecton in the Finsbury projects, including a health centre (1938) and the school and housing programme that was interrupted in 1939. During WWII the firm assisted the Air Ministry as consultant and contractor in providing rational air raid shelters, industrial projects and marine work. Between 1944–46 Arup was finally assigned to implement and install aluminium demountable houses of one and two storeys and hangars, developed since 1938, for the Ministry of Works following the 1943 Memorandum for the Directorate of Post-War Building. The project led Arup to prepare an article on reinforced concrete and box-frame construction for Jane Drew (1911–96) and Trevor Dannatt (1920–) for the first issue of the *Architect's Year Book*. However, none of the mass-housing plans of Arup were implemented and in 1945 he became professor at Imperial College and in 1946 he established himself exclusively as an architects' engineering consultant with a commission for a bus station in Dublin (1945–49) and the support from Fry & Drew who tried to secure him work overseas, such as the report on "Kuwait Building Program" (1946–47) that prompted a visit to Kuwait in December 1946 to select the future location of Al-Ahamdi. In 1948 he finally established

Ove Arup & Partners; structural engineering consultants that became a leading firm all over the world to this day. From 1963 the firm expanded in scope to all design disciplines, including architecture.

Source: Jones, Peter, *Ove Arup. Masterbuilder of the Twentieth Century*, Yale University Press, 2006

Jackson, Iain; Holland, Jessica, *The Architecture of Edwin Maxwell Fry and Jane Drew: Twentieth Century Architecture, Pioneer Modernism and the Tropics*, Ashgate Publishing, Ltd., 2014

PACIFIC CONSULTANTS INTERNATIONAL

Fukujiro Hirayama (1888–1962), civil engineer and officer of the former South Manchurian Railway returned back to Japan after WWII participating in the post-war reconstruction effort. Hirayama became a common presence at the "Tuesday Club Advisory Office" (1949–51), with regular meetings on and during Japan's post-war reconstruction, organised by the Shiraishi brothers in Tokyo. The meetings had a strong western orientation with the need to establish a US corporate institution for consulting engineers became the major motivation among those participating. In 1951 Pacific Consultants Inc. was eventually established through equal investments from Muneki Shiraishi, E. Floor and Antonín Reimann (1888–1976) and was registered in the United States. The last was a Czech-American architect who studied at the Polytechnic Institute of Prague (1909) under Josef Schultz (1840–1917) and Jan Koula (1855–1919) who completed his degree in Trieste (1910) and travelled to New York where he worked for Cass Gilbert (1859–1934) before joining Frank Lloyd Wright's offices. In 1919 he travelled to Japan to supervise the construction of the former Imperial Hotel in Tokyo and after two years established his own practice there. After WWI he partnered with Ladislav Leland Rado (1909–1993). However, the business venture did not last long and in 1954 was dissolved giving birth to Pacific Consultants Co., Ltd. with Japanese capital and partners and Hirayama as the corporation president. During its operation the corporation kept a horizontal hierarchy and collaborated with many of the well-known Japanese designers such as Kenzo Tange and Asabuki in Kuwait and Kisho Kurokawa in Saudi Arabia. After 1967 with an increased number of works outside Japan, Pacific Consultants International was established. One of the referenced projects in the region apart from the Kuwait and Saudi Arabia projects, commissioned largely by the Japanese Arab Oil Co. (AOC established in 1958, since 2002 named Kuwait Gulf Oil Co.), was the Dubai Municipality completed in 1979 and designed in association with the Civic Design Studio. In Kuwait the design agency was commissioned by AOC for the Kuwait Institute for Scientific Research Laboratories and Offices (1967–70 with Asabuki Architects), for the Institute of Social and Economic Planning in the Middle East (Arab Planning Institute) and the Kuwait University Science Annex, built between 1967–70 in association with Japan City Planning Inc. In the following years the agency took part in several planning and large scale projects such as the "Urban Study Within Kuwait City" (1974–75 with Japan City Planning Inc.) and was awarded with a second prize for an international competition for Low-Income Housing, eventually Riqqa, in association with Toshikagaku Institute (1970).

Source: Pacific Consultants Co. online platform http://www.pacific.co.jp/e/

PAN ARAB CONSULTING ENGINEERS (PACE)

Pan Arab Consulting Engineers was established in 1968 by Hamid Shuaib (1932–94), the Assistant Director for Technical Affairs of the Municipality, Charles Haddad (1934–), Head of Municipality Planning division and Sabah Al Rayes (1939–), Kuwait Ministry of Foreign Affairs Ministry Advisor and Executive Secretary of Kuwait Society of Engineers. The firm in the first years was more related to privately developed mixed housing schemes, basing the practice on the strong knowledge of the planning and normative procedures combined with the technical and organisational support of IQC and T-Consult. With the termination of IQC venture, PACE developed a series of work during the 1970s based on a very well educated and solid architectural and engineering staff. Buildings such as the Kuwait Shipping Co. HQ (1971–73), an Office and Commercial Building (1972–74) developed with Abdulaziz Duaij (1938–), and several office towers in Sharq are examples of the firm design capacity. During these years PACE established the most relevant design associations with TAC and SOM, first for the Kuwait Fund for the Advancement of Science and the Souqs, with the second for several bank headquarters and also often internationally, with several commissions in Saudi Arabia, Bahrain and Abu Dhabi.

Source: Charles Haddad résumé and interview in Kuwait Apr. 2014

PACE Company Profile, 2013

de Gruyter, Walter, *Who's Who in the Arab World 2007–2008*, Publitec Publications, Beirut 2007

PERKINS & WILL PARTNERSHIP

Lawrence B. Perkins (1907–97) and Philip Will (1906–85), were both graduates of Cornell University in 1930, and a few years training in Chicago and New York. Upon visiting the Century of Progress Exposition (1933) in Chicago led by Louis Skidmore (1897–1962), Perkins persuaded Will to stay in Chicago and join him working for General Houses Inc., a specialised firm in the design of prefabricated steel homes. In 1935 they started a practice and one year later, were joined by E. Todd Wheeler (1906–1987), a graduate of the University of Illinois (1929)

who became a specialist in hospitals. The firm Perkins, Wheeler & Will became a successful practice and in 1938 joined Eliel and Eero Saarinen in the awarded Crow Island School project in Winnetka, in the US. In 1946, upon Wheeler's departure, the firm was named Perkins & Will Partnership, in 1949 was commissioned by Cornell University and by the mid-1950s was the leader in the school-design field in the US with 372 school projects in 24 states. During this period Perkins published two books on school design and planning, *Schools* (1949) and *Workplace for Learning* (1957). In 1957 Wheeler rejoined the firm and the firm developed a special expertise in hospitals and health centres. However the most famous works of the firm were the Chicago Towers for the First National Bank in Chicago (1964–69) and for the US Gypsum Building completed in 1963. In the same year the firm won its first significant international project – the National College of Agriculture in Chapingo, Mexico and ten years later opened the first branch outside the country in Tehran (1973). The office in Tehran gave the firm exposure in the Middle-East market and during the late 1970s the firm was commissioned for several projects in the region, including Kuwait. The collaboration with Dar Al-Handasah on Kuwait projects ultimately led, in 1985, to Dar Al-Handasah buying out the company.

Source: Kamin, Blair, "Lawrence B. Perkins, Architectural Pioneer," obituary, *the Chicago Tribune*, Dec. 4, 1997

Dunlap, David W., "Lawrence Perkins, 90, Architect Who Loved Building Schools," obituary, *The New York Times*, Dec. 6, 1997

Heise, Kenan, "Philip Will Jr., 79, Top City Architect," obituary, *the Chicago Tribune*, Oct. 24, 1985

Perkins & Will company history time-line online: http://history.perkinswill.com/

PIETILÄ, REIMA AND RAILI

Frans Reima Ilmari Pietilä (1923–93) graduated from the Polytechnic Institute in Helsinki (1945–53) with professors that included Olli Pöyry (1912–73) and J.S. Sirén (1889–1961), the author of Eduskuntatalo, the Parliament of Finland building (1924–31). Following the first prize and completion of the Finnish Pavilion for Expo '58, Pietilä won the commission for a church in Tampere, Finland (1959–66) initiating his collaboration with Raili Paatelainen (1926–), his future partner (1960) and wife (1961). Raili graduated from the same school three years later. With their practice established the work developed included the Dipoli Student Centre (1961–66) at the new campus of the Polytechnic Institute in Helsinki – today Aalto University, the most well-known building after Alvar Aalto's (1898–1976) main building (1965) and library (1969). The Suvikumpu housing complex (1967–69) in Tapiola, and first prize in the competition for Finnish Embassy in New Delhi (1980–86) brought international exposure. In 1968 they were invited in Kuwait for the "Urban Form Study of the Old Town" (1968–69) and later to

further develop the extension of the Seif Palace, which included the design of the Minister of Foreign Affairs (1973–83). During these years both joined Team X meetings: 1973 in Berlin and in 1974 in Rotterdam. Pietilä developed a faculty career as a Professor of Architecture at Oulu University from 1973 to 1979.

Source: Connah, Roger, *Reima Pietilä. Centro Dipoli, Otaniemi*, Universale di Architettura, Testo & Imagine, Torino, 1998

Connah, Roger, *Finland: Modern Architectures in History*, Reaktion Books, 2006

Pietilä, Reima; Connah, Roger; Tango Mäntyniemi, *The Architecture of the Official Residence of the President of Finland. Tasavallan presidentin virka-asunnon arkkitehtuuri*, Painatuskeskus, 1994

Pietilä, Reima; Quantrill, Malcolm, *Pietilä, Reima, Architecture, Context and Modernism*, Rizzoli, 1985

PROJECT PLANNING ASSOCIATES LTD. PPAL

Born in Nanjing, China, Macklin L. Hancock (1925–2010) earned a Bachelor's degree in Agriculture from the Ontario Agricultural College (now the University of Guelph) in 1949 and pursued further his studies at Harvard University in planning and landscape (1949–50). At Graduate School he met Walter Gropius (1883–1969) and Dean G. Holmes Perkins (1904–2003) who wrote the charter and organised the Middle East Technical University in Ankara, Turkey in 1956. Hancock's first major project, under his newly established firm, Hancock, Little & Calvert, for the New Community of Don Mills, Toronto (1952–56) led to international recognition as a landscape architect and town planner. In 1956 Hancock and his seven colleagues at Don Mills, established the Project Planning Associates, Ltd. and Hancock, Little & Calvert, organised to provide a fully integrated consulting service on an international scale, including planners and designers, infrastructure and transportation engineers, landscape architects, and environmental and socio-economic specialists. Hancock was the president of the firm for more than 45 years. In 1959 Don Mills was part of the third "Urban Design" conference at Harvard and Hancock eventually became faculty in the same university. He was also developing an extensive body of work for waterfronts in Monaco and Kuwait where the firm worked from 1961 to 1979. In 1967 the firm accomplished the plan for the International and Universal Exhibition of Montréal (1963–68). In those years they worked with Josep Lluis Sert in the new plan for the University of Guelph (1963–74). Hancock is recognised to this day as central figure of landscape and planning in Canada for being, during his practice years, the president, director and secretary-general of all related institutions and boards in the country. In Kuwait PPAL developed an extensive body of work after the Kuwait Waterfront Competition (1961) and consequent Waterfront Development (1964–66), such as the Kuwait Beach Clubs (1972–76), Failaka Doha Harbours and Ras

Al-Salmiya Ferry Terminal (1973–1976), Soor Gardens (1977–82), partially built excluding the Museum and the preliminary studies for Al-Khiran Development (1978–84).

Source: Macklin Hancock/Project Planning Associates Ltd. Fonds Archive, Special Collection at University of Guelph, Toronto, Canada

Macklin Hancock/Project Planning Associates Ltd. biographies, The Cultural Landscape Foundation, Canada

Minutes of the Senate Meeting of February 11, 1969 at the University of Guelph, University of Guelph, Toronto, Canada

Interview with Charles Rewin Burkhead by Yona R. Owens, SCRC Series: Lewis Clarke Oral Histories Project, 2008

RAGLAN SQUIRE & PARTNERS

Raglan Squire (1912–2004), son of Sir John C. Squire, a renowned British poet and critic, established a practice in 1937 and during WWII served with the Royal Engineers. He was also part of the RIBA Reconstruction Committee. In 1948 he founded Raglan Squire & Partners with the most prestigious commission being the redevelopment of Eaton Square in Belgravia. Four years later the firm was commissioned to design the Engineering College at Rangoon University. He considered the Assembly Hall of this college, together with the Nat Mauk Technical High School in Yangon, Burma (1952–56), among his finest works. This experience opened doors to a series of other works all over the Middle East and Singapore where today the firm still operates under the name RSP Architects Planners & Engineers since 1981. Among the most significant projects in the region are the Hilton Hotels in Tehran, Tunis, Nicosia and Bahrain.

Source: Raglan Squire, obituary, *The Telegraph*, London, Jun. 2, 2004

Squire, Raglan, *Portrait of an Architect*, Colin Smythe Ltd., 1984

REIDY, AFFONSO

Affonso Eduardo Reidy (1909–64), a Brazilian architect born in Paris, graduated in Architecture from the National School of Fine Arts in Rio de Janeiro where he also taught, first as assistant to Gregori Warchavchik, who brought Modernist theory to Brazil after a degree in Rome and an apprenticeship with Marcello Piacentini. As intern Reidy collaborated with Donat Alfred Agache, an important French planner, on the Urban Renewal Plan of Rio. Reidy's first work, the Albergue da Boa Vontade (1931), a hostel for the homeless, developed with Gerson Pompeu Pinheiro (1910–1978) was featured in MoMA's New York exhibition in 1943 "Brazil Builds: Architecture New and Old, 1652–1942." In 1936 he became part of the Lucio Costa design team, along with others such as Oscar Niemeyer, who later developed the Ministry of Education and Health building in Rio, under the guidance of Le Corbusier. During the three decades of practice Reidi worked as public servant, first for the Municipality, then for the General Secretary of Public Works where he was director of the Departments of Popular Housing and Urbanism. During this period Reidy developed the Theatres of Armando Gonzaga (1950) and Marechal Hermes (1950), and several housing complexes including the well-known project Complex of Pedregulho (1946–55). The latter was acclaimed by Max Bill, in his "Report on Brazil" for *Architectural Review* in 1954, by Walter Gropius, Ernesto Rogers and Siegfried Giedion during the II Bienal of Sao Paulo jury, by Kenzo Tange during the III Bienal and by Le Corbusier during a visit in 1962. In the last part of his career, Reidy developed with the landscape architect Roberto Burle Marx, the project for Parque do Flamengo (1953–1962), the Museum of Modern Art (1953–67) in Rio de Janeiro and the competition for Kuwait National Museum in 1960.

Source: Fraser, Valerie, *Building the New World: Studies in the Modern Architecture of Latin America, 1930–1960*, Verso, 2000

Bonduki, Nabil (ed.), *Affonso Eduardo Reidy*, Editorial Blau & Instituto Lina Bo e P. M. Bardi, São Paulo, 2000

REMI LOPEZ & ASSOCIATES

Rémi Marie Alfred Lopez (1939–), son of Raymond Lopez (1904–1966), a well-known Parisian architect, urbanist and professor, graduated in Architecture from l'École Nationale Supérieure des Beaux-Arts de Paris (1961–64) under Louis Arretche's (1905–1991) Atelier. Following graduation he was hired in his father's practice and upon his father's death continued the collaboration with Jean Prouvé and the fascination for the use of aluminium in building façades. In 1967 Lopez became the Curator for Architecture at the Salon d'Automne at the Grand Palais in Paris. From 1967 to 1977 he developed the massive urban plan and the consequent five, 18-storey housing towers of La Beaucaire in Toloun, which included a shopping centre, a stadium and various public facilities. During this period Remi Lopez & Associates developed several projects outside France including the Amiri Hospital extension (1975) and the Credit & Savings Bank Headquarters (1970–77) in Kuwait as well as the Technical and Industrial Institute in Jeddah, Saudi Arabia (1975) and the Hôtel Métropole renovation and extension in Hanoi, Vietnam. In France the major works during these years were Le Centre Hospitalier Universitaire de Liège (1973) and the Centre Culturel et Sportif André Malraux in Le Mesnil-le-Roi using Jean Prouvé's aluminium roof framing and curtain walls for the façades. Between 1993–96 Lopez was the president of the French Chamber of Architects at the Conseil National de l'Ordre des Architectes.

Source: Morelli, Bruno J.; Bron, C., *Assemblies and Homes of the Period 1945/1975 in the Territory of Toulon Provence Méditerranée*, Direction Régionale Des Affaires Culturelles Provence-Alpes-Côte d'Azur (DRAC PACA), October, 2008

"Das Werk von Robert Maillart im Salon d'Automne 1967 in Paris," in *Schweizerische Bauzeitung*, n. 85, 1967

"Remi Lopez & Associates, Three projects: 1, Technical and Industrial Institute in Jiddah, Saudi Arabia. 2, Amiri Hospital in Kuwait. 3, Savings and Credit Bank in Kuwait," in *Recherché & Architecture*, 1975, pp. 25–30

RENDEL, PALMER & TRITTON (RP&T)

James Meadows Rendel (1799–1856) grandson of architect John Meadows, a well-known architect of his day (died in 1791), after an education in Civil Engineering initiated his practice as a surveyor in London having by then, his first experience with bridge engineering. About 1822 he established in Plymouth his own practice dedicated to the construction of roads and suspended bridges in the area. In about 1838 he was awarded with his first overseas commission, the implementation of similar bridges over the Hooghly River distributary of the Ganges River in West Bengal, India. He soon became the expert in harbour construction methods, applying a comprehensive system of hydraulic machinery, including Portland and Holyhead. From 1913, upon acquisition, the company was renamed Rendel, Palmer & Tritton Partnership and by the 1930s had acted as consulting engineers for 31,000 of the 33,000 miles of railway and 200 major bridges in the Indian sub-continent. The company operated by then mainly from Colonial India, but was able to keep its relevance in the UK with the construction of Waterloo Bridge (1937–44). After the Indian independence and the Suez crisis it kept working in the Gulf, mainly on road infrastructure and port facilities, including the North Pear in Mena Abdullah, Ahmadi Kuwait (1957–59), and in 1971 designed the famous Thames Barrier completed by Richard Costain contracting in 1984. In the following year it merged with High-Point, a specialist financial, contractual and management consultancy firm and became known as High-Point Rendel Limited until today.

Source: Allinson, Ken, *London's Contemporary Architecture*, Routledge, 2007

James Meadows Rendel Obituary, 1857 by Grace's Guide to British Industrial History web platform

Skempton, A. W., *A Biographical Dictionary of Civil Engineers in Great Britain and Ireland: 1500–1830*, Thomas Telford, 2002

RICHARD COSTAIN (MIDDLE EAST) CO. LTD.

Contracting company established in 1865 by Richard Costain (1839–1902), became known all over UK for housing construction. Dolphin Square (1935) in London is the best known project of this type. In the same decade the first commissions overseas include the Trans-Iranian Railway (1939) and the refinery at Abadan in 1938. During WWII the company was fundamental in the construction of the *Mulberry* floating concrete port that gave the Allies the logistics support across the Channel in the days following the D-Day invasion. In the post-war period the company was present in some of the most famous architectural work, such as the Festival of Britain Complex by Fry & Drew. The projects in Kuwait were the first in the region, a connection that remains until now with the influential Kharafi construction family holding a major stake in the company. This included the airports in Bahrain and Dubai (1960), and the world's largest dry dock and the Middle East's largest deep water port in Dubai. In recent years the firm has remained highly visible with prestigious projects such as the Thames Barrier (1984), the Channel Tunnel (1994), Hong Kong Airport Platform (1997), the restoration London's St. Pancras Station (2006) and other London Underground Stations.

Source: Bowley, Marion, *The British Building Industry*, 1966

Costain online platform: http://costain.com/who-we-are/our-history/;

ROTH, ALFRED

Alfred Roth (1903–1998) with a degree in Architecture from ETH Zurich (1925) started his practice collaborating with his former professor, Karl Moser (1860–1936), the first president of CIAM at Chateau de La Sarraz in 1928. The professor recommended Roth to Le Corbusier and Pierre Jeanneret and in 1926 he was appointed site manager for the two houses in Stuttgart's Weißenhofsiedlung and collaborated in the initial developments of the Palais des Nations in Geneva. The experience in Stuttgart brought Roth closer to international architectural and artistic personalities such as Piet Mondrian. In 1928 he met Ingrid Wallberg (1880–1965) and they established a practice in Gothenburg, which was to last for two years. Both represented the co-operative HSB at the Stockholm Exhibition (1930) with interiors such as kitchenettes and other compact living solutions. Sune Lindstrom was to be in charge of the HSB housing programme upon Roth's departure. In 1931 Roth joined his cousin Emil Roth (1893–1980) at the site of the Werkbundsiedlung Neubühl in Zurich (1928–32). Later the two joined Marcel Breuer (1902–1981) in the commission for Sigfried Giedion Doldertalhäuser houses in Zurich (1935–36). During this period Roth completed his first school building, Kappeli in Zurich (1932). In 1940 he published his first publication *Die Neue Architektur* and later became the editor of *Das Werk* (1943–57). In 1949 he initiated an academic career at George Washington University in St. Louis and in 1950 he published the influential *Das neue Schulhaus* (the New School). In the USA he completed a school in St. Louis and taught at the Graduate School of Design, Harvard (1953) before returning to Switzerland where he was a professor at ETH between 1957–71. During the 1960s Roth provided consultancy in educational facilities design and implementation for different agencies in Macedonia, following the Skopje earthquake, and also for Jordan and Kuwait. In association with Alvar Aalto he developed the commercial complexes of Schönbühl in Lucerne (1967–70) and Bank Sabbagh (1964–70) built by Al Hani Construction & Trading Company in Beirut. Until the 1980s Roth was still involved with prefabricated schools and commercial buildings in Kuwait such as the Hotel Intercontinental (1980) proposal for Salmiya.

Source: Roth, Alfred; von Moos, Stanislaus, *Architect of Continuity*, Waser Verlag, Zürich, 1985

Winiger, Alex, *Bestandesbeschrieb Alfred Roth*, in Website des gta Archivs / ETH Zürich, Mai 2011, www.archiv.gta. arch.ethz.ch/nachlaesse-vorlaesse/roth-alfred

SABA GEORGE SHIBER

Born in Jerusalem, Shiber (1923–1968) obtained a first degree in Civil Engineering at the American University of Beirut (1944) and a Bachelor's in Architecture from the Egyptian University of Cairo (1946). Following completion of his Master's in City Planning at the MIT in 1948 he served as instructor of Architecture at the Kansas State College of Agriculture and Applied Science and eventually developed a career as a professor holding the Chair of the City Planning Department at Rensselaer Polytechnic Institute, in Troy, New York, between 1949–51. He completed his PhD in "City and Regional Planning" with Prof. John W. Reps at Cornell University (1956) where he became interested in emerging concepts such as "site planning" and "urban design" as opposed to the pragmatism of "city planning." His interests of planning ranged from touristic and recreational to industrial and urban preservation. Appointed as Chief of the Technical Bureau of the National Reconstruction Authority of Lebanon he was to be in Beirut the following three years working from 1959 with the recently established engineering firm Associated Consulting Engineers (ACE) by the three ex-partners of Kamal Shair. During this period Shiber contributed to the establishment of the Association for the Maintenance of Ancient Residences with Assem Salam, and worked with Michel Écochard in the Plan for Saida, and with Sami Abdul Baki, who eventually recommended Shiber for the position of city planning advisor to the Kuwait Government. He was also Planning Advisor for the Municipality of Damascus and for the Ministry of Urban and Rural Affairs of Syria. In 1960 Shiber initiated his service at the Department of Public Works in Kuwait, later transferred to the Development Board and finally to the Municipality as "the planning expert." Along this period, characterised by intensive construction activity, Shiber implemented a new strategy for the city's urban development, intensively described on his well-known publication *The Kuwait Urbanization* (1964). In 1963 he was awarded the title; "Arab of the Year" by the *Middle East Business Digest*. He was featured on the cover of the December issue, which also gave an extensive account of the architecture, city planning, regional development, and public administration career in the Arab world of "Mr. Arab Planner," as has he became known from then. During this period Shiber established an interesting relationship with Doxiadis becoming the Kuwait correspondent for *Ekistics*. In 1964 he retired due to illness and returned to Lebanon, but remained very active with international congresses and encounters, becoming the Vice-President of the Afro-Asian Housing Organization in 1967 and Kuwait's representative of UN Housing Building and Planning Committee from early 1968 up to his death in the summer of the same year.

Source: Nasr, Joe, "Saba Shiber, 'Mr. Arab Planner'. Parcours professionnel d'un urbaniste au Moyen-Orient," in *Géocarrefour*, v. 80, n. 3, 2005, pp. 197–206

Shiber, Saba George, *Kuwait Urbanization, Documentation, Analysis, Critique*, Kuwait Government Printing Press, Kuwait, 1964, p. 643

Shiber, Saba George, *Recent Arab City Growth*, Kuwait Government Printing Press, Kuwait, 1968, p. 831

Students Work, Cornell University Archive

SABAH ABI-HANNA

Sabah Abi-Hanna (1929–), received a Bachelor's in Architectural Engineering from the American University of Beirut (1959) with Prof. Assem Salam one year after his first experience in Kuwait as intern in the Road Department of the Department of Public Works. He returned to Kuwait where he served at the Planning Division of the Department of Public Works, being later transferred to the Municipality. During this period Sabah was responsible for building inspection and construction license approvals. He discussed with Charles Haddad, a fellow graduate of AUB who worked in Kuwait since 1956, the possibility of a design partnership. (Delta would have been the name). But Charles opted instead for a Master's at Yale and Sabah moved on with his practice. His first commissions were related to domestic environments of some members of the ruling family. The first corporate commissions were from the National Bank of Kuwait (NBK), the Association of Cloth Merchants for CBD Area 9, and Kuwait Public Transportation Company (KPTC), eventually with some role in the Mirqab Bus Terminal. In 1968 the commission for the residential complex Loulou'a Al-Marzouq (1968–71) and Messilah Beach Hotel (1970–74) opened the opportunity for the first commission abroad, the Sharjah Carlton Hotel in the UAE. In 1972 with Salem Al-Marzouq, Sabah's practice was expanded into a partnership, Salem Al-Marzouk & Sabah Abi-Hanna (SSH).

Source: Mneimneh, Dina H., *Becoming an Architect: A Look at Architectural Education at the American University of Beirut*, FEASAC, Faculty of Engineering and Architecture, American University of Beirut, 2013

Sweet, Rod (ed.), *SSH Design: The First 50 Years*, Al-Khat Printing Press, Kuwait, 2012

SABAH MOHAMMED AMIN AL-RAYES

Sabah Al Rayes (1939–), B.Sc in Civil Engineering with a minor in Architecture and Metallurgy from Indiana Institute of Technology (1965), he returned to Kuwait in the same year to work for the Ministry of Public Works. He was one the founders of PACE where he served in the role of Managing Director from 1968. During the following years (1968–73) he was Advisor to the Kuwait Ministry of Foreign Affairs Aid Programme for Developing Countries, Executive Secretary of Kuwait Society of Engineers from its foundation in 1967, Director of Kuwait National Industries Co. (1973–76), Director of Gulf Real Estate Development Co. (1976–80), Director of United Gulf Bank of Bahrain (1981–86), Director of Arab Life Insurance Co. of Jordan (1981–87), Chairman of Kuwait Precious Metals Co. (1982–86), Vice-Chairman of Tunis International Bank (1982–85), Vice-Chairman Kuwait Department Stores. He is an honorary Doctor in Civil Engineering, Indiana Institute of Technology (1984). Upon retirement he left PACE.

Source: Gedeon, Charles G., *Who's Who in the Arab World 2007–2008*, Publitec Publications, Beirut, 2007

SAMI ABDUL BAKI ARCHITECTS

Sami Abdul Baki, also known as Sami Abd El Baqi (1925–), has a degree in Civil Engineering from AUB (1947), a Master's in Architecture from University of Munich, a Master's in Law from Cairo University and a PhD in Economics from LSE. He was among the first members of the Beirut Society of Engineers (1950). With a practice established in Beirut he integrated the first group of professors into the recently founded degree of Architecture at AUB (1952). The only reference to his work are the Martyrs Statue (1952–58), the Amatoury Building in Hamra Street, the Druze Community House in Beirut and an apartment building for Joseph Shader, former Minister of Finance and Planning. The implementation of the monument was to lead to a big controversy in the city and finally the Italian sculptor Mazzacurati was called to cast in bronze a statue with four human figures. To this day, Baki remains connected to this episode being for the last 40 years the president of the League for Honouring the Martyrs. During this period he met Saba George Shiber, the new Chief of the Technical Bureau of the National Reconstruction Authority. However, his major known works are in Kuwait, where he was appointed by Sheikh Fahad Al-Salem Al-Sabah in 1953 as Chief-Engineer in the Public Works Department. The Kuwait Municipality Buildings Complex (1959–62) and the Ministries of Finance and Information are well-known and credited to Mr. Baki. Less known are the roles in the International Air Terminal renovation and some other ministry buildings such as the Defence Ministry and the Prime Minister's Diwan. During this period Baki partnered with Ernst Van Drop (1920–2003), who had a firm in Bonn, Germany. In 1962 he returned to Lebanon to run for parliamentary elections and was eventually part of the Lebanese Council of Ministers. During this period he was involved in the supervision of Sidon (Saida) and Tripoli stadiums for the first Arab Football Cup (1963).

Source: Volk, Lucia, *Memorials and Martyrs in Modern Lebanon*, Indiana University Press, 2010

http://www.mcaleb.org/ar/mahrajanalkitab/
mahrajan2011/72-takrim-dr-sami-3abdelbaki.html

SALEM AL-MARZOUQ & SABAH ABI-HANNA (SSH)

Following the completion of Loulou'a Al-Marzouq (1968–71), Sabah Abi-Hanna (1939–) met Salem al-Marzouq, a highway engineer educated in the US and elected to Kuwait's National Assembly in the same year. Soon, Sabah Abi-Hanna & Associates became Salem Al-Marzouq & Sabah Abi-Hanna WLL and the scale of the firm's scope expanded from building design into planning and large infrastructure design. Salem Al-Marzouq was instrumental in providing new opportunities. During this period the firm enlarged its capacity and work force substantially, and was able to develop complex and large architectural projects, such as those in Salem Al-Mubarak Street. However, the relationship with Shankland Cox Partnership (SCP) and other large international companies such as SOM and W.S. Atkins, in several planning projects, including the first review on the Kuwait Master Plan, was to transform the firm into an international corporate design consultancy that is still active to these days.

Source: Sweet, Rod (ed.), *SSH Design: The First 50 years*, Al-Khat Printing Press, Kuwait, 2012

SAM JAMPEL & PARTNERS

Sam Jampel graduated in Civil Engineering and established his practice in London in 1960. Four years later, with John Davison he established Jampel & Davison Consulting Engineers. During the first 20 years the company was mainly involved in the design and supervision of the construction of small roads and bridges in the UK. By the end of the 1970s Paul Bell and George Pelentrides had joined the firm and became partners after 1981 of Jampel Davison & Bell Ltd. In this period and throughout the 1980s the firm was primarily involved in providing structural engineering consultancy to small architectural practices including Michael Carapetian Associates and Brian Meeking Associates, mainly on residential buildings. With Brian Meeking the firm was eventually responsible for the structural design of several houses listed on the UK Modern House Index and the well-known Greenwich Theatre in London.

Source: Perkin, George, "Town House Terraces, House in Blackheath," in *Concrete Quarterly* (CQ), The Cement and Concrete Association, n.154, Autumn 1987

Hope, Alice, *Town Houses*, B.T. Batsford, 1963

UK Modern House Index database by Martin Hugh and others, online platform, http://ukmoho.co.uk/

SASAKI ASSOCIATES

Hideo Sasaki (1919–2000) initiated studies in Business Administration with a minor in art at the University of California, Los Angeles in 1939 and transferred to University College Berkeley where planning was taught in the Landscape Architecture Department. During WWII he was internee in a Japanese Americans camp and only completed his Bachelor's degree in Landscape Architecture at the University of Illinois in 1946 under Stanley Hart White (1891–1979), referred to as the inventor of the green wall, and Karl B. Lohmann (1887–1963). In 1948 he completed his Master's in Landscape Architecture at the Harvard Graduate School of Design. He commenced his practice at Skidmore, Owings & Merrill (SOM) and taught at the University of Illinois and Harvard. In 1953 he established Sasaki Associates and between 1958–68 was the head of the landscape architecture department at Harvard GSD. During this period he developed a body of work with different practices including SOM, Eero Saarinen and Associates for the Bell Labs Holmdel Complex (1962), Pietro Belluschi (1899–1994) advisor to the US Embassy in Baghdad (1961) and J.L. Sert (1902–83) who designed it, I.M. Pei (1917–) and Paul Rudolph (1918–97). He was also a jury member for the Joint Banking Centre competition in Kuwait (1976) among other projects. As lead designer, the completion of One Maritime Plaza, San Francisco (1964) and the Greenacre Park, New York (1971) may have been a factor in the competition selection (1976) and consequent award of Kuwait Waterfront project that was to last from 1978–88. The firm is still active and operating internationally.

Source: Raver, Anne, "Hideo Sasaki, 80, Influential Landscape Architect, Dies," *The New York Times*, Sep. 25, 2000

SAYYED KARIM

Degree in Architecture from University of Zurich (ETH) in 1932, followed by a Master's in Urban Planning and PhD under Otto Rudolf Salvisberg's mentoring (1938) in the same institution. After returning back to Egypt, Sayyed Karim established the magazine *Majallat al-'Imarah* (between 1939–50; 1952–59 also titled *Emara, Alemara Alefoun*). The magazine presented contemporary architecture in pre-war and post-war Cairo, but also served as a vehicle for Karim's practice exposure. Articles such as "If Cairo Were Destroyed?" (1945), provided provocative publicity to trigger large-scale commissions. Between 1947–64 as UN consultant he worked on

New Baghdad (1947) Damascus Airport and Al Zahra suburb (1947), Jeddah Master Plan (1948), the Al-Malaz Housing Plan (1953) for Riyadh and 'Greater Cairo' (1953). As consultant he produced reports on all the main plans that had been produced in the region during those years, including Kuwait First Master Plan in 1952. After the 1956 crisis the relationship with the Arab Contractors and Nasser were consolidated and Karim was commissioned for Port Said's reconstruction (1957) and Nasr City (1956–58).

Source: ETH Studio Basel Contemporary City Institute, *The Middle East Studio*, Winter Semester 2010

Elshahed, Mohamed, "Port Said 1957: Egyptian Modernism Unfurled", in *Portal 9*, n. 1 "The Imagined," Autumn 2012

Elshahed, Mohamed, *Downtown as seen by a Modernist*, *Downtown Cairo*, Jovis Verlag, 2015

Volait, Mercedes, *L'architecture moderne en Egypte et la revue al-'Imara (1939–1959)*, Centre d'études et de documentation économique, juridique et sociale (CEDEJ), Cairo, 1988

SCOTT & WILSON, KIRKPATRICK & PARTNERS

Sir Cyril Kirkpatrick (1872–1957), the chief engineer to the Port of London Authority from 1913 to 1924, established Kirkpatrick & Partners that specialised in docks, harbours and sea defences in the same year. During WWII, Kirkpatrick advised Richard Costain in the construction of the Mulberry floating concrete port that gave the Allies the logistical support across the Channel in the days following the D-Day Invasion. Following the war, the engineers William S. Scott (1855–1950) and Dr. Guthlac Wilson (1902–53), an authority on soil mechanics with a S.M. from Harvard and PhD from London Univ., founded Scott & Wilson. In 1948 they were appointed with the Leslie Martin design team (Peter Moro and Edwin Williams) as structural and mechanical engineers for the Royal Festival Hall centrepiece of the Festival of Britain. Before the opening of the hall in 1951 they merged with Kirkpatrick & Partners. The firm grew through acquisitions over the following decades to 2010 when the Scott Wilson Group was acquired by URS Corporation.

Source: "Guthlac Wilson (1902–1953)," obituary, in *The Engineer*, Jan.–Jun. 1953, Index, *British Industrial History*

"Sir Cyril Reginald Sutton Kirkpatrick, 1872–1957," obituary, in *ICE Proceedings*, v. 9, n. 1, Jan. 1, 1958, pp. 127–128

Banham, Mary; Hillier, Bevis (eds.), *A Tonic to the Nation: The Festival of Britain, 1951*, Thames & Hudson, London 1976

SKIDMORE, OWINGS & MERRILL

Louis Skidmore (1897–1962) graduated from MIT (1924) after studies in Architecture at the BAC (1921) and a degree in Electric Engineering at Bradley Polytechnic Institute (1917). Supported by dean William Emerson

(1873–57), who served as director of the Bureau of Construction of the American Red Cross in Paris during the war and a graduate from the École Nationale Supérieure des Beaux-Arts, Skidmore won a travelling scholarship to Europe (1927–29), one year ahead of Philip Johnson (1906–2005) and Louis Kahn (1901–1974) for the European Modernism tours. Eventually, Skidmore spent more of his time between Paris and Rome where he met Raymond Hood (1881–1934). Hood became significant in Skidmore's establishment in Chicago after 1929 and appointed, first as assistant and later as the chief-architect of the Century of Progress Exposition scheduled for 1933 in Chicago. For the "Chicago's World Fair" Nathaniel Owings (1903–1984) joined the team after practice experience in New York and the graduation from Cornell University. In 1936 the two established a design firm in Chicago; Skidmore & Owings. One year later the firm opened in New York to assist the American Radiator Company in designing a new office building and Gordon Bunshaft (1909–1990) was hired. Bunshaft joined after a two year travelling scholarship to Europe (1935–37) concluding his studies at MIT, B. Arch (1933) and M. Arch (1935) and was strongly influenced by the work of Le Corbusier and Willem Dudok. In 1939 they won the contract for the New York World's Fair and the engineer John Ogden Merrill (1896–1975), trained in Civil Engineering at Wisconsin (1914–17) and Architecture at MIT (1919–21), joined the firm as partner, thus establishing Skidmore, Owings & Merrill. After WWII the firm was awarded the design of the Lever House in New York City (1949–50), the H.J. Heinz Plant in Pittsburgh (1948–50) and several other large building developments that were exhibited at MoMA, New York in 1950. By then, Bunshaft was one of the seven new partners and was responsible for the majority of the firm's design up to the 1960s. Following the efforts of his dean William Emerson and Robert Van Nice in surveying Hagia Sophia, the American firm was awarded with the Hilton Hotel in Istanbul, Turkey (1953–1959) in association with Sedad Hakki Eldem (1908–88). During the coming years the firm was successful in the Middle East and in 1976–77 commissions for the Joint Banking Centre in Kuwait and the National Commercial Bank in Jeddah, Saudi Arabia confirmed the company's reputation in the region, despite the departure of all the original partners, including Bunshaft, who retired after the completion of these projects in 1982. Since then the firm has gone through successive management reforms and continues operating all over the world including the Gulf.

Source: Adams, Nicholas, *Skidmore, Owings & Merrill: SOM dal 1936*, Electa, Milano, 2006

The completion of the John Hancock Center in Chicago in 1970, under Bruce Graham (1925–2010), consolidated Skidmore, Owings & Merrill's reputation for high-rise building. In 1969 the firm's New York office was awarded with the construction of Tour Fiat (Areva) in Paris (1972–74) and consequently with its surroundings the Quartier Gambetta (La Défense), including office buildings, apartments, shopping arcade and parking for 3,000 cars. In 1973 the firm opened an office in Paris under the partner David Hughes (1918–2007), who had been the project manager in charge of the office in Bonn, Germany, during the American consulate project in the 1950s, known as the "German programme." According to Jacques Guiton this last project prompted the establishment of SOM's Paris branch at Boulevard du Montparnasse. However the office did not last long and in June 1974 the staff returned back to New York. During this nine-month period SOM's drawings for Souq Al-Kuwait and Souq Al-Kabeer (1973–76) in Kuwait were issued from this office. The strong involvement of Francis Bouygues in the Paris projects and his firm's special interest in markets such as Kuwait after 1973, led to the establishment of Bouygues Off-Shore (BOS) and several construction commissions.

Source: David, H., Paid Notice: "Deaths Hughes," *The New York Times*, Jun. 28, 2007

Loeffler, Jane C., *The Architecture of Diplomacy: Building America's Embassies*, Princeton Architectural Press, 1998

Guiton, Jacques, *A Life in Three Lands: Memoirs of an Architect*, Branden Books, 1991

SMITHSON, ALISON AND PETER

Alison Margaret Gill (1928–93) and Peter Denham Smithson (1923–03), both graduated from the School of Architecture of the University of Durham in the UK. During WWII Peter was forced to interrupt his studies and enlist in the Queen Victoria's Own Madras Sappers and Miners, serving in India and Burma where he had the first contact with the East. After the completion of his degree in Newcastle (1948) Peter enrolled at the Royal Academy of Arts in London where an exhibition on *The Art of India and Pakistan* was displayed and with great success. There, Peter eventually met Hugh Casson (1910–99) who was appointed the same year as director of architecture for the Festival of Britain. Casson was eventually influential in recommending the young Peter to Leslie Martin (1908–2000) for a post with the London County Council (LCC). Alison, with whom Peter was married in 1949, graduated from Durham in the same year and joined the Schools' Division of the LCC. Both had submitted an entry for the Hunstanton Secondary Modern School (1950–54) competition, which they won and were commissioned for the full design. They left London County Council and established their own practice in 1950. In the following years their proposals for Coventry Cathedral (1951), Golden Lane (1952) and Sheffield University (1953) competitions did not result in actual commissions, but established their reputation in the UK. In 1953 they join the CIAM congresses for the first time. At the ninth CIAM congress in Aix-en-Provence they presented the "urban re-identification" poster display, attacking the functional segregation of the Athens Charter. With the Dutch group led by Jacob Bakema they organised the tenth CIAM congress and the first Team X in Dubrovnik (1956). The House of the Future (1956), the Sugden House (1956), their own weekend home in Fonthill (1959–82) and the Iraq Airways branch in London (1960) were fundamental in their research. In 1959 Peter and Alison were commissioned for the Economist offices, off St. James's Street in central London. The project was completed in 1964 and was instrumental in gaining other major commissions in the following years; this was apart from their thought and knowledge they related actively in several publications (especially Alison) and through their teaching careers. The British Embassy in Brasilia (1964, never built), Garden Building at St. Hilda's College in Oxford (1967–70) and Robin Hood Gardens (1966–72) were their major building achievements before being invited to Kuwait in 1968. Their work in Kuwait, until 1973, did not result in actual building commissions, but had a strong impact in the post Oil Embargo era building production of the country.

Source: Klemek, Christopher, *The Transatlantic Collapse of Urban Renewal: Postwar Urbanism from New York to Berlin*, University of Chicago Press, 2011

Rowntree, Diana, "Peter Denham Smithson," obituary, *The Guardian*, Mar. 4, 2003

STEINBÜCHEL-RHEINWALL, RAMBALD VON

Steinbüchel-Rheinwall (1902–1990), studied in Munich and Berlin, completed his studies under Hans Poelzig in 1926. During this first year Rambald worked for Peter Behrens and Hans Poelzig. In 1930 he established his practice in Berlin and joined as member the Deutscher Werkbund. The first commission was for Stadtwerke-Haus in his hometown of Graz, where he joined the Sezession Graz until 1933. In 1931 he joined Taut, Mendelsohn, Gropius, among others, at the Berliner Bauausstellung "Sonne, Luft und Haus für Alle." After WWII he moved to Frankfurt and converted the practice into a commercial consultancy well-known for hotel, industrial and office work, including Lufthansa travel agencies.

Source: Antje Senarclens de Grancy, *Rambald Von Steinbüchel-Rheinwall Architekt, 1902–1990*, City of Graz online platform: http://www.graz.at/cms/beitrag/10096242/1869835/

Senarclens de Grancy, Antje, *Keine Würfelwelt. Architekturpositionen einer "bodenständigen" Moderne Graz 1918–1938*, Graz, Haus der Architektur, 2007

STUDIO NERVI

Pier Luigi Nervi (1891–1979) with a degree in Civil Engineering from Bologna (1913) commenced his practice working with concrete construction companies. In 1920 he established his own construction company in Rome, the Società Ing. Nervi e Nebbiosi. Upon the commission for the Cinema Augusteo in Naples and the seating for the Municipal Stadium in Florence (1930–32), Nervi changed partner and then incorporated the Società Ing. Nervi e Bartoli. With Bartoli came the first large commission from the Italian Aviation Company for eight airplane hangars in Orvieto, Orbetello and Torre del Lago (1935–42) where the technique of spatial construction of large geodetic roof structures and prefabricated elements were used. Nervi became Professor of Construction Techniques and Material Technology at the Faculty of Architecture in Rome in 1946, where he taught until 1961. During the 1950s and 1960s he completed various important projects, including the Pirelli Tower in Milan, the UNESCO Headquarters in Paris (for Marcel Breuer and Bernard Zehrfuss with Antonio Nervi), the Olympic Complex in Rome (the Palazzetto dello Sport, the Corso Francia viaduct and the Flaminio Stadium), the Palazzo del Lavoro in Turin (with Gino Covre and Antonio Nervi), the George Washington Bus Station in New York, the Risorgimento Bridge in Verona, the Stock Exchange Tower in Montreal (collaboration with Luigi Moretti), St. Mary's Cathedral in San Francisco and the Papal Audience Hall in Vatican City (with Antonio Nervi). In these years the well-known Studio Nervi S.p.A. was invited for two major competitions in Kuwait, the Kuwait Sports Centre (1968–69) and the Kuwait National Assembly (1971–72).

Source: Desideri, Paolo, *Pier Luigi Nervi*, Zanichelli, Bologna, 1983

SUTOUR, JACQUES

Jacques Sutour was a graduate in Architecture from the late 1940s and after 10 years of practice experience in Paris applied to the national French company Postes, Télégraphes et Téléphones (PTT) Architectural department. Sutour spent the majority of his career at PTT developing radio, television and telecom administration and operation buildings all over France as well as outside to include the Algiers Radio Television Centre and Kuwait Radio Television Centre (1968–78). In his years of service at PTT, Sutour was also involved in the construction, repair and renovation of hotels, central offices, telegraph and telephone and other special buildings under the administration of PTT.

Source: Postes, Télégraphes et Téléphones (PTT) architects staff selection and evaluation report from 1923–1968 online: https://www.siv.archives-nationales.culture.gouv.fr/siv/

TANGE, KENZO (URTEC)

Kenzo Tange (1913–2005), graduated from the Architecture Department in the Faculty of Engineering of Tokyo Imperial University (1938). After experience with Mayekawa Kunio, a former collaborator of Le Corbusier, he returned to Graduate School. In 1946 he become Assistant Professor and established the Tange Laboratory. His students at the Lab conducted mostly urban analyses. They were Sachio Otani, Atsushi Shimokobe, Fumihiko Maki, Koji Kamiya, Arata Isozaki, Kisho Kurokawa, Yoshio Taniguchi and Taneo Oki, among others. In parallel with his academic life, Tange developed an architectural practice responsible for numerous public buildings during the post-war reconstruction including the City of Hiroshima and the Peace Centre. His interest on city planning led to Tange's doctorate (1959) titled "Spatial Structure in a Large City," the establishment of URTEC (acronym for urban architect) in 1957 and to the "Plan for Tokyo 1960" (1959). The city was selected for the 1964 Olympic Games and Tange was commissioned to design the stadium. At the same time Tange's team worked on the reconstruction of St. Maria Cathedral in Tokyo (1961–64) destroyed during the war. One of the most relevant projects was the Yamanishi Broadcasting and Press Centre in Kofu, Japan completed in 1966. In the same year Tange's team was commissioned to work on the plan for the reconstruction of Skopje (1966) after the 1963 earthquake. Such experience led in 1967 to the commissioning of several works outside Japan including the Fiera District Towers in Bologna and Librino, a town for 60,000 in Catania. In the following year the competitions for the Sports Centres in Riyadh (1969) and Kuwait (1968) were entered in collaboration with Frei Otto. The experience with Frei Otto in Kuwait was to lead to vast collaborations worldwide, such as the Arctic City Study (1970–71), which involved beside Otto, also Ewald Bubner and Ove Arup. In the Gulf Region, the collaborations ware extended through the Pacific International Consultants Corporation in projects such as the Kuwait International Air Terminal (1967–81), the University of Yarmouk (1976–85) in Amman, Jordan and Al-Khayriyya Complex in Riyadh, completed in 1982. Other projects came by direct invitation from governments such as the Political and Administrative Centre of Tehran in the Abbas Abad Hills (1973–74), the Pilgrims Settlement in the Mina Valley in Mecca (1974), the Tehran Hotel (1976), the Japanese Embassy in Riyadh (1985) and the Kuwait Embassy in Tokyo (1968–70). After being awarded with the Pritzker Prize in 1987, Tange designed the Gulf University in Manama, Bahrain.

Source: Kultermann, Udo (ed.), "Kenzo Tange: 1946–1969: arquitectura y urbanismo," Gustavo Gili, Barcelona, 1970

Abbas Abad new city centre, "*The Work of Kenzo Tange & URTEC during the 70s*", Japan Architect 51, nos. 8–9, special issue, Aug.– Sep. 1976, pp. 9–104

Khosravi, Hamed, *Politics of DeMonst(e)ration*, in *San Rocco 6, Collaboration*, Spring 2013

TECHNICAL STUDIES BUREAU (TEST)

The Technical Studies Bureau was established in 1965 by Fareed Khoursheed, with a Bachelor's degree from the University of Colorado in Civil Engineering (1949–52). By 1971 the company was established in Kuwait with support from Al-Nsif family who awarded Khoursheed for a trial intervention in the Sheraton Hotel, "trapezoidal pool and a restaurant." After terminating relations with PACE, Iraq Consult (IQC) was also an important factor in further developing the role of TEST in Kuwait, together both companies' ventures in three of the Kuwait Sport Clubs (1970–74) and for the Al-Qabas Newspaper Headquarters (1972). During this period Sami Al-Bader, a graduate from Baghdad University and a former collaborator with Hisham Munir, led the office as local partner and developed a strong relationship with the Sudanese architect Abdalla Sabbar (1939–) from Colin Buchanan & Partners and some of IQC seniors such as Maath Alousi (1938–) and Safa H. Killidar, a graduate from Oregon School of Architecture in 1964 and a relative of Rifat Chadirji's (1926–) colleague Farkhondeh Killidar (1937–). In 1973 Abdalla Sabbar, a graduate of the Tropical Studies Department at the AA (1971) and with a Master's in Urban & Regional Planning from MIT (1973), while working for Colin Buchanan & Partners in the Regional Plan for Kurdistan and the Urban Development Plan for Erbil Citadel started a strong working relationship with Alousi that eventually led to the establishment of a partnership. Following the Oil Embargo (1973) and the rise of the Ba'ath Party in Iraq, upon Sami al-Bader suggestion, Alousi led the establishment of Technical Studies Bureau (TEST) office in Beirut with Khoursheed, Killidar and Sabbar as partners. In the same year new branches were established from Beirut in Baghdad, Muscat, Dubai and later Dammam (KSA). Between 1974 and 1980 the planning and urban studies part of the firm was led by Abdalla Sabbar, working on Sharq, Hawally and Salmiya District Centres (1971–80) in Kuwait and Deira Creek Corniche (1974–78) in Dubai; while the Architecture Department was led by Maath Alousi, first from Beirut and later from Athens (1976–80). During this period the most well-known buildings completed were the Embassy of the United Arab Emirates in Oman (1976–79), the Kuwaiti Embassy building in Khartoum, Sudan (1975–1977), the Banking Studies Centre (1976–80), the Al Qabas Newspaper Headquarters extension (1976–77) and the Ministry of Planning Head Offices (1980–82) in Kuwait. In 1980 Alousi established Alousi Associates Technical Studies Bureau TEST-Baghdad and Khoursheed proceeded with TEST-International, based in the UAE. Both offices are still operative today.

Source: Khoursheed, Fareed, "Letter to the Editor," *Life Magazine*, Mar. 28, 1949, and *Life Magazine*, Apr. 18, 1949

Maath Al-Alousi interview, Aug. 12, 2015

THE ARCHITECTS COLLABORATIVE

The Architects Collaborative (TAC) was established in 1945 by eight architects including Walter Gropius (1883–1969) and was the practice through which Gropius operated for nearly half of his professional career. Referred by many as the "Cambridge School," by the 1970s, the practice based in Harvard Square had more than 380 employees, being eventually the largest dedicated architectural practice in the United States at the time. The firm's early involvement in the Middle East, beginning with a commission to design the University of Baghdad after 1957, led to more than 25 years of work in the Gulf states, including projects in Kuwait, Saudi Arabia, Iraq, and the United Arab Emirates. The financial and political conflict in the region in the early 1980s led to the fall of TAC after 1983, eventually leading to the firm's bankruptcy in 1995. Former partners and employees succeeded in establishing new practices that after TAC's fall in the region emerged with some reputation, such as the Cambridge Seven Associates (1962–), Benjamin Thompson and Associates (1966–) and Charles Gibson Design (1979–), who developed architectural signage, murals, and banners for many of the TAC's projects in Kuwait, and even independent practices as Michael Francis Gebhart (1990–) that has worked since then for many of the local consultants in Kuwait.

Source: Kubo, Michael, "The Cambridge School: What went on at 46 Brattle Street," in *American Gropius*, v. 16, n. 3, summer 2013, p. 7

THURFJELL CONSULT

January Thurfjell (1924–2000) completed his studies in the Naval School of Härnösand (1942) and his architectural degree at the Chalmers Technical School, the former Arts & Crafts School of Gothenburg in 1949, both in Sweden. In Gothenburg he met Helge Zimdal, who became professor at the Technical School immediately after Thurfjell's graduation and eventually Sigurd Lewerentz, who was still supervising the works at the Town Hall extension on behalf of Gunnar Asplund, and the Sune Lindstrom who was then the Regional Planning Director in Gothenburg (1940–1944). At the time, the HSB Society Apartments (1929–30) from Alfred Roth and Ingrid Wallberg were still important references for those studying architecture and eventually had an impact on Thurfjell's interest for mass-produced housing. As young graduate he pursued further studies in architecture at the Royal Academy of Stockholm and eventually met Sven Markelius, at the time working for the city as planner, developing the city's satellite housing schemes. In 1954 he moved back to his hometown and three years later, founded his practice Thurfjells Arkitektkontor AB. By the 1960s he had established offices in Stockholm, Gothenburg and Malmö and became one of the main consultants to the World Bank's housing policy, the "Million Programme" for Sweden between 1965–74. For that the firm, Thurfjell Consult (T Consult), developed large housing schemes where the units were fabricated in wood. The concept was brought into Kuwait but never succeed, as happened in several other locations around the world. However, out of this experience T Consult became one of the first design associates of PACE, developing projects such as the Al-Ahli Bank of Kuwait Head Offices tower, built in 1968–73.

Source: Thurfjell, Jan, *Nästan allt om strömming: recepten*, Cewe-förlaget, Bjästa, 1994

TRIPE AND WAKEHAM PARTNERSHIP

The Tripe and Wakeham Partnership practice was founded by Philip Oliver George Wakeham (ARIBA 1933) and Anthony Charles Tripe (AA 1932, ARIBA 1934) in 1950. The firm's work in the UK extended from factories and warehouses to schools, housing, post offices, prisons and other public facilities. Works for the Royal Navy, the Royal Air Force and the Army were a major portion of it, such as the messing facilities in Chelsea (1962), Sutton Coalfield and Chattenden and the Polaris Base at Faslane. Abroad, the consultancy was commissioned for embassy buildings, schools, banks, power stations and military installations. During most of the second half of the 20th century they had permanent offices in Kuwait, Abu Dhabi, Aden and Cyprus. In Kuwait from 1952 they developed a series of educational facilities. Between1953–54 the later AA faculty member, David Oakley (1958–63) was one of the design team members for Kuwait Technical College. The firm returned to Kuwait some decades later as an associate of CTHA for KOC Computer and Training Centre (1979–83). Among the most famous projects are the Royal Assurance Company HQ (1972–76), St. John's School in Cyprus (1972), the Factory Canteen for Marconi Space and Defence, Neston and the National Nuclear Corporation UK, also in Cheshire.

Source: Tripe and Wakeham Partnership Corporate brochure for Kuwait, 1983

Home, Robert, "Knowledge Networks and Postcolonial careering: David Oakley (1927–2003)," in *ABE Journal*, 2013 online, http://abe.revues.org/812

UNICONSULT AB

Uniconsult AB is the international design subsidiary of the Swedish firm Contekton Architects and Planners AB established in 1966. Upon the Swedish government's investment in the expansion of health centres and hospitals, Contekton created an hospital design department with multidisciplinary specialists. In 1970 the company was involved in a series of competitions for hospital and hospital campuses all over Africa and the Middle East. Tomas Saagpakk, a fresh graduate in Architecture from the Royal Institute of Technology led the international practice Uniconsult until 1982. During this period the firm was involved in the design of hospitals in Nigeria, Libya (Tripoli 1973–75), Algeria (Constantine, Algiers and Oran 1976–80), and several design competitions including Kuwait Hospitals (Mubarak Al-Kabeer, Al-Adan, Al-Jahra, Al-Farwaniya) in 1972–73 and Military Hospital in Baghdad, Iraq (1980). During this period projects were completed for a hotel in UAE and several commissions for Aramco in Saudi Arabia, including Riyadh Sports Centre in Al-Qurayyat and the town planning of several cities near the border with Iraq.

Source: Contekton Architects and Planners AB profile online: http://www.contekton.org/

Murolen, Pentti, *Ihmistä ei voi suunnitella, kiveä voi! Raportti Suomalaisesta ja kansainvälisestä liikennesuunnittelusta, en. Man cannot plan – stone can!*, B&M Architects, Helsinki, 2012

Leonard, Barry (ed.), *Technology-transfer to the Middle East*, Diane Publishing, 1984

UNITED ENGINEERING AND TECHNICAL CONSULTANTS LIMITED (UNETEC)

United Engineering and Technical Consult-ants Limited (UNETEC), was founded in Kuwait in 1977 by Yousef K. Shuhaibar as a subsidiary of Kuwait Engineering, Operation & Management Co KSC (KEOMAC), estab-lished in 1975 with Salem Mussallam and Jassem Qattan as mechanical and industrial engineering consultants. Yousef Shuhaibar had a Bachelor's degree in Civil Engineering from Ohio Northern University (1960–64), a Master's from The University of New Mexico (1964–44) and a PhD from the Uni-versity of Arizona (1970–72). Among the company's first projects in Kuwait were the Kuwait Disabled Sports Club in Hawally that included hotel and administration buildings (today the Continental Hotel and Kuwait Olympic Committee HQ), the Hospital Moni-toring Centre at the Sabah Hospital Campus and the former USSR Embassy in Kuwait. During the 1980s other commissions were awarded including the residential buildings of Bu Shagara Residential Complex and Marina Commercial Building in Sharjah, UAE and several Kuwaiti Embassy buildings in Algiers, Pretoria, Moscow and Tehran. After the war the firm was responsible for several building refurbishments including the Al-Rehab Commercial Complex (1971–72) and the completion of the Telecommunication Centre and Antenna Tower (1981–95).

Source: UNETEC company profile, online, http://www.uneteckuwait.com/about.html

Bricault, G. C. (ed.), *Major Companies of the Arab World 1990/91*, Springer Science & Business Media, 2012

UTZON, JØRN

Jørn Oberg Utzon (1918–2008) graduated from the Royal Danish Academy of Fine Arts in Copenhagen (1942) under Steen Ejler Rasmussen (1898–1990). He started his practice with Hakon Ahlberg (1891–1984) in Stockholm collaborating in the design of numerous hospitals and eventually worked in Gunnar Asplund's (1885–1940) office with Paul Hedqvist (1895–1977). During this period Utzon established a strong working relationship with Arne Korsmo (1900–68) who later became the Norwegian representative at CIAM and after WWII moved to Helsinki for a six-month internship with Alvar Aalto (1898–1976). From 1946 he travelled extensively with his former colleague, Tobias Faber (1915–2010) visiting Paris where he met Fernand Leger, Le Corbusier and the sculptor Henri Laurens; also travelling to Morocco, Mexico and the United States after winning two travelling scholarships in 1948 and later to China, Japan, India, and Australia. In 1950 he established his own architectural firm to develop the water tower in Savaneke (1946–52) and in 1957 won the competition for the Opera House in Sydney (1959–73) with Leslie Martin (1908–2000) and Eero Saarinen (1910–61) in the competition jury. In the following year Utzon was commissioned by Jorgen Saxild (1891–1975), co-founder of Kampsax, responsible for projects such as the Trans-Iranian Railway (1933–38), to design in collaboration with Hans Munk Hansen (1929–) the branch of Iran's National Bank, Bank Melli Iran, in the university area of Tehran (1959–61). During the following years Utzon won several other commissions in the region such as the Grotto Theatre in Jeita, Lebanon (1968–70) commissioned by Dar Al-Handasah, and the competition entry for Jeddah Stadium in 1967, upon the invitation of Omar Azzam (1930–). In 1968 Azzam and Martin were instrumental in inviting Utzon to the design competition for the Kuwait National Assembly. Four years later he was awarded the first prize. Utzon was also won the Pritzker Prize in 2003.

Source: Weston, R., *Utzon: Inspiration, Vision, Architecture*, Edition Bløndal, Hellerup, 2002

Lund, N.O., *Jørn Utzon*, Verlag Anton Pustet, Salzburg-Munchen, 1999

Sharp, Dennis, "Jørn Utzon: Award-winning architect who designed the Sydney Opera House," obituary, *The Independent*, Dec. 3, 2008

"Jørn Utzon," obituary, *The Telegraph*, Nov. 29, 2008

VBB (VATTENBYGGNADSBYRÅN/ SWECO)

Johan Gustaf Richert (1857–1934), an engineer and politician who graduated from the Royal Institute of Technology in Stockholm (1876) in Engineering, joined the Department of Public Works first in Stockholm (1880–81) and then in Gothenburg (1881–97) where he gained experience in water distribution and storage. With his practice established in the capital since 1897 and professor at the Royal Institute of Technology (1898–1911), Richert founded the AB Vattenbyggnadsbyrån, as a firm specialised in water buildings. The first commission was for St. Petersburg (1903) and the first major work in Sweden was the water supply and distribution system for Gothenburg where Richert applied techniques for the collection of ground water. During the implementation Richert eventually met briefly the young Sune Lindström (1906 –1989) who was to become the Regional Planning Director in Gothenburg (1940–44) prior being hired by VBB with Gunnar Lindman (1912–2000). The system was only completed in 1946 after the death of Richert and in the same year the architect Harald Mjöberg (1916–98), disciple of Gunnar Asplund, was incorporated as urban planner, together with Stig Egnell and under Lindman responsibilty for the design and coordination of the Master Plan for Rumaithiya approved by Kuwait Municipality in 1962. The same team was to develop a proposal for the coastal strip of Kuwait before 1965. Lindstrom who graduated from the same school of Richert in 1931, with a short sabbatical to study one semester at the Bauhaus, was the chief architect and the main designer, responsible for projects such as the water tower in Örebro (1954–58). In the following year Lindstrom started teaching at the Chalmers University of Technology (1959–69), he was professor at the Royal Institute of Technology in Stockholm (1938–47) and holding lead positions in several institutions such as expert for the Council of Urban Planning (1955–59) and later Director at the Nordic Institute of Urban Planning (1967–69). With the increasing demand of projects abroad in 1964 Mjöberg became the chief architect in charge of major projects outside Sweden, such as the Abu Simbel temples relocation (1964–68), a concept developed by Fry & Drew and Ove Arup (1962), following the Aswan High Dam, also designed by VBB in the initial stages. The dam would eventually be designed by the Soviet Hydroproject Institute and built by Osman Ahmed Osman's Arab Contractors, that were at the time also building the Municipality Complex in Kuwait (1959–1962). Following the discovery of a fresh water source in the northern Kuwait (1962–1963), the government decided to commence a vast programme of water infrastructure and in 1965 VBB was commissioned to design a system of water towers (1965–76) including the Abraj Al-Kuwait (1965–77) under Sune Lindstrom's lead, followed by his son Joe. The latter graduated in 1973 and joined on the site Stig Egnell, an experienced planner working for VBB in Kuwait since his graduation (Chalmers University, 1960), on projects such as the Rumaithiya Neighbourhood Master Plan (1962–64), the Low-Income Housing Scheme for Rumaithiya (1964–65) with Ohlsson & Skarne's AB, the Coastal Strip Development Plan (1982–85). Egnell became Vice-President of the company after 1981. From then the team would be assigned for an identical commission in Saudi Arabia for Jeddah Water Tower (1980). After 1997 the company was re-named Sweco, a name already in use during the construction of the towers in Kuwait, as VBB's brand for foreign operations.

Source: The Swedish Centre for Architecture and Design

Report for The Aga Khan Award for Architecture, 1980 http://www.akdn.org/architecture/pdf/0159_Kuw.pdf

Indebetou, Govert and Hylander, Erik (ed.), *Swedish Teknologföreningen 1861 – 1936*. Biographies. Part 2. Date of the years 1885 – 1914. Alongside appendages: List of persons graduated from the Technological Institute of Technology, Stockholm,1937, p. 1261

Löwgren, Eva (ed.): *Who is it. Swedish biographical handbook 1973*, Stockholm, 1972

Andersson, Henrik O.; Bedoire, Fredric, *Stockholm buildings. A Book on Architecture and Cityscape of Stockholm*, Stockholm, 1988

Bjørn, Malene, *The Light & Airy. How It All Began in 1945*, Baltic Books, Växjö, 2013

Engfors, Christina, *Asplund – Architect, friend and colleague*, Arkitektur Forlag Stockholm, 1990

Stig, Egnell, *Harald Mjöberg*, Nekrolog i Dagens Nyheter

WATSON, NEWTON

Newton Frank Watson (1923–2002) was an expert on environmental studies, the Haden/Pilkington Professor of Environmental Design and Engineering at the Bartlett School of Architecture and Planning, University College of London, Dean of the Faculty of Environmental Studies between 1986–88 and Head of Bartlett School of Architecture and Planning, University College of London (1985–88). Among his several consultancies in support to partner designers, the most significant were the Stock Exchange Building (1978–86) and the Zoo extension (1981–82), both in Kuwait.

Source: Watson, Newton Frank (1923–2002), obituary, *Oxford Index Who Was Who*, Nov. 2014, online platform *http://oxfordindex.oup.com/view/10.1093/ww/9780199540884.013.U39061*

WEIDLINGER ASSOCIATES

Paul Weidlinger (1915–99) was a graduate from ETH Zurich in Civil Engineering before WWII. Weidlinger moved to US and in 1949 established the structural design consultancy Weidlinger Associates, which is still operating to this day. During 1950s–60s Weidlinger collaborated with Marcel Breuer, Gordon Bunschaft (SOM), Walter Gropius, Eero Saarinen and José Luis Sert. Weidlinger's first notable structural works were for SOM's "German Programme" of consulates during the 1950s and the Beinecke Library in New Haven, Connecticut (1958–63). Other important works were the CBS Tower in New York City (1963–65) by Eero Saarinen, the John Hancock Tower in Boston by Henry N. Cobb of I. M. Pei & Partners (1968–76) and the National Aquarium in Baltimore by Peter Chermayeff of Cambridge Seven Associates (1976–81).

Source: Paid Notice: Deaths Weidlinger, Paul, *The New York Times*, Sep. 8, 1999

Weidlinger Associates, company profile, online: http://www.wai.com/history.aspx

WHITE YOUNG PARTNERS

Ron Young and Terence White graduated as civil engineers and established the practice White Young and Partners in 1964. Their first project in the Middle East was awarded by Sir Basil Spence in Kuwait; the Law Courts (1976–83). After that the company rapidly expanded all over the Gulf and in 1997 merged with Ernest Green and Partners Holdings PLC to form White Young Green (WYG), an environmental consultancy based today in the UK and with local representation in Qatar, Saudi Arabia and the UAE.

Source: White Young Green corporate profile online: http://www.wyg.com/uploads/files/pdfs/WYG-media-pack.pdf

WILSON, MASON AND PARTNERS

James Mollison Wilson (1887–1965), after a first collaboration with Sir Edwin Lutyens' (1869–1944) offices in New Delhi (1913–16), the architect and planner was hired as head of the Public Works Department in Baghdad. Until 1926, Wilson and Harold Mason (both with degrees from Liverpool University in Planning and Architecture) developed several public buildings in Iraq, such as the Ahl Al-Bayt University (1921–24) and Baghdad Archaeology Museum, inaugurated by Gertrude Bell in 1926. With the establishment of Wilson, Mason and Partners in London the first commissions for the oil sector came from APOC (Anglo-Persian Oil Company) in Abadan, for the General Hospital and for the Technical College. In Iraq the Port Directorate Offices in Basra (1927–29) is a major work. In 1944 Wilson was assigned as the oil company's official architect in charge of the master plans of different oil towns in Iran, Iraq and was later hired by KOC for Ahmadi (1947). In Ahmadi, apart from the plan, the main buildings were assigned to the firm with the exception of the health and entertainment facilities. From these the KOC Head Offices, guesthouse and the two mosques are the most prominent. During this period the commission for Baghdad Railway Station (1947–51) became the firm's reference work in the region.

Source: Pieri, Caecilia, *Baghdad Arts Deco: Architectural Brickwork, 1920–1950*, American University in Cairo Press, Cairo, 2010

Crinson, Mark, "Abadan: Planning and Architecture under the Anglo-Iranian Oil Company," in *Planning Perspectives* 12, n. 3, 1997, pp. 341–359

WS ATKINS & PARTNERS (WSA&P)

Sir William Sydney Albert Atkins (1902–1989) gained a degree in Engineering from University College, London and trained as a draughtsman at E. Graham Wood on Sydney Harbour Bridge for Oscar Faber Consulting Engineers. In 1938 he established WS Atkins & Partners and in 1945 was invited by the South Wales Iron & Steel Co. to discuss plans to extend the Abbey Steelworks at Port Talbot (1952). In 1967 Atkins received its first commission to deliver work in the Middle East. In 1979 Atkins opened a branch in Dubai. Atkins was awarded the Sir William Larke Medal for designing the first ever building to be erected using plastic theory and was dubbed Knight Bachelor upon retirement in 1982.

Source: Atkins online platform: http://www.atkinsglobal.com/en-gb/about-the-group

SELECTED BIBLIOGRAPHY

Suggested further reading

ARTICLES

Al-Ragam, Asseel, "Critical Nostalgia: Kuwait Urban Modernity and Alison and Peter Smithson's Kuwait Urban Study and Mat-Building," in *Journal of Architecture,* 2015, v. 20, n. 1, pp. 1–20

Christensen, Peter, "The 'Inventive Jump': Curiosity, Culture and Islamicate Form in the Works of Peter and Allison Smithson," in *International Journal of Islamic Architecture*, 2014, v. 3, n. 1, pp. 43–68

Ardalan, Nader, "Towards Sustainable Urbanism in the Persian Gulf: Analysis of the Past," in *International Journal of Islamic Architecture*, 2014, v. 3, n. 1, pp. 171–186

Al-Nakib, Farah, "Kuwait's Modern Spectacle: Oil Wealth and the Making of a New Capital City, 1950-1990," in *Comparative Studies of South Asia, Africa and Middle East*, 2013, v. 33, n. 1, pp. 7–25

Al-Shalfan, Sharifa, "The Right to Housing in Kuwait: an Urban Injustice in a Socially just system. Kuwait Programme on Development, Governance and Globalisation in the Gulf States," research paper, London School of Economics and Political Science, London, May 2013, n. 28, pp. 4–31

Kubo, Michael "'Oil-Slick': Middle Eastern Economy and Late-Modern Aesthetics," in *Dis-appearing Non-West* Conference, Columbia, May 2012

Al-Ragam, Asseel, "Representation and Ideology in Postcolonial Urban Development: the Arabian Gulf," in *Journal of Architecture*, 2011, v. 16, n. 4, pp.455–469

Al-Ragam, Asseel "The Destruction of Modernist Heritage: The Myth of Al-Sawaber," in *Journal of Architectural Education*, 2011, v. 67, n. 2, pp. 234–252

Hjertholm, Helge, "Kuwait National Assembly," in *Arkitektur*, 2008, v. 90, n. 4, p. 73

Mahgoub, Yasser, "Architecture and the expression of cultural identity in Kuwait", in *The Journal of Architecture*, 2007, v. 12, n. 2, pp. 165–182

Anderson, Richard; Al-Bader, Jawaher, "Recent Kuwaiti Architecture: Regionalism vs. Globalization," in *Journal of Architectural & Planning Research*, 2006, v. 23, n. 2, pp.134–146

Khattab, Omar, "In Search of Local Image for the Arab City: the Case of Kuwait City," in *Tall Buildings and Urban Habitat. Cities in the Third Millennium,* Spon Press, London and New York, 2001, pp. 379–393

Khattab, Omar; Al-Mumin, Adil, "The Evolution of Public Housing Policies in Kuwait from 1960s to 1990s," in *International Journal for Housing Science & Its Applications*, 2000, v. 24, n. 4, pp. 353–360

Slessor, Catherine, "On the Waterfront," in *Architectural Review*, Mar. 1998, v. 203, n. 1213, pp. 42–45

"Arne Jacobsen: Edificios públicos; Public buildings," in *2G Revista internacional de Arquitectura; International Architecture Review*, 1997, n. 4, pp. 1–144

Kroloff, Reed, "Building Diplomacy," in *Architecture*, 1996, v. 85, n. 1, pp. 115–117

Sutherland, Graeme, "Climate Register: four Projects by A + P Smithson," in *AA files*, Summer 1995, n. 29, pp. 72–77

"Europe's Door," in *World Architecture*, 1995, n. 33, pp. 78–79

Richards, Kristen, "Back to Work. Kuwait National Assembly," in *Interiors*, Jan. 1993, v. 152, n. 1, p. 18

Taylor, Brian Brace, "Kuwait City Waterfront Development," in *Mimar: Architecture in Development*, Mar. 1990, v. 10, n. 1(34), pp. 12–20

Shuaib, Hamid, "Urban Development of Kuwait," in *Alam Albena*, 1989, n. 98, pp. 4–5

Sultan, Ghazi, "Kuwait: Design for the Arabian Gulf Region," *in Architecture & Design*, May-Jun. 1989, v. 5, n. 4, pp. 90–97

Baird, Timothy, "The Kuwait Conference Center," in *Landscape Design*, Feb. 1988, n. 171, pp. 43–47

Sultan, Ghazi, "An Architect from Kuwait," in *Albenaa*, Dec. 1987– Jan. 1988, v. 7, n. 38, pp. 10–11, 23–29

Makiya, Mohammed Saleh, "Islamic Architecture and Modernism," in *Albenaa*, Dec. 1985 – Jan.1986, v. 5, n. 26, pp. 69–73

"American Designers in Arabia," in *Middle East Construction*, Aug. 1985, v. 10, n. 8, pp. 37–43

Salvin, Meave, "Three Kuwaiti Banks of High Interest on Single Site by Skidmore, Owings & Merrill," in *Middle East Construction*, Aug. 1985, v. 10, n. 8, pp. 37–43

Randall, Janice, "Sief Palace Area Buildings," in *Mimar 16: Architecture in Development*, edited by Hasan-Uddin Khan, 1985, pp. 28–35

Al-Bahar, Huda, "Contemporary Kuwaiti Houses," in *Mimar 15: Architecture in Development*, Jan.–Mar. 1985, pp. 63–72

Al-Abad, Badi, "Contemporary Architecture," in *Arts & the Islamic World*, Spring 1985, v. 3, n. 1, pp. 60–66

Antoniou, Jim, "Plan for Amiri Diwan in Kuwait," in *Middle East Construction*, Jul. 1984, v. 9, n. 7, p. 19

Parkyn, Neil, "The Arab Consultants: Sabah Al-Rayes," in *Middle East Construction*, Feb. 1984, v. 9, n. 2, pp. 25–28

"Kuwait International Air Terminal Building, Kuwait, 1967–1979; Architects: Kenzo Tange and URTEC," in *Space Design*, Sept. 1983, n. 9(228), pp. 48–59

"The Kuwait Chancery in Washington, D.C.: a Total-design Project by Skidmore, Owings & Merrill-New York Blending Expressions of Islamic Culture with Western Technology," in *Interior Design*, Aug. 1983, v. 54, n. 8, pp. 152–157

Clouten, Neville, "Kuwait: Brilliant Desert Complex by Architects from a Frigid Arctic Climate," in *Architecture: The AIA Journal*, Aug. 1983, v. 72, n. 8, pp. 144–145

"Islamic Jewel in a Modernist Box," in *Architecture: The AIA Journal*, Jul.1983, pp. 34–41

Clouten, Neville; Pietilä, Reima, "Sief Palace Area Building, Kuwait," in *Architecture & Urbanism*, Jun. 1983, n. 6(153), pp. 26–50

Parkyn, Neil, "Winning the Numbers Game," in *Middle East Construction*, Apr. 1982, v. 7 n. 4, p. 10

"Joint-banking Centre for Kuwait City," in *Middle East Construction*, Mar. 1982, v. 7, n. 3, p. 67

"Materials in Context," in *Middle East Construction*, Feb. 1982, v. 7, n. 2, p. 51

"Preview '82. Embassy, Kuwait," in *Architectural Review*, Jan. 1982, v. 171, n. 1019, p. 34

"Multi-purpose Building at the Centre of Kuwait: Residential, Commercial, Parking," in *Alam Albena,* Apr. 1981, v. 1, n. 9, pp. 28–29

"Salmiya District Centre, Kuwait," in *Albenaa*, 1981, v. 2, n. 12, pp. 48–51

"Kuwait Towers," in *Mimar: Architecture in Development*, Oct.-Sep. 1981, n. 2, pp.40–41

"Post Office Sorting Complex and Offices in Kuwait," in *Mur Vivant*, 1981, n. 60, pp. 99–102

"Hospitals at Farwaniya and Al Jahra on the Outskirts of Kuwait," in *Mur Vivant*, 1981, n. 60, pp. 30–32

"Kuwait Law Courts; Architects: Sir Basil Spence International Partnership, with Fitzroy Robinson Partnership," in *Middle East Construction*, Sep. 1980, v. 5, n. 9, pp. 84–85

"Olympic Skating Rink in Kuwait," in *Mur Vivant*, 1980, n. 56, pp. 30–32

Morris, Tony, "Precast Concrete's Middle East Future: Al-Mothaida Car Park," in *Middle East Architectural Design*, May–Jun. 1979, v. 2, n. 4, pp. 24–25

Blee, Anthony; Relph-Knight, Lynda, "Sunshine and the Rule of Law: Kuwaiti Law Courts Scheme, Originally a Winning Design for a Limited Competition in 1976, but Much Modified Since", in *Building Design*, June 20 1980, n. 501, pp. 22–25

Erickson, Arthur, "Projects in Kuwait and Saudi Arabia," in *Places of Public Gathering in Islam: Proceedings of Seminar Five from the series Architectural Transformations in the Islamic World*, Amman, Jordan, May 4–7, 1980. The Aga Khan Award for Architecture, Philadelphia, 1980, pp. 87–92

"Kuwait Stock Exchange - the Gulf's First Custom designed Stock Market Building," in *Middle East Construction*, Sep. 1979, v. 4, n. 9, pp. 67–69

"Sawaber Housing, Kuwait," in *Canadian Architect*, Aug. 1979, v. 24, n. 8, pp. 42–43

"Kuwait Central Bank, Kuwait; Architects: Dissing and Weitling," in *Domus*, Jun. 1979, n. 595, pp. 46–47

"Middle East Structures: Meriden Hotel, Safat, Kuwait," in *Consulting Engineer*, Jun. 1979, v. 43, n. 6, p. 51

"Middle East," in *Architectural Design*, May-Jun. 1979

"Kuwait Mosque," in *Albenaa*, Feb.-Mar. 1979, v. 1, n. 1, pp. 14–15

Rykwert, Joseph, "Kuwait," in *Lotus International*, Mar. 1978, n. 18, pp. 126–135

"Rantapalatsialieen Rakennukset, Kuwait," in *Arkkitehti*, 1978, v. 76, n. 2, pp. 22–27

Siatt, Wayne, "Mideast Market Viewed as Long Term", in *Building Design & Construction*, Jan. 1977

Vago, Pierre, "Les modèles exportés," *Architecture Française*, Dec. 1976, n. 400, pp. 64–79

Tange, Kenzo, "Works of Kenzo Tange and URTEC," in *Japan Architects*, Aug.–Sep. 1976 v. 51, n. 8–9(234), pp. 9–112

"Prefabricatable School Building System," in *Bauen und Wohnen*, Jul.-Aug. 1976, v. 30, n. 7–8, pp. 259–262

Jamal, Karim, "Destruction of the Middle East?," in *Architects' Journal*, Jul. 1976, v. 164, n. 30, Jul. 1976, pp. 161–162

"Covered Market," in *Mideast Markets*, Chase, Jun. 1976, p. 7

"Large Mixed Development to Be Built in Kuwait," in *Building Design*, Jun. 1975, n. 255, p. 9

"Remi Lopez & Associates, Three Projects: 1, Technical and Industrial Institute in Jiddah, Saudi Arabia. 2, Amiri Hospital in Kuwait. 3, Savings and Credit Bank in Kuwait," in *Recherche & Architecture*, 1975, n. 23, pp. 25–30

"United Pre-Fab Building Company," in *Building Design*, Jun. 20, 1975

"Ministries in the 'Souq'," in *Bauen und Wohnen*, Feb. 1975, v. 29, n. 2, pp. 54–57

"Proposals for Restructuring Kuwait," in *Architectural Review*, Sep. 1974, v. 156, pp. 178–182

Sultan, Ghazi, "Kuwait," in *The Architects' Journal,* 1974, v. 160, pp. 792–794

Jamal, Karim, "Immigrant Workers' Settlements in Kuwait," in *Architectural Design*, Jul. 1974, v. 44, n. 7, pp. 408-413

Buchanan, Colin, "Kuwait," in *Architects' Journal*, May 1974, v. 159, n. 21, pp. 1131–1132

Jamal, Karim, "Kuwait: a Salutory Tale," in *Architects' Journal*, Dec. 1973, v. 158, n. 50, pp. 1452–1457

"Kuwait: Mädchen-Sekundarschule; Kindergarten," in *Werk*, 1973, v. 60, n. 11, pp. 1358–1361

"Alfred Roth: Girl's Secondary School, Kuwait," in *A & U: Architecture & Urbanism*, Sep. 1973, v. 3, n. 9, pp. 79–82

"Kuwait National Assembly Competition; Competition Entry by Sir Basil Spence, Bonnington & Collins," in *Building Design*, Feb. 1973, n. 137, pp. 16–17

"Frei Otto at Work," in *Architectural Design*, Mar. 1971, v. 41, pp. 137–167

"Kuwait: Area of Expansion and Opportunity," in *Building*, Feb. 1971, v. 220, n. 8, pp. 79–80, 83

Portoghesi, Paolo, "Il non finito come alternativa: un'opera inedita di Kenzo Tange, l'ambasciata del Kuwait a Tokyo," in *Controspazio*, Jun.–Jul. 1970, v. 2, n. 6–7, pp. 2–12

"Kuwait Sports Center," in *Architectural Design*, Mar. 1970, v. 40, n. 3, pp. 134–137

"Women's Hospital, Kuwait," in *Architectural Review*, Apr. 1969, v. 145, pp. 291–294

"Lebanese Engineering Achievements," in *Al-Mouhandess*, special, 1968, pp.168–172

"Nationalbanken i Kuwait," in *Arkitektur*, Apr. 1968, v. 12, n. 2, pp. 53–55

"Tripe & Wakeham," in *Building*, Feb. 1967, p. 81

El-Mallakh, Ragaei, "Planning in a Capital Surplus Economy: Kuwait," in *Land Economics*, Nov. 1966, v. 42, n. 4, pp. 425–440

Füeg, Franz, "Schulbauten, Ecoles, Schools," in *Bauen und Wohnen*, Apr. 1966, v. 20, p. 123

Shiber, Saba George, "Saga of Kuwait Planning: a Critique," in *Ekistics*, Jan. 1966, v. 21, n. 122, pp. 51–58

"Tripe & Wakeham," in *Builder*, Apr. 1964, p. 792

Écochard, Michel "Plans for a National Museum in Kuwait," in *Museum: a Quarterly Review*, 1964, v. 17, n. 3, pp. 146–151

"Proposed Institute for Physically Handicapped Children, Kuwait," in *Interbuild*, Jan. 1963, pp. 18–22

"Chlorine Plant," in *Al-Mouhandess,* Nov. 1963, n. 1, pp. 17–21

Écochard, Michel, "National Museum, Kuwait," in *Architectural Design*, v. 32, Apr. 1962, p. 209

"Affonso Eduardo Reidy," in *Baukunst und Werkform*, Jan. 1962, v. 15, pp. 3–29

"Palace in the Persian Gulf," in *Architectural Review*, Dec. 1960, pp. 424–428

"Kuwait State Development Projects," in *The Kuwaiti*, 26 Mar. 1959

"Grande albergo a Kuwait," in *Domus*, Mar. 1959, n. 352, p. 6

"Hotel in Kuwait," in *Architectural Design*, Nov. 1958, v. 28, pp. 460–461

Abuhamdeh, Said, "Kuwait," in *Middle East Forum*, Apr. 1958, pp. 20–21

"Architecture in the Middle East," in *Architectural Design*, Mar. 1957, v. 27, pp. 72–108

"Kuwait," in *Architecture and Building News*, Jul. 12 1956, v. 210, pp. 72–73

"Power Station at Kuwait," in *Architectural Review*, Jul. 1956, v. 120, pp. 9–12

Banks, R. L., "Notes on a Visit to Kuwait," in *Town Planning Review*, Apr. 1955, v. 26, pp. 48–50

Mac Farlane, Peter W., "Planning an Arab Town: Kuwait on the Persian Gulf," in *Town Planning Institute Journal*, Apr. 1954, v. 40, pp. 110-113

Architectural Design, Special Issue. Number on tropical buildings: Section on hot, dry climates, e.g., Kuwait, Borneo, North Nigeria, Rangoon-Burma, French West Africa, Oct. 1953, pp. 272–281

"Naif Avenue, Kuwait," in *Architectural Review*, Feb. 1953, v. 113, p. 126

THESES

Alissa, Reem I. R., "Building for Oil: Corporate Colonialism, Nationalism and Urban Modernity in Ahmadi, 1946–1992." University of California, Berkeley, 2012. PhD diss.

Dalsoglio, Martino, "La Lezione dell' architettura Islamica. Regioni, forme e protagonisti." Politecnico di Milano, 2012. Master's thesis.

Soares, Sara Saragoça, "The Identity of Modern Heritage: Kuwait City." Faculdade de Arquitectura da Universidade Técnica de Lisboa, 2012. Master's thesis.

Al-Nakib, Farah, "Kuwait City: Urbanization, the Built Environment and the Urban Experience Before and After Oil (1716–1986)." SOAS, 2011. PhD diss.

Albaqshi, Muhannad A., "The Social Production of Space: Kuwait's Spatial History." Illinois Institute of Technology, 2010. PhD diss.

Solomita, Pasqualino, "Pier Luigi Nervi: forma e sezione nel tema della cupola." Università degli Studi di Bologna, 2010. PhD diss.

Alajmi, Mohammed, "History of Architecture in Kuwait: The Evolution of Kuwaiti Traditional Architecture Prior to the Discovery of Oil." The University of Nebraska – Lincoln, 2009. PhD diss.

Al-Jassar, Mohammad, "Constancy and Change in Contemporary Kuwait City: The Socio-Cultural Dimensions of the Kuwait Courtyard and Diwaniyya." The University of Wisconsin – Milwaukee, 2009. PhD diss.

Al-Ragam, Asseel, "Towards a Critique of an Architectural Nahdha: A Kuwaiti Example." University of Pennsylvania, 2008. PhD diss.

Sadik, Rula Muhammad, "Nation-Building and Housing Policy: A Comparative Analysis of Urban Housing Development in Kuwait, Jordan, and Lebanon." University of California, Berkeley, 1996. PhD diss.

Al-Mutawa, Yasmin, "Landscape Design Guidelines for Kuwait." University of Arizona, 1993. Master's thesis.

Beshir, Tarek, "Architecture Beyond Cultural Politics: Western Practice in the Arabian Peninsula." MIT, 1993. Master's thesis.

Al-Mosully, Suhair A., "Revitalizing Kuwait's Empty City Center", MIT, 1992. Master's thesis.

Fawzi Abdo, Muhammad, "The Urbanization of Kuwait since 1950: Planning, Progress and Issue." University of Durham, 1988. PhD diss.

PUBLICATIONS

Bjorn, Malene, *The Light & Air. How it All Began in Sweden in 1945,* transl. Eva Lindstrom, Baltic Books, Växjö, 2013

El-Wakil, Leila, *Hassan Fathy dans son temps*, inFolio, Gollion and Paris, 2013

Sweet, Rod (ed.), *SSH Design. The First Fifty Years*, Al-Khat Printing Press, Kuwait, 2011

Al-Ghunaim, Abdullah Y.; Ali Rais, Ali Gholoum (eds.), *Kuwait in Postcards,* Centre for Research and Studies on Kuwait, Kuwait, 2009

Utzon, Jørn; Nisses, Børge (eds.), *Jørn Utzon Logbook IV/Kuwait National Assembly. Prefab*, Edition Blondal, Hellerup 2008

Serageldin, Ismail, *Hassan Fathy*, Bibliotheca Alexandrina, Alexandria, 2007

Al-Bassam, Anne, *Footsteps in the Sand: Kuwait and Her Neighbors, 1700–2003*, the Kuwait Bookshops Co. Ltd., Kuwait, 2004

Makiya, Kanan, *Post-Islamic Classicism: A Visual Essay on the Architecture of Mohamed Makiya*, Saqi Book, London, 2001

Binder, Georges, *Montois Partners: Selected and Current Works*, Images Publishing Ltd., Hong Kong, 2001

Frampton, Kenneth; Correa, Charles; Robson, David (eds.), *Modernity and Community: Architecture in the Islamic World: The Aga Khan Award for Architecture,* Thames and Hudson, London, 2001

Smithson, Peter and Alison, *The Charged Void: Architecture*, The Monacelli Press, New York, 2001

Al-Hijji, Yacoub, *Old Kuwait*, Center for Research and Studies for Kuwait, Kuwait, 2001

Kultermann, Udo, *Contemporary Architecture in the Arab State: Renaissance of a Region*, McGraw-Hill, New York, 1999

Abdul Reda, Haidar Mirza; Kuruvilla Varghese (eds.), *Kuwait Liberation Tower. A Profile*, Kuwait, 1999

Bettinotti, Massimo (ed.), *Kenzo Tange, 1946–1996: Architecture and Urban Design*, Electa, Milan, 1996

Kuwait Facts and Figure, Ministry of Information, Kuwait, 1996

Vale, Lawrence J., *Architecture, Power and National Identity*, Yale University Press, New Haven, 1992

Ali, Evangelia Simos. *Kuwait Historical Preservation Study-Old Kuwait Town*, vol. 1, Kuwait Municipality, Kuwait, 1988

Santuccio, Salvatore, *Luigi Moretti*, Zanichelli, Bologna, 1986

Chadirji, Rifat, *Concepts and Influences: Towards a Regionalized International Architecture*, KPI, London and New York, 1986

Al-Mutawa, Subhi, *Kuwait City Parks: A Critical Review of Their Design, Facilities, Programs, and Management*, KPI, London, 1985

Roth, Alfred, *Alfred Roth: Architekt der Kontinuität*, Waser Verlag für Kunst und Architektur, Zürich, 1985

Morris, Anthony Edwin James, *John R. Harris Architects*, Hurtwood, Westerham, 1984

Squire, Raglan, *Portrait of an Architect*, Colin Smythe, Gerrards Cross, 1984

Gardiner, Stephen, *Kuwait, the Making of a City*, Longman, Harlow, 1983

Al-Tehaih, S., *Housing Service in the State of Kuwait. A Study Submitted to His Highness the Amir*, Kuwait Govt. Press, Kuwait, 1981

Jargy, Marie Georges, *Koweit, les mystères d'un destin,* Hachette, Tours, 1980

Shaw, Ralph, *Kuwait*, Macmillan London Limited, London and Basingstoke, 1976

Smithson, Peter and Alison, *Without Rhetoric: An Architectural Aesthetic 1955–1972*, the MIT Press, Cambridge, 1974

Shiber, George, Saba, *Recent Arab City Growth*, Kuwait Govt. Printing Press, Kuwait, 1969

Kuwait Today. A Welfare State, Quality Publication Ltd, Nairobi, 1965

Shiber, George, Saba, *The Kuwait Urbanization*, Kuwait Govt. Printing Press, Kuwait, 1964

CREDITS

Image copyrights

All drawings, graphics and diagrams are produced by the research team (Copyright © MAK 2015), except where noted. All actual pictures are by Nelson Garrido (Copyright © NGP 2015) except where noted.

WATER DISTILLATION PLANT AND POWER STATION A AND B

1. KOC Archive, Kuwait

4, 5. Private Archive, Kuwait

6, 7. Watercolours by C. A. Farey & Adams, RIBA Library, Drawings Collection, London

SHUWAIKH SECONDARY SCHOOL

1, 3, 5. KOC Archive, Kuwait

2, 4. Project drawings. Kuwait Municipal Archive, Kuwait

PUBLIC SCHOOLS

1. National Council for Culture, Arts and Letters Archive, Kuwait

3, 4, 6, 7. C. T. Haddad Private Archive, Kuwait

5. KOC Archive, Kuwait

SULAIBIKHAT HOSPITAL

1. Shiber, George, Saba, *The Kuwait Urbanization*, Kuwait Govt. Printing Press, 1964

SHEIKH JABER AL-ALI'S PALACE

1, 2, 3, 4, 5, 6. "Palace in the Persian Gulf," in *Architectural Review*, Dec. 1960, pp. 424–428. (Photos Hugo B. R. Galway)

THUNAYAN AL-GHANIM BUILDING

1. "Architecture in the Middle East," in *Architectural Design*, 1957 Mar., v. 27, pp. 72–108

2. Private Archive, Kuwait

MINISTRY OF INFORMATION AND GUIDANCE

5, 6. Al-Kuwait Magazine, 1965

GIRLS' SECONDARY SCHOOL

1. Colin Buchanan, Second Master Plan documentation, 1968–72. Kuwait Municipal Archive, Kuwait

MUBARAKYA SCHOOL

2, 3. National Council for Culture, Arts and Letters Archive, Kuwait

4. Postcard from Al-Ghunaim, Abdullah Y.; Ali Rais, Ali Gholoum (eds.), *Kuwait in Postcards*, Centre for Research and Studies on Kuwait, Kuwait, 2009

5. Colin Buchanan, Second Master Plan documentation, 1968–72. Kuwait Municipal Archive, Kuwait

CINEMAS

1, 2, 4. Al-Kuwait Magazine, 1974

3, 9. KOC Archive, Kuwait

5, 6, 7. PACE Archive 69024, Kuwait. Copyright © Pace 2015

8. Al-Bana Magazine, 1971

10 top, 10 bottom left. Postcard from Al-Ghunaim, Abdullah Y.; Ali Rais, Ali Gholoum (eds.), *Kuwait in Postcards*, Centre for Research and Studies on Kuwait, Kuwait, 2009. (photo Ezmat Sheikh)

10 bottom right. Al-Kuwait Magazine, 1974

GOVERNMENT HOTEL

1. Photo of the scale model. Kuwait Municipal Archive, Kuwait

AL-SABAH HOSPITAL

1. Al-Kuwait Magazine, 1966

2. C.A.T. Archive, Beirut

3, 6. Al-Kuwait Magazine, 1972

4. Al-Kuwait Magazine, 1964

5. Colin Buchanan, Second Master Plan documentation, 1968–72. Kuwait Municipal Archive, Kuwait

MUNICIPAL COMPLEX

1. Al-Kuwait Magazine, 1959

2. Tor Eigeland/*Saudi Aramco World*/ SAWDIA

ANWAR AL SABAH COMPLEX, PHASE I AND II

1, 5. Project drawings. Kuwait Municipal Archive, Kuwait

AL-SALAM PALACE

2. Postcard, from Al-Ghunaim, Abdullah Y.; Ali Rais, Ali Gholoum (eds.), *Kuwait in Postcards*, Centre for Research and Studies on Kuwait, Kuwait, 2009. (photo Ezmat Sheikh)

3, 4, 5. Photos by the authors

KUWAIT NATIONAL MUSEUM COMPETITION

1, 2, 3, 4. *ArkiDes*, Swedish Centre for Architecture and Design, Stockholm

5, 6, 7, 8. Nikšić Olujić, Ivana, *Zdravko Bregovac – The Catalogue of the Personal Archive*, Izdanje HAZU Hrvatski Musej Arhitikturi, 2015

10, 11, 12. Kuwait Municipal Archive, Kuwait

KUWAIT NATIONAL MUSEUM

1, 2, 4, 7, 9. Kuwait Municipal Archive, Kuwait

3. National Council for Culture, Arts and Letters Archive, Kuwait

5. Redrawing of KNM by Alia Farid

6. Écochard, Michel "Plans for a National Museum in Kuwait", in *Museum: a Quarterly Review*, 1964, v.17, n. 3, pp. 146–150

8. Irene Perlman/*Saudi Aramco World*/ SAWDIA

WATERFRONT COMPETITION

1. Shiber, George, Saba, *The Kuwait Urbanization*, Kuwait Govt. Printing Press, 1964

2. BBPR, "The Future Development for the Old City of Kuwait – Report 1969," Kuwait Municipal Archive, Kuwait

3. "Kuwait Water Front. In the report of Scott & Wilson Kirkpatrick & Co. London. October 1961" Reproduced and published by Centre for Research and Studies on Kuwait, Kuwait, 2008

CBD AREA 1/AREA 2

1, 4. Shiber, George, Saba, *The Kuwait Urbanization*, Kuwait Govt. Printing Press, 1964

2, 6. KOC Archive, Kuwait

3. Photo by the authors

7. Postcard, from Al-Ghunaim, Abdullah Y.; Ali Rais, Ali Gholoum (eds.), *Kuwait in Postcards*, Centre for Research and Studies on Kuwait, Kuwait, 2009

9. Tor Eigeland/*Saudi Aramco World*/ SAWDIA

CBD AREA 3

1, 3. Al-Kuwait Magazine, 1968

2. Colin Buchanan, Second Master Plan documentation, 1968–72. Kuwait Municipal Archive, Kuwait

4, 5. Shiber, George, Saba, *The Kuwait Urbanization*, Kuwait Govt. Printing Press, 1964.

6. Al-Kuwait Magazine, Feb. 1964

NATIONAL BANK HEADQUARTERS

1, 3. Postcards from Al-Ghunaim, Abdullah Y.; Ali Rais, Ali Gholoum (eds.), *Kuwait in Postcards*, Centre for Research and Studies on Kuwait, Kuwait, 2009

2. Antony Irving's drawings, Arab Centre for Architecture, Beirut

4. Photo by the authors

GULF BANK

1, 2, 3. Project drawings. Kuwait Municipal Archive, Kuwait

4. Photo by the authors

5. Burnett H. Moody /*Saudi Aramco World*/ SAWDIA

KNPC OFFICE BUILDING

4. KOC Archive, Kuwait

CHAMBER OF COMMERCE & INDUSTRY

4, 6. Burnett H. Moody/*Saudi Aramco World*/ SAWDIA

5. Photo by the authors

SHERATON HOTEL AND EXTENSION

1, 2. Sheraton Hotel Kuwait, building repository, Kuwait

4. Project drawings. Kuwait Municipal Archive, Kuwait

5, 6. PACE Archive 75275, Kuwait. Copyright©Pace 2015

CBD AREA 9

1. Shiber, George, Saba, *The Kuwait Urbanization*, Kuwait Govt. Printing Press, 1964

3, 4, 5, 6, 13. Project drawings. Kuwait Municipal Archive, Kuwait

7. Al-Kuwait Magazine, 1969

9. Tor Eigeland/*Saudi Aramco World*/ SAWDIA

12. Al-Kuwait Magazine, Feb. 1972

INSTITUTE FOR PHYSICALLY HANDICAPPED

1, 2, 3, 5, 6, 7, 8. "Proposed Institute for Physically Handicapped Children, Kuwait", in *Interbuild*, Jan. 1963, pp. 18–22

4. Colin Buchanan, Second Master Plan documentation, 1968–72. Kuwait Municipal Archive, Kuwait

STANDARD SCHOOLS

1. Colin Buchanan, Second Master Plan documentation,1968–72. Kuwait Municipal Archive, Kuwait

2, 3. ETH – gta archiv, Zürich. Alfred Roth 0164-131/ PrototypeSchulen

FAHED AL-SALEM MOSQUE

1, 5, 6. Photos by the authors

2, 3, 4. SSH Archive, Kuwait

LOW-INCOME AND RURAL HOUSING PROJECTS

1. C.T. Haddad Private Archive, Kuwait

2, 3. Tor Eigeland/*Saudi Aramco World*/ SAWDIA

4. Al-Kuwait Magazine, Jul. 1976

5. Shiber, George, Saba, *Recent Arab City Growth*, Kuwait Govt. Printing Press, 1969

6, 7, 8, 9, 10, 11, 12. Archivio Centrale dello Stato, Roma. ACS_MOR_Progetti_271_1969

HASSAWI RESIDENTIAL COMPLEXES

1, 2, 3, 4. PACE Archive, Kuwait. 68001. Copyright © Pace 2015

KUWAIT SOCIETY OF ENGINEERS

1, 2, 3, 4. PACE Archive 71092, Kuwait. Copyright © Pace 2015

5, 6. Chadirji Foundation, Beirut

7, 8, 9, 10. Archivio Centrale dello Stato, Roma. ACS_MOR_Progetti_266_1968

INTERMEDIATE SCHOOL FOR GIRLS

1, 2, 3, 4, 5, 6, 7. ETH – gta archiv, Zürich. Alfred Roth 131-0162 / Mädchen-Sekundarschule

EIGHT AUTOMATIC BAKERY UNITS

1. Project drawings. Kuwait Municipal Archive, Kuwait

2. Al-Kuwait Magazine, Jun. 1969

FEMALE STUDENTS' HOUSING – COLLEGE OF EDUCATION

1. Al-Bahar Magazine

2. Photo by the authors

CENTRAL BANK OF KUWAIT

1, 2, 3, 5, 7. Aga Khan Award for Architecture. IAA7505, IAA7507, IAA7511 © AKAA/Courtesy of architect (photographer)

4. Photo by the authors

6. Dissing + Weitling Architecture a/s, Copenhagen

AL-AHLI BANK

1, 2, 3, 4. PACE Archive 68005, Kuwait. Copyright © Pace 2015

COMMERCIAL BANK OF KUWAIT

1. Postcard from Al-Ghunaim, Abdullah Y.; Ali Rais, Ali Gholoum (eds.), *Kuwait in Postcards*, Centre for Research and Studies on Kuwait, Kuwait, 2009

2, 3, 4, 5. Project drawings. Kuwait Municipal Archive, Kuwait

EMBASSY OF THE STATE OF KUWAIT AND CHANCELLERY

1, 2, 3, 4. *Controspazio*, Jun.–Jul.1970, v. 2, n. 6–7, pp. 2–12

KUWAIT INTERNATIONAL AIR TERMINAL

1, 2, 3. Aga Khan Award for Architecture. IAA7537, IAA7544, IAA7542 © Courtesy of architect/Courtesy of Kenzo Tange (photographer)

KUWAIT SPORTS CENTRE

1, 2, 3, 4. Columbia University, Avery Library, Drawings & Archives, Collection Felix Candela, Architectural Records & Papers 1950–84, Rolls A059.29 and 30

5, 6, 7, 8, 9, 10. MAXXI Museo Nazionale delle Arti del XXI secolo, Roma. Collezione MAXXI Architettura. Archivio Pier Luigi Nervi, Nervi-1. AP/225 – Kuwait Sport Centre: FO6732, FO6733, FO6739, FO6743, FO6771, FO6772

11, 12, 13. "Kuwait Sports Centre", in *Architectural Design*, Mar. 1970, v. 40, n. 3, pp. 134–137 (photo O. Murai)

WATER TOWERS

1, 2, 3, 4. *Aga Khan Award for Architecture Report,* 1980

5. Photo by Alia Farid

ABRAJ AL-KUWAIT

8. Malene Bjørn Archive, Stockholm

9. Tor Eigeland/*Saudi Aramco World*/ SAWDIA

FOUR "URBAN FORM STUDIES FOR THE OLD CITY"

1, 3. BBPR, "The Future Development for the Old City of Kuwait – Report 1969," Kuwait Municipal Archive, Kuwait

2, 7, 8, 9. Reima and Raili Pietilä, "The Task of Searching The Form for the New Capital –1969," Centre for Research and Studies on Kuwait

4. G. Candilis, "Reflections on the Development of the City of Kuwait," Private Archive, Kuwait

5, 6. The Alison and Peter Smithson Archive, Frances Loeb Library, Special Collections, Graduate School of Design, Harvard University

FOUR DEMONSTRATION AREAS

1, 2, 3. BBPR, "The Future Development for the Old City of Kuwait – Report 1969". Kuwait Municipal Archive, Kuwait

4, 5, 6, 7, 8. Vago, Pierre, "Les modèles exportés", *Architecture*, Dec. 1976, n. 400

9, 10. Reima and Raili Pietilä, "The Task of Searching The Form For The New Capital –1969," Centre for Research and Studies on Kuwait, Kuwait

11. Colin Buchanan, Second Master Plan documentation, 1968–72. Kuwait Municipal Archive, Kuwait

12, 13, 14, 15, 16. The Alison and Peter Smithson Archive. Courtesy of the Frances Loeb Library, Graduate School of Design, Harvard University

NATIONAL ASSEMBLY COMPETITION

1, 2. Chadirji Foundation, Beirut

3, 4, 5, 6, 7. B. V. Doshi Archive, Vastu-Shilpa Foundation, Sangath, Ahmedabad

8, 9, 10, 11. "Kuwait National Assembly Competition; Competition Entry by Sir Basil Spence, Bonnington & Collins" in *Building Design*, Feb. 1973, n.137, pp. 16–17

KUWAIT NATIONAL ASSEMBLY

2, 3, Aga Khan Award for Architecture, IAA7528, IAA7531, © AKAA/Courtesy of architect (photographer)

4. Edition Bløndal

KUWAIT SPORT CLUBS

1, 2, 3. Project drawings. Kuwait Municipal Archive, Kuwait

4, 5. Maath Alousi Private Archive, Limassol

GULF BANK HEADQUARTERS

1, 2. Gulf Bank Corporate Archive, Kuwait

SAVINGS & CREDIT BANK MAIN OFFICES

1, 2 and other unnumbered photos. PACE Archive 75242, Kuwait. Copyright © Pace 2015

SALEM AL-MUBARAK STREET

1, 2, 3, 6. Maath Alousi Private Archive, Limassol

4, 7. SSH Archive, Kuwait

5. KOC Archive, Kuwait

KUWAIT SHIPPING COMPANY HEADQUARTERS

1, 2, 3 and the unnumbered photos at top right corner. PACE Archive 69031, Kuwait. Copyright © Pace 2015

HILTON HOTEL

1, 3. PACE Archive 74218, Kuwait. Copyright © Pace 2015

4. Photo by Gustavo Ferrari

SHEIKH NASSER PALACE

1, 2. Photos by the authors

3. Tor Eigeland/*Saudi Aramco World*/ SAWDIA

SHEIKHA FATIMA MOHAMED ALI'S MOSQUE

1, 2, 3. Project drawings. Kuwait Municipal Archive

UNITED CENTRE HOUSING PROJECT

1. Aga Khan Visual Archive AKVA, Aga Khan Documentation Center, MIT – Cambridge, © TAC, The Architects Collaborative, Inc. (photographer), 126322, Box 9 Slide 147

2, 3. © "Fonds Candilis. SIAF/Cité de l'architecture et du patrimoine/Archives d'architecture du XXe siècle" 236 Ifa, Chapitre H. Projets et réalisations au Moyen Orient, 1970–1978. CANGE-H-71. Ensemble rèsidentiel, Kuwait City (Koweït)

LOULOU'A AL-MARZOUQ

1, 2, 4, 5. Pad 10 Architects, Kuwait

3. SSH Archive, Kuwait

6. Photo by the authors

KINDERGARTEN

1, 2, 3, 4, 5. ETH – gta archiv, Zürich. Alfred Roth 131-0163 / Kindergarten Mansouria

SIEF PALACE EXTENSION, MINISTRY OF FOREIGN AFFAIRS

2, 3, 4, 5, 6, 7. Aga Khan Award for Architecture. IAA7592, IAA7594, IAA7590, IAA7600, IAA7588, IAA7589, IAA7596, © Courtesy of architect/Reima Pietila (photographer)

KUWAIT AIRWAYS

1. Project drawing. Kuwait Municipal Archive, Kuwait

2, 3. Shiber, George, Saba, *The Kuwait Urbanization*, Kuwait Govt. Printing Press, 1964

4, 5, 6. Photos by the authors

SOUQ AL-KUWAIT

1. Project drawings. Kuwait Municipal Archive, Kuwait

SOUQ AL-KABEER

2, 3. Project drawings. Kuwait Municipal Archive, Kuwait

SOUQ AL-SAFAT

1, 3. Project drawings. Kuwait Municipal Archive, Kuwait

4, 5. Aga Khan Visual Archive AKVA, Aga Khan Documentation Center, MIT – Cambridge, © TAC, The Architects Collaborative, Inc. (photographer) 165477 Box 72 Slide 91; 165483 Box 72 Slide 97

SOUQ AL-MANAKH

2. Project diagram. Kuwait Municipal Archive, Kuwait

SOUQ AL-WATANIYA

4, 5, 6. Aga Khan Visual Archive AKVA, Aga Khan Documentation Center, MIT – Cambridge, © TAC, The Architects Collaborative, Inc. (photographer); 165485 Box 72 Slide 99; 165498 Box 72 Slide 112; 165495 Box 72 Slide 109

7, 8. PACE Archive, Kuwait. Copyright © Pace 2015

SOUQ AL-WATIYA

1, 2, 3, 4. PACE Archive 74208, Kuwait. Copyright © Pace 2015

SOUQ AL-MUTTAHEDA AND AL-MASSEEL

1, 2, 3, 6, 7, 8, 9, 10. United Real Estate Company (Photos N. Garrido)

4, 5. KEO Archive, Kuwait

HOSPITALS. MUBARAK AL-KABEER, AL-ADAN, AL-JAHRA

2, 3, 4. © Fonds Dossiers d'œuvres de la direction de l'Architecture et de l'Urbanisme (DAU). SIAF/Cité de l'architecture et du patrimoine/Archives d'architecture du XXe siècle. 133 Ifa, DAU-AART-ND-07. Dossier AART-ATEA (Forgia, Léon). Hôpital, Farwaniya (Koweit)

KUWAIT FUND FOR ARAB ECONOMIC DEVELOPMENT

1, 8, 9, 14, 15. PACE Archive 75260, Kuwait. Copyright © Pace 2015

11, 12, 13, 15. Kuwait Municipal Archive

NUGRA COMMERCIAL AND RESIDENTIAL COMPLEX

1, 2, 4, 5. PACE Archive 75247-80467, Kuwait. Copyright © Pace 2015

DASMAN COMPLEX

1, 2, 3, 4, 5. Project drawings. Kuwait Municipal Archive, Kuwait

BANKING STUDIES INSTITUTE

1, 2. Maath Alousi Private Archive, Limassol

JOINT BANKING CENTRE

2, 3. PACE Archive 76032, Kuwait. Copyright © Pace 2015

KUWAIT LAW COURTS

1. "Kuwait Law Courts; Architects: Sir Basil Spence International Partnership, with Fitzroy Robinson Partnership", in *Middle East Construction*, Sep. 1980, v. 5, n. 9, pp. 84–85

2. Project drawing. Kuwait Municipal Archive, Kuwait

MIDEAST MARKET

1, 2. Marcel Breuer papers, Archives of American Art, Smithsonian Institution, Washington DC

GOLD MARKET

1, 2, 3, 4, 5. PACE Archive 76309, Kuwait. Copyright © Pace 2015

SALHIYA COMMERCIAL PROJECT AND LE MERIDIEN HOTEL

1. "Middle East Structures: Meriden Hotel, Safat, Kuwait," in *Consulting Engineer,* Jun. 1979 v. 43, n. 6, p. 51

KUWAIT STATE MOSQUE

1, 2, 3, 4, 5. Aga Khan Award for Architecture. IAA7567, IAA7552 © AKAA/Courtesy of architect (photographer)

6, 7. United Real Estate Company (Photos N. Garrido)

8. Project drawing. Kuwait Municipal Archive, Kuwait

STOCK EXCHANGE

1, 2, 3, 4, 5. KEO Archive, Kuwait

IRANIAN EMBASSY IN KUWAIT

1. "Preview '82. Embassy, Kuwait; Architects: Michael Carapetian Associates", in *Architectural Review*, Jan. 1982, v. 171, n. 1019, p. 34

KUWAIT NATIONAL THEATRE COMPETITION

1, 2. RIBA, Drawings Collection, London

3. K. Wiśniowsky Private Archive, Kuwait

AL-SABAH HOUSE

1, 3, 4, 5. IHF2316, IHF2319, IHF2312, IHF2314 © Aga Khan Trust for Culture/A. Albek and M. Niksarli (photographer)

2. Private collection, Kuwait

AL-SAWABER HOUSING COMPLEX

1, 2, 3, 4, 5. "The Sawaber Project, National Housing Authority Kuwait: Development Study, Part C. Arthur Erickson Architects, Canada, May 1977," Kuwait Municipal Archive, Kuwait

Photos by Abdulaziz Al-Khandari. Aerial photo by N. Garrido

AL-MUTHANNA COMPLEX

1. KEO Archive, Kuwait

2, 4. Project drawing. Kuwait Municipal Archive, Kuwait

AWQAF COMMERCIAL COMPLEX

1. Project drawing. Kuwait Municipal Archive, Kuwait

WATERFRONT

1, 3, 6, 11. Taylor, Brian Brace, "Kuwait City Waterfront development" in *Mimar: Architecture in Development*, Mar. 1990, v. 10, n. 1(34), pp. 12–20. © Concept Media Ltd. / Aga Khan Trust for Culture

7. KEO Archive, Kuwait

12. G. Sultan, KEO, KTEC, F. James and Municipality of Kuwait, "Evaluation of Phase 1 and 2", in the *Waterfront project, Phase 5*, 1989. Kuwait Municipal Archive, Kuwait

HILTON AREA APARTMENTS

1, 2, 3, 4, 5. Project drawings. Kuwait Municipal Archive, Kuwait

OFFICE TOWERS

1, 2, 3, 4, 5, 7, 8, 9, 10. 11, 12, 13, 14, 15, 18, 19, 20, 21. PACE Archive, Kuwait.78410, 78409, 73188, 79434, 79435, Copyright © Pace 2015

17, 22. Photos by the authors

FINTAS TOWN CENTRE

1, 2, 3. John Bland Canadian Architecture Collection, Rare Books and Special Collections, McGill University Library

MINISTRIES COMPLEX

1, 2. Project drawings. Kuwait Municipal Archive, Kuwait

3. Photo by Gustavo Ferrari

KUWAIT RADIO TELEVISION CENTRE

1. Photo by Gustavo Ferrari

2, 3, 4, 5. Kuwait Radio Television Centre. Dossier. Centre for Research and Studies on Kuwait, Kuwait

KUWAIT INSTITUTE FOR SCIENTIFIC RESEARCH (KISR)

1. Unesco Report "Kuwait: Establishment of a Petroleum and Petrochemical Division, Kuwait Institute for Scientific Research, Jan.–Mar. 1968" by T. Rifai

2. Al-Kuwait Magazine, Sep. 1973

3, 4, 5. PACE Archive, Kuwait. 79427, Copyright © Pace 2015

COMMERCIAL BANK OF KUWAIT OPERATIONS CENTER

5. PACE Archive 79452, Kuwait. Copyright © Pace 2015

ALGHANIM INDUSTRIES HEADQUARTERS

2. KEO Archive, Kuwait

KOC COMPUTER & TRAINING CENTRE

1, 2, 3, 4, 6. C. T. Haddad Private Archive, Kuwait

5. Morris, A. E. J., "Offices. A Review of Layouts, Fittings and Furnishings", in *Middle East Construction*, Mar. 1982, p. 57

AL-AHLI BANK HEADQUARTERS

2, 3, 4. PACE Archive 79456, Kuwait. Copyright © Pace 2015

DERWAZAH ABDULRAZAQ AND SAFAT SQUARE

1, 7. BBPR, Proposal for Safat Square, 1977. Kuwait Municipal Archive, Kuwait

2, 4, 5, 6. Devecom; IN.CO, "Safat Square. Preliminary Design Report," Jan. 1982, Kuwait Municipal Archive, Kuwait

3. Al-Kuwait Magazine, April 1988

CENTRE FOR PHYSICAL MEDICINE AND REHABILITATION

1, 2, 3, 4. Project drawings. Kuwait Municipal Archive, Kuwait

UNITED ARAB SHIPPING COMPANY HEADQUARTERS

1, 2, 3, 4, 5. PACE Archive 80461, Kuwait. Copyright © Pace 2015

CONFERENCE CENTRE

1. Izdavač, Neimar V., ArhArt broj 3, jesen 2011. ArhArt, magazin za arhitekturu i umetnost, broj3 (Autum 2011). Izdavač, Neimar V.; Design & Prepress, Max Nova Creative

2. Aga Khan Award for Architecture, IAA3571 © Courtesy of architect/Gustavo Ferrari (photographer)

3, 4. KEO Archive, Kuwait

5. SSH Archive, Kuwait

INTERCONTINENTAL HOTEL

1, 2, 3, 4. ETH – gta archiv, Zürich. Alfred Roth 131-0178/ Hotel in al Salmiya

SHEIKH NASSER AL-SABAH MOSQUE

1, 2, 3. Montois Partners Architects Archive, Belgium. Peter Mandl Private Archive, Belgium

KUWAIT ZOO EXTENSION AND RENOVATION

1, 2, 3, 4, 5, 6, 7. KEO Archive, Kuwait

TELECOMMUNICATION CENTRE AND ANTENNA TOWER

1, 2. Project drawings. Kuwait Municipal Archive, Kuwait

KUWAIT FOUNDATION FOR THE ADVANCEMENT OF SCIENCES

3. Aga Khan Visual Archive AKVA, Aga Khan Documentation Center, MIT – Cambridge, © TAC, The Architects Collaborative, Inc. (photographer), 165503 Box 72, Slide 116, 117

4, 5. PACE Archive, Kuwait. Copyright © Pace 2015

MIRQAB TRANSPORTATION CENTRE

1, 4. "Report Val in Kuwait," by Matra Transportation Branch in St. Quentin en Yvelines, May 1984

2, 5. Shuaib, H. (ed.), "Planning and Urban Development in Kuwait, Kuwait Municipality," 1977

3. Tor Eigeland/*Saudi Aramco World*/ SAWDIA

6. SSH Archive, Kuwait

AL-BALOUSH BUS STATION

1, 3. Al-Kuwait Magazine, Jul. 1965

PORT AUTHORITY HEADQUARTERS

1. K. Wiśniowski Private Archive, Kuwait

KUWAIT INSURANCE COMPANY

1, 2, 3, 4, 5, 6. Canadian Center for Architecture Collection, Montréal, Canada, AP022.S2.SS2.D20Y